PHILIP'S

G000127557

STREET

West Kent

Chatham, Dartford, Gillingham, Maidstone, Royal Tunbridge Wells

www.philips-maps.co.uk
First published in 1989 by Philip's
a division of Octopus Publishing Group Ltd
www.octopusbooks.co.uk
Endeavour House 189 Shaftesbury Avenue
London WC2H 8JY
An Hachette UK Company
www.hachette.co.uk

Fourth edition 2010
First impression 2010
WKTDA

ISBN 978-1-84907-021-8 (pocket)

© Philip's 2010

Ordnance Survey®

This product includes mapping data licensed from
Ordnance Survey® with the permission of the
Controller of Her Majesty's Stationery Office.
© Crown copyright 2010. All rights reserved.
Licence number 100011710.

Contents

II   Mobile safety cameras

III   **Key to map symbols**

IV   **Key to map pages**

VI   **Route planning**

VIII   Major administrative and Postcode boundaries

1   **Street maps** at 2⅔ inches to 1 mile

200   **Index** of towns, villages, streets, hospitals, industrial estates, railway stations, schools, shopping centres, universities and places of interest

Digital Data

The exceptionally high-quality mapping found in this atlas is available as digital data in TIFF format, which is easily convertible to other bitmapped (raster) image formats.

The index is also available in digital form as a standard database table. It contains all the details found in the printed index together with the National Grid reference for the map square in which each entry is named.

For further information and to discuss your requirements, please contact
philips@mapsinternational.co.uk

Mobile safety cameras

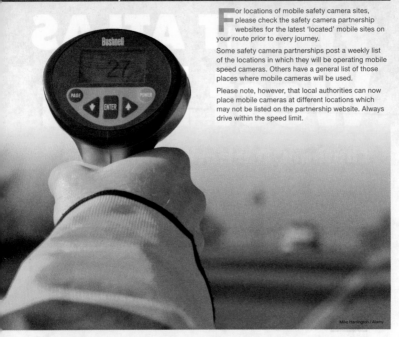

For locations of mobile safety camera sites, please check the safety camera partnership websites for the latest 'located' mobile sites on your route prior to every journey.

Some safety camera partnerships post a weekly list of the locations in which they will be operating mobile speed cameras. Others have a general list of those places where mobile cameras will be used.

Please note, however, that local authorities can now place mobile cameras at different locations which may not be listed on the partnership website. Always drive within the speed limit.

Mike Harrington / Alamy

Useful websites

Kent and Medway Safety Camera Partnership
www.kmscp.org

London Safety Camera Partnership
www.lscp.org.uk

Surrey Safety Camera Partnership
www.surrey-safecam.org

Sussex Safer Roads Partnership
www.sussexsaferroads.gov.uk

Further information
www.dvla.gov.uk
www.thinkroadsafety.gov.uk
www.dft.gov.uk
www.road-safe.org

Key to map symbols

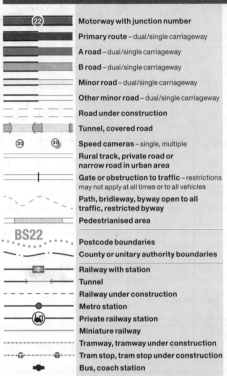

Motorway with junction number

Primary route – dual/single carriageway

A road – dual/single carriageway

B road – dual/single carriageway

Minor road – dual/single carriageway

Other minor road – dual/single carriageway

Road under construction

Tunnel, covered road

Speed cameras – single, multiple

Rural track, private road or narrow road in urban area

Gate or obstruction to traffic – restrictions may not apply at all times or to all vehicles

Path, bridleway, byway open to all traffic, restricted byway

Pedestrianised area

Postcode boundaries

County or unitary authority boundaries

Railway with station

Tunnel

Railway under construction

Metro station

Private railway station

Miniature railway

Tramway, tramway under construction

Tram stop, tram stop under construction

Bus, coach station

Ambulance station

Coastguard station

Fire station

Police station

Accident and Emergency entrance to hospital

Hospital

Place of worship

Information centre – open all year

Shopping centre, parking

Park and Ride, Post Office

Camping site, caravan site

Golf course, picnic site

Church / ROMAN FORT   Non-Roman antiquity, Roman antiquity

Univ   Important buildings, schools, colleges, universities and hospitals

Woods, built-up area

River Medway   Water name

River, weir

Stream

Canal, lock, tunnel

Water

Tidal water

58 ◄ 87 / 246   Adjoining page indicators and overlap bands – the colour of the arrow and band indicates the scale of the adjoining or overlapping page (see scale below)

The dark grey border on the inside edge of some pages indicates that the mapping does not continue onto the adjacent page

The small numbers around the edges of the maps identify the 1-kilometre National Grid lines

Abbreviations

Acad	Academy	Meml	Memorial
Allot Gdns	Allotments	Mon	Monument
Cemy	Cemetery	Mus	Museum
C Ctr	Civic centre	Obsy	Observatory
CH	Club house	Pal	Royal palace
Coll	College	PH	Public house
Crem	Crematorium	Recn Gd	Recreation ground
Ent	Enterprise	Resr	Reservoir
Ex H	Exhibition hall	Ret Pk	Retail park
Ind Est	Industrial Estate	Sch	School
IRB Sta	Inshore rescue boat station	Sh Ctr	Shopping centre
Inst	Institute	TH	Town hall / house
Ct	Law court	Trad Est	Trading estate
L Ctr	Leisure centre	Univ	University
LC	Level crossing	W Twr	Water tower
Liby	Library	Wks	Works
Mkt	Market	YH	Youth hostel

The map scale on the pages numbered in blue is 2⅔ inches to 1 mile
4.2 cm to 1 km • 1:23 810

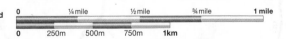

| 0 | ¼ mile | ½ mile | ¾ mile | 1 mile |
| 0 | 250m | 500m | 750m | 1km |

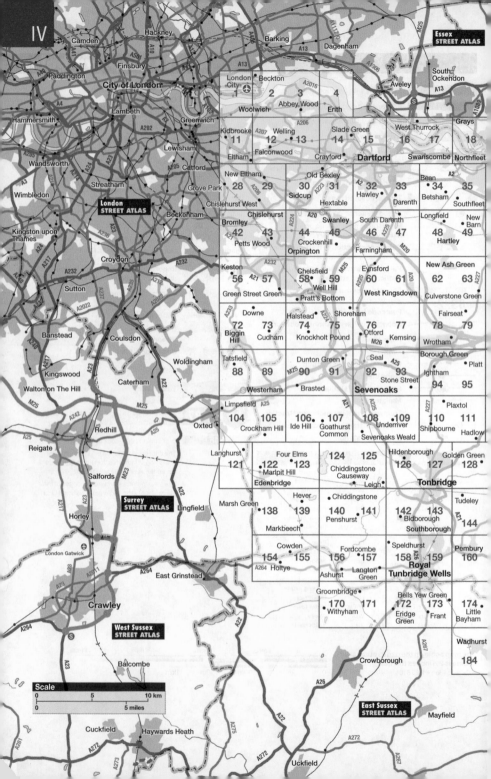

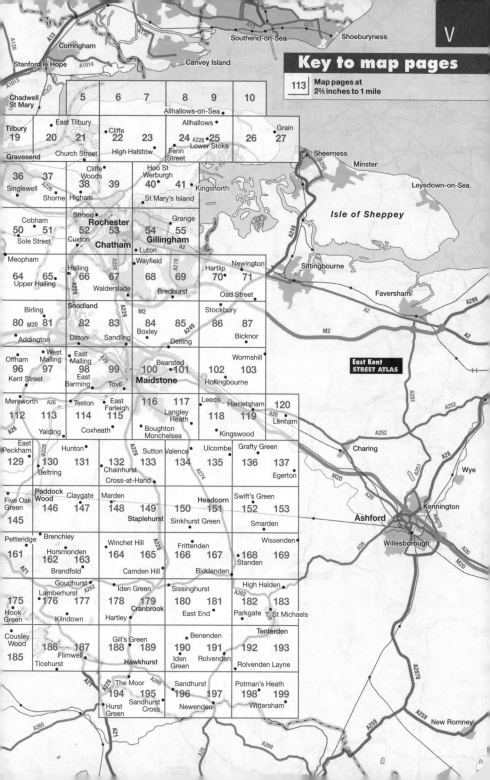

Key to map pages

113 | Map pages at 2⅔ inches to 1 mile

V

East Kent STREET ATLAS

Route Planning

Scale

0		5	10 km
0		5 miles	

Major administrative and Postcode boundaries

Scale

County and unitary authority boundaries
District boundaries
Postcode boundaries
Area covered by Philip's street atlases of Kent

0   5   10   15 km
0   5   10 miles

TQ TR

Greater London
Essex
Southend-on-Sea
Thurrock
Surrey
West Sussex
East Sussex

Thanet
Dover
Canterbury
Shepway
Swale
Ashford
Medway
Gravesham
Tonbridge & Malling
Maidstone
Sevenoaks
Dartford
Tunbridge Wells

Kent

Margate, Broadstairs, Ramsgate, Minster, Birchington, Herne Bay, Whitstable, Sandwich, Deal, St Margaret's at Cliffe, Dover, Wingham, Aylesham, Folkestone, Hawkinge, Hythe, Petham, Canterbury, Chilham, Wye, New Romney, Lydd, Faversham, Queenborough, Grain, Cliffe Woods, Rochester, Gillingham, Chatham, Sittingbourne, Newington, Ashford, Bethersden, Hamstreet, Tenterden, Lenham, Headcorn, Maidstone, Loose, Wateringbury, Aylesford, Snodland, Addington, Meopham, Gravesend, Tilbury, Dartford, Swanley, Hartley, Eynsford, Otford, Sevenoaks, Westerham, Edenbridge, Bromley, Orpington, Lewisham, Eltham, Woolwich, Wrotham, Hadlow, Tonbridge, Royal Tunbridge Wells, Staplehurst, Cranbrook, Hawkhurst, Wadhurst, Groombridge

CT11, CT10, CT9, CT8, CT7, CT6, CT5, CT2, CT1, CT3, CT4, CT12, CT13, CT14, CT15, CT16, CT17, CT18, CT19, CT20, CT21

TN25, TN24, TN23, TN26, TN27, TN30, TN31, TN29, TN28, TN17, TN18, TN32, TN19, TN12, TN2, TN3, TN5, TN1, TN4, TN9, TN10, TN11, TN13, TN14, TN15, TN16, TN8, TN7, TN6, RH19, RH7, RH8, CR6

ME11, ME12, ME10, ME9, ME13, ME3, ME2, ME4, ME5, ME1, ME7, ME8, ME6, ME14, ME15, ME16, ME17, ME18, ME19, ME20

DA10, DA11, DA12, DA13, DA2, DA3, DA4, DA1, DA5, DA6, DA7, DA8, DA9, DA14, DA15, DA16, DA17, DA18

SE28, SE2, SE18, SE7, SE3, SE12, SE9, E13, SE6, BR8, BR5, BR6, BR1, BR2, BR7, BR4, BR3

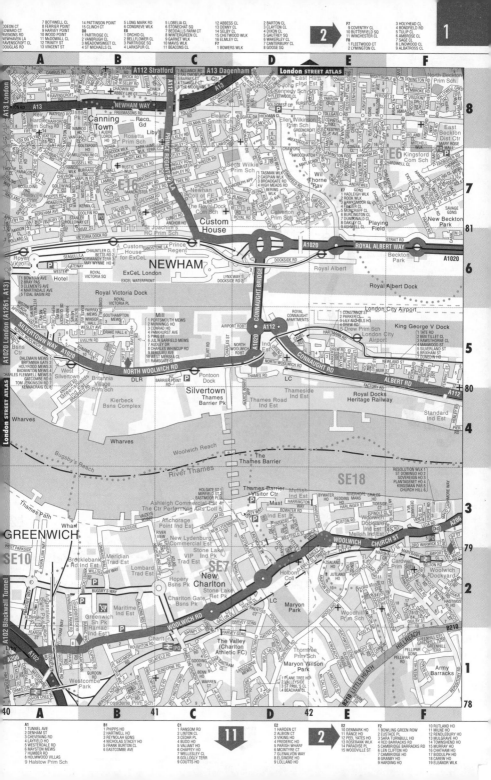

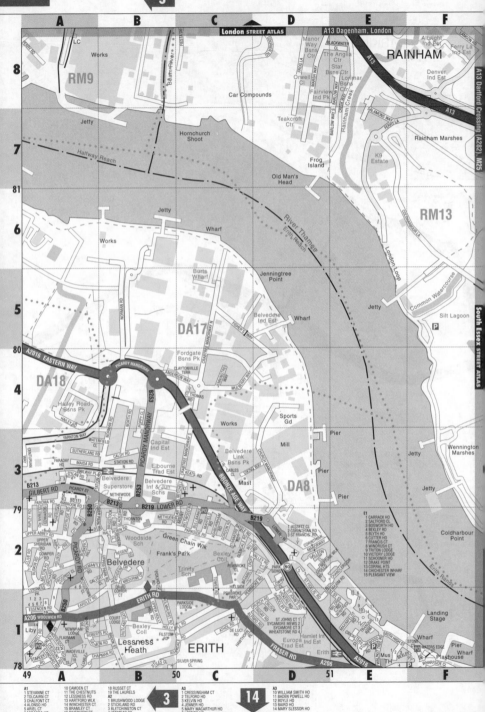

A1
1 STEVANNE CT
2 TOLCAIRN CT
3 CHALFONT CT
4 ALONSO HO
5 ARIEL CT
6 MIRANDA HO
7 PROSPERO HO
8 SMARDEN CL
9 BERKHAMPSTEAD RD

10 CAMDEN CT
11 THE CHESTNUTS
12 LESSNESS RD
13 HARTFORD WLK
14 WINCHESTER CT
15 BRAMLEY CT
16 RIVERVIEW CT
17 Lessness Heath Prim Sch

18 RUSSET CT
19 THE LAURELS

A2
1 BRUSHWOOD LODGE
2 STICKLAND RD
3 BLETCHINGTON CT
4 VENMEAD CT
5 MITRE CT
6 CHAPELSITE CT

A3
1 CRESSINGHAM CT
2 TELFORD HO
3 KELVIN HO
4 JENNER HO
5 MARY MACARTHUR HO
6 LENNOX HO
7 KEIR HARDY HO
8 MONARCH RD
9 ELIZABETH GARRETT ANDERSON HO

A3
10 WILLIAM SMITH HO
11 BADEN POWELL HO
12 BOYLE HO
13 BAIRD HO
14 MARY SLESSOR HO

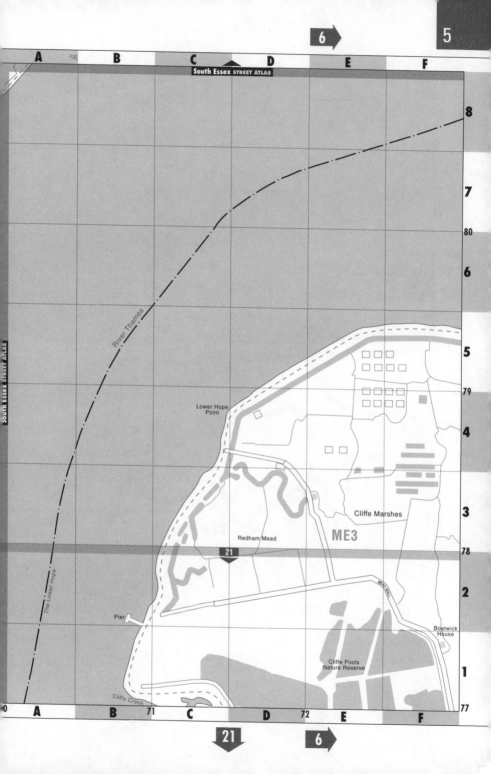

South Essex STREET ATLAS

SOUTH ESSEX STREET ATLAS

River Thames

The Lower Hope

Lower Hope Point

Cliffe Marshes

ME3

Redham Mead

21

Pier

MORE HILL

Boatwick House

Cliffe Pools Nature Reserve

Cliffe Creek

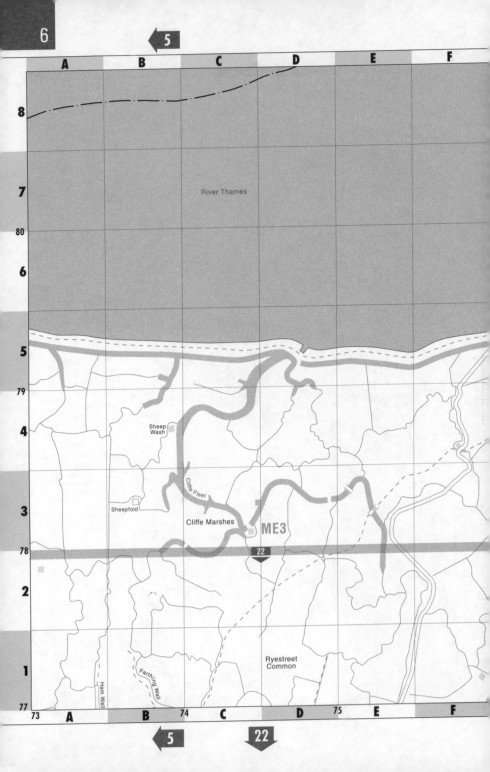

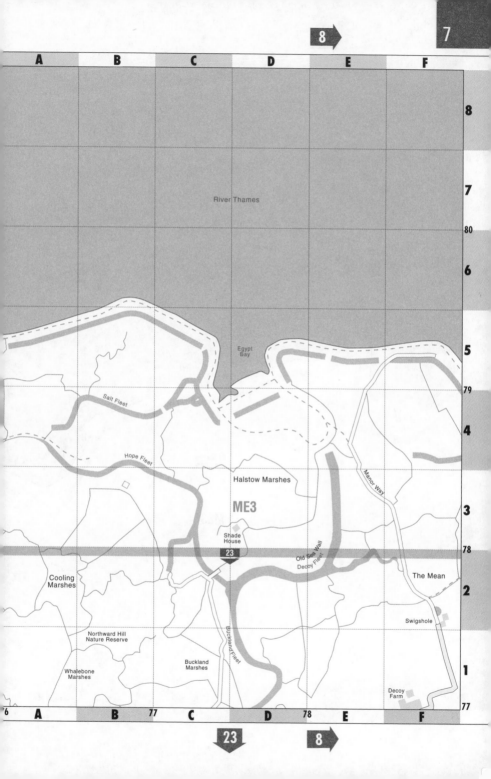

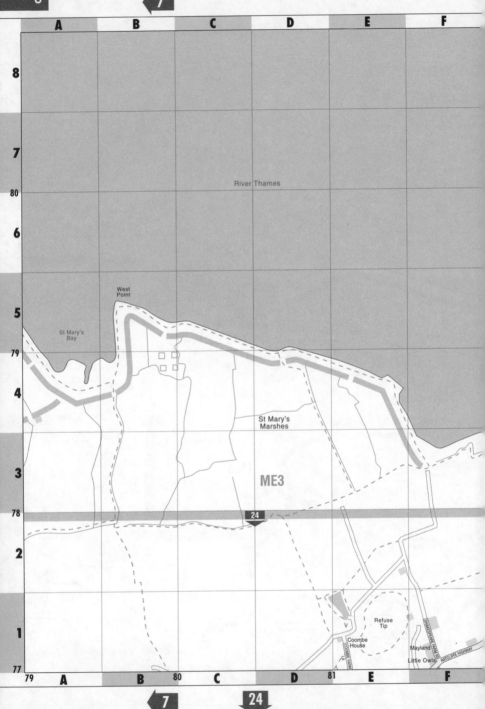

7

A B C D E F

8

7

80

6

River Thames

5

West
Point

St Mary's
Bay

79

4

St Mary's
Marshes

3

ME3

78

24

2

1

Refuse
Tip

V

Coombe
House

Mayland

77

Little Owls

79 A B 80 C D 81 E F

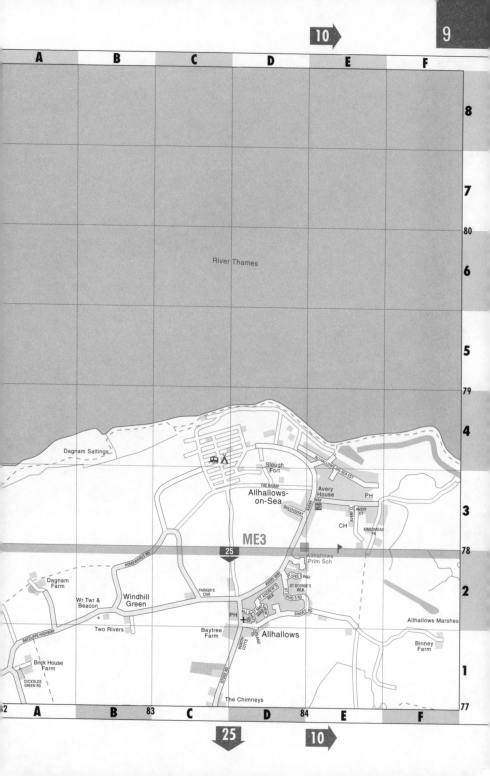

A   B   C   D   E   F

8

7

80

River Thames

6

5

79

4

Dagnam Saltings

Slough
Fort

THE BRIMP

Allhallows-
on-Sea

ALLHALLOWS-ON-SEA EST

Avery
House

AVERY WAY

PH

PO

QUEENSWAY

AVERY CL

AVERY CT

CH

KINGSMEAD PK

3

ME3

78

25

HOMEWARDS RD

Allhallows
Prim Sch

Dagnam
Farm

Wr Twr &
Beacon

Windhill
Green

PARKER'S
CNR

AVERY WAY

ST ANDREW'S WAY

ST LUKE'S WAY

ST GEORGE'S
WLK

ST DAVID'S RD

BINNEY RD

Allhallows Marshes

2

Two Rivers

RATCLIFFE HIGHWAY

Brick House
Farm

CUCKOLDS
GREEN RD

PH

ALL SAINTS WAY

BAPTY COTTS

Baytree
Farm

STOKE RD

Allhallows

The Chimneys

Binney
Farm

1

A B C D E F

8

7

80

6

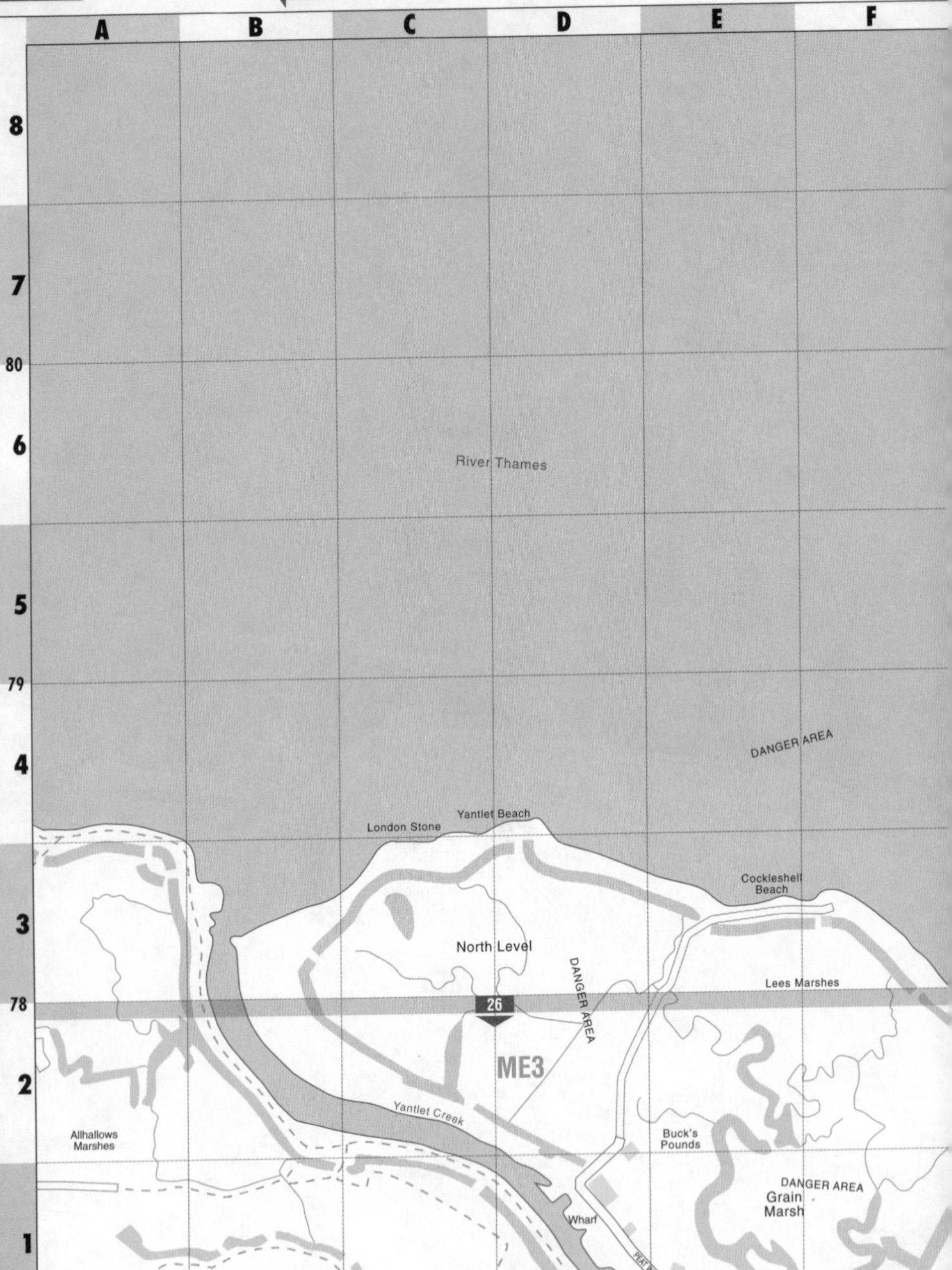

River Thames

5

79

4

DANGER AREA

Yantlet Beach

London Stone

Cockleshell
Beach

3

North Level

DANGER AREA

Lees Marshes

78

26

ME3

Buck's
Pounds

2

Yantlet Creek

Allhallows
Marshes

DANGER AREA
Grain
Marsh

1

Wharf

WEST
LA

77

85 A B 86 C D 87 E F

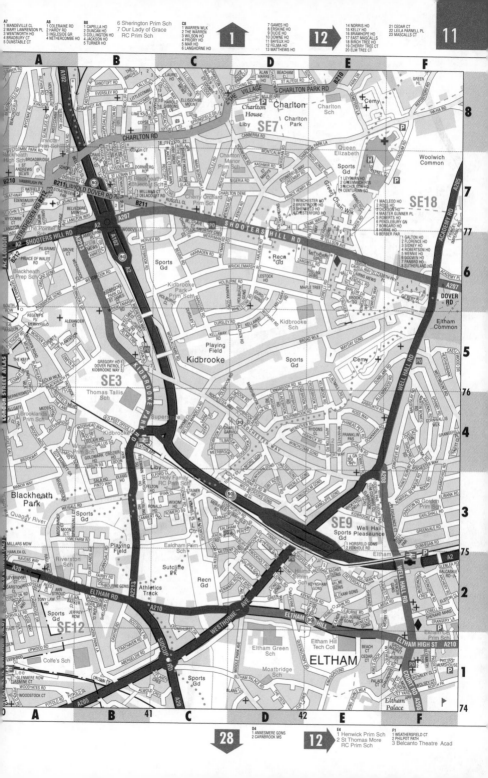

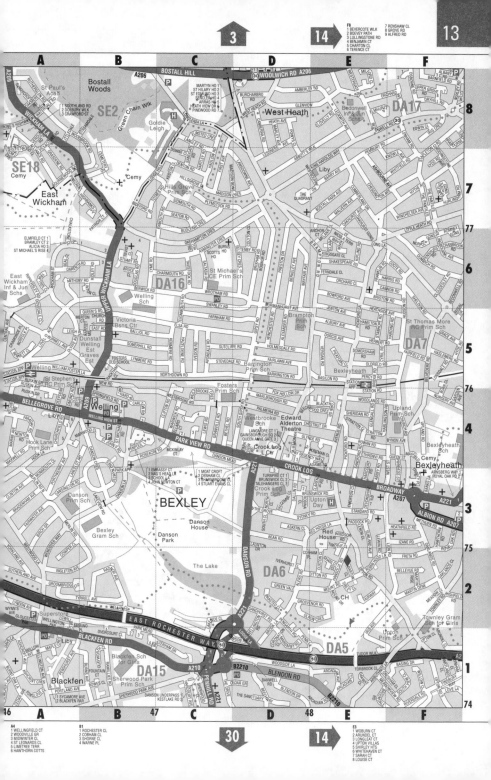

D1
1 ESSEX RD
2 CHADWICK CT
3 FROBISHER CT
4 CLEVES VIEW
5 PRIORY CT
6 WESTGATE HO
7 TWISTLETON CT
8 CONSTANCE GR
9 CRAWFORD AVE

10 CRITCHLEY AVE
11 Our Lady's RC
  Prim Sch

E1
1 THE CLOISTERS
2 COPPERFIELDS
3 BULLACE LA
4 CHURCH VIEW
5 Orchard Sh Ctr
6 Copperfields
  Sh Ctr

F1
1 LAVINIA RD
2 LAMPLIGHTERS CL

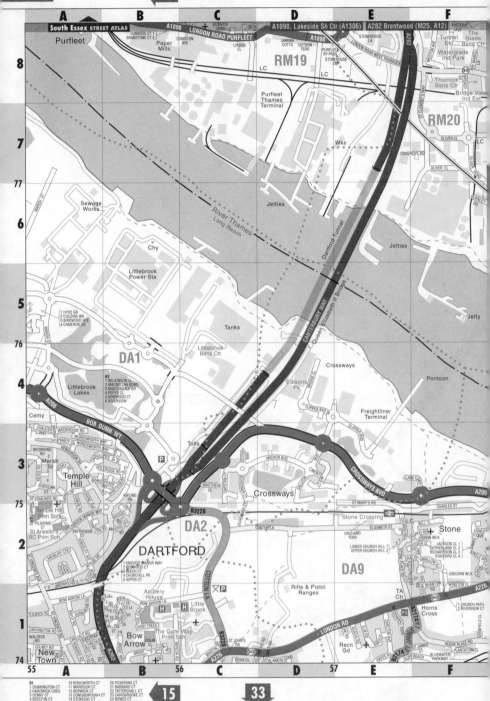

South Essex STREET ATLAS

Purfleet

A1090

LONDON ROAD PURFLEET

A1090, Lakeside Sh Ctr (A1306)

A282 Brentwood (M25, A12)

RM19

Purfleet
Thames
Terminal

River Thames
Long Reach

RM20

Thurrock
Bsns Ctr

Bridge View
Ind Est

Waterglade
Ind Park

Tunnel
Est

The
Glade
Bsns Ctr

Wks

Jetties

Dartford Tunnel

Jetties

Jetty

Sewage
Works

Chy

Littlebrook
Power Sta

Tanks

Littlebrook
Bsns Ctr

Crossways

Pontoon

DA1

1 HYDE GR
2 COUZINS WK
3 BIRDWOOD AVE
4 CAMERON DR

A3
1 WILKINSON CL
2 MACMILLAN GDNS
3 NIGHTINGALE GR
4 PEPYS CL
5 NORWOOD CT
6 RIVERVIEW

Littlebrook
Lakes

Littlebrook
Lakes

Cemy

Edisons
Pk

Freightliner
Terminal

BOB DUNN WY

A206

Tolls

Tolls

CROSSWAYS BVD

A206

Marsh
St

Temple
Hill

St EDMUNDS RD

Temple Hill
Prim Sch

PILGRIMS

St Anselm's
RC Prim Sch

DA2

Crossways

Stone Crossing

Stone

LOWER CHURCH HILL
UPPER CHURCH HILL

DA9

DARTFORD

1 KNIGHTS MANOR WAY
2 BEDWOOD CT
3 BEECH CT
4 CHURCHILL PK
5 ASPEN CT

Archery
House

P

Little
Brook

Rifle & Pistol
Ranges

TA
Ctr

Horns
Cross

Bow
Arrow

New
Town

The Gate Way
Prim Sch

H

H

St JOHN'S RD

B3228

LONDON RD

ALAMEIN GDNS

Recn
Gd

B2174

Bluewater
Parkway

Horns
Cross

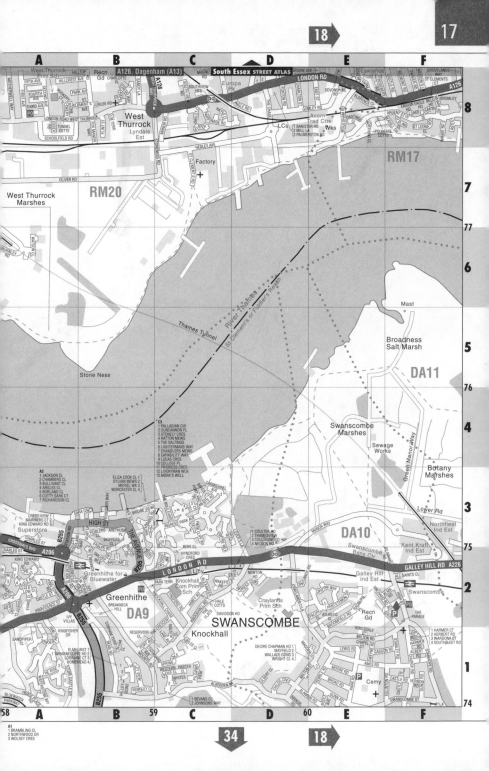

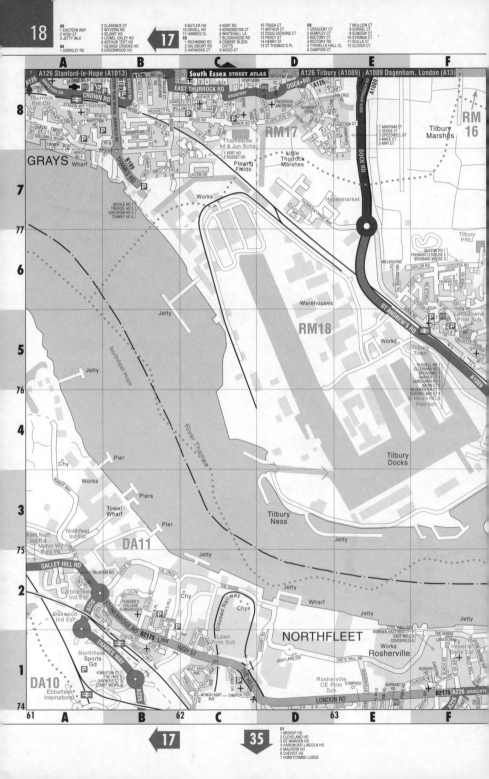

A8
1 EASTERN WAY
2 HIGH ST
3 JETTY WLK

B8
1 DARNLEY RD

2 CLARENCE CT
3 WYVERN HO
4 SEJANT HO
5 LIONEL OXLEY HO
6 ARTHUR TOFT HO
7 GEORGE CROOKS HO
8 GREENWOOD HO

9 BUTLER HO
10 DAVALL HO
11 HAWKES CL

C8
1 RICHMOND RD
2 SALISBURY RD
3 HARWOOD CT

4 KENT RD
5 KENSINGTON CT
6 WHITEHALL LA
7 BLOCKHOUSE RD
8 CEMENT BLOCK COTTS
9 WOOD ST

10 TRASA CT
11 ARTHUR CT
12 DOUG SIDDONS CT
13 PERCY ST
14 HENRY ST
15 ST THOMAS'S PL

D8
1 CRESCENT CT
2 KEMPLEY CT
3 RECTORY CT
4 RECTORY RD
5 TYRRELLS HALL CL
6 CAMPION CT

7 MULLEIN CT
8 SORREL CT
9 SUNDEW CT
10 SYRINGA CT
11 SCILLA CT
12 CLOVER CT

South Essex STREET ATLAS

D1
1 MENDIP HO
2 CLEVELAND HO
3 DE WARREN HO
4 HAREWOOD LINCOLN HO
5 MALVERN HO
6 CHEVIOT HO
7 HONEYCOMBE LODGE

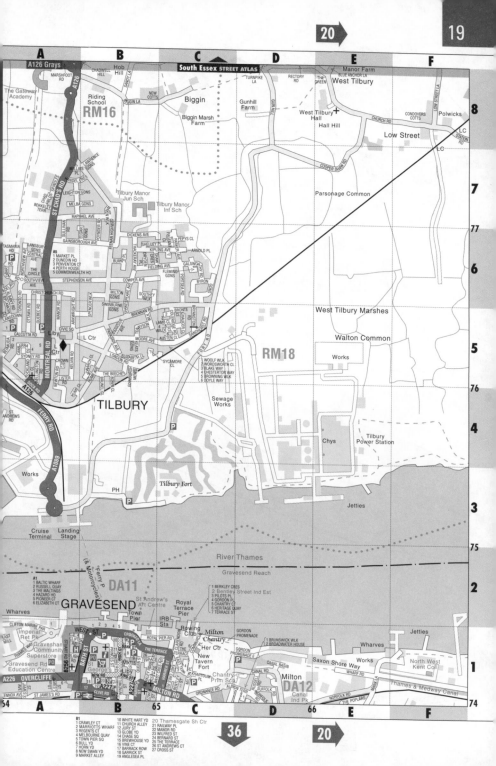

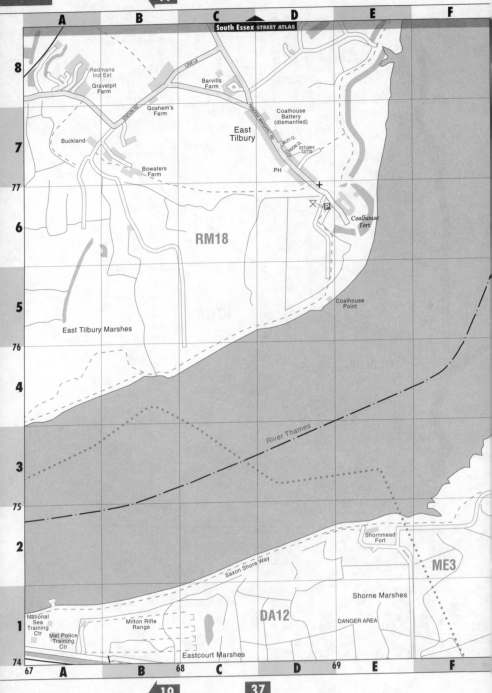

South Essex STREET ATLAS

A **B** **C** **D** **E** **F**

8

Redmans
Ind Est
Gravelpit
Farm

LOVE LA

Barvills
Farm

Goshem's
Farm

STATION RD

Coalhouse
Battery
(dismantled)

East
Tilbury

7

Buckland

Bowaters
Farm

PRINCESS MARGARET RD

LINLEY CL
LONDON CL
ESTUARY
COTTS

PH

77

RM18

Coalhouse
Fort

6

Coalhouse
Point

5

East Tilbury Marshes

76

4

River Thames

3

75

Shornmead
Fort

2

Saxon Shore Way

ME3

Shorne Marshes

DA12

1

National
Sea
Training
Ctr

Met Police
Training
Ctr

Milton Rifle
Range

DANGER AREA

Eastcourt Marshes

74

67 **A** **B** 68 **C** **D** 69 **E** **F**

← 19

37 ↓

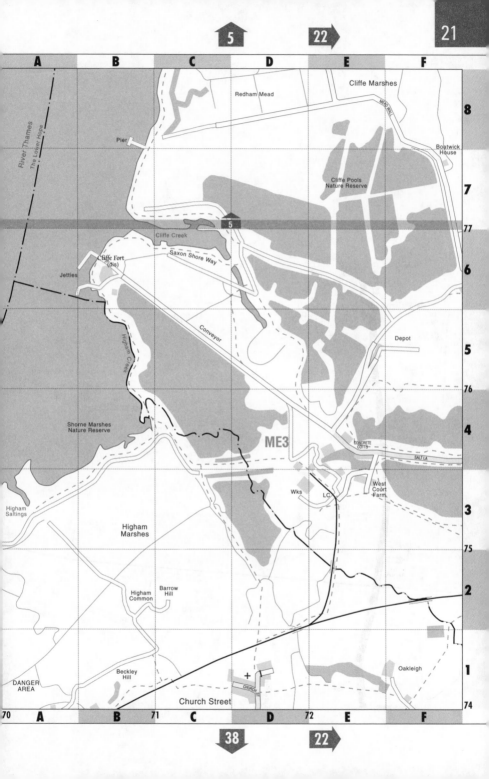

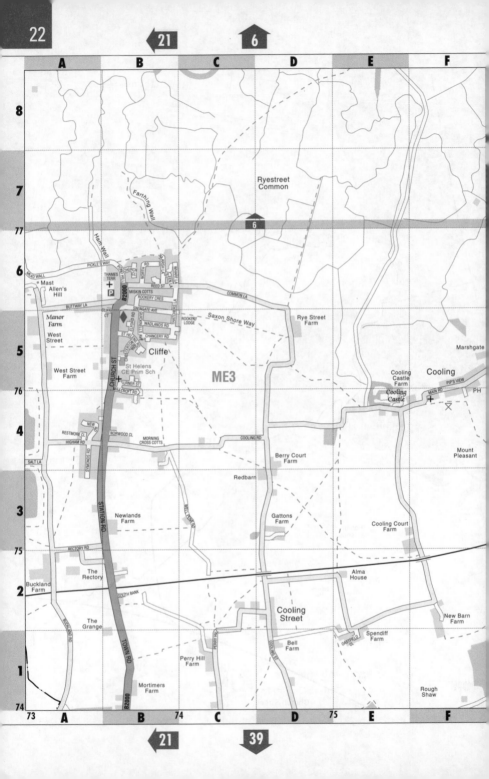

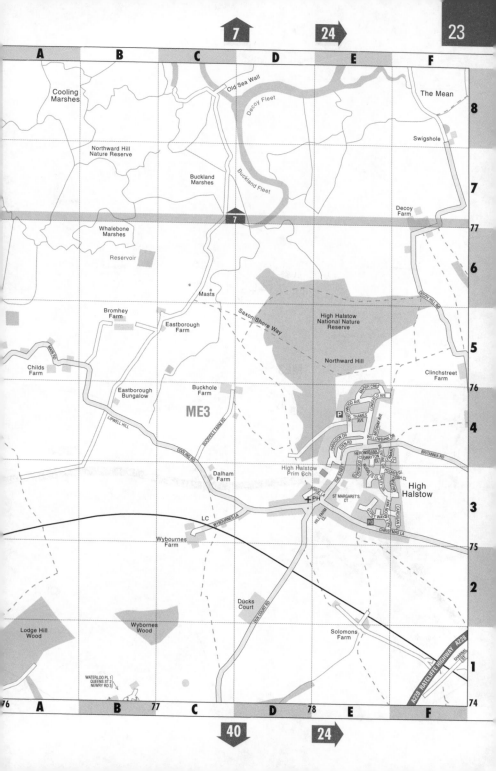

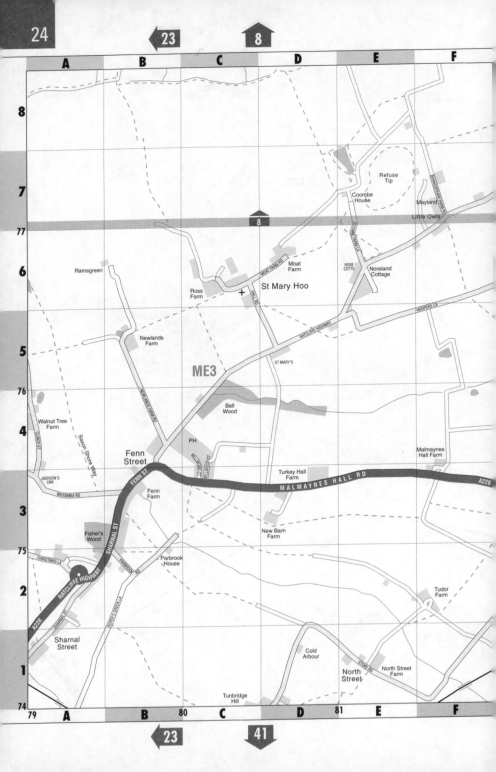

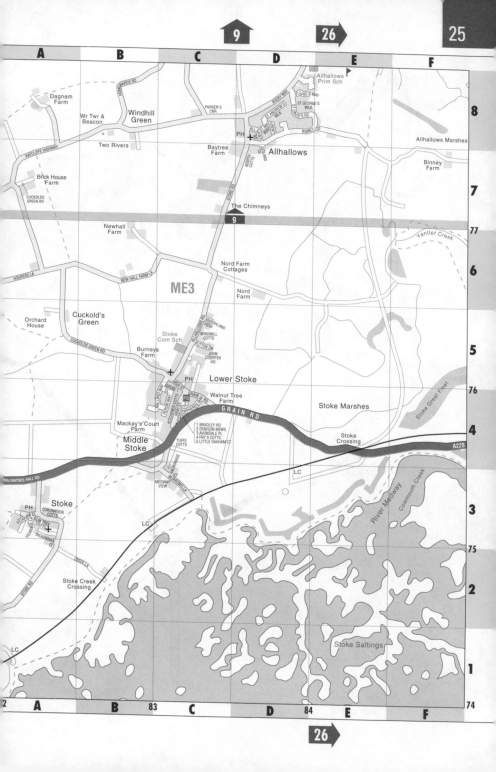

A B C D E F

Dagnam Farm
Wr Twr & Beacon
Windhill Green
PARKER'S CNR
Allhallows Prim Sch
ST JAMES'S WAY
AVERY WAY
ST GEORGE'S WLK
ST ANDREW'S
ST DAVID'S RD
Allhallows Marshes
8

Two Rivers
Baytree Farm
PH
ALL SAINTS RD
BINNEY RD
Allhallows
Binney Farm

RATCLIFFE HIGHWAY
Brick House Farm
CUCKOLDS GREEN RD
The Chimneys
9
Yantlet Creek
77

Newhall Farm
HOOPERS LA
NEW HALL FARM LA
Nord Farm Cottages
7

6

Orchard House
Cuckold's Green
CUCKOLDS GREEN RD
Burneys Farm
ME3
Stoke Com Sch
ALLHALLOWS RD
MARSHLAND VIEW
WINDMILL COTTS
SUTTON DR
JOHN COOPPER HO
Nord Farm
5

PH
Lower Stoke
Walnut Tree Farm
Stoke Marshes
Stoke Great Fleet
76

HIGH ST
GRAIN RD
KITCHENER COTTS
1 BRADLEY HO
2 DENISON MEWS
3 AVONDALE PL
4 FRY'S COTTS
5 LITTLE OAKHAM CT
GRAIN RD
Stoke Crossing
A228
4

Mackay's Court Farm
Middle Stoke
TUFFS COTTS
ANCHORAGE
BIRCHOMS LA
MEDWAY VIEW
LC
River Medway
Colemouth Creek
3

MALMAYNES HALL RD
PH
Stoke
CORONATION COTTS
VICARAGE CL
ELM TREE COTTS
VICARAGE RD
DICKENSON CL
LC
75

CREEK LA
STOKE RD
Stoke Creek Crossing
2

LC
Stoke Saltings
1

74

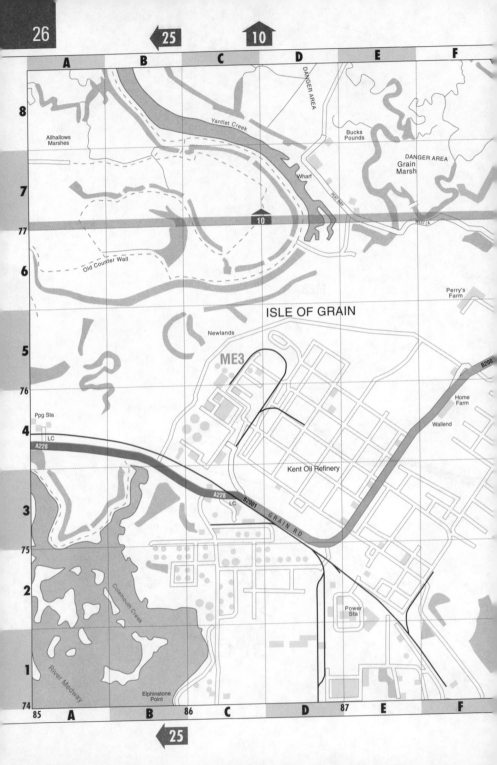

A   B   C   D   E   F

8

Allhallows
Marshes

Yantlet Creek

DANGER AREA

Bucks
Pounds

DANGER AREA
Grain
Marsh

7

Wharf

FERRY RD

10

WESTA

77

Old Counter Wall

6

Perry's
Farm

ISLE OF GRAIN

Newlands

5

ME3

B200

76

Home
Farm

Ppg Sta

Wallend

4

LC

A228

A228

LC

B2001

Kent Oil Refinery

GRAIN RD

3

75

Colemouth Creek

2

Power
Sta

River Medway

1

Elphinstone
Point

74

85   A   B   86   C   D   87   E   F

A   B   C   D   E   F

8

River Thames   Grain Spit

7

77

DANGER AREA

Works

Rose Court
Farm

Grain

HIGH ST
B2001
PANELL RD
FRY CL
PH
WEST LA

St James'
CE Prim Sch

6

Lib'y
Edinburgh Rd
Coronation Rd
Corinthian
Ct
Rivenhall Cl
ST JAMES
PIN DEAL RD
SHELDRAKE CL
COASTGUARD
COTTS
Jetty

GRAIN RD

Whitehouse
Farm

SMITHFIELD RD

5

76

ME3

POWER STATION RD

Grain
Tower

PORT VICTORIA RD

4

Smithfield
Marshes

Garrison
Point

Chy

Grain
Power
Station

LB
Sta
GARRISON RD
SLIPWAY RD
BOATHOUSE
RD
Docks
ANCHOR LA
SHORESIDE

SHEERNESS

3

Jetty   Sheerness
Harbour Est
GREAT BASIN RD

75

House Fleet

River Medway

2

Piers

ME12

Cockleshell
Hard   Jetty

1

The
Lappel

Horseshoe
Point

8   A   B   89   C   D   90   E   F   74

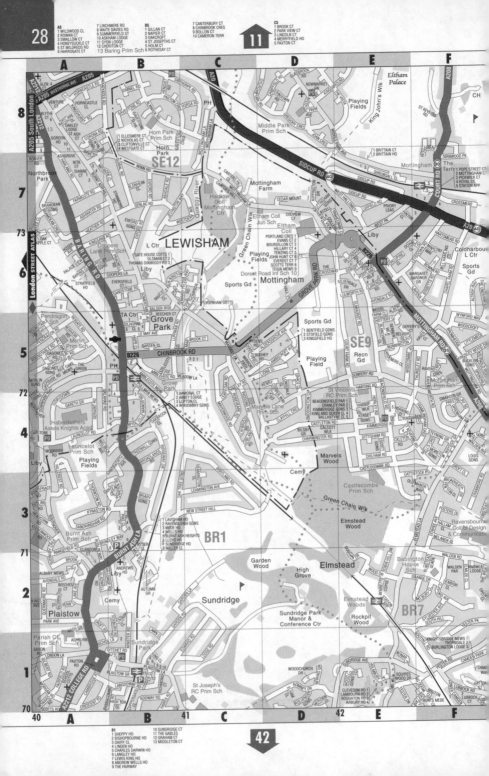

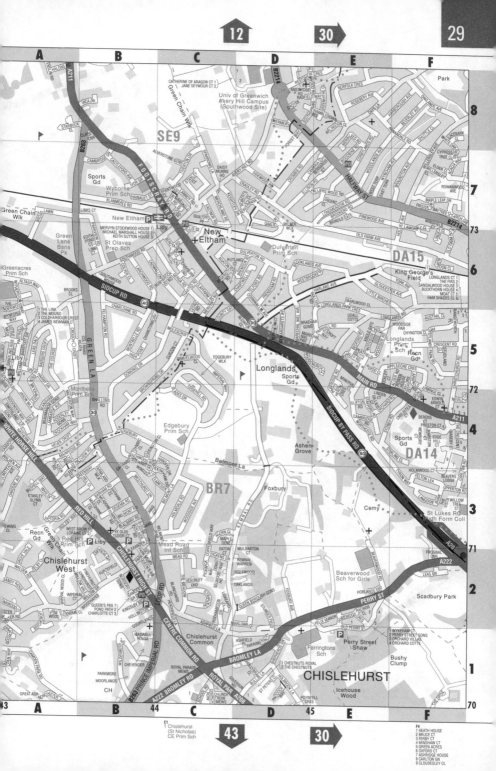

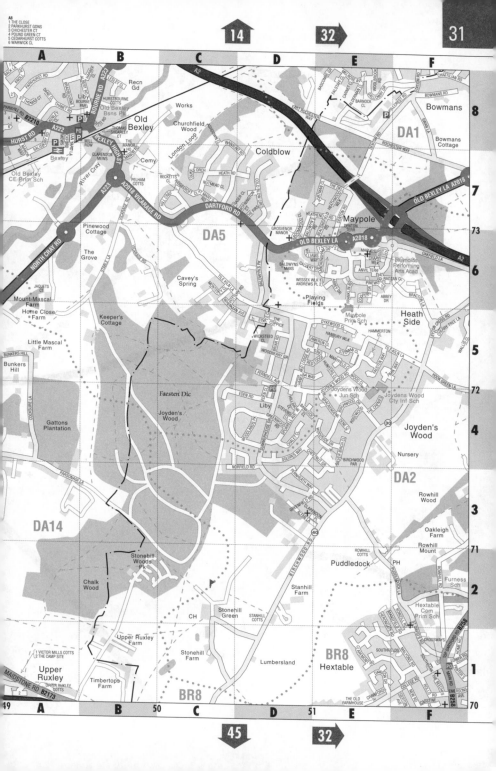

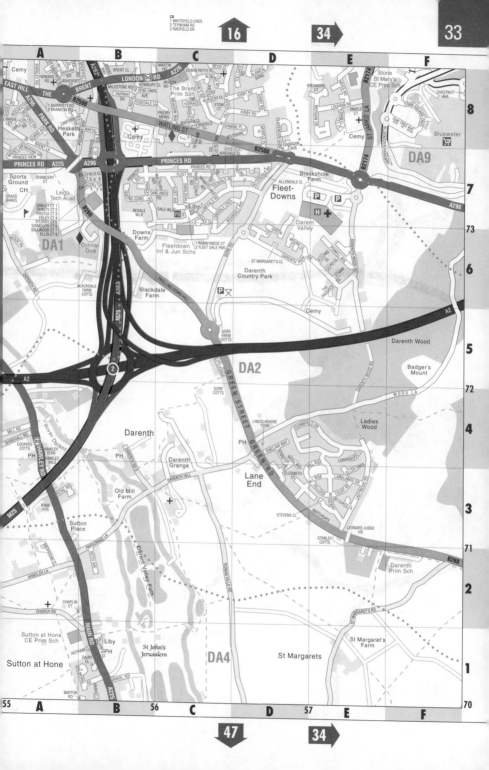

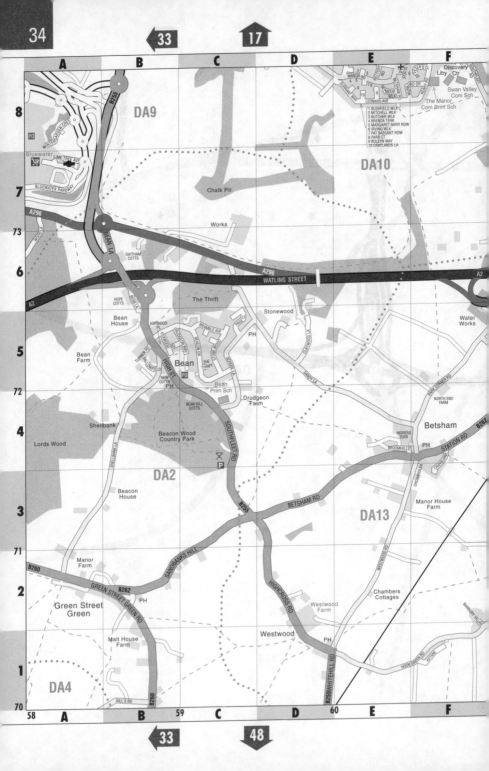

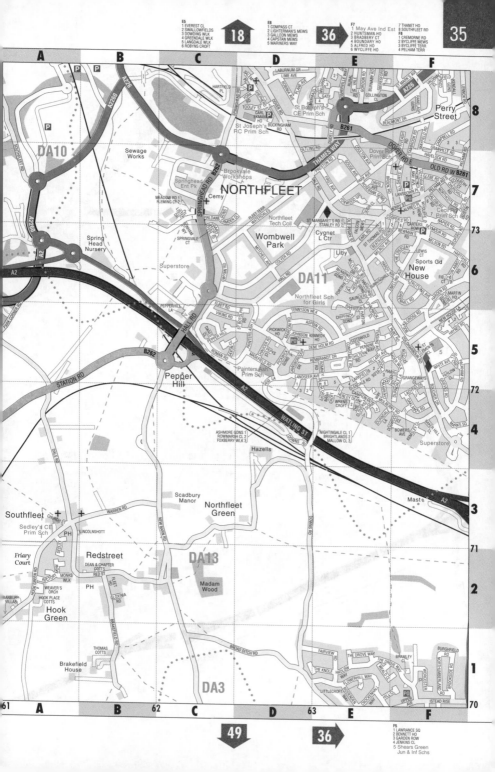

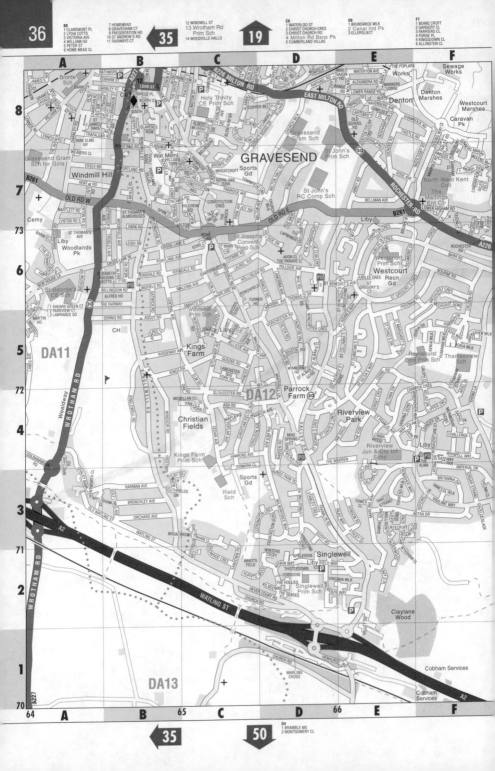

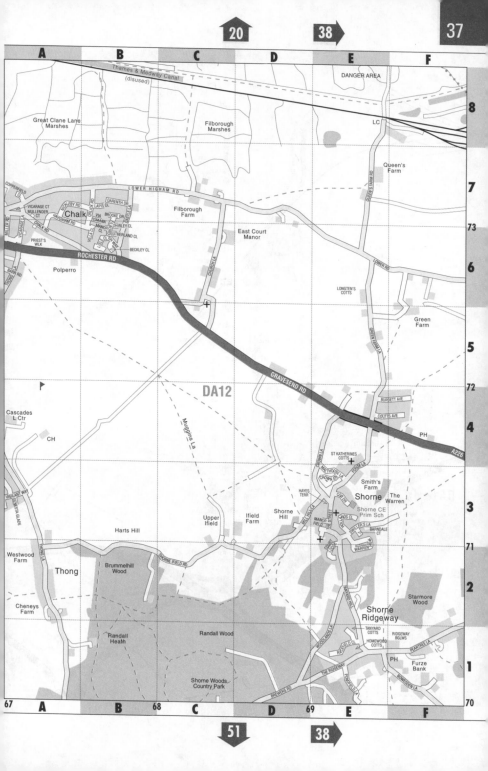

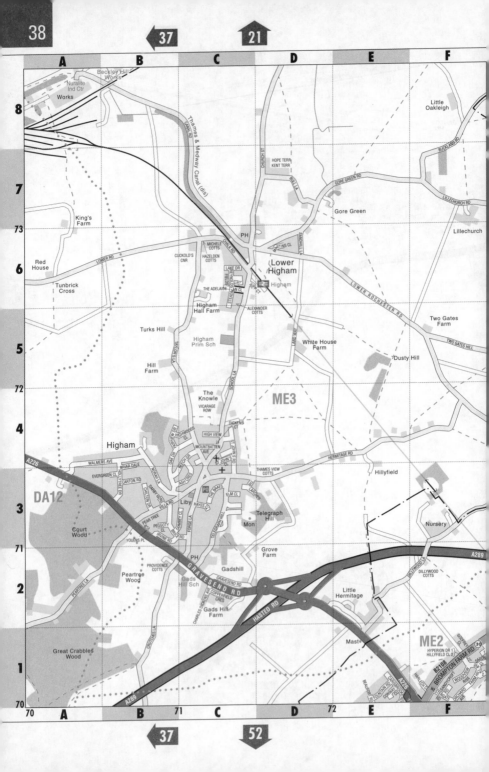

A B C D E F

8

Nuralite Ind Ctr
Works
Beckley Hill Works

Little Oakleigh

7

King's Farm

Thames & Medway Canal (dis)

Hope Terr
Kent Terr

Gore Green Rd

Gore Green

Lillechurch Rd

Buckland Rd

73

Lillechurch

PH

MICHELE COTTS

Red House

Lower Rd

CUCKOLD'S CNR

HAZELDEN COTTS

Gatlins Cl

6

Tunbrick Cross

THE ADELAIDE

LAKE DRI

Lower Higham

Higham

Lower Rochester Rd

Two Gates Farm

ELM CL

Higham Hall Farm

ALEXANDER COTTS

White House Farm

Dusty Hill

Two Gates Hill

5

Turks Hill

Higham Prim Sch

ME3

Hill Farm

72

The Knowle

VICARAGE ROW

4

HIGH VIEW

DICKENS CT

Higham

MOUNTBATTEN AVE

HERMITAGE RD

Hillyfield

WALMERS AVE

BRIAR DALE

THAMES VIEW COTTS

DA12

EVERGREEN CL

CARTON RD

Liby

THE BRAES

ELM CL

Nursery

3

Court Wood

PEAR TREE

DARBY GDNS

P.O.

HAYES CT

Mon

Telegraph Hill

A289

71

PEGGOTY

YOUENS PL

Grove Farm

DILLYWOOD COTTS

Peartree Wood

PROVIDENCE COTTS

PH

GRAVESEND RD

Gadshill

GADS HILL

COPPERFIELD CRES

Little Hermitage

2

PORTHILL LA

Gads Hill Sch

GRAVESEND RD

Gads Hill Farm

HASTED RD

Mast

ME2

HYPERION DR 1
HILLYFIELD CL 2

B2108

BROMPTON FARM RD

1

Great Crabbles Wood

A289

70

A B 71 C D 72 E F

39
23

A B C D E F

8

Depot

Deangate Ridge Sports Gd

Deangate Wood

Deangate

CH

A228

7

Tile Barn Farm

73

Chattenden Farm

Mill Farm

Mast

6

Sundown

PH

RATCLIFFE HIGHWAY

Stonebridge

ME3

Street Farm Cotts

Hoo St Werburgh

The Hundred of Hoo Sch

Hoo St Werburgh Prim Sch

Marlborough Ctr

Jennifer Ct

5

1 NURSERY GDNS
2 BUTT HAW CL

Broad Street

MAIN RD

ST WERBURGH

P
PO

Lib y

72

HAIG VILLAS

MAIN RD

A229

BROADWOOD

ARMYTAGE CL 1
EVEREST MEWS 2

BRANTA FIELDS

CHURCH FARM CL

ABBOTS COURT RD

WHITE HOUSE CL

4

SEARCHLIGHT HTS

Cockham Farm

Saxon Shore Way

Hoo Lodge

Arethusa Venture Ctr

ME2

Saxon Shore Way

Cockham Wood

Gull Down Plantation

Hoo Marina Park

Works

CARRIAGE LA

3

P

Lower Upnor

Hoo Marina

CYPRESS RD 1
GLOVER RD 2
MARINE DR

PIER RD

GALLEON WAY

71

Upnor Reach

River Medway

Pier

ME4

St Mary's Island CE Prim Sch

Finsborough Ness

ME3

Hoo Salt Marsh

2

EGRET CL 1
PARTRIDGE DR 2
MEADOWSWEET VW 3
ASTER DR 4
TEALOFT 5
EASTVIEW 6

7 TAPPAN DR
8 HENRIETTA CH
9 LITTLE VICTORY MOUNT

THE PINNACLES

Short Reach

ME7

1

Marina

St Mary's Island

Hoo Ness

HAVEN WAY 1
THE WHIMBRELS 2
WILLOWHERB CL 3
DEWBERRY CL 4

70

DOCK HEAD RD

76 A B 77 C D 78 E F

A B C D E F

8

7

73

6

5

72

4

3

71

2

1

70

Roper's Farm

White Hall Farm

Saxon Shore Way

ROPER'S STREET LA

STOKE RD

Beluncle Farm

BELUNCLE VILLAS

BETA RD

JETTY RD

MAIN RD

Kingsnorth Ind Est

Works

ROPER'S ST LA

STURDEE COTTS

STOKE RD

JACOB LA

ESHOCK RD

ME3

Kingsnorth

Abbots Court

Saxon Shore Way

Sewage Works

Mast

Power Station

Damhead Creek

Hoo Flats

Jetty

Long Reach

River Medway

Middle Creek

Pinup Reach

Darnet Ness

Darnet Fort

ME3

Bishop Saltings

ME3

South Yantlet Creek

Hoo Fort

Folly Point

ME7

ME7

Gillingham Reach

Nor Marsh

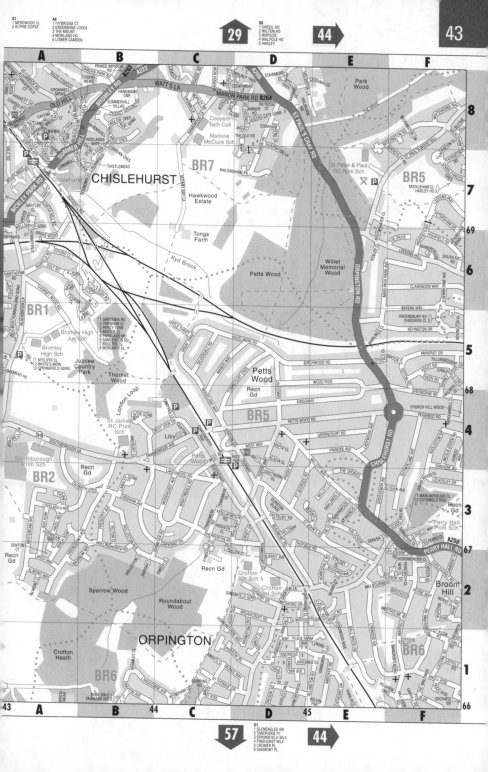

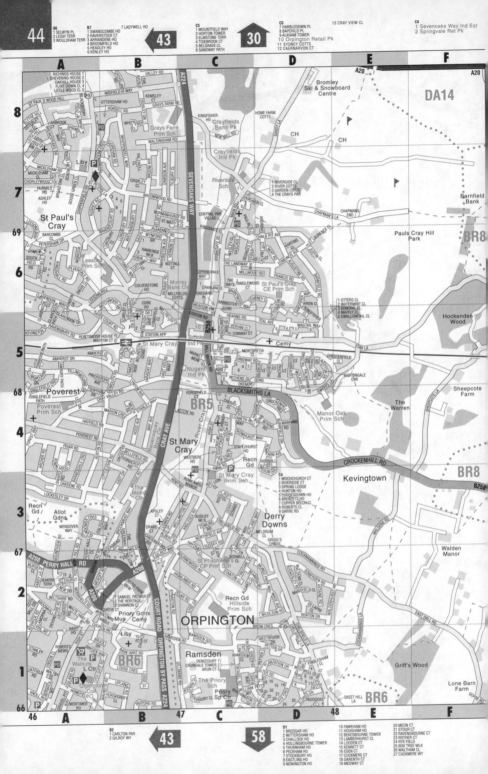

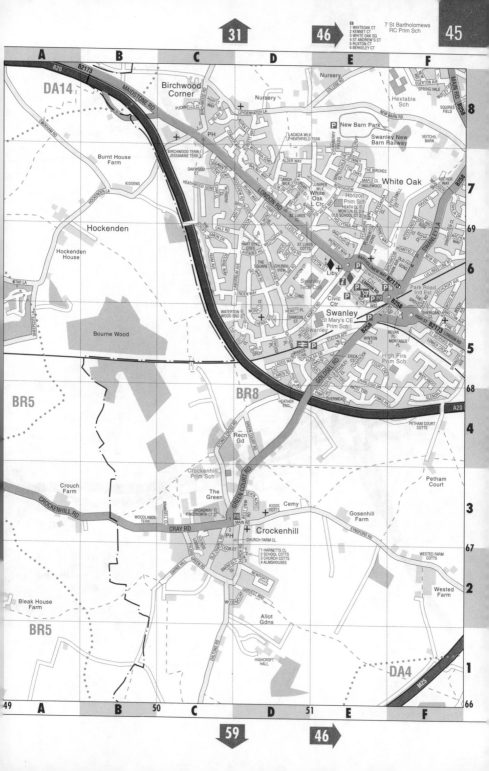

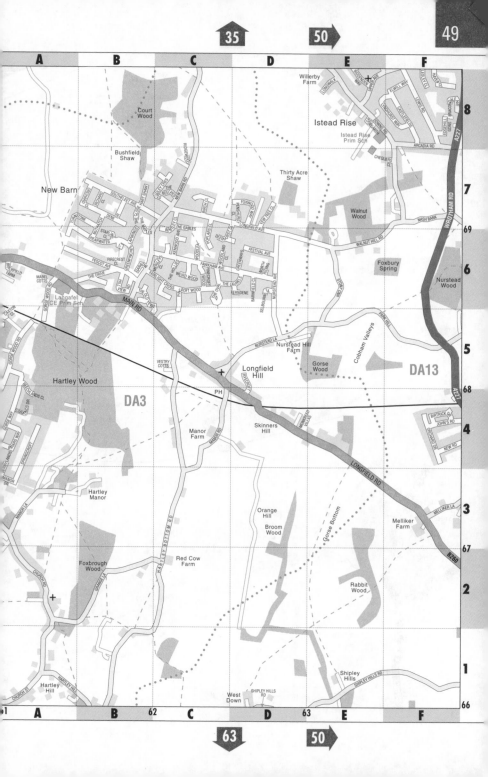

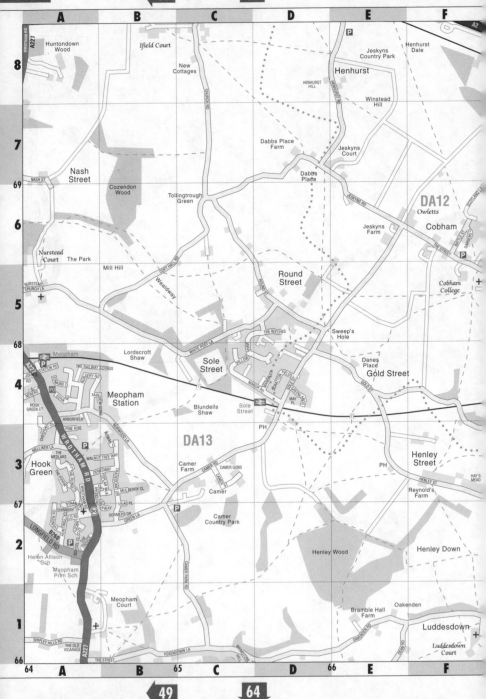

A B C D E F

8

Huntondown Wood

Ifield Court

New Cottages

Henhurst

Jeskyns Country Park

Henhurst Dale

HENHURST HILL

Winstead Hill

7

Nash Street

Cozendon Wood

Tollingtrough Green

Dabbs Place Farm

Jeskyns Court

69

NASH ST

Dabbs Place

DA12

Owletts

6

Nurstead Court

The Park

Mill Hill

Wealdway

Jeskyns Farm

Cobham

THE STREET

Round Street

Cobham College

5

NURSTEAD CHURCH LA

Sweep's Hole

68

Meopham

Lordscroft Shaw

THE BECHES

Danes Place

Gold Street

4

STATION RD

The Railway Sidings

Meopham Station

Sole Street

Blundells Shaw

Sole Street

Gold Street

Henley Street

HENLEY ST

HAY'S MEAD

3

Hook Green

THE MEDLARS

Walnut Tree Way

Camer Farm

CAMER RD

Camer Gdns

Camer

PH

Reynold's Farm

67

CHINNERY

Camer Country Park

2

Helen Allison Sch

Meopham Prm Sch

Henley Wood

Henley Down

1

Meopham Court

Bramble Hall Farm

Oakenden

Luddesdown

66

SHIPLEY MILLS RD

THE OLD VICARAGE

A227

THE STREET

FOXENDOWN LA

Luddesdown Court

64 A B 65 C D 66 E F

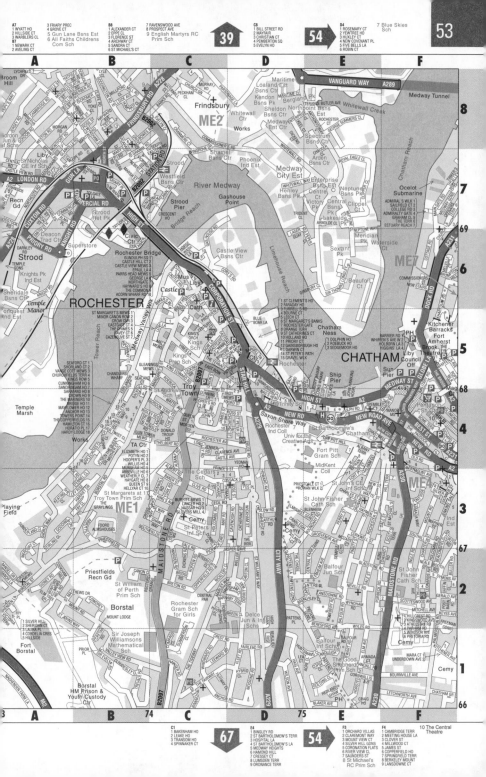

C7
1 AUGUSTA HO
2 ANNVERA HO
3 SUNDERLAND HO
4 LATIMER PL
5 HUNTERS CT
6 KING WILLIAM RD

7 FORSYTH CT

53

40

D6
1 Burnt Oak
Prim Sch

A3
1 OTWAY TERR
2 LEOPOLD RD
3 All SAINTS CE
   Prim Sch
4 New Road
   Prim Sch

A6
1 VICTORY MANOR
2 TEMERAIRE MANOR
3 BARFLEUR MANOR
4 MIDDLE ST
5 CAMPERDOWN MANOR
6 RIVER ST
7 DAWSON CT
8 MCCUDDEN ROW

9 PERIE ROW
10 PLEASANT ROW
11 HORNIM CL
12 MELVILLE CT
13 FLAXMANS CT
14 MANOR HO
15 ESMONDE HO
16 CONWAY HALL
17 THE CUT

53

B2
1 PORTLAND ST
2 LISTMAS RD
3 BRIGHT RD
4 COBDEN RD
5 SAILMAKERS CT
6 EVORG HO
7 CAULKERS HO
8 THE ENDEAVOUR FOYER

68

B3
1 SEYMOUR RD
2 HARE ST
3 SHORT ST
4 PICCADILLY APARTMENTS
5 WEALDEN CT
6 OCELOT CT
7 LEONARD RD
8 CONSTITUTION HILL

C6
1 PADSTOW MANOR
2 CAMBORNE MANOR
3 REDRUTH MANOR
4 PENRYN MANOR
5 AUSTELL MANOR
6 TINTAGEL MANOR
7 GRAND CT
8 DEANE CT
9 WILL ADAMS CT

10 CHATSWORTH RD
11 PHOENIX CT

12 Skinner Street Prim Sch

A B C D E F

8
7
69
6
5
68
4
3
67
2
66
1

River Medway
Gillingham Reach

Nor Marsh

Copperhouse Marshes

Ferol Peak

Cinque Port Marshes

DANES HILL

Horrid Hill

Walnut Tree Farm

Saxon Shore Way

B2004

Grange

Mill Hill

THE SPIERS

Sharp's Green

Visitor Ctr

ME7

Lower Twydall

LOWER RAINHAM RD

Riverside Country Park

Mariners Farm

Bloors Wharf

East Kent STREET ATLAS

Allot Gdns

Grace Manor

FITZGILBERT

1 BUTTERMERE CL
2 PENRITH CT
3 KESWICK CT
4 BRAITHWAITE CT

Cemy

Sports Fields

Little London Farm

MANOR CT

LITTLE YORK MEWS

1 BISHOPBOURNE GN
2 HEADCORN RD
3 DENTON GN

Pump Farm

PH

Bloors Place

WEST MOTNEY WAY

B2004

ITD WAY

Beechings Way Ind Ctr

LITTLEBURNE AVE

Lower Rainham

Featherby Inf Sch
Featherby Jun Sch

Liby

1 FORDWICH GN
2 BONNINGTON GN
3 SELLINGE GN

BEECHINGS WAY

WOOTTON VIEW

Twydall

Twydall Jun Sch
Twydall Inf Sch
PIKEFIELDS
WOODCHURCH RD

ABSALOM

Rainham Mark Gram Sch

Thames View Inf Sch

Thames View Jun Sch

THE WILLOWS

Lower Rainham

St Thomas of Canterbury RC Prim Sch

1 TATSFIELD CL
2 KESTON CT
3 Danecourt Com Sch

SOVEREIGN BLVD

NORFOLK CL

ME8

Cozenton Park

CHILTON

Rainham

The Ice Bowl

SHERMAN CL

A2

Superstore

LONDON RD

Spalshes L Ctr

Liby

HIGH ST A2

STATION RD

B2004

Works

BOSTON GDNS

Playing Fields

A B C D E F
80 81

F1
1 CREVEQUER CHAMBERS
2 Rainham Sh Ctr
3 GRESHAM CL
4 HARRISON CT
5 MAPLINS CL
6 SIGNAL CT
7 SUFFOLK CT

London Street Atlas

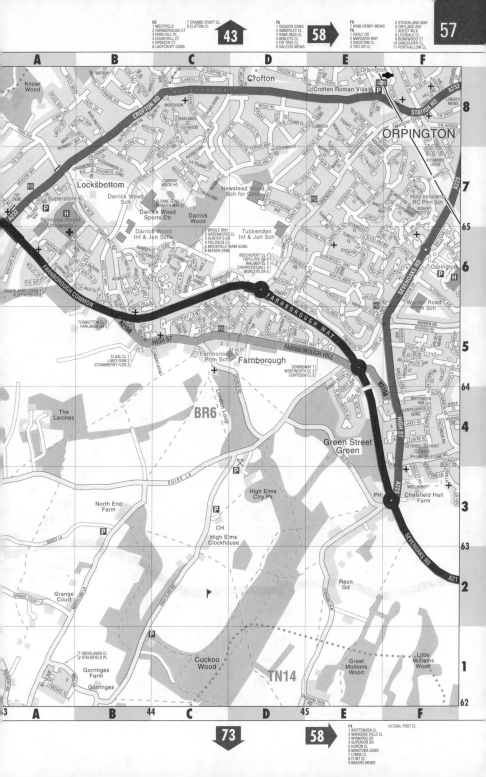

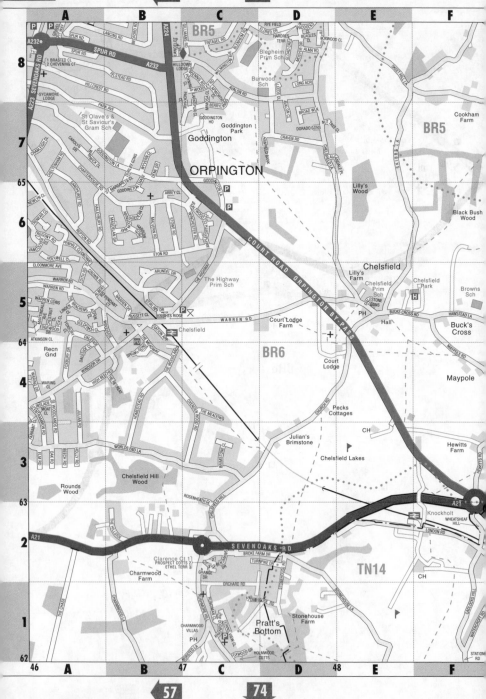

59
46

	A	B	C	D	E	F

8

Hulberry

Eagle Heights
Wildlife Park

Hulberry
Farm

LULLINGSTONE LA

CRACKHALL LA

SPARPENNELL LA

Anthony Roper
Prim Sch

Eynsford
Castle

HIGH ST

A225

TOWER CROFT

PRIORY FIELDS

ALTON
COTTS

FERN BANK

Home
Farm

RIVERSIDE

Recn
Gd

P

PH

WILLOW
TERR

ELIZABETH
COTTS
FOUNTAIN

PARSONAGE
BANK

KNIGHT
FIELD

Eynsford

MALT SHOVEL
COTTS

7

HILLCROFT

WALNUT CL

STATION RD

CHURCH

POLLYHAUGH

Pollyhaugh
Farm

65

LULLINGSTONE
ROMAN VILLA
(rems of)

P

Newbarn
Farm

ST MARTIN'S DR

Eynsford

EYNSFORD RISE

6

Lullingstone Park
Farm

Lullingstone Park

BOWER LA

5

*Lullingstone
Castle*

Darent Valley Path

River Darent

P

Robsacks

Chalkhurst

DA4

Chalkhurst
Wood

Park
House
Farm

PARK HOUSE
COTTS

Park
House

64

Lullingstone Pk
Visitor Ctr

P

CASTLE RD

Lower Austin
Lodge Farm

UPPER AUSTIN LODGE RD

Hartnips
Wood

4

REDMANS LA

Castle
Farm

The
Birches

3

UPPER AUSTIN
LODGE FARM
COTTS

63

CASTLE FARM RD

Upper Austin
Lodge

CH

2

Rifle
Range

Preston Hill
Plantation

1

Preston
Farm

TN14

DANGER
AREA

A225

Round
Hill

TN15

Lower
Wood

62

52	A		53	C		54	E		F

59
76

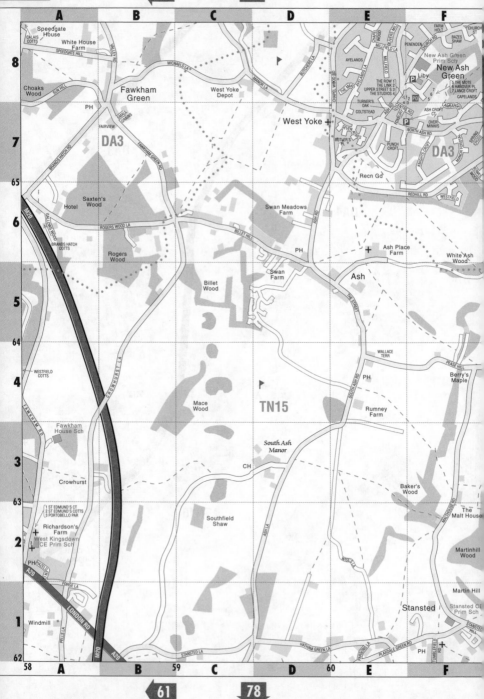

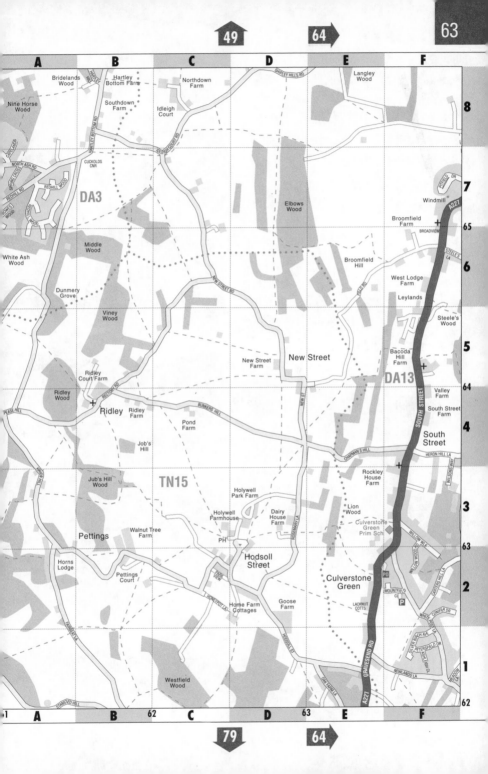

A · B · C · D · E · F

8

Meopham Sch
L Ctr
Liby
Meophum
Sch
LOMER
FARM
MEADFIELD RD
ARNOLD AVE
GLENHEIM CL
WARWICK
WROTHAM RD
A227
OAKMEAD
GREENVILLE RD

Meopham

Foxendown

The
Larches

Brimstone
Wood

Dene
Manor

Rid Ridge

7

MILLERS WAY
KENT
TERR
A221
CRICKET DRS DR

WELLINGTON
COTTS

Dunstan
Wood

Wood Hill
Farm

65

Meopham
Green

STEELE LA

Dilmer
Wood

6

WHITEPOST LA

Waares Meadow
Farm

HORN'S OAK RD

Nutfield
Farm

Merry
Hill

Purvil
Wood

Strawberry
Hill

Rochester
Forest

Coomb Hill
Farm

5

David
Street

Priestwood

CHANDLER'S HILL

Priestwood
Green

DEAN LA

PLUG LA

Lenniker
Wood

Ham
Farm

Great Buckland
Farm

LOCKYERS HILL

64

Haddocks
Wood

PRIESTWOOD RD

Eastfield
Farm

DA13

LUCAS RD

Luxon Wood

Great
Buckland

4

HERON HILL LA

Dean
Mead

Lie
Wood

+

3

Beechen
Wood

LUCKS LA

SCHOOL LA

Harvel House
Farm

ST PRIMUS LA
HORNFIELD
COTTS
PH
HARVEL ST
PH
Harvel
Upper
Harvel

Harvel Hill
Farm

Little Delmar
Farm

Wealdway

Boughurst Street
Farm

Holly
Hill

63

2

Ridge
Wood

HARVEL LA

LETWOOD RD

1

MEADOW LA
BEECHWOOD DR
BEECHWOOD RD

Sparrowhaugh
Farm

HIGHVIEW

HARVEL RD

Swanswood
Farm

Poundgate

Wealdway

Daniel
Chambers

WHITE HORSE RD

North
Downs Way

62

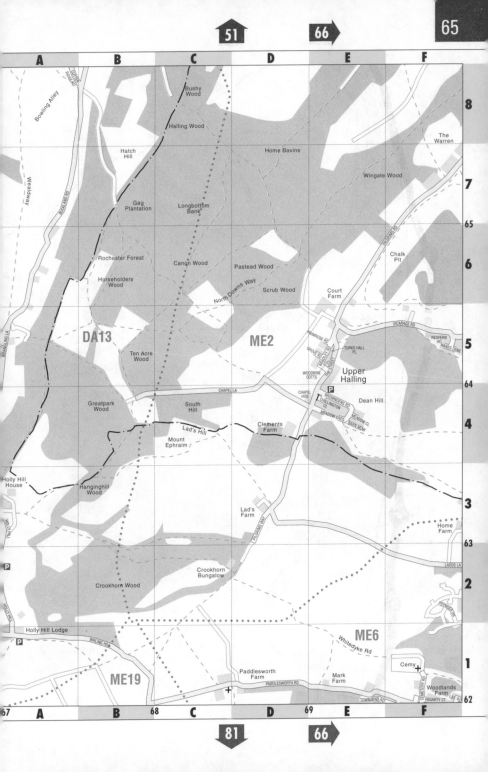

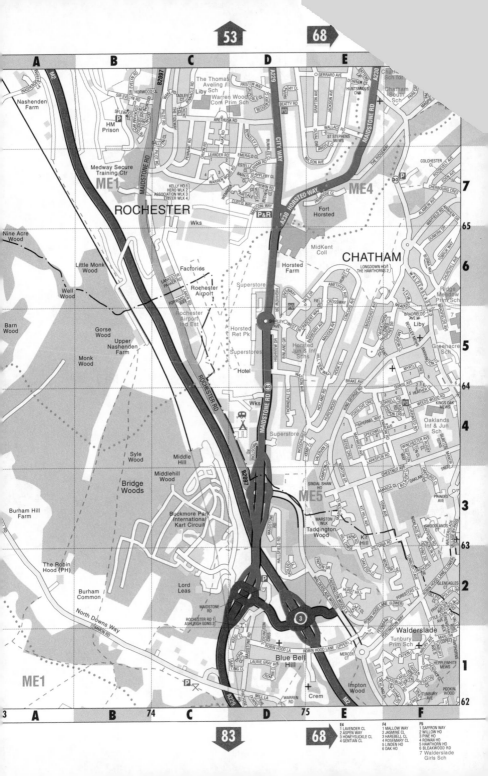

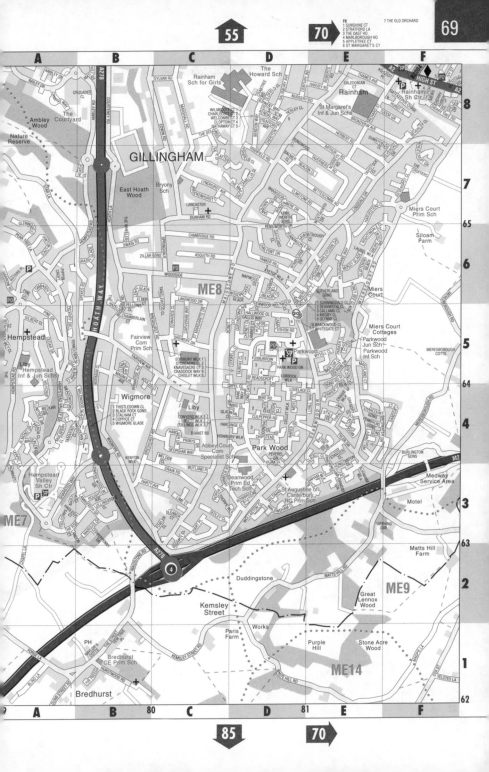

East Kent STREET ATLAS

A   B   C   D   E   F

8

Church View Farm
Bog Farm
Wardwell Wood
Oak Hill Farm

Cemy
Newington Ent Ctr
Mill Hill
Rook Wood
Rook Lodge

7

Newington Prim Sch
1 ST MARY'S PL
2 EDWINS PL
3 ST MARK'S CL
4 ST STEPHEN'S CU
5 ST MATTHEW'S CL
6 ST MARTINS CL
VICARAGE CT
DENHAM RD
WESTWOOD WLK
Newington

Cold Harbour

65

LONDON RD
LONDON RD
PO
P

HIGH ST
Pond Farm
Newington
Keycol Hill

6

THE TRACES
1 RED ROBIN COTTS
2 CHERRY HILL CT
3 ALBION PL
Ellen's PL
BOYCES HILL
Keycol
ROOK LA

PEAR TREE WLK
BRAMLEY CL
Newington Manor
KEYCOL HILL
A2 Sittingbourne
A2

OLD MAIDSTONE RD

5

Cranbrook Wood
A249
A249 Sheerness

PH

Gwelo Farm
Standard Hill
ME9
CHESTNUT ST

64

Chesley Farm
WORMDALE RD
Wormdale Farm
Cold Store
Chestnut Street
Borden CE Prim Sch

East Kent STREET ATLAS

4

Chesley
Rock Meadows
Sunnyhill
LIMEPITS CROSS

3

Thrognall Farm
CH
DANAWAY COTTS
Danaway
MASTINFIELD GDNS
Munsgore Farm

63

Eyehorn Farm
Pond Farm

2

WOODGATE LA
Woodgate Farm
Vinson Farm
Oad Street
DUVARD'S

1

Church Wood
A249
Stockbury Valley
Bowl Reed
M2
Plough and Harrow (PH)

62

A   B   C   D   E   F
86   87

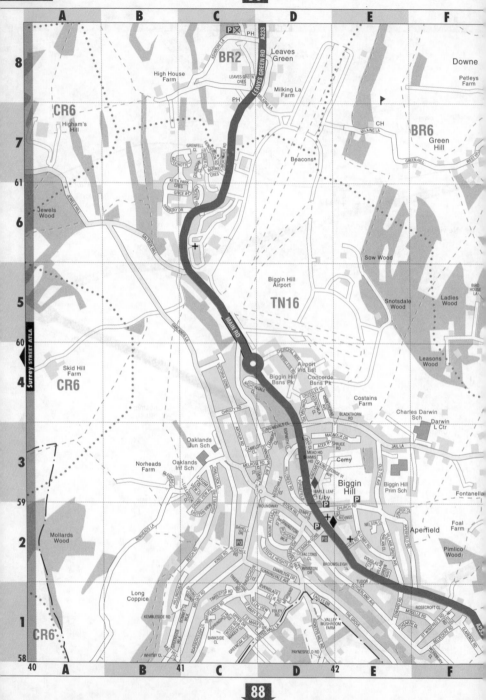

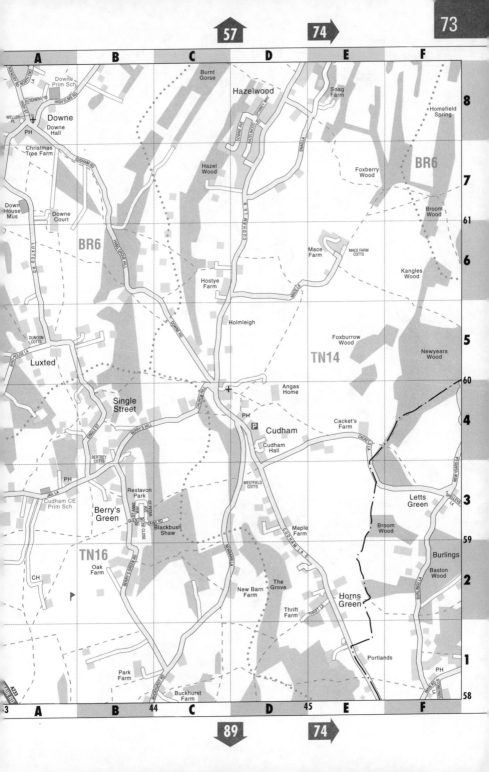

8

7

61

6

5

60

4

3

59

2

1

58

A 46 B 47 C D 48 E F

THE CHASE

Norsted Manor Farm

High Wood

Newlands Wood

NEW HILL LA

Jockey's Wood

Shelleys

SHELLEYS LA

The Mount

BRASTED LA

Charm Wood

CHURCHFIELD LA

NORSTED LA

Fairtrough Farm

BR6

Lower Brooms Wood

The Washneys

WASHNEYS RD

Hayman's Wood

PENDRIS LA

Court Lodge

Knockholt

St Katharines Knockholt CE Prim Sch

PH

Mast

LAMBARDES CL

Pratts Bottom Prim Sch

HOOKWOOD COTTS

Hook Wood

FORT HILL

RUSHMORE HILL

BYRS HILL

Rushmore Hill Farm

Perry Wood

SINGLE'S CROSS LA

Piece Wood

Blueberry Farm

BLUEBERRY LA

MAIN RD

Chine Farm

CHINE FARM PL

Ash Platt

KNOCKHOLT LA

Pratt's Grove

Birthday Wood

HOOKWOOD RD

FOX & HOUNDS HILL

Nurseries

SINGLE'S CROSS

TN14

Knockholt Pound

POUND LA

Nurseries

ELMTREE COTTS

P

PH

Mast

The Grange

North Downs Way

Sand Banks

Park Wood

Sundridge Hill Farm

SANDHILL

TIMBERDELL LA

CHURCH RD

STERLING AV

The Old Rectory

Village House

Halstead Prim Sch

SOUTHGATE RD

PARKSIDE

KNOCKHOLT RD

Halstead

Warren Court Farm

BEALTREE LA

Park Farm

HUNTERS WLK

HALSTEAD LA

Homevale Cotts

WAYLANDS CL

+ PH

JUBILEE TERR

HARROW RD

CRAYFIELDS LA

Old London Rd

HAMPTON COTTS

Park House

YEW TREE COTTS

SHOREHAM LA

PH

PO

THE MEADOWS

KILNWOOD

Curry Farm

BIRCHWOOD DR

Lees Wood

COACH DR

Minny Wood

CORNFIELD LA

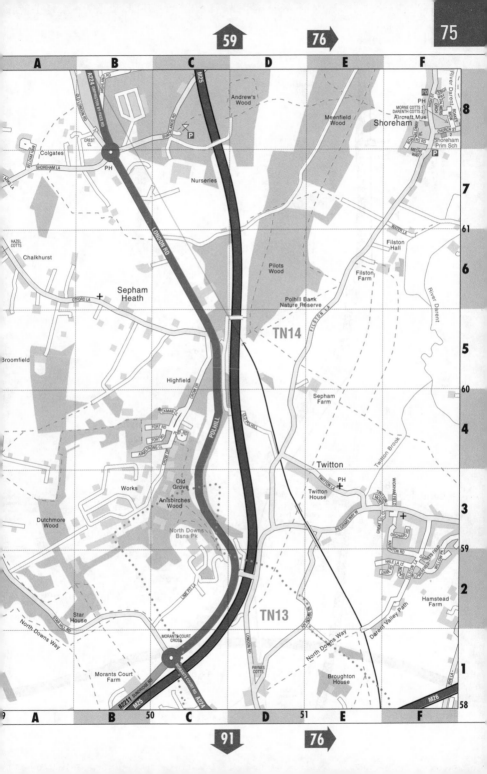

A B C D E F

River Darent
PO
PH
MORNE COTTS 1
DARENTH COTTS 2
Aircraft Mus
Shoreham
CHURCH ST
Shoreham
Prim Sch
MISC WAY 2
P

Andrew's
Wood

Meenfield
Wood

Nurseries

WATER LA

Filston
Hall

HAZEL
COTTS
Chalkhurst

Sepham
Heath

Pilots
Wood

Filston
Farm

FILSTON LA

Polhill Bank
Nature Reserve

River Darent

TN14

Broomfield

Highfield

Sepham
Farm

ECKMAN CL
FORT RD
FORT
ARMSTRONG CL

POLHILL

OLD POLHILL

Twitton Brook

Twitton

Works

Old
Grove

Antsbirches
Wood

LIME PIT LA

North Downs
Bsns Pk

TWITTON LA

PH
Twitton
House

WICKHAMFIELD

PILGRIMS WAY W

Dutchmore
Wood

ORCHARD

KIPPINGTON RD

Hamstead
Farm

North Downs Way

Star
House

MORANTS COURT
CROSS

Morants Court
Farm

LONDON RD

PAYNES
COTTS

North Downs Way

Darent Valley Path

Broughton
House

B2211 BUNGHOUSE RD

M25

A224

M26

London Rd

A224 ORPINGTON BY-PASS RD

OLD LONDON RD

SHOREHAM LA

CROWN DR

CHILSA LA

OTFORD LA

SHORLANDS RD

M25

Colgates

CREST CL

PH

8
7
61
6
5
60
4
3
59
2
1
58

75
60

A B C D E F

DA4

8

CHAPEL ALLEY COTTS
CHURCH COTTS
CHURCH ST
SHOREHAM RD
Shoreham
STATION RD
CH

Dunstall Priory

Dunstall Woods

Austin Spring

Romney Street Farm

7

River Darent

White Hill

JACKEDEN LA

Dunstall Farm

Rose Cottage Farm

MAGPIE BOTTOM

61

Home Farm

Whitehill Farm

Warren Farm

Doctor's Wood

Eastdown

Darent Valley Path

6

Sevenacre Stubs

Highfield

5

Lower Barn

60

TN14

Mast

Greenhill Wood

Mount Farm

Paine's Farm

Great Wood

TN15

GREENHILL RD

HILLYDEAL RD

BIRCHIN CROSS RD

4

Hillydeal Wood

North Downs Way

Otford Mount

St Michaels Sch

Rowdow Wood

Shore. Hill

COOMBE RD

SHOREHAM RD

Park Farm

Russell House Sch

STATION RD

Otford

PILGRIMS WAY E

Kemsing Down Nature Reserve

3

Otford

PH
Liby
HIGH ST
Otford Prim Sch
COLETS ORCH
STATION PPP

Bishop's Palace (remains of)

PILGRIMS WAY

CHALKWAYS

SHOREHILL CT

COPPERFIEL ORCH

59

SHINECROFT

BUBBLESTONE RD

THE BUTTS

River Darent

THE PARADE 1
BARCLAY FIELD 2

DYNES RD

NORMAN

EDGAR RD

NIGHTINGALE RD

COPPERFIELDS CL

WEST END

2

Oxenhill Shaw

Liby

Kemsing

1

M26

OTFORD RD

A225

Ladds House

Childsbridge House

M2

58

52 A 53 B C 54 D E F

75
92

A B C D E F

8

HOLLYWOOD LA

Pells Farm

Hollands Farm

TUMBLEFIELD EST

PELL LA

PLAXDALE GREEN RD

Cox's Wood

7

Gravelpit Wood

Peckham Wood

Plaxdale Green Farm

Stansted Lodge Farm

TUMBLEFIELD RD

BENNETT LA

PELL LA

M20

A20

61

ST CLERE HILL RD

Thrift Wood

WROTHAM HILL RD

6

KNOCK MILL LA

Terry's Lodge Farm

TERRY'S LODGE RD

LONDON RD

PH

Hotel

LABOUR-IN-VAIN RD

Labour-in-vain

WT Sta

Tower Ind Est

5

Birches Wood

Mast

Cooper's Wood

Long Wood

OLD COACH RD

Butts Hill Wood

60

OLD TERRY'S LODGE RD

Exedown

2

TN15

A20

M20

4

Chalk Pit Wood

EXEDOWN RD

White Hill

North Downs Way

HOWLANDS CT 8

HOWLANDS 2

OLD LONDON RD

PILGRIMS WAY

Pilgrims Way

Blacksole Field

BATTLE RISE

WEST ST

WOODWORTH RD

COURT MDW

COURTYARD GDNS

OTFORDS HL

7

COURT MDW

3

KEMSING RD

New House Farm

WEST ST

RANGID HILL WAY

BABCOCK

6

5

Wrotham

59

FEN POND RD

2

Yaldham Manor

Martin Spring Wood

M26

1

M26

Westlands Farm

Potters Mede

58

Hook Wood

TELSTON MDW

A B 59 C D 60 E F

F3
1 THORNDYKE WAY
2 THOMAS WYATT WAY
3 BLACKSOLE RD
4 NEW WLK
5 RIGGS WAY
6 MOUNTAIN CL
7 St George's CE
  Prim Sch

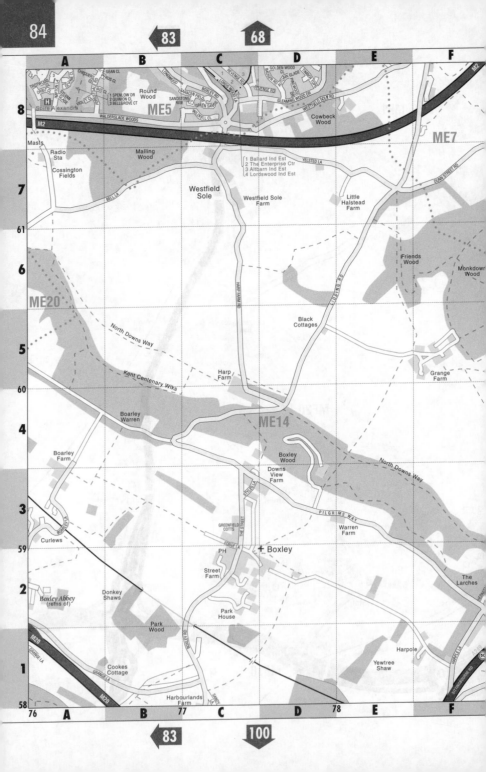

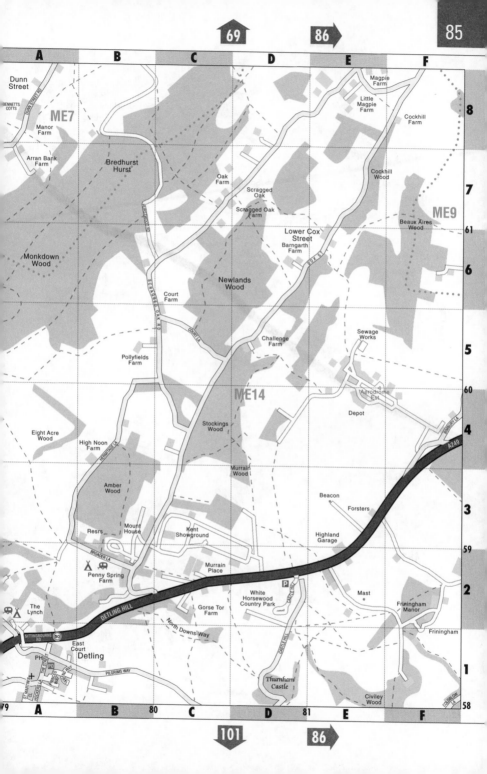

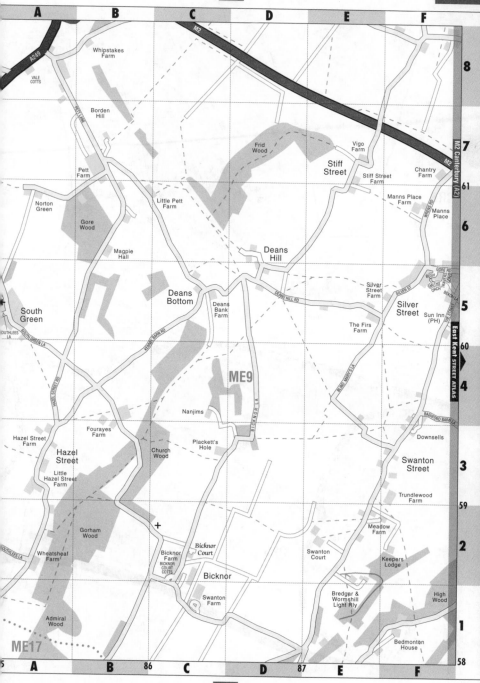

A   B   C   D   E   F

8

M2

A249

VALE
COTTS

Whipstakes
Farm

Borden
Hill

7

PETT LANE

Frid
Wood

Vigo
Farm

Stiff
Street

Stiff Street
Farm

Chantry
Farm

M2 Canterbury (A2)

M2

Pett
Farm

61

Little Pett
Farm

Manns Place
Farm

WEENS RD

Manns
Place

Norton
Green

Gore
Wood

6

Magpie
Hall

Deans
Hill

GORE RD

BUSH
TRAPS CL

SMITHS
ORCH

BIXON LA

Deans
Bottom

Deans
Bank
Farm

DEANS HILL RD

Silver
Street
Farm

SILVER ST

Silver
Street

South
Green

BOURNE BARN RD

ME9

The Firs
Farm

Sun Inn
(PH)

East Kent STREET ATLAS

5

OUTHLEES
LA

SOUTH GREEN LA

60

HAZEL STREET RD

Nanjims

BICKNOR LA

BLIND MARY LA

4

Fourayes
Farm

Plackett's
Hole

BADMOND BARN LA

Downsells

Hazel Street
Farm

Church
Wood

Swanton
Street

3

Hazel
Street

Little
Hazel Street
Farm

Trundlewood
Farm

59

Gorham
Wood

Meadow
Farm

2

OUTHLEES LA

Wheatsheaf
Farm

Bicknor
Farm

Bicknor
Court

BICKNOR
COURT
COTTS

Swanton
Court

Keepers
Lodge

Bicknor

Swanton
Farm

Bredgar &
Wormshill
Light Rly

High
Wood

1

Admiral
Wood

ME17

Bedmonten
House

58

5   A   B   86   C   D   87   E   F

A B C D E F

8

PH
South Street
Withins Wood
Shellem Wood
Cudham Frith
Scott's Lodge
TN14

A233
MAIN RD

7

Southwood
Buckhurst
Bombers Farm
Cudham Grange
Joeland's Wood

57

GRAYS RD
SILVERSTED LA

6

Tor Croft
PH
Hawley's Corner
Gray's Farm
North Downs Way
Hogtrough Hill

WESTERHAM HILL

Little Betsom's Farm
Pilgrim House

5

Betsom's Hill
THE AVENUE

56

Hill Park
PILGRIMS' WAY
Betsons Farm
TN16
Holywell Shaw

4

Gaysham Farm
Force Green
FORCE GREEN FARM COTTS
M25

3

Hartley Wood
LONDON RD
BEGGARS LA
Charmans Farm

55

Westerham Wood
CROYDON RD
A25
A233

2

Churchill CE Prim Sch
Court Lodge
Churchill Bsns Ctr

Green Croft
Westerham
P
P
Quebec Ho
Dunsdale House
BRASTED RD
The Granary
Valence Sch

1

Squerryes Sand Pit
A25
QUEBEC SQ

54

A B C D E F

10 QUEBEC SQ

D1
1 HORTONS WAY
2 MARKET WAY
3 MORETON ALMHOUSES
4 AUSTIN CT
5 ST MARY'S CT
6 DUNCANS COTTS
7 FULLERS HILL
8 WINTERTON CT
9 QUEBEC COTTS

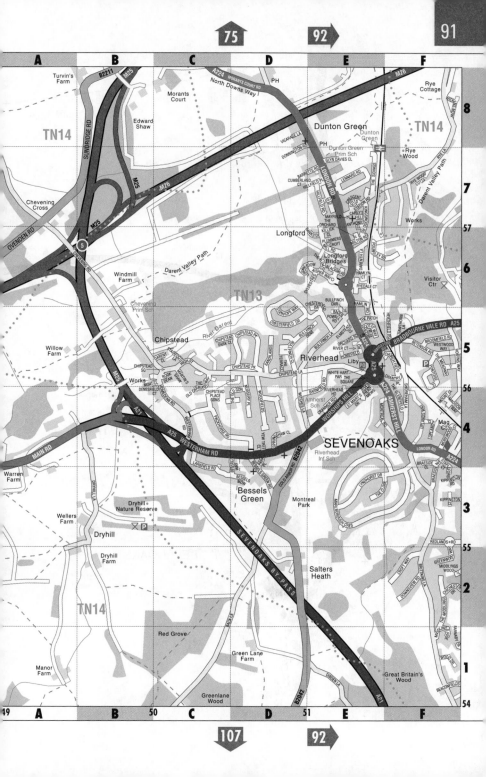

← 91
76 ↑

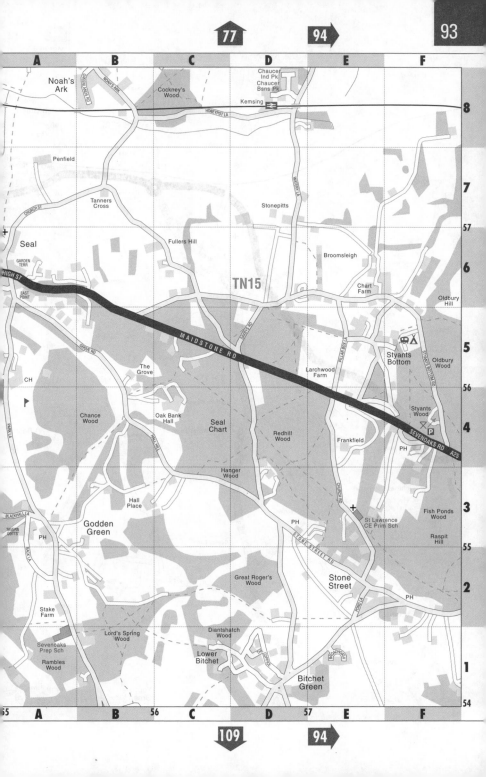

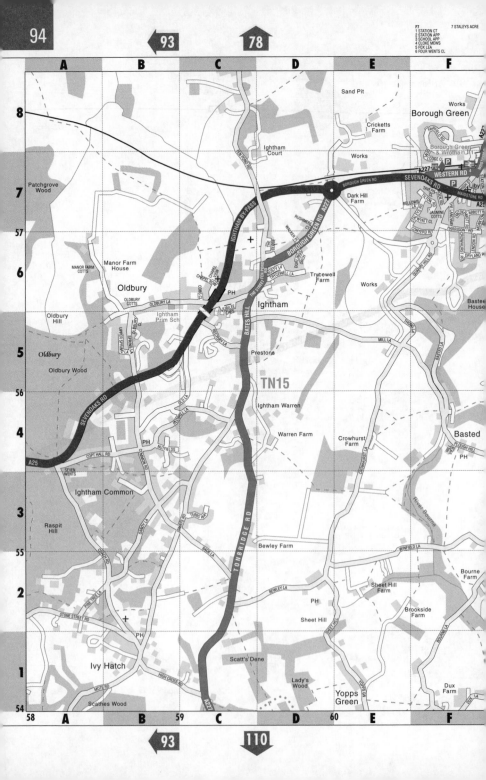

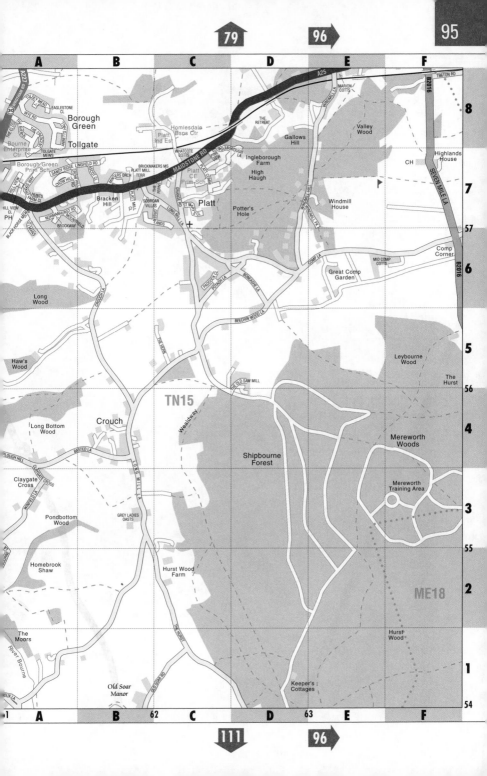

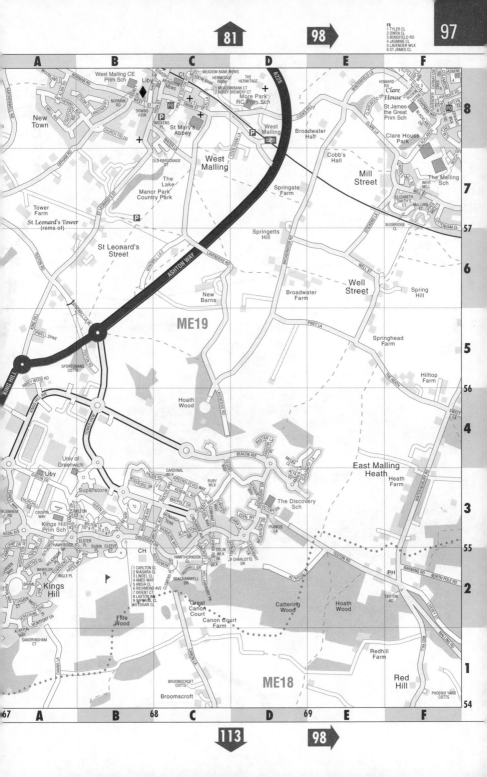

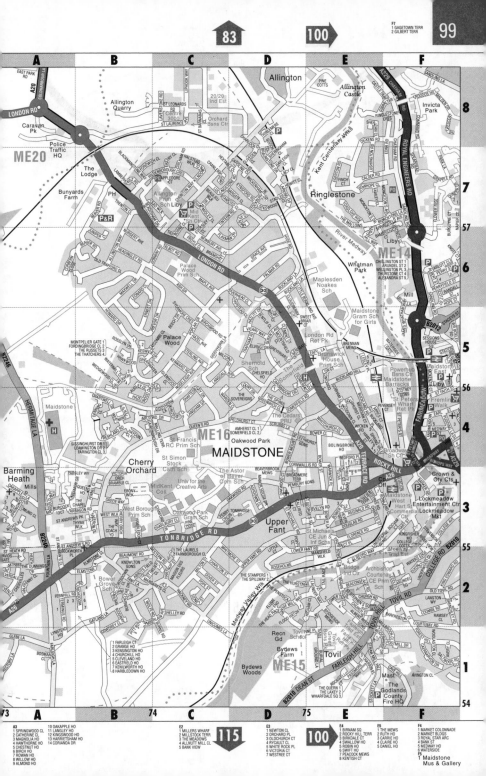

A3
1 SPRINGWOOD CL
2 CATHERINE CL
3 MAGNOLIA HO
4 HAWTHORNE HO
5 CHESTNUT HO
6 BIRCH HO
7 ROWAN HO
8 WILLOW HO
9 ALMOND HO
10 OAKAPPLE HO
11 LANGLEY HO
12 KINGSWOOD HO
13 HARRIETSHAM HO
14 CORIANDA DR

E2
1 MILLERS WHARF
2 ORCHARD PL
3 THE MEADOWS
4 ALLNUTT MILL CL
5 BANK VIEW

115

E3
1 NEWTON CL
2 ORCHARD PL
3 OLDCHURCH CT
4 RYCAULT CL
5 WHITE ROCK PL
6 VICTORIA CT
7 WESTREE CT

100

E4
1 BIRNAM SQ
2 ROCKY HILL TERR
3 BIRKDALE CT
4 SWALLOW HO
5 ROBIN HO
6 SWIFT HO
7 PEACOCK MEWS
8 KENTISH CT

E5
1 THE MEWS
2 RUTH HO
3 CARRIE HO
4 CLAIRE HO
5 DANIEL HO

F4
1 MARKET COLONNADE
2 MARKET BLDGS
3 ROYAL STAR ARC
4 BANK ST
5 MEDWAY HO
6 WATERSIDE

F5
1 Maidstone
Mus & Gallery

A5
1 MANDEVILLE CT
2 GRUNDALE
3 WALMER CT
4 PRIORY GATE
5 STARNES CT
6 KILBURN HO
7 LADBROOKE HO
8 LAMBARD HO
9 WINCHESTER PL
10 LOWER BOXLEY RD

99

A6
1 TELFORD HO
2 WALSHAW HO
3 WALSINGHAM HO

84

A7
1 ADEN TERR
2 BARBADOS TERR
3 CANADA HO
4 NORWAY TERR
5 MALTA TERR
6 LIBYA TERR
7 KENYA TERR
8 HONDURAS TERR

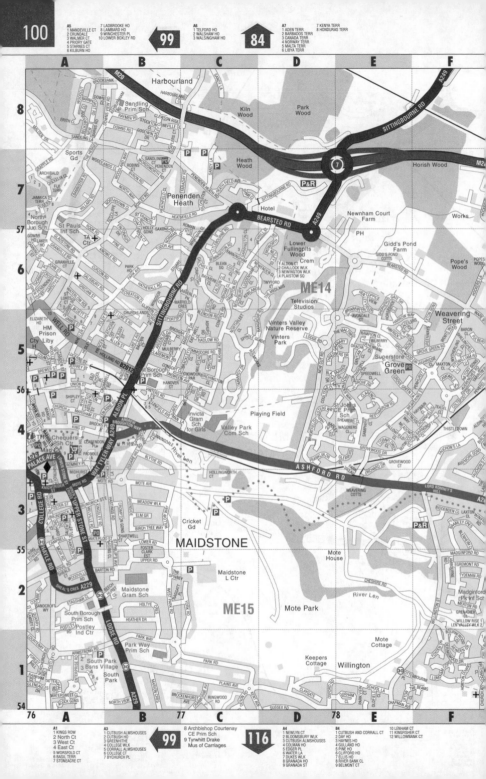

A1
1 KINGS ROW
2 NORTH CT
3 WEST CT
4 EAST CT
5 WORSFOLD CT
6 BASIL TERR
7 STONEACRE CT

A3
1 CUTBUSH ALMSHOUSES
2 CUTBUSH HO
3 GREENHITHE
4 COLLEGE WLK
5 CORRALL ALMSHOUSES
6 COLLEGE CT
7 BYCHURCH PL

99

8 Archbishop Courtenay
CE Prim Sch
9 Tyrwhitt Drake
Mus of Carriages

116

A4
1 NEWLYN CT
2 BLOOMSBURY WLK
3 CUTBUSH ALMSHOUSES
4 COLMAN HO
5 EDGER PL
6 WATER LA
7 DUKES WLK
8 GRANADA HO
9 GRANADA ST

B4
1 CUTBUSH AND CORRALL CT
2 DAY HO
3 HAYNES HO
4 GULLAND HO
5 PINE HO
6 CLIFFORD HO
7 ELLIS HO
8 RIVER BANK CL
9 BELMONT CT

10 LENHAM CT
11 KINGFISHER CT
12 WILLOWBANK CT

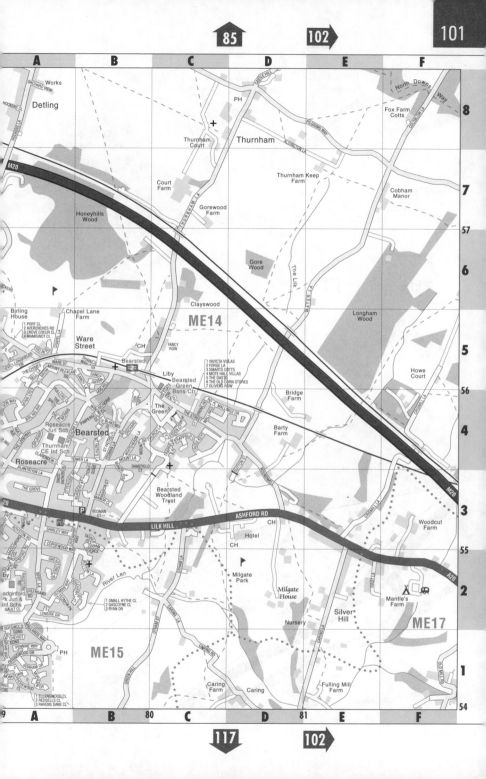

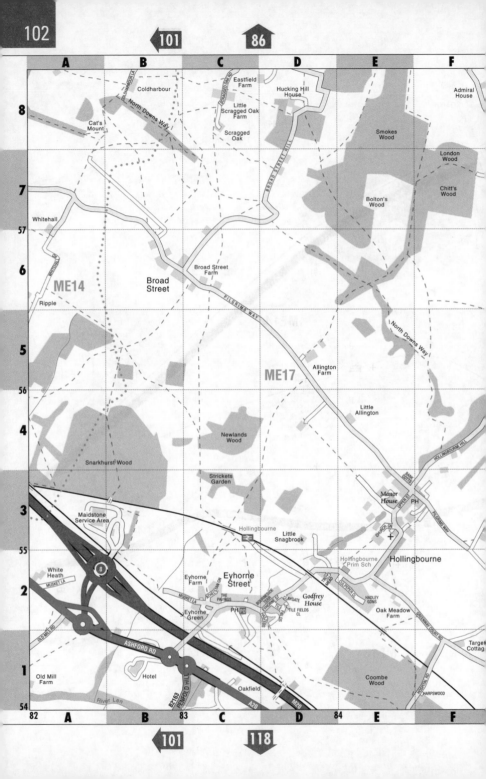

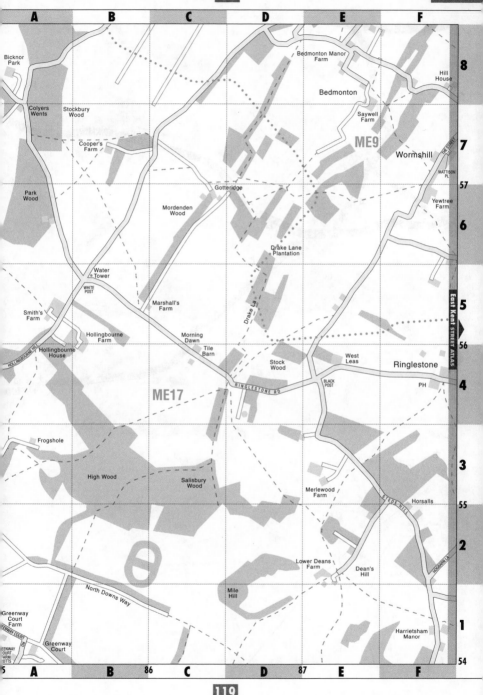

89
106
122
106

← 105
90 ↑

	A	B	C	D	E	F

8

Valence Wood

Vines Gate

Great Wood

BIRCHFIELD

Foxwold

7

Brasted Chart

Quornden Wood

PIPER'S GREEN RD

Penn Farm

53

Stanhope wood

Round Wood

Quornden

6

Frenchstreet Farm

Parson's Marsh

Phillippines

CANONS WK

Great Norman Street Farm

Cordons Farm

TN16

Weardale

EMMETTS RD

The Chart

Emmetts Garden

5

Scords Wood

CREASEY'S ROW

52

PH

TN14

MOUNT PLEASANT

Greensand Way

Ide Hill CE Prim Sch

Ide Hill

4

P

Toy's Hill

Ide Hill

B2042

HANGING BANK

Castle Grove

3

Toy's Hill

Quinten Wood

The Guzzle

PUDDLEDOCK LA

Bardogs

51

Puddlelock

IDE HILL RD

Oakwood Lodge

2

Ties Wood

Toy's Hill Wood

Tanhouse Wood

Round Wood

Henden Manor

1

TN8

Tan House

Obriss Farm

50

Boons Wood

B2042

| 46 | A | B | 47 | C | D | 48 | E | F |

← 105
123 ↓

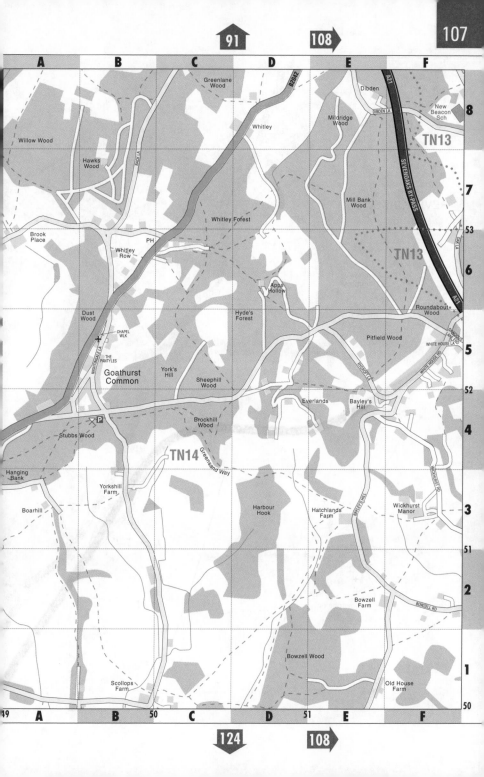

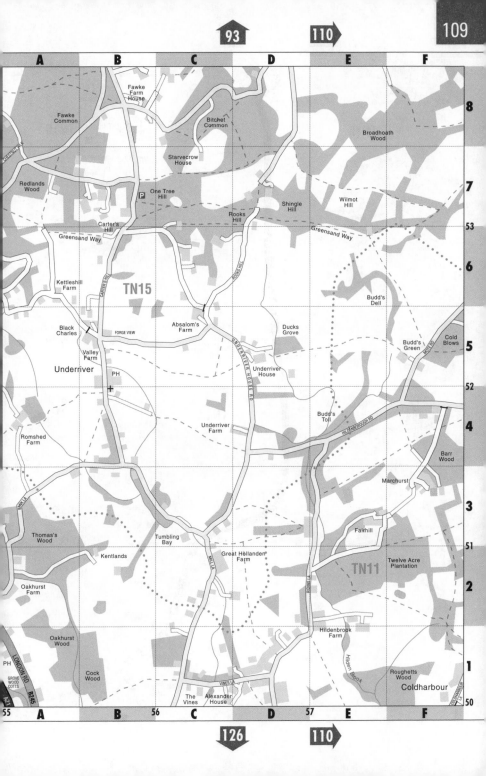

A B C D E F

8
7
53
6
5
52
4
3
51
2
50

TN15

Mote
Cotts
Mote Farm
Ightham
Mote
South Seers
Wood
Fatting
Pen
Cold
Blows
Peacock
Wood
West Green
Farm
Tinley Lodge
Farm
Cold Harbour
Toll
Coldharbour
Farm

A227 TONBRIDGE RD
High Beeches
Fairlawne
PLAXTOL LA
Fairlawne
Park
Home
Coverts
Greensand Way
Shipbourne
PH
The
Common
Hotel
LADY VANE CL
Shipbourne
Prim Sch
Woodhall
Farm
HILDENBOROUGH RD
UPPER GREEN RD
NEW
COTTS
UPPER GREEN LA
BACK LA
TN11
Hoad
Common
The
Hoad
Kiln
Wood
Point
Wood
Scrambles
STUMBLE HILL
IGHTHAM RD
SHIPBOURNE RD
Dene Park
Farm
Lodge
Wood
Dene
Park
Pen Stream
SPRINGWOOD
HALL
HIGH LA
A227
Upper Lodge
Wood
Fox
Wood
Dene
Park
Golden Stable
Wood
NORTH
FRITH PK
ASH LA
CH

Plaxtol
TN15
FREE HILL
GRANGE HILL
DUX HILL
The
Grange
ST HILDAS
THE STREET
CHURCH
ROW
Plaxtol
Prim Sch
RED LION
PO
WHEELWRIGHTS
PH
Almhouses
SCHOOL LA
Brakybank
Wood
Fairlawne Home
Farm
The
Alders
REDES LA
HAMPTONS RD
WHITE POST
CNR
Claygate
Hookwood
House
Dene
Park
PATTENDEN RD
GLASSMILL LA
P
COLDHARBOUR LA

58 59 60

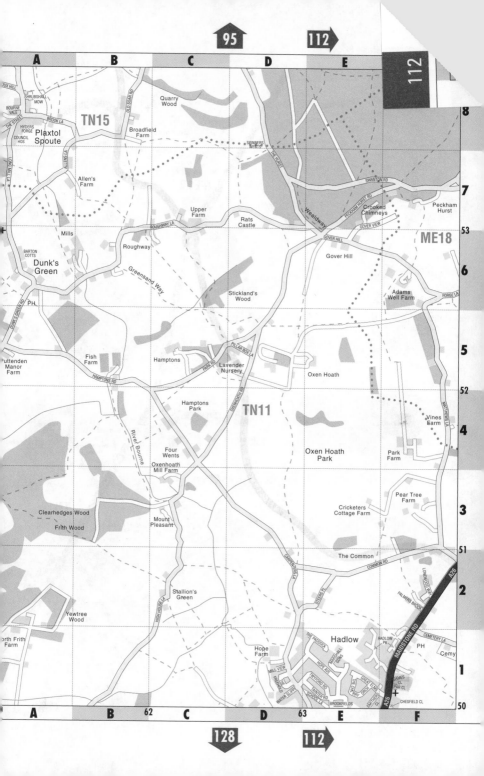

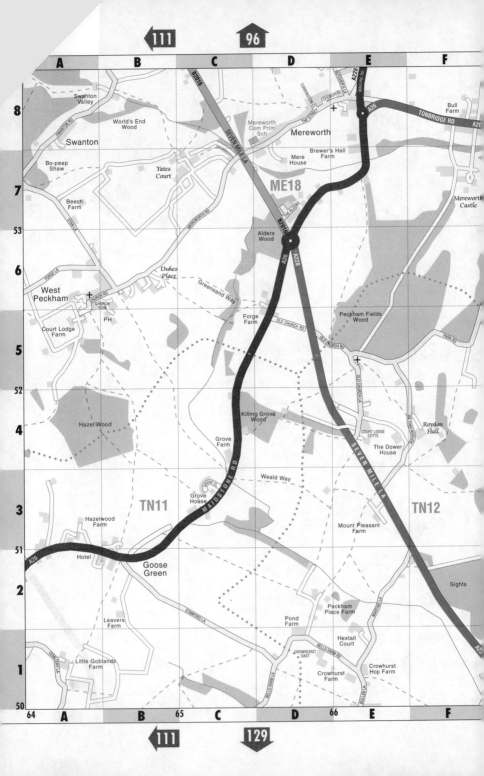

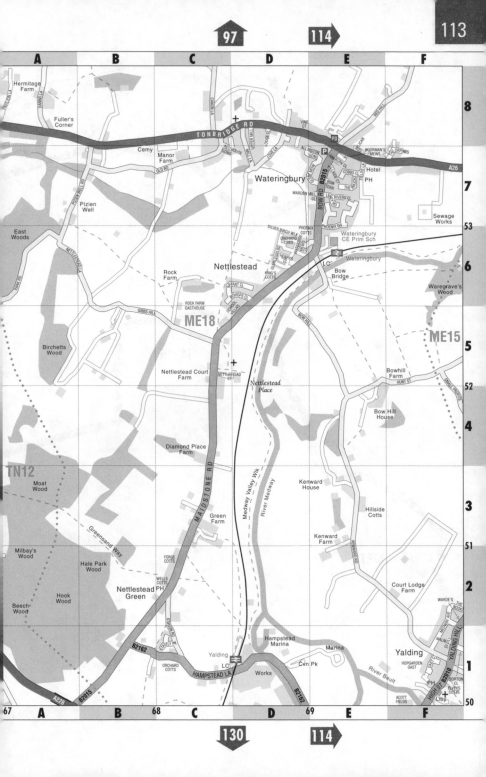

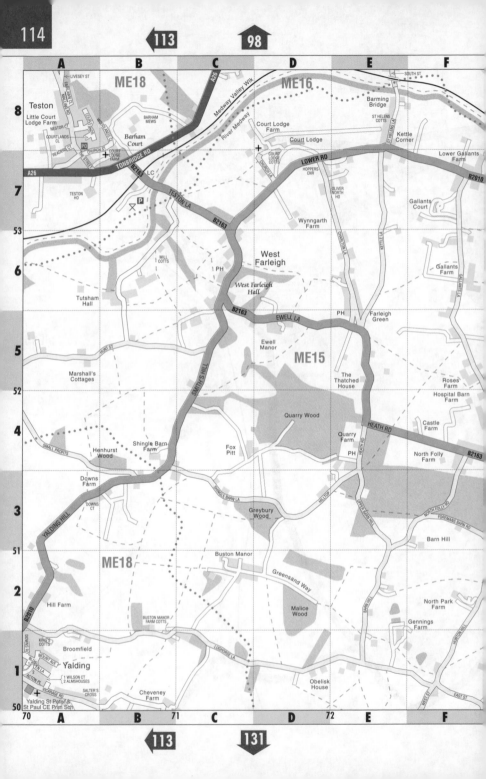

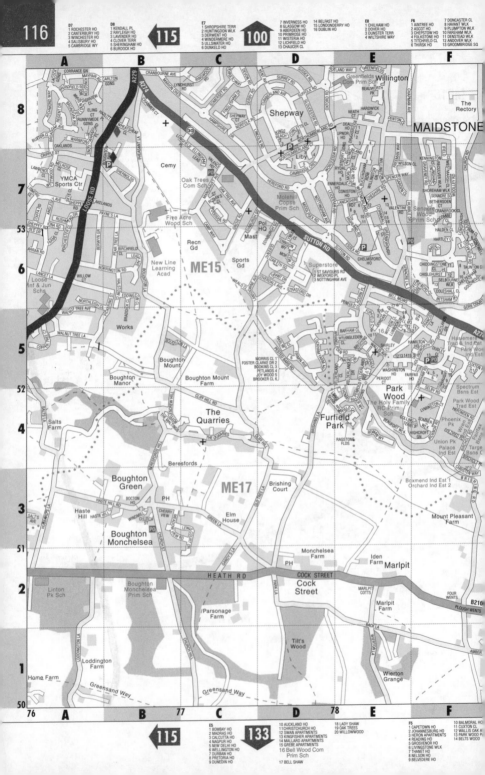

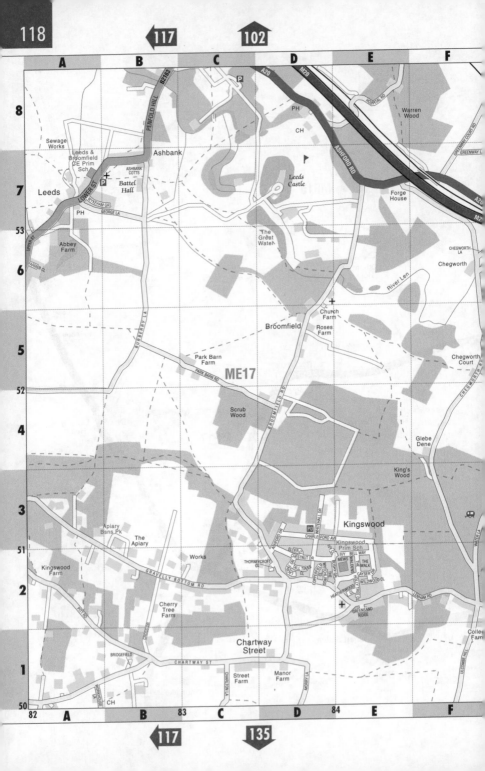

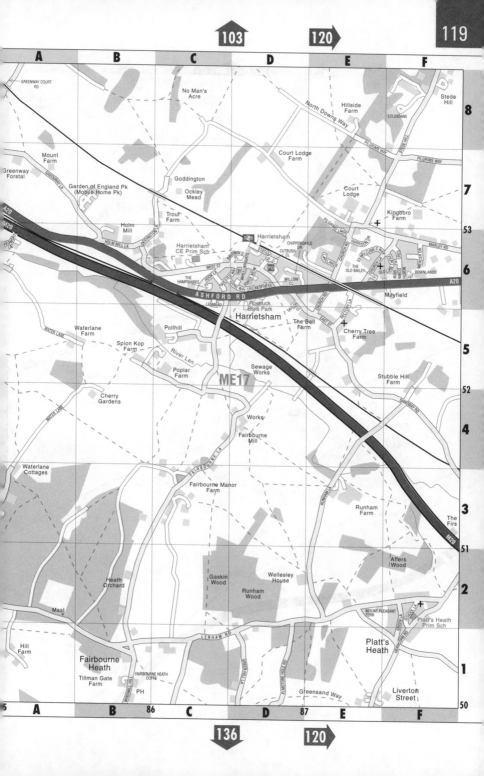

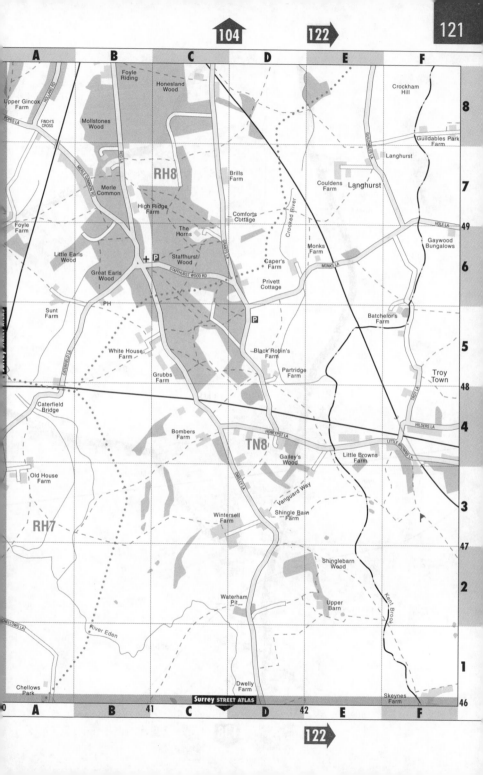

121 105

C1
1 CRANBROOK MEWS
2 HOLMDEN CT
3 THE OLD SCHOOL HO
4 LINGFIELD MEWS
5 FLORENCE COTTS
6 MONT ST AIGNAN WAY

D3
1 STACKFIELD
2 WOODPECKER CL
3 MAGPIE GN
4 SORRELL CL
5 SPEEDWELL CL
6 ROWFIELD
7 SMITHY FIELD
8 BRIAR CL
9 FOXGLOVE CL

10 BROOK CT
11 TEMPLARS CT
12 HOPGARDEN CL
13 CLOVER WLK

121 138

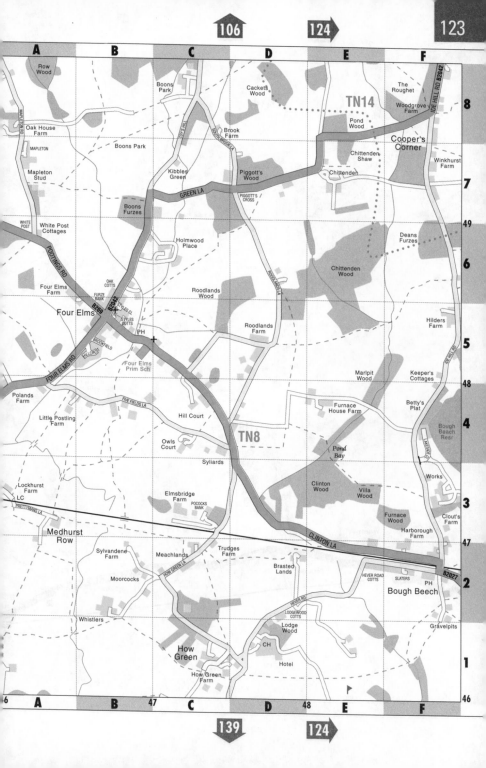

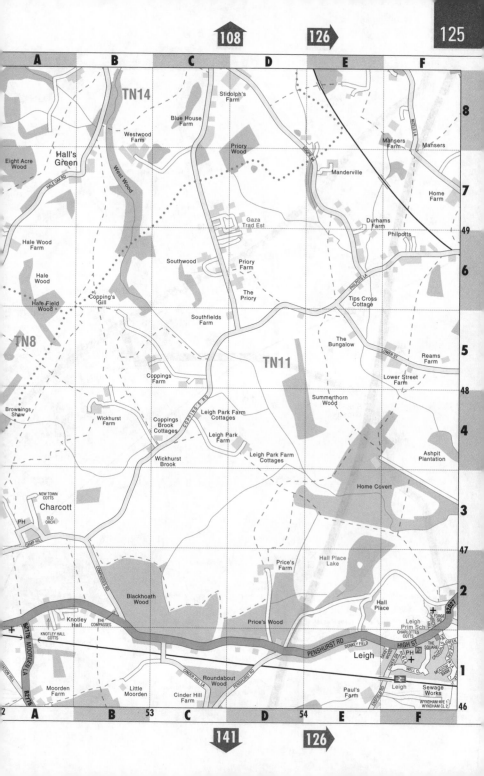

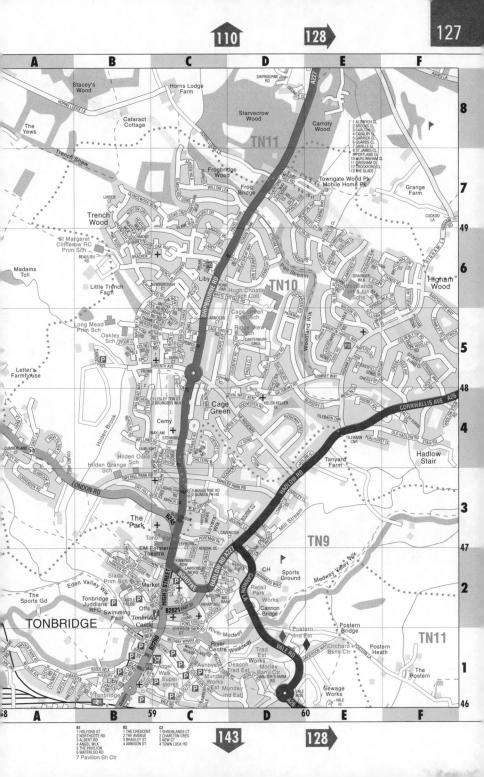

TN11

TN10

TN9

TN11

TONBRIDGE

1 ALDWYCH CL
2 BROOKS CL
3 CARLTON CL
4 CAVALRY CL
5 GARRICK CL
6 GUARDS CL
7 SAVILLE CL
8 ST JAMES CL
9 PORTLAND CL
10 HURLINGHAM CL
11 GRESHAM CL
12 CROCKFORD CL
13 THE GLADE

B1
1 HOLFORD ST
2 NORTHCOTE RD
3 ALBERT RD
4 ANGEL WLK
5 THE PAVILION
6 WATERLOO RD
7 Pavilion Sh Ctr

B2
1 THE CRESCENT
2 THE AVENUE
3 BRADLEY ST
4 ANNISON ST

C2
1 SHRUBLANDS CT
2 CHARLTON CRES
3 NEW CT
4 TOWN LOCK HO

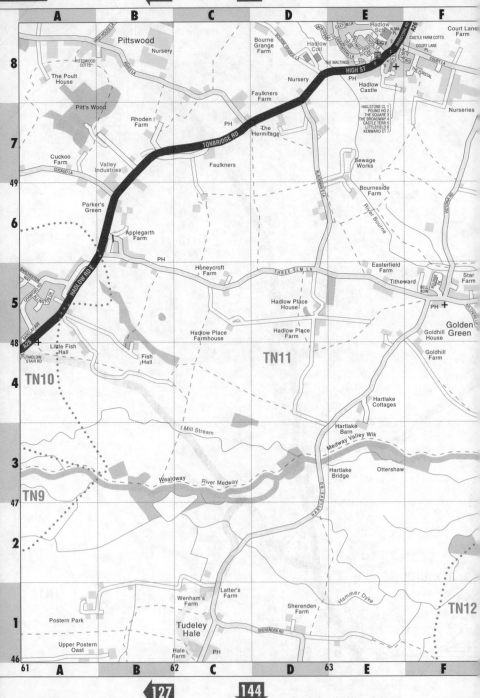

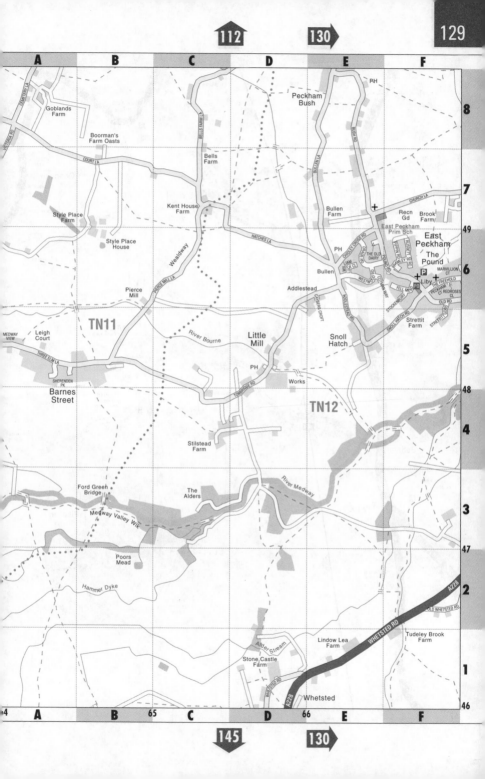

129 113

	A	B	C	D	E	F

8

Borough's Oak Farm

Works

ACOTT FIELDS

HIGH ST

The Lees

PH

LEES RD

Twyford Bridge

Greensand Way

PO

KILLICKS COTTS

LYNGS CL

A228

MAIDSTONE RD

SEVEN MILE LA

Ppg Sta

Parsonage Farmhouse

HAMPSTEAD LA

B2162

Tea Pot Island

P

Lees House

River Beult

BENOVER RD

B2162

PH

▽

PH

BOYLE WAY

7

Hale Street

Smythers Green Farm

HALE CT

HOP BINE CL

PATTENDEN GDNS

BARDSLEY CL

CHURCH LA

HALE CT

SMITHERS LA

SMITHERS CT

River Medway

LC

LEES RD

Yalding Organic Centre

Congelow

Congelow Farm

Nightingale Farm

ST MICHAELS LA

49

CAPEL CT

Arnold's Lodge Farm

Medway Valley Walk

Uptons Farm

Mill Place Barn

6

WHITEWATER GDNS

GOLDING CL

CROWN ACRES

OLD RD

MEDWAY FARM RD

PH

Sewage Works

Woodfalls Ind Est

Manor Farm

PINKHAM GDNS

Branbridges

Arnolds Bsns Pk

ME18

5

Branbridges Ind Est

Stoneham Cottages

PH

MEADOW VIEW COTTS

Laddingford

ST MARYS CL

Peacock Farm

BRANBRIDGES RD

TONBRIDGE RD

Little Budds Farm

Laddingford St Mary's CE Prim Sch

ST MARYS CL

48

LC

Laddingford Farm

Laddingford Farm Ind Est

CLAYGATE RD

Foxden Farm

4

BELTRING RD

PH

Beltring

LC

West Pike Fish Farm

East Pikefish Farm

Beltring

3

Hop Farm Family Park

PH

P

TN12

Woodlands

DARMAN LA

GREEN ST

Pikefish

River Teise

EMMETTS HILL LA

PETERS LA

47

Lily Hoo

B2162

WHETSTED RD

OLD WHETSTED RD

A228

Darman Bridge

2

MAIDSTONE RD

Beltring House

Little Darman Farm

Darman Oast

1

LC

High Lees Farm

WAGON LA

Great Fowlehall Farm

Fowle Hall

NEWBRIDGE LA

46

B2160

LUCKS LA

67	A	B	68	C	D	69	E	F

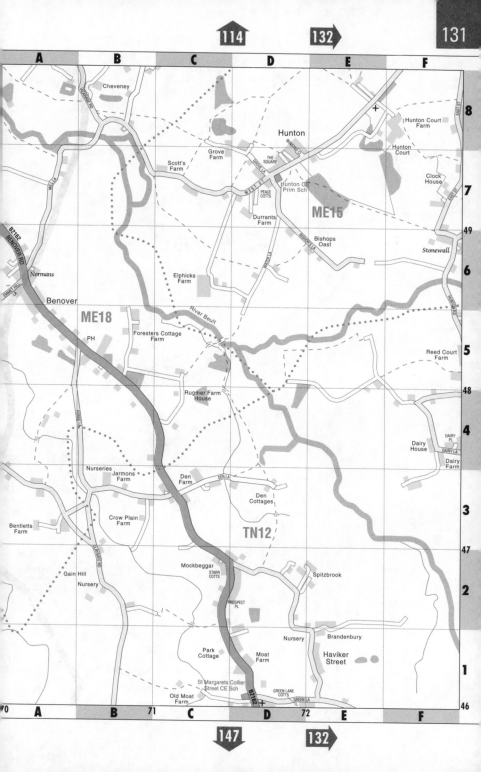

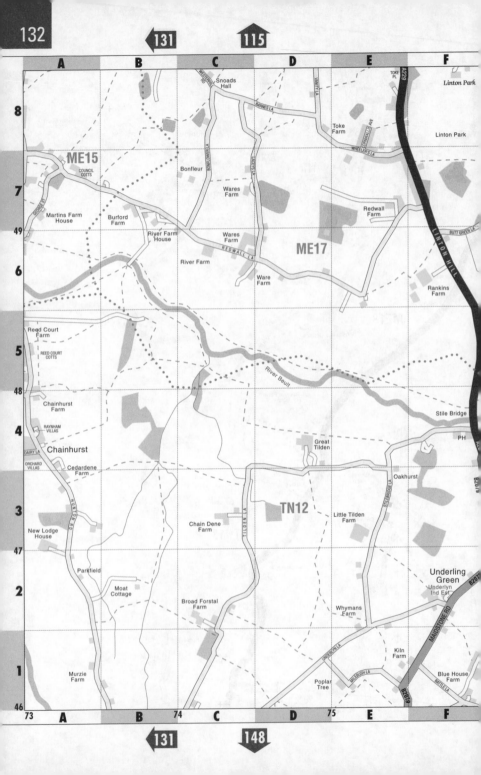

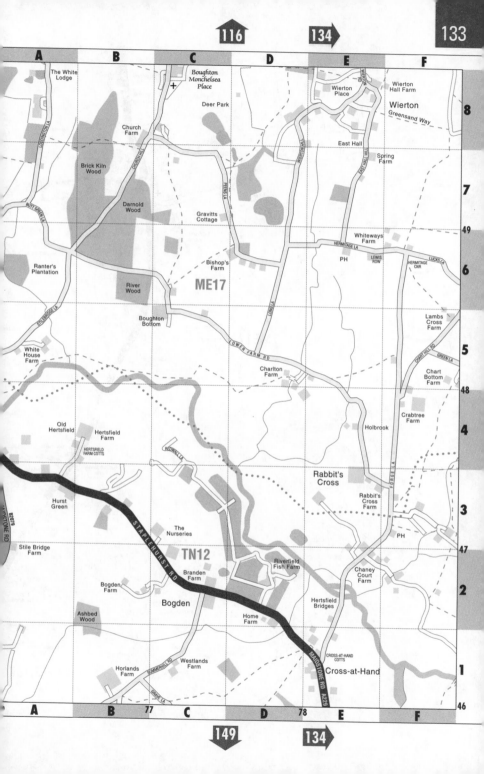

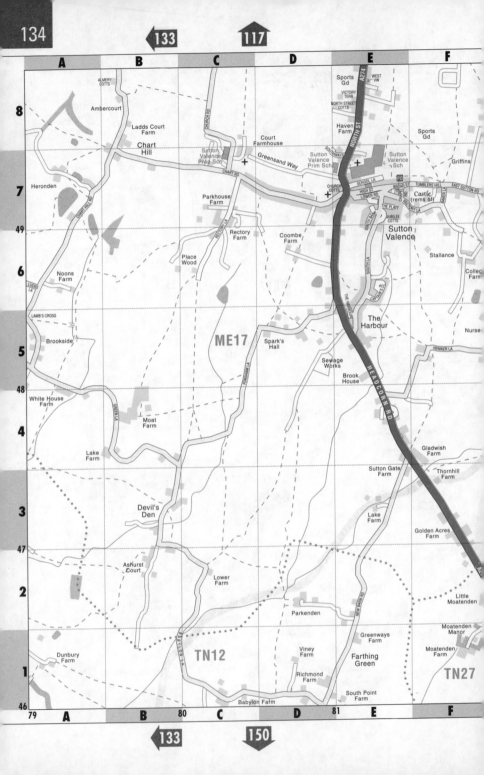

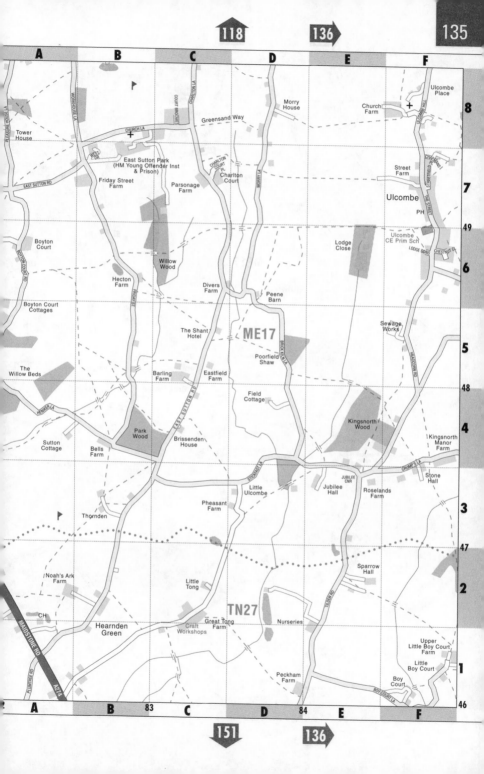

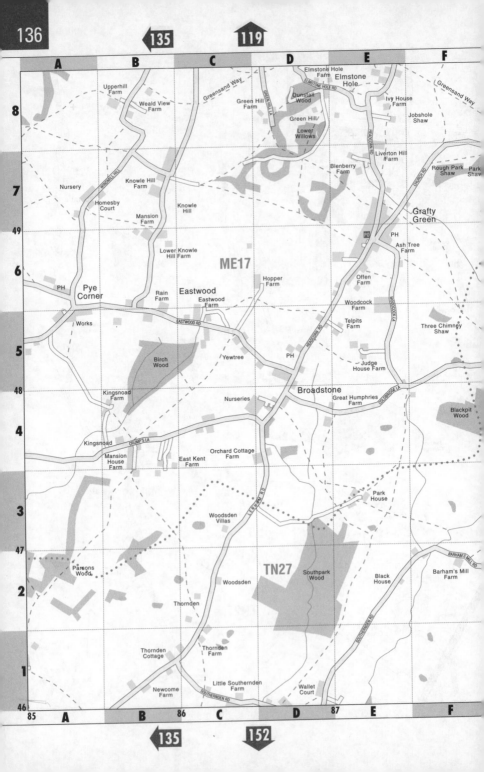

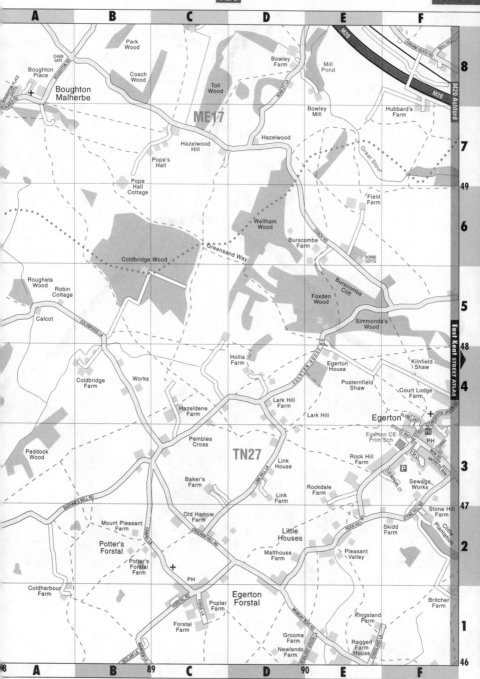

A B C D E F

8

M20

M20 Ashford

Boughton
Place

CHAIN
GATE

Boughton
Malherbe

Park
Wood

Coach
Wood

Toll
Wood

Bowley
Farm

Mill
Pond

Bowley
Mill

Hubbard's
Farm

ME17

7

49

Hazelwood
Hill

Hazelwood

Pope's
Hall

Great Stour

Field
Farm

Pope
Hall
Cottage

Wellham
Wood

Greensand Way

Coldbridge Wood

Burscombe
Farm

6

DORNE
COTTS

Roughets
Wood

Robin
Cottage

Burscombe
Cliff

5

Calcot

COLDBRIDGE LA

Foxden
Wood

Simmonds's
Wood

48

Coldbridge
Farm

Works

Hollis
Farm

Egerton
House

Kilnfield
Shaw

Posternfield
Shaw

Court Lodge
Farm

4

Hazeldene
Farm

Lark Hill
Farm

Lark Hill

Egerton

Egerton CE
Prim Sch

PH

Pembles
Cross

TN27

Link
House

Rock Hill
Farm

Sewage
Works

Paddock
Wood

Baker's
Farm

Link
Farm

Rockdale
Farm

P

Stone Hill
Farm

3

47

BARDYAM'S MILL RD

Old Harrow
Farm

CHEQUERS LA

Mount Pleasant
Farm

Little
Houses

Skidd
Farm

Cliffe
Plantation

2

Potter's
Forstal

Potter's
Forstal
Farm

PH

Malthouse
Farm

Pleasant
Valley

ROCK HILL RD

Coldharbour
Farm

FORSTAL RD

LYING LA

Poplar
Farm

Egerton
Forstal

Kingsland
Farm

Britcher
Farm

1

REDLAND LA

WARDEN LA

Forstal
Farm

Groome
Farm

Newlands
Farm

Ragged
Farm
House

46

A 89 B C D 90 E F

A **B** **C** **D** **E** **F**

LINGFIELD RD

COOMBES CL
CORBETTS WAY
B2026
HIGH ST
MONT ST AIGNAN WAY

Edenbridge

River Eden

KATHERINE RD

LUCILINA DR 1
TANNERS MEAD 2
DOGGETTS CL 3
SIX PENNY CL 4
VICTORIA COTTS 5
KATHERINE VILLAS 6
VICTORIA RD 7
TEKRAM CL 8

VICTORIA CL

Delaware Farm

Kent Brook

Warsop Trad Est

Edenbridge Trad Ct

HEVER RD

DELAWARE COTTS

8

MILL HILL

Edenbridge War Meml

MEAD RD
EDEN VILLAS

7

Devil's Den

Eden Valley Wlk

River Eden

45

Gabriel's Farm

Gabriel's Manor

DEN CROSS

Old Barn Farm

Eden Valley Wlk

LYDENS LA

6

B2028

Lydens Farm

MARSH GREEN RD

Dencross Farm

HARTFIELD RD

Leydens Farm

5

PH

MILL LA

Marsh Green

TN8

Leydens House

Brook Street Farm

44

Old Chiswell Hall

SHENDEN LA

TOMANS RD

4

MOOR LA

B2028

Christmas Place

Christmas Mill

Shernden Oast Farm

Little Brookstreet

Stickhill Wood

B2026

SHENDEN LA

Smoaky Cottage

Marsh Green Wood

Gilridge Wood

Howletts Farm

3

New Barns Farm

GREYBURY LA

Birches Wood

Clatfields

Ockhams

Cobhambury Farm Stud

43

2

Middleroom Wood

Greybury Farm

Greybury Furzes

Shernden Wood

Cobhambury Wood

Round House Farm

RH7

Gilridge

SPORE LA

1

Reynolds Wood

MOOR LA

Greybury Wood

Ash Plantation

Beechenwood Farm

42

43 **A** **B** **44** **C** **D** **45** **E** **F**

Surrey STREET ATLAS

A B C D E F

8

Swansnest Island
River Eden

Sixteen Acre Island

Polebrook Farm

Hever Bridge
Hever Castle

7

Hever Rd
Brocas Farm

Hever Gardens

45

Brocas Cottages

Park Wood

P
PH
Hever CE Prim Sch
Hever

6

Hever
Newhouse Farm
Hever Grange

The Red House

Tangle Wood

PARSON'S CROFT

Lockskinners Farm

Hever Warren

PH
Dyehurst Bridge

5

Fell House
Meechlands Farm
Pigdown

44

Dogpits

TN8 Newtown

4

PARK PL

Stick Hill

Greenland Farm

Wilderness Farm

Heathen Street

Wychwood Fruit Farm

Markbeech Wood

Newtye Hurst

3

St Andrew's Convent Eden Hall

43

HARTFIELD RD

Buckhurst Farm

Bramsell's Farm

Buck Hurst

PH
Markbeech

Buckhurst Farm

2

PH
Cowden Pound
Falconhurst

Horseshoe Green

PH
SPODE LA

Lord's Land Wood

Horseshoe Green Farm

Bilton's Gill

1

B2026
Lambert Cottage Wood

Edells

42

A B C D E F

139
124

A B C D E F

8

River Eden

Mill Shaw

Somerden Green

Vexour Bridge

The Grove

River Eden

7

Gilwyns

Chiddingstone

Larkin's Farm

Hampkins Hill

Vexour

PH

Chiddingstone Castle

Chiddingstone CE Prim Sch

45

Chantlers

6

THRESHER FIELD

Moor Wood

Hill Hoath

Clappers Shaw

Hill Hoath Farm

Eden Valley Wlk

BOURNE ROW

Weller's Town

Mounters

SOUTH ROW

TN8

5

The Slips

Gillridge

Doubleton Farm House

44

Sliders

Stock Wood

Robins Land

Lew Cross Farm

Wat Stock

TN11

4

Trugger's Gill

Russell's Wood

Salmans Farm

River Eden

The Warren

3

Trugger's Farm

PH

Hoath Corner

Yewtree Wood

Harden Cottage

Puckden Wood

Harden Farmhouse

The Grove

43

Oakenden Farm

Vine Cottage

2

Chiddingstone Hoath

Oakenden

Stonewall Wood

Courtlands Wood

South Park Wood

Hoath House

Brookers Farm House

The Rangers

Stonewall Park

PH

BOTTLE HOUSE COTTS

COLDHARBOUR RD

1

42

49 A B 50 C D 51 E F

TN9

Brook Street Farm

Straight Mile
Eden Valley Wlk

Haysden Water

Haysden Country Park

LOWER HAYSDEN LA

Lower Haysden

PH

TN11

Chartfield

Manor Farm

TONBRIDGE BY-PASS

UPPER HAYSDEN LA

Ensfield

Great Hayesden Farm

Fosters Farm

Fishpond Farm

Upper Hayesden

ENSFIELD RD

Coxon Wood

New Plantation

Wealdway

Home Farm

Beechy Toll

Birch Wood

Hawk's Wood

Judd's Wood

Broadfield

Seals Wood

Waghorn's Wood

B2176

Bidborough Corner

Home Farm

BIDBOROUGH RIDGE

THE CRESCENT

DAHNLEY DR

TN4

B2176

Printstile

PENSHURST RD

GATEHOUSE FARM COTTS

PH

THE GLEBE

ST LAWRENCE AVE

LONDON RD

VAUXHALL LA

Windmill (dis)

BIDBOROUGH CT

MILL CT

HIGH ST

GREAT HALL DR

MANOR FIELDS

TN3

Old Farmhouse

The Grange

SPRING LA

Bidborough

Bidborough CE Prim Sch

Birch Wood

Meadows Sch

Brock's Wood

Sewage Works

FARM HOLLOW WAY

Cemy

Southborough Common

Tonbridge Wells Circular Wlk

HEATHVIEW

Holden House

Bentham Farm

Birchett's Wood

Stockland Green

STOCKLAND GREEN RD

BENTHAM HILL

Modest Corner

The Park

SIR DAVID'S

WOOLLEY RD

Speldhurst Wood

Scriventon

F2
1 PENNINGTON MANOR
2 CASTLE ST
3 DRAPER ST
4 SHEFFIELD RD

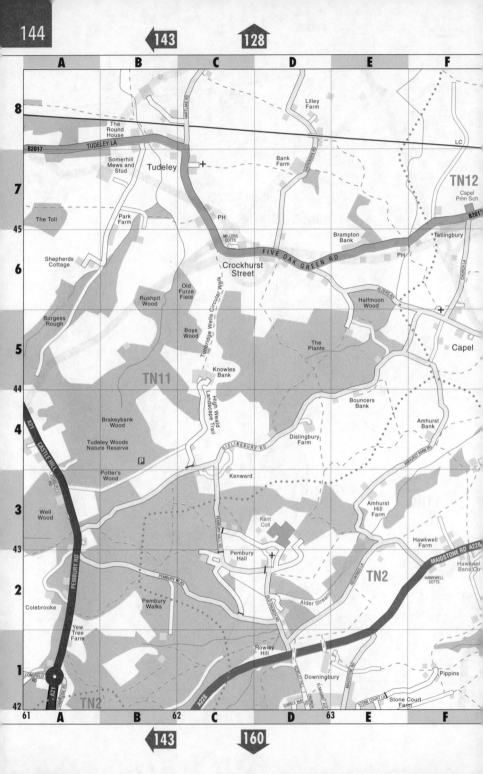

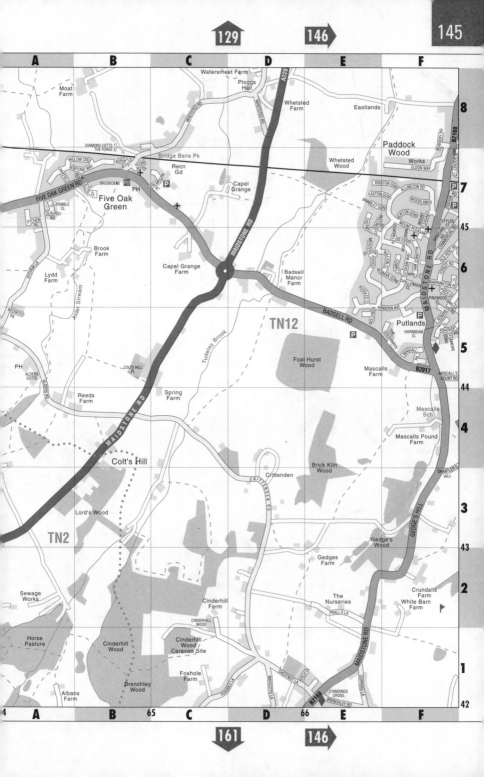

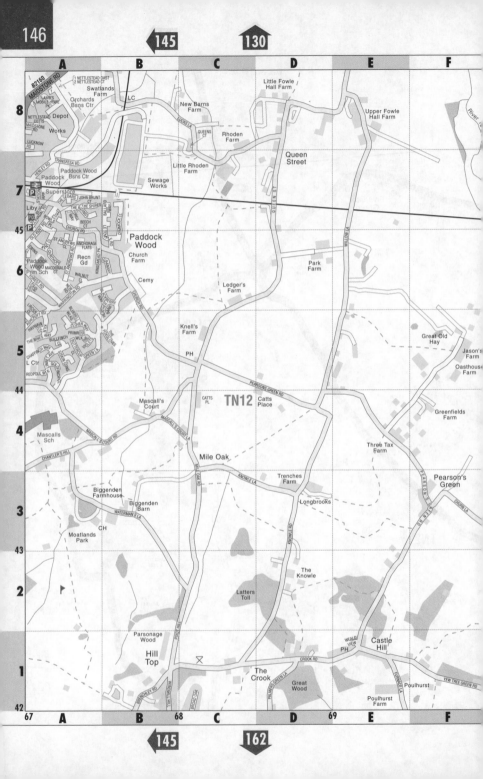

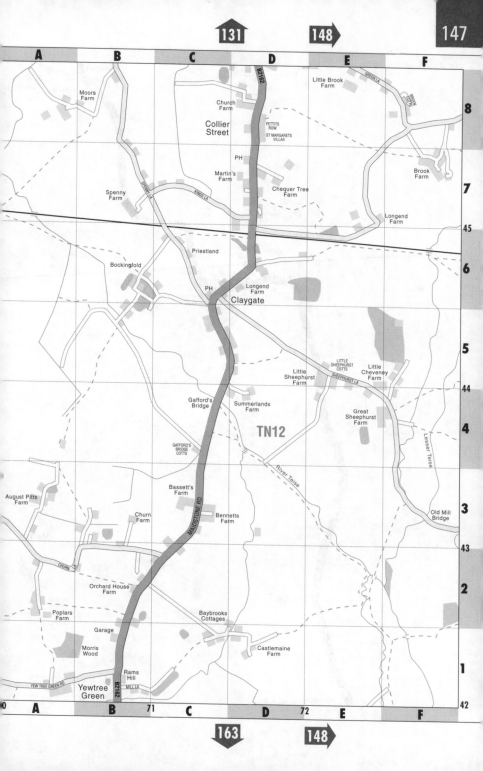

147
132

A | B | C | D | E | F

Spitz Bridge
Mill Farm
HUNTON RD
Gatehouse Farm
ELGIN LA
UNDERLYN LA
Foundation Farm
Little Mill Farm Cotts
Target Farm
Copt Hall Farm

Milebush
B2079
ST ANN'S GREEN LA
Milebush Farm
St Ann's Green

8

Little Pattenden

Marden Grange

The Old Vicarage Sch

7

Whealbarrow Park Est

PATTENDEN LA

Guardian Ind Est

Church Farm

Cemy

MAIDSTONE RD

Bridgehurst Wood

45

Crest Ind Est

Marden

6

Turkey Farmhouse

MILGATE CL
GOUDHURST RD
STANLEY RD
OVERDENS WAY
MEDWAY COTTS
WEST END
CHURCH GN
BALLARD
CL
PROVIDENCE CHAPEL
CHANTRY
THE CL
HIGH ST
RAILWAY COTTS
EASON VILLAS
The Old MKT
HOWLAND COTTS
Moatlands Farm

Marden Prim Sch
THE COCKPIT
MAYNARD
SUTTON CT
STANLEY RD
OAK-TREE CL
STANLEY RD
JAMES WK
HOWLAND RD
Hall House
Holders Farm

5

Marden

Gravelpit Farm House
Westfield House
BROOKLYN VILLAS
WESTFIELD VILLAS
SPRINGROVE COTTS
STANHAM SQ
1 ALLENS
2 MAPLESDEN
3 ALBION COTTS
4 CLAREMONT PL
COPPER LA
Little Mountain Farm

44

TN12

4

Roughlands Farm
Poulters Hall
PLAIN RD
Cannon Farm
THORN RD
Longridge Farm

3

The Plain
Thorn Farm

Beech Farm
SHEEPHURST LA
Marden Beech
Widehurst
Marden Thorn

43

Beale Farm

2

Cornwells Farm
Springfield
Susans Farm

1

Great Cheveney Farm
Widehurst Wood
Wilden Wood
WILSLEY PARK RD
Tavern Farm
Forstal Farm
Cockle Wood

Great Cheveney House
B2079
SHERENDEN LA

42

73 | A | B | 74 | C | D | 75 | E | F

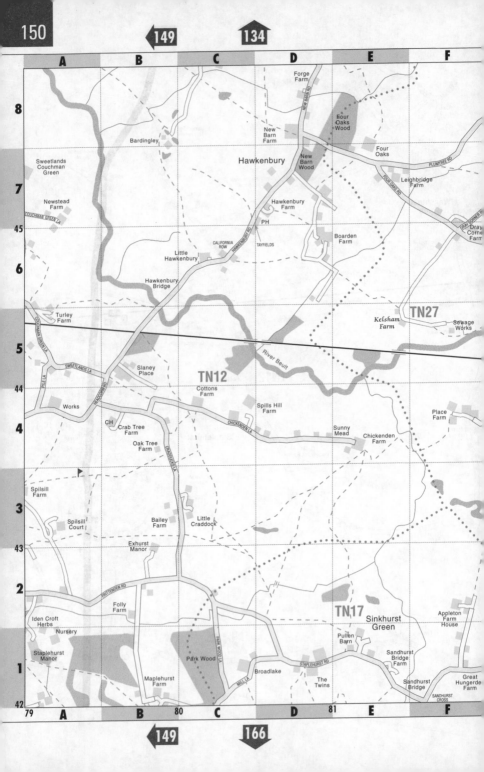

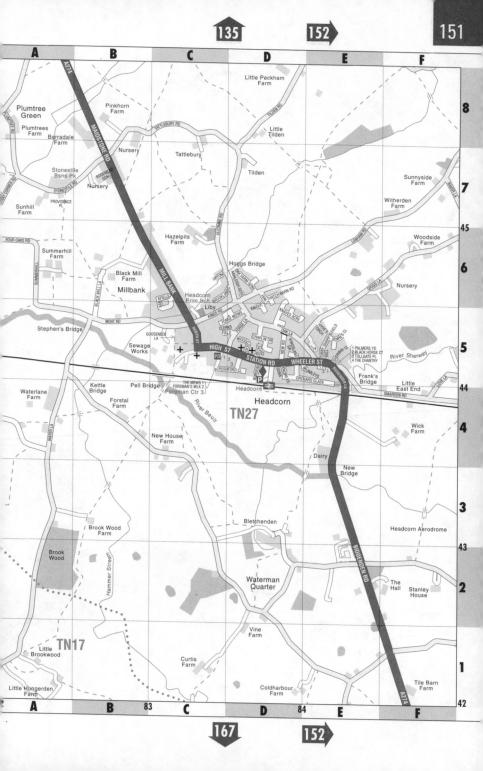

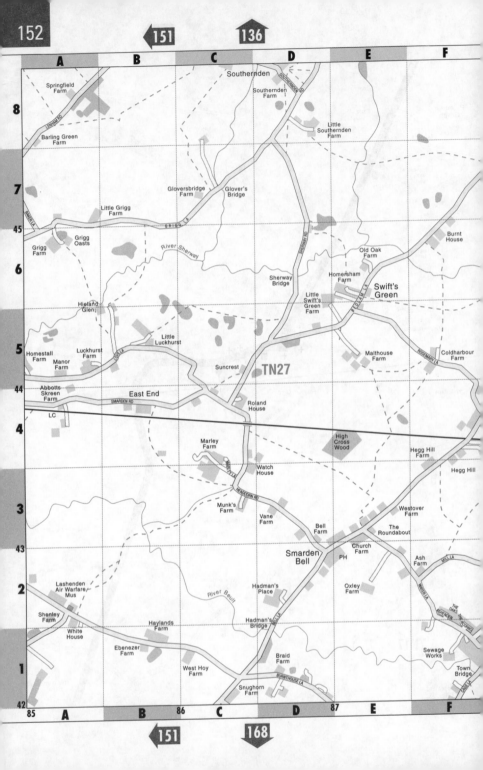

A B C D E F

Clark Hill Farm

Box Farm

Newland Green

Oak's Farm

Appleby Farm

Little Mundy Bois Farm

Heronsdale

8

Wanden Farm

Acorn Wood

Shaw Farm

Munday Bois

Weeks Farm

Wanden

Little Wanden

Alfred Wood

PH

Kingsden Farm

Wheeler Wood

Watersheet Farm

Woodland Farm

7

45

Stace Wood

Frith Wood

Frith Farm

Kite Farm

P

6

Park Farm

Dering Wood

Giles Farm

School Wood

Clover Farm

The Quarter

TN27

Oaklands

5

Cousins Farm

Roughland Wood

Hodges Farm

Roughlands

44

Berry Court

4

Dering Lodge

Mount Pleasant Farm

Ash Plantation

Mainey Wood

Woodside Farm

3

New House Farm

Little Biddenden Green Farm

Tilden Field Hassock

Maltman's Hill

Tolhurst Farm

PH

43

Baker's Bridge

PLUCKLEY RD

Biddenden Green

Dering Farm

Mainey Wood

2

Round Wood

Little Wood

Snapmill

Smarden Prim Sch

HASLEWOOD CL

THE STREET

PH

Gain Bridge

River Beult

TN26

PO

Romden

Romden Bridge

Dadson Farm

Smarden

The Gorse

Vesper Hawk Farm

Romden Castle

Tuesnoad Farm

1

42

A B 89 C D 90 E F

155
140

8

Birchcope Shaw

Frienden Gill

Coldharbour

Westfield House

COLDHARBOUR RD

Cook's Wood

NUNNERY LA

Bassett's Mill

TN8

Finch Green

White Post

Harts

SANDFIEL RD

7

BASSETTS LA

Frienden Farm

Blacklands Wood

Hartsland Farm

Bassett's Farm

Prinkham

TN11

WALTER'S GREEN RD

41

Top Hill Wood

Walter's Green

6

Hobbs Hill Farm

Pilbeams

Kent Water

BRADLEY RD

Nore Farm

Sussex Border Path

Chafford Bridge

Hedge Barto Trailer Pk

CHAFFORD COTTS

5

CH

THE PADDOCK

Tollhurst Farm

Willett's Farm

40

Salehurst

Stephnett's Farm

Blackham

River Medway

CARRIERS LA

WILLETTS LA

WILLETTS COTTS

TEASLEY MEAD

4

Chafford Park

Cousins Shaw

Pound Farm

Teasley Mead

TN3

Ashurst Wood

3

Stable Cottage

ASHURST RD

A26

A264

Ashurst Bridge

MILLSTREAM CT

ASHURST HILL

Manor Court Farm

39

Highfields Park

Ashurst

Ashurst

Jessup's Farm

OLD HSE LA

2

Lodgefield Wood

Lodgefield Farm

Weald way

1

Lords Wood

TN7

Clay Shaw

Old Woodland Wood

Minepit Wood

38

155
170

B4
1 MOLYNEUX ALMSHOUSES
2 SIMMONDS CT
3 GLADSTONE RD
4 SPRING GDNS
5 SOUTHWOOD BLDGS
6 St Pauls CE
Prim Sch

F1
1 Broadwater Down
Prim Sch

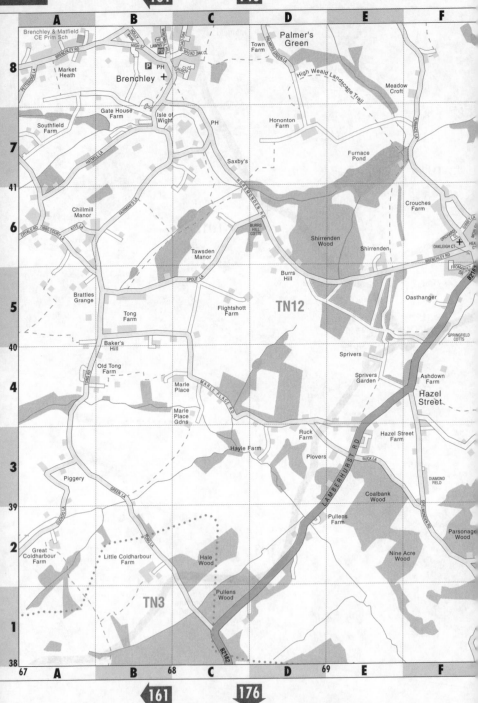

161
146

A   **B**   **C**   **D**   **E**   **F**

Brenchley & Matfield
CE Prim Sch

Palmer's
Green

Town
Farm

8

Market
Heath

THE
LAWNS
PO

BROAD OAK CL.

Meadow
Croft

P PH

Brenchley

CHURCH

High Weald Landscape Trail

Gate House
Farm

Isle of
Wight

PH

Hononton
Farm

Southfield
Farm

7

Saxby's

Furnace
Pond

41

Chillmill
Manor

Crouches
Farm

6

BURRS
HILL
COTTS

Shirrenden
Wood

ORCHARD
CE
OAKLEIGH CT.

Tawsden
Manor

Shirrenden

BRENCHLEY RD

FROMANDS DR

Burrs
Hill

SPOUT LA

Brattles
Grange

Flightshott
Farm

TN12

Oasthanger

5

Tong
Farm

SPRINGFIELD
COTTS

Baker's
Hill

40

Sprivers

Old Tong
Farm

Sprivers
Garden

Ashdown
Farm

4

Marle
Place

Hazel
Street

MARLE PLACE RD

Marle
Place
Gdns

Ruck
Farm

Hazel Street
Farm

LAMBERHURST RD

Hayle Farm

Plovers

RUCK LA

DIAMOND
FIELD

3

Piggery

GREEN LA

Coalbank
Wood

39

Pullens
Farm

Parsonage
Wood

Great
Coldharbour
Farm

2

Little Coldharbour
Farm

Hale
Wood

Nine Acre
Wood

TN3

Pullens
Wood

B2162

1

38

161
176

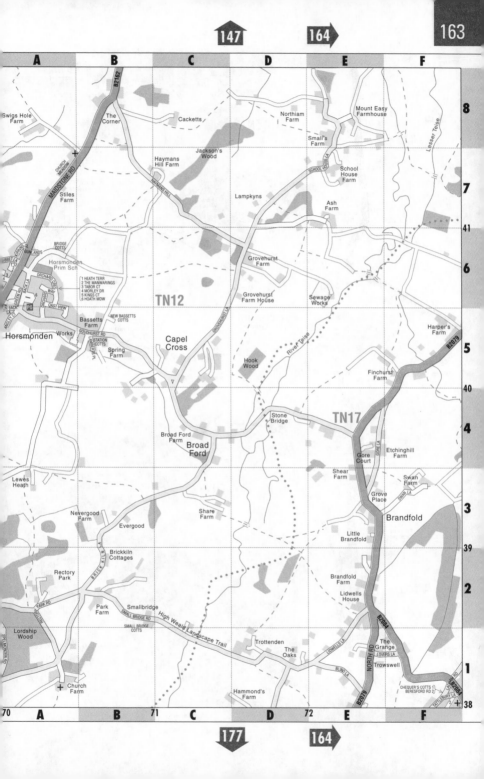

163
148

A B C D E F

8

Five Oak Green La
Plain Farm
Love's Farm
B2079
Huggins Farm
SHERENDEN LA
Sherenden Wood
Hobbs Wood
TN12
Tanner House

7

Mount Pleasant
ASH TREE COTTS
Love's Wood
Mab's Wood
Little Harts Heath
WILSLEY PARK RD
Dodges Farm
Harts Heath Farm

41

Winchet Hill
Pookhill Wood
Hush Heath Manor
HUSHEATH HILL
Husheath Farm

6

B2079
SUMMERFIELD
Mallions Farm
Curtisden Green
Ladysden Farm
Bethany Sch
Great Horden Farm
Little Horden Farm

5

Sewage Works
MILL RD
Blantyre House (HM Prison)
Worms Hill

40

Combourne Farm
Broadoak Wood
ROUND GREEN COTTS

4

Little Combourne Cottages
Round Green

Bockingfold Farm
Bakers Farm
Bakers Corner
TN17
Spring Wood

3

Footway Cottages
Woodfield
LADHAM RD
MILE LA

39

Blue Barn Farm
Colliers' Green

2

Ladham House
Knight's Hole
Colliers' Green CE Prim Sch
MARDEN RD
Colliers' Green Farm

Ladham Farm Cottages
Cherry Gardens Farm
Lynx Park

1

MOREBREDDIS COTTS
Sewage Works
Old Park Wood

38

73 A B 74 C D 75 E F

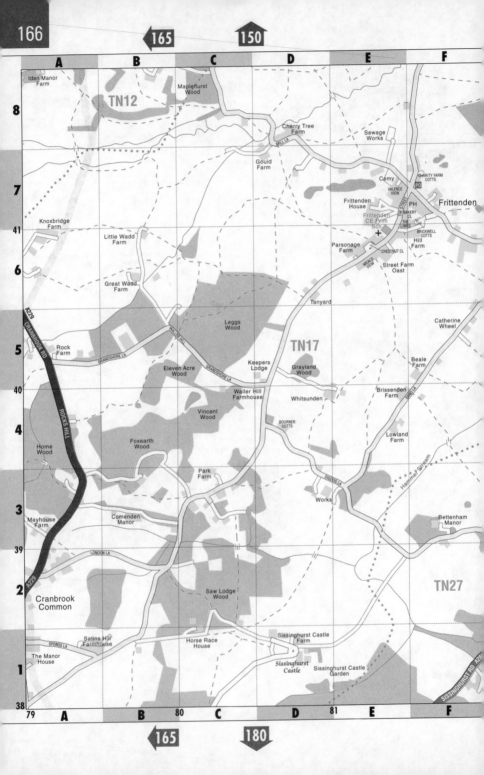

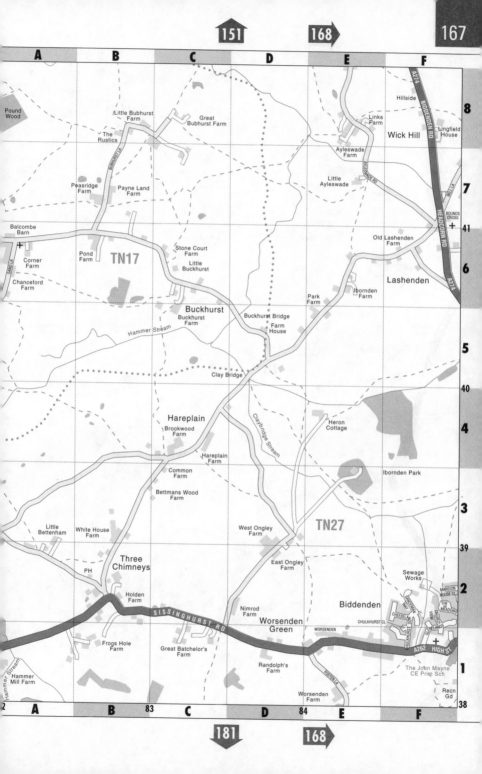

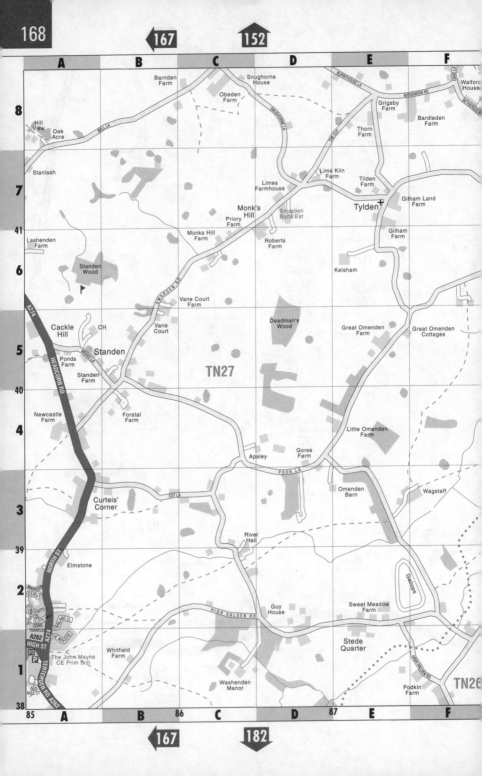

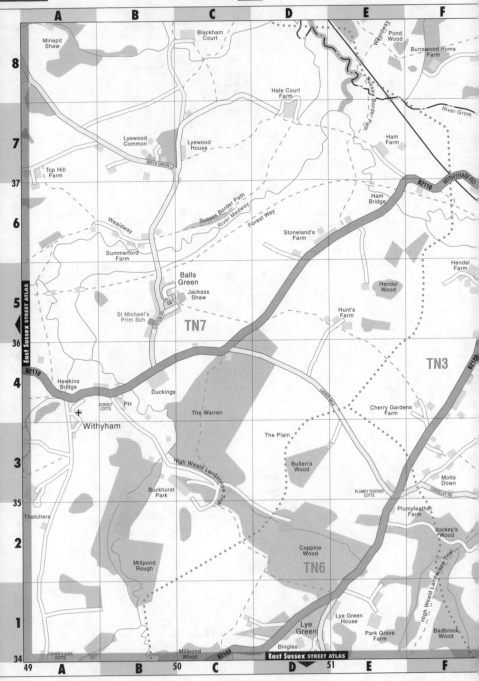

Minepit
Shaw

Blackham
Court

Waldway

Pond
Wood

Burrswood Home
Farm

Hale Court
Farm

River Grom

Sussex Border Path

Lyewood
Common

Lyewood
House

Ham
Farm

Top Hill
Farm

BEECH GREEN LA

Withyham Rd

B2110

37

Ham
Bridge

Sussex Border Path

Wealdway

River Medway

Forest Way

Stoneland's
Farm

Hendal
Farm

Summerford
Farm

Balls
Green

Jackass
Shaw

Hendal
Wood

St Michael's
Prim Sch

BALLS
GN

SCHOOL RD

TN7

Hunt's
Farm

TN3

B2188

36

B2110

Hewkins
Bridge

Duckings

LADIES MILE

Cherry Gardens
Farm

DORSET
COTTS

PH

The Warren

Withyham

The Plain

Motts
Down

High Weald Landscape Trail

Bullen's
Wood

PLUMEY FEATHER
COTTS

CORSELEY RD

Buckhurst
Park

35

Plumyfeather
Farm

Thatchers

Jockey's
Wood

Millpond
Rough

Coppice
Wood

TN6

High Weald Landscape Trail

Lye Green
House

Lye
Green

Park Grove
Farm

Badbrook
Wood

Bingles

Millpond
Wood

B2188

FISHER'S GATE
COTTS

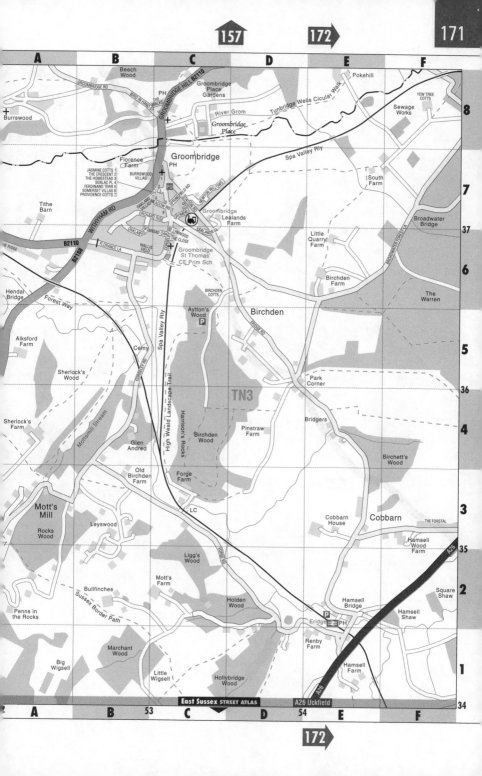

A B C D E F

8

Burrswood

Beech Wood

Groombridge Place Gardens

Pokehill

YEW TREE COTTS

River Grom

Sewage Works

GROOMBRIDGE HILL B2110

GROOMBRIDGE RD

BIRD IN HAND LA

PH

Tunbridge Wells Cicular Walk

Groombridge Place

Groombridge

PH

Spa Valley Rly

7

Florence Farm

PH

JASMINE COTTS 1
THE CRESCENT 2
THE HOMESTEAD 3
SENLAC PL 4
FERDINAND TERR 5
SOMERSET VILLAS 6
PROVIDENCE COTTS 7

BURRSWOOD VILLAS

FOXTHORN RD

MORTON WILLOWS

South Farm

37

Tithe Barn

WITHYHAM RD

OAKLAND VILLAS
ORCHARD RISE
THE MEADOW RD

Groombridge Lealands Farm

Little Quarry Farm

Broadwater Bridge

B2110

B2110

OAKLANDS

FLORANCE LA

BROAD OAK RD

LYNWOOD

THE CLOSE

WALLIS FIELD

LEA LANDS

BROADWATER FOREST LA

6

RIDGE

Hendal Bridge

Forest Way

Groombridge St Thomas' CE Prim Sch

BIRCHDEN COTTS

Birchden Farm

The Warren

Alksford Farm

Aytton's Wood P

Birchden

Cemy

Spa Valley Rly

CORSELEY RD

Sherlock's Wood

RIDGE RD

5

Sherlock's Farm

High Weald Landscape Trail

Motts Mill Stream

Park Corner

36

Glen Andred

Harrison's Rocks

Birchden Wood

Pinstraw Farm

Bridgers

TN3

4

Old Birchden Farm

Birchett's Wood

Forge Farm

FORGE RD

LC

3

Mott's Mill

Leyswood

Cobbarn House

Cobbarn

THE FORSTAL

Rocks Wood

Ligg's Wood

Hamsell Wood Farm

A26

35

Bullfinches

Mott's Farm

Sussex Border Path

Holden Wood

Hamsell Bridge

Square Shaw

2

Penns in the Rocks

P

Eridge ≡≡ PH

Hamsell Shaw

Marchant Wood

Renby Farm

Big Wigsell

Little Wigsell

Hollybridge Wood

Hamsell Farm

A26

1

A B 53 C D 54 E F 34

Spa Valley Rly

Ramslye
Wood

TN4

Ramslye
Farm

RAMSLYE RD

EASTLANDS RD

EDGE RD

COURT
ROYAL

KENTISH GDNS

BROADWATER
ICT

SCHOOL
WAY

STUART CL

FURNIVAL PL

BROADMEAD

ANDREWS

GIBSON PL

BROADOAK

ST GEORGE'S PL

NEVIL RD

ST GEORGE'S DR

1 LEICESTER DR
2 DEVONSHIRE CL
3 BROADMEAD AV

DEVONSHIRE CL

BAINFIELD RD

ST MARK'S RD

Strawberry
Hill

BROADWATER
DOWN

HARGATE

STRAWBERRY CL

Broadwater
Down

TN2

8

Ruffet
Wood

LOOSE LA

The Firs

BROADWATER FOREST LA

7

Broadwater
Forest

Spratsbrook
Farm

Strawberry
Hill Farm

Sprat's Brook

Hargate
Forest

37

Broadwater
Lodge

Fintree
Plantation

6

The Warren

The
Roundabouts

BUNNY LA

Bohemia

5

Whitehill
Wood

36

Eridge
Rocks

TN3

Warren
Farm

PH

+

WARREN FARM LA

4

Eridge
Park

Eridge
Park

Eridge
Green

3

A26

Crown
House

Mill
Wood

35

Steel
Bridge

Keepers
Cottages

2

Steel Bridge
Farm

High Weald Landscape Trail

Forge
Wood

Eridge
Old Park

1

Bushy
Wood

Bushy
Shaw

Great Robbins
Shaw

34

55   A   B   56   C   D   57   E   F

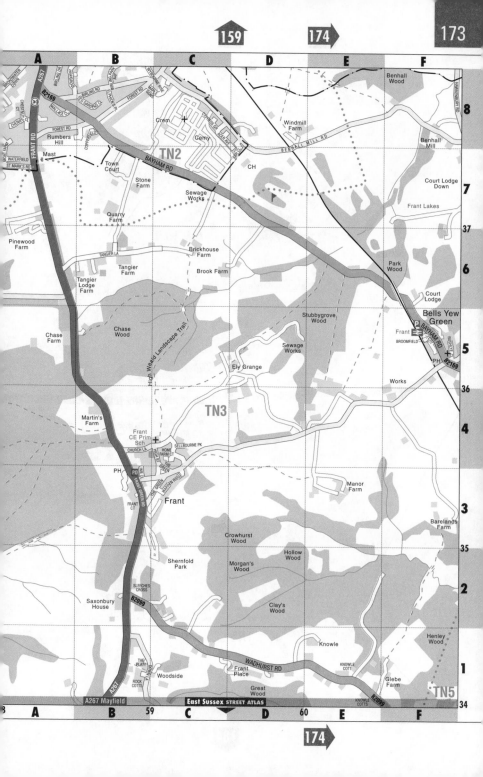

175
162

8

37

7

6

36

37

5

36

4

35

3

2

1

34

67

68

69

A   B   C   D   E   F

TN12

Stunts Wood

Hayden Wood

B2162

LAMBERHURST RD

Windmill Farm

The Horizon Farm

Pittsgate Farm

East Wood

Parsonage Wood

A262

Forstal Farm

Grantham Hall Farm

A262

Crooked Wood

Finchcocks Bridge

The Priory Farm

CHURCH RD

CH

Finchcocks Farm

The Priory

COURT LODGE FLATS

MOUNT PLEASANT LA

PARSONAGE HILL

SCHOOL HILL

HOPGARDEN CL

MANOR COTTS

BREWER ST

Lamberhurst

Foxbury Wood

Little Scotney Farm

CLIVEDON

THE BROADWAY

1 CROWN HO
2 STAR HO

PH

River Teise

Pierce Barn

B2100

ROSE COTTS

HIGH ST

P

PEARSE PL

Broadham Wood

Lamberhurst St Mary's CE-Prim Sch

TN3

Vineyard

TOWN HILL

SPRAY HILL

Down Farmhouse

Ridge Farm

PH

Invicta House

B2169 FURNACE LA

EAST RD

DAINE'S LA

Spray Hill Farm

TN17

FURNACE AVE

PH

B2162

Scotney Castle Gdns

Kilndown

PROSPECT COTTS

THE SLADE

TEISE ACRE

The Down

B2169

P

Scotney Castle (rems of)

HIGHDOWN COTTS 1
WOODSIDE 2

WEST RD

Kilndown

Slade Farm

Whiskett's Farm

BEWL RD

CHURCH RD

CHICKS L

RIVER BEWL

B2100

River Bewl

POP ROW COT

SWEET BOURNE

Bewl Bridge

Bewlbridge

Wiskett's Wood

Bewl Bridge Farm

Kilndown Poultry Farm

TN5

R.W. BRIDGE RD

TN5

Water Treatment Works

Nursery Farm

A21

175
186

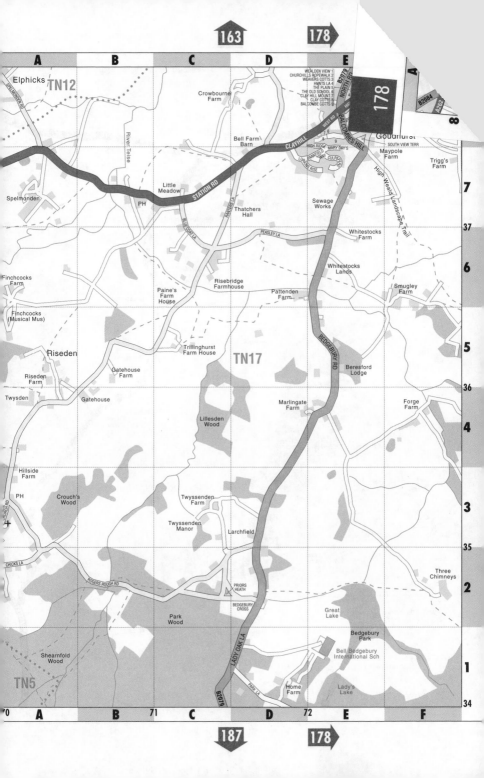

A B C D E A 8

Elphicks TN12
Crowbourne Farm

WEALDEN VIEW 1
CHURCHILLS ROPEWALK 2
WEAVERS COTTS 3
HINTS LA 4
THE PLAIN 5
THE OLD SCHOOL 6
CLAY HILL MOUNT 7
CLAY COTTS 8
BALCOMBE COTTS 9

B2079
NORTH RD
HIGH ST
WEST RD
BALCOMBES HILL
CLAYHILL

B2084
A262

Bell Farm Barn
Goudhurst
SOUTH VIEW TERR
Maypole Farm

HIGH RIDGE
HANWELL WAY
LUKINS RISE
MARY DAY'S
CULPEPERS

178

Trigg's Farm

River Teise
Little Meadow
STATION RD
PH
PLANTERS LA
Thatchers Hall
BLUEBELL LA
PEASLEY LA

Sewage Works

Whitestocks Farm

High Weald Landscape Trail

7
37
6

Spelmonden

Finchcocks Farm
Finchcocks (Musical Mus)

Paine's Farm House
Risebridge Farmhouse
Pattenden Farm

Whitestocks Lands

Smugley Farm

BEDGEBURY RD

5

Riseden
Gatehouse Farm
Trillinghurst Farm House
TN17

Beresford Lodge

36

Riseden Farm
Twysden
Gatehouse
Lillesden Wood
Marlingate Farm

Forge Farm

4

Hillside Farm
PH
Crouch's Wood

Twyssenden Farm
Twyssenden Manor
Larchfield

3
35

CHICKS LA
ROGERS ROUGH RD

PRIORS HEATH
BEDGEBURY CROSS

Three Chimneys

2

Park Wood

LADY OAK LA
PARK LA

Great Lake

Bedgebury Park
Bell Bedgebury International Sch

Shearnfold Wood
TN5

Home Farm
Lady's Lake

B2079

1
34

A 71 B C 72 D E F

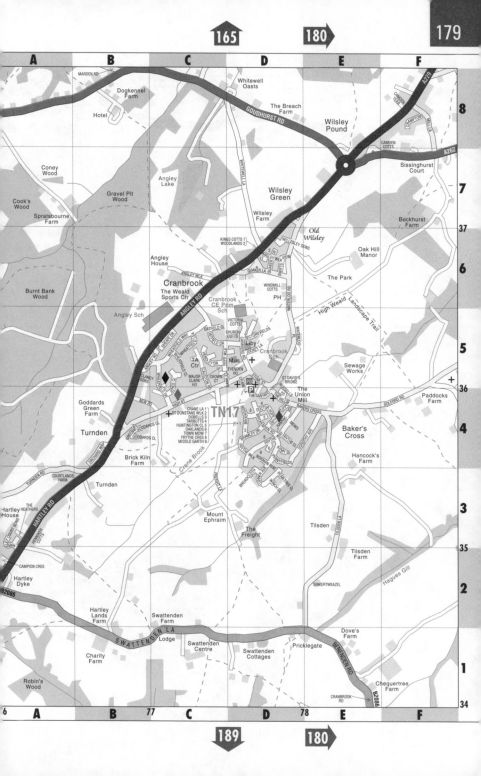

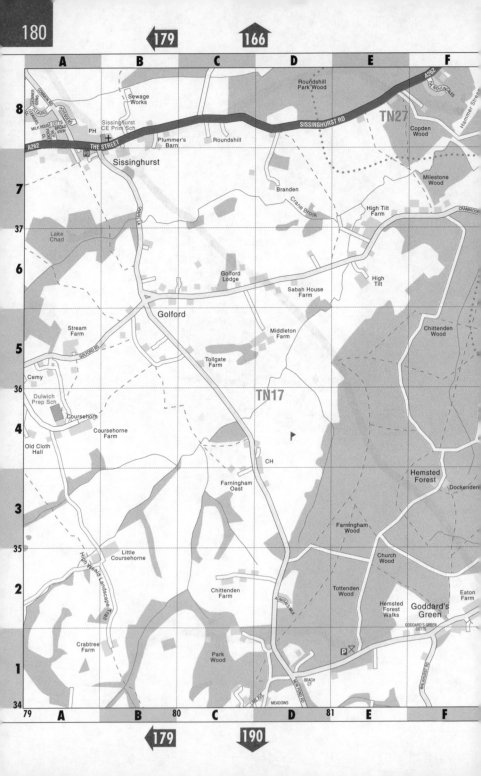

181
168

A **B** **C** **D** **E** **F**

TN26

8 Randolph's
Dashmonden
Hook Wood
Podkin Wood
Crailyn
Crampton House

WOOLPACK CNR
7 WOOLPACK COTTS
TENTERDEN RD
Fredith Farm
Sportsman Farm
St Michael's Court

37 Bowland
Duesden
Greenfields Sch
1 BEECH WLK
2 ASH CRES
Lotland Farm

6 Goldwell Wood
TN27
Golden Fleece
Goldwell
BIDDENDEN RD
A262
High Chimney Farm

Bugglesden

5 Newhouse Farm
Barnfield Wood
Haffenden Farm
GRIBBLE BRIDGE LA

36 Biddenden Vineyards & Cider Works
CH
Children's Farm

4 Sandpit Wood
Reader's Bridge
Brook Farm

3 Short's Wood
Gribble Wood
Penhill
TN30
Silcocks Farm
Short's Farm
Millpond Farm
Honour Farm
GRANGE RD
Flight Wood

35 Boundary Farm
MILLPOND LA

2 Parkgate
Twisden Farm
Rosedown Wood
Pott's Wood
Coombe Farm

Parkgate Farm
CRANBROOK RD
Goodshill Farm
Patt's Farm

1 Goods Hill House Farm

34 TN17
85 **A** **B** 86 **C** **D** 87 **E** **F**

181
192

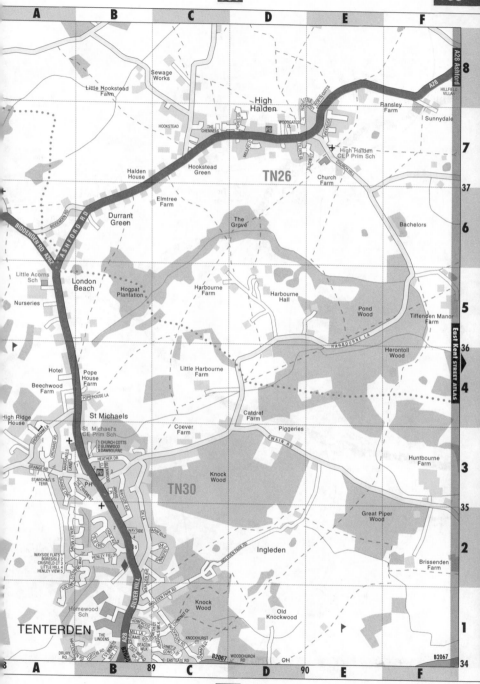

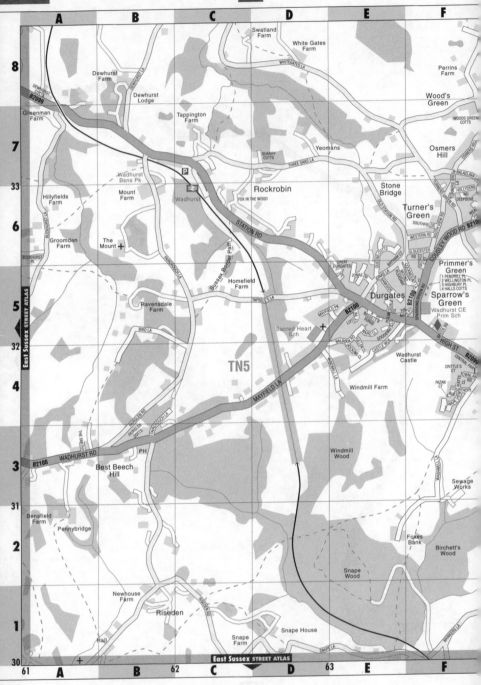

A   B   C   D   E   F

8

Swatland
Farm

White Gates
Farm

Perrins
Farm

WHITEGATES LA

Dewhurst
Farm

Wood's
Green

Dewhurst
Lodge

WOODS GREEN
COTTS

DEWHURST
COTTS

B2099

Tappington
Farm

Osmers
Hill

Greenman
Farm

7

QUARRY
COTTS

Yeomans

THREE OAKS LA

Stone
Bridge

33

P

Wadhurst
Bsns Pk

Turner's
Green

Hillyfields
Farm

Mount
Farm

Wadhurst

Rockrobin

FOX IN THE WOOD

OLD STATION RD

SOUTHFIELDS

WESTERN RD

6

STATION RD

COWLEY WOOD RD B2099

Groomden
Farm

The
Mount

GLOUCESTER
RD

Primmer's
Green

Sussex Border Path

SANDHURST LA

GREAT
DURGATES

JONAS DO

QUEENS RD

PLEASANT

1 PENDRILL PL
2 WELLINGTON PL
3 HIGHBURY
4 HALLS COTTS

BUCKHURST LA

BUCKHURST
PL

Homefield
Farm

Durgates

Sparrow's
Green

5

Ravensdale
Farm

TAPSELL'S LA

B2100

Wadhurst CE
Prim Sch

BIRD LA

MATFIELD PK

BASSETT'S
FORGE

32

Sacred Heart
Sch

LITTLE

Wadhurst
Castle

HIGH ST   B2099

TN5

BALDOCK

CASTLE WK

CENTRAL
RD

CRITTLE'S
CT

FAZAN
CT

COURTHOPE

TOWNLAND

4

MAYFIELD LA

WINDMILL LA

Windmill Farm

SNAPE

ACKERS RD

FAIRCROSS LA

FARRIDEN
COTTS

Windmill
Wood

WASHWELL LA

Sewage
Works

3

B2100   WADHURST RD

THE MARSH

PH

Best Beech
Hill

31

Bensfield
Farm

Pennybridge

Foxes
Bank

Birchett's
Wood

2

Snape
Wood

Newhouse
Farm

SNAPE LA

RISEDEN RD

1

Riseden

Snape House

Snape
Farm

Hall

30

East Sussex STREET ATLAS

61   A   B   62   C   D   63   E   F

East Sussex STREET ATLAS

TN3

River Bewl

Cats Wood

Beal Barn Gardens

BEWL BRIDGE LA

Bewl Water Visitor Ctr

Slipway

Chingley Wood

Hook Farm

Activities Ctr

Hook House

Chingley Manor

A21

Stonecrouch

Bewl Water Nature Reserve

Sussex Border Path

Bewl Water

Beaumans Oast

Greenwoods

OLDHALL LA

BARDEN'S LA

Hazelhurst Farm

Rosemary Farmhouse

Overy's Farm

Norwoods Farm

Overy's Farmhouse

Birchetts Point

Rowley

UPPER HAZELHURST

Bakers & Strakes Farm

TN5

HUNTLEY MILL

TURTON HILL

Borders Farm

Walter's Farm

BORDERS LA

Burnt Lodge

Three Leg Cross

THREE LEG CROSS RD

PH

TALLIS LA

Upper Tolhurst

CORONATION COTTS

Broomden

BURNT LODGE LA

BIRCHETTS LA

Windmill Hill

Ticehurst

Steellands Farm

Dale Hill

CROSS LA

VINEYARD LA

Ticehurst House

Landscapes Farm

Pickforde

PH

1 FRANT COTTS
2 CHAPEL PL
3 MAREPIT GDNS
4 REEVES TERR
5 LAVENDER GDNS
6 LOWER ST MARY'S

STEELLANDS RISE

PH

Ridgeway Farm

HIGH ST

CROSS LANE GDNS

NEWINGTON CT

P

PH

Brick Kiln Farm

HILLBURN GDNS

HAZELWOOD COTTS

SPRINGFIELDS

ST MARY'S LA

PO

ST MARY'S LA

AGNES RISE

LOWER ST MARY'S

MEADOWSIDE COTTS

UPPER PLATTS

LOWER PLATTS

RIDGESIDE AVE

B2099

B2099

B2087

189
180

A B C D E F

8

New House

Coggers

Benenden Sch

Walkhurst Farm

Apple Pie Farm

Mount's Farm

New Pond

Sewage Works

7

B2086 MOUNTS HILL

ORANGE LA

WALKHURST RD

WALKHURST COTTS

33

NORTONS CL
PO
1 CHERRYFIELDS
2 BARRACK ROW

THE STREET

KINGSFORD COTTS

FEOFFE COTTS

RISEDEN LA

HARMSWORTH CT

STEPNEIGH FIELD CH

1 CHURCHILL HO
2 KENNEDY HO

Babbes Farm

RIDDLES LA

The Green

6

NINEHAM LA

Collingwood Grange

Benenden CE Prim Sch

Benenden

DINGHURST CL

PULLINGTON COTTS

BENENDEN RD

B2086

Scullsgate House

Pullington Farm

5

NINEHAM RD

Iden Green Farm

Stream Farm

OLD WEAVERS COTTS

Ramsden Farm

SANDERS LA

High Weald Landscape Trail

32

GOLDHURST RD

Frame Farm

TN17

CLAREMONT PL

CHAPEL LA

PH

4

Sarnden

Yewtree Farm

CORNFIELD COTTS

Sewage Works

Iden Green

Moor Wood

Broom Hill

Reed Wood

IVYPLAN COTTS

MEDWAY COTTS

WOODCOCK LA

Nurseries

3

Depot

MILL ST

PH

Standen Wood

Dingleden

31

Eaglesden

Trafford Farm

DINGLESIDE LA

2

Campion House

BAKERS LA

Wandle Mill

DOCK LA

Mount Wood

Old Standen

Cattstord

SANDERS LA

1

TN18

Standen Street

Springhill Farm

HOPEHOUSE LA

Bankside Farm

30

79 A 80 B C D 81 E F

189
196

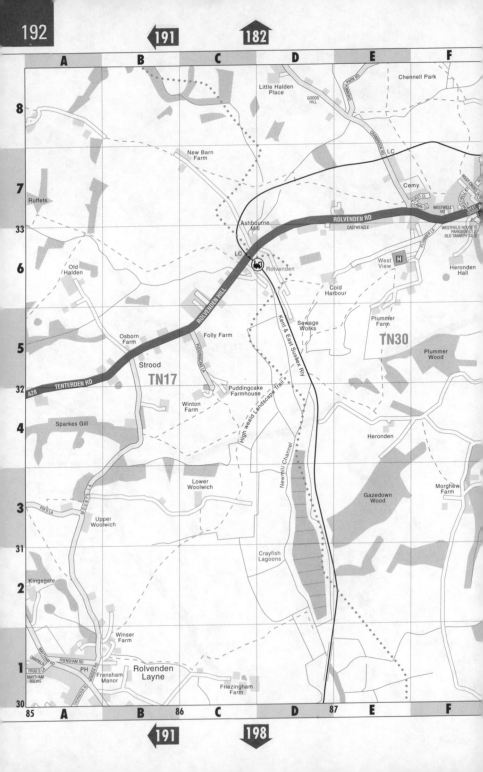

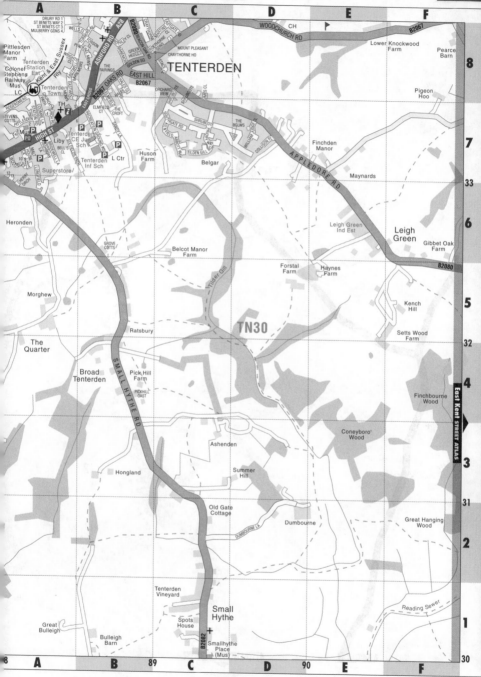

A7
1 PITTLESDEN PL
2 PARK VIEW TERR
3 STATION MEWS
4 ST MILDREDS CL
5 EASTWELL
6 SAYERS LA

DRURY RD 1
ST BENETS WAY 2
ST BENETS CT 3
MULBERRY GDNS 4

7 THEATRE SQ
8 BELLS LA
9 BURGESS ROW
10 MAYOR'S PL
11 CEDAR CT
12 BENNETTS MEWS
13 AUSTENS ORCH

14 ROGERSMEAD

WOODCHURCH RD
CH
B2067

Lower Knockwood
Farm

Pearce
Barn

8

Pittlesden
Manor
Farm

Colonel
Stephens
Railway
Mus
LC

Tenterden
Station
East

Kent & East Sussex

MOUNT PLEASANT
CRAYTHORNE HO

TENTERDEN

EAST HILL

B2067

Pigeon
Hoo

Tenterden
Town

ORCHARD
VIEW

THE
IGLWS

Finchden
Manor

ASHFORD RD

B2080

328

WELLS CL

OAKS RD

THE
FAIRINGS

GOLDEN SQ

GREEN
HEDGES
CL

MARTINS

Herenden

Tenterden
CE Jun
Sch

Liby

Tenterden
Inf Sch

L Ctr

Huson
Farm

Belgar

APPLEDORE RD

Maynards

33

HIGH ST

Superstore

Mus

STEVENS
COTTS

ELMFIELD
CT

THE
CROFT

SHRUBCOTE

SHOEGATE RD

TILDEN GILL

COLLISON PL

WILLIAM

Leigh Green
Ind Est

Leigh
Green

Gibbet Oak
Farm

B2080

6

Grove
Cotts

Belcot Manor
Farm

Forstal
Farm

Haynes
Farm

Kench
Hill

5

Morghew

Tilder Gill

TN30

Setts Wood
Farm

32

The
Quarter

Ratsbury

Pick Hill
Farm

PICKHILL
OAST

Finchbourne
Wood

4

SMALL HYTHE RD

Broad
Tenterden

Coneyboro'
Wood

East Kent STREET ATLAS

Hongland

Ashenden

Summer
Hill

3

31

Old Gate
Cottage

DUMBOURNE LA

Dumbourne

Great Hanging
Wood

2

Reading Sewer

Tenterden
Vineyard

Small
Hythe

1

Great
Bulleigh

Spots
House

Bulleigh
Barn

B2082

Smallhythe
Place
(Mus)

30

A   B   89   C   D   90   E   F

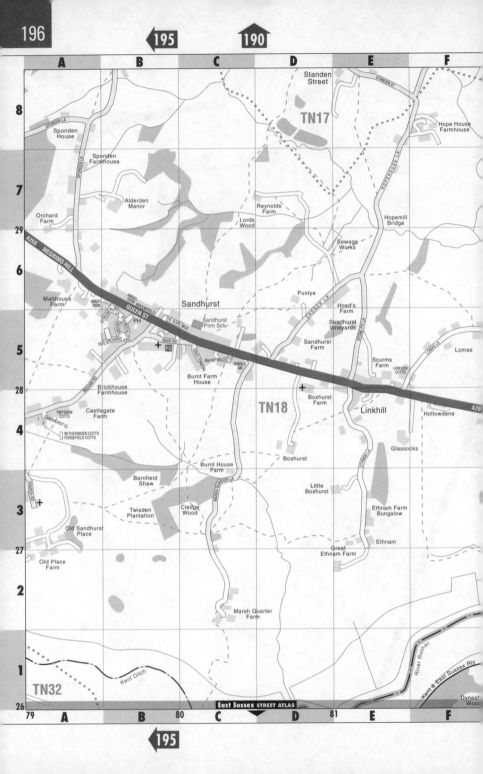

A   B   C   D   E   F

8

Standen Street

TN17

Hope House Farmhouse

SPONDEN LA

Sponden House

Sponden Farmhouse

7

Alderden Manor

Reynolds Farm

Lords Wood

Hopemill Bridge

Orchard Farm

HOPEMILL LA

29

A268   MEGRIMS HILL

Sewage Works

6

Malthouse Farm

Angel Tier Brookfield

ANGEL ROW

Puxtye

Hoad's Farm

QUEEN ST

Sandhurst

PH

THE RICHE WLK

Sandhurst Prim Sch

Sandhurst Vineyards

CROUCH LA

STONE PIT LA

OLD ORCHARD RD

BACK RD

LOMAS LA

5

PO

OAST TERMINAL

BURNT HOUSE

RUNGLE GN

Sandhurst Farm

Scurms Farm

Lomas

Burnt Farm House

Linkden Cotts

BODIAM RD

28

Brickhouse Farmhouse

Boxhurst Farm

TN18

Linkhill

A26

Hollowdene

TWYSDEN COTTS

Castlegate Farm

SANDHURST CL

1 2

4

1 BETHERINDEN COTTS
2 FORGEFIELD COTTS

Boxhurst

Glassocks

ETHNAM LA

Barnfield Shaw

Burnt House Farm

Little Boxhurst

CHURCH RD

MARSH QUARTER LA

3

Twisden Plantation

Cledge Wood

Ethnam Farm Bungalow

Old Sandhurst Place

27

Ethnam

Old Place Farm

Great Ethnam Farm

2

Marsh Quarter Farm

River Rother

1

Kent-&-East Sussex Rly

TN32

Kent Ditch

26

Dynest Wood

79   A   B   80   C   D   81   E   F

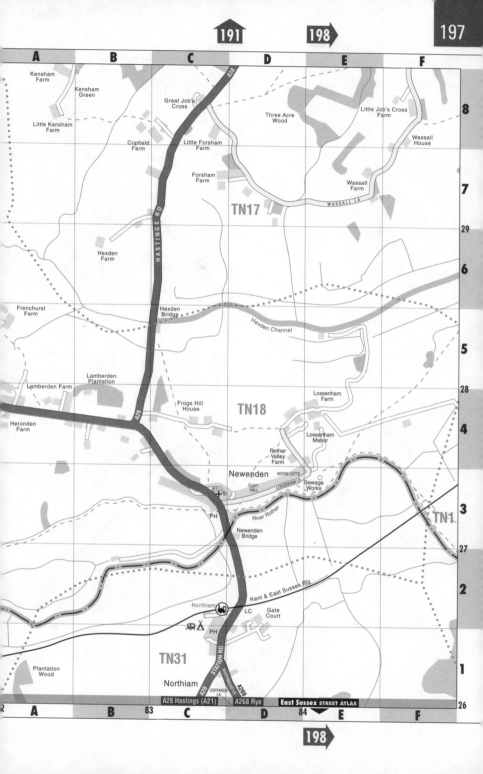

← 197

↑ 192

A	B	C	D	E	F

8

THORNDEN CT
THORNDEN LA
Thornden
Farmhouse

Sewage
Works

Lowden
Farm

Hillgate
Farm

Britcher's

7

MAYTHAM RD

Lambsland
Farm

29

Ingles

TN17

Tench Pit

LC

Wittersham
Road

6

Newmill Channel

Marsh
Wood

Castle
Toll

Maytham
Farm

Kent & East Sussex Rly

5

Pumping
Station

Reading Sewer

TN30

28

TN18

WITTERSHAM RD

Potman's
Heath

Hexden Channel

Spurban
Farm

Moons
Green
Farm

4

Maytham
Wharf

Oxney
Farm

New Barn
Farmhouse

Bush Wall

River Rother

Potman's Heath Channel

Maytham Sewer

Wittersham Sewer

3

27

Methersham
Farm

Wet Level

2

TN31

Otter Channel

Brickhurst
Wood

1

Methersham
Wood

26

A	B	C	D	E	F
85	86		87		

← 197

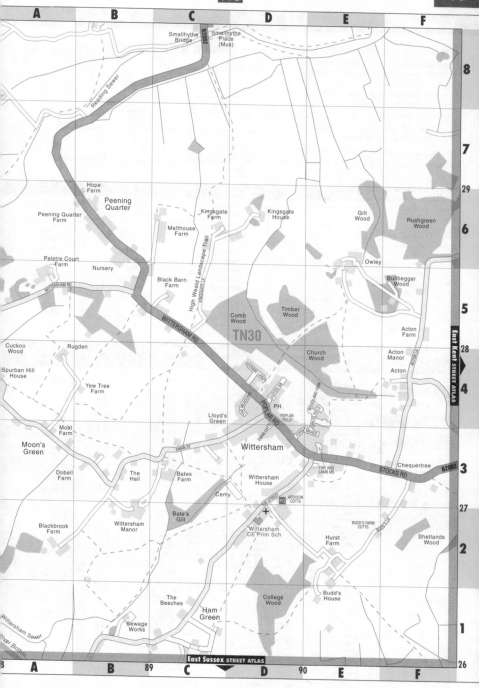

Index

Place name May be abbreviated on the map

Location number Present when a number indicates the place's position in a crowded area of mapping

Locality, town or village Shown when more than one place has the same name

Postcode district District for the indexed place

Page and grid square Page number and grid reference for the standard mapping

Church Rd **6** Beckenham BR2..........**53** C6

Cities, towns and villages are listed in CAPITAL LETTERS

Public and commercial buildings are highlighted in magenta   **Places of interest** are highlighted in blue with a star★

Abbreviations used in the index

Acad	Academy	Comm	Common	Gd	Ground	L	Leisure	Prom	Promenade
App	Approach	Cott	Cottage	Gdn	Garden	La	Lane	Rd	Road
Arc	Arcade	Cres	Crescent	Gn	Green	Liby	Library	Recn	Recreation
Ave	Avenue	Cswy	Causeway	Gr	Grove	Mdw	Meadow	Ret	Retail
Bglw	Bungalow	Ct	Court	H	Hall	Meml	Memorial	Sh	Shopping
Bldg	Building	Ctr	Centre	Ho	House	Mkt	Market	Sq	Square
Bsns, Bus	Business	Ctry	Country	Hospl	Hospital	Mus	Museum	St	Street
Bvd	Boulevard	Cty	County	HQ	Headquarters	Orch	Orchard	Sta	Station
Cath	Cathedral	Dr	Drive	Hts	Heights	Pal	Palace	Terr	Terrace
Cir	Circus	Dro	Drove	Ind	Industrial	Par	Parade	TH	Town Hall
Cl	Close	Ed	Education	Inst	Institute	Pas	Passage	Univ	University
Cnr	Corner	Emb	Embankment	Int	International	Pk	Park	Wk, Wlk	Walk
Coll	College	Est	Estate	Intc	Interchange	Pl	Place	Wr	Water
Com	Community	Ex	Exhibition	Junc	Junction	Prec	Precinct	Yd	Yard

Index of towns, villages, streets, hospitals, industrial estates, railway stations, schools, shopping centres, universities and places of interest

200 20/–Ald

20/20 Ind Est ME16..... 99 C8

A

Aaron Hill Rd E6............. 2 A8
Abberley Pk ME14..... 100 C6
Abbess Cl 12 E6............ 1 E8
Abbeville Ho ME1......... 53 C4
Abbey Brewery Ct ME19 . 97 C8
Abbey Cl BR6................. 58 B6
Abbey Court Sch ME2... 52 E8
Abbey Cres DA17 .... 4 A2
Abbey Dr
  Maypole DA2.............. 31 E6
  Maypole DA3.............. 31 E6
Abbey Gate Cotts ME14... 83 F2
Abbey Gdns BR7 .... 43 A8
Abbey Gr SE2................. 3 B2
Abbeyhill Rd DA15 .... 30 C6
Abbey Ho SE2................ 3 D1
Abbey Life Ct E13.......... 1 B8
Abbey Lodge SE12 .... 28 B4
Abbey Mount DA17........ 3 F1
Abbey Pl DA1................ 15 D2
Abbey Rd
  Bexley DA6, DA7.......... 3 E3
  Erith DA17.................. 55 A2
  Gillingham ME8......... 36 E7
  Gravesend DA12......... 52 F8
  Rochester ME2 .... 52 F8
  Swanscombe DA9...... 17 C2
ABBEY WOOD............... 3 B3
Abbey Terr SE2.............. 3 C2
ABBEY WOOD............... 3 B3
Abbey Wood Rd
  Kings Hill ME19......... 97 A5
  Woolwich SE2............. 3 C2
Abbey Wood Sch SE2 .... 3 A3
Abbey Wood Sta SE2 .... 3 C3
Abbots Cl BR5............... 43 C1
Abbots Court Rd ME3 ... 40 F4
Abbots Field
  Gravesend DA12......... 36 C2
  Maidstone ME16........ 92 B2
Abbotswood Ct 7 DA7... 3 E3
Abbott Rd T15............. 94 F7
Abbotts Cl
  Rochester ME1........... 53 B3
  Swanley BR8.............. 46 A5
  Woolwich SE28........... 3 C6

Abbott's Wlk DA7......... 13 D7
Abbott Way TN30........ 193 C7
Aberdeen Ho 9 ME15... 116 E7
Aberford Gdns SE18..... 11 E6
Abergeldie Rd SE12..... 11 B1
Abery Dr ME20............. 82 B4
Abery St SE18................ 2 E2
Abigail Cres ME5.......... 68 A1
Abingdon Mews ME19... 97 C8
Abingdon Rd ME16....... 98 F2
Abingdon Way BR6........ 58 B6
Abinger Cl BR1............. 42 E6
Abinger Dr ME5............ 68 D2
Absalom Ct ME8........... 55 C2
Acacia Cl BR5............... 43 D4
Acacia Ct DA11............ 36 A8
Acacia Rd
  Dartford DA1............. 32 D7
  Stone DA9.................. 16 E1
Acacia Way DA15.......... 29 F7
Acacia Wlk BR8............ 45 D7
Academy Dr ME7.......... 54 F1
Academy Pl SE18......... 12 A6
Academy Rd SE18........ 11 F7
Acer Ave TN2.............. 173 C8
Acer Rd TN16.............. 72 D3
Achilles Rd ME5........... 68 C2
Acland Cl SE18............ 12 D7
Acorn Cl
  Chislehurst BR7......... 29 C3
  Five Oak Green TN12.. 145 B7
Acorn Gr ME20............. 98 D8
Acorn Ind Pk BR1......... 15 A2
Acorn Pl ME15............ 116 E6
Acorn Rd
  Crayford DA1............. 14 F2
  Gillingham ME7......... 54 F4
Acorns The
  Sevenoaks TN13......... 92 A4
  Smarden TN27.......... 152 F1
Acorn Trad Ctr RM20.... 17 E8
Acorn Way
  Hurst Green TN19...... 194 A3
  Orpington BR6........... 57 B6
Acorn Wharf Rd ME1.... 53 C6
Acott Fields ME18....... 130 F8
Acre Cl ME1.................. 47 A3
Acre Gr ME2................. 66 A4
Acres Rise TN5........... 186 E1
Acton La TN30............ 199 F4
Acton Pl ME18............ 114 A1
Acworth Ho 1 SE18..... 12 B8
Acworth Pl DA1............ 15 C1

Adam Cl ME17............ 115 D3
Airport Ind Est TN16 ... 72 D4
Airport Rdbt E16........... 1 D5
Adamson Rd E16........... 1 A7
Adams Sq DA6............. 13 E4
Adbert Dr ME15.......... 115 B4
Adcot Wlk 7 BR6.......... 57 F6
Adderley Gdns SE9...... 29 A4
ADDINGTON................ 80 C3
Addington La ME19 ...... 80 B4
Addison Cl
  Orpington BR5........... 43 C3
  West Malling ME19..... 81 F1
Addison Cotts TN30.... 199 D3
Addison Dr SE12.......... 11 B2
Addison Rd BR2........... 42 D4
Addlestead Rd TN12... 129 E6
Adelaide Cl
  Chislehurst BR7......... 29 B3
  Gillingham ME7......... 54 C4
  Tilbury RM18.............. 18 F5
Adelaide The ME3........ 38 C6
Aden Terr 1 ME14...... 100 A7
Adisham Dr ME16......... 99 B7
Admaston Rd SE18..... 12 C8
Admers Way 2 DA13... 80 B8
Admers Wood 1 DA13.. 80 B8
Admiral Cl BR5............. 44 D5
Admiral Rd TN16......... 17 D1
Admiral Moore Dr ME20.. 82 F1
Admirals Ct E6.............. 2 B7
Admiral Seymour Rd SE9.. 11 F3
Admirals Wlk
  Chatham ME5.............. 68 B3
  Goddard's Green TN17. 180 C2
  Swanscombe DA9........ 17 B2
  Tenterden TN30......... 183 C1
Admiral's Wlk ME4....... 53 F7
Admiralty Rd ME24...... 39 F1
Admiralty Terr
  Chatham ME7............. 54 A7
  Rochester ME2.......... 39 F1
Admiral Way ME11....... 97 A1
Aerodrome Est ME14.... 85 E4
Afghan Rd ME4............ 53 E4
Agate Cl E16................ 1 D7
Agaton Rd SE9............. 29 C6
Agnes Cl E6.................. 2 A6
Ailsa Cl ME1................ 52 F2
Ailsa Mews ME1........... 52 F2
Ainsdale Cl BR6............ 43 D1
Aintree Cl DA12........... 36 B5
Aintree Ho 1 ME15..... 116 F6
Aintree Rd ME5............ 68 C3

Airedale Cl DA2............ 33 C7
Aisher Rd SE28............. 3 C6
Aisher Way TN13......... 91 E6
Ajax Rd ME1................ 67 C8
Akehurst La TN13......... 92 C2
Alabama St SE18......... 12 E7
Alamein Ave ME5......... 67 F7
Alamein Gdns DA2....... 33 D8
Alamein Rd DA10......... 17 D1
Alanbrooke DA12......... 36 C8
Alan Cl DA1................. 15 C3
Alan Marre Ho SE7....... 11 D8
Alanthus Cl SE12......... 11 A1
Alban Cres DA4............ 47 A1
Albany Cl
  Sidcup DA5................ 30 D8
  Tonbridge TN9.......... 143 D7
Albany Hill TN2.......... 159 C5
Albany Mews BR1........ 28 A2
Albany Park Sta DA5 ... 30 D6
Albany Rd
  Bexley DA5.................. 13 F8
  Chatham ME4............. 54 B2
  Chislehurst BR7......... 29 B3
  Gillingham ME7......... 54 C4
  Rochester ME1........... 53 C4
  Sidcup DA5................. 30 C8
  Tilbury RM18.............. 19 A6
Albany St ME14.......... 100 B5
Albany Terr
  Chatham ME5............. 53 E4
  Gillingham ME7......... 54 C4
Albatross Ave ME2....... 52 C6
Albatross Cl 9 E6......... 1 F8
Albatross St SE18........ 12 E7
Albemarle Rd ME5....... 68 C2
Alberta Rd DA8............ 14 C6
Albert Basin Way E16.... 2 C6
Albert Cotts TN1......... 159 B4
Albert Ho SE28.............. 2 C3
Albert Manor ME7........ 54 B5
Albert Murray Cl DA12.. 36 C8
Albert Pl ME2.............. 53 B7
Albert Rd
  Bromley, Bromley Common
    BR2........................ 42 D4
  Bromley, Mottingham SE9.. 28 E5
  Chatham ME4............. 54 A3
  Dartford DA2............. 32 C5
  Erith DA17.................. 3 F1
  Gillingham ME7......... 54 C4

Albert Rd continued
  Newham E16................ 1 F5
  Orpington BR5............ 44 B3
  Orpington, Green Street Green
    BR6........................ 58 A5
  Rochester ME1........... 53 C3
  Sidcup DA5................. 31 B8
  Swanscombe DA10....... 17 F1
  3 Tonbridge TN9...... 127 B1
Albert Reed Gdns ME15.. 99 C8
Albert St
  Maidstone ME14........ 99 F6
  Royal Tunbridge Wells
    TN1....................... 159 B4
Albert Wlk E16............. 2 B4
Albion Cotts TN12..... 148 D5
Albion Ct 8 SE18.......... 1 E2
Albion Ho E16............... 2 B5
Albion Mews TN1....... 159 C5
Albion Pl
  Chattenden ME2......... 40 A3
  Maidstone ME14....... 100 B4
  Newington ME9.......... 71 B6
Albion Rd
  Bexley DA6................. 14 A3
  Chatham ME5............. 68 B2
  Gravesend DA12......... 36 C8
  Marden TN12............ 148 D5
  Royal Tunbridge Wells
    TN1....................... 159 C5
Albion Terr DA12......... 19 D1
Albion Way TN16.......... 84 B7
Albright Ind Est RM13... 4 F8
Albury Ave DA7........... 13 E5
Albury Cl ME5.............. 68 C2
Albyfield BR1............... 42 F6
Alchins Cotts ME17.... 115 E2
Alconbury DA6............ 14 B2
Aldeburgh Pl SE10........ 1 A1
Aldeburgh St SE10........ 1 A1
Alder Cl TN4.............. 143 D1
Alder La TN17............ 191 C1
Alder Lodge TN4........ 158 E4
Alderman Cl DA1.......... 31 B8
Aldermary Rd BR1....... 42 A8
Alderney Rd DA8........... 9 C5
Alder Rd DA14............. 29 C5
Alders Cotts TN12....... 145 A5
Aldersgrove Ave SE9.... 28 D5
Aldershot Rd ME5........ 68 A7
Alders Meadow ME1... 126 F2
Alders Rd TN11, TN12.. 144 E6
Alders The ME18.......... 99 C6

Alder Way BR8. . . . . 45 D7
Alderwick Rd ME18. . . . . . 97 C3
Alderwood Prim Sch SE9. 12 E1
Alderwood Rd SE9. . . . . . . 12 D1
Aldington La ME14. . . . . 101 D8
Aldington Rd
  Greenwich SE18 . . . . 1 D3
  Maidstone ME14. . . . . . 100 F4
ALDON. 80 B1
Aldon Cl ME14. . . . . 100 C6
Aldon Ct ME14. . . . . 100 C6
Aldon La ME19. . . . . 96 C8
Aldwick Cl SE9 . . . . 29 D5
Aldwych Cl TN10. . . . . . . 127 D7
Alen Sq TN12 . . . . 149 F4
Alers Rd DA6 . . . . 13 D2
Alestan Beck Rd E16. . . . . . 1 D7
Alexander Cl
  Hayes BR2. . . . . 42 A1
  Sidcup DA14 . . . . 12 E1
Alexander Cotts ME2. . . . 38 C6
Alexander Ct
  Greenwich SE3 . . . . 11 B5
  [1] Rochester ME2. . . . . . 53 B8
  [2] Royal Tunbridge Wells
    TN1. . . . . 159 A4
Alexander Gr ME18. . . . . . 97 A4
Alexander McLeod Prim Sch
  SE2 . . . . 3 B1
Alexander Rd
  Bexley DA7. . . . . 13 D5
  Chislehurst BR7. . . . . . . 29 B3
  Swanscombe DA9. . . . . . 17 C2
Alexandra Ave ME7 . . . . . 54 E4
Alexandra Glen ME5 . . . . 68 A1
Alexandra Rd
  Biggin Hill TN16. . . . . . . 88 B8
  Chatham ME4. . . . . 54 B2
  Erith DA8. . . . . 14 F8
  Gravesend DA12. . . . . . . 36 E8
  Tilbury RM18. . . . . 18 F5
  Tonbridge TN9 . . . . 143 B8
Alexandra St
  Maidstone ME14 . . . . . . 99 F6
  Newham E16 . . . . 1 A7
Alexandra Wlk DA4 . . . . . 47 E7
Alex Hughes Cl ME6. . . . . 81 F6
Alfa Cl ME19. . . . . 97 D3
Alfan La DA2 . . . . 31 D3
Alford Ho [6] SE18. . . . . . 12 B8
Alford Rd DA8 . . . . 4 C1
Alford Snell Lodge 7 . 159 D2
Alford Cl ME4. . . . . 54 B2
Alfred Ho
  Gravesend DA11. . . . . . . 36 B6
  [5] Northfleet DA11. . . . . 35 F7
Alfred Pl TN1. . . . . 35 F7
Alfred Rd
  Erith DA17. . . . . 3 F1
  Gravesend DA11 . . . . . . 36 B6
  Hawley DA2. . . . . 32 B6
Alfred St RM17 . . . . 18 C8
Alfriston Cl DA1. . . . . 14 E1
Alfriston Gr ME19 . . . . . . 97 C3
Alice Thompson Cl SE12. . 28 D1
Alicia Ho DA16. . . . . 13 B6
Alison Cl E6 . . . . 2 A2
Alkerden La DA9, DA10. . . 17 C1
Alkham Rd ME14. . . . . . . 100 C6
Alkham Tower [9] BR5. . . 44 C5
Allan Cl TN4. . . . . 158 C4
Allandale Pl ME1. . . . . . . 58 D7
Allandale Rd TN2 . . . . . . 159 D7
Allard Cl BR5 . . . . 44 C2
Allenby Rd
  Biggin Hill TN16. . . . . . . 72 E2
  Woolwich SE28 . . . . 2 C3
Allen Cl ME5. . . . . 68 C6
Allendale Cl DA2. . . . . 33 D7
Allen Gardiner Ho 3 . 159 C3
Allens CI 148 D5
Allens La TN15, TN11. . . 111 A7
Allens Mead DA12. . . . . . 36 F7
Allen St ME14. . . . . 100 B5
Allenswood Rd SE9 . . . . . 11 F5
All Faiths Childrens Com Sch
  [6] ME2. . . . . 53 B7
ALLHALLOWS 9 D1
ALLHALLOWS-ON-SEA 8 A1
Allhallows-on-Sea East
  ME3 . . . . 9 E4
Allhallows Prim Sch ME3. . 9 D2
Allhallows Rd
  Lower Stoke ME3. . . . . . 25 C5
  Newham E6 . . . . 1 E7
Alliance Rd
  Newham E13 . . . . 1 C8
  Woolwich SE18 . . . . 13 A7
Alliance Way TN12 . . . . . 145 F6
ALLINGTON 99 D8
Allington Cl [1] DA12. . . . 36 F7
Allington Dr
  Rochester ME1 . . . . 52 E8
  Tonbridge TN10 . . . . . . 128 A5
Allington Gdns ME18. . . . 113 E7
Allington Prim Sch ME16. . 99 F7
Allington Rd
  Orpington BR6. . . . . 38 A5
  Paddock Wood TN12 . . . 145 F7
Allington Way ME16. . . . . 99 B6
Allison Ave ME7 . . . . 54 E1
Allnutt Mill Cl [4] ME15. . 99 E2
Allotment La TN13. . . . . . 92 C5
All Saints CE Prim Sch [3]
  ME4. . . . . 54 A3

All Saints Cl DA10. . . . . . 17 F2
All Saints Rd
  Allhallows ME3 . . . . 9 D2
  Hawkhurst TN18 . . . . . 189 A1
  Royal Tunbridge Wells
    TN4. . . . . 159 B6
All Saints' Rd DA11. . . . . 35 F7
All Saints Rise TN4. . . . . 159 A6
Allsworth Cl ME9 . . . . 71 B6
Alma Pl
  Hadlow TN11. . . . . 128 E8
  Rochester ME2 . . . . 53 A7
Alma Rd
  Eccles ME20 . . . . 82 F6
  Orpington BR5. . . . . 58 D8
  Sidcup DA14 . . . . 30 A5
  Swanscombe DA9. . . . . . 17 F2
  West Malling ME19. . . . . 97 A8
Alma The DA12 . . . . 36 F4
Almery Cotts ME17. . . . . 134 B8
Almond Cl BR2. . . . . 43 A2
Almond Dr BR8. . . . . 45 D7
Almond Gr ME7. . . . . 69 A4
Almond Ho [7] ME16. . . . . 99 B3
Almond Rd DA2. . . . . 33 C8
Almshouses ME14. . . . . . 101 A4
Almond Way BR2 . . . . 43 A2
Almon Pl ME1. . . . . 53 D5
Almshouses
  Crockenhill BR8 . . . . 45 D2
  Penshurst TN11. . . . . . 141 C4
  [10] Tonbridge TN9 . . . 143 B8
  Yalding ME18. . . . . 114 A1
Alms Row TN16. . . . . 90 B3
Alnwick Ct [8] DA2. . . . . . 16 B1
Alnwick Rd
  Eltham SE12. . . . . 28 B8
  Newham E16 . . . . 1 C7
Alonso Ho [4] DA17. . . . . . 4 A1
Alpine Bsns Ctr E6. . . . . . 2 A8
Alpine Copse [2] BR1. . . . 43 A7
Alpine Way E6. . . . . 2 A8
Alsike Rd DA18 . . . . 3 E3
Altash Way SE9 . . . . 29 A6
Altbarn Ind Est ME5. . . . . 84 C8
Alton Ave ME19. . . . . 97 A3
Alton Cl DA5. . . . . 30 E7
Alton Cotts DA4. . . . . 60 E8
Alverstone Gdns SE9 . . . . 29 C7
Alwold Cres SE12 . . . . 11 C1
Amanda Cl ME5. . . . . 67 F3
Amar Ct SE18 . . . . 2 F2
Amardeep Ct SE18. . . . . . . 2 F1
Ambassador Ho E6 . . . . . . 1 F8
Amber Ct ME7. . . . . 54 D5
Amber La ME17. . . . . 117 A1
Amber Lane ME19. . . . . . . 97 D3
Amberleaze Dr TN2 . . . . 160 D6
Amberley Cl
  [2] Orpington BR6. . . . . 57 F5
  Tonbridge TN9 . . . . 143 A8
Amberley Ct
  Royal Tunbridge Wells
    TN4. . . . . 159 C8
  Sidcup DA14 . . . . 30 C3
Amberley Rd SE2 . . . . 13 D8
Amber Way ME17. . . . . . . 117 B1
Amblecote Cl SE12. . . . . . 28 B5
Amblecote Mdw SE12. . . . 28 B5
Amblecote Rd SE12. . . . . . 28 B5
Ambleside Rd DA7 . . . . . . 14 A5
Ambley Gn ME8. . . . . 69 A8
Ambley Rd ME8. . . . . 69 B8
Ambley Wood Nature
  Reserve* ME7, ME8 . . . . 69 A8
Ambrook Rd [4] 4 A3
Ambrose Cl
  Crayford DA1. . . . . 15 A3
  [6] Newham E6 . . . . 1 F8
  Orpington BR5. . . . . 57 F7
Ambrose Hill ME5. . . . . . . 54 C2
Amels Hill ME9 . . . . 86 F8
Ames Ave ME14. . . . . 101 A4
Amesbury Rd BR1. . . . . . . 42 D6
Ames Rd DA10. . . . . 17 E1
Ames Way ME19 . . . . 97 A3
Amethyst Ave ME5 . . . . . . 67 E6
Amherst Cl
  Maidstone ME16. . . . . . . 99 D4
  Orpington BR5. . . . . 44 A5
Amherst Dr BR5 . . . . 44 A5
Amherst Hill
  Chatham ME7. . . . . 54 A6
  Sevenoaks TN13 . . . . . . 91 F4
Amherst Prim Sch TN13 . . 91 F4
Amherst Rd
  Rochester ME1 . . . . 53 D3
  Royal Tunbridge Wells
    TN4. . . . . 159 A5
  Sevenoaks TN13 . . . . . . 92 B5
Amherst Redoubt ME4 . . . 54 A5
Amhurst Bank Rd TN2, TN11,
  TN12 . . . . 144 F4
Amhurst Wlk SE28 . . . . . . 3 A5
Amies Ho ME15 . . . . 115 F3
Ampleforth Cl BR6. . . . . . 58 C6
Ampleforth Rd SE2 . . . . . . 3 C4
Amsbury Rd ME15, ME17. . 115 B2
Amshurst Villas ME15 . . . 115 A4
Ancaster St SE18. . . . . . . 12 E7
Anchorage Cl ME1 . . . . . . 53 C3
Anchorage Flats TN12. . . 146 A6
Anchorage Point Ind Est
  SE7. . . . . 1 C3
Anchor Bay Ind Est DA8. . 15 A8
Anchor Bvd DA2. . . . . 16 D3
Anchor Ct DA7. . . . . 13 E6

Anchor Ho
  Newham E16 . . . . 1 C7
  Rochester ME1 . . . . 53 B4
Anchor & Hope La SE7 . . . 1 C2
Anchor La ME12. . . . . 27 F3
Anchor Rd ME1. . . . . 53 C1
Ancona Rd SE18 . . . . 2 D1
Andace Pk BR1 . . . . 42 C8
Anderson Way DA7. . . . . . . 4 B4
Andorra Ct BR1. . . . . 42 C8
Andover Ave E16. . . . . 1 D7
Andover Rd BR6 . . . . 43 E1
Andover Wlk [12] ME15 . . 116 F6
Andrew Broughton Way
  ME14 . . . . 100 B4
Andrew Cl
  Dartford DA1 . . . . 14 D2
Andrews Gdns E6 . . . . 1 E7
Andrew Manor ME7 . . . . . 54 C6
Andrew Rd TN4 . . . . 159 C8
Andrews Cl
  Orpington BR5. . . . . 44 A6
  Royal Tunbridge Wells
    TN2 . . . . 159 D5
Andrews Pl DA2 . . . . 31 E6
Andrew Wells Ho [8] BR1. . 28 E1
Andringham Lodge [7]
  BR1. . . . . 42 B8
Andwell Cl SE2 . . . . 3 B4
Anerley Cl ME16 . . . . 99 D7
Angelica Dr E6 . . . . 2 A8
Angel La TN9 . . . . 127 B1
Angel Row TN18 . . . . 196 B5
Angel Terr TN18 . . . . 196 B6
Angel Walk Shop Ctr
  TN9. . . . . 127 C1
Angel Wlk [4] TN9 . . . . . 127 B1
Angerstein Bsns Pk SE10. . 1 A2
Angle Rd RM20 . . . . 17 D8
Anglesea Ave SE18. . . . . . 2 B2
Anglesea Pl [10] DA11 . . . 19 B1
Anglesea Rd
  Orpington BR5. . . . . 44 C3
  Woolwich SE18 . . . . 2 B2
Anglesey Ave ME15 . . . . . 116 A7
Anglesey Cl ME15. . . . . . . 68 B7
Angley Ct TN12. . . . . 163 A5
Angley Rd TN17. . . . . 179 C6
Angley Sch TN17. . . . . . . 179 C5
Angley Wlk TN17 . . . . . . 179 C6
Anglia Ctr The RM13 . . . . 4 E8
Anglian Ind Est IG11 . . . . 3 A8
Anglo Saxon Ho DA12 . . . 36 E8
Ankerdine Cres SE18 . . . . 12 B6
Annandale Rd DA15 . . . . . 29 F8
Anne of Cleves Rd DA1. . . 15 D1
Annesley Rd SE3 . . . . 11 B6
Annesmere Gardens [1]
  SE3 . . . . 11 A2
Annetts Hall TN15 . . . . . . 95 A8
Annex The BR8 . . . . 46 B6
Annie Rd ME6 . . . . 81 F6
Annison Street [4] TN9 . . 127 B2
Ann St SE18 . . . . 2 D2
Ann Stroud Ct SE12 . . . . . 11 A2
Annvera Ho ME7 . . . . 54 C7
Ansell Ave ME4 . . . . 54 A1
Ansia Cl ME19 . . . . 97 B3
Anson Ave ME19 . . . . 96 F3
Anson Cl ME5. . . . . 68 C6
Anson Pl SE28 . . . . 2 D4
Anstridge Rd SE9 . . . . 12 D1
Antelope Rd SE18 . . . . 1 F3
Anthony Cl TN13 . . . . 91 E7
Anthony Rd DA16 . . . . 13 A6
Anthony Roper Prim Sch
  DA4. . . . . 60 E8
Anthonys La BR8 . . . . 46 A8
Anthonys Way ME2. . . . . . 53 E8
Anvil Terr DA2 . . . . 31 E6
Aperfield Rd
  Biggin Hill TN16. . . . . . . 72 E2
  Erith DA8. . . . . 14 F8
Apiary Bsns Pk
  ME17. . . . . 118 B3
Apollo Ave BR1 . . . . 42 B8
Apollo Ho ME5. . . . . 68 A6
Apollo Way
  Erith SE28 . . . . 4 D2
  St Mary's Island ME4 . . . 40 C2
  [3] Woolwich SE28 . . . . . 2 D7
Appleby Cl
  Orpington BR5. . . . . 43 E2
  Rochester ME1 . . . . 67 D7
Appleby Rd E16. . . . . 1 A7
Apple Cl ME6. . . . . 82 A6
Applecross Cl ME1 . . . . . . 53 B8
Apple Ct TN12 . . . . 145 F6
Appledore Ave DA7. . . . . . 14 D5
Appledore Rd DA2. . . . . . . 42 A4
Appledore Cres DA14 . . . . 29 F5
Appledore Ct ME16. . . . . . 99 C7
Appledore Rd
  Gillingham ME8. . . . . . . 55 A3
  Tenterden TN30. . . . . . 193 F7
Applegarth Dr DA1. . . . . . 32 F6
Applegarth Ho DA14. . . . . 14 F5
Applegarth Rd SE28 . . . . . 3 D5
Apple Orch SE28 . . . . 45 D5
Appleshaw Cl DA11. . . . . . 36 A3
Appleton Cl DA7. . . . . 14 C5
Appleton Dr DA2. . . . . 32 B5
Appleton La DA2 . . . . 41 E6
Appletons TN11. . . . . 128 E8
Apple Tree Ct [5] ME8 . . . 98 F2
Appletree Ct [5] ME8 . . . . 69 F8
Appold St DA8 . . . . 14 F8

Approach Rd CR6, TN16. . . 88 B5
Approach The BR6. . . . . . . 57 F8
April Cl ME4. . . . . 54 A1
Apsledene DA12 . . . . 36 D2
Apsley Cl BR5 . . . . 44 B3
Apsley Ct TN4 . . . . 158 D4
Aragon Cl BR2. . . . . 42 F1
Arborfield DA13 . . . . 50 A4
Arbroath Rd SE9 . . . . 11 E4
Arbrook Cl BR5. . . . . 44 A6
Arbrook Ct BR5. . . . . 44 A6
Arbury Ho BR1. . . . . 28 E1
Arbuthnot La DA5. . . . . . . 13 E1
Arcade The [2] SE9 . . . . . 12 A1
Arcadian Ave DA5. . . . . . . 13 E1
Arcadian Cl DA5. . . . . 13 E1
Arcadian Rd DA5. . . . . 13 E1
Arcadia Rd DA13. . . . . 49 F8
Archbishop Courtenay CE
  Prim Sch (Tovil Site)
  ME15. . . . . 99 E2
Archbishop Courtenay CE
  Prim Sch (Town Site)
  ME15. . . . . 100 A3
Archbishops Cres ME7 . . . 55 A5
Archer Ho ME3 . . . . 39 F6
Archer Rd
  Chatham ME5. . . . . 68 B6
  Orpington BR5. . . . . 44 A4
Archer Way ME8 . . . . 46 A7
Archery Cl ME3 . . . . 39 B7
Archery House Hospl DA2 16 B1
Archery Rd SE9 . . . . 11 F2
Archibald Ho ME14. . . . . 100 A7
Archway Ct
  Dartford DA1 . . . . 32 D8
  [4] Rochester ME2. . . . . 53 B8
Arden Bsns Ctr ME2. . . . . 53 E7
Arden Cl SE28 . . . . 3 D7
Arden Gr BR6. . . . . 57 B6
Ardenlee Dr ME14. . . . . . 100 B5
Arden St ME7. . . . . 54 C6
Arethusa Pl DA9 . . . . 17 B2
Arethusa Rd ME1 . . . . 67 C8
Arethusa Venture Ctr★
  ME2. . . . . 40 A3
Argali Ho [3] DA18. . . . . . 3 E3
Argent St RM17 . . . . 18 B7
Argles Cl [4] DA12 . . . . . . 17 A2
Argyle Cl ME1. . . . . 67 E8
Argyle Rd
  Newham E16 . . . . 1 B7
  Royal Tunbridge Wells
    TN4. . . . . 143 A2
  Sevenoaks TN13 . . . . . . 92 B2
Argyll Rd SE18 . . . . 2 C3
Ariel Cl DA12. . . . . 36 F4
Ariel Ct [8] DA17 . . . . 4 A1
Arkwright Rd RM18 . . . . . 19 A5
Arlington Cl DA15 . . . . . . 29 E8
Arlott Cl ME14 . . . . 99 F6
Armada Ct ME4. . . . . 53 E1
Armada Way
  Chatham ME4. . . . . 53 F3
  Newham E6 . . . . 2 C7
Armitage Pl [4] TN18 . . . 188 F2
Armoury Dr DA12 . . . . . . 36 C8
Armstrong Cl
  Badgers Mount TN14. . . . 75 B4
  Bromley BR1. . . . . 42 E6
  Newham E6 . . . . 1 F7
Armstrong Rd
  Maidstone ME15. . . . . . 100 A1
  Woolwich SE18 . . . . 2 E1
Armytage Cl ME3 . . . . 40 E4
Arne Ct TN10 . . . . 127 E6
Arne Gr BR6. . . . . 57 F7
Arnhem Dr ME5. . . . . 67 F7
Arnold Ave DA13 . . . . 64 B8
Arnold Cl ME2 . . . . 53 E7
Arnold Pl RM18 . . . . 19 C6
Arnold Rd DA12 . . . . 36 D6
Arnolds Business Park
  TN12 . . . . 130 A5
Arnolds Ct TN10 . . . . 127 C5
Arnolds La DA4 . . . . 33 A2
Arnott Cl SE28 . . . . 3 C5
Arnsberg Way DA6, DA7. . 14 A3
Arnside Rd DA7. . . . . 14 A6
Arran Cl DA8 . . . . 14 D8
Arandene Ho [3] BR5 . . . . 44 B7
Arran Gn ME2 . . . . 52 C6
Arran Rd ME15 . . . . 116 A6
Arras Ho
  Bexley SE2. . . . . 13 D8
  Erith SE2 . . . . 3 D1
Arsenal Rd SE9 . . . . 11 F4
Arsenal Way SE18. . . . . . . 2 C3
Artemis Cl DA12 . . . . 36 E8
Arthur Cl [8] RM17 . . . . . 18 C8
Arthur Gr SE18. . . . . 2 C2
Arthur Rd
  Biggin Hill TN16. . . . . . . 72 C3
  Gillingham ME8. . . . . . . 69 E7
  Rochester ME1 . . . . 53 D3
Arthur Ruxley Est DA14. . 30 D2
Arthur St
  Erith DA8 . . . . 14 F7
  Gravesend DA11 . . . . . . 36 A8
  Grays RM17. . . . . 18 C8
Arthur Street W DA11. . . . 36 A8
Arthur Toft Ho [6] RM17 . . 18 B8
Artillery Ho SE18. . . . . 2 A1
Artillery Row DA12. . . . . . 36 C8
Artington Cl BR6. . . . . 57 C6
Artisan Cl E6 . . . . 2 B6
Arun Cl BR5 . . . . 44 C1

Arundel DA14. . . . . 30 A3
Arundel Cl
  Bexley DA5. . . . . 13 F1
  Chatham ME5. . . . . 68 D1
  Tonbridge TN9 . . . . 143 A8
Arundel Ct [2] DA6 . . . . . 13 E3
Arundel Dr BR6. . . . . 58 B5
Arundel Ho TN1. . . . . 159 A3
Arundel Rd
  Dartford DA1. . . . . 15 C3
  Royal Tunbridge Wells
    TN1. . . . . 159 B2
Arundel Sq ME14 . . . . 99 F2
Arundel St ME14 . . . . 99 F6
Ascot Cl
  Borough Green TN15 . . . 95 B7
  Chatham ME5. . . . . 68 C2
Ascot Ct
  Bromley BR1. . . . . 42 E7
  Sidcup DA5 . . . . 30 F8
Ascot Ho [2] ME15 . . . . . 116 F6
Ascot Rd
  Gravesend DA12 . . . . . . 36 B5
  Orpington BR5. . . . . 43 F5
ASH 62 E5
ASHBANK 118 B7
Ashbank Cotts ME17 . . . 118 B7
Ashbee Cl ME6. . . . . 82 A7
Ashbourne Ave DA7 . . . . . 13 E7
Ashbourne Ct TN4 . . . . . 158 D4
Ashbourne Rise BR6 . . . . 57 E6
Ashburn Cl BR1. . . . . 28 A1
Ashburnham Cl TN13 . . . 108 C8
Ashburnham Rd
  Erith DA17. . . . . 4 C2
  Maidstone ME14 . . . . . . 100 B8
  Tonbridge TN10. . . . . . . 127 C3
Ashburn Mews ME7. . . . . 54 E3
Ashburton Rd E16. . . . . . . 1 A7
Ashby Cl ME2. . . . . 66 A4
Ashby's Cl TN8. . . . . 138 D8
Ashbys Yd TN9. . . . . 127 C1
Ash Cl
  Aylesford ME20 . . . . 82 E1
  Chatham ME5. . . . . 54 C1
  Edenbridge TN8 . . . . . . 122 B1
  Gillingham ME8 . . . . 55 B3
  Orpington BR5. . . . . 43 D0
  Royal Tunbridge Wells
    TN2. . . . . 173 D7
  Sidcup DA14 . . . . 30 B5
  Swanley BR8 . . . . 45 D7
Ashcombe Dr TN8 . . . . . . 122 B4
Ash Cres
  Biddenden TN27. . . . . . 182 D7
  Higham ME3 . . . . 38 C3
Ashcroft Ave DA15 . . . . . . 13 A1
Ashcroft Cres DA15 . . . . . 13 A1
Ashcroft Ct
  Dartford DA1. . . . . 33 A8
  [5] Chatham ME5 . . . . . . 12 A1
Ash Croft Ct DA3. . . . . . . 62 F7
Ashcroft Rd
  Paddock Wood TN12 . . . 146 A5
  Rochester ME2 . . . . 39 B2
Ash Ct SE12 . . . . 28 B8
Ashdale Rd SE12. . . . . 28 B7
Ashden Wlk TN10 . . . . . . 127 C7
Ashdown Cl
  Coldblow DA5 . . . . 31 C8
  Maidstone ME16 . . . . . . 99 D3
  Royal Tunbridge Wells
    TN4. . . . . 158 F4
Ashen E6. . . . . 2 A7
Ashenden TN27 . . . . 152 F2
Ashenden Cl ME2 . . . . . . 39 C2
Ashenden Wlk TN2. . . . . 159 E8
Ashen Dr DA1. . . . . 15 A1
Ashen Grove Mobile Home
  Pk TN15. . . . . 61 B1
Ashen Grove Rd TN15 . . . 61 B1
Asher Reeds TN3 . . . . . . 158 A4
Ashes La
  Plaxtol TN11. . . . . 110 F1
  Tonbridge TN11. . . . . . 128 B8
Ashfield La BR7. . . . . 29 C1
Ashfield Pl BR7. . . . . 29 D1
Ashford Dr ME17 . . . . . . 118 D3
Ashford Rd
  Harrietsham ME17. . . . . 119 C6
  Maidstone, Grove Green
    ME14 . . . . 100 D4
  Maidstone ME14 . . . . . . 100 D3
  Tenterden, Durrant Green TN26,
    TN30. . . . . 183 A6
  Tenterden TN30 . . . . . . 193 B8
Ash Gr ME16. . . . . 99 C6
Ashgrove SE12. . . . . 28 A7
Ashgrove Rd TN13 . . . . . 108 B7
Ashgrove Sch BR1 . . . . . . 42 B7
Ash Ho BR5. . . . . 44 C5
Ash Keys DA13. . . . . 80 B8
Ash La TN15 . . . . 62 D2
Ashlar Pl [4] SE18 . . . . . . 2 B2
Ashleigh Cl DA13. . . . . . . 63 F1
Ashleigh Commercial Est
  SE18 . . . . 1 D1
Ashleigh Gdns
  Chatham ME5. . . . . 67 D1
  Headcorn TN27 . . . . . . 151 D6
Ashley Cl TN13. . . . . 92 B3
Ashley Gdns
  Orpington BR6. . . . . 57 E5
  Rusthall TN4. . . . . 158 C5
Ashley Ho BR5. . . . . 44 A7

Ashley Park Cl TN4......158 C5
Ashley Pk TN4......158 C5
Ashley Rd
　Gillingham ME8......55 C2
　Sevenoaks TN13......92 B3
　Tonbridge TN11......126 E5
Ashly Ct 22 DA14......30 A5
Ashmead Cl ME5......68 C3
Ashmead Gate BR1......42 C8
Ashmill Bsns Pk ME17......120 F6
Ashmore Gdns DA11......35 D5
Ashmore Gr DA16......12 E4
Ashmore La BR2......72 C8
Ash Platt TN15......92 E6
Ash Rd
　Dartford DA1......32 D7
　Gravesend DA12......36 C4
　Hartley DA3......52 A7
　Hawley DA2......32 F4
　New Ash Green DA3, TN15......62 E7
　Orpington BR6......57 F3
　Rochester ME2......52 F6
　Westerham TN16......89 E2
Ashridge Cres SE18......12 C7
Ashridge House 7 DA14......29 F4
Ash Row BR2......42 A8
Ashton Way ME19......97 C6
Ashtree Cl BR6......57 B6
Ash Tree Cl TN15......61 F2
Ash Tree Cotts TN12......164 B7
Ash Tree Dr TN15......61 F2
Ash Tree La ME5......54 D1
ASHURST......156 D2
Ashurst Cl DA1......1 C4
Ashurst Hill TN3......156 D2
Ashurst Pl ME8......69 E8
Ashurst Rd
　Maidstone ME14......100 C5
　Stone Cross TN3......157 B2
Ashurst Sta TN3......156 D2
Ashwater Rd SE12......23 A5
Ashwell Cl 3 E6......1 E7
Ashwood Cl ME3......39 C7
Ashwood Pl DA2......34 B5
Ashworth Ave TN15......61 D3
Askern Cl DA6......13 D3
Askews Farm La RM17,
　RM20......17 E8
Askham Lodge 19 SE12......28 A8
Aslop Rd DA11......35 E5
Aspen Cl
　Orpington BR6......58 A5
　Swanley BR8......45 D8
Aspen Copse BR1......42 F7
Aspen Gn DA1......16 A2
Aspen Ho 2 DA15......30 A5
Aspen Way
　2 Gillingham ME7......67 E4
　Royal Tunbridge Wells
　TN4......143 C1
Aspian Dr ME17......115 D3
Asquith Rd ME8......69 C6
Association Wlk ME1......67 C7
Aster Dr ME4......40 B3
Aster Rd ME3......40 E3
Astley RM17......17 F8
Astley St ME14......100 A4
Aston Cl
　Chatham ME5......68 A2
　Sidcup DA14......30 A5
Astor Ct E16......1 C7
Astor of Hever Com Sch The
　ME16......90 C3
Astor Rd TN15......111 E5
Astra Dr DA12......36 F3
Atcost Rd IG11......3 A8
Athelstan Gn ME17......102 C2
Athelstan Rd ME4......53 F2
Athelstan Way BR5......44 A8
Athill Ct TN13......92 C5
Athol Rd DA8......4 C1
Atkinson Ct BR6......58 A5
Atkinson Rd E16......1 C8
Atlanta Ct ME4......53 D3
Atlantic Cl DA10......17 E2
Atlantis Ave E16......2 C6
Atlas Gdns SE7......1 C2
Atlas Rd DA1......15 F4
Atterbury Cl TN16......96 D1
Attlee Dr DA1......16 D1
Attlee Rd SE28......3 B6
Attwaters La TN18......189 C6
Auckland Cl ME18......19 A5
Auckland Ho 10 ME15......116 E5
Auckland Rd TN1......159 C5
Auden Rd ME20......82 A3
Auden Ave
　Gillingham ME7......54 E1
　Tonbridge TN9......126 F2
Audley Cl ME16......99 B5
Audley Dr E16......1 B5
Audley Rise TN9......126 F1
Audley Wlk BR5......44 C3
Audre Lorde Ho E16......1 B8
Audrey Sturley Ct TN4......158 D4
Auger Cl ME7......70 E5
Augusta Cl 1 ME7......54 C7
Augustine Rd TN10......127 C3
Augustine Rd
　Gravesend DA12......36 C8
　Orpington BR5......44 D6
Aultmore Ct TN2......159 D3
Austell Manor 8 ME7......54 C6

Austen Cl
　Swanscombe DA9......17 C1
　Tilbury RM18......19 C5
Austen Ct 5 ME17......117 E6
Austen Gdns DA1......15 F3
Austen Rd DA8......14 B7
Austens Orch 13 TN30......193 A7
Austen Way ME20......81 F4
Austin Ave BR2......42 E4
Austin Cl ME5......54 E2
Austin Ct 4 TN16......89 D1
Austin Rd
　Northfleet DA11......35 F7
　Orpington BR5......44 A4
Austral Cl DA15......29 F5
Autumn Glade ME5......84 D8
Autumn Gr BR1......28 B2
Avalon Cl BR6......58 D7
Avalon Rd BR5, BR6......58 C8
Avard Gdns BR6......57 C6
Avards Cl TN18......194 E8
Avebury Ave TN9......127 B1
Avebury Rd BR6......57 D7
Aveley Cl DA8......14 F8
Aveling Cl ME3......40 D6
Aveling Ct 2 ME2......53 B7
Avenons Rd 1 E13......1 A8
Avenue du Puy TN9......127 C1
Avenue Rd
　Bexley DA7, DA6......13 E4
　Erith DA8......14 E7
　Sevenoaks TN13......92 C3
　Tatsfield TN16......88 E7
Avenue The
　Aylesford ME20......82 E1
　Biggin Hill TN16......88 F5
　Borough Green TN15......95 A8
　Bromley BR1......42 D6
　Gravesend DA11......36 A8
　Hill Park TN16......89 A4
　Orpington BR6......57 F8
　Orpington, Keston Mark
　BR2......56 D7
　Orpington, St Paul's Cray
　BR5......30 B1
　Sidcup DA5......30 D8
　St Mary's Island ME4......40 C2
　Swanscombe DA9......17 B2
　2 Tonbridge TN9......127 B2
Averenches Rd ME14......100 F5
Avery Cl
　Allhallows-on-Sea ME3......9 E3
　Maidstone ME15......99 F1
Avery Ct ME3......9 E3
AVERY HILL......12 C1
Avery Hill Rd SE9......29 D7
Avery La ME15, ME17......117 D2
Avery Way
　Allhallows ME3......9 D2
　Dartford DA1......32 F6
Aviemore Gdns ME14......100 F4
Avington Cl ME15......99 F1
Avocet Mews SE28......2 D3
Avocet Wlk ME5......68 C2
Avon Cl
　Gravesend DA12......36 D6
　Tonbridge TN10......127 C5
Avon Ct DA14......30 B5
Avondale Ct ME4......100 E5
Avondale Pl ME3......25 C4
Avondale Rd
　Bexley DA16......13 C5
　Bromley, Mottingham SE9......28 E6
　Bromley, Plaistow BR1......28 A2
　Gillingham ME7......54 D5
Avonmouth Rd DA1......15 D2
Avon St TN1......159 C5
Avonstowe Cl ME8......57 C7
Awliscombe Rd DA16......12 F5
Axford St ME8......70 A8
Axminster Cres DA16......13 C6
Axtaine Rd BR5......44 D2
Axtane DA13......34 F1
Axtane Cl DA4......47 C8
Aycliffe Cl BR1......42 F5
Ayelands DA3......62 E8
Ayelands La DA3......62 E8
Ayers Cotts BR8......32 E2
Aylesbury Rd BR2......42 A6
AYLESFORD......82 E2
Aylesford Cres ME8......55 B4
Aylesford Prim Sch ME20......82 D1
Aylesford Sch & Sports Coll
　ME20......82 D1
Aylesford Sta ME20......82 D2
Aylesham Rd BR6......43 F2
Aylewade Rd TN27......167 E7
Aynscombe Angle BR6......44 A2
Azalea Dr BR8......45 E5

B

Babbacombe Rd BR1......28 B1
Babb's La TN17......190 A6
Babington House Sch
　BR7......27 E5
Babylon La ME17, TN12......134 B1
Backfields ME3......53 B4
Back La
　Godden Green TN15......93 A2
　Goudhurst TN17......177 E8
　Horsmonden TN12......163 A4
　Ightham TN15......94 C2
　Maidstone ME17......116 E1
　Sevenoaks TN13, TN14......91 C1
　Shipbourne TN11......110 D4
　Sidcup DA5......31 A8

Back Rd
　Sandhurst TN18......196 B5
　Sidcup DA14......30 A4
Back St ME17......117 E6
Baden Powell Ho 11 DA17......4 A3
Baden Powell Rd TN13......91 E5
Baden Rd ME7......54 D7
Bader Cres ME5......68 A7
Bader Wlk DA11......35 F5
Badger Rd ME5......68 A7
Badgers Copse BR6......57 F8
Badgers Croft SE9......29 A5
Badgers Holt TN2......159 E5
BADGERS MOUNT......59 B1
Badgers Rd TN14......59 B1
Badgers Rise TN14......59 A1
Badlow Cl DA8......14 E7
Badminton Mews E16......1 A5
Badsell Rd TN12......145 E5
Baffin Cl ME4......53 F2
Bagshaw Ho 6 BR1......42 A8
Bailey Cl SE28......2 E5
Bailey Dr ME7......55 A1
Baird Ho 13 DA17......4 A3
Bakenham Ho 1 ME1......53 C1
Baker Beall Ct DA14......14 B4
Baker Cres DA1......32 D8
Baker Hill Cl DA11......35 F4
Baker La
　Headcorn TN27......151 F7
　Sutton Valence ME17......134 F7
Baker Rd SE18......11 E7
Bakers Ave TN15......61 E3
BAKER'S CROSS......179 E4
Bakers Cross TN17......179 E4
Bakers Mews 8 BR6......57 F4
Baker St
　Burham ME1......66 F1
　Rochester ME1......53 C3
Baker's Wlk ME1......53 C6
Bakery Cl TN17......166 E7
Bakery Cotts ME14......83 E3
Balaclava La TN5......185 A6
Balcaskie Rd SE9......11 F2
Balchen Rd SE3......11 D5
Balcombe Cl DA6......13 D3
Balcombe Cotts TN17......177 E8
Balcombes Hill TN17......177 E8
Balder Rise SE12......28 B6
Baldock Rd TN5......184 E4
Baldwin's Pl ME17......119 D6
Baldwyns Mans DA2......31 D6
Baldwyn's Pk DA5......31 D6
Baldwyn's Rd DA5......31 D6
Balfour Inf Sch ME1......53 E1
Balfour Jun Sch ME4......53 E2
Balfour Rd
　Bromley BR2......42 D4
　Chatham ME4......53 E1
Balgowan St SE18......2 F2
Ballamore Rd BR1......28 A5
Ballantyne Cl SE9......28 E4
Ballard Bsns Pk ME2......52 F5
Ballard Cl TN12......148 C6
Ballard Ct 20 DA14......30 A5
Ballard Ind Est ME5......84 C8
Ballards La RH8......104 C6
Ballard Way TN12......146 B7
Ballens Rd ME5......68 C3
Balliol Rd DA16......13 B5
Ball's Cotts ME3......39 F4
Ball's Gn TN7......170 B5
BALLS GREEN......170 C5
Balmer Cl ME8......69 D4
Balmoral Ct SE12......28 D4
Balmoral Gdns DA5......30 F8
Balmoral Ho 10 ME15......116 F5
Balmoral Rd
　Gillingham ME7......54 D5
　Sutton at Hone DA4......33 B1
Balmoral Trad Est E6......2 F8
Baltic Ho TN1......159 B5
Baltic Rd TN9......133 A7
Baltic Wharf 1 DA11......19 A1
Baltimore Pl DA16......12 F5
Bambridge Ct ME14......99 F6
Banbury Villas DA13......34 F1
Banchory Rd SE3......11 B7
Bandside DA8......48 E5
Bancroft Gdns BR6......57 F8
Bancroft La ME19......97 C2
Bancroft Rd TN15......78 F3
Bangor Rd ME2......52 D6
Banister Ho RM20......17 D8
Bank Cotts ME17......102 E3
Bankfields TN27......151 C5
Bankfield Way TN17......177 E7
Bank Ho TN15......79 A3
Bank Hos DA2......33 A3
Bank La TN1, TN15......109 A3
Bankside
　Chatham ME5......68 B8
　Durgates TN5......184 E5
　Northfleet DA11......18 C1
　Sevenoaks TN13......91 E6
Bankside Cl
　Biggin Hill TN16......72 C1
　Joyden's Wood DA5......31 D4
Bank St
　Chatham ME4......53 B3
　Cranbrook TN17......179 C5
　Gravesend DA12......19 B1
　Maidstone ME14......100 C2
　Sevenoaks TN13......91 D6
　Tonbridge TN9......127 C2
Bank View 5 ME15......99 E2

Banky Mdw ME16......98 F3
BANNER FARM......159 C2
Banner Farm Rd TN2......159 B2
Banning St ME2......53 B8
Bannister Gdns BR5......44 C6
Bannister Rd ME14......100 A7
Bannockburn Prim Sch
　SE18......2 F2
Bannockburn Rd SE18......2 F2
Banstead Ct 3 BR1......42 B6
Banstead Rd DA5......13 D1
Bapchild Pl 11 BR5......44 C5
Barbados Terr 2 ME14......100 A7
Barberry Ave ME5......67 E5
Barcham Ct ME15......115 F5
Barchester Way TN10......127 F6
Barclay Ave TN10......128 A5
Barclay Field TN5......176 E2
Barcombe Cl BR5......44 A6
Bardell Terr ME1......53 D5
Barden Ct ME14......100 B5
BARDEN PARK......126 F1
Barden Park Rd TN9......127 A1
Barden Rd
　Penshurst TN3......141 F2
　Speldhurst TN3......158 A8
　Tonbridge TN9......127 B1
Bardsley Cl TN12......130 A7
Barfield DA4......47 B8
Barfield Rd BR1, BR7......43 A6
Barfleur Manor 3 ME7......54 A6
Barfreston Cl ME14......99 F2
Bargate Cl SE18......2 F1
Barge Ct DA9......17 C3
Bargehouse Rd E16......2 B4
Bargrove Rd ME14......100 C5
Barham Cl
　Chislehurst BR7......29 B3
　Gravesend DA12......36 B7
　Maidstone ME15......116 E5
　Orpington BR2......42 E1
Barham Ct BR2......42 E1
Barham Ct* ME18......114 B8
Barham Mews ME18......114 B8
Barham Rd
　Chislehurst BR7......29 B3
　Dartford DA1......33 A8
Barham's Mill Rd TN27......137 B3
Baring Cl SE12......28 A6
Baring Prim Sch 13 SE12......28 A8
Baring Rd SE12......28 A6
Barker Rd ME16......99 F3
Bark Hart Rd BR6......44 B1
BARKING......3 B8
Barkis Cl ME1......67 D7
Barkway Dr BR6......57 A6
Barleycorn ME19......81 E1
Barleycorn Dr ME8......69 E6
Barley Fields ME14......100 D4
Barleymow Cl ME5......68 C7
Barling Cl ME5......68 E1
Barlow Cl ME8......69 E5
Barlow Dr SE18......11 E6
Barlow Way RM13......4 E8
Barlow Way S RM13......4 E7
BARMING HEATH......99 A3
Barming Prim Sch ME16......98 F2
Barming Rd ME18......97 F2
Barming Sta ME16......98 F6
Barnaby Terr ME1......53 D2
Barnard Cl
　Chislehurst BR7......43 D8
　Woolwich SE18......2 A3
Barnard Ct
　Chatham ME4......54 A2
　21 Dartford DA2......16 B1
Barncroft Cl ME14......100 F4
Barncroft Dr ME7......68 F4
Barndale Ct DA12......37 E3
Barned Ct ME14......98 F2
BARNEHURST......14 D4
Barnehurst Ave DA7, DA8......14 C6
Barnehurst Cl DA8......14 C6
Barnehurst Inf Sch DA8......14 C5
Barnehurst Jun Sch DA8......14 C5
Barnehurst Rd DA7......14 C5
Barnehurst Sta DA7......14 D5
Barn End Ctr DA2......32 C5
Barn End Dr DA2......32 C5
Barn End La DA2......32 C4
BARNES CRAY......15 B3
Barnes Cray Prim Sch
　DA1......15 A3
Barnes Cray Rd DA1......15 A3
Barnes Ct E16......1 C8
Barnesdale Cres BR5......44 A4
Barnes La ME17......132 D8
Barnes St E13......1 A7
BARNES STREET......129 A4
Barnes Wlk TN13......148 D6
Barnet Dr BR2......56 E8
Barnett Cl DA8......14 F5
Barnetts Cl TN4......143 C1
Barnetts Rd TN11......126 A2
Barnetts Way TN4......159 C8
Barnet Wood Rd BR2......56 C8
Barney Cl SE7......1 C1
Barnfield
　Chatham ME5......68 A8
　Gravesend DA11......36 A6
　Royal Tunbridge Wells
　TN2......172 F7
　Tenterden TN30......183 C2
Barnfield Cl
　Crockenhill BR8......45 C2
　New Barn DA3......49 D6
　Stone DA9......16 F1
Barnfield Cres TN15......76 E2

Barnfield Gdns SE18......12 B8
Barnfield Rd
　Bexley DA17......13 F8
　Orpington BR5......44 D6
　Sevenoaks TN13......91 E4
　Tatsfield TN16......88 E8
　Woolwich SE18......12 B8
Barnfield Way RH8......104 A2
Barnham Dr SE28......2 F5
Barn Hill ME15......114 C2
Barnhill Ave BR2......42 A4
Barnhurst Rd ME14......100 A8
Barn Mdw
　Staplehurst TN12......149 E4
　Upper Halling TN12......65 E4
Barnock Cl DA1......31 E8
Barnsole Inf Sch ME7......54 E4
Barnsole Jun Sch ME7......54 E4
Barnsole Rd ME7......54 C5
Barnwell Pl ME7......54 C5
Barnwell Rd DA1......15 F4
Barnwood Cl ME1......67 B8
Baron Cl
　Gillingham ME7......54 E7
　Maidstone ME14......100 F5
Barons Ct TN4......149 C7
Barrack Cnr TN13......92 C4
Barrack Rd ME4......54 B8
Barrack Row
　Benenden TN17......190 D6
　11 Gravesend DA11......19 B1
Barrel Arch Cl TN12......148 C6
Barretts Green Cotts 8
　TN18......189 A2
Barretts Rd
　Hawkhurst TN18......189 A2
　Sevenoaks TN13......91 E7
Barrie Dr 7 ME20......81 F4
Barrier Point Rd E16......1 C5
Barrier Rd ME4......53 F5
Barrington Cl ME5......67 F5
Barrington Prim Sch DA7......13 D5
Barrington Rd DA7......13 D5
Barrington Villas SE18......12 A6
Barrowfields ME5......68 D1
Barrow La TN3......157 F2
Barr Rd DA12......36 F6
Barry Ave DA7......13 E7
Barry Cl BR6......57 F7
Barry Rd E6......1 E7
Barth Mews SE18......2 E2
Bartholomew Way BR8......45 E6
Barth Rd SE18......2 E2
Bartlett Cl ME5......68 C1
Bartlett Rd
　Gravesend DA11......36 A7
　Westerham TN16......89 C1
Bartley Mill Rd TN3......174 F3
Barton Cl
　Bexley DA6......13 E2
　2 Newham E6......1 F7
Barton Cotts TN11......111 A6
Barton Rd
　Maidstone ME15......100 A2
　Rochester ME2......53 A7
　Sidcup DA14......30 E2
　Sutton at Hone DA4......47 B8
Bartons Cotts TN16......90 C3
Barwell Cres TN16......72 C7
Bascombe Gr DA1......14 E1
Basden Cotts 2 TN18......189 A2
Baseing Cl E6......2 A6
Basi Cl ME2......39 C1
Basildon Rd SE2......3 A1
Basilon Rd DA7......13 E5
Basil Terr 6 ME15......100 A1
Basing Cl ME15......100 B3
Basing Dr DA5......13 F1
Basket Gdns SE9......11 E2
Basmere Cl ME14......100 C6
Bassant Rd SE18......12 F8
Bassetts Cl BR6......57 B6
Bassett's Forge TN5......184 E5
Bassant La TN8, TN11......156 C7
Bassetts Way BR6......57 B6
BASTED......94 F4
Basted La
　Basted TN15......94 F5
　Crouch TN15......95 B4
Bastien Lane ME19......97 D4
Bastion Rd SE2......3 A1
Bath Hard ME1......53 D5
Bath Rd DA1......32 B8
Baths Rd BR2......42 D5
Bath St DA11......19 B1
Bathurst Cl TN12......149 E4
Bathurst Rd TN12......149 E3
Bathway 13 SE18......2 A2
Batten Cl E6......1 F7
Battery Rd SE28......2 E4
Battlefields TN5......78 F3
Battle La TN12......149 A8
Battle Rd DA8, DA17......4 C2
Battlesmere Rd ME3......39 B8

Battle St DA12 . . . . 50 F6
Batt's Rd DA12 . . . . 51 A4
Baugh Rd DA14 . . . . 30 C3
Baxter Cl BR1 . . . . 43 B6
Baxter Rd E16 . . . . 1 C7
Baxter Way ME19 . . . . 97 C3
Bayard Ct DA6 . . . . 14 B3
Bay Cl ME3 . . . . 40 E3
Bayeux Gdns ME7 . . . . 55 A5
Bayeux Ho ☒ SE7 . . . . 11 C8
Bayfield Rd SE9 . . . . 11 D3
Bayhall Rd TN2 . . . . 159 C3
Bayham Ct TN5 . . . . 184 E6
Bayham Old Abbey (rems
of)★ TN3 . . . . 175 B5
Bayham Rd
  Bells Yew Green TN3 . . . 174 B4
  Royal Tunbridge Wells TN2,
  TN3 . . . . 173 C7
  Sevenoaks TN13 . . . . 92 D4
Bayley's Hill TN14 . . . . . . 107 E3
Bayley Wlk SE2 . . . . 3 E1
Bayliss Ave SE28 . . . . 3 C6
Bayly Rd DA1 . . . . 16 A1
Bay Manor La RM20 . . . . . 16 F8
Bay Rd BR6 . . . . 44 C6
Baynham Cl DA5 . . . . 13 F1
Bays The BR5 . . . . 44 C6
Bayswater Dr ME8 . . . . 69 E4
Bay The DA13 . . . . 80 A8
Baytree Cl
  Bromley BR1 . . . . 42 D8
  Sidcup DA15 . . . . 29 F7
Bay Trees Ho18 . . . . 104 B2
Baywell ME10 . . . . 81 E2
Bazes Shaw DA3 . . . . 62 F8
Beacham Cl SE7 . . . . 11 D8
Beachamwell Dr ME19 . . . . 97 C2
Beach Ct
  Eltham SE9 . . . . 11 E1
  Goddard's Green TN17 . . 180 D1
Beacon Ave ME19 . . . . 97 D4
Beacon Cl ME8 . . . . 69 D7
Beacon Dr DA2 . . . . 34 C5
Beaconfields TN13 . . . . 92 A1
BEACON HILL 191 A5
Beacon Hill La TN17 . . . . . 191 B6
Beacon Hill La ME3 . . . . . . 39 F4
Beacon Oak Rd TN30 . . . . 193 B8
Beacon Rd
  Chatham ME5 . . . . 54 C2
  Erith DA8 . . . . 15 B7
  Lenham ME17 . . . . 120 C5
Beacon Rise TN13 . . . . 92 A1
Beacon Row TN15 . . . . 61 F2
Beacons Cl 11 . . . . 1 E8
Beaconsfield Ave ME14 . . . . 54 E5
Beaconsfield Cl SE3 . . . . . . 11 A8
Beaconsfield Par SE9 . . . . . 28 E4
Beaconsfield Rd
  Bromley, Mottingham SE9 . . 28 E4
  Bromley, Widmore BR1 . . 42 D6
  Chatham ME4 . . . . 53 F3
  Greenwich SE3 . . . . 11 A8
  Maidstone ME15 . . . . 99 E2
  Maypole DA5 . . . . 31 E6
  New Eltham ME7 . . . . . . 115 C2
Beacon Wlk TN30 . . . . . . 183 B1
Beacon Wood Ctry Pk★
  DA2 . . . . 34 B4
Beadon Rd BR2 . . . . 42 A4
Beagles Cl BR5 . . . . 58 D8
Beagles Wood Rd TN2 . . . 160 E7
Beal Cl DA16 . . . . 13 A6
BEAL'S GREEN 189 A4
Beaman Cl TN17 . . . . 177 F8
Beamish Rd BR5 . . . . 44 C2
Beams The ME15 . . . . 100 F1
Bean 34 C5
Beane Croft DA12 . . . . 36 F7
Bean Hill Cotts DA3 . . . . . . 34 C4
Bean La DA2 . . . . 34 B6
Bean Prim Sch DA2 . . . . . . 34 C4
Bean Rd
  Bexley DA6 . . . . 13 D3
  Swanscombe DA9 . . . . . . 17 B1
Beanshaw SE9 . . . . 29 A4
BEARSTED 101 B4
Bearsted Cl ME8 . . . . 55 B3
Bearsted Green Bsns Ctr
  ME14 . . . . 101 C4
Bearsted Rd ME14 . . . . . . 100 E6
Bearsted Sta ME14 . . . . . . 101 B5
Bearsted Woodland Trust★
  ME14 . . . . 101 C3
Beaton Cl DA9 . . . . 17 B2
Beatrice Gdns DA11 . . . . . . 35 E6
Beatty Ave ME7 . . . . 54 F4
Beatty Cotts ME3 . . . . 9 D1
Beatty Rd ME1 . . . . 67 D8
Beaufighter Rd ME19 . . . . . 96 E3
Beaufort E6 . . . . 2 A8
Beaufort Ct ME2 . . . . 53 E6
Beaufort Rd ME2 . . . . 52 E8
Beaufort Wlk ME15 . . . . . . 116 E4
Beaulieu Ave E16 . . . . 1 A5
Beaulieu Cl
  Tonbridge TN10 . . . . . . 127 B4
  Tonbridge TN10, TN11 . . 127 B6
Beaulieu Rise ME1 . . . . 53 D1
Beaulieu Wlk ME16 . . . . . . 99 C7
Beaumanor Gdns SE9 . . . . . 29 A4
Beaumont Dr DA11 . . . . . . 35 F8
Beaumont Rd
  Maidstone ME16 . . . . 99 B2
  Orpington BR5 . . . . 43 D3
Beauworth Pk ME15 . . . . . 116 E8
Beaverbank Rd SE9 . . . . . . 29 D7

Beaverbrook Mews ME16. 99 D3
Beaver Rd ME16 . . . . 99 B7
Beavers Lodge DA14 . . . . . 29 F3
Beaverwood Rd BR7 . . . . . . 29 E2
Beaverwood Sch for Girls
  BR7 . . . . 29 E2
Beaver Zoological Gdns &
  Reptile Rescue Ctr★
  TN16 . . . . 88 B5
Bebbington Rd ☒ SE18 . . . . 2 E2
Beblets Cl ◢ BR6 . . . . 57 F5
Beckenham Dr ME16 . . . . . 99 D7
Becket Ct
  Headcorn TN27 . . . . . . 151 D5
  ☒ Tonbridge TN9 . . . . . 143 B8
Beckets Field TN11 . . . . . . 141 A3
Beckets Pl TN14 . . . . 76 C3
Beckett Cl DA17 . . . . 3 F3
Becketts Cl
  Coldblow DA5 . . . . 31 C7
  Orpington BR6 . . . . 57 F7
Beckford Dr BR5 . . . . 43 D2
Beckley Cl DA12 . . . . 36 C7
Beckley Hill Works ME2 . . . 38 B8
Beckley Mews ME5 . . . . 67 F5
Beckman Dr TN14 . . . . 75 C4
Beckshourne Cl ME14 . . . . 100 A8
Becks Rd DA14 . . . . 30 A5
BECKTON 2 A8
Beckton Park Sta E6 . . . . . . 1 F6
Beckton Rd E16 . . . . 1 A8
Beckton Ret Pk E6 . . . . 2 A8
Beckton Sta E6 . . . . 2 A8
Beckworth Pl ME16 . . . . . . 99 B2
Becton Pl DA8 . . . . 14 C6
Bedale Wlk DA2 . . . . 33 B7
Beddalls Farm Ct 7 E6 . . . . 1 E8
Beddington Gdn BR5 . . . . . 43 F8
Beddington Rd BR5 . . . . . . 43 F8
Beddlestead La CR6 . . . . . . 88 A6
Beddow Way ME20 . . . . . . 83 B3
Bedens Rd DA14 . . . . 30 E3
Bedford Ave ME8 . . . . 55 D1
Bedford Pl ME16 . . . . 99 E4
Bedford Rd
  Dartford DA1 . . . . 33 A8
  Northfleet DA11 . . . . 35 F6
  Orpington BR6 . . . . 44 B1
  Royal Tunbridge Wells
  TN4 . . . . 143 A1
  Sidcup DA15 . . . . 29 E5
Bedford Sq DA3 . . . . 48 E6
Bedford Terr 18 TN1 . . . . . 159 A2
Bedgebury Cl
  Maidstone ME14 . . . . . . 100 C6
  Rochester ME1 . . . . 67 D8
Bedgebury Cross TN17 . . . 177 D2
Bedgebury National
  Pinetum★ TN17 . . . . 187 E8
Bedgebury Rd
  Eltham SE9 . . . . 11 D3
  Goudhurst TN17 . . . . . . 177 E5
Bedivere Rd BR1 . . . . 28 A5
Bedlam La TN27 . . . . 152 E6
BEDMONTON 103 E8
Bedonwell Inf Sch DA17 . . . 13 E8
Bedonwell Jun Sch DA17 . . 13 E8
Bedonwell Rd
  Bexley, Bexleyheath DA7 . 13 F6
  Bexley, West Heath DA7,
  DA17 . . . . 13 E8
Bedwell Rd DA17 . . . . 4 A1
Bedwin Cl ME1 . . . . 67 D7
Beeby Rd E16 . . . . 1 B8
Beecham Rd TN10 . . . . . . 127 E6
Beech Ave
  Sidcup DA15 . . . . 30 A8
  Swanley BR8 . . . . 45 F5
  Tatsfield TN16 . . . . 88 D8
Beech Cl
  Beech Copse BR1 . . . . . . 42 F7
Beechcroft BR7 . . . . 29 A1
Beechcroft Ave DA7 . . . . . . 14 D5
Beechcroft Cl BR6 . . . . 57 D6
Beechcroft Rd BR6 . . . . 57 D6
Beech Ct
  Dartford DA1 . . . . 16 A1
  Paddock Wood TN12 . . . 146 A2
  Royal Tunbridge Wells
  TN2 . . . . 159 D4
Beech Dell BR2 . . . . 56 F6
Beech Dr ME3 . . . . 99 C5
Beechen Bank Rd ME5 . . . . 68 A1
Beechenlea La BR8 . . . . 46 B6
Beechen Ct SE12 . . . . 28 B5
Beeches St BR1 . . . . 28 A2
Beeches The
  Aylesford ME20 . . . . 82 E1
  Chatham ME5 . . . . 68 A4
  Hextable BR8 . . . . 31 F1
  New Barn DA3 . . . . 49 C7
  Royal Tunbridge Wells
  TN2 . . . . 159 D5
  Sole Street DA13 . . . . . . 50 D5
  The Moor TN18 . . . . . . 194 E7
  Tilbury RM18 . . . . 19 B5
Beechfield Cotts 6 BR2 . . . 42 C7
Beechfield Rd
  Bromley BR1 . . . . 42 C7
  Erith DA8 . . . . 14 E7
Beech Gr ME3 . . . . 38 C4
Beech Green La
  Cowden TN7 . . . . 155 F1
  Withyham TN7 . . . . 170 B7
Beech Haven Ct DA1 . . . . . 14 D2
Beechhill Rd SE9 . . . . 12 A2
Beech Ho 7 ME8 . . . . 30 A5
Beech Hurst TN2 . . . . 160 D7

Beech Hurst Cl ME15 . . . . 100 B2
Beeching Rd ME5 . . . . 68 B3
Beechings Gn ME8 . . . . 55 C3
Beechings Way ME8 . . . . . . 55 C3
Beechings Way Ind Ctr
  ME8 . . . . 55 B4
Beechin Wood La TN15 . . . 95 D5
Beechlands Cl DA3 . . . . 49 A4
Beech Manor ME2 . . . . . . 159 D3
Beech Mast DA13 . . . . 80 A8
Beechmont Rd TN13 . . . . . 108 B6
Beechmont Rise TN13 . . . . 127 B6
Beechmore Dr ME5 . . . . . . 68 A2
Beech Rd
  Biggin Hill TN16 . . . . 72 C2
  Dartford DA1 . . . . 32 D7
  East Malling ME19 . . . . . 97 F7
  Herne Pound ME18 . . . . . 96 D2
  Hoo St Werburgh ME3 . . . 40 E3
  Newenden TN18 . . . . . . 197 C3
  Orpington BR6 . . . . 58 A3
  Rochester ME2 . . . . 52 F6
  Sevenoaks TN13 . . . . 92 B2
Beech St TN1 . . . . 159 B4
Beechway
  Meopham Station DA13 . . 50 B2
  Sidcup DA5 . . . . 13 D1
Beech Wlk
  Biddenden TN27 . . . . . . 182 D7
  Crayford DA1 . . . . 15 A3
Beechwood Ave
  Gillingham ME8 . . . . 54 D2
  Orpington BR6 . . . . 57 E4
Beechwood Cres DA7 . . . . . 13 E4
Beechwood Dr
  Culverstone Green DA13 . . 64 A1
  Orpington BR6 . . . . 56 D6
Beechwood Gdns DA3 . . . . 64 A1
Beechwood Mews TN2 . . . 159 C3
Beechwood Rd ME16 . . . . . 98 F3
Beechwood Rise BR7 . . . . . 29 B4
Beechwood Sacred Heart
  Sch TN2 . . . . 159 E4
Beechy Lees Rd TN14 . . . . . 76 E3
Beeken Dene BR6 . . . . 57 C6
Beesfield La DA4 . . . . 47 A1
Beeston Ct 4 DA1 . . . . 16 B1
Begbie Rd SE3 . . . . 11 C6
Beggars La TN16 . . . . 89 E3
Begonia Ave ME8 . . . . 55 C2
Beke Rd ME8 . . . . 69 D4
Bekesbourne Tower 12
  BR5 . . . . 44 D1
Belcanto Theatre Acad 3
  SE9 . . . . 11 F1
Beldam Haw TN14 . . . . 75 A8
Belfast Ho 10 ME15 . . . . . 116 A8
Belfield Rd TN2 . . . . 160 D6
Belford Gr SE18 . . . . 2 A2
Belfry Dr ME3 . . . . 40 E6
Belgrave Cl 5 BR5 . . . . 44 C5
Belgrave Cl SE7 . . . . 11 C7
Belgrave Rd TN1 . . . . 159 B4
Belgrave St ME20 . . . . 82 F6
Belgrave 5 TN1 . . . . 159 A2
Bellarmine Cl SE28 . . . . 2 F4
Bell Bedgebury International
  Sch TN17 . . . . 177 E1
Bell Cl DA9 . . . . 16 F2
Bell Cres ME1 . . . . 82 F8
Bellefield Rd BR5 . . . . 44 B4
Bellegrove Cl DA16 . . . . . . 12 F5
Bellegrove Par DA16 . . . . . 12 E5
Bellegrove Rd DA16 . . . . . . 12 E5
Bellevue Rd DA6 . . . . 13 F2
Belle Vue Rd BR6 . . . . 57 A1
Bell Farm Gdns ME16 . . . . 98 F2
Bellfield Cl SE3 . . . . 11 B7
Bellflower Cl 2 E6 . . . . 1 E8
Bell Gdns BR5 . . . . 44 C4
Bellgrove Ct ME5 . . . . 84 A8
Bell Ho
  Erith SE2 . . . . 3 D1
  Grays RM17 . . . . 17 F8
Bellingham Way ME20 . . . . 82 B3
Bell La
  Burham ME1 . . . . 82 F8
  Chatham ME1 . . . . 84 B7
  Larkfield ME20 . . . . 82 B2
  Maidstone ME14 . . . . . . 101 A5
  Newham E16 . . . . 1 A5
  Standen TN27 . . . . 168 B8
  Staplehurst TN12 . . . . . 149 E3
Bellman Ave DA12 . . . . 36 E7
Bell Mdw ME15 . . . . 116 A6
Bellows La TN15 . . . . 94 F7
Bell Rd ME15 . . . . 116 A6
Belring Cl DA17 . . . . 14 A8
Bell Row TN11 . . . . 128 F5
Bell's Cl TN30 . . . . 193 A7
Bells Farm La TN11 . . . . . 129 C8
Bells Farm Rd TN11 . . . . . 112 D1
Bell Shaw 17 ME15 . . . . . . 116 E5
Bells La LB TN30 . . . . 193 A7
Bell's La ME1 . . . . 60 E6
Bell St SE18 . . . . 11 E6
BELLS YEW GREEN 173 F5
Bell Water Gate SE18 . . . . . 2 A3
Bell Way ME17 . . . . 118 C2
Bellwood Ct ME4 . . . . 24 C3
Bell Wood Prim Sch 16
  ME15 . . . . 116 E5
Belmont Ave DA16 . . . . 12 E4
Belmont Cl ME16 . . . . 98 F2
Belmont Ct 8 ME15 . . . . . 100 B4
Belmont Par BR7 . . . . 29 C3

Belmont Prim Sch DA8. . . . 14 A7
Belmont Rd
  Chislehurst BR7 . . . . 29 B3
  Erith DA8 . . . . 14 B6
  Gillingham ME7 . . . . 54 C4
  Grays RM17 . . . . 17 F8
Belson Rd SE18 . . . . 1 F2
Beltana Dr DA12 . . . . 36 E4
Belton Rd DA14 . . . . 30 A4
BELTRING 130 A4
Beltring Rd
  Beltring TN12, ME18 . . . 130 B4
  Royal Tunbridge Wells
  TN4 . . . . 159 A6
Beltring Sta TN12 . . . . 130 B4
Belts Wood 14 ME15 . . . . . 116 F5
Beltwood Rd DA17 . . . . 4 C2
Beluncle Villas ME3 . . . . . . 41 C7
BELVEDERE 4 B2
Belvedere Cl DA12 . . . . 36 C7
Belvedere Ct DA17 . . . . 4 A3
Belvedere Ho 9 ME15 . . . . 116 F5
Belvedere Inf Sch DA17 . . . . 4 D5
Belvedere Inf Sch DA17 . . . . 4 A3
Belvedere Jun Sch DA17 . . . 4 B3
Belvedere Link Bsns Pk
  DA17 . . . . 4 B4
Belvedere Mews SE3 . . . . . 11 B7
Belvedere Rd
  Bexley DA7 . . . . 13 F5
  Biggin Hill TN16 . . . . 72 F1
  Erith DA8 . . . . 3 D5
Belvedere Sta DA17 . . . . 4 B3
Belvoir Cl SE9 . . . . 28 E5
Benares Rd SE18 . . . . 2 F2
Benden Cl TN12 . . . . 136 C7
Bendmore Ave SE2 . . . . 3 A2
Bendon Way ME8 . . . . 69 D8
Benedict Cl
  9 Erith DA17 . . . . 3 E3
  Halling ME2 . . . . 66 B4
  Orpington BR6 . . . . 57 E7
Benedict House Prep School
  DA5 . . . . 30 A5
BENENDEN 190 E6
Benenden CE Prim Sch
  TN17 . . . . 190 D6
Benenden Hospl TN17 . . . 181 C3
Benenden Manor ME5 . . . . 55 B3
Benenden Rd
  Benenden TN17 . . . . . . 191 B4
  Cranbrook TN17 . . . . . . 179 E1
  Fosten Green TN27 . . . . 181 F5
  Rochester ME2 . . . . 39 C1
Benenden Sch TN17 . . . . . 190 C8
Benhall Mill Rd TN2, TN3 . 173 D8
Benjamin Ct 4 DA17 . . . . . 173 D8
Benn Cl RH8 . . . . 104 A1
Bennett Cl DA16 . . . . 13 A5
Bennett Ct 5 ME5 . . . . 48 F1
Bennett Ho 8 DA11 . . . . . . 35 F5
Bennett Memorial Diocesan
  Sch TN4 . . . . 158 E6
Bennetts Ave ME15 . . . . . . 78 C7
Bennetts Copse BR7 . . . . . . 28 E2
Bennetts Cotts ME7 . . . . . . 76 E3
Bennetts Mews 12 TN30 . . 193 A7
Bennett Way DA2 . . . . 33 D3
Benn Ho SE7 . . . . 1 C1
BENOVER 131 A6
Benover Rd ME18 . . . . 130 F7
Benson Rd RM17 . . . . 18 C8
Bensted Cl ME15 . . . . 131 D7
Bentfield Gdns SE9 . . . . . . 28 D5
Bentham Hill TN3, TN4 . . 142 D1
Bentham Rd SE28 . . . . 3 B5
Ben Tillet Cl E16 . . . . 1 F5
Bentley Cl
  Aylesford ME20 . . . . 82 F1
  Chatham ME5 . . . . 68 D2
  New Barn DA3 . . . . 49 C7
Bentleys Bglws TN15 . . . . . 92 F7
Bentley's Mdw TN15 . . . . . 92 F7
Benton Rd BR6 . . . . 51 F6
Bentley Street Ind Est
  DA12 . . . . 19 C1
Bentlif Cl ME16 . . . . 99 D5
Berber Parade SE18 . . . . . . 11 E6
Berber Rd ME2 . . . . 53 B8
Bercta Rd SE9 . . . . 29 C6
Bere Cl DA9 . . . . 17 C2
Berengrave La ME8 . . . . 55 F2
Berens Ct ME2 . . . . 25 E4
Berens Rd BR5 . . . . 44 D4
Berens Way BR5 . . . . 43 F6
Beresford Ave ME1 . . . . 53 E2
Beresford Cl TN17 . . . . . . 176 F2
Beresford Dr BR1 . . . . 42 E6
Beresford Rd
  Gillingham ME7 . . . . 54 D4
  Goudhurst TN17 . . . . . . 163 F1
  Kit's Coty ME20 . . . . 83 D7
  Northfleet DA11 . . . . 35 E8
Beresfords Hill ME17 . . . . 116 B4
Beresford Square Market Pl
  SE18 . . . . 2 B3
Beresford St SE18 . . . . 2 B3
Berger Cl BR5 . . . . 43 E3
Bergland Pk ME2 . . . . 53 D8
Bering Wlk E16 . . . . 1 D7
Berkeley Ave ME8 . . . . 13 D6
Berkeley Cl
  Orpington BR5 . . . . 43 E2
  Pembury TN2 . . . . 160 E7
Berkeley Cres DA11 . . . . . . 67 D8
Berkeley Ct 6 BR8 . . . . 45 E6
Berkeley Mount 8 ME4 . . . . 53 F4

Berkeley Rd 7 TN1 . . . . . . 159 A2
Berkeley Terr RM18 . . . . . . 19 A7
Berkhampstead Rd 9
  DA17 . . . . 4 A1
Berkeley Cl DA14 . . . . 19 C1
Berkley Rd DA12 . . . . 19 B1
Berkshire Cl ME5 . . . . 68 C8
Bermuda Rd RM18 . . . . . . 19 A5
Bernal Cl SE28 . . . . 3 D6
Bernard Ashley Dr SE7 . . . 1 B1
Bernards Cl DA15 . . . . 29 E7
Bernard St 24 DA12 . . . . . . 19 B1
BERNER'S HILL 187 A2
Berner's Hill TN5 . . . . 187 A3
Bernersmede SE3 . . . . 11 A4
Berryfield Cl BR1 . . . . 42 E7
Berryhill SE9 . . . . 12 B3
Berryhill Gdns SE9 . . . . 12 B3
Berrylands
  Hartley DA3 . . . . 49 A3
  Orpington BR6 . . . . 58 C7
Berry Rd ME3 . . . . 40 E3
BERRY'S GREEN 73 B3
Berry's Green Rd TN16 . . . . 73 B2
Berry's Hill TN16 . . . . 73 B4
Bertha Hollamby Ct DA14 . . 30 C3
Bertha James Ct ME2 . . . . . 42 B5
Bertrand Way SE28 . . . . 3 C6
Bert Reilly Ho 1 SE18 . . . . . 2 D1
Bertrey Ct TN16 . . . . 73 B3
Berwick Cres DA15 . . . . . . 12 E1
Berwick Ct 12 DA2 . . . . 16 B1
Berwick Rd
  Bexley DA16 . . . . 13 B6
  Newham E16 . . . . 1 C7
Berwick Way
  Orpington BR6 . . . . 44 A1
  Rochester ME2 . . . . 39 C1
  Sevenoaks TN14 . . . . 92 B7
Berwyn Gr ME15 . . . . 116 A6
Beryl Ave E6 . . . . 1 E8
Beryl Ho 8 SE18 . . . . 2 F1
Besant Ct 8 SE28 . . . . 3 B6
BESSELS GREEN 91 D3
Bessels Green Rd TN13 . . . . 91 D3
Bessels Meadow TN13 . . . . 91 D3
Bessels Way TN13 . . . . 91 D4
Bessie Lansbury Cl E6 . . . . . 2 A7
BEST BEECH HILL 184 B3
Best Rd ME4 . . . . 53 F4
Beta Rd ME3 . . . . 34 D7
Betenson Ave TN13 . . . . . . 91 F5
Bethany Sch TN17 . . . . . . 164 B5
Bethel Rd
  Bexley DA16 . . . . 13 C4
  Sevenoaks TN13 . . . . 92 D4
Betherinden Cotts TN18 . . 196 A4
Bethersden Ct ME15 . . . . . 116 F7
Bethersden Rd TN27,
  TN26 . . . . 169 C5
Beths Gram Sch DA5 . . . . . 14 B1
Betjeman Cl ME20 . . . . 81 F3
Betony Gdns ME14 . . . . . . 100 F5
BETSHAM 34 F4
Betsham Rd
  Betsham DA13 . . . . 34 D3
  Erith DA8 . . . . 14 F7
  Maidstone ME15 . . . . . . 116 F6
  Swanscombe DA10 . . . . . 34 E8
Betteridge Cl ME5 . . . . 68 A2
Betterton Dr DA14 . . . . 30 E6
Bettescombe Rd ME8 . . . . . 69 E7
Betts Rd E16 . . . . 1 B6
Beulah Rd TN1 . . . . 159 C4
Beult Mdw TN27 . . . . 153 A1
Beult Rd DA1 . . . . 15 A3
Bevan Pl BR8 . . . . 45 F5
Bevan Rd SE2 . . . . 3 B1
Bevans Cl DA9 . . . . 17 C1
Bevercote Wlk 1 DA17 . . . 13 F8
Beveridge Ct 1 SE28 . . . . 3 B6
Beverley Cl ME8 . . . . 29 F8
Beverley Cres TN9 . . . . . . 142 F7
Beverley Ct 8 DA14 . . . . . . 30 B4
Beverley Rd
  Bexley DA7 . . . . 14 C5
  Maidstone ME16 . . . . 98 F2
  Orpington BR2 . . . . 56 E8
Bevile Ho RM17 . . . . 18 B7
Bevis Cl DA2 . . . . 33 C8
BEWLBRIDGE 176 D1
Bewl Bridge Cl TN5 . . . . . 187 B3
Bewlbridge La
  Lamberhurst TN3, TN5 . . 176 B1
  Lower Cousley Wood TN5 . 185 F8
Bewley La TN15 . . . . 94 D2
Bewl Water Nature Reserve★
  TN5 . . . . 186 B8
Bewl Water Visitor Ctr★
  TN3 . . . . 186 B8
Bexhill Dr RM17 . . . . 17 F8
BEXLEY 13 C3
Bexley Cl DA1 . . . . 14 E2
Bexley Coll
  Erith DA17 . . . . 4 B1
  Erith DA17 . . . . 47 C5
Bexley Cotts DA4 . . . . 47 C5
Bexley Gram Sch DA16 . . . 13 B3
Bexley High St DA5 . . . . . . 31 B7
Bexley La
  Crayford DA1 . . . . 14 E2

Bexley La *continued*
Sidcup DA14 . . . . 30 C5
Bexley Rd
Eltham SE9 . . . . 12 C2
 4 Erith DA8 . . . . 4 E1
Erith, Northumberland Heath
DA8 . . . . 14 C8
Bexley Sta DA5 . . . . 31 A7
BICKLEY 42 F7
Bickley Cres BR1 . . . . 42 E5
Bickley Ct **2** BR1 . . . . 42 E6
Bickley Park Pre Prep School
BR1 . . . . 42 D6
Bickley Park Prep Sch
BR1 . . . . 42 E6
Bickley Park Rd BR1 . . . . . 42 F6
Bickley Prim Sch BR1 . . . . 42 C7
Bickley Rd
Bromley BR1 . . . . 42 E7
 5 Tonbridge TN9 . . . . . . 143 B8
Bickley Sta BR1 . . . . 42 E6
Bickmore Way TN9 . . . . . . 127 D3
BICKNOR 87 C2
Bicknor Court Cotts ME9 . 87 C2
Bicknor Rd
Maidstone ME14 . . . . 116 F4
Orpington BR5 . . . . 43 F2
BIDBOROUGH 142 D3
Bidborough CE Prim Sch
TN3 . . . . 142 D3
Bidborough Ct TN3 . . . . . . 142 B3
Bidborough Ridge TN4 . . 142 E4
BIDDENDEN 167 E2
Biddenden CE Prim Sch
ME15 . . . . 100 F3
Biddenden Gn TN27 . . . . . 153 B2
Biddenden La TN27 . . . . . 151 E5
Biddenden Rd
Headcorn TN27 . . . . 151 E2
Tenterden TN30 . . . . 182 E6
Tylden TN27 . . . . 168 F8
Biddenden Vineyards & Cider
Works* TN27 . . . . 182 A5
Biddenden Way
Eltham SE9 . . . . 29 A4
Istead Rise DA13 . . . . 35 E1
Biddulph Ho **17** SE18 . . . . 1 F2
Bideford Rd DA16 . . . . 13 B7
BIGGIN 19 C8
Biggin Hill Airport TN16 . 72 E3
Biggin Hill Bsns Pk TN16 . 72 D4
Biggin Hill Prim Sch
TN16 . . . . 72 E3
Biggin La RM16 . . . . 19 B8
Bignell Rd SE18 . . . . 2 B1
Bilberry Cl ME14 . . . . 100 E5
Billet Hill TN15 . . . . 62 C6
Billings DA3 . . . . 48 F3
Bill Street Rd **1** ME2 . . . 33 C8
Bilsby Gr SE9 . . . . 28 D4
Bilsington Cl ME5 . . . . 68 B5
Bilton Rd DA8 . . . . 15 A8
Bimbury La ME14, ME9 . . 86 A5
Bines The TN12 . . . . 146 A5
Bingham Point **5** SE18 . . 2 B2
Bingham Rd ME2 . . . . 39 C1
Bingley Ct ME6 . . . . 81 F8
Bingley Rd
Newham E16 . . . . 1 C7
 1 Rochester ME1 . . . . . 53 E4
Binland Gr ME5 . . . . 67 D5
Binnacle Rd ME1 . . . . 67 C8
Binney Rd ME3 . . . . 9 D2
Binsey Wlk **1** SE2 . . . . . . 3 C4
Birbetts Rd ME3 . . . . 28 F6
Birch Cl
Eynsford DA4 . . . . 60 D7
Matfield TN12 . . . . 145 D1
New Barn DA3 . . . . 49 C7
Royal Tunbridge Wells
TN2 . . . . 159 D7
Sevenoaks TN13 . . . . 92 B4
Tonbridge TN11 . . . . 126 D4
Birch Cres ME20 . . . . 98 D8
BIRCHDEN 171 D5
Birchden Cotts TN3 . . . . . 171 C6
Birchdene Dr SE28 . . . . . . 3 A5
Birch Dr ME5 . . . . 68 D1
Birches The
Greenwich SE7 . . . . 11 B8
Orpington BR6 . . . . 57 A6
Swanley BR8 . . . . 45 E7
Tonbridge TN9 . . . . 143 B7
Birchetts Ave TN3 . . . . . . 157 E3
BIRCHETT'S GREEN 185 F3
Birchetts Green La TN5 . 186 A2
Birchfield TN14 . . . . 106 E8
Birchfield ME15 . . . . 116 B6
Birchfields ME5 . . . . 68 A3
Birch Gr
Bexley DA16 . . . . 13 A3
Gillingham ME7 . . . . 69 A4
Birch Ho **6** ME16 . . . . . . 99 A3
Birchin Cross Rd TN15 . . . 77 A5
Birchington Cl
Bexley DA7 . . . . 14 B6
Maidstone ME14 . . . . 100 C5
Orpington BR5 . . . . 44 C1
Birch Kiln Cotts TN5 . . . . 185 A6
Birch Mead BR6 . . . . 57 A8
Birchmere Bsns Pk SE28 . . 3 A4
Bircholme TN2 . . . . 159 D7
Bircholt Rd ME15 . . . . 116 F4

Birch Pl
Sevenoaks TN13 . . . . 92 A3
Stone DA9 . . . . 16 E1
Birch Rd
Hoo St Werburgh ME3 . . 40 E3
Paddock Wood TN12 . . . 146 A6
Birch Row BR2 . . . . 43 A3
Birch Tree Ho **11** SE7 . . . 11 C8
Birch Tree Way ME15 . . . 100 B3
Birchway TN15 . . . . 61 F2
Birch Way TN2 . . . . 159 D7
Birchwood Ave
Bidborough TN4 . . . . 142 E3
Sidcup DA14 . . . . 30 C5
BIRCHWOOD CORNER . . . 45 C8
Birchwood Dr DA2 . . . . . . 31 E4
Birchwood La TN14 . . . . . 74 F4
Birchwood Par DA2 . . . . . 31 E4
Birchwood Park Ave BR8 . 45 F6
Birchwood Rd
Joyden's Wood DA2, BR8 . 31 D3
Maidstone ME16 . . . . 99 C5
Orpington BR5 . . . . 43 E5
Birchwood Terr BR8 . . . . . 45 C8
Birdbrook Rd SE3 . . . . 11 C4
Bird Coll (Birkbeck Ctr)
DA15 . . . . 30 A5
Birdham Cl BR1 . . . . 42 E4
Bird House La BR6 . . . . . . 73 A5
Bird in Hand La BR1 . . . . . 42 D7
Bird in Hand St TN3 . . . . 171 E2
Bird La TN5 . . . . 184 B5
Birdwood Ave DA1 . . . . . . 16 A5
Birkbeck Prim Sch DA14 . 30 A5
Birkbeck Rd DA14 . . . . . . 30 A5
Birkdale TN1 . . . . 159 B6
Birkdale Cl
Erith SE28 . . . . 3 D7
Orpington BR6 . . . . 43 D2
Birkdale Ct **8** ME16 . . . . 99 E4
Birkdale Rd SE2 . . . . 3 A2
Birken Rd TN2 . . . . 159 D6
Birkhall Cl ME5 . . . . 68 A5
BIRLING 81 C6
Birling Ave
Gillingham ME8 . . . . 55 C5
Maidstone ME14 . . . . 101 A4
Birling Ct ME14 . . . . 101 A4
Birling Dr TN2 . . . . 159 D1
Birling Hill DA13, ME19,
ME6 . . . . 81 B1
Birling Park Ave TN2 . . . 173 B8
Birling Pk ME19 . . . . 81 F5
Birling Rd
Bexley DA8 . . . . 14 E6
Leybourne ME19 . . . . 81 C3
Royal Tunbridge Wells
TN2 . . . . 173 B8
Ryarsh ME19 . . . . 81 A5
Snodland ME6 . . . . 81 F7
Birnam Sq **1** ME16 . . . . . 99 E4
Birtrick Dr DA13 . . . . 49 F4
Bishopbourne Gn ME8 . . 55 B4
Bishop Butt Cl BR6 . . . . . . 57 F7
Bishop John Robinson CE
Prim Sch SE28 . . . . 3 C6
Bishop Justus CE Sch
BR2 . . . . 42 E2
Bishop Ridley CE Prim Sch
DA16 . . . . 12 E3
Bishops Ave BR1 . . . . 42 C6
Bishopsbourne Ho **2** BR1 28 B1
Bishops Cl
Eltham SE9 . . . . 29 C6
Nettlestead ME18 . . . . . . 113 D6
Bishops Ct
Royal Tunbridge Wells
TN4 . . . . 158 F3
Stone DA9 . . . . 16 E2
BISHOP'S DOWN 158 E3
Bishop's Down TN4 . . . . 158 F3
Bishop's Down Park Rd
TN4 . . . . 158 F4
Bishop's Down Prim Sch
TN4 . . . . 158 E3
Bishop's Down Rd TN4 . . 158 F3
Bishops Gn BR1 . . . . 42 C8
Bishops La TN17 . . . . 171 E8
Bishop's La ME1 . . . . 131 D6
Bishops Mews TN9 . . . . . 143 C8
Bishops Oak Ride TN10 . 127 C6
Bishops Way ME15 . . . . . 91 F5
Bishops Wlk
Chislehurst BR7 . . . . 43 C8
Rochester ME1 . . . . 53 C5
BITCHET GREEN 93 D1
Blackberry Field BR5 . . . . 44 A8
Blackberry Way TN12 . . 146 B6
Blackbrook La BR1, BR2 . . 43 A5
BLACK CHARLES 109 A5
Blackdale Farm Cotts
DA1 . . . . 33 B6
Black Eagle Cl TN16 . . . . 105 C4
BLACKFEN 13 A1
Blackfen Par DA16 . . . . . . 13 A1
Blackfen Rd DA15 . . . . . . 13 B1
Blackhall La TN15 . . . . . . 92 E3
BLACKHAM 156 A4
Blackheath Bluecoat Sch
SE3 . . . . 11 B7
Blackheath High Sch SE3 11 A7
BLACKHEATH PARK 11 A3
Blackheath Pk SE3 . . . . . . 11 A5
Blackheath Prep Sch SE3 11 A4
Black Horse La TN27 . . . 151 E5
Blackheath Mews TN15 . 160 C6
Black Horse Rd DA15 . . . . 29 F6

Black Horse Rd 14 DA14 . 30 A4
BLACKHURST 159 F5
Blackhurst La TN2 . . . . . . 159 F6
Blacklands ME19 . . . . 97 F7
Blacklands Dr ME19 . . . . . 97 F8
Black Lion L Ctr ME4 . . . . 54 B6
Blackman Cl ME3 . . . . 40 D7
Blackmans Cl DA1 . . . . . . 32 C7
Blackman's La TN11 . . . . 128 D6
Blackmanstone Way
ME16 . . . . 99 B7
Blackmead TN13 . . . . 91 E6
Black Mill La TN27 . . . . . 151 B6
Blackness La BR2 . . . . 56 D2
Black Post ME17 . . . . 133 D7
Black Rock Gdns ME7 . . . 69 B4
Blacksmith Dr ME14 . . . 100 D5
Blacksmiths Field TN27 . 195 C1
Blacksmiths La BR5 . . . . . 44 C4
Blacksmith's La TN5 . . . . 185 A5
Blacksole La TN15 . . . . . . 78 F3
Blacksole Rd **3** TN15 . . . 78 F3
Black's Yd TN13 . . . . 92 C2
Blackthorn Ave
Chatham ME5 . . . . 68 A3
Royal Tunbridge Wells
TN4 . . . . 143 C1
Blackthorn Cl TN15 . . . . . 61 F2
Blackthorn Dr ME20 . . . . 82 B2
Blackthorne Rd ME8 . . . . 70 B8
Blackthorn Rd DA17 . . . . 13 E4
Blackwater Cl RM13 . . . . . 4 E8
Bladindon Dr DA5 . . . . . . 30 D8
Blainey Ho ME3 . . . . 39 F6
Blair Cl DA15 . . . . 12 E2
Blair Dr TN13 . . . . 92 B4
Blake Cl DA16 . . . . 12 E6
Blake Dr **8** ME20 . . . . . . 61 A6
Blake Gdns DA1 . . . . 15 F3
Blakemore Way DA17 . . . 3 E3
Blakeney Cl ME14 . . . . . . 101 B4
Blaker Ave ME1 . . . . 53 E1
Blaker Ct SE7 . . . . 11 C7
Blake Way
Royal Tunbridge Wells
TN2 . . . . 159 D7
Tilbury RM18 . . . . 19 C5
Blanchard Cl SE9 . . . . 28 E5
Blanchard Ho BR7 . . . . . . 29 C2
Bland St SE9 . . . . 11 D3
Blanmerle Rd SE9 . . . . . . 29 B7
Blann St SE9 . . . . 11 D1
Blatchford Cl ME19 . . . . . 81 F1
Blatchington Rd TN1 . . . 159 B1
Bleak Hill La SE18 . . . . . . 12 F8
Bleakwood Rd **8** ME5 . . 67 F5
Blean Rd ME8 . . . . 55 C2
Blean Sq ME14 . . . . 100 C6
Bledlow Cl SE28 . . . . 3 C6
Blendon Dr DA5 . . . . 13 D1
Blendon Rd
Maidstone ME14 . . . . 100 C5
Sidcup DA5 . . . . 13 D1
Blendon Terr SE18 . . . . . . 12 C8
Blendon Ho ME4 . . . . 53 E2
Blenheim Cl
Dartford DA1 . . . . 15 C1
Lewisham SE12 . . . . 28 B7
Maidstone ME15 . . . . 100 F3
Meopham DA13 . . . . 64 B8
Blenheim Ct
Chatham ME4 . . . . 53 E3
Sidcup DA15 . . . . 29 D5
Blenheim Gr DA12 . . . . . . 36 C8
Blenheim Ho SE18 . . . . . . 2 B2
Blenheim Prim Sch BR6 . 58 C8
Blenheim Rd
Bromley BR1 . . . . 42 E5
Dartford DA1 . . . . 15 C1
Kings Hill ME19 . . . . 97 A3
Orpington BR5, BR6 . . . . 58 C8
Sidcup DA15 . . . . 30 C7
Blenheim Way TN5 . . . . . 187 C3
Bletchington Ct **3** DA17 . . 4 A2
Blewbury Ho **3** SE2 . . . . 3 C4
Bligh Inf Sch ME1 . . . . . . 52 C7
Bligh Jun Sch ME1 . . . . . . 52 C7
Bligh Rd DA11 . . . . 19 A1
Bligh's Ct TN13 . . . . 92 B2
Bligh's Rd TN13 . . . . 92 B2
Bligh's Wlk TN13 . . . . 92 C2
Bligh Way ME2 . . . . 52 D6
Blind La
Bredhurst ME7 . . . . 69 A1
Gillingham ME7 . . . . 68 F1
Goudhurst TN17 . . . . 163 E1
Blind Mary's La ME9 . . . . 87 E4
Bliss Way TN10 . . . . 127 C5
Blithdale Rd SE2 . . . . 3 A2
Blockhouse Rd **7** RM17 . 18 C8
Blockmakers Ct ME4 . . . . 54 B1
Bloomfield Rd
Bromley BR2 . . . . 42 D4
Woolwich SE18 . . . . 2 B1
Bloomfield Terr TN16 . . . 89 E2
Bloomsbury Wlk **2**
ME15 . . . . 100 A4
Bloors La ME8 . . . . 55 D1
Bloors Wharf Rd ME7 . . . 55 F4
Blowers Hill Cott TN3 . . 158 B8
Blowers Hill TN6 . . . . . . 155 D8
Blowers Wood Gr ME7 . . 69 B3
Bloxam Gdns SE9 . . . . . . 11 E2
Blue Anchor La RM18 . . . 19 E8
Bluebell Cl
Gillingham ME7 . . . . 54 F6

Bluebell Cl *continued*
Orpington BR6 . . . . 57 C8
BLUE BELL HILL 67 D1
Bluebell Wlks TN12 . . . . 146 A5
Blueberry La TN14 . . . . . . 74 C4
Bluebird Way SE28 . . . . . . 2 D4
Blue Boar La ME1 . . . . 53 D5
Blue Chalet Ind Pk TN15 . 61 D4
Blue Coat La TN17 . . . . . 177 C6
Bluehouse Gdns RH8 . . . 104 A3
Bluehouse La RH8 . . . . . . 104 A8
Blue Skies Sch **7** ME1 . . 53 D4
Bluett St ME14 . . . . 100 A5
Bluewater Parkway DA9 . 33 E8
Bluewater Sta *(for* DA9 . . 33 F8
Blunden La ME18 . . . . . . 114 A1
Blunts Rd SE9 . . . . 12 A2
Blythe Cl SE12 . . . . 28 A8
Blythe Hill BR5 . . . . 44 A8
Blythe Rd ME15 . . . . 100 B4
Blyth Ho **5** DA8 . . . . 4 E1
Blyth Rd SE28 . . . . 3 C6
Boakes Mdw TN14 . . . . . . 75 F8
Boarders La TN5 . . . . 186 C3
Boarley Cl ME14 . . . . 83 F1
Boarley La ME14 . . . . 83 F2
Boathouse Rd ME12 . . . . . 27 F3
Bob Dunn Way DA1 . . . . . 16 A3
Bocking Cl TN5 . . . . 184 E4
Bockingford La ME15 . . . 115 F8
Bocton Ho ME17 . . . . 116 B3
BODIAM 195 D1
Bodiam Cl ME8 . . . . 55 C3
Bodiam Ct ME16 . . . . 99 F3
Bodiam Rd TN18, TN32 . 195 F3
Bodkins Ct ME17 . . . . 116 D5
Bodle Ave DA10 . . . . 17 E1
Bodmin Cl BR5 . . . . 44 C1
Bodsham Cres ME15 . . . 101 B3
Boevey Path
 2 Bexley DA17 . . . . 13 F8
Erith DA17 . . . . 3 F1
Bogarde Dr ME2 . . . . 39 B2
BOGDEN 133 C2
Bogey La BR6 . . . . 57 A3
Bognor Rd DA16 . . . . 13 D6
Boley Hill ME1 . . . . 53 C6
Boleyn Rd TN15 . . . . 76 E2
Boleyn Way DA10 . . . . . . 34 E8
Bolingbroke Ho ME16 . . . 99 E3
Bollon Cl **9** SE12 . . . . 28 B5
Bolner Cl ME5 . . . . 67 F2
Bombay Ho **1** ME15 . . . 116 E5
Bombers La TN16 . . . . 89 D7
Bonar Pl BR7 . . . . 28 E1
Bonaventure Ct DA12 . . . 36 F4
Bonchester Cl BR7 . . . . . . 29 A1
Bond Cl TN14 . . . . 74 D4
Bondfield Cl TN4 . . . . 143 A1
Bondfield Ho SE18 . . . . . . 12 A7
Bondfield Rd
 3 East Malling ME19 . . 97 F8
 4 Newham E6 . . . . 1 F8
Bondfield Wlk DA1 . . . . . . 15 F4
Bond Rd ME8 . . . . 69 E5
Bond St RM17 . . . . 18 C8
Boneashe La TN15 . . . . . . 95 D6
Boneta Rd SE18 . . . . 1 F3
Bonflower La ME17 . . . . . 132 C2
Bonham Way ME2 . . . . . . 39 C1
Bonney Way BR8 . . . . 45 E6
Bonnington Gn ME8 . . . . 55 C3
Bonnington Rd ME14 . . . 100 C6
Bonnington Twr BR2 . . . . 42 E3
Boorman's Mews ME18 . . 113 E7
Bootham Ct SE18 . . . . 52 D5
Booth Cl
Snodland ME6 . . . . 66 A2
 3 Woolwich SE28 . . . . 3 B6
Booth Rd ME4 . . . . 53 F2
Borden CE Prim Sch ME9 71 F3
Bordyke TN9 . . . . 127 C2
Boreham Ave E16 . . . . 1 A7
Boresisle TN30 . . . . 183 B2
Borgard Ho SE18 . . . . 11 E6
Borgard Rd SE18 . . . . 1 F2
Borkwood Cl **8** BR6 . . . . 57 F6
Borkwood Pk BR6 . . . . . . 57 F6
Borkwood Way BR6 . . . . . 57 E6
Borland Cl **5** DA9 . . . . . . 17 A2
BOROUGH GREEN 94 F8
Borough Green Prim Sch
TN15 . . . . 95 A8
Borough Green Rd
Borough Green TN15 . . . . 94 E7
Ightham TN15 . . . . 94 D6
Wrotham TN15 . . . . 79 A1
Borough Green & Wrotham
Sta TN15 . . . . 94 F7
Borough Rd
Gillingham ME7 . . . . 54 D4
Tilbury TN16 . . . . 88 D6
BORSTAL 53 B2
Borstal Mews ME1 . . . . . . 53 A2
Borstal Rd ME1 . . . . 53 B3
Borstal St ME1 . . . . 53 B3
Borton Cl ME8 . . . . 118 F1
Boscobel Cl BR1 . . . . 42 F4
Bosman Ct ME16 . . . . 99 A1
Bostall Hill SE2 . . . . 3 A1
Bostall La SE2 . . . . 3 B1
Bostall Manorway SE2 . . 3 B2
Bostall Park Ave DA7 . . . 13 E7
Bostall Rd BR5 . . . . 30 B1
Boston Gdns ME8 . . . . . . 55 C1
Boston Rd ME5 . . . . 68 C2
Bosville Ave TN13 . . . . . . 83 F4
Bosville Dr TN13 . . . . 92 A4

Bosville Rd TN13 . . . . 92 A4
Boswell Cl BR5 . . . . 44 C3
Boswell Ho BR2 . . . . 42 D4
Bosworth Ho **3** DA8 . . . . . 4 E1
Botany TN9 . . . . 127 C1
Botany Bay La BR7 . . . . . 43 C7
Botha Rd E13 . . . . 1 C8
Bothwell Cl **7** E16 . . . . . . 1 A8
Botsom La TN15 . . . . 61 D4
Bottle House Cotts TN11 140 F1
Bottlescrew Hill ME17 . . 116 B4
Bott Rd DA2 . . . . 32 F4
Boucher Dr DA11 . . . . 35 F4
BOUGH BEECH 123 F2
Bough Beech Nature
Reserve* TN14 . . . . 124 B7
Boughton Cl ME8 . . . . 55 B3
BOUGHTON GREEN 116 B3
Boughton Ho BR1 . . . . . . 28 E1
Boughton La ME15 . . . . . 116 B6
BOUGHTON MALHERBE . 137 A8
BOUGHTON
MONCHELSEA 116 B3
Boughton Monchelsea
Place* ME17 . . . . 133 C8
Boughton Monchelsea Prim
Sch ME17 . . . . 116 B2
Boughton Par ME15 . . . . 116 A7
Boughton Place Cotts
ME17 . . . . 137 A8
Boughton Rd
Sandway ME17 . . . . 120 B2
Woolwich SE28 . . . . 2 E3
Boulevard The DA9 . . . . . 17 C3
Boulter Cl BR1 . . . . 43 D5
Boulthurst Way RH8 . . . 104 B3
Boultwood Rd E6 . . . . 1 F7
Boundary Ho **6** DA11 . . 35 F7
Boundary Rd
Chatham ME4 . . . . 53 E3
Royal Tunbridge Wells
TN2 . . . . 159 D1
Sidcup DA15 . . . . 12 E2
Boundary St **2** DA8 . . . . 14 F7
Boundary The TN3 . . . . . 158 B3
Bounds Cross TN27 . . . . . 167 F7
Bounds Oak Way TN4 . . 142 E3
Bounds The ME20 . . . . . . 82 E1
Bourchier Cl TN13 . . . . . . 92 B1
Bourdillon Ct SE9 . . . . . . 28 E6
Bournbrook Rd SE3, SE9 . 11 D4
Bourne Cl TN9 . . . . 127 D3
Bourne Ct ME1 . . . . 53 D5
Bourne Ent Ctr TN15 . . . 95 A7
Bourne Grange La TN11 . 128 D8
Bourne Ind Pk DA1 . . . . . 14 E2
Bourne La
Cranbrook TN32 . . . . 194 F1
Plaxtol TN15 . . . . 94 F1
Sandhurst Cross TN18 . . 195 E4
Tonbridge TN9 . . . . 127 D3
Bourne Mead DA5 . . . . . . 14 D2
Bourne Par DA5 . . . . 31 B8
Bourne Pk TN11 . . . . 128 F5
Bourne Rd
Bexley DA1, DA5 . . . . 14 D2
Bromley BR2 . . . . 42 F6
Gravesend DA12 . . . . 36 F6
Sidcup DA5 . . . . 31 B8
Bourne Row TN8 . . . . . . 140 D6
Bourneside Terr ME17 . . 102 D2
Bourne Vale
Hayes BR2 . . . . 42 A2
Plaxtol Spoute TN15 . . . 111 A8
Bourne Way
Hayes BR2 . . . . 56 A8
Swanley BR8 . . . . 45 C6
Bournewood Cl ME15 . . 100 F1
Bournewood Rd
Orpington BR5 . . . . 44 C2
Woolwich SE18, SE2 . . . . 13 A7
Bournville Ave ME4 . . . . . 53 F1
Bovarde Ave ME19 . . . . . 97 C3
BOW ARROW 16 A1
Bow Arrow La DA1 . . . . . . 16 A1
Bowater Pl SE3 . . . . 11 B7
Bowater Rd SE18 . . . . 1 D3
Bowen Rd TN4 . . . . 158 B4
Bower Cl ME16 . . . . 99 E4
Bower Gn ME5 . . . . 68 C1
Bower Grove Sch ME5 . . . 99 B2
Bower La
Eynsford DA4 . . . . 60 F6
Maidstone ME16 . . . . 99 E3
Bower Mount Rd ME16 . . 99 D3
Bower Pl ME16 . . . . 99 E3
Bower Rd BR8 . . . . 32 A2
Bowers Ave DA11 . . . . . . 35 F4
Bowers Ho ME7 . . . . 54 E7
Bowers Rd TN14 . . . . 75 F8
Bower St ME16 . . . . 99 E4
Bowers Wlk **1** E6 . . . . 1 F7
Bower Terr ME16 . . . . 99 E3
Bower Wlk TN12 . . . . 149 E3
Bowes Cl DA15 . . . . 13 B1
Bowes Ct **24** DA2 . . . . . . 16 B1
Bowesden La DA12 . . . . . 37 A2
Bowes Rd ME8 . . . . 53 B8
Bowes Wood DA3 . . . . . . 62 F7
Bowford Ave DA7 . . . . . . 13 C6
Bow Hill ME18 . . . . 113 D5
Bowley La ME17 . . . . 137 D8
Bowling Green Row 1
SE18 . . . . 1 F2
Bowls Pl TN12 . . . . 146 A2

Bowman Ave E16 . . . . 1 A6
Bowman Cl ME5 . . . . 68 C5
BOWMANS 31 F8
Bowmans Rd DA1 . . . . 31 F8
Bowmead SE9 . . . . 28 F6
Bown Cl RM18 . . . . 19 B5
Bowness Rd DA7 . . . . 14 B5
Bow Rd ME18 . . . . 113 E7
Bow Terr ME18 . . . . 113 E7
Bowyer Cl 1 F8
Bowzell Rd TN14 . . . . 108 A2
Boxgrove Prim Sch SE2 . . . 3 C3
Boxgrove Rd SE2 . . . . 3 C3
BOXLEY 84 D2
Boxley Cl ME14 . . . . 100 B8
Boxley Rd
  Chatham ME5 . . . . 68 B2
  Maidstone ME14 . . . . 84 B2
Boxley St E16 . . . . 1 B5
Boxmend Ind Est ME15 . . 116 F3
Boxshall Rd 7 SE18 . . . . . 12 B8
Box Tree Wlk 25 BR5 . . . . 44 D1
Boyard Rd SE18 . . . . 2 B1
Boyces Hill ME9 . . . . 71 D6
Boy Court La TN27 . . . . . 135 F1
Boyle Ho 7 DA17 . . . . 4 A3
Boyle Way TN12 . . . . 130 B7
Boyne Pk TN4 . . . . 148 B5
Boyton Court Rd ME17 . . 135 A6
Brabourne Ave ME15 . . . 116 F8
Brabourne Cres DA7 . . . . . 13 F8
Bracken Cl
  Newham E6 . . . . 1 F8
  Royal Tunbridge Wells
  TN2 . . . . 159 C5
Brackendene DA2, DA5 . . . 31 E4
Bracken Hill ME5 . . . . 68 A1
Bracken Lea ME5 . . . . 54 C1
Bracken Rd TN12 . . . . . . 159 E5
Bracken Wlk TN10 . . . . . 127 B6
Brackley Cl ME14 . . . . . . 100 C5
Brackwood Cl ME8 . . . . . 69 F5
Bracondale Ave DA13 . . . . 49 F8
Bracondale Rd SE2 . . . . . . 3 A2
Bracton La DA2 . . . . 31 F6
Bradbery Cl 3 DA11 . . . . . 35 F7
Bradbourne Ct TN13 . . . . 92 B6
Bradbourne La ME20 . . . . 82 B1
Bradbourne Park Rd
  TN13 . . . . 92 A4
Bradbourne Parkway
  ME19 . . . . 82 A1
Bradbourne Rd
  Grays RM17 . . . . 18 B8
  Sevenoaks TN13 . . . . 92 B5
  Sidcup DA5 . . . . 31 A8
Bradbourne Sch The
  TN13 . . . . 92 A6
Bradbourne Vale Rd TN13,
  TN14 . . . . 92 A5
Bradbury Cl 4 SE3 . . . . . 11 A7
Braddick Cl ME15 . . . . . 116 B6
Bradenham Ave DA16 . . . 13 A3
Bradfield Rd E16 . . . . 1 B4
Bradfields Ave ME5 . . . . . 67 F5
Bradfields Avenue W ME5 67 F5
Bradfields FE Ctr ME5 . . . 54 B5
Bradfields Sch ME5 . . . . . 68 A6
Bradford Cl BR2 . . . . 42 F1
Bradfords Cl ME4 . . . . 40 B2
Bradford St TN9 . . . . 127 B1
Bradley House ME3 . . . . . 25 C4
Bradley Rd
  Ashurst TN3 . . . . 156 D5
  Upper Halling ME2 . . . . . 60 C5
Bradley St 3 TN9 . . . . . . 127 B2
Bradley Stone Rd E6 . . . . . 1 F8
Brady Dr BR1 . . . . 43 A6
Bradymead E6 . . . . 2 B7
Braeburn Way ME19 . . . . . 97 C3
Braemar Ave DA7 . . . . 14 C3
Braemar Gdns DA15 . . . . . 29 C5
Braeside Ave TN13 . . . . . . 91 F3
Braeside Cl TN13 . . . . 91 F4
Braeside Cres DA7 . . . . . . 14 C3
Braes The ME3 . . . . 38 C3
Braesyde Cl DA17 . . . . 3 F2
Braithwaite Ct ME7 . . . . . 55 A5
Brake Ave ME5 . . . . 67 E5
Brakefield Rd DA13 . . . . . 35 B1
Brakes PI TN15 . . . . 61 A4
Bramber Cl 9 DA2 . . . . . . 16 B1
Bramble Ave DA2 . . . . 34 C5
Bramble Bank DA13 . . . . . 79 F7
Bramblebury Rd SE18 . . . . 2 C1
Bramble Cl
  Hurst Green RH8 . . . . . . 104 B2
  Maidstone ME16 . . . . 99 B3
  Tonbridge TN11 . . . . . . 126 F4
Bramble Croft DA8 . . . . . . 4 C2
Brambledown
  Chatham ME5 . . . . 68 B8
  Hartley DA3 . . . . 48 F5
Bramblefield Cl DA3 . . . . . 48 E6
Bramble La TN13 . . . . . . 108 B7
Bramble Mews 1 DA12 . . 36 D4
Bramble Reed La TN12 . . 161 B7
Brambletree Cotts ME1 . . 52 E2
Brambletree Cres ME1 . . 52 F2
Bramble Wlk TN2 . . . . . . 159 D7
Brambling 1 BR9 . . . . 17 A1
Bramdean Cres SE12 . . . . 28 A7
Bramdean Gdns SE12 . . . . 28 A7
Bramham Ho 16 SE7 . . . . 11 C8
Bramhope La SE7 . . . . 11 B8
Bramis Ho TN16 . . . . 72 D3

Bramley Cl
  Istead Rise DA13 . . . . . . 70 B8
  Newington ME9 . . . . 35 F1
  Orpington BR6 . . . . 71 A5
  Swanley BR8 . . . . 45 E5
Bramley Cres ME15 . . . . . 100 F3
Bramley Ct
  Bexley DA16 . . . . 13 B6
  15 Erith DA17 . . . . 4 A1
  Marden TN12 . . . . 148 B6
Bramley Dr TN17 . . . . . . 179 D4
Bramley Gdns
  Coxheath ME17 . . . . 115 C3
  Paddock Wood TN12 . . . 145 E2
Bramley PI DA1 . . . . 15 A3
Bramley Rd
  East Peckham TN12 . . . . 129 F6
  Snodland ME6 . . . . 82 A8
Bramley Rise ME2 . . . . 52 E8
Bramleys TN27 . . . . 151 D5
Bramley Way ME19 . . . . . . 97 A2
  Brampton Prim Sch DA7 . 13 D5
Brampton Rd DA7 . . . . 13 E6
Bramshot Ave SE3, SE7 . . 11 B8
Bramshott Cl ME14 . . . . . 99 C6
BRANBRIDGES 130 A5
Branbridges Ind Est
  TN12 . . . . 130 A5
Branbridges Rd TN12 . . . 130 B4
BRANDFOLD 163 F3
Brandon Rd DA1 . . . . 33 A8
Brandon St DA11 . . . . 36 B8
Brandreth Rd E6 . . . . 1 F7
Brands Hatch Circuit ✱ . . 61 F6
Brands Hatch Cotts DA3 . 62 A6
Brands Hatch Rd DA3 . . . . 62 A7
Branham Ho 1 SE18 . . . . . 2 B1
Bransell Cl BR8 . . . . 45 C3
Bransgore Cl ME8 . . . . 69 D7
Branston Cres BR5 . . . . . . 43 D1
Branstone Ct RM19 . . . . . . 16 B8
Brantala Fields ME3 . . . . . 40 E4
Brantingham Cl TN9 . . . . 142 F7
Branton Rd DA9 . . . . 16 F1
Brantwood Cl ME18 . . . . . 14 C7
Brantwood Rd DA7 . . . . . . 14 B4
Brantwood Way BR5 . . . . . 44 C6
Brasenose Rd ME7 . . . . . . 54 E4
Brassey CI RH8 . . . . 104 A6
Brassey Dr ME20 . . . . 98 D8
Brassey Hill RH8 . . . . 104 A6
Brassey Rd RH8 . . . . 104 A6
BRASTED 90 C3
BRASTED CHART 106 B7
Brasted Cl
  Bexley DA6 . . . . 13 D2
  Orpington BR6 . . . . 58 A8
Brasted Ct
  Brasted TN16 . . . . 90 D2
  Rochester ME2 . . . . 39 A1
Brasted Hill TN14 . . . . 90 A7
Brasted Hill Rd TN16 . . . . 90 C5
Brasted La TN14 . . . . 74 A1
Brasted Rd
  Erith DA8 . . . . 14 E7
  Westerham TN16 . . . . 89 E1
Brattle Farm Mus ✱
  TN12 . . . . 149 D1
Brattle Wood TN13 . . . . . 108 C6
Braundton Ave DA15 . . . . 29 F7
Braunstone Dr ME16 . . . . 99 D7
Bray Gdns ME15 . . . . 115 F5
Bray Pas E16 . . . . 1 A6
Braywood Rd SE9 . . . . 12 D3
BREACH 79 C1
Breach Rd RM20 . . . . 16 F8
Breakneck Hill DA9 . . . . . 17 B2
Breakspears Dr BR5 . . . . . 44 A8
Bream Cl ME20 . . . . 82 A5
Breaside Prep Sch BR1 . . . 42 D8
Breckonmead BR1 . . . . . . 42 C7
Brecon Ct 7 SE12 . . . . . . 12 A1
Bredgar Cl ME14 . . . . . . 100 C5
Bredgar Ho 1 BR5 . . . . . . 44 D1
Bredgar Rd ME8 . . . . 55 B4
Bredgar & Wormshill Light
  Rly ✱ ME9 . . . . 87 E1
BREDHURST 69 B1
Bredhurst CE Prim Sch
  ME7 . . . . 69 B1
Bredhurst Rd ME8 . . . . . . 69 B4
Breedon Ave TN4 . . . . . . 142 F1
Bremner Cl BR8 . . . . 46 A5
BRENCHLEY 162 B8
Brenchley Ave DA11 . . . . . 36 B3
Brenchley Cl
  Chislehurst BR7 . . . . 43 A8
  Rochester ME1 . . . . 53 D2
Brenchley & Matfield CE
  Prim Sch TN12 . . . . . . 162 A8
Brenchley Rd
  Gillingham ME8 . . . . 55 B2
  Horsmonden TN12 . . . . 162 F6
  Maidstone ME15 . . . . 99 F2
  Matfield TN12 . . . . 161 F8
  St Paul's Cray BR5 . . . . . 43 F7
Brenda Ct 4 DA14 . . . . . . 30 A4
Brenda Terr DA10 . . . . 34 E8
Brendon 18 DA14 . . . . 30 A4
Brendon Ave ME5 . . . . 68 A3
Brendon Cl
  Bexley DA8 . . . . 14 E6
  Royal Tunbridge Wells
  TN2 . . . . 159 D5
Brendon Rd SE9 . . . . 29 D6
Brenley Gdns SE9 . . . . 11 D3

Brennan Ct ME7 . . . . 54 D6
Brennan Mews ME16 . . . . 99 E5
Brennan Rd RM18 . . . . 19 B5
Brent Cl
  Chatham ME5 . . . . 67 E5
  Dartford DA2 . . . . 16 B1
  Sidcup DA15 . . . . 30 E7
Brentfield Rd DA1 . . . . 33 B8
Brent La DA1 . . . . 33 A7
Brentlands Dr DA1 . . . . . . 33 A7
Brentor Ct TN12 . . . . 159 D8
Brent Prim Sch The DA2 . . 33 C8
Brent Rd
  Newham E16 . . . . 1 A8
  Woolwich SE18 . . . . 12 B7
Brent The
  Dartford DA1 . . . . 33 B8
  Tonbridge TN10 . . . . . . 127 C6
Brent Way DA2 . . . . 16 B1
Brentwood Cl SE9 . . . . 29 C7
Brentwood Ho SE18 . . . . . 11 D7
Brenzett Cl ME5 . . . . 68 B5
Brenzett Ho 8 BR5 . . . . . . 44 C4
Bretaneby TN15 . . . . 92 F6
Bretland Ct TN4 . . . . 158 D4
Bretland Rd TN4 . . . . 158 D4
Breton Rd ME1 . . . . 53 C2
Brett Wlk ME8 . . . . 69 D4
Brewer Rd ME3 . . . . 39 B7
Brewers Field DA2 . . . . . . 32 C4
Brewers Rd DA12 . . . . 51 C8
Brewer St
  Lamberhurst TN3 . . . . . 176 A5
  Maidstone ME14 . . . . . . 100 A5
Brewery La TN13 . . . . 92 C2
Brewery Rd
  Orpington BR6 . . . . 42 E1
  Woolwich SE18 . . . . 2 D1
Brewhouse Rd SE18 . . . . . 1 F2
Brewhouse Yd 3 DA12 . . 19 B1
Brian Cres TN4 . . . . 159 B8
Briar Cl
  Larkfield ME20 . . . . 82 A2
  8 Marplit Hill TN8 . . . . 122 D3
Briar Dale ME3 . . . . 38 B4
Briar Fields ME14 . . . . . . 100 E5
Briar Rd DA5 . . . . 31 D5
Briars Cross ME6 . . . . . . 104 D5
Briars The TN15 . . . . 61 D4
Briars Way DA3 . . . . 49 A4
Briarswood Way BR6 . . . . 57 F5
Briar Wlk TN10 . . . . 127 C6
Briary Ct DA14 . . . . 30 B3
Briary Gdns BR1 . . . . 28 B3
Brice Rd ME3 . . . . 38 B3
Brick Ct RM17 . . . . 18 A8
Brickenden Rd TN17 . . . . 179 B8
Brickfield Cotts SE18 . . . . 12 F8
Brickfield Farm DA3 . . . . . 49 A6
Brickfield Farm Gdns
  BR6 . . . . 57 C6
Brickfields
  Pembury TN2 . . . . 160 E8
  West Malling ME19 . . . . . 81 B1
Brick Kiln La
  Horsmonden TN12 . . . . 163 B2
  Limpsfield RH8 . . . . 104 C5
  Ulcombe ME17 . . . . 135 D5
Brickmakers Meadows
  TN15 . . . . 95 C7
Brickwell Cotts TN17 . . . 166 F6
Brickworks Cl TN9 . . . . . . 143 B7
Bridewell La TN30 . . . . . . 193 A7
Bridge Cl
  Dartford DA2 . . . . 16 D4
  Tonbridge TN9 . . . . 143 C8
Bridge Cotts SE12 . . . . . . 163 A6
Bridge Ct
  20 Dartford DA2 . . . . 16 B1
  Grays RM17 . . . . 18 B8
Bridgefield Rd ME17 . . . . 118 B1
Bridge Ho
  Rochester ME1 . . . . 53 B4
  Royal Tunbridge Wells
  TN4 . . . . 159 B5
Bridge Ind Ctr ME15 . . . . 99 E2
Bridgeland Rd E16 . . . . 1 A6
Bridge Mill Way ME15 . . . 99 D2
Bridgen Rd DA5 . . . . 30 E8
Bridge PI ME20 . . . . 82 F2
Bridge Rd
  Bexley DA7 . . . . 13 E5
  Erith DA8 . . . . 14 F6
  Gillingham ME7 . . . . 54 C7
  Grays RM17 . . . . 18 B8
  Orpington BR5 . . . . 44 B3
  Rochester ME1 . . . . 53 C2
Bridges Dr DA1 . . . . 16 B2
Bridgeside Mews ME15 . . 99 E2
Bridge St ME15 . . . . 115 F5
Bridge View DA9 . . . . 17 B3
Bridge View Ind Est RM20 16 B8
Bridgewater Cl BR7 . . . . . 43 E6
Bridgewater Rd E19 . . . . . 81 E2
Bridle Way BR6 . . . . 57 C6
Bridlington St ME14 . . . . . 99 F4
Bridlington Ct TN16 . . . . . 88 B8
Brier Cl ME5 . . . . 68 C8
Bright Cl DA17 . . . . 3 D2
Bright Ct 33 SE28 . . . . 3 C5
Brightlands DA1 . . . . 33 C4
Bright Rd 3 ME4 . . . . 54 B2
Bright Ridge TN4 . . . . . . 158 B8
Brigstock Rd DA17 . . . . . . 4 B2
Brimpsfield Cl SE2 . . . . . . 3 B3
Brimp The ME3 . . . . 9 D3
Brimstone Cl BR6 . . . . 58 C3

Brimstone Hill DA13 . . . . . 64 D8
Brindle Gate DA15 . . . . . . 29 E7
Brindle's Field TN9 . . . . . 143 A7
Brindle Way ME5 . . . . 68 C1
Brindley Cl DA7 . . . . 14 B4
Brindley Way BR1 . . . . 28 A3
Brinkcroft CI SE2 . . . . 3 A2
Brinkers La TN5 . . . . 185 A2
Brinklow Cres SE18 . . . . . 12 B7
Brionne Gdns TN9 . . . . . 143 D8
Brisbane Ho MR18 . . . . . . 18 F6
Brisbane Ho ME4 . . . . 54 A3
Briset Rd SE9 . . . . 11 D3
Brishing Cl ME15 . . . . . . 116 E5
Brishing La ME17 . . . . . . 116 F4
Brishing Rd ME15, ME17 . 116 F3
Brisley's Row ME1 . . . . . . 66 F1
Brissenden Cl ME2 . . . . . . 40 A3
Bristol Cl ME2 . . . . 52 D5
Bristol Rd DA12 . . . . 36 D5
Bristow Rd DA7 . . . . 13 E6
Britannia Cl
  Erith DA8 . . . . 14 F8
  Halling ME2 . . . . 66 A4
Britannia Dr DA12 . . . . . . 36 F3
Britannia Gate 1 E16 . . . . 1 A5
Britannia Ho ME3 . . . . 24 A3
Britannia Village Prim Sch
  E16 . . . . 1 B5
Britannia Ct SE9 . . . . 28 E7
Brittain Ho SE9 . . . . 28 E7
Brittains La TN13 . . . . 91 F2
Britten Cl TN10 . . . . 127 F6
Britten Par BR6 . . . . 57 F4
Britton St ME5 . . . . 54 B5
Brixham Rd DA16 . . . . 13 D6
Brixham St E16 . . . . 2 A5
Broadbridge Cl SE3 . . . . . 11 A7
Broadclcth TN17 . . . . 179 D3
Broadcroft TN2 . . . . 172 F8
Broadcroft Rd BR5 . . . . . . 43 D2
Broad Ditch Rd DA13 . . . . 35 D1
Broader La ME14 . . . . 85 B2
Broadfield Rd ME15 . . . . . 116 A8
Broadgate Rd E16 . . . . 1 D7
Broad Gr FN2 . . . . 159 A1
Broadheath Dr BR7 . . . . . 28 F3
Broadhoath TN15 . . . . 93 E1
Broad La
  Dartford DA2 . . . . 32 B4
  Fordcombe TN3 . . . . . . 157 A4
Broadlands Dr ME5 . . . . . . 68 B4
Broadlands Rd BR1 . . . . . . 28 B4
Broad Lawn SE9 . . . . 29 A7
Broadmead TN2 . . . . 172 F8
Broadmead Ave TN2 . . . . 172 F8
Broadmere Terr ME16 . . . 99 D3
Broadoak ME19 . . . . 81 E2
Broad Oak
  Brenchley TN12 . . . . . . 162 C8
  Groombridge TN3 . . . . . 171 C6
Broadoak Ave ME15 . . . . 116 A8
Broadoak Cl DA4 . . . . 33 A2
Broad Oak Cl
  Brenchley TN12 . . . . . . 162 C8
  Orpington BR5 . . . . 44 A7
  Royal Tunbridge Wells
  TN2 . . . . 158 F1
Broadoak Rd DA8 . . . . 14 D7
Broad Rd DA10 . . . . 17 B5
Broadreach Coll SE28 . . . . 2 F4
Broad St ME17 . . . . 134 E7
BROADSTONE 136 D4
BROAD STREET
  Hoo St Werburgh 40 B5
  Maidstone 102 B6
Broad Street Hill ME17 . . 102 D7
BROAD TENTERDEN 193 B4
Broadview DA13 . . . . 63 F6
Broadview Ave ME8 . . . . . 69 E8
Broadwater La TN2 . . . . . 172 E8
BROADWATER DOWN . . . 172 E7
Broadwater Down 172 E7
Broadwater Down Prim Sch
  8 TN2 . . . . 158 F1
Broadwater Forest La
  TN3 . . . . 172 B7
Broadwater Gdns BR6 . . . 57 C6
Broadwater Ho DA12 . . . . 19 D1
Broadwater La TN2, TN4 . 158 F1
Broadwater Rd
  East Malling ME19 . . . . . 97 D6
  Woolwich SE18 . . . . 2 D3
Broadwater Rise TN2 . . . 158 F1
Broadway
  Bexley DA6 . . . . 13 F3
  Crockenhill BR8 . . . . 45 C3
  Gillingham ME8 . . . . 55 A3
  Grays RM17 . . . . 18 C8
  Limpsfield RH8 . . . . 104 B5
  Maidstone ME14 . . . . 99 F4
  Tilbury RM18 . . . . 18 F5
Broadway St Ctr ME16 . . 99 F4
Broadway The
  Hadlow TN11 . . . . 128 E8
  Lamberhurst TN3 . . . . . 176 B5
Broad Wlk
  Eltham SE3, SE9 . . . . 11 E5
  Orpington BR6 . . . . 58 D7
  Sevenoaks TN15 . . . . . . 108 E7
Broadwood DA11 . . . . 36 B3
Broadwood Rd ME4 . . . . . 40 A4
Brockbank Cl ME5 . . . . . . 68 A1
Brockdene Dr BR2 . . . . . . 56 D6

Bow–Bro 205

Brockenhurst Ave ME15 . 100 C1
Brockenhurst Cl ME8 . . . . 69 C7
Brocklebank Ho 7 E16 . . . 2 A5
Brocklebank Rd SE7 . . . . . 1 B2
Brocklebank Rd Ind Est
  SE7 . . . . 1 B2
Brock Rd E13 . . . . 1 B8
Brockway TN15 . . . . 95 A7
Brockwell Cl BR5 . . . . 43 F4
Brodrick Gr SE2 . . . . 3 B2
Brogden Cres ME17 . . . . 117 F7
Broke Farm Dr BR6 . . . . . 58 C2
Brokes Way TN4 . . . . 159 B8
Brome Ho SE18 . . . . 11 E6
Brome Rd SE9 . . . . 11 F4
Bromford Cl RH8 . . . . . . 104 A2
Bromhedge SE9 . . . . 28 F5
Bromholm Rd SE2 . . . . 3 B3
BROMLEY 42 B6
Bromley RM17 . . . . 17 F8
Bromley Cl ME5 . . . . 68 B4
Bromley Coll 13 BR2 . . . . 42 A8
Bromley Coll of FE & HE
  (Rookery Lane Campus)
  BR2 . . . . 42 D3
Bromley Comm BR2 . . . . . 42 D3
BROMLEY COMMON 42 E3
Bromley High Junior Sch
  BR1 . . . . 43 D5
Bromley High Sch BR1 . . . 43 A5
Bromley Ind Ctr BR1 . . . . 42 D6
Bromley La BR7 . . . . 29 D1
Bromley Manor Mans 3
  BR2 . . . . 42 A6
Bromley Mus ✱ BR6 . . . . 44 B2
Bromley North Sta BR1 . . 42 A8
Bromley Rd ME4 . . . . 53 F6
Bromley South Sta BR1 . . 42 A8
BROMPTON 54 A5
Brompton Dr DA8 . . . . 15 B7
Brompton Farm Rd ME2 . 39 A2
Brompton Hill ME4 . . . . . . 53 F6
Brompton La ME2 . . . . 53 A8
Brompton Rd ME7 . . . . . . 54 B6
Brompton Westbrook Prim
  Sch ME7 . . . . 54 A5
Bronington Cl ME5 . . . . . . 68 A5
Bronte Cl
  Cliffe Woods ME3 . . . . . . 39 B7
  Erith DA8 . . . . 14 B7
  Lunsford ME20 . . . . 81 F3
  Tilbury RM18 . . . . 19 C5
Bronte Gr DA1 . . . . 15 F3
Bronte Sch DA11 . . . . 36 A8
Bronte View DA12 . . . . . . 36 C7
Bronze Age Way DA8, DA17 4 C3
Brookbank ME14 . . . . 100 A8
Brook Cotts
  Collier Street TN12 . . . . 147 F8
  East Farleigh ME15 . . . . 115 C7
Brook Ct
  1 Lewisham SE12 . . . . . . 28 C5
  10 Marplit Hill TN8 . . . 122 D3
Brookdale Rd DA5 . . . . . . 13 E1
Brookdene TN12 . . . . 145 B7
Brookdene Rd SE18 . . . . . 2 F2
Brooke Dr DA12 . . . . 37 B7
Brookend Rd DA15 . . . . . . 29 C7
Brookes Cl ME17 . . . . . . 116 D5
Brookes PI ME9 . . . . 71 B6
Brookfield
  Four Elms TN8 . . . . 123 B5
  Kemsing TN15 . . . . 76 E2
  Sandhurst TN18 . . . . . . 196 B5
Brookfield Ave ME20 . . . . 82 A4
Brookfield Ct TN4 . . . . . . 143 A1
Brookfield Inf Sch ME20 . 82 A2
Brookfield Jun Sch ME20 . 82 A2
Brookfields TN11 . . . . . . 111 E1
Brook Hill Cl SE18 . . . . . . 2 B1
Brookhill Rd SE18 . . . . 2 B1
Brookhurst Gdns TN4 . . . 142 E3
Brook La
  Bexley DA5 . . . . 13 D2
  Bromley BR1 . . . . 28 A2
  Greenwich SE3 . . . . 11 B5
  Plaxtol Spoute TN15 . . . 111 A8
  Snodland ME6 . . . . 82 A6
  Tonbridge TN9 . . . . 127 D2
BROOKLANDS 32 F7
Brooklands
  Dartford DA1 . . . . 32 E7
  Headcorn TN27 . . . . 151 C6
  Royal Tunbridge Wells
  TN2 . . . . 159 D7
Brooklands Ave DA15 . . . . 29 D7
Brooklands Farm Cl TN3 157 A6
Brooklands Pk SE3 . . . . . . 11 A4
Brooklands Prim Sch SE3 11 A4
Brooklands Rd ME20 . . . . 82 A4
Brooklyn Paddock ME7 . . 54 D6
Brooklyn Rd BR2 . . . . 42 D4
Brooklyn Villas TN12 . . . 148 C5
Brookmead TN11 . . . . . . 126 E4
Brookmead Ave BR1 . . . . 42 F4
Brookmead Cl BR5 . . . . . . 44 B3
Brookmead Rd ME3 . . . . . 39 B7
Brookmead Way BR5 . . . . 44 B3
Brook Rd DA1 . . . . 33 A6
Brook Rd
  Lunsford ME20 . . . . 81 F4
  Northfleet DA11 . . . . 35 E7
  Royal Tunbridge Wells
  TN2 . . . . 159 D7
  Swanley BR8 . . . . 45 D7

Brooks Cl
Eltham SE9 . . . . 29 A6
Staplehurst TN12 . . . . 149 E4
Tonbridge TN10 . . . . . 127 E7
Brookside
Cranbrook TN17 . . . . . 179 D4
Hoo St Werburgh ME3 . . 40 E5
Orpington BR6 . . . . . . 43 F2
Brookside Rd DA13 . . 33 F1
Brooks Pl ME14 . . . . 100 A4
Brook Sq SE18 . . . . . 11 E6
Brook St
Erith DA8 . . . . 14 B7
Snodland ME6 . . . . 82 B8
Tonbridge TN9 . . . . . . 143 A8
BROOK STREET 143 A8
Brook The ME4 . . . . . 54 A4
Brook Vale TN3 . . . . 187 E3
Brookvale Workshops
DA11 . . . . 35 C7
Brookway SE3 . . . . . 11 A4
Broom Ave BR5 . . . . . 44 B7
Broom Cl BR2 . . . . . . 42 E3
Broomcroft Rd ME8 . . 55 F2
BROOMFIELD 118 D5
Broomfield TN3 . . . . 173 F5
Broomfield Ho 4 BR5 . 44 B7
Broomfield Rd
Bexley DA6 . . . . 14 A2
Kingswood ME17 . . . . 118 D4
Sevenoaks TN13 . . . . . 91 F5
Swanscombe DA10 . . . . 27 F2
Broomfields DA3 . . . . 48 E4
BROOM HILL 47 C3
Broomhill Bank Sch TN3 158 C6
Broom Hill Cotts TN6 . 187 B3
Broomhill Park Rd TN4 . 158 F8
Broomhill Rd
Dartford DA1 . . . . 15 B1
Orpington BR6 . . . . . . 44 A1
Royal Tunbridge Wells
TN3 . . . . 158 D7
Broom Hill Rd ME2 . . . 52 F8
Broomhill Rise DA6 . . 14 A2
Broomhills TN13 . . . . 34 E4
Broom La TN3 . . . . . 157 F1
Broomlands La RH8 . . 104 E8
Broomleigh 5 BR1 . . . 42 A8
Broom Mead DA6 . . . . 14 A2
Broom Pk TN3 . . . . . 157 E3
Broomscroft Cotts ME18 97 C1
Broomshaw Rd ME16 . . 98 F3
Broomsleigh TN16 . . . 72 E2
Broomwood Cl DA5 . . . 31 D6
Broomwood Rd BR5 . . . 44 B7
Brougham Ct 5 DA2 . . 16 B1
Broughton Rd
Orpington BR6 . . . . . . 57 D8
Otford TN14 . . . . 76 A3
Brow Cl BR5 . . . . 44 D2
Brow Cres BR5 . . . . . 44 D2
Brownden Rd ME2 . . . . 65 E4
Brownelow Copse ME5 . 68 B1
Brownhill Cl ME5 . . . . 68 A4
Browning Cl
Bexley DA5 . . . . 13 B6
6 Lunsford ME20 . . . . 81 F4
Browning Rd DA1 . . . . 15 D5
Browning Wlk RM18 . . 19 C5
Brown Rd DA12 . . . . . 36 E7
Brownspring Dr SE9 . . 28 B5
Browns Sch BR6 . . . . . 58 F5
Brown St ME8 . . . . . . 55 F1
Broxbourne Rd BR6 . . 43 F2
Bruce Cl DA16 . . . . . 13 B6
Bruce Ct 2 DA15 . . . 29 F4
Bruce Gr DA1 . . . . . . 44 A1
Bruces Wharf Rd RM17 . 18 A8
Brucks The ME18 . . . . 113 E7
Brummel Cl DA7 . . . . 14 C4
Brunel Cl RM18 . . . . . 19 E4
Brunel Cl ME16 . . . . . 99 D5
Brunel Way ME4 . . . . 54 A7
Brungers Wlk TN10 . . . 127 B5
Brunswick Cl DA6 . . . 13 D3
Brunswick House Prim Sch
ME16 . . . . 99 E5
Brunswick Rd DA6 . . . 13 E3
Brunswick St ME15 . . . 100 A3
Brunswick Terr TN1 . . 159 A2
Brunswick St E
ME15 . . . . 100 A3
Brunswick Wlk 1 DA2 . 36 D8
Bruton Cl BR7 . . . . . . 28 F1
Bryanston Rd RM18 . . . 19 C5
Bryant Cl ME18 . . . . . 113 D6
Bryant Rd ME2 . . . . . 53 A7
Bryant St ME4 . . . . . . 54 A3
Bryony Sch ME8 . . . . . 55 C7
Bubblestone Rd TN14 . . 76 B3
Buchurst La TN17 . . . 167 B7
Buckden Cl SE12 . . . . 11 A1
Buckham Thorns Rd TN16 89 C1
Buckhole Farm Rd ME23 23 C4
BUCKHURST 167 C5
Buckhurst Ave TN13 . . 92 C2
Buckhurst La
Rockrobin TN3 . . . . . 184 A6
Sevenoaks TN13 . . . . . 92 C2
Buckhurst Pl TN5 . . . 184 A6
Buckhurst Rd TN16 . . . 89 B7
Buckingham Ave DA16 . 12 E3

Buckingham Cl BR5 . . 43 E2
Buckingham Dr ME7 . . 29 C3
Buckingham Rd
Gillingham ME7 . . . . . 54 D5
Northfleet DA11 . . . . . 35 D8
Royal Tunbridge Wells
TN1 . . . . 159 B2
Buckingham Row ME15 . 116 E7
Buckland Cl ME5 . . . . 68 A2
BUCKLAND HILL 175 A1
Buckland Hill ME16 . . 99 E5
Buckland La ME16 . . . 99 D6
Buckland Rd ME14 . . . 99 E4
Buckland Rd
Cliffe Woods ME3 . . . . 39 A8
Luddesdown DA13 . . . . 65 A7
Maidstone ME16 . . . . . 99 E4
Orpington BR6 . . . . . . 57 E6
Buckler Gdns SE9 . . . 28 F5
Bucklers Ct DA17 . . . 3 D2
Buckles Ct DA17 . . . . 3 D2
Buckley Cl DA1 . . . . . 14 F5
Buckmore Pk-International
Kart Circuit ME5 . . . 67 C3
BUCK'S CROSS 58 F5
Bucks Cross Rd
Chelsfield BR6 . . . . . . 58 E5
Northfleet DA11 . . . . . 35 F5
Buckthorn House DA15 . 29 A3
Buckwheat Ct DA18 . . . 3 D3
Budd Ho 4 SE7 . . . . . 1 C1
Budd's Farm Cotts TN30 199 E2
Budd's La TN30 . . . . . 199 F3
Budgin's Hill BR6 . . . 74 C8
Budleigh Cres DA16 . . 13 C6
Bugglesden Rd TN27,
TN30 . . . . 182 D5
Bugsby's Way SE10, SE7 . 1 B2
Bullace La 3 ME1 . . . 61 C2
Bullbanks Rd DA17 . . . 4 C1
Bulldog Rd ME5 . . . . . 68 B2
Bullen La TN12 . . . . . 129 F7
Buller Rd ME4 . . . . . . 53 F2
Bullers Ct DA14 . . . . 30 E3
Bullers Wood Dr BR7 . . 42 E8
Bullers Wood Sch BR7 . 42 E8
Bull Fields ME4 . . . . 82 A8
Bullfinch Cl
Paddock Wood TN12 . . . 146 A5
Sevenoaks TN13 . . . . . 91 D5
Bullfinch Cnr TN13 . . . 91 E5
Bullfinch Dene TN13 . . 91 D5
Bullfinch La TN13 . . . 91 E5
Bull Hill
Horton Kirby DA4 . . . . 47 C5
Lenham ME17 . . . . . . 137 F8
BULLINGSTONE 157 F7
Bullingstone Cotts TN3 157 F7
Bullingstone La TN3 . . 157 F7
Bullion Cl TN12 . . . . 145 F6
Bullivant Cl 3 DA9 . . 17 A2
Bull La
Chislehurst BR7 . . . . . 29 D1
Eccles ME20 . . . . 82 F5
Lower Higham ME3 . . . . 38 D7
Wrotham TN15 . . . . . . 79 A3
Yelsted ME9 . . . . 70 E2
Bull Lane Cotts
Hook Green TN3 . . . . . 175 C4
Yelsted ME9 . . . . 70 E1
Bull Orch ME16 . . . . . 98 F2
Bull Rd ME14 . . . . . . 81 C5
Bulls Pl TN2 . . . . . . 160 D6
Bull Yd 3 DA11 . . . . 19 B1
Bulrush Cl ME5 . . . . . 67 F3
Bumbles Cl ME1 . . . . . 67 D7
Bungalows The TN30 . . 193 F7
Bunkers Hill
New Ash Green TN15 . . . 63 C4
Sidcup DA14 . . . . 30 F5
Bunker's Hill DA17 . . . 4 A2
Bunny La TN3 . . . . . . 172 E5
Bunters Hill Rd ME3 . . 39 B4
Bunton St 3 SE18 . . . 2 A3
Burberry La ME17 . . . . 118 B5
Burcharbro Rd SE2 . . . 13 D8
Burch Rd DA11 . . . . . 18 F1
Burdens TN27 . . . . . . 151 D5
Burdett Ave DA12 . . . . 37 F4
Burdett Cl DA14 . . . . 30 E3
Burdett Rd TN4 . . . . . 158 B4
Burdock Ho ME1 . . . . . 116 D8
Burford Rd BR1 . . . . . 42 E5
Burgate Cl DA1 . . . . . 14 F4
Burgess Hall Dr ME17 . 117 F6
Burgess Rd 5 TN1 . . . 53 B7
Burgess Row 3 TN30 . . 193 F7
Burghclere Dr ME16 . . . 99 B2
Burghfield Rd DA13 . . . 35 F1
Burgoyne Ct ME14 . . . . 99 F7
BURHAM 66 B8
Burham CE Prim Sch ME1 82 F8
Burham Rd ME1 . . . . . 66 B8
Burial Ground La ME15 . 99 E1
Burleigh Ave DA15 . . . 23 F7
Burleigh Cl ME2 . . . . 52 E8
Burleigh Dr ME14 . . . . 83 F1
Burley Rd E16 . . . . . . 1 C8
Burlings La TN14 . . . . 73 F2
Burlington Cl
6 Newham E6 . . . . . . 1 E7
Orpington BR6 . . . . . . 57 B8
Burlington Gdns ME8 . . 69 E4
Burlington Lodge BR7 . 28 F1
Burman Cl DA2 . . . . . 33 C8
Burmarsh Cl ME5 . . . . 68 B5
Burma Way ME5 . . . . . 67 F6

Burnaby Rd DA11 . . . . 18 E1
Burnell Ave DA16 . . . . 13 A5
Burnett Rd DA8 . . . . . 15 D8
Burnham Cres DA1 . . . 15 C3
Burnham Rd
Dartford DA1 . . . . 15 C3
Sidcup DA14 . . . . 30 E6
Burnham Trad Est DA1 . 15 D3
Burnham Wlk ME8 . . . . 69 E3
Burnley Rd RM20 . . . . 17 A6
Burns Ave DA15 . . . . . 13 B1
Burns Cl
Bexley DA16 . . . . 12 F6
Erith DA8 . . . . 14 F6
Burns Cres TN9 . . . . . 143 A7
Burns Ho DA16 . . . . . 13 C6
Burns Pl RM18 . . . . . 19 B6
Burns Rd ME7 . . . . . . 54 C7
Burn's Rd ME7 . . . . . . 54 C7
Burnt Ash Heights BR1 . 28 B3
Burnt Ash Hill BR1 . . . 28 B3
Burnt Ash Hill SE12 . . . 28 B3
Burnt Ash La BR1, SE12 . 28 B3
Burnt Ash Prim Sch BR1 28 A3
Burntash Rd ME20 . . . . 98 F8
Burnt House Cl
Rochester ME2 . . . . . . 39 C2
Sandhurst TN18 . . . . . 196 C5
Burnthouse La TN27 . . . 152 D1
Burnt House La
Dartford DA2 . . . . 32 F5
Dartford DA2 . . . . 32 F4
Langton Green TN3 . . . . 158 A5
Burnt Lodge La TN5 . . . 186 B2
Burnt Oak Jun Sch DA15 30 A7
Burnt Oak La DA15 . . . 13 A1
Burnt Oak Prim Sch 1
ME7 . . . . 54 D6
Burnt Oak Terr ME7 . . . 54 D6
Burntwood Gr TN13 . . . 108 B8
Burntwood Rd TN13 . . . 108 B7
Burrage Gr SE18 . . . . 2 C2
Burrage Pl SE18 . . . . 2 B1
Burrage Rd SE18 . . . . 2 C1
Burrard Rd E16 . . . . . 1 B7
Burr Bank Terr DA2 . . . 32 C4
Burr Cl DA7 . . . . 13 F4
Burrfield Dr BR5 . . . . 44 D4
Burritt Mews ME1 . . . . 53 C3
Burrows La ME3 . . . . . 25 C3
Burrs Hill Cotts TN12 . 162 D6
Burrswood Villas TN3 . 171 B7
Bursdon Cl DA15 . . . . 29 F6
Burslem Rd TN2 . . . . . 159 E7
Bursted Wood Prim Sch
DA7 . . . . 14 B5
Burston Rd ME14 . . . . 115 B2
Burton Cl ME3 . . . . . . 39 C3
Burt Rd E16 . . . . 1 C5
Burts Wharf DA17 . . . . 4 C5
Burwash Ct BR5 . . . . . 44 C4
Burwash Rd SE18 . . . . 2 D1
Burwood Ave BR2 . . . . 42 B1
Burwood Ho SE9 . . . . . 29 C7
Burwood Sch BR6 . . . . 58 D8
Busbridge Ho ME19 . . . 97 F7
Busbridge Rd ME6 . . . . 81 E7
Bus Bridge Rd ME15 . . 115 E6
Bus Depot ME1 . . . . . 67 F5
Bushell Way BR7 . . . . 29 A3
Bushey Cl ME15 . . . . . 15 A6
Bushey Ho SE9 . . . . . . 28 C5
Bushey Lees DA15 . . . . 12 F1
Bushfield Wlk DA10 . . . 34 E8
Bushmeadow Rd ME8 . . 55 F2
Bushmoor Cres SE18 . . . 12 B6
Bush Rd
Cuxton ME2 . . . . 52 B2
East Peckham TN12 . . . . 129 E8
Bush Row ME20 . . . . . 83 A3
Bushy Gill TN3 . . . . . 158 A3
Bushy Gr ME17 . . . . . 118 D2
Business Acad Bexley The
DA18 . . . . 3 E4
BUSS'S GREEN 175 A2
Buston Manor Farm Cotts
ME18 . . . . 114 B2
Busty La TN15 . . . . . . 94 D6
Butcher Cl TN12 . . . . . 149 E3
Butcher La TN15 . . . . . 62 D8
Butcher's La ME19 . . . . 96 D1
Butchers Rd E16 . . . . . 1 A7
Butcher Yd BR6 . . . . . 73 A8
Butcher Wlk DA10 . . . . 34 E8
Butler Ho 3 RM17 . . . 18 B8
Butler's Cotts DA7 . . . 14 A5
Butler's Pl DA3 . . . . . 62 E7
Buttercup Cl TN12 . . . 146 A5
Butterfield Mews 16 SE18 12 B8
Butterfield Sq 10 E6 . 1 F7
Butterfly Ave DA1 . . . 32 F6
Butterfly La SE9 . . . . 29 B7
Buttermere Rd BR5 . . . 44 D5
Butt Green La ME17 . . . 133 A7
Butt Haw Cl ME3 . . . . 40 E5
Buttmarsh Cl SE18 . . . 2 B1
Button Cl ME3 . . . . . . 25 C5
Button Ho ME3 . . . . . . 39 F6
Button La ME15 . . . . . 101 B2
Button St BR8, DA4 . . . 46 A5
Butts La TN5 . . . . 185 C7
Butts The TN4 . . . . . . 76 B2
Buttway La ME3 . . . . . 22 A6
Buxton Cl
Chatham ME5 . . . . 68 D1
Loose ME15 . . . . 116 A8
Buxton Rd DA8 . . . . . . 14 D7

Buzzard Creek Ind Est
IG11 . . . . 3 A8
Bychurch Pl 7 ME15 . 100 A3
Bycliffe Mews 2 DA11 . 35 F8
Bycliffe Terr 3 DA11 . 35 F8
Byland Cl SE2 . . . . . . 9 D3
Byng Rd TN4 . . . . 158 F5
Bynon Ave DA7 . . . . . 13 F4
Byrneside TN11 . . . . . 126 E4
Byron Cl SE28 . . . . . . 3 C5
Byron Dr DA8 . . . . 14 B7
Byron Gdns RM18 . . . . 19 C6
Byron Prim Sch ME7 . . 54 C3
Byron Rd
Dartford DA1 . . . . 16 B3
Gillingham ME7 . . . . . 54 C3
Maidstone ME14 . . . . . 100 B7
Bywater Ho SE18 . . . . 1 E3

C

Cabbage Stalk La TN4 . 158 E2
Cables Cl DA8 . . . . . . 4 C3
Cacket's La TN14 . . . . 73 E4
CACKLE HILL 168 A5
Cade La TN13 . . . . . . 108 C7
Cadlocks Hill TN14 . . . 58 F1
Cadman Cl ME2 . . . . . 52 E8
Cadogan Ave DA2 . . . . 33 D8
Cadogan Gdns 6 DA11 . 159 B4
Cadogan Rd SE18 . . . . 2 C3
Cadwallon Rd SE9 . . . . 29 C6
Caerleon Cl DA14 . . . . 30 C3
Caerleon Terr SE2 . . . 3 B2
Caernarvon Cl
Erith DA8 . . . . 14 D7
8 Orpington BR5 . . . . 44 C5
Caernarvon Dr ME15 . . 99 F1
CAGE GREEN 127 C4
Cage Green Prim Sch
TN10 . . . . 127 D5
Cage Green Rd TN10 . . 127 C5
Cage La TN27 . . . . . . 152 F1
Cagney Cl ME3 . . . . . . 39 C3
Cairns Cl DA1 . . . . . . 15 D2
Cairns Mews SE18 . . . . 11 E6
Caistor Rd TN9 . . . . . 127 F1
Caithness Gdns DA15 . . 12 F1
Calais Cotts DA3 . . . . 62 A8
Calcott Wlk SE9 . . . . . 28 D4
Calcroft Ave DA9 . . . . 17 C2
Calcutta Ho 6 ME15 . . 116 E5
Calcutta Rd RM18 . . . . 19 A5
Calder Rd ME14 . . . . . 99 E7
Calderwood DA12 . . . . 36 E2
Calderwood St SE18 . . . 2 A2
Caldew Ave ME8 . . . . . 55 C1
Caldy Rd DA17 . . . . . . 4 B3
Caledonian Cl ME8 . . . 69 E8
Calehill Cl ME14 . . . . 100 C6
Caley Rd TN2 . . . . 159 D7
Calfstock La DA4 . . . . 46 F5
California Row TN12 . . 150 C6
Caling Croft TN15 . . . 48 F1
Caliph Cl DA12 . . . . . 36 F1
Callams Cl ME8 . . . . . 69 D6
Callaways La ME9 . . . . 71 B6
Callis Ct ME10 . . . . . . 99 D3
Callisto Cl SE28 . . . . . 3 C5
Callis Way ME8 . . . . . 69 D5
Calshot Ct 17 DA2 . . . 16 B1
Calverley Ct TN1 . . . . 159 C3
Calverley Park Cres 1
TN1 . . . . 159 B3
Calverley Park Gdns
TN1 . . . . 159 C4
Calverley Pk TN1 . . . . 159 B3
Calverley Rd TN1 . . . . 159 B3
Calverley St TN1 . . . . 159 B4
Calvert Cl
Erith DA17 . . . . 4 B1
Sidcup DA14 . . . . 30 E2
Calvert Dr DA2 . . . . . 31 D6
Calverton Prim Sch E16 . 1 D7
Calvin Cl BR5 . . . . . . 44 D6
Calydon Rd SE7 . . . . . 1 B1
Cambert Way SE3 . . . . 11 B3
Camberwell La TN14 . . 106 F4
Camborne Manor 2 ME7 54 C6
Camborne Rd
Bexley DA16 . . . . 12 F5
Sidcup DA14 . . . . 30 C5
Cambrai Rd BR6 . . . . . 43 F2
Cambria Ave ME1 . . . . 52 F2
Cambria Cl DA15 . . . . 29 E7
Cambria Cres DA12 . . . 36 F4
Cambria Ho 2 DA8 . . . 14 E7
Cambrian Gr DA11 . . . . 36 A8
Cambrian Rd TN4 . . . . 159 C7
Cambridge Ave DA16 . . 13 B1
Cambridge Barracks 8
SE18 . . . . 1 F2
Cambridge Cres ME15 . . 116 D7
Cambridge Dr SE12 . . . 11 A2
Cambridge Gdns TN2 . . 159 B2
Cambridge Gn SE9 . . . . 29 B7
Cambridge Ho 7 SE18 . 2 B1
Cambridge Rd
Bromley BR1 . . . . 28 A1
Gillingham ME8 . . . . . 69 C6
Rochester ME2 . . . . . . 53 A8
Sidcup DA14 . . . . 29 E4
Cambridge Row SE18 . . 2 B1
Cambridge St TN2 . . . . 159 C3
Cambridge Terr 1 ME4 . 53 F4
Cambridge Way 5
ME15 . . . . 116 D7
Cambus Rd E16 . . . . . 1 A8

Camdale Rd SE18 . . . . 12 F7
Camden Ave TN2 . . . . 160 C6
Camden Cl
Chatham ME5 . . . . 68 B5
Chislehurst BR7 . . . . . 43 C8
Northfleet DA11 . . . . . 35 C7
Camden Cotts TN17 . . . 179 F8
Camden Ct
10 Erith DA17 . . . . . . 4 A1
Pembury TN2 . . . . 160 D6
2 Royal Tunbridge Wells
TN1 . . . . 159 B4
Camden Gr BR7 . . . . . 29 B2
CAMDEN HILL 165 F2
Camden Hill TN2 . . . . 159 B3
CAMDEN PARK 159 C2
Camden Park Rd BR7 . . 29 A1
Camden Pk TN2 . . . . . 159 C2
Camden Rd
Gillingham ME7 . . . . . 54 D7
Royal Tunbridge Wells
TN1 . . . . 159 B4
Sevenoaks TN13 . . . . . 92 B5
Sidcup DA15 . . . . 30 F8
Camden St ME14 . . . . . 100 A5
Camden Terr
Seal TN15 . . . . 92 F6
Sissinghurst TN17 . . . . 179 F8
Camden Way BR7 . . . . 29 A1
Camellia Cl ME8 . . . . . 69 D7
Camelot Cl
Biggin Hill TN16 . . . . . 72 C3
Woolwich SE28 . . . . . . 1 F4
Camel Rd E16 . . . . . . 1 E5
Camer Ctry Pk★ DA13 . 50 C2
Camer Gdns DA13 . . . . 50 C3
Cameron Cl
Chatham ME5 . . . . 68 B8
Joyden's Wood DA5 . . . 31 E5
Cameron Dr DA1 . . . . . 16 A5
Cameron Rd BR2 . . . . . 42 A4
Camerons 4 TN18 . . . . 189 E2
Camer Park Rd DA13 . . 50 C2
Camer Rd DA13 . . . . . 50 C3
Camer St DA13 . . . . . 50 C3
Camomile Dr ME14 . . . 100 F5
Campbell Cl SE18 . . . . 12 A6
Campbell Ho ME3 . . . . 39 F6
Campbell Rd
Maidstone ME15 . . . . . 100 A3
Northfleet DA11 . . . . . 35 F8
TN4 . . . . 159 A6
Camperdown Manor 5
ME7 . . . . 54 A6
Campfield Rd SE9 . . . . 28 D8
Camp Hill TN11 . . . . . 125 A3
Camp Hill Cotts TN11 . 124 F2
Campion Cl
Chatham ME5 . . . . 67 E3
Newham E6 . . . . 1 F6
Northfleet DA11 . . . . . 35 E4
Campion Cres TN17 . . . 179 A2
Campion Ct 6 RM17 . . 18 D8
Campion Pl SE28 . . . . 3 B5
Campleshon Rd ME9 . . 69 D5
Camp Site The DA14 . . 31 A1
Camps Way ME8 . . . . . 69 A8
Camp Way ME8 . . . . . 116 C6
Camrose Ave DA8 . . . . 14 B8
Camrose St SE2 . . . . . 3 A2
Canada Farm Rd DA4 . . 48 A6
Canada Rd DA8 . . . . . 10 A7
Canadian Ave SE6 . . . . 54 F4
Canadian Rd ME7 . . . . 54 F4
Canal Basin DA12 . . . . 19 D1
Canal Ind Pk 2 DA12 . . 36 D8
Canal Rd
Gravesend DA12 . . . . . 19 D1
Higham ME3 . . . . 38 C8
Rochester ME2 . . . . . . 53 C7
Canberra Rd
Bexley DA7 . . . . 13 D8
Greenwich SE7 . . . . . . 11 D8
Canberra Sq RM18 . . . . 19 A5
Canbury Path BR5 . . . . 44 A5
Canning St ME14 . . . . 100 A6
CANNING TOWN 1 B8
Cannon Bridge Works
TN9 . . . . 127 D2
Cannon La TN9 . . . . . 127 D2
Cannon Pl SE7 . . . . . . 1 E1
Cannon Rd DA7 . . . . . 13 F6
Canon Cl ME1 . . . . . . 53 B2
Canon Jeffreys Ct 13
TN18 . . . . 188 F2
Canon La ME18 . . . . . 97 C1
Canon Rd BR1 . . . . . . 42 A6
Canons Wlk TN16 . . . . 106 B6
Cansiron La TN7, TN8 . 154 E2
Canterbury Ave DA15 . . 30 C6
Canterbury Christ Church
Univ (Medway Campus)
ME4 . . . . 54 B8
Canterbury Cl
Dartford DA1 . . . . 33 A8
4 Newham E6 . . . . . . 1 F7
Canterbury Cres TN10 . . 127 D5
Canterbury Ct 7 SE12 . 28 B5
Canterbury Ho
6 Erith DA18 . . . . . . 14 F7
2 Maidstone ME15 . . . 116 D7
Canterbury Rd
Gravesend DA12 . . . . . 36 C6
Pembury TN2 . . . . 160 E6
Canterbury St ME7 . . . 54 C4

Canterbury Way DA1, DA2,
RM20 . . . . 16 D5
Cantwell Ho SE18 . . . . 12 B7
Cantwell Rd SE18 . . . . 12 B7
Capability Way **3** DA9 . . . 17 C3
CAPEL 144 F5
Capel Cl
 Gillingham ME8 . . . . 69 D4
 Orpington BR2 . . . . 42 E1
CAPEL CROSS 163 C5
Capella Ho **3** SE7 . . . . . . 11 B8
Capell Cl ME17 . . . . 115 C3
Capel Pl DA2 . . . . 32 C4
Capel Prim Sch TN12 . . . 144 F7
Capetown Ho **1** ME15 . . 116 F5
Capital Ind Est DA17 . . . . . . 4 B3
Capstan Ct DA2 . . . . 16 C3
Capstan Ctr RM18 . . . . 18 D7
Capstan Mews **4** DA11 . . 35 E8
CAPSTONE 68 E7
Capstone Farm Ctry Pk★
 ME7 . . . . 68 D5
Capstone Rd
 Chatham ME5 . . . . 54 D1
 Gillingham ME7 . . . . 68 F6
 Lewisham BR1 . . . . 28 A4
Captain's Cl ME17 . . . . . . 134 E6
Capulet Mews E16 . . . . 1 A5
Caraway Cl E13 . . . . 1 B8
Cardens Rd ME3 . . . . 39 B8
Cardiff St SE18 . . . . 12 E7
Cardigan Rd ME23 . . . . . . 23 F3
Cardinal Cl
 Chislehurst BR7 . . . . 43 D8
 Tonbridge TN9 . . . . 143 D8
Cardinal Wlk ME19 . . . . . . 97 C3
Cardwell Prim Sch SE18 . . . 1 F2
Carew Ho **10** SE18 . . . . 1 F2
Carew Way BR5 . . . . 44 C1
Carey Ct DA6 . . . . 14 B2
Carey's Field TN13 . . . . . . 91 E7
Caring La ME14, ME17 . . . 101 E1
Caring Rd ME15, ME17 . . 101 C1
Carisbrooke Ave DA5 . . . . . 30 D7
Carisbrooke Ct
 2 Dartford DA2 . . . . 16 B1
 20 Sidcup DA14 . . . . 30 A4
Carisbrooke Dr ME16 . . . . 99 C4
Carisbrooke Rd
 Bromley BR1 . . . . 42 C5
 Rochester ME2 . . . . 38 E1
Carleton Pl DA4 . . . . 47 C5
Carleton Rd DA1 . . . . 33 A8
Carlisle Cl ME2 . . . . 52 C6
Carlisle Rd DA1 . . . . 16 A1
Carlton Ave
 Gillingham ME7 . . . . 54 E4
 Stone DA9 . . . . 16 E1
Carlton Cl
 Kings Hill ME19 . . . . 97 B3
 Tonbridge TN10 . . . . . . 127 E7
Carlton Cres
 Chatham ME5 . . . . 68 D8
 Royal Tunbridge Wells
 TN1 . . . . 159 C4
Carlton Gn **3** DA14 . . . . . 29 F4
Carlton Par **1** BR5 . . . . . . 44 B2
Carlton Rd
 Bexley DA16 . . . . 13 B4
 Erith DA8 . . . . 14 C8
 Royal Tunbridge Wells
 TN1 . . . . 159 C4
 Sidcup DA14 . . . . 29 F3
Carlyle Ave BR1 . . . . 42 D6
Carlyle Rd SE28 . . . . 3 C6
Carman's Cl ME15, ME17 . 115 F3
Carmelite Way DA3 . . . . . . 48 F4
Carmichael Ave DA9 . . . . . 17 C3
Carnation Cl **1** ME9 . . . . . 82 A1
Carnation Cres ME19 . . . . 81 F1
Carnation Rd ME2 . . . . 52 D7
Carnation St SE2 . . . . 3 B1
Cranbrook Mews **3** S . . 11 D4
Cranbrook Rd SE3 . . . . 11 D4
Carnecke Gdns SE9 . . . . . . 11 E2
Carnet Cl DA1 . . . . 31 E8
Carnoustie Cl SE28 . . . . 3 D7
Caroline Cres ME16 . . . . . . 99 D7
Carolyn Dr BR6 . . . . 58 A7
Carp Cl ME20 . . . . 82 A4
Carpeaux Cl ME4 . . . . 54 B4
Carpenters Cl ME1 . . . . 53 E2
Carpenters Ct BR1 . . . . 42 D7
Carpenters La TN11 . . . . . 111 D2
Carpinus Ct ME5 . . . . 68 B1
Carrack Ho **1** DA8 . . . . 4 E1
Carr Gr SE18 . . . . 1 E2
Carr Ho DA1 . . . . 14 E2
Carriageway The TN16 . . . 90 D1
Carrick Dr TN13 . . . . 92 B4
Carrie Ho **3** ME16 . . . . 99 E5
Carriers Pl TN3 . . . . 156 B4
Carriers Rd TN17 . . . . 179 D5
Carrill Way DA17 . . . . 3 D3
Carrington DA14 . . . . 30 A3
Carrington Cl ME7 . . . . 54 F6
Carrington Rd DA1 . . . . . . 16 F1
Carroll Cl ME2 . . . . 66 A4
Carroll Gdns SE28 . . . . . . 81 F3
Carronade Pl SE28 . . . . 2 D3
Carsington Gdns DA1 . . . . 32 D6
Carson Rd E16 . . . . 1 A8
Carston Cl SE12 . . . . 11 A2
Carter Ave TN15 . . . . 61 D3

Carter's Hill
 Bromley ME9 . . . . 28 C7
 Underriver TN15 . . . . . . 109 B6
Carters Hill Cl SE9 . . . . . . 28 C7
Carters Hill La DA13 . . . . . 63 F2
Carters Row DA11 . . . . 35 F6
Cartmel Rd DA7 . . . . 14 A6
Carton Cl ME1 . . . . 53 D2
Carton Rd ME3 . . . . 38 B3
Carville Ave TN4 . . . . 142 F1
Carvoran Way ME8 . . . . . . 69 D4
Cascade Cl BR5 . . . . 44 C6
Cascades L Ctr DA12 . . . . 37 A4
Caspian Way DA10 . . . . . . 17 E2
Caspian Wlk E16 . . . . 1 D7
Cassilda Rd SE2 . . . . 3 A2
Cassine Ct BR8 . . . . 31 F1
Castalia Ct DA1 . . . . 15 F4
Casterbridge Rd SE3 . . . . . 11 A4
Castlefield **3** ME1 . . . . . . 22 E1
Castle Ave ME1 . . . . 53 C4
Castilion Prim Sch SE28 . . . 3 C7
Castlecombe Prim Sch
 SE9 . . . . 28 E3
Castlecombe Rd SE9 . . . . . 28 E4
Castle Dene ME14 . . . . 99 F8
Castle Dr TN15 . . . . 76 E2
Castle Farm Cotts TN11 . 128 F8
Castle Farm Rd TN14 . . . . 60 A3
Castlefields DA13 . . . . 49 F8
Castle Fields TN9 . . . . 127 B2
Castleford Ave SE9 . . . . . . 23 B7
CASTLE HILL 146 E1
Castle Hill
 Hartley TN3 . . . . 48 E4
 Rochester ME1 . . . . 53 C6
 Thurnham ME14 . . . . . . 85 D1
 Tonbridge TN11 . . . . . . 143 D4
Castle Hill Ct ME1 . . . . 53 C6
Castle Hurst TN32 . . . . . . 195 B1
Castle La DA12 . . . . 37 B6
Castlemaine Ave ME7 . . . . 54 F8
Castle Rd
 Chatham ME4 . . . . 54 B2
 Eynsford DA4 . . . . 60 C5
 Grays RM17 . . . . 17 F8
 Maidstone ME16 . . . . . . 99 D7
 Royal Tunbridge Wells
 TN4 . . . . 159 A3
 Swanscombe DA10 . . . . . 17 A3
Castle St
 Rochester ME2 . . . . 39 E1
 2 Royal Tunbridge Wells,
 Sion TN1 . . . . 159 A2
 3 Royal Tunbridge Wells,
 Southborough TN4 . . . . 142 F2
 Stone DA9 . . . . 17 A2
 Swanscombe DA10 . . . . . 17 F1
 Tonbridge TN9 . . . . 127 C2
 Wouldham ME1 . . . . 66 C4
Castle Terr
 Hadlow TN11 . . . . 128 E8
 Hawkhurst TN18 . . . . . 188 F3
Castleton Ave DA7 . . . . . . 14 D5
Castleton Rd SE9 . . . . 28 E3
Castle View Bsns Ctr ME1 53 C6
Castle View Mews ME1 . . . 53 C6
Castle View Rd ME2 . . . . . 53 A7
Castle Way ME19 . . . . 88 E7
Castle Wlk TN5 . . . . 184 E4
Castlewood Dr SE9 . . . . . . 11 F5
Castweazle TN30 . . . . 192 E6
Caterfield La RH7, RH8 . . 121 A5
Cates Ct TN12 . . . . 130 A7
Cathcart Dr BR6 . . . . 43 E1
Catherine Cl **2** ME1 . . . . . 99 A3
Catherine of Aragon Ct
 DA15 . . . . 29 D8
Catherine Pl **7** TN1 . . . . 159 B4
Catherine St ME1 . . . . 53 D3
Catkin Cl ME9 . . . . 67 F1
Catlyn Cl ME19 . . . . 98 A8
Catterick Rd ME5 . . . . 68 D2
Cattistock Rd SE28 . . . . . . 28 F3
Catts Alley ME6 . . . . 82 A3
Catts Pl TN12 . . . . 146 C4
Caulkers Ho **7** ME4 . . . . . 54 B2
Causton Rd TN17 . . . . 179 C6
Cavalry Ct TN10 . . . . 127 E7
Cave Hill ME15 . . . . 99 F1
Cavell Cres DA1 . . . . 16 A3
Cavendish Ave
 Bexley DA16 . . . . 12 F4
 Erith DA8 . . . . 14 C8
 Gillingham ME7 . . . . 54 E6
 Sevenoaks TN13 . . . . . . 92 A5
 Sidcup DA15 . . . . 24 A2
Cavendish Cl TN10 . . . . . . 127 D7
Cavendish Ct TN9 . . . . . . 127 D2
Cavendish Dr TN2 . . . . . . 159 B1
Cavendish Place BR1 . . . . . 42 F6
Cavendish Rd ME1 . . . . . . 53 D3
Cavendish Sq DA3 . . . . 48 D6
Cavendish Way ME15 . . . 101 B3
Caversham Rd ME8 . . . . . . 55 F1
Caveside Cl BR7 . . . . 43 A8
Caxton Cl
 Hartley DA3 . . . . 48 F5
 Tenterden TN30 . . . . . . 192 F7
Caxton Ho RH8 . . . . 104 F3
Caxton La
 Hadlow TN11 . . . . 128 E8
 The Chart RH8 . . . . 104 E4
Cayser Dr ME17 . . . . 118 E2
Caysers Croft TN12 . . . . . 129 E6
Cazeneuve St ME1 . . . . . . 53 C5

Cecil Ave
 Gillingham ME8 . . . . 55 A2
 Rochester ME2 . . . . 53 B8
Cecil Burns Cl TN2 . . . . . 159 D2
Cecil Kidby Ho TN2 . . . . 159 F6
Cecil Rd
 Northfleet DA11 . . . . 35 F7
 Rochester ME2 . . . . 53 C3
Cecil Road Prim Sch
 DA11 . . . . 35 F7
Cecil Way BR2 . . . . 42 A1
Cedar Ave
 Gravesend DA12 . . . . 36 C4
 Sidcup DA15 . . . . 30 A8
Cedar Cl
 Ditton ME20 . . . . 98 D8
 Meopham Station DA13 . . 50 A3
 Orpington BR2 . . . . 56 E7
 Swanley BR8 . . . . 45 C7
Cedar Copse BR1 . . . . 42 F7
Cedar Cres
 Orpington BR2 . . . . 56 E7
 Tonbridge TN10 . . . . . . 127 C7
Cedar Ct
 Eltham SE9 . . . . 11 E1
 21 Greenwich SE7 . . . . . 11 D5
 Maidstone ME14 . . . . . 100 B5
 Royal Tunbridge Wells
 TN4 . . . . 159 A5
 11 Tenterden TN30 . . . . 193 A7
Cedar Dr
 Edenbridge TN8 . . . . . . 122 B2
 Maidstone ME16 . . . . . . 98 E2
 Sutton at Hone DA4 . . . . 47 B7
Cedar Gdns ME9 . . . . 86 E8
Cedar Gr
 Gillingham ME7 . . . . 69 A5
 Sidcup DA5 . . . . 13 D1
Cedar Ho TN4 . . . . 158 E4
Cedarhurst Cotts **3** DA5 . 31 A8
Cedarhurst Dr SE9 . . . . . . 11 C2
Cedar La TN27 . . . . 182 D7
Cedar Lodge TN4 . . . . 158 F3
Cedarmore Ct BR7 . . . . . . 43 C8
Cedar Mount **3** SE7 . . . . . 1 C1
Cedar Rd
 Bromley BR1 . . . . 42 C7
 Dartford DA1 . . . . 32 D7
 Erith DA8 . . . . 15 A6
 Hoo St Werburgh ME3 . . 40 E3
 Rochester ME2 . . . . 52 F6
Cedar Ridge TN2 . . . . 159 D5
Cedars PRU The ME16 . . . 99 D4
Cedars Sch The ME1 . . . . 103 C3
Cedars The TN12 . . . . 146 A7
Cedar Terrace Rd TN13 . . . 92 A4
Cedarwood Ho ME15 . . . . 115 B6
Cedric Rd SE9 . . . . 29 C5
Celandine Dr SE28 . . . . 3 B5
Celestine Cl ME5 . . . . 68 A1
Celia Ave TN15 . . . . 61 E3
Cellini Walk ME11 . . . . . . 97 C2
Cement Block Cotts **8**
 RM17 . . . . 18 C8
Cemetery La
 Hadlow TN11 . . . . 112 A1
 Woolwich SE7 . . . . 11 E8
Cemetery Rd
 Halling ME2 . . . . 66 A4
 Snodland ME6 . . . . 65 F1
 Woolwich SE2 . . . . 3 C3
Centenary Rd DA4 . . . . . . 47 A2
Central Ave
 Bexley DA16 . . . . 13 A5
 Chatham ME4 . . . . 54 B8
 Gravesend DA12 . . . . 36 B5
 Tilbury RM18 . . . . 19 A6
 Welling DA16 . . . . 13 A5
Central Bsns Pk ME2 . . . . . 53 E7
Central Ct **3** SE18 . . . . 2 B2
Central Lodge TN15 . . . . . 79 E6
Central Par
 Rochester ME1 . . . . 53 D2
 Sidcup DA15 . . . . 30 A5
 Wadhurst TN5 . . . . 184 F4
Central Park Gdns ME4 . . . 53 E7
Central Par Villas BR5 . . . 44 C7
Central Rd
 Dartford DA1 . . . . 15 E2
 New Hythe ME20 . . . . . . 82 B4
 Rochester ME2 . . . . 53 E7
Central Terr ME3 . . . . 39 F6
Central Theatre The★ **10**
 ME4 . . . . 53 F4
Central Way SE28 . . . . 3 B6
Centre 2000 ME16 . . . . . . 99 C8
Centre Common Rd BR7 . . 29 C1
Centre Ct ME2 . . . . 53 B7
Centre Performing Arts Coll
 The SE18 . . . . 1 D3
Centre Rd DA3 . . . . 62 E7
Centurian Square SE18 . . . 11 E7
Centurion Sq DA18 . . . . . . 4 A3
Centurion Cl ME18 . . . . . . 54 F1
Century Ct ME1 . . . . 53 C5
Century Rd ME8 . . . . 69 D8
Ceres Rd SE18 . . . . 2 F2
Cerne Rd DA12 . . . . 36 E5
Cervia Way DA12 . . . . 36 F5
Chada Ave ME7 . . . . 54 E3
Chadd Dr BR1 . . . . 42 E6
Chadfields RM18 . . . . 19 A7
Chadwell Hill RM17 . . . . . 18 C8
Chadwick Cl DA11 . . . . . . 35 E5
Chadwick Ct
 2 Dartford DA1 . . . . 15 D1
 4 Woolwich SE28 . . . . . . 3 B5
Chadwick Way SE28 . . . . . . 3 D6

Chadwin Rd E13 . . . . 1 B8
Chaffey Ho **6** SE7 . . . . 1 C1
Chaffinch Cl ME15 . . . . . . 68 A7
Chaffinch Way TN12 . . . . 146 A5
Chafford Cotts TN3 . . . . . 156 F5
Chafford La TN3 . . . . 156 F5
Chain Gate ME17 . . . . . . 137 A8
CHAINHURST 132 A4
Chalcombe Rd SE2 . . . . 3 B3
Chalet Cl DA5 . . . . 31 D4
Chalfont Ct **3** DA17 . . . . . . 4 A1
Chalfont Dr TN27 . . . . . . 151 D5
Chalgrove Mews ME7 . . . . 66 A5
Chalice Way DA9 . . . . 16 F2
CHALK 37 A7
Chalk Ave TN30 . . . . 183 C8
Chalk Ct RM17 . . . . 18 A8
Chalkenden Ave ME8 . . . . 55 A2
Chalkers Way ME8 . . . . . . 55 B4
Chalket La TN2 . . . . 160 C5
Chalk La TN17 . . . . 178 E7
Chalklin Business Park
 TN2 . . . . 159 E8
Chalk Pit Ave BR5 . . . . . . 44 D6
Chalk Pit Hill ME4 . . . . . . 54 A3
Chalk Rd
 Chalk DA12 . . . . 37 A6
 Lower Higham ME3 . . . . 38 C6
 Newham E13 . . . . 1 C8
Chalkstone Cl DA16 . . . . . 13 A6
Chalkways TN5 . . . . 76 F3
Chalky Bank DA1 . . . . 36 A3
Chalky Bank Rd ME8 . . . . 55 F2
Chalky Rd ME9 . . . . 86 C6
Challenge Cl DA12 . . . . . . 36 F4
Challenger Cl TN12 . . . . . 145 F6
Challock Cl TN16 . . . . 72 C3
Challock Ho
 3 Erith DA8 . . . . 14 F7
 2 Orpington BR5 . . . . . . 44 D1
Challock Wlk ME14 . . . . . 100 C6
Chalmers Way ME8 . . . . . . 55 A4
Chamberlain Ave ME16 . . . 99 C2
Chamberlain Cl **5** SE28 . . . 3 D2
Chamberlain Cres BR4 . . . 36 A3
Chamberlain Ho E16 . . . . . 69 B5
Chamberlain Rd ME4 . . . . 54 B2
Chambers Ave DA14 . . . . . 30 E2
Chambers Cl **3** DA9 . . . . . 17 A2
Champions Dr TN8 . . . . . 122 B2
Chancel Cl TN15 . . . . 61 E3
Chancellor Ho TN4 . . . . . 158 F3
Chancellor Way TN13 . . . . 92 A5
Chancelot Rd SE2 . . . . 3 B2
Chancery Cl DA1 . . . . 33 A7
Chancery La ME15 . . . . . . 100 B3
Chancery Rd ME3 . . . . 22 B5
Chanctonbury Cl SE9 . . . . 29 B5
Chandler Ave E16 . . . . 1 A8
Chandlers Dr DA8 . . . . 4 E2
Chandler's Hill DA13 . . . . 64 C5
Chandlers Mews **2** DA9 . 17 C3
Chandler's Rd DA13 . . . . . 64 C5
Chandlers Wharf ME1 . . . . 53 B5
Chandos Rd TN1 . . . . 159 B1
Chantler's Mead TN8 . . . . 155 A5
Chantry Ave DA3 . . . . 48 E3
Chantry Cl
 Sidcup DA14 . . . . 30 E3
 Woolwich SE2 . . . . 3 C3
Chantry Ct DA12 . . . . 19 C1
Chantry Her Ctr★ DA12 . . 19 C1
Chantry La BR2 . . . . 42 D4
Chantry Pl
 Marden TN12 . . . . 148 C6
 Sevenoaks TN13 . . . . . . 91 F5
Chantry Prim Sch DA12 . . 19 C1
Chantry Rd TN12 . . . . 148 C5
Chantry The TN2 . . . . 151 E5
Chapel Alley Cotts TN14 . . 76 A8
Chapel Cl
 Crayford DA1 . . . . 14 E2
 Ryarsh ME19 . . . . 80 F5
 West Thurrock RM20 . . . 17 B8
Chapel Cotts ME17 . . . . . 117 F5
Chapel Ct DA10 . . . . 17 E1
Chapel Farm Rd SE9 . . . . . 28 F6
Chapel Field Cotts DA4 . . 47 B8
Chapel Hill DA1 . . . . 14 E2
Chapel Hos ME7 . . . . 83 A5
Chapel La
 Bredhurst ME7 . . . . 69 A2
 Egerton Forstal TN27 . . 137 B2
 Gillingham ME7 . . . . 69 A4
 Iden Green TN17 . . . . . 190 C4
 Maidstone ME14 . . . . . 101 A5
 Sissinghurst TN17 . . . . 180 B7
 Staplehurst TN12 . . . . . 149 F3
 Upper Halling ME2 . . . . 65 C4
Chapel Row
 East Malling ME19 . . . . . 98 A6
 Ryarsh ME19 . . . . 80 F5
Chapel The ME16 . . . . 99 B3
Chapel View TN15 . . . . . . 94 C6

Chapel Wlk
 Goathurst Common
 TN14 . . . . 107 B5
 Maypole DA2 . . . . 31 E6
Chapel Wood DA3 . . . . . . 62 E8
Chapel Wood Rd DA3,
 TN15 . . . . 62 E8
Chaplin Cl ME3 . . . . 39 C3
Chaplin Ct DA4 . . . . 33 A2
Chaplin Dr TN27 . . . . 151 D5
Chapman Ave ME15 . . . . 116 E8
Chapman Rd DA17 . . . . 4 B1
Chapmans Cl TN14 . . . . . . 90 E3
Chapmans End BR5 . . . . . 44 E7
Chapman's Hill DA13, TN15 63 A4
Chapman's La
 Orpington BR5, BR8 . . . 44 D7
 Swanley BR8 . . . . 45 A7
Chapmans Pl ME17 . . . . . 135 F7
Chapmans Rd TN14 . . . . . 90 E3
Chapman Way
 East Malling ME19 . . . . . 97 F8
 Royal Tunbridge Wells
 TN2 . . . . 159 C8
Chapter Rd ME2 . . . . 52 F8
Chapter Sch ME2 . . . . 52 D7
CHARCOTT 125 A3
Chardwell Cl E6 . . . . 1 F7
Charford Rd E16 . . . . 1 A8
Charing Cl BR6 . . . . 57 F6
Charing Ho **3** DA8 . . . . . . 14 F7
Charing Rd ME8 . . . . 55 B3
Chariot Way ME7 . . . . 52 F4
Charity Farm Cotts TN17 166 F7
Charlbury Cl ME15 . . . . . . 99 C3
Charldane Rd SE9 . . . . 29 B5
Charles Busby Ct ME20 . . 82 F1
Charlecote Cl
 Sidcup DA14 . . . . 30 B4
 Snodland ME6 . . . . 82 A8
Charles Ct
 Erith DA8 . . . . 14 E8
 Royal Tunbridge Wells
 TN2 . . . . 159 C3
Charles Darwin Ho **5**
 BR1 . . . . 28 B1
Charles Darwin Sch TN16 . 72 F3
Charles Dickens Ave ME3 . 38 C2
Charles Dr ME2 . . . . 52 B2
Charlesfield SE9 . . . . 28 C5
Charles Flemwell Mews
 E16 . . . . 1 A5
Charlesford Ave ME17 . . . 118 D3
Charles Garvice Ct SE3 . . . 11 D4
Charles Grinling Wlk SE18 . 2 A2
Charles Rd TN14 . . . . 59 B1
Charles St
 Chatham ME4 . . . . 53 E3
 Grays RM17 . . . . 18 C8
 Maidstone ME16 . . . . . . 99 E3
 Newham E16 . . . . 1 C5
 Rochester ME2 . . . . 53 A7
 Royal Tunbridge Wells
 TN4 . . . . 159 A8
 Stone DA9 . . . . 16 F2
Charles Street Ctr The
 TN4 . . . . 159 A8
Charles Whincup Rd E16 . . 1 B5
Charlewille Rd DA14 . . . . . 14 C7
Charlock Cl ME16 . . . . 99 D8
Charlotte Cl
 Bexley DA6 . . . . 13 C2
 Chatham ME5 . . . . 68 B6
 Charlotte Ct BR7 . . . . . . 29 B2
Charlotte Dr
 Gillingham ME8 . . . . 55 C1
 Kings Hill ME19 . . . . 97 D3
Charlotte Park Ave BR1 . . 42 E6
Charlotte Pl RM20 . . . . . . 17 B8
Charlottes Cl TN11 . . . . . 125 F1
CHARLTON 11 D8
Charlton Church La SE7 . . . 1 C1
Charlton Court Rd ME17 . 135 C7
Charlton Cres **2** TN9 . . . 127 C2
Charlton Dene SE7 . . . . . . 11 D7
Charlton Dr TN16 . . . . 72 D2
Charlton Gate Bsns Pk SE7 1 C2
Charlton La
 Chartway Street ME17 . . 118 C1
 Greenwich SE7 . . . . 1 C1
 Sutton Valence ME17 . . 135 C8
 West Farleigh ME15 . . . 114 E6
Charlton Manor ME7 . . . . 54 B5
Charlton Manor Prim Sch
 SE7 . . . . 11 D7
Charlton Park La SE7 . . . . 11 E8
Charlton Park Rd SE7 . . . . 11 D8
Charlton Rd SE3, SE7 . . . . 11 B8
Charlton Sch SE7 . . . . 11 E8
Charlton St
 Grain ME3 . . . . 21 B2
 Maidstone ME16 . . . . . . 99 C2
Charlton Sta SE7 . . . . 1 C1
Charlton's Way TN4 . . . . . 158 E1
Charminster Rd SE9 . . . . . 28 D4
Charmouth Rd DA16 . . . . 13 C6
Charnwood La BR6 . . . . . . 58 B1
Charnwood Villas BR6 . . . 58 C1
Charne The TN14 . . . . 76 A2
Charnock BR8 . . . . 45 E5
Chart Cnr ME17 . . . . 117 B1
Charter Dr DA5 . . . . 24 A8
Charterhouse Dr TN13 . . . 92 A4
Charterhouse Rd BR6 . . . . 58 A6

Charter St
Chatham ME4. . . . . 53 F2
Gillingham ME7 . . . . 54 C7
CHART HILL 134 B8
Chart Hill Rd
Chart Sutton ME17 . . . . . . 117 B1
Sutton Valence ME17. . . . 134 A7
Chart Hills CI SE28 . . . . 3 E7
Chart La TN16 . . . . 106 B7
Charton CI 3 DA17 . . . . . . 13 F8
Chart PI ME8 . . . . 69 C3
Chart Rd ME17 . . . . 134 C7
CHART SUTTON 117 B1
Chart Sutton Bsns Est
ME17. . . . . 117 B2
Chart View TN15 . . . . 77 B2
Chartway TN13 . . . . 92 C3
Chartway St ME17. . . . . . . 118 C1
CHARTWAY STREET 118 C1
Chartwell Bsns Ctr BR1 . . 42 D6
Chartwell* TN16 . . . . 105 F4
Chartwell CI
Rochester ME2 . . . . 39 B1
Sidcup SE9 . . . . 29 D6
Chartwell Ct
Chatham ME4. . . . . 53 E4
Maidstone ME15 . . . . 100 B3
Chartwell Dr
Maidstone ME16 . . . . 99 B4
Orpington BR6 . . . . 57 D5
Chase Sq 10 DA11. . . . . . . 19 B1
Chase The
Bexley DA7 . . . . 14 B4
Bromley BR1 . . . . 42 B6
Chatham ME4. . . . . 53 D2
Gillingham ME8 . . . . 55 A2
Kemsing TN15 . . . . 76 E3
Pratt's Bottom BR6 . . . . . 58 A1
Tonbridge TN10 . . . . 117 C8
West Thurrock RM20. . . . 17 D8
Chastilian Rd DA1. . . . . . . 32 A8
Chatfield Way ME19. . . . . 82 B1
CHATHAM 53 E5
Chatham Ave BR2. . . . . . . 42 A2
Chatham CI SE18 . . . . 2 B3
Chatham Gr ME4. . . . . 53 F1
Chatham Gram Sch for Boys
ME4. . . . . 67 F8
Chatham Gram Sch for Girls
ME5. . . . . 54 C2
Chatham Hill ME4. . . . . . . 54 B3
Chatham Hill Rd TN14. . . . 92 C6
Chatham Ho 16 SE18 . . . . . . 1 F2
Chatham Rd
Kit's Coty ME20 . . . . 83 D6
Maidstone ME14 . . . . 83 E1
Sandling ME14. . . . . 83 E4
Chatham Ski Ctr ME7 . . . . 68 E6
Chatham South ME4. . . . . 67 F8
Chatham St ME4. . . . . 53 E4
Chatsworth Ave
Bromley BR1 . . . . 28 B4
Sidcup DA15. . . . . 30 A7
Chatsworth Dr ME2 . . . . . 39 B1
Chatsworth Ho 3 BR2 . . . 42 A1
Chatsworth Inf Sch DA15. 30 A7
Chatsworth Par BR5 . . . . . 43 C4
Chatsworth Rd
Dartford DA1. . . . . 15 C3
10 Gillingham ME7 . . . . . 54 C6
CHATTENDEN 39 F4
Chattenden Ct ME14 . . . . 100 B6
Chattenden La ME3 . . . . . 39 F5
Chattenden Prim Sch
ME3. . . . . 39 F4
Chattenden Terr ME3 . . . . 39 F4
Chatterton Rd BR2. . . . . . 42 D4
Chatwell Ct ME7 . . . . 54 C5
Chaucer Bsns Pk TN15 . . . 93 D8
Chaucer CI
18 Maidstone ME15 . . . . 116 E7
Rochester ME2 . . . . 53 E8
Tilbury RM18. . . . . 19 C5
Chaucer Gdns TN9 . . . . . 142 F7
Chaucer Ind Pk TN15. . . . 93 D8
Chaucer Pk DA1. . . . . 32 F8
Chaucer Rd
Bexley DA16 . . . . 12 F6
Gillingham ME7 . . . . 54 D3
Northfleet DA11. . . . . 35 D5
Sidcup DA15. . . . . 30 C7
Chaucer Way
Dartford DA1. . . . . 16 A3
New Hythe ME20. . . . . . . 82 A3
Chaundrye CI SE9. . . . . . . 11 F1
Chauntler CI E16. . . . . 1 B6
Chave Rd DA2 . . . . 32 E5
Cheeselands TN27 . . . . . 167 F2
Cheffins Ho ME2 . . . . 54 E7
Chegwell Dr ME5 . . . . 68 B4
Chegworth La ME17 . . . . 119 A6
Chegworth Rd ME17 . . . . 118 F5
Cheldoc Rise ME4. . . . . . . 40 C2
Chellows La RM7 . . . . 121 A1
Chelmar Rd ME7 . . . . 54 B4
Chelmsford CI E6. . . . . 1 F7
Chelmsford Ho ME15. . . . 116 E6
Chelmsford Rd ME2. . . . . 52 D6
Chelsea Ct 6 BR1 . . . . 42 E6
CHELSFIELD 58 E5
Chelsfield Hill BR6. . . . . . . 58 C2
Chelsfield La
Badgers Mount BR6, TN14. . 59 B2
Chelsfield BR5, BR6. . . . . 58 D7

Chelsfield La continued
Orpington BR5. . . . . 44 D1
Chelsfield Park Hospl
BR6. . . . . 58 F5
Chelsfield Prim Sch BR6. 58 E5
Chelsfield Rd BR5. . . . . . . 44 C3
Chelsfield Sta BR6. . . . . . 58 B5
Chelsiter Ct DA14 . . . . . . 29 F4
Chelsworth Dr SE18. . . . . 12 D8
Cheltenham CI
Gravesend DA12 . . . . 36 C3
Maidstone ME15 . . . . . . 116 F6
Cheltenham Rd BR6. . . . . 58 A7
Cheney CI ME8. . . . . 69 D5
Chenies CI TN2 . . . . 173 A8
Chenies The
Joyden's Wood DA2. . . . . 31 E4
Orpington BR6. . . . . 43 E3
Chennel Park Rd TN30. . . 182 E1
Chennels The TN26 . . . . . 183 C7
Chepstow Ho 3 ME15. . . 116 F6
Chequers CI
Chatham ME5. . . . . 84 A8
Istead Rise DA13. . . . . . . 49 F7
Orpington BR5. . . . . 43 F5
Chequer's Cotts TN17 . . 177 F8
Chequers Ct ME2 . . . . . . 39 A1
Chequers Hill Cotts TN8. 124 A2
Chequers La RM9 . . . . 4 A8
Chequers Sh Ctr ME15 . . 100 A4
Cherbourg Cres ME5. . . . 67 F7
Cherbury Ct SE28 . . . . 3 D7
Cheriton Ave BR2 . . . . . . 42 A4
Cheriton Ct 12 SE22 . . . . 28 A8
Cheriton Dr SE18 . . . . 12 D8
Cheriton Rd ME8 . . . . 69 D8
Cheriton Way ME16 . . . . . 99 C7
Cherries The ME16. . . . . . 99 A2
Cherry Amber CI ME8 . . . 69 F8
Cherry Ave BR8. . . . . 45 D5
Cherry CI ME17 . . . . 120 C5
Cherrycot Hill BR6. . . . . . 57 D6
Cherrycot Rise BR6. . . . . 57 C6
Cherry Ct DA14. . . . . 30 B5
Cherrydown Rd DA14. . . . 30 D6
Cherryfields TN17. . . . . . 190 D6
Cherry Gr TN10. . . . . 127 E5
Cherry Hill Ct ME9 . . . . . . 71 B6
Cherry Orch
Ditton ME20. . . . . 98 C8
Greenwich SE7 . . . . 11 C8
Tenterden TN30 . . . . 193 A6
CHERRY ORCHARD 99 B4
Cherry Orchard CI BR5 . . 44 C4
Cherry Orchard Prim Sch
SE7. . . . . 11 C7
Cherry Orchard Way
ME16. . . . . 99 B4
Cherry Rd ME3. . . . . 40 E3
Cherry Tree CI RM17 . . . . 18 C8
Cherry Tree Ct 15 ME17. . 117 B1
Cherry Tree Gr TN15 . . . . 61 B1
Cherry Tree La DA2 . . . . . 31 F5
Cherry Tree Rd
Gillingham ME8 . . . . 69 F8
Royal Tunbridge Wells
TN2. . . . . 158 A3
Tonbridge TN10 . . . . 127 D7
Cherry Trees DA3. . . . . . . 48 F4
Cherry View ME17 . . . . . 116 B3
Cherry Wlk BR2. . . . . 42 A1
Cherrywood Dr DA11. . . . 35 E5
Cherwell CI TN10 . . . . . . 127 B4
Chervil Mews SE28. . . . . . . 3 B5
Chester Ave TN2 . . . . 159 D2
Chester CI ME2 . . . . 52 D6
Chesterfield CI BR5. . . . . 44 D5
Chesterfield Dr
Dartford DA1. . . . . 15 B2
Sevenoaks TN13 . . . . 91 D5
Chesterford Ho SE18. . . . 11 D7
Chester Rd
Gillingham ME7 . . . . 54 C7
Sidcup DA15. . . . . 12 E2
Chestnut Ave
Chatham ME5. . . . . 67 F3
Hill Park TN16 . . . . 89 A6
Royal Tunbridge Wells
TN4. . . . . 159 B8
Staplehurst TN12. . . . . . 149 F4
Stone DA9 . . . . 33 F8
Tatsfield TN16 . . . . 88 E5
Chestnut CI
Edenbridge TN8 . . . . . . 122 B2
Frittenden TN17. . . . . . . 166 E6
Kings Hill ME19 . . . . 97 A2
Northfleet DA11. . . . . 18 F1

Chestnut CI continued
Orpington BR6. . . . . 58 A5
Royal Tunbridge Wells
TN4. . . . . 159 B8
Sidcup DA15. . . . . 30 A6
Tenterden TN30 . . . . 183 C1
Ulcombe ME17. . . . . 135 F6
Chestnut Copse RH8 . . . 106 B2
Chestnut Dr
Bexley DA7 . . . . 13 E4
Coxheath ME17 . . . . 115 B3
Kingswood ME17 . . . . . . 118 D2
Chestnut Gr DA2. . . . . . . 31 E4
Chestnut Ho 5 ME16. . . . 99 A3
Chestnut La
Matfield TN12 . . . . 145 D1
Sevenoaks TN13 . . . . 92 B3
Vigo Village DA13 . . . . . . 80 B8
Chestnut PI TN8 . . . . 155 A6
Chestnut Rd
Dartford DA1. . . . . 32 D7
Rochester ME2 . . . . 52 E6
Chestnut Rise SE18 . . . . . . 2 E1
Chestnuts Royal BR7 . . . . 29 D1
Chestnut St ME9 . . . . 71 E4
Chestnuts The
Addington ME19 . . . . 80 C3
Chislehurst BR7. . . . . 29 D1
7 Erith DA17. . . . . 3 F1
The Moor TN18 . . . . 194 F8
Woolwich SE18 . . . . 12 B6
CHESTNUT STREET 71 E4
Chestnut Wlk
Larkfield ME20. . . . . 82 B2
Sevenoaks TN15 . . . . . . 108 F6
Tonbridge TN9 . . . . 126 F2
Chestnut Wood La ME9. . 71 E3
Cheswick Ct DA8. . . . . . . 14 E5
Chesworth CI DA8. . . . . . 14 E5
Chetney CI ME2 . . . . 52 C7
Chetwood Wlk 16 E6 . . . . . 1 E8
Chevender BR7. . . . . 29 B1
Cheveney Wlk 2 BR2 . . . 42 A6
CHEVENING 90 F8
Chevening CI ME5 . . . . . . 68 A5
Chevening Ct BR6. . . . . . . 58 A8
Chevening House BR5. . . 44 A4
Chevening La TN14 . . . . . 74 E3
Chevening Prim Sch TN13 91 B5
Chevening Rd
3 Greenwich SE10. . . . . . 1 A1
Sevenoaks TN13, TN14 . . 91 B6
Sundridge TN14. . . . . 90 F4
Chevenings The DA14. . . 30 C5
Cheviot CI
Bexley DA7 . . . . 14 E5
Tonbridge TN9 . . . . 127 C4
Cheviot Gdns ME5 . . . . . 101 A1
Cheviot Ho 6 DA11 . . . . . 18 D1
Chevron CI E16 . . . . 1 A7
Chevron Ho RM17. . . . . . 18 B7
Cheyne CI BR2. . . . . 56 E7
Cheyne Wlk
Longfield DA3. . . . . 48 D6
Meopham DA13 . . . . 64 A8
Chicago Ave ME7 . . . . . . 54 F5
Chichester CI
Gillingham ME8 . . . . 70 A8
Greenwich SE3 . . . . 11 C6
Newham E6 . . . . 1 E7
Chichester Ct 3 DA15. . . 31 A8
Chichester Dr TN13. . . . . 91 F2
Chichester Rd
Stone DA9 . . . . 16 F1
Tonbridge TN9 . . . . 143 A8
Chichester Rise DA12 . . . 36 C4
Chichester Wharf 14 DA8. . . 4 E1
Chickenden La NT17. . . . 150 C4
Chickfield Gdns 4 ME5. . . 54 C2
Chicks La TN17 . . . . 176 F2
CHIDDINGSTONE 140 A7
Chiddingstone Ave DA7. . 13 F7
Chiddingstone Castle*
TN8. . . . . 140 B7
CHIDDINGSTONE
CAUSEWAY 124 F2
Chiddingstone CE Prim Sch
TN8. . . . . 140 A7
Chiddingstone CI ME15. . 116 F6
CHIDDINGSTONE
HOATH 140 A2
Chidley Cross Rd TN12 . . 129 E6
Chieveley Dr TN2 . . . . . . 159 D1
Chieveley Par DA7 . . . . . . 14 B4
Chieveley Rd DA7 . . . . . . 14 B4
Chiffinch Gdns DA11. . . . 35 E5
Childbridge La ME17 . . . 135 A8
Childsbridge Way TN15 . . 92 F7
Childs Cres DA10 . . . . 17 D1
Childscroft Rd ME8 . . . . . 55 F2
Childs Way TN15. . . . . . . 78 F3
Chilham CI
Chatham ME4. . . . . 53 E3
Sidcup DA15. . . . . 30 F8
Chilham Ho
1 Maidstone ME15 . . . . 116 E8
Rochester ME2 . . . . 39 C1
Chilham Rd
Bromley SE9 . . . . 28 E4
Gillingham ME8 . . . . 55 A3
Maidstone ME15 . . . . 99 C7
Chilham Way BR2. . . . . . 42 A2
Chillington CI ME2 . . . . . 65 E4
Chillington St ME14 . . . . 99 F6
Chilliwack Rd ME3 . . . . . 39 F5
Chilston CI TN4 . . . . 159 A5

Chilston Rd
Lenham ME17 . . . . 120 D5
Royal Tunbridge Wells
TN4. . . . . 159 A5
Chiltenhurst TN8 . . . . . . 122 A2
Chiltern CI
Bexley DA7 . . . . 14 E6
Maidstone ME15 . . . . . . 100 F1
Chiltern Ct 11 SE9 . . . . . 12 A1
Chiltern Rd DA11 . . . . . . 35 E5
Chilterns DA. 30 A3
Chiltern Way TN2 . . . . . . 127 C4
Chiltern WIk TN2 . . . . . . 159 D4
Chilton CI ME8. . . . . 55 E1
Chilton Dr ME3 . . . . 38 B3
Chimes The
Hoo St Werburgh ME3. . . 40 E6
Maidstone ME14 . . . . . . 101 A5
Rochester ME1 . . . . 53 C5
Chinbrook Cres 8 SE12. . 28 B5
Chinbrook Rd SE12 . . . . . 28 B5
Chine Farm Rd TN14. . . . 74 D3
Chinnery Ct DA13. . . . . . 50 A2
Chippendale CI ME5 . . . . 67 F1
Chippendayle Dr ME17 . 119 D2
Chipperfield Rd BR5 . . . . 44 A7
CHIPSTEAD 91 C5
Chipstead CI ME16. . . . . 99 D6
Chipstead La TN13. . . . . . 91 D5
Chipstead Park CI TN13 . 91 C5
Chipstead Pk TN13 . . . . . 91 D5
Chipstead Place Gdns
TN13. . . . . 91 C4
Chipstead Rd
Erith DA8. . . . . 14 E7
Gillingham ME8 . . . . 69 D4
Chipstead Sq TN13. . . . . 91 C5
CHISLEHURST 43 B7
Chislehurst Caves* TN8. . 43 A8
Chislehurst CI ME15. . . . 116 F6
Chislehurst High St BR7. . 29 B2
Chislehurst Rd
Bromley BR1, BR2. . . . . . 42 E8
Orpington, Petts Wood BR5,
BR6. . . . . 43 E4
Sidcup DA14 . . . . 30 A3
Chislehurst & Sidcup Gram
Sch DA15. . . . . 30 B6
Chislehurst Sta BR7. . . . . 43 A7
Chislehurst (St Nicholas) CE
Prim Sch 11 BR7 . . . . . 29 C1
CHISLEHURST WEST 29 A2
Chislet Wlk ME8 . . . . 69 D5
Chislet Sq SE3 . . . . 11 B5
Chorleywood Cres BR5. . 44 A7
Christchurch Ave 14 E8
Christ Church Ave 1
TN1. . . . . 159 A2
Christ Church CE Sch
SE18 . . . . 12 A6
Christ Church Cres 2
DA12 . . . . 36 C8
Christ Church CE Sch
ME15. . . . . 116 C5
Christ Church Prim Sch
DA8. . . . . 14 D8
Christchurch Rd
Dartford DA1. . . . . 15 C1
Sidcup DA15. . . . . 29 F5
Tilbury RM18. . . . . 19 A6
Christ Church Rd 3 DA12 36 C8
Christen Way ME15,
ME17. . . . . 116 F3
Christian Ct 3 ME2 . . . . . 53 C8
CHRISTIAN FIELDS 36 C4
Christian Fields Ave DA12 36 C4
Christie CI ME5. . . . . 68 B6
Christie Dr 3 ME20 . . . . . 81 F4
Christie Ho DA6. . . . . 14 B2
Christies Ave TN14 . . . . . 59 B1
Christmas La ME23. . . . . . 23 F3
Christmas St ME7 . . . . . . 54 E7
Christmas Tree Farm*
BR6. . . . . 73 A7
Christopher CI DA15 . . . . 12 F2
Christy Rd TN16. . . . . 72 C4
Chudleigh 7 DA14 . . . . . . 30 B4
Chulkhurst TN27 . . . . . . 167 F1
Chulkhurst CI TN27 . . . . 167 F1
Church Alley 11 DA11. . . . 19 B1
Church Ave DA14 . . . . . . 30 B3
Churchbury Rd SE9 . . . . . 28 D8
Church CI
Brenchley TN12 . . . . 162 C8
Cliffe ME3 . . . . 22 B6
Mereworth ME18. . . . . . 112 D8
Church Cotts
Cranbrook TN17. . . . . . . 179 D5
Crockenhill BR8. . . . . 45 D2
Shoreham TN14. . . . . 76 A8
Sutton Valence ME17. . . 134 E7
Tenterden TN30 . . . . 183 B3
Church Cres ME17 . . . . . 119 F6
Church Ct DA2. . . . . 32 D5
Church Farm CI
Crockenhill BR8. . . . . 45 D3
Hoo St Werburgh ME3. . . 40 E4
Churchfield
Hadlow ME19 . . . . 80 D3
Edenbridge TN8 . . . . . . 122 D1

Church Fields ME19. . . . . 97 B8
Churchfields Terr ME1 . . . 53 B4
Church Gn
Hollingbourne ME17 . . . 102 E3
Marden TN12. . . . . 148 C6
Rochester ME2 . . . . 53 C8
Staplehurst TN12. . . . . . 149 E2
Church Hill
Chatham ME5. . . . . 54 C2
Crayford DA1. . . . . 14 E3
Cudham TN14, TN16. . . . 73 C4
Dartford DA2. . . . . 32 D6
High Halden TN26 . . . . . 183 E7
Leigh TN11. . . . . 125 F2
Linton ME17 . . . . 133 B7
Loose ME17 . . . . 116 C1
Orpington BR6. . . . . 44 A2
Plaxtol TN15. . . . . 110 E8
Stockbury ME9. . . . . 86 F7
Stone DA9 . . . . 16 E2
Tatsfield TN16 . . . . 88 D5
Church Hill Wood BR5. . . 43 F4
Church Hyde SE18 . . . . . . 12 E8
Churchill Ave ME5 . . . . . . 54 C2
Churchill Bsns Ctr TN16. . 89 D1
Churchill CE Prim Sch
TN16. . . . . 89 C2
Churchill CI DA1 . . . . 33 B7
Churchill Cotts ME17 . . . 117 F6
Churchill Ct
4 Orpington BR6 . . . . . . 57 C5
Westerham TN16. . . . . . . 89 D1
Churchill Ho
Benenden TN17. . . . . . . 190 E6
Maidstone ME16 . . . . . . 99 B2
6 Woolwich SE18. . . . . . . 2 B2
Churchill Pk DA1 . . . . 16 A2
Churchill Rd
Grays RM17. . . . . 18 D3
Horton Kirby DA4. . . . . . 47 C5
Newham E16 . . . . 1 C7
Northfleet DA11. . . . . 35 F7
Churchill Sq ME19 . . . . . 97 A3
Churchills Ropewalk
TN17 . . . . 177 E8
Churchill Theatre* BR1 . 42 A7
Churchill Way
Biggin Hill TN16 . . . . 72 D4
Bromley BR1 . . . . 42 A7
Churchin CI TN16 . . . . . . 72 C7
Church La
Capel TN2. . . . . 144 F6
Chalk DA12 . . . . 37 C6
Chatham ME4. . . . . 53 F6
Chislehurst BR7. . . . . 43 C8
East Peckham TN12. . . . 129 F7
Frant TN3. . . . . 173 B4
Harrietsham ME17. . . . . 119 E6
Kemsing TN15 . . . . 77 B2
Maidstone, Bearsted
ME14. . . . . 101 C4
Maidstone ME16 . . . . 98 E1
Newington ME9 . . . . 71 B6
Orpington BR2. . . . . 42 E1
Stockbury ME9. . . . . 86 E8
Sutton Valence ME17. . . 135 B8
Tonbridge TN9 . . . . 127 C2
Trottiscliffe ME19 . . . . . . 80 B5
West Farleigh ME15 . . . 114 D7
Churchlands ME14 . . . . . 100 B5
Church Manorway DA8. . . 4 D3
Church Manor Way SE18,
SE2. . . . . 3 A2
Church Meadow TN12. . 163 A7
Church Mews ME8 . . . . . . 69 E8
Church Path
Gillingham ME7 . . . . 54 E6
Northfleet DA11. . . . . 18 C1
Stone DA9 . . . . 16 F1
Church Rd
Bexley DA7, DA6 . . . . 13 F4
Bexley, Welling DA16 . . . 13 B5
Biggin Hill TN16. . . . . 72 E2
Bitchet Green TN15. . . . . 93 E3
Brasted TN16. . . . . 90 B3
Bromley BR1, BR2 . . . . . 42 A7
Chart Sutton ME17 . . . . 117 C5
Chelsfield BR6 . . . . 58 D4
Crockenhill BR8. . . . . 45 D2
Erith DA8 . . . . 4 D1
Goudhurst TN17. . . . . . . 177 F8
Grafty Green ME17 . . . . 136 F7
Gravesend DA12, DA13. . 36 D1
Halstead TN14. . . . . 74 F7
Harrietsham ME17. . . . . 119 E6
Hartley DA3. . . . . 49 A2
Hawley DA4. . . . . 32 F1
Henhurst DA13 . . . . 50 C8
Hucking ME17 . . . . 86 E1
Kilndown TN17. . . . . 176 F3
Lamberhurst TN3 . . . . . . 176 C6
Maidstone ME15 . . . . . . 116 F7
Maidstone, Tovil ME15. . . 99 E2
Offham ME18. . . . . 96 D8
Orpington BR6. . . . . 57 D5
Orpington, Keston BR2 . . 56 D3
Paddock Wood TN12. . . 146 B6
Pembury TN2 . . . . 144 D1
Pembury TN2. . . . . 160 D8
Royal Tunbridge Wells,
Southborough TN4 . . . 142 F2
Royal Tunbridge Wells
TN1. . . . . 159 A3
Ryarsh ME19 . . . . 81 A3
Sandhurst Cross TN18. . . 195 F4
Seal TN15. . . . . 92 F6
Sevenoaks Weald TN14 . . 108 B3

Church Rd continued
Sidcup DA14 . . . . 30 A4
Stone DA9 . . . . 16 F2
Sundridge TN14 . . . . 90 E2
Sutton at Hone DA4 . . . . 33 A4
Sutton Valence ME17 . . . . . . 134 C8
Swanley Village BR8 . . . . 46 D8
Swanscombe DA10 . . . . 17 F1
Tenterden TN30 . . . . 193 A7
Tilbury RM18 . . . . 18 F6
Tonbridge TN11 . . . . 126 D6
West Kingsdown TN15 . . . . . . 61 E3
West Peckham ME18 . . . . . . 112 A6
West Tilbury RM18 . . . . 19 E8
Church Row
Chislehurst BR7 . . . . 43 C8
Plaxtol TN15 . . . . 110 E8
Snodland ME6 . . . . 82 A7
West Peckham ME18 . . . . . . 112 B6
Church Row Mews BR7 . . 29 C1
Churchsettle La TN5 . . . . 185 C5
Churchside DA3 . . . . 80 A8
Churchside Cl TN16 . . . . . . 72 C2
Church Sq ME17 . . . . 120 D5
Church St
Burham ME1 . . . . 66 F1
Chatham ME4 . . . . 54 A4
Cliffe ME3 . . . . 22 B5
Cowden TN8 . . . . 155 B5
Edenbridge TN8 . . . . 122 D1
Gillingham ME7 . . . . 54 E6
Grays RM17 . . . . 18 C8
Hadlow TN11 . . . . 118 D8
Hoo St Werburgh ME3 . . . . . . 40 E5
Lower Higham ME3 . . . . 38 D7
Maidstone, Boughton
Monchelsea ME17 . . . . 116 B2
Maidstone, Loose ME15 . . . . 115 F5
Maidstone ME14 . . . . 100 E4
Maidstone, Tovil ME15 . . . . . . 99 E2
Newham E16 . . . . 2 B5
Northfleet DA13 . . . . 35 A3
Rochester ME1 . . . . 53 D4
Seal TN15 . . . . 93 A7
Shoreham TN14 . . . . 76 A8
Teston ME18 . . . . 114 A8
Ticehurst TN5 . . . . 186 D1
Tonbridge TN9 . . . . 127 C2
Westerham TN16 . . . . 185 A4
CHURCH STREET 21 C1
Church Street
Hartley DA3 . . . . 49 A1
New Ash Green DA3 . . . . 62 F8
Church Terr ME5 . . . . 54 C2
Church Trad Est DA8 . . . . . 15 A7
Church View
Biddenden TN27 . . . . 167 F2
4 Dartford DA1 . . . . 15 E1
Swanley BR8 . . . . 45 D6
Church Wlk
Dartford DA2 . . . . 32 D5
East Malling ME19 . . . . 98 A7
Eynsford DA4 . . . . 60 E7
Gravesend DA12 . . . . 36 D7
4 Gravesend DA12 . . . . 36 D7
City Way ME1 . . . . 53 C5
Churchyard Cotts TN8 . . 158 A8
Churn La TN12 . . . . 147 A2
Chute ME8 . . . . 69 D4
Chyngton Cl DA15 . . . . 29 F5
Cimba Wood DA12 . . . . 36 E4
CINDER HILL 141 C8
Cinder Hill La TN11 . . . . . 145 C2
Cinderhill Wood TN11 . . 145 C2
Cinderhill Wood Cotts On Site
TN12 . . . . 145 C1
Cinnabar Cl ME5 . . . . 61 A1
Cinnamon Gr ME16 . . . . . . 99 A3
Circle The RM18 . . . . 19 A6
Circular Way SE18 . . . . 12 A8
Cirrus Cres DA12 . . . . 36 E3
City Way ME1 . . . . 53 C5
Civic Sq RM18 . . . . 19 A5
Civic Way TN1 . . . . 159 A3
CJ Gallards Almshouses
TN4 . . . . 159 A8
Clacket La
Tatsfield TN16 . . . . 88 C2
Westerham TN16 . . . . 105 A8
Clacketts Farm ME14 . . . . . 96 F7
Claire Ho 3 ME16 . . . . 99 E5
Clancy Gdns TN12 . . . . . . 179 B5
Clandon Cl BR1 . . . . 28 A2
Clandon Rd ME8 . . . . 49 D6
Clanricarde Gdns 1
TN1 . . . . 159 A3
Clanricarde Rd 2 TN1 . . . 159 A3
Claphatch La TN5 . . . . 186 A5
Clapper La TN12 . . . . 149 D6
Clara Pl SE18 . . . . 2 A2
Clare Ave TN9 . . . . 126 F1
Clare Cnr SE9 . . . . 23 B8
Clare Cswy DA9 . . . . 16 F3
Clare Ct BR7 . . . . 42 F8
Clare La ME19 . . . . 97 E8
Claremont Cl
Newham E16 . . . . 2 A5
Orpington BR6 . . . . 57 A6
Claremont Cres DA1 . . . . . 14 E3
Claremont Ct 4 TN2 . . . . 159 C7
Claremont Gdns TN2 . . . . 159 B2
Claremont Pl
1 Gravesend DA11 . . . . 36 B8
Maidstone ME16 . . . . 99 A3
Marden TN12 . . . . 138 C6
Claremont Prim Sch
TN2 . . . . 159 B2
Claremont Rd
Bromley BR1 . . . . 42 F5

Claremont Rd continued
Hextable BR8 . . . . 31 E1
Maidstone ME14 . . . . 100 B5
Royal Tunbridge Wells
TN1 . . . . 159 B2
Claremont St E16 . . . . 2 A4
Claremont Way 2 ME4 . . . 53 F3
Clarence Ave
Bromley BR1 . . . . 42 E5
Rochester ME1 . . . . 53 C4
Clarence Cres DA14 . . . . . . 30 B5
Clarence Ct
2 Grays RM17 . . . . 18 B8
Maidstone ME14 . . . . 100 E4
Clarence Ct ME8 . . . . 58 C2
Clarence Lodge TN1 . . . . 159 A3
Clarence Pl DA12 . . . . 36 B7
Clarence Rd
Bexley DA6 . . . . 13 E3
Biggin Hill TN16 . . . . 72 F1
Bromley, Mottingham SE9 . . 28 E6
Bromley, Widmore BR1 . . . . . 42 E6
Chatham ME4 . . . . 54 B2
Grays RM17 . . . . 18 B8
Royal Tunbridge Wells
TN1 . . . . 159 A3
Sidcup DA14 . . . . 30 B5
Clarence Row
Gravesend DA12 . . . . 36 B8
Royal Tunbridge Wells
TN1 . . . . 159 A3
Clarendon Cl
Maidstone ME14 . . . . 101 A4
Orpington BR5 . . . . 44 A6
Clarendon Ct TN13 . . . . . . 92 A2
Clarendon Dr ME2 . . . . 39 A1
Clarendon Gdns
Dartford DA2 . . . . 33 D8
Royal Tunbridge Wells
TN2 . . . . 159 A1
Clarendon Gn BR5 . . . . 44 A5
Clarendon Gr BR5 . . . . 44 A5
Clarendon Mews DA5 . . . . 31 B7
Clarendon Path BR5 . . . . . 44 A6
Clarendon Pl
Joyden's Wood DA2 . . . . 31 E3
Maidstone ME14 . . . . 100 A4
Sevenoaks TN13 . . . . 92 A2
Clarendon Rd
Gravesend DA12 . . . . 19 C1
Sevenoaks TN13 . . . . 92 A2
Clarendon Way
Royal Tunbridge Wells
TN1 . . . . 159 A1
St Paul's Cray BR5, BR7 . . . . 43 F6
Claret Ho TN13 . . . . 92 B3
Clarewell Rd BR5 . . . . 57 C8
Clare Way
Bexley DA7 . . . . 13 E6
Sevenoaks TN13 . . . . 108 C3
Clarewood Dr ME19 . . . . . . 97 E8
Claridge TN1 . . . . 159 A2
Claridge Ct ME7 . . . . 68 F4
Clarkbourne Dr RM17 . . . . 18 D8
Clark Cl DA8 . . . . 15 A6
Clarkes Green Rd TN15 . . . 77 B5
Clark Mews ME20 . . . . 82 F1
Clarks La
Halstead TN14 . . . . 74 F7
Titsey CR6, RH8, TN14, TN16 . 88 C4
Clarks Yard TN5 . . . . 187 A3
Clark's Yd TN5 . . . . 187 A3
Claston Cl DA1 . . . . 14 E3
Clavadal Rd TN12 . . . . 146 A7
Clavell Cl ME8 . . . . 69 E4
Claybridge Rd SE12 . . . . . . 28 C4
Clay Cotts TN17 . . . . 177 E8
Claydown Mews SE18 . . . . . 2 A1
Clayfarm Rd SE9 . . . . 29 C6
CLAYGATE 147 D6
Claygate
Eyhorne Street ME17 . . . . . . 102 D2
Maidstone ME15 . . . . 100 D1
Claygate Cross TN15 . . . . . 95 A3
Claygate Cl TN11 . . . . 110 F4
Claygate Rd TN12 . . . . 139 E4
Clayhall TN17 . . . . 177 D8
Clayhill Cres SE9 . . . . 28 D4
Clay Hill Mount TN17 . . . . 177 E8
Clay Hill Rd TN17 . . . . 175 D6
Claymill Ho 2 SE18 . . . . 2 C1
Clayton Cl 3 E6 . . . . 1 F7
Clayton Croft Rd DA2 . . . . 32 A6
Clayton's La TN3 . . . . 156 E2
Claytonville Terr DA17 . . . . 4 C4
Clay Wood Cl BR6 . . . . 43 E2
Claywood La DA2 . . . . 34 D5
Clayworth Cl DA15 . . . . 13 B1
Cleanthus Cl SE18 . . . . 12 B6
Cleanthus Rd SE18 . . . . . . 12 B6
Clearheart Lane ME19 . . . . 97 D3
Clearway ME19 . . . . 80 A1
Clearways Bsns Est TN11 . 61 E3
Clearways Mobile Home Pk
TN11 . . . . 61 D3
Cleave Ave ME4 . . . . 57 E4
Cleave Rd ME7 . . . . 54 E3
Cleavers TN17 . . . . 180 A8
Cleavers La TN17 . . . . 180 A8
Cleavesland ME18 . . . . 130 E5
Cleeve Ave TN2 . . . . 159 D2
Cleeve Ct ME19 . . . . 97 B3
Cleeve Park Gdns DA14 . . . 30 B6
Cleeve Park Sch DA14 . . . . 30 C5
Clegg Ho SE3 . . . . 11 B3
Clematis Ave ME8 . . . . 69 B5
Clemens Pl ME19 . . . . 97 C2
Clement Ct ME16 . . . . 99 D5

Clements Ave E16 . . . . 1 A6
Clement St BR8, DA4 . . . . . . 32 E2
CLEMENT STREET 32 D2
Cleminson St DA14 . . . . 30 D2
Clenches Farm La TN13 . . . 92 A1
Clenches Farm Rd TN13 . . . 92 A1
Clendon Way SE18 . . . . 2 D2
Clerks Field TN27 . . . . 151 D5
Clermont Cl ME7 . . . . 48 C4
Clevedon Ho BR1 . . . . 28 E1
Cleveland TN2 . . . . 159 D4
Cleveland Ho
Maidstone ME16 . . . . 99 B2
2 Northfleet DA11 . . . . 18 D1
Cleveland Rd
Bexley DA16 . . . . 12 F5
Gillingham ME7 . . . . 54 D6
Clevely Cl SE7 . . . . 1 D2
Cleve Rd DA14 . . . . 30 D5
Cleves Rd ME15 . . . . 76 E2
Cleves View 4 DA1 . . . . 15 D1
Clewer Ho 8 SE2 . . . . 3 D4
Clewson Rise ME14 . . . . . . 100 B8
CLIFFE 22 B5
Cliffe ME3 . . . . 22 B5
Cliffe Pools Nature Reserve★
ME3 . . . . 5 E1
Cliffe Rd ME2 . . . . 39 A1
CLIFFE WOODS 39 C8
Cliffe Woods Cty Prim Sch
ME3 . . . . 39 C8
Clifford Ave ME7 . . . . 48 E2
Clifford Ho 6 ME14 . . . . . . 100 B4
Clifford Way ME15 . . . . 99 E2
Cliff Reach DA9 . . . . 16 F1
Clifton Cl
Maidstone ME14 . . . . 100 B5
8 Orpington BR6 . . . . 57 C5
Rochester ME2 . . . . 52 F7
Clifton Cotts TN2 . . . . 159 D8
Clifton Gr DA11 . . . . 13 A1
Clifton Marine Par DA11 . . 18 F1
Clifton PI TN1 . . . . 159 B2
Clifton Rd
Bexley DA16 . . . . 13 C4
Gillingham ME7 . . . . 54 C7
Gravesend DA11 . . . . 19 A1
Royal Tunbridge Wells
TN2 . . . . 159 C7
Sidcup DA14 . . . . 29 E4
Cliftonville Ct SE12 . . . . . . 28 A7
Clinch Cl 8 E16 . . . . 1 A8
Clinch St ME3 . . . . 24 A4
Clinton Ave
Bexley DA16 . . . . 13 A3
Rochester ME2 . . . . 52 E8
Clinton Bsns Ctr TN12 . . . 149 F5
Clinton Cl ME17 . . . . 115 B3
Clinton La TN8 . . . . 123 E3
Clipper Boulevard W DA2 . 16 D4
Clipper Bvd DA9 . . . . 16 E3
Clipper Cres DA12 . . . . 36 F4
Clipper Cl ME2 . . . . 53 E7
Clive Ave DA1 . . . . 14 F1
Cliveden Cl ME4 . . . . 99 D7
Clivedon Ct TN3 . . . . 176 B5
Clive Ho ME20 . . . . 98 F8
Clive Rd
Erith DA17 . . . . 4 A2
Gravesend DA11 . . . . 19 B1
Rochester ME1 . . . . 53 C3
Clock Ho The DA15 . . . . 30 A7
Clockhouse TN12 . . . . 159 F6
Clock House La TN13 . . . . . 92 A4
Clock House Rise ME17 . . . 115 C2
Clock Tower Mews
Snodland ME6 . . . . 66 A1
Woolwich SE28 . . . . 3 C5
Cloisterham Rd ME1 . . . . . . 67 D7
Cloisters Ave BR2 . . . . 42 F4
Cloisters Ct DA7 . . . . 14 B4
Cloisters The
1 Dartford DA1 . . . . 15 E1
Lenham ME17 . . . . 120 C5
Clopton Ct ME8 . . . . 69 D8
Close The
Addington ME19 . . . . 80 C2
Birling ME19 . . . . 81 B5
Borough Green TN15 . . . . 95 A8
Bough Beech TN8 . . . . 124 A2
Cudham TN16 . . . . 73 B3
Dartford DA2 . . . . 32 D5
Groombridge TN3 . . . . 171 C6
Ightham TN15 . . . . 94 C6
New Barn DA3 . . . . 49 B7
Orpington BR5 . . . . 43 E3
Rochester ME1 . . . . 53 C4
Royal Tunbridge Wells
TN2 . . . . 159 C8
Sevenoaks TN13 . . . . 110 A8
Sidcup DA14 . . . . 30 B3
1 Sidcup, Old Bexley DA5 . . . 30 B3
Cloth Hall Gdns TN27 . . . . 168 A2
Clothier Ho SE7 . . . . 1 B1
Clothworkers Rd SE18 . . . . 12 D7
Cloudberry Cl ME16 . . . . . . 99 D6
Cloudesley Cl
Sidcup DA14 . . . . 53 B1
8 Sidcup DA14 . . . . 29 F4
Cloudesley Rd
Bexley DA7 . . . . 13 F6
Erith DA8 . . . . 14 F6
Clovelly Rd DA7 . . . . 13 E8

Clovelly Way BR6 . . . . 43 F3
Clover Bank View ME5 . . . . 68 B6
Clover Cl 17 RM17 . . . . 18 C8
Cloverdale Gdns DA15 . . . . 12 F1
Clover Rd ME3 . . . . 40 E3
Clover St 3 ME4 . . . . 53 F4
Clovers The DA11 . . . . 35 E4
Clover Terr 4 ME15 . . . . . . 116 D8
Clover Way TN12 . . . . 146 A5
Clover Wlk 8 TN9 . . . . 122 D3
Club Cotts TN11 . . . . 126 D8
Club Gardens Rd BR2 . . . . . 42 A2
Clyde Rd TN10 . . . . 127 C6
Clydesdale Ho DA18 . . . . 3 E4
Clydon Cl DA8 . . . . 14 E8
**C M Booth Collection of
Historic Vehicles (Mus)★**
TN17 . . . . 191 E4
Coach Dr The DA13 . . . . . . 79 E7
Coach & Horses Pas 8
TN2 . . . . 159 A2
Coach House Mews 8
BR1 . . . . 42 A6
Coach Rd
Egerton ME17, TN27 . . . . . . 137 E6
Ightham TN15 . . . . 94 B2
Rusthall TN4 . . . . 158 C3
Coach Yd The ME16 . . . . . . 99 B3
Coal Ct RM17 . . . . 18 A8
Coalhouse Fort★ RM18 . . . 20 E6
Coal Post Cl BR6 . . . . 57 F4
Coastguard Cotts ME3 . . . . 27 B5
Coates Hill Rd BR1 . . . . 43 A7
COBBARN 171 F3
Cobb Cl ME2 . . . . 52 D8
Cobbets Way TN8 . . . . 138 C8
Cobbett Cl ME19 . . . . 97 F8
Cobbett Rd SE9 . . . . 11 E4
Cobbett's Ride TN2 . . . . . . 158 F1
Cobblestones ME7 . . . . 68 F5
Cobbs Cl
Paddock Wood TN12 . . . . . . 145 F6
Wateringbury ME18 . . . . 113 E7
Cobden Ct
Bromley BR2 . . . . 42 C5
9 Woolwich SE28 . . . . 3 C5
Cobden Rd
4 Chatham ME4 . . . . 54 B2
Orpington BR6 . . . . 57 D6
Sevenoaks TN13 . . . . 92 C4
Cobdown CI ME20 . . . . 82 C2
Cob Dr DA12 . . . . 37 E3
Cobfield ME17 . . . . 117 A1
COBHAM 50 F6
Cobham Cl
Bromley BR2 . . . . 42 E2
Maidstone ME16 . . . . 99 E4
Rochester ME2 . . . . 52 E7
2 Sidcup DA15 . . . . 13 B1
Cobham Coll★ DA12 . . . . . 50 F5
Cobham Dr ME19 . . . . 97 C3
Cobham Hall Sch DA12 . . . 51 C6
Cobham Ho 4 DA11 . . . . . . 18 C1
Cobham PI DA6 . . . . 13 D2
Cobham Prim Sch DA12 . . . 51 A5
Cobham Rise ME7 . . . . 54 F5
Cobham St DA11 . . . . 36 B8
Cobham Terr DA9 . . . . 17 B1
Cobland Rd SE12 . . . . 28 C4
Cobs Cl TN15 . . . . 72 A3
Cobsdene DA12 . . . . 36 D2
Cobtree Cl ME5 . . . . 68 C8
Cobtree Rd ME17 . . . . 115 C3
Cobtree Wharf ME20 . . . . . 83 C2
Cochrane Dr DA1 . . . . 15 D1
Cockerhurst Rd TN14 . . . . . 59 E2
Cockmannings La BR5 . . . . 44 E1
Cockmannings Rd BR5 . . . . 44 D2
Cockmount La TN5 . . . . . . 184 F5
Cockpit The TN12 . . . . 148 C5
Cocksett Ave BR6 . . . . 57 E4
COCKSHOT 188 F1
Cock St ME17 . . . . 116 D2
COCK STREET 116 D2
Cocksure La DA14 . . . . 31 A4
Codown Sports Club
ME20 . . . . 82 C2
Codrington Cres DA12 . . . . 36 D3
Codrington Gdns DA12 . . . . 36 D3
Coe's Green ME3 . . . . 40 A4
Cogate Rd TN12 . . . . 145 E6
Cokers Yd TN4 . . . . 143 A1
Colchester Cl ME5 . . . . 68 A7
Cold Arbor Rd TN13 . . . . . . 91 D3
COLDBLOW 31 D7
Cold Blow Cres DA5 . . . . . . 31 D7
Coldblow La ME14 . . . . 86 A2
Coldbridge La TN27 . . . . . . 137 B5
COLDHARBOUR 109 F1
Coldharbour Rd
Forstal ME20 . . . . 83 A1
Hucking ME14, ME9 . . . . 86 B1
Rainham RM13 . . . . 4 F6
Shipbourne TN11 . . . . 110 A2
Tonbridge TN11 . . . . 126 F2
Cold Harbour La ME19 . . . . 71 F6
Coldharbour L Ctr SE9 . . . . 28 F6
Coldharbour Rd
Gravesend DA11 . . . . 36 A4
Iden Green TN17 . . . . 190 B4
Northfleet DA11 . . . . 35 F5
Coldred Rd ME15 . . . . 116 F4

Coldrum La ME19 . . . . 80 C6
Coldrum Long Barrow★
ME19 . . . . 80 C6
Coldshott RH8 . . . . 104 A3
Colebrooke Ct DA14 . . . . . . 30 B4
Colebrook Ind Est TN2 . . . 143 E1
Colebrook Rd TN4 . . . . 159 C8
Colebrook St 1 DA8 . . . . . . 14 F8
Cole Cl SE28 . . . . 3 B5
Colegate Dr ME14 . . . . 101 C4
Coleman Rd DA17 . . . . 4 A2
Colemans Heath SE9 . . . . . 29 B5
Colepits Wood Rd SE9 . . . . 12 D2
Coleraine Rd 1 SE3 . . . . 11 A8
Coleridge Cl 4 ME20 . . . . . . 81 F4
Coleridge Rd
Dartford DA1 . . . . 16 B3
Tilbury RM18 . . . . 19 C5
Coleridge Way BR6 . . . . 44 A3
Coles Ct TN2 . . . . 159 C3
Colesdane ME17 . . . . 119 E8
Coleshall Cl ME15 . . . . 116 F6
Cole La TN16 . . . . 90 C4
Cole Terr ME17 . . . . 120 C4
Colets Orch TN14 . . . . 76 B3
Colewood Dr ME2 . . . . 52 B8
Colfe's Sch SE12 . . . . 11 B1
Colin Blythe Rd TN10 . . . . 127 F5
Colin Chapman Way DA3 . . 61 E6
Colin Cl DA2 . . . . 16 E1
College Ave
Gillingham ME7 . . . . 54 B4
Maidstone ME15 . . . . 99 F3
Tonbridge TN9 . . . . 143 A7
College Cotts ME16 . . . . 99 F3
College Ct 6 ME15 . . . . 100 A3
College Dr TN2 . . . . 159 D4
College Gn 10 BR1 . . . . 42 A8
College Pl 9 DA9 . . . . 17 C3
College Rd
Bromley BR2 . . . . 28 A1
Chatham ME4 . . . . 54 A7
Hextable BR8 . . . . 31 F1
Maidstone ME15 . . . . 99 F2
New Hythe ME20 . . . . 82 B3
Northfleet DA11 . . . . 18 B2
College View SE9 . . . . 28 D7
College Wlk 4 ME15 . . . . . . 100 A3
College Yd ME1 . . . . 53 C6
Coller Cres DA2 . . . . 33 E3
Collet Rd TN15 . . . . 76 E2
Collet Wlk ME8 . . . . 69 D4
Collier Cl 6 . . . . 2 A6
COLLIERS' GREEN 164 F2
Colliers' Green Cte Prim Sch
TN17 . . . . 164 F2
Colliers Shaw BR2 . . . . 56 D5
COLLIER STREET 147 C8
Collindale Ave
Erith DA8 . . . . 14 B8
Sidcup DA15 . . . . 30 A7
Colling Cl ME19 . . . . 82 A1
Collings Wlk ME8 . . . . 69 D4
Collington Cl DA11 . . . . 35 E8
Collington Ho 3 TN1 . . . . . 159 C8
Collington Terr ME15 . . . . 116 E4
Collingwood Ho 7 TN18 . . 17 D2
Collingwood Ind Est
ME17 . . . . 117 C2
Collingwood Rd ME20 . . . . 83 C7
Colison Pl TN30 . . . . 193 D7
Collis St ME2 . . . . 53 A8
Colman Ho 4 ME14 . . . . . . 100 A4
Colman Rd E16 . . . . 1 C8
Colne Rd TN10 . . . . 127 B5
Colney Rd DA1 . . . . 15 F1
Colonade The 10 TN18 . . . 189 A2
Colonel Stephens Rly Mus★
TN30 . . . . 193 A8
Colonel Stephens Way
TN30 . . . . 183 B2
Colonel's Way TN4 . . . . . . 143 A2
Coltness Cres SE2 . . . . 3 B1
Coltsfoot Ct RM17 . . . . 18 D8
Coltsfoot Dr ME14 . . . . 100 F4
Coltsfoot Ho E16 . . . . 1 B8
Coltsfoot La RH8 . . . . 104 A1
COLT'S HILL 145 B4
Colts Hill Pl TN12 . . . . 145 B5
Coltstead DA3 . . . . 62 E7
Columbia Wharf Rd RM17 . 18 A8
Columbine Ave E6 . . . . 1 E8
Columbine Cl
Rochester ME2 . . . . 52 E7
West Malling ME19 . . . . 81 F1
Columbine Rd
East Malling ME19 . . . . 97 F8
Rochester ME2 . . . . 52 E7
Columbus Sq DA8 . . . . 14 F8
Colveiw Ct SE9 . . . . 28 D7
Colyer Cl SE9 . . . . 29 B6
Colyer Ho SE2 . . . . 3 D1
Colyer Rd DA11 . . . . 35 D6
Colyers Cl DA8 . . . . 14 D6
Colyers La DA8 . . . . 14 C6
Colyers Prim Sch DA8 . . . . 14 D6
Colyers Wlk DA8 . . . . 14 E6
Colyton Cl DA16 . . . . 13 C6
Combe Bank Cotts TN14 . . 90 D5
Combe Bank Dr TN14 . . . . . 90 C6
Combe Bank Farm TN14 . . 90 C6
Combe Bank Sch TN14 . . . . 90 E4
Combedale Rd SE10 . . . . 1 A1
Combeside SE18 . . . . 12 F7
Combwell Cres SE2 . . . . 3 A3

Comforts Farm Ave RH8. 104 A3
Comfrey Ct RM17 . . . . 18 D8
Command Rd ME14 . . . . . . 99 F8
Commerce Way TN8 . . . 122 C3
Commercial PI DA12 . . . 19 C1
Commercial Rd
  Paddock Wood TN12 . . . . 145 F6
  Rochester ME2 . . . . 53 B7
  Royal Tunbridge Wells
    TN1. . . . . 159 B5
  Tonbridge TN9 . . . . 143 C8
Commissioners Ct ME4. . 53 F6
Commissioner's Rd ME2. . 53 C8
Commodore Rd ME14 . . . 100 C5
Common La
  Cliffe ME3 . . . . 22 C6
  Dartford DA2 . . . . 32 B5
Common Rd
  Burham ME6 . . . . 67 B1
  Cliffe Woods ME3 . . . . 39 B5
  Hadlow TN11 . . . . 111 E2
  Ightham TN15 . . . . 94 B4
  Sissinghurst TN17 . . . . . . 180 A8
Commonside BR2 . . . . 56 C6
Common The ME1 . . . . 53 C6
Common View TN4. . . . . 158 C4
Common Wall ME3. . . . . . 22 D6
Commonwealth Ho 5
  RM18 . . . . 19 A5
Commonwealth Way SE2. . 3 C1
Commority Rd DA13. . . . . 80 B8
Compass Cl ME1. . . . . 23 C2
Compass Ct DA11 . . . . 18 E1
Compass Ctr ME4 . . . . 54 A8
Compasses Rd TN11 . . . 125 B2
Comp La TN15 . . . . 95 E6
Compton Cl ME5 . . . . 68 D2
Compton PI DA8 . . . . 14 F8
Concord Ave ME5. . . . . . . 67 E5
Concord Cl
  Paddock Wood TN12 . . . . 145 E7
  Royal Tunbridge Wells
    TN2. . . . . 159 C4
Concorde Dr E6 . . . . 1 F8
Concrete Cotts ME4 . . . . . 21 E4
Condover Cres SE18 . . . . . 12 B7
Condovers Cotts RM18 . . . 19 F8
Conduit Rd SE18 . . . . 2 B1
Coneyburrow Rd TN2 . . . 159 E5
Conference Rd SE2 . . . . 3 C2
Congelow Rd 130 F7
Conghurst La TN18 . . . . 195 B6
Congou Gr SE18 . . . . 2 C1
Congo Rd SE18 . . . . 2 C1
Congress Rd SE2 . . . . 3 C2
Congreve Rd SE9 . . . . 11 F4
Congreve Wlk 6 E16 . . . . . 1 D8
Conifer Ave DA3 . . . . 48 E3
Conifer Cl BR6. . . . . 57 D6
Conifer Dr
  Chatham ME5. . . . . 68 D1
  Culverstone Green DA13. . 63 F2
Conifer Way ME8 . . . . 48 C8
Conisborough Ct 13 DA2 . 16 B1
Coniscliffe Cl BR7. . . . . . . 43 A8
Coniston Ave
  Bexley DA16 . . . . 12 E4
  Purfleet RM19 . . . . 16 C8
  Royal Tunbridge Wells
    TN4. . . . . 158 E5
Coniston Cl
  Bexley DA7 . . . . 14 C6
  Dartford DA1 . . . . 32 B7
  Erith DA8 . . . . 14 E7
  Gillingham ME7 . . . . 55 A6
Coniston Ho ME15 . . . . . . 91 D2
Coniston Rd DA7. . . . . 14 C6
Connaught Bridge E16. . . . 1 D6
Connaught Ct ME15 . . . . 116 F4
Connaught Mews
  2 Chatham ME4. . . . . 54 C2
  Woolwich SE18 . . . . 2 A1
Connaught Rd
  Chatham ME4. . . . . 54 C2
  Gillingham ME7 . . . . 54 D5
  Newham, Silvertown E16. . 1 D5
  Woolwich SE18 . . . . 2 B1
Connaught Way TN4 . . . 158 F5
Connections Business Park
  TN14 . . . . 92 C7
Conqueror Ind Est ME2. . 55 A6
Conquest Ind Est ME2. . . 53 A5
Conrad Cl ME8 . . . . 49 C6
Consort Cl ME14 . . . . 100 B5
Constable Ave E16. . . . . . . 1 B5
Constable Mews BR1. . . . 42 B7
Constable Rd
  Northfleet DA11. . . . . 35 E5
  Tonbridge TN10 . . . . 127 E5
Constance Gr 8 DA1 . . . . 15 D1
Constance St E16 . . . . 1 E5
Constitutional Hill Rd
  TN4 . . . . 142 F1
Constitution Cres DA12. . 36 B7
Constitution Hill
  8 Chatham ME5. . . . . 54 B3
  Gravesend DA12 . . . . 36 C7
  Snodland ME6 . . . . 60 A8
Constitution Hill Rd ME5 . . 54 B2
Constitution Rise SE18 . . 12 A6
Consul Gdns BR8 . . . . 32 A1
Contessa Cl BR6 . . . . 57 E5

Convalescent La TN17. . . 165 F2
Conway Cl ME2 . . . . 38 E1
Conway Ct BR5 . . . . 44 C5
Conway Gdns RM17 . . . . . 18 B7
Conway Hall 10 ME7. . . . . 54 A6
Conway Mews ME7 . . . . . . 54 A6
Conway Prim Sch 5 SE18. . 2 E2
Conway Rd
  Maidstone ME16 . . . . 99 C6
  Woolwich SE18 . . . . 2 E2
Conyerd Rd TN15 . . . . 94 F6
Conyers Wlk ME8 . . . . 69 D4
Cooden Cl BR1. . . . . 28 B1
Cook Cl ME5. . . . . 68 C6
Cookham Dene Cl BR7 . . . 43 D8
Cookham Hill ME1 . . . . 53 A2
Cookham Rd DA14, BR8 . . 45 A8
Cookham Wood Rd ME1. . 67 B8
Cookhill Rd SE2. . . . . 3 B3
Cookson Gr DA8 . . . . 14 B7
Cook Sq DA8 . . . . 14 F7
Cooks Wharf ME1. . . . . . . 53 E4
Coolfin Rd E16. . . . . 1 B7
Cooling 22 F5
Cooling Castle ★ ME3 . . . 22 E4
Cooling Cl ME14 . . . . 100 C6
Cooling Comm ME3 . . . . . 39 D8
Cooling Rd
  Cliffe ME3 . . . . 22 C4
  High Halstow ME23. . . . . . 23 C4
  Rochester ME2 . . . . 39 B2
Cooling St ME3 . . . . 22 D1
COOLING STREET. 22 D2
Coombe Ave TN14 . . . . 92 B7
Coombe Cl
  Chatham ME5. . . . . 68 B3
  Snodland ME6 . . . . 81 F6
Coombe Ct TN14 . . . . 92 B7
Coombe Farm La ME3 . . . 24 E6
Coombe La TN30. . . . . . . 193 A7
Coombe Lands TN30 . . . . 199 D6
Coombe Lea ME1 . . . . 42 E6
Coombe Lodge SE7 . . . . . . 11 C8
Coombe Rd
  Gravesend DA12 . . . . 36 C6
  Hoo St Werburgh ME3. . . 40 E5
  Maidstone ME15 . . . . 99 F2
  Otford TN14. . . . . 76 C4
Coomb Field TN8 . . . . . . 138 C8
Coombfield Dr DA2 . . . . . 33 D4
Cooper Cl DA9 . . . . 16 C4
Cooper Ct SE18 . . . . 12 B8
Cooper Rd
  Chatham ME5. . . . . 68 B3
  Snodland ME6 . . . . 81 F6
Coopers Cl DA4 . . . . 47 D8
COOPER'S CORNER. 123 F8
Coopers Cotts DA2 . . . . . . 33 A4
Coopers Dr DA2 . . . . 31 E6
Cooper Shaw Rd RM18 . . 19 F7
Coopers La
  Lewisham SE12 . . . . 28 B6
  Poundsbridge TN11, TN3. . 157 C7
Coopers Lane Prim Sch
  SE12 . . . . 28 B6
Cooper's Rd DA11. . . . . . . 35 F7
Coopers Tech Coll BR7 . . . 43 C8
Coote Rd DA7 . . . . 13 F6
Copenhagen Rd ME7 . . . . 54 C4
Copley Dene BR1 . . . . 42 D8
Coppards La TN31 . . . . . . 197 D1
Copper Beech Cl
  7 Orpington BR5 . . . . 44 C4
Copper Beech View TN9. 143 A8
Copperfield Cl
  Chalk DA12 . . . . 37 A7
  Kingswood ME17 . . . . 118 D2
Copperfield Cres ME3 . . . 38 C2
Copperfield Ct DA1 . . . . . . 14 E2
Copperfield Dr ME17 . . . 117 E4
Copperfield Ho 6 ME4. . . 53 F4
Copperfield Rd
  Erith SE28 . . . . 3 C7
  Rochester ME1 . . . . 53 C2
Copperfields
  2 Dartford DA1 . . . . 15 E1
  Kemsing TN15 . . . . 76 F2
  Royal Tunbridge Wells
    TN2. . . . . 173 B8
Copperfields Cl ME3 . . . . . 76 F2
Copperfields Orch TN15 . . 76 F2
Copperfields Sh Ctr 6
  DA1. . . . . 15 E1
Copperfields The ME1 . . . 53 B4
Copperfields Wlk TN15. . . 76 F2
Copperfield Way BR7 . . . 29 C2
Coppergate ME7 . . . . 48 E3
Coppergate Cl BR1 . . . . . . 42 B8
Copperhouse La ME7. . . . 55 B6
Copperhouse Rd ME2 . . . 52 C7
Copper La TN12. . . . . 148 E5
Copperpenny Dr ME7 . . . 69 B3
Coppers Ct TN4 . . . . 159 A8
Coppers Cl TN12. . . . . . . 145 E1
Copper Tree Ct ME15 . . . 116 A5
Copper Tree Wlk ME5 . . . 68 C1
Coppice Ct ME7 . . . . 69 A4
Coppice Rd ME5 . . . . 68 C2
Coppice The
  Aylesford ME20 . . . . 82 E1
  Bitchet Green TN15. . . . . . 93 D1
  Joyden's Wood DA5. . . . . 31 D5
  Pembury TN2 . . . . 160 D7
Coppice View ME14. . . . . 100 E6
Copping's Rd TN11 . . . . . 125 C4
Copse Bank TN15 . . . . 92 F7

Copse Cl
  Greenwich SE7 . . . . 11 B8
  Rochester ME1 . . . . 53 E1
Copsehill ME19 . . . . 81 E2
Copse Rd TN11 . . . . 126 E4
Copse Side DA3. . . . . 48 E6
Copse The
  Hoo St Werburgh ME3. . . 40 E3
  Tatsfield TN16. . . . . 88 C7
Copsewood Cl DA15. . . . . 12 E1
Copsewood Way ME15 . . 101 A3
Coptefield Dr DA17 . . . . . . 3 E3
Copt Hall TN18. . . . . 197 D3
Copthall Ave TN18 . . . . . 189 A1
Copt Hall Rd
  Ightham TN15 . . . . 94 A4
  Sole Street DA13. . . . . 50 B5
Copthorne Ave BR2 . . . . . 56 F8
Coralline Wlk 4 SE2 . . . . . 3 C4
Coral Pk ME14 . . . . 100 B5
Corben Cl ME14 . . . . 99 B6
Corbridge No SE2 . . . . 3 C3
Corbylands Rd DA15 . . . . 29 E7
Cordelia Cres ME1 . . . . 52 F2
Corelli Rd SE18, SE3 . . . . . 11 E6
Corhaven Ho ME4 . . . . . . 14 C7
Corianda Dr 14 ME6. . . . . 99 A3
Corinthian Ct ME3 . . . . . . 27 B5
Corinthian Manorway DA8. 4 D2
Corinthian Rd DA8 . . . . 4 D2
Cork Ho BR5. . . . . 44 B6
Cork La TN12. . . . . 165 D3
Cork St ME20 . . . . 82 F6
Corkwell St ME4 . . . . 53 F3
Cormorant Cl ME2 . . . . . . 52 C7
Cornel Ho 4 DA15 . . . . . . 30 A5
Cornelia PI DA8. . . . . 14 E8
Cornell Cl DA14 . . . . 30 E2
Corner Farm Rd TN12. . . 149 E4
Corner Gn SE3 . . . . 11 A5
Cornfield Way TN10 . . . . 127 D6
Cornflower Ct ME14. . . . . 100 E4
Cornford Cl
  Hayes BR2. . . . . 42 A4
  Pembury TN2 . . . . 160 B6
Cornford La TN2 . . . . 160 B5
Cornford Pk TN2 . . . . 160 C6
Cornforth Cl TN12 . . . . . . 149 F4
Corn Mill Dr BR6. . . . . 44 A2
Cornwall Ave DA16. . . . . . 12 E4
Cornwall Cl ME15 . . . . . . 116 E7
Cornwall Cres ME1. . . . . . 66 D4
Cornwall Dr BR5. . . . . 30 C1
Cornwallis Ave
  Chatham ME4. . . . . 53 E1
  Gillingham ME8 . . . . 55 A4
  Linton ME17. . . . . 132 E8
  Sidcup SE9 . . . . 23 D6
  Tonbridge TN10 . . . . 127 F4
Cornwallis Cl DA8. . . . . . . 14 F8
Cornwallis Cotts ME17 . . 115 E2
Cornwallis Ho
  Maidstone ME16 . . . . 99 D4
  Woolwich SE18 . . . . 2 B3
Cornwallis Rdbt ME16 . . . 55 A4
Cornwallis Sch ME15. . . . 115 F2
Cornwallis Wlk SE9 . . . . . 11 F4
Cornwall Rd
  Dartford DA1. . . . . 15 F4
  Gillingham ME7 . . . . 54 D6
  Rochester ME1 . . . . 53 C3
Cornwell Ave DA12. . . . . . 36 C5
Corona Rd SE12. . . . . 28 A8
Corona Terr ME6 . . . . 81 F6
Coronation Cl DA5 . . . . . . 13 D1
Coronation Cotts
  Stoke ME3 . . . . 25 A3
  Ticehurst TN5 . . . . 186 F2
Coronation Ct DA8 . . . . . . 14 F8
Coronation Flats 5 ME4 . 53 F3
Coronation Rd
  Chatham ME5. . . . . 54 C2
  Grain ME3 . . . . 27 B5
Corporation Rd ME7. . . . . 54 D7
Corporation St ME1 . . . . . 53 C6
Corral Cl ME5 . . . . 54 D2
Corral Hts 11 DA8 . . . . 4 E1
Corral Almshouses 1
  ME15. . . . . 100 A3
Corrance Gn ME15 . . . . . . 116 A8
Correnden Rd TN10 . . . . 127 A3
Corseley Rd TN3 . . . . 171 B5
Cortland Cl DA1 . . . . 14 E1
Cory's Rd ME1. . . . . 53 D6
Cosgrove Rd RM20 . . . . . . 16 F7
Cossack St ME1. . . . . 53 D3
Cossington Rd ME5 . . . . . 68 B1
Costells Mdw TN16. . . . . . 86 C7
Cot La TN27 . . . . 168 B3
Cotleigh Ave DA5 . . . . 30 B6
Cotmandene Cres BR5 . . . 44 A7
Cotman's Ash La TN15 . . 77 D4
Cotman Way TN12 . . . . . . 129 E6
Coton Rd DA16 . . . . 13 A4
Cotswold Cl DA7 . . . . 14 E5
Cotswold Gdns ME15 . . . 101 A2
Cotswold Rd DA11 . . . . . . 35 E5
Cotswold Rise BR6 . . . . . . 43 F3
Cottage Ave BR2. . . . . 42 E1
Cottage Field Cl DA14 . . . 30 C7
Cottage Ind Est ME20 . . . 83 B2
Cottall Ave ME4 . . . . 53 F2
Cottenham Cl ME19 . . . . . 97 F7
Cotton La DA2, DA9 . . . . . 16 C2
Couchman Green La
  TN12 . . . . 149 F7
Coulman St ME7 . . . . 54 D5

Coulter Ho DA9. . . . . 17 C2
Coulters Cl ME14. . . . . . . 100 D5
Coulton Ave DA11. . . . . . . 35 E7
Council Ave DA11. . . . . . . 18 C1
Council Cotts
  Chainhurst ME15 . . . . . . 132 A7
  Chiddingstone Causeway
    TN11. . . . . 141 A8
  Coxheath ME15 . . . . 115 A4
Council Mos TN15. . . . . . 111 A8
Countess of Thanet's
  Almshouses TN8 . . . . . . 154 F3
County Gate SE9 . . . . 29 C5
County Gr ME19. . . . . 97 B8
County Ho SE18. . . . . 12 A8
County Rd
  Maidstone ME14 . . . . 100 A5
  Newham E6 . . . . 2 B8
Coupland PI SE18. . . . . 2 C1
Courier Rd RM13. . . . . 4 D8
Course The SE9. . . . . 29 A5
Courtaulds Cl SE28. . . . . . . 3 A5
Court Ave DA17 . . . . 3 F1
Court Broomes ME17. . . . 135 C8
Court Cl ME16 . . . . 99 D8
Courtenay Rd ME15 . . . . . 99 F2
Courtenay Rd ME8 . . . . . . 69 B8
Courtenwell TN3. . . . . 157 F4
Court Farm Rd SE9 . . . . . 28 E5
Courtfield Ave ME5 . . . . . 68 A3
Courthope TN12 . . . . 146 A6
Courthope Ave TN5 . . . . . 184 F4
Court La
  Detling ME14 . . . . 85 C5
  Hadlow TN11 . . . . 129 B7
Courtland Gr SE28 . . . . 3 D6
Courtlands
  Chislehurst BR7 . . . . 29 B2
  Teston ME18 . . . . 114 A8
  Tonbridge TN10 . . . . 127 A3
Courtlands Ave SE12 . . . . 11 B2
Courtlands Cl ME18 . . . . . 114 A8
Courtlands Farm TN17 . . 179 A3
Court Lane Pl TN11 . . . . . 128 F8
Courtlet Dr DA8 . . . . 14 B6
Court Lodge
  Erith DA17. . . . . 4 A1
  Shorne DA12 . . . . 37 E2
Court Lodge Cotts
  East Farleigh ME15 . . . . . 115 A7
  Horton Kirby DA4. . . . . . . 47 C6
  Mereworth ME18 . . . . 112 C4
  West Farleigh ME15 . . . . 114 D7
Court Lodge Farm ME18. 114 B7
Court Lodge Flats TN3 . . 176 C6
Court Lodge Rd ME7 . . . . 54 F6
Court Mdw
  Gillingham ME8 . . . . 55 B2
  Wrotham TN15. . . . . 78 F3
Court Mews DA11 . . . . 18 B1
Court Rd
  Burham ME1 . . . . 82 F8
  Dartford DA2. . . . . 33 E3
  Eltham SE9 . . . . 28 F7
  Royal Tunbridge Wells
    TN4. . . . . 158 F4
**Court Rd (Orpington By-
Pass)**
  Chelsfield BR6, TN14 . . . . 58 D5
  Orpington BR6. . . . . 44 B2
Court Royal TN2 . . . . 172 E8
Court St BR1 . . . . 42 A7
Courtstreet BR1 . . . . 42 A7
Courtwood Dr TN13 . . . . . 92 A3
Courtyard Gdns TN15. . . . 78 F3
Courtyard Mews BR5. . . . 30 A1
Courtyard The ME8. . . . . . 69 A8
Courtyard The
  Watts's Cross TN11 . . . . . 126 A7
  Westerham TN16. . . . . . . 105 D8
Court Yd SE9 . . . . 11 F3
Cousley Wood BR6. . . . . . 185 C7
Cousley Wood Rd TN5. . . 185 C7
Couthurst Rd SE3 . . . . 11 B7
Coutts Ave DA12 . . . . 37 E4
Coutts Ho 9 SE7 . . . . 1 C1
Couzins Walk DA1 . . . . . . 16 A5
Covelees Wall E6 . . . . 2 A7
Coventry Cl
  9 Newham E6 . . . . 1 F7
  Rochester ME2 . . . . 52 D6
Coventry Rd TN10. . . . . . 127 D5
Coverdale Ave ME15 . . . . 116 D6
Coverdale Cl ME5 . . . . 68 B7
Covert The
  Chatham ME5. . . . . 68 B1
  Orpington BR6. . . . . 43 E3
  Vigo Village DA13 . . . . 79 E7
Covesfield DA11 . . . . 35 F8
Covet Wood Cl BR5 . . . . . 43 F3
Covey Hall Rd ME6 . . . . . . 66 A1
Cowan Cl E6. . . . . 1 E8
Cowbeck Cl ME8. . . . . 69 D6
COWDEN 155 A6
Cowden Cl TN18 . . . . 194 E8
Cowden Cross TN8 . . . . . 155 A7
Cowden La TN18 . . . . 194 E7
Cowden Mews TN8. . . . . . 155 A5
COWDEN POUND 139 B2
Cowden Rd
  Maidstone ME14 . . . . 100 C5
  Orpington BR6. . . . . 57 F5
Cowden Sta TN8 . . . . 155 D8
Cowdrey Cl
  Maidstone ME16 . . . . 99 B2
  Rochester ME1 . . . . 53 B2
Cowdrey Ct DA1 . . . . 32 B8

Cowdreys TN9 . . . . 143 C8
Cowen Ho 4 SE18 . . . . 12 B8
Cow La TN8 . . . . 139 D1
Cow Leaze E6 . . . . 2 A7
Cowley Ave DA9 . . . . 17 A2
Cowper Ave RM18. . . . . . . 19 B6
Cowper Cl
  Bexley DA16 . . . . 13 A2
  Bromley BR2 . . . . 42 D5
Cowper Rd
  Bromley BR2 . . . . 42 D5
  Erith DA17 . . . . 4 A2
  Gillingham ME7 . . . . 54 D3
Cowstead La ME9 . . . . 70 D3
Cowstead Rd ME9. . . . . . . 70 D2
Cox Gdns ME8 . . . . 55 A2
COXHEATH 115 C2
Coxheath Prim Sch
  ME17. . . . . 115 C3
Coxmount Rd SE7. . . . . 1 D1
Cox's Cl ME6 . . . . 81 F8
Cox St ME14 . . . . 85 E6
Coxwell Rd SE18 . . . . 2 D1
Cozenton Cl ME8. . . . . 49 F3
Crabbs Croft Cl 7 BR6. . . 57 C5
Crabtree Cl ME19 . . . . 97 A2
Crabtree Manorway N
  DA17 . . . . 4 C3
Crabtree Manorway S
  DA17 . . . . 4 C3
Crabtree Rd ME8. . . . . 69 D8
Crabtree Way ME8 . . . . . . 69 D8
Caddock Way ME15 . . . . . 69 D5
Cradducks La TN12 . . . . . 150 B4
Cradles Rd ME9 . . . . 70 C2
Cradley Rd SE9 . . . . 29 F7
Craft Workshops TN27. . 135 C1
Cragie Wlk ME8. . . . . 69 E4
Craigerne Rd SE3 . . . . 11 B7
Craig Ho
  Greenwich SE3 . . . . 11 B7
  Rochester ME1 . . . . 53 E1
Craigholm SE18. . . . . 12 A6
Craigie Ct DA1. . . . . 33 A8
Craigton Rd SE9 . . . . 11 F3
Crales Ho SE18 . . . . 1 E3
Cramonde Pl DA16. . . . . . 13 A5
Cramptons TN17 . . . . 179 F8
Crampton's Rd TN14 . . . . 92 B7
Cranborne Ave ME15. . . . 100 C1
Cranbourne Ave ME15. . . 116 B8
CRANBROOK 179 C6
Cranbrook CE Prim Sch
  TN17. . . . . 179 D5
Cranbrook Cl
  Gillingham ME8 . . . . 55 C7
  Hayes BR2. . . . . 42 A3
Cranbrook Mews ME15 . . 116 F7
CRANBROOK COMMON . . 162 F8
Cranbrook Ho 1 DA8 . . . . 14 F7
Cranbrook Mews 3 TN18 . 122 C1
Cranbrook Mus★ TN17 . . 179 C5
Cranbrook Rd
  Benenden TN17 . . . . 189 F8
  Bexley DA7 . . . . 13 F6
  Fosten Green TN27 . . . . . 181 C6
  Goudhurst TN17 . . . . 178 A8
  Hawkhurst TN18 . . . . 188 F4
  Knox Bridge TN12, TN17 . 165 F7
  Parkgate TN30 . . . . 182 C1
  Tenterden TN30 . . . . 192 F7
Cranbrook Sch TN17 . . . . 179 D5
Crandalls TN11 . . . . 125 F1
Cranden Wlk DA4 . . . . 47 E7
Crane Ho 11 SE18 . . . . . . 188 F2
Crane House Gdns 10
  TN18 . . . . 188 F2
Crane La TN17 . . . . 179 D5
Cranford Cl ME18 . . . . 55 D1
Cranford Ho DA1 . . . . 15 A2
Cranford Mews BR2. . . . . 42 E4
Cranford Rd
  Dartford DA1. . . . . 32 E7
  Tonbridge TN10 . . . . 128 A5
Cranham Sq TN12. . . . . . 148 C5
Cranleigh Cl
  Orpington BR6. . . . . 58 A7
  Sidcup DA5 . . . . 14 B1
Cranleigh Dr BR8 . . . . 45 E5
Cranleigh Gdns
  Chatham ME5. . . . . 53 D3
  Maidstone ME16 . . . . 99 C7
Cranley Par SE9 . . . . 28 E4
Cranley Rd E13 . . . . 1 B8
Cranmer Ct ME15 . . . . . . 116 B8
Cranmere Ct ME2 . . . . 53 C8
Cranmer Rd TN13 . . . . 91 E4
Cranmore Rd BR7. . . . . . . 28 F3
Cranstone Ct 16 DA4 . . . . 30 B4
Cranwell Rd TN4. . . . . . . 158 C4
Crates Yd TN4 . . . . 159 A5
Crathie Rd SE12 . . . . 11 B1
Craven Rd BR6. . . . . 58 D7
Crawford Ave 9 DA1. . . . . 15 D1
Crawford Cl SE18 . . . . 13 A8
Crawford Way ME5 . . . . . . 53 D1
Crawley Ct TN13 . . . . 91 B1
Crawshay Cl TN13. . . . . . . 92 A4
Cray Ave BR5 . . . . 44 B4
Cray Bldgs DA14 . . . . 30 C2
Craybrooke Rd DA14 . . . . 30 B4
Crayburne DA13 . . . . 34 F4
Craybury End SE9 . . . . 29 C6
Cray Cl DA1 . . . . 15 E4
Craydene Rd DA8 . . . . 14 F6
Crayfields Bsns Pk BR5. . 44 C7
Crayfields Ind Pk BR5 . . . 44 C7
CRAYFORD 14 D1

rayford Cl
Maidstone ME14 100 C6
Newham E6 1 E7
rayford Commercial Ctr
DA1 14 E1
rayford High St DA1 14 E2
rayford Ind Est DA1 14 F2
rayford L Ctr DA2 14 E1
rayford Rd DA1 14 F2
rayford Sta DA1 14 E1
rayford Way DA1 15 A3
raylands BR5 44 C6
raylands La DA10 17 D2
raylands Lane DA10 34 E8
raylands Prim Sch DA10 17 D2
raylands Sq DA10 17 D2
rayleigh Terr DA14 30 C2
raymill Sq DA1 14 F5
ray Rd
Crockenhill BR8 45 C3
Erith DA17 14 A8
Sidcup DA14 30 C2
rayside Ind Est DA1 15 B3
rays Par The BR5 44 C7
raythorne TN30 193 B8
raythorne Ho TN30 193 B8
ray Valley Rd BR5 44 B4
ray View Cl 13 BR5 44 C5
reasey's Row TN14 106 E5
redenhall Dr BR2 42 F1
redo Way RM20 17 B8
reek La ME3 25 B2
REEKMOUTH 2 F8
reek The DA11 18 B2
reek Way RM13 4 E8
remorne Rd 1 DA11 35 F8
rendon Pk TN4 159 A8
rescent Ave RM17 18 D8
rescent Cotts TN13 91 E7
rescent Ct
1 Grays RM17 18 D8
Sidcup DA15 30 A5
rescent Dr BR5 43 C3
rescent Gdns BR8 45 C7
rescent Ho ME2 53 C7
rescent Rd
Bromley BR1 28 A1
Erith DA8 14 F8
Royal Tunbridge Wells
TN1 159 B3
Sidcup DA15 29 F5
Woolwich SE18 2 B2
rescent The
Bidborough TN4 142 E4
Borough Green TN15 95 A8
Groombridge TN3 171 C7
Longfield DA3 48 E6
Maidstone ME14 99 F8
Northfleet DA11 35 F6
Sevenoaks TN13 92 D6
Sidcup DA5 30 C8
Sidcup DA14 29 F4
St Mary's Island ME4 40 B1
Swanscombe DA9 17 C2
1 Tonbridge TN9 127 B2
Crescent Way
Chatham ME5 67 D5
Orpington BR6 57 E5
Cressey Ct 7 ME4 53 E4
Cressingham Ct 1 DA17 4 A3
Crest Ave RM17 18 B7
Crest Cl TN14 75 B8
Crest Ind Est TN12 148 C6
Crest Rd ME1 53 C1
Crest View DA9 17 A3
Crest View Dr BR5 43 C4
Crestway ME5 68 B8
Crete Hall Rd DA11 18 E1
Creton St SE18 2 A3
Creve Coeur Cl ME14 101 A5
Crevequer Chambers 1
ME8 55 F1
Cricketers Cl
Bells Yew Green TN3 174 A5
Erith DA8 4 E1
Harrietsham ME17 119 D6
Cricketers Dr DA13 64 A7
Cricket Ground Rd BR7 43 B8
Cripple Hill TN26 169 D1
Cripple St ME15 116 A7
Crisfield Ct TN30 183 B2
Crismill La ME14 101 F4
Crispe Cl ME8 69 D4
Crispin Ct ME17 115 C3
Crispin Rd ME2 52 E8
Crispin Way ME19 97 A3
Critchley Ave 10 DA1 15 D1
Crittall's Cnr DA14 30 C1
Crittenden Bglws ME15 115 A4
Crittenden Cotts ME15 115 A4
Crittenden Rd TN12 145 D3
Crittle's Ct TN5 184 F4
Crockenhall Way DA13 35 E1
CROCKENHILL 45 D3
Crockenhill Hill BR5 44 D4
Crockenhill La BR8, DA4 46 C2
Crockenhill Prim Sch
BR8 45 C3
Crockenhill Rd BR5, BR8 44 E4
Crocken Hill Rd TN27 137 C2
Crockers Hatch Cnr TN3 157 D2
Crockford Cl TN10 127 E7
CROCKHAM HILL 105 C2
Crockham Hill CE Prim Sch
TN8 105 C2
Crockham Way SE9 29 A4
CROCKHURST STREET 144 C6

Croft Cl
Bromley BR7 28 F3
Chatham ME5 68 C1
Erith DA17 3 F1
Tonbridge TN10 127 F5
Croft Ct TN8 122 C1
Crofters The ME8 69 F7
Croft Gdns ME17 120 D4
Croft La TN8 122 C1
CROFTON 57 D8
Crofton Ave
Orpington BR5, BR6 57 C8
Sidcup DA5 30 D8
Crofton Inf Sch BR5 43 D2
Crofton Jun Sch BR5 43 D2
Crofton La BR5, BR6 43 D2
Crofton Rd BR6 57 B8
Crofton Roman Villa*
BR6 57 E8
Croft Rd
Bromley BR1 28 A2
Westerham TN16 89 C1
Croftside DA13 80 A8
Croft The
Leybourne ME19 81 E2
Swanley BR8 45 C6
Tenterden TN30 193 B7
Croft Way
Sevenoaks TN13 91 F2
Sidcup DA15 29 E5
Cromarty Ct 8 BR1 42 C7
Crombie Rd DA15 29 D7
Cromer Pl 5 BR6 43 D1
Cromer Rd ME2 53 B8
Cromer St TN9 127 A1
Cromford Cl BR6 57 E7
Cromlix Cl BR7 43 B7
Crompton Gdns ME15 100 B3
Cromwell Ave BR2 42 B5
Cromwell Cl BR2 42 B5
Cromwell Mews BR7 43 A8
Cromwell Rd
Maidstone ME14 100 B5
Royal Tunbridge Wells
TN2 159 C3
Cromwell Terr ME4 54 A3
Cronin Cl 2 ME20 81 F4
Crooked La DA11, DA12 19 B1
Crook Log DA6 13 D3
Crook Log L Ctr DA6 13 D4
Crook Log Prim Sch DA6 13 D3
Crook Rd TN12 146 D1
Crookston Rd SE9 12 A4
Croombridge Dr ME7 54 F6
Croombs Rd E16 1 C8
Crosby House DA1 15 A1
Crosier Cl SE3 11 E6
Crosley Rd ME7 54 D3
CROSS-AT-HAND 133 E1
Cross-at-Hand Cotts
TN12 133 E2
Crossbrook Rd SE3 11 E4
Cross Ct 11 SE28 3 B6
Cross Dr ME17 118 B1
Crossfield Walk ME6 66 A2
Cross Keys
Maidstone ME14 101 C4
Sevenoaks TN13 108 A8
Cross Keys Cl TN13 108 A8
Cross La
Sidcup DA5 30 F8
Ticehurst TN5 186 D2
Cross Lane E DA12 36 B6
Cross Lane Gdns TN5 186 D1
Cross Lane W DA11 36 B6
Crossley Cl TN16 72 D4
Crossmead SE9 28 F7
Cross Rd
Dartford DA1 15 C1
Hawley DA2 32 F4
Northfleet DA11 18 F1
Orpington, Keston Mark BR2 56 E8
Orpington, St Mary Cray
BR5 44 B4
Sidcup DA14 30 B4
Cross St
Chatham ME4 54 A4
Erith DA8 14 E8
Gillingham ME7 54 C6
27 Gravesend DA12 19 B1
Maidstone ME14 100 A6
Rochester ME2 53 B8
Crossway
Chatham ME5 67 E6
Erith SE28 3 D7
Orpington BR5 43 D4
Cross Way ME1 53 C3
CROSSWAYS 16 D3
Crossways
Chart Sutton ME17 117 B1
Hextable BR8 31 F1
Tatsfield TN16 88 C7
Crossways Bvd DA2, DA9 16 E3
Crossways Ct TN16 88 C7
Crossway The
Bromley SE9 28 D6
Royal Tunbridge Wells
TN4 158 D2
CROUCH 95 B4
Crouch Croft SE9 29 A5
Crouch House Cotts TN8 122 B2
Crouch House Rd TN8 122 B2
Crouch La
Crouch TN15 95 B6
Linkhill TN18 196 D6
Crow Cnr ME1 53 C5
Crowden Way SE28 3 C6
CROWDLEHAM 77 D2

Crow Dr TN14 75 C4
Crowfoot Cl SE28 2 E5
Crow Hill TN15 95 A7
Crow Hill Rd TN15 95 A7
Crowhurst La
Basted TN15 94 E4
West Kingsdown TN15 62 B4
Crowhurst Oast TN12 112 D1
Crowhurst Rd TN15 94 F6
Crowhurst Way BR5 44 C4
Crow La ME1 53 C5
Crown Acres TN12 130 A6
Crown Cl BR6 58 A6
Crown Ct
Bromley BR2 42 E4
Cranbrook TN17 179 C5
Eltham SE12 11 B1
Tilbury RM18 19 A5
Crownfields
Maidstone ME14 100 F4
Sevenoaks TN13 92 B2
Crown Gn DA12 37 E3
Crown Ho
Lamberhurst TN3 176 B5
Rochester ME1 53 B4
Crown La
Bromley BR2 42 D4
Chislehurst BR7 43 C8
Shorne DA12 37 E4
Crown Lane Spur BR2 42 D3
Crown Rd
Grays RM17 18 A8
Marlpit Hill TN8 122 D4
Orpington BR6 58 A5
Shoreham TN14 59 F1
Crown St ME7 54 D6
Crown Woods La SE18 12 B5
Crown Woods Sch SE9 12 C2
Crown Woods Way SE9 12 D2
Crowther Cl TN12 149 E4
Croxley Cl BR5 44 B7
Croxley Gn BR5 44 B8
Croyde Cl DA15 29 D8
Croydon Cl ME5 68 C4
Croydon Rd
Hayes BR2, BR4, BR6 56 C7
Tatsfield TN16 88 F3
Westerham TN16 89 B2
Crozier Ho SE3 11 B4
Cruden Rd DA12 36 F6
Crumpsall St SE2 3 C2
Crump's La ME17 136 B4
Crundale 2 ME14 100 A5
Crundale Rd ME8 55 C3
Crundale Tower BR5 44 C1
Crundwell Rd TN4 142 F1
Crusader Cl ME8 69 B8
Crusader Ct DA1 15 F3
Crusoe Rd DA8 4 D1
Crutches La ME3, ME2 38 B1
Cryals Ct TN12 161 E5
Cryals Rd TN12 161 D5
Crystal Ho 2 SE18 2 F1
Cuckmere Ct 17 BR5 44 D1
Cuckmere Way 27 BR5 44 D1
Cuckolds Cnr DA3 63 B7
Cuckold's Cnr
Lower Higham ME3 38 C6
Staplehurst TN12 149 F4
CUCKOLD'S GREEN 25 A5
Cuckolds Green Rd ME3 25 B5
Cuckoo La
Lamberhurst TN12 162 A2
Tonbridge TN11 128 A7
Cuckoowood Ave ME14 83 F1
CUDHAM 73 D4
Cudham CE Prim Sch
TN16 73 A3
Cudham Cl ME14 100 C6
Cudham Lane N TN14 73 D7
Cudham Lane S TN14 73 D2
Cudham Park Rd TN14 57 E1
Cudham Rd
Downe BR6 73 B7
Tatsfield TN16 88 E8
Cuff Cres SE9 11 D1
Cugley Rd DA2 33 C8
Culcroft DA3 48 F6
Culpeper Cl
Hollingbourne ME17 102 E2
Rochester ME2 53 E6
Culpepers TN17 177 E7
Culpepper Rd
Coxheath ME17 115 B3
Gillingham ME8 69 D4
Culverden Ave TN4 159 A6
Culverden Down TN4 158 F5
Culverden Park Rd TN4 158 F5
Culverden Pk TN4 158 F5
Culverden Sq TN4 159 A5
Culverden St TN1 159 A4
CULVERSTONE GREEN 63 E2
Culverstone Green Prim Sch
DA13 63 F3
Culverstone Ho BR5 44 B6
Culverton Ct 19 DA14 30 A4
Culvey Cl DA3 48 E4
Cumberland Ave
Bexley DA16 12 F3
Gravesend DA12 36 C8
Maidstone ME15 116 D8
Cumberland Cotts 23
TN1 159 A2
Cumberland Ct
Sevenoaks TN13 91 E7
Tonbridge TN10 127 A4
Cumberland Dr
Dartford DA1 32 F8

Cumberland Dr *continued*
Erith DA7 13 E7
Cumberland Gdns 10
TN1 159 A2
Cumberland Ho SE28 2 D4
Cumberland Mews 12
TN1 159 A2
Cumberland Rd
Chatham ME4, ME7 54 B7
Gillingham ME7 54 C7
Newham E13 1 B8
Cumberland Villas 5
DA12 36 C8
Cumberland Wlk TN1 159 A2
Cumberland Yd 11 TN1 159 A2
Cumbrian Ave DA7 14 E5
Cundy Rd E16 1 C7
Cunningham Cl TN4 159 B7
Cunningham Cres ME5 68 A8
Cunningham Ho ME1 53 B4
Cunningham Rd TN4 159 B7
Cupar Pl ME3 40 B8
Cupola Cl BR1 28 B3
Curates Wlk DA2 32 D5
Curlew Cl SE28 3 D6
Curlew Cres ME2 52 C6
Curlews The DA12 36 D6
Curran Ave DA15 12 F2
Currie Rd TN4 159 A5
CURTEIS' CORNER 168 A3
Curteis Rd TN30 183 B1
Curtis Ct BR6 44 A2
CURTISDEN GREEN 164 C5
Curtismill Cl BR5 44 B6
Curtismill Way BR5 44 B6
Curtis Way
Rochester ME1 67 D7
7 Woolwich SE28 3 B6
Curzon Cl BR6 57 D6
Curzon Ct SE9 29 C5
Curzon Dr RM17 18 C7
Curzon Rd
Chatham ME4 53 F3
Maidstone ME14 100 A6
CUSTOM HOUSE 1 C7
Custom House for Excel Sta
E16 1 B6
Cutbush Almshouses 1
ME15 100 A3
Cutbush Cl ME17 119 D6
Cutbush & Corrall Ct 1
ME14 100 B4
Cutbush Ho 2 ME15 100 A3
Cutmore St DA11 36 B8
Cutter Cl ME2 39 F3
Cutter Ho 6 DA8 4 E1
Cutter Ridge Rd DA13 51 A1
Cut The
17 Chatham ME4/ME7 54 A6
Tylden TN27 168 E8
Cutty Sark Ct 6 DA9 17 A2
CUXTON 52 B2
Cuxton BR5 43 C4
Cuxton Cl
Bexley DA6 13 E2
11 Maidstone ME15 116 F5
Cuxton Com Inf Sch ME2 52 B2
Cuxton Com Jun Sch ME2 52 B2
Cuxton Ind Est ME2 52 C2
Cuxton Rd
Maidstone ME15 116 F5
Rochester ME2 52 F5
Cuxton Sta ME2 52 C2
Cyclamen Rd BR8 45 D5
Cygnet Cl ME20 82 A2
Cygnet Gdns DA11 35 F6
Cygnet L Ctr DA11 35 E6
Cygnet Rd ME5 68 C2
Cypress Ave ME3 40 E3
Cypress Ct ME7 54 F6
Cypress Gr TN2 173 C8
Cypress Rd ME2 39 C1
Cypress Tree Cl DA15 29 F7
CYPRUS 2 B6
Cyprus Pl E6 2 A6
Cyprus Sta E6 2 A6
Cyril Hall Ct DA11 18 F1
Cyril John Gange Lodge
TN2 159 D2
Cyril Lodge 6 DA14 30 A4
Cyril Rd
Bexley DA7 13 E5
Orpington BR6 44 A2

D

Dabbling Cl DA8 15 B7
Daerwood Cl BR2 42 F1
Daffodil Rd ME2 52 E7
Dagmar Rd ME4 54 B2
Dagonet Gdns BR1 28 A5
Dagonet Rd BR1 28 A5
Dahlia Dr BR8 45 F7
Dahlia Rd SE2 3 B2
Dainton Cl 2 BR1 42 B8
Daintons Cotts 2 TN18 188 F2
Dairsie Ct 4 BR1 42 C7
Dairsie Rd SE9 12 A4
Dairy Cl
3 Bromley BR1 28 B1
Sutton at Hone DA4 33 B1
Dairy La
Chainhurst TN12 131 F4
Crockham Hill TN8 105 B1
Woolwich SE18 1 F2
Dairy Pl TN12 131 F4
Daisy Munns Ho SE9 29 C7

Dajen Bsns Pk ME4 54 C1
Dalberg Way SE2 3 D3
Dale Cl
Crayford DA1 14 F1
Greenwich SE3 11 A4
Dale Ct
Bromley BR1 42 D6
Chatham ME5 68 A2
Dale End DA1 14 F1
Dalemain Mews E16 1 A5
Dale Rd
Crayford DA1 14 F1
Northfleet DA13 35 A4
Rochester ME1 53 C3
Swanley BR8 45 C6
Daleside BR6 58 A5
Daleside Cl BR6 58 A4
Dale St
Chatham ME4 53 E2
Royal Tunbridge Wells
TN1 159 B4
Dale The BR2 56 D6
Dale View DA8 14 F5
Dale Wlk DA2 33 C7
Dale Wood Rd BR6 43 E1
Dalison Ct ME2 66 B4
Dallin Rd
Bexley DA6 13 D3
Woolwich SE18 12 B7
Dalmeny Rd DA8 14 B6
Dalton Cl BR6 57 E7
Daltons Rd BR6, BR8 59 C7
Dalton St ME7 54 C6
Daly Dr BR1 43 A6
Damiem Cl ME4 54 A2
Damigos Rd DA12 36 F7
Damon Cl DA14 30 B5
Damon Ct DA14 30 B5
Damson Ct BR8 45 D5
Damson Dr ME3 40 E3
DANAWAY 71 C3
Danaway Cotts ME9 71 C3
Dando Cres SE3 11 B4
Dane Cl
Chatham ME5 68 C2
Hartlip ME9 70 D6
Orpington BR6 57 D5
Sidcup DA5 31 A8
Danecourt Com Sch ME8 55 A2
Dane Ct ME17 115 C2
Danefield Ct ME14 101 B4
Danehill Wlk DA14 30 A5
Dane La ME9 70 D6
Danemore TN30 193 B8
Dane Pk ME15 115 C6
Dane Rd TN14 75 F2
Danes Cl DA11 35 C5
Danescombe SE12 28 A7
Danes Hill ME7 55 A6
Daniel Ho 5 ME16 99 E5
Danns La ME18, ME19 97 A1
Dansington Rd DA16 13 A3
Danson Cres DA16 13 B4
Danson House* DA6 13 C3
Danson La DA16 13 B3
Danson Mead DA16 13 C4
Danson Prim Sch DA16 13 A3
Danson Rd
Bexley DA5 13 D1
Bexley DA5, DA6 13 D2
Danson Underpass DA5 13 C1
Danson Way ME8 55 D2
Danvers Rd TN9 127 B1
Darby Gdns ME3 38 B3
Darby's La TN5 185 B2
D'arcy Pl BR2 42 A5
Darent Cl TN13 91 C5
DARENTH 33 B4
Darenth Ave TN10 127 C5
Darenth Cotts TN14 75 F8
Darenth Ct 18 BR5 44 D1
Darenth Ctry Pk* DA2 33 D6
Darenth Dr DA12 37 B7
Darenth Gdns TN16 89 D1
Darenth Hill DA2 33 C3
Darenth La TN13 91 E6
Darenth Park Ave DA2 33 D6
Darenth Prim Sch DA2 33 E2
Darenth Rd
Bexley DA16 13 A6
Dartford DA1 32 F7
Darenth Rd S DA2 33 B4
Darenth Rise ME5 68 B3
Darenth Way TN14 76 A8
Darenth Wood Rd DA2 33 E6
Darent Ind Pk DA8 15 D8
Darent Mead DA4 47 B8
Darent Valley Hospl DA2 33 E7
Dargate Cl ME16 99 D7
Dargets Rd ME5 68 A3
DARLAND 68 E8
Darland Ave ME7 54 E1
Darland Ho SE9 12 D1
Darlton Cl DA1 14 F4
Darman La TN12, ME18 130 D3
Darnets Field TN14 75 F2
Darnley Cl ME2 52 D6
Darnley Ct DA11 36 A8
Darnley Dr TN4 142 E4
Darnley Rd
Gravesend DA11 36 A8
1 Grays RM17 18 B8
Rochester ME2 52 E6
Darnley St DA11 36 B8
Darns Hill BR8 45 C2

Darrick Wood Ho BR6 . . . . . 57 C7
Darrick Wood Inf & Jun Schs
  BR6 . . . . 57 B6
Darrick Wood Rd BR6 . . . 57 D8
Darrick Wood Sports Ctr
  BR6 . . . . 57 B7
Dart Cl ME2 . . . . 52 F7
DARTFORD 15 E2
Dartford Borough Mus★
  DA1 . . . . 32 E8
Dartford Gram Sch DA1 . . 15 C1
Dartford Gram Sch for Girls
  DA1 . . . . 32 C8
Dartford Rd
  Coldblow DA5 . . . . 31 C7
  Dartford DA1 . . . . 15 B1
  Farningham DA4 . . . . 47 A5
  Sevenoaks TN13 . . . . 92 C3
Dartford Sta DA1 . . . . 15 E1
Dartford Technology Coll
  DA1 . . . . 32 C8
Dartford Trad Pk DA1 . . 32 F6
Dartmouth Rd BR2 . . . . . . 42 A2
Darwin Cl DA7 . . . . 57 D5
Darwin Ct
  Eltham SE9 . . . . 12 A1
  Rochester ME1 . . . . 53 D5
Darwin Dr TN10 . . . . 127 D6
Darwin L Ctr TN16 . . . . . . 72 F3
Darwin Rd
  Bexley DA16 . . . . 12 F4
  Tilbury RM18 . . . . 18 F6
Dashmonden Cl ME2 . . . . 39 C2
Dashwood Cl DA6 . . . . 14 A2
Dashwood Rd DA11 . . . . . . 36 A6
Davall Ho ⑩ RM17 . . . . . . 18 B8
Davema Cl BR7 . . . . 43 A8
Davenport Ave ME15 . . . . 106 E4
Davenport Rd DA14 . . . . . . 30 E6
Davey Ct ME1 . . . . 53 C5
David Coffer Ct DA17 . . . . 4 B2
David Ho ㉓ DA14 . . . . 30 A5
David Ramsey Ho SE18 . . . 2 D2
Davidson Ho DA9 . . . . 17 C2
DAVID STREET 64 B5
Davis Ave DA11 . . . . 12 C5
Davis Cl TN13 . . . . 92 C5
Davis Way DA14 . . . . 30 E2
Davy's Pl DA12 . . . . 36 E2
Dawbourne TN30 . . . . . . 183 B3
Dawell Dr TN16 . . . . 72 C2
Dawes Cl
  Stone DA9 . . . . 16 F2
  Tonbridge TN9 . . . . 127 D3
Dawes St SE17 . . . . 54 C5
Dawn Ave ME18 . . . . 97 D3
Dawson Ave BR5 . . . . 44 B7
Dawson Cl SE18 . . . . 2 C2
Dawson Ct ⑦ ME7 . . . . . . 54 A6
Dawson Dr BR8 . . . . 31 E1
Day Ho ② ME14 . . . . 100 B8
Days La DA15 . . . . 29 E8
Days Lane Prim Sch DA15 12 F1
Dayton Dr DA8 . . . . 15 D8
Deacon Cl ME2 . . . . 52 E8
Deacon Ind Est ME20 . . . . 83 A2
Deacons Leas BR6 . . . . 57 D6
Deacon Trad Ctr ME2 . . . . 53 A6
Deacon Trad Est TN9 . . . 127 D1
Deakin Leas TN9 . . . . 143 B7
Deakins Terr BR6 . . . . 44 A2
Deal Ho ME15 . . . . 116 E8
Dean & Chapter Cotts
  DA13 . . . . 35 B2
Deane Ct ⑧ ME4 . . . . 54 C6
Deanery Rd TN8 . . . . 105 C2
Dean La DA13 . . . . 64 C5
Dean Rd
  Luddesdown DA13 . . . . . . 64 E8
  Rochester ME2 . . . . 52 F8
  Woolwich SE28 . . . . 3 A6
DEANS BOTTOM 87 C5
Deans Ct ⑦ TN9 . . . . 143 B8
Deansfield Prim Sch SE9 . 12 A4
DEANS HILL 87 D6
Deans St ME15 . . . . 115 C6
DEAN STREET 115 D7
Deanwood Cl ME8 . . . . . . 69 D6
Deanwood Dr ME8 . . . . . . 69 E4
Deanwood Prim Education
  Tech Sch ME8 . . . . 69 D3
Debrabant Cl DA8 . . . . 14 D8
Decimus Pl TN1 . . . . 59 B4
Decoy Hill Rd ME23 . . . . . 23 F6
Deepdene TN5 . . . . 185 A6
Deepdene Rd DA16 . . . . . . 13 A4
Deerhurst Cl DA3 . . . . 49 C6
Deerhurst Gdns ME16 . . . 99 D4
Deering Cl ME4 . . . . 40 B2
Deerleap La TN14 . . . . 74 E6
Defence Cl SE28 . . . . 2 E5
Defiance Wlk SE18 . . . . 1 F3
Defiant Cl ME6 . . . . 68 B6
Defoe Cl
  Chatham ME5 . . . . 68 B6
  Erith DA8 . . . . 14 F6
Degema Rd BR7 . . . . 29 B3
De Haviland Dr ⑧ SE18 . . 2 B1
Deirdre Chapman Ho DA10 17 E1
Delacourt Rd SE3 . . . . 5 B7
Delafield Rd SE7 . . . . 1 C1
Delagarde Rd TN16 . . . . . 89 C1
Delamere Gdns ③ ME6 . . 82 A8

Delamere Rd ME6 . . . . 82 A8
De Lapre Cl BR5 . . . . 44 D2
Delarue Cl TN11 . . . . 127 D8
Delaware Cotts TN8 . . . . 138 F8
Delce Jun & Inf Schs
  ME1 . . . . 53 D2
Delce Rd ME1 . . . . 53 D4
Delisle Rd SE28 . . . . 2 E4
Delius Dr TN10 . . . . 127 F6
Dell Dr TN2 . . . . 159 D4
Dell The
  Maypole DA5 . . . . 31 E7
  Swanscombe DA9 . . . . . . 17 B2
  Woolwich SE2 . . . . 3 A1
Delme Cres SE3 . . . . 11 B5
Delmonden La TN18 . . . . 194 C8
Delmonden Rd TN18 . . . . 188 B1
De Luci Rd DA8 . . . . 4 C1
De Lucy Prim Sch SE2 . . . 3 B4
De Lucy St SE2 . . . . 3 B2
Delvan Cl SE18 . . . . 12 A7
Delves Ave TN2 . . . . 159 C1
Demelza Cl ME2 . . . . 52 A2
De Mere Cl ME8 . . . . 69 D6
Denbeigh Dr TN10 . . . . . 127 D6
Denberry Dr DA14 . . . . . . 30 B5
Denbigh Ave ME8 . . . . 55 D1
Denbigh Cl BR7 . . . . 28 F2
Denbigh Rd BR1 . . . . 42 F7
Den Cross TN8 . . . . 138 D6
Dene Ave DA15 . . . . 30 B8
Dene Cl DA2 . . . . 31 A6
Denecourt BR5 . . . . 44 C1
Dene Dr
  New Barn DA3 . . . . 49 B7
  Orpington BR6 . . . . 58 B7
Dene Holm Rd DA11 . . . . 35 E5
Dene Lodge DA14 TN15 . . 94 F7
Dene Rd DA1 . . . . 32 F8
Denesfield Ct TN13 . . . . . 91 C4
Denesway DA13 . . . . 50 B3
Dene The TN13 . . . . 92 B1
Dene Way TN3 . . . . 158 A7
Dene Wlk DA3 . . . . 48 E6
Denham Cl DA16 . . . . 13 C4
Denham Rd ME7 . . . . 71 B7
Denham St ② SE10 . . . . . . 1 A1
Denison Mews ME3 . . . . . 25 C4
Deniston Ave DA5 . . . . . . 30 E7
Den La TN12 . . . . 131 C3
Denmark Ho ⑩ SE18 . . . . 1 E2
Denmark Rd BR1 . . . . 42 B8
Denmark St E13 . . . . 1 A8
Dennard Way BR6 . . . . . . 57 A6
Dennettsland Rd TN8 . . 105 C1
Denning Cl ME16 . . . . . . 99 B4
Dennington Ct ⑨ DA1 . . 143 A2
Dennis Cadman Ho ME20 . 82 F1
Dennis Rd DA11 . . . . 36 B5
Dennis Wilcocks Cl ME9 . 71 B6
DENNY BOTTOM 158 E4
Denny Cl ⑪ E6 . . . . 1 E8
Denny Ct ⑬ DA2 . . . . 16 B1
Denstead Wlk ⑪ ME15 . 116 F6
DENTON 36 E8
Denton Cl ME15 . . . . 116 E8
Denton Court Rd DA12 . . 36 E8
Denton Ct BR2 . . . . 43 A2
Denton Gn ME8 . . . . 55 B4
Denton Rd
  Bexley DA16 . . . . 13 C7
  Dartford DA1 . . . . 31 E8
  Maypole DA5 . . . . 31 E7
Denton St DA12 . . . . 36 E8
Denton Terr DA5 . . . . 31 E6
Denver Cl BR6 . . . . 43 E3
Denver Rd DA1 . . . . 32 A8
De Quincey Mews E16 . . . 1 A5
Derby Cl TN11 . . . . 126 E6
Derby Rd
  Gillingham ME8 . . . . 54 E2
  Grays RM17 . . . . 18 C8
  Maidstone ME15 . . . . . . 116 A8
Derby Road Bridge RM17 . 18 B8
Derifall Cl E6 . . . . 1 F8
Dering Way DA12 . . . . 36 F7
Deringwood Dr ME15 . . 100 F1
Dernier Rd TN10, TN9 . . 127 C4
Derrick Gdns SE7 . . . . 1 C3
DERRY DOWNS 44 D3
Derry Downs BR5 . . . . 44 C3
Derwent Cl DA1 . . . . 32 B7
Derwent Cres DA7 . . . . . . 14 A5
Derwent Dr
  Orpington BR5 . . . . 43 D2
  Royal Tunbridge Wells
  TN4 . . . . 158 E5
Derwent Ho ⑩ ME15 . . . 116 E7
Derwent Rd TN10 . . . . . . 127 C6
Derwent Way ME8 . . . . . . 69 D8
Detillens La RH8 . . . . 104 A5
DETLING 85 B1
Detling Cl ME8 . . . . 55 C2
Detling Hill ME14 . . . . . . 85 B2
Detling Rd
  Bromley BR1 . . . . 28 A3
  Erith DA8 . . . . 14 D7
  Northfleet DA11 . . . . 35 D7
Devalls Cl E6 . . . . 2 A6
Devenish Rd SE2 . . . . 3 A4
DEVIL'S DEN 134 B3
Devon Cl
  Chatham ME5 . . . . 68 C7
  Gillingham ME8 . . . . 55 F1
Devon Ct DA4 . . . . 47 B8

Devon Rd
  Maidstone ME15 . . . . . . 116 C8
  Sutton at Hone DA4 . . . . 47 C8
Devonshire Ave DA1 . . . . 15 B1
Devonshire Cl TN2 . . . . . 172 F8
Devonshire Rd
  Bexley DA6 . . . . 13 E3
  Bromley SE9 . . . . 28 E6
  Gillingham ME8 . . . . 54 D7
  Gravesend DA12 . . . . 36 B6
  Newham E16 . . . . 1 B7
  Orpington BR6 . . . . 44 A2
  West Thurrock RM20 . . . . 17 E8
Devonshire Sq BR2 . . . . . 42 B5
De Warren Ho ② DA11 . . 18 D1
Dewberry Cl ME4 . . . . 40 B1
Dewberry Gdns E6 . . . . . . 1 E8
Dewhurst Cotts TN5 . . . 184 A8
Dewhurst La TN5 . . . . . . 184 B8
De Winter Ho TN13 . . . . . 92 A3
Dewlands Ave DA2 . . . . . . 33 B8
Dexter Ho ② DA18 . . . . . . 3 E3
Dhekelia Cl ME14 . . . . . . 100 A7
Dial Cl
  Gillingham ME7 . . . . 54 F6
  Swanscombe DA9 . . . . . . 17 D2
Dial Rd ME7 . . . . 54 F6
Diameter Rd BR5 . . . . 43 C3
Diamond Cotts TN12 . . . 145 B7
Diamond Field TN12 . . . 162 F3
Diana Cl DA14 . . . . 30 C6
Diana Ct DA8 . . . . 14 A2
Diana Rd ME4 . . . . 54 A2
Dianne Ct SE12 . . . . 28 A7
Dianthus Cl SE2 . . . . 3 B1
Dibden La TN13, TN14 . . 107 E8
Dickens Ave
  Dartford DA1 . . . . 16 A3
  Tilbury RM18 . . . . 19 B6
Dickens Cl
  Erith DA8 . . . . 14 B7
  Hartley DA3 . . . . 48 F4
  Langley Heath ME17 . . . 117 C4
Dickens Ct
  Higham ME3 . . . . 38 C4
  Rochester ME1 . . . . 53 D8
  Staplehurst TN12 . . . . . . 149 F5
Dickens Dr
  Chislehurst BR7 . . . . 29 C2
  West Malling ME19 . . . . . 81 F1
Dickens Ho ③ DA17 . . . . . 3 F1
Dickensian Cl ME3 . . . . . . 25 A2
Dickens Rd
  Gravesend DA12 . . . . 36 E7
  Maidstone ME14 . . . . 99 B8
  Rochester ME1 . . . . 53 C2
Dickens Way ⑱ ME15 . . 189 A2
Dickens World★ ME4 . . . 54 A8
Dickley La ME17 . . . . 120 A6
Dickson Rd SE18 . . . . 11 C6
Dickson St SE9 . . . . 11 E4
Digdog La TN12, TN17 . . 166 D3
Diggerland★ ME2 . . . . . . 52 F4
Dignals Cl ME8 . . . . 55 D5
Dilhorne Ct SE12 . . . . 28 B5
Dillon Way TN2 . . . . 159 D7
Dillywood Cotts ME3 . . . 38 F2
Dilly Wood Fields ME3 . . 39 A3
Dillywood La ME3 . . . . . . 38 F2
Dimmock Cl TN12 . . . . . 146 B7
Dingleden La TN17 . . . . . 190 F2
Dippers Cl TN11 . . . . 7 B2
Discovery Dr ME19 . . . . . 97 B3
Discovery Prim Sch SE28 . 2 E6
Discovery Rd ME15 . . . . 101 B2
Discovery Sch The ME18 . 97 D3
Dislingbury Rd TN11 . . . 144 C4
Disraeli Cl
  Maidstone ME15 . . . . . . 116 C5
  Woolwich SE28 . . . . 3 C5
Dittisham Rd SE9 . . . . 28 E4
DITTON 82 C1
Ditton CE Jun Sch ME20 . 82 C1
Ditton Court Cl ME20 . . . 82 B1
Ditton Pl ME20 . . . . 82 B1
Ditton Heritage Ctr &
  Victorian Classroom★ ◼
  ME20 . . . . 82 C1
Ditton Inf Sch ME20 . . . . 82 C1
Ditton Rd DA6 . . . . 14 A2
Dixon Cl
  Maidstone ME15 . . . . 99 F2
  ④ Newham E6 . . . . 1 F7
Dixon Ho SE2 . . . . 3 C1
Dixwell Cl ME8 . . . . 69 D5
Dobell Rd SE9 . . . . 11 F2
Dobells TN17 . . . . 179 D4
Dobson Rd DA12 . . . . 36 F2
Dock Approach Rd RM17 . 18 E8
Dock Head Rd
  Chatham ME4 . . . . 54 A8
  St Mary's Island ME4 . . . 40 A1
Docklands Light Railway
  E16 . . . . 1 E8
Dockland St E16 . . . . 2 A5
Dock Rd
  Chatham ME4 . . . . 53 F6
  Grays RM17 . . . . 18 D8
  Tilbury RM18 . . . . 18 F1
Dockside Outlet Ctr ME4 . 54 A8
Dockside Rd E16 . . . . 1 F6
Doctor Hope's Rd TN17 . 179 D4
Doddington Cl ME16 . . . . 99 F5
Doddington Rd ME8 . . . . 55 D3
Dodd Rd TN10 . . . . 127 C5
Dog Cotts RH19 . . . . 154 B1
Doggetts Cl SE26 . . . . . . 138 C8

Doggetts Row ME3 . . . . . . 27 B6
Dogwood Cl
  Chatham ME5 . . . . 68 D1
  Northfleet DA11 . . . . 35 F4
Dolphin Cl SE28 . . . . 3 D7
Dolphin Dr ME8 . . . . 69 E5
Dolphin Ho ME1 . . . . 53 C3
Dombey Cl
  Higham ME3 . . . . 38 C3
  Rochester ME1 . . . . 53 C3
Domonic Dr SE9 . . . . 29 B5
Donald Biggs Dr DA12 . . 36 D8
Donaldson Rd SE18 . . . . . 12 A6
Donald Troup Ho ME1 . . . 53 C4
Doncaster Cl ⑦ ME15 . . 116 F6
Donet Cl ME8 . . . . 69 C5
Dongola Rd ME2 . . . . 39 B1
Donkey Field TN11 . . . . . 125 E1
Donkey La DA4 . . . . 61 B8
Donnington Ct ⑪ DA2 . . 16 B1
Donnington Rd TN13 . . . . 99 D1
Doon Brae TN4 . . . . 143 A2
Dorado Gdns BR6 . . . . 58 D7
Doran Gr SE18 . . . . 12 F7
Dorchester Cl
  Cliffe Woods ME3 . . . . . . 39 B7
  Dartford DA1 . . . . 32 F7
  Orpington BR5 . . . . 38 A6
Dorchester Rd DA12 . . . . 36 D5
Dorcis Ave DA7 . . . . 13 E5
Doria Dr DA12 . . . . 36 F5
Doric Ave TN4 . . . . 142 F1
Doric Cl TN4 . . . . 142 F1
Dorin Ct TN2 . . . . 159 C3
Doris Ave DA8 . . . . 14 C6
Dorking Rd ME1 . . . . 159 C6
Dormers Dr DA13 . . . . 50 B2
Dornberg Cl SE3 . . . . 11 A7
Dornberg Rd SE3 . . . . 11 A6
Dorndon Dr TN3 . . . . 158 A4
Dornden Gdns ME5 . . . . . 68 B2
Dorne Cotts TN27 . . . . . . 137 C6
Dorney Rise BR5 . . . . 43 F5
Dorothy Ave TN17 . . . . . 179 E4
Dorothy Evans Cl DA7 . . 14 B3
Dorrit Way
  Chislehurst BR7 . . . . 29 C2
  Rochester ME1 . . . . 53 D2
Dorset Ave DA16 . . . . 12 F3
Dorset Cotts TN7 . . . . . . 170 B4
Dorset Cres DA12 . . . . 36 E4
Dorset Rd
  Bromley SE9 . . . . 28 E6
  Royal Tunbridge Wells
  TN2 . . . . 159 D2
Dorset Road Inf Sch SE9 . 28 E6
Dorset Sq ME8 . . . . 55 D1
Dorset Sq TN13 . . . . 92 C2
Dorset Way ME15 . . . . . . 116 C8
Dorton Coll of FE TN15 . . 92 F5
Dorton Dr TN15 . . . . 92 F5
Dorton House Sch (for the
  Blind) TN15 . . . . 92 F5
Dorville Rd SE12 . . . . 11 A2
Dothill Rd SE18 . . . . 12 C7
Dotterel Cl ME5 . . . . 68 D2
Doubleton La TN11 . . . . . 141 A4
Douglas Almshouses
  ME17 . . . . 120 D5
Douglas Bldgs TN12 . . . . 149 E5
Douglas Cl TN16 . . . . 72 E2
Douglas Rd
  Bexley DA16 . . . . 13 B6
  Lenham ME17 . . . . 120 D5
  Maidstone ME16 . . . . 99 E3
  ⑥ Newham E16 . . . . 1 A8
  Tonbridge TN9 . . . . 143 B7
Doug Siddons Ct ⑫ RM17 18 C8
Douro Stables ME4 . . . . . 159 A4
Doust Way ME1 . . . . 53 D5
Dove App E6 . . . . 1 E8
Dove Cl ME5 . . . . 68 B6
Dovedale Cl DA16 . . . . 13 A5
Dovedale Rd DA2 . . . . 33 C7
Doveney Cl BR5 . . . . 44 D6
Dover Cl DA2 . . . . 33 C2
Dover Ho
  ② Maidstone ME15 . . . . 116 E8
  Rochester ME2 . . . . 39 C1
Dover Patrol SE3 . . . . 11 B5
Dover Rd
  Northfleet DA11 . . . . 35 D8
  Woolwich DA16 . . . . 12 C5
  Dover Road Com Prim Sch
  DA11 . . . . 35 E7
Dover Road E DA11 . . . . . 35 F7
Dover St ME16 . . . . 99 C2
Doves Cl BR2 . . . . 56 B8
Dowding Ho TN16 . . . . . 145 F6
Dowding Rd TN16 . . . . . . 72 D2
Dowding Way TN2 . . . . . 143 E1
Dowding Wlk DA11 . . . . . 35 F5
Dower Ho The DA14 . . . . 30 F5
Dower House Cres TN4 . 142 E3
Dowgate Cl TN9 . . . . 143 D7
Dowlerville Rd BR6 . . . . . 57 F4
Dowling Cl ME6 . . . . 81 E7
Dowling Ho DA17 . . . . 3 F3
Downage The DA11 . . . . . 36 A6
Downash Ct TN5 . . . . 187 A3
Downash Ho TN5 . . . . . . 187 A3
Down Ave TN3 . . . . 176 A4
Downbank Ave DA7 . . . . . 14 D5
Downderry Lavender
  Nursery★ TN11 . . . . . . 111 D5
Downderry Way ME20 . . 82 B1

DOWNE 73 A8
Downe Ave TN14 . . . . 73 D8
Downe Cl DA16 . . . . 13 C7
Downe Ho ⑩ SE7 . . . . 11 C8
Downend 12 B7
Downe Prim Sch BR6 . . . . 73 A8
Downer Ct ME1 . . . . 67 E8
Downe Rd
  Cudham BR6, TN14 . . . . . 73 C5
  Farthing Street BR2 . . . . . 56 E2
Downham Way BR1 . . . . . 28 A6
Down House Mus★ BR6 . . 73 A7
Downings E6 . . . . 2 A7
Down La TN3 . . . . 173 B1
Downlands ME17 . . . . . . 119 F6
Downland Wlk ME5 . . . . . 68 A5
Downleys Cl SE9 . . . . 28 F6
Downman Rd SE9 . . . . 11 E4
Downs Ave
  Bromley BR7 . . . . 28 F3
  Dartford DA1 . . . . 33 A8
Downs Cl ME14 . . . . 100 B8
Down's Ct TN12 . . . . 151 E5
Downs Cl ME18 . . . . 114 B3
Downside ME2 . . . . 53 A7
Downsland Ho ME2 . . . . . 52 C2
Downs Rd
  Istead Rise DA13 . . . . 35 D3
  Maidstone ME14 . . . . . . 100 B8
  Yalding ME18 . . . . 114 A1
Downs View ME5 . . . . 67 D1
Downs Valley DA3 . . . . . . 48 E5
Downsview
  Chatham ME5 . . . . 68 C8
  Trottiscliffe ME19 . . . . . . 80 A5
Downs View
  Burham ME1 . . . . 66 F1
  West Malling ME19 . . . . . 97 B8
Downsview Cl BR8 . . . . . . 45 F6
Downs View Cl BR6 . . . . . 58 C1
Downsview Prim Sch BR8 46 A6
Downsview Rd TN13 . . . . 91 F2
Downs View Rd ME14 . . 100 B8
Downsway BR6 . . . . 57 E5
Downsway Cl DA3 . . . . . . 79 F8
Downton Cotts TN18 . . . 195 F4
Doyle Cl DA8 . . . . 14 B6
Doyle Way RM18 . . . . 19 C5
Drage Rd TN12 . . . . 129 E6
Drake Cres SE28 . . . . 3 C7
Drake Ct BR5 . . . . 44 B3
Drake Hall E16 . . . . 1 B5
Drake Mews ⑨ BR2 . . . . . 42 C5
Drake Point ⑫ DA8 . . . . . 4 E1
Drake's Ave ME2 . . . . 52 F8
Drake's Ave ME2 . . . . 52 F8
Draper Cl DA17 . . . . 3 F2
Draper Ct BR1 . . . . 42 E5
Draper St ⑧ TN4 . . . . . . 142 F2
Drawbridge Cl ME15 . . . 116 E8
Drawell Cl SE18 . . . . 2 E1
Dray Corner Rd TN27 . . . 150 F7
Dray Ct TN11 . . . . 128 E8
Drays Cotts DA4 . . . . 47 B5
Drayton Ave BR6 . . . . 43 B1
Drayton Cl ME23 . . . . 23 E4
Drayton Rd TN9 . . . . 143 C8
Drewery Dr ME8 . . . . 69 C5
Drew Prim Sch E16 . . . . . . 1 E5
Drew Rd E16 . . . . 1 E5
Driffield Gdns TN9 . . . . . 142 F7
Drift The BR2 . . . . 56 D7
Drive The
  Ashurst TN3 . . . . 156 F5
  Bexley DA5 . . . . 30 D8
  Chislehurst BR7 . . . . 43 E8
  Erith DA8 . . . . 14 B8
  Gravesend DA12 . . . . 36 E4
  New Barn DA3 . . . . 49 B6
  Orpington BR6 . . . . 57 F8
  Royal Tunbridge Wells
  TN2 . . . . 159 B1
  Sevenoaks TN13 . . . . 92 B3
  Sidcup DA14 . . . . 30 B4
  St Paul's Cray BR7 . . . . . 43 F6
  Tonbridge TN9 . . . . 143 B7
Dryden Ct TN10 . . . . 127 C4
Dryden Rd DA16 . . . . 127 C4
Dryden Pl RM18 . . . . 19 B6
Dryden Rd DA16 . . . . 12 F6
Dryden Way BR6 . . . . 44 A1
DRYHILL 82 C3
Dryhill La TN14 . . . . 91 B3
Dryhill Nature Reserve★
  TN14 . . . . 91 B3
Dryhill Park Cres TN10 . 127 C3
Dryhill Rd DA17 . . . . 7 F8
Dryland Ave ⑥ BR6 . . . . 57 F6
Dryland Rd
  Borough Green TN15 . . . . 94 F6
  Snodland ME6 . . . . 81 F8
Dublin Ho ⑩ ME15 . . . . 116 F7
Duchess Cl ME2 . . . . 52 E8
Duchess of Kent Ct The
  ME20 . . . . 82 B3
Duchess of Kent Dr ME5 . 68 B3
Duchess' Wlk TN15 . . . . . 92 E2
Ducie Ho ⑨ SE7 . . . . 11 C8
Ducketts Rd DA1 . . . . 14 F2
Duddington Cl SE9 . . . . . 28 D4
Dudley Rd DA11 . . . . 35 E8

udley Cl ME15...........116 F5
udley Keen Ct TN9...143 E8
udley Lodge TN2 ....159 C4
udley Rd TN1...........159 A4
udsbury Rd
Dartford DA1..............15 B2
Sidcup DA14............30 B2
uggan Dr BR7............28 E2
uke of Wellington Ave SE18,
SE28......................2 C3
ukes Meadow TN11...124 F2
ukes Meadow Dr ME7..68 F6
ukes Orch SE3............31 C7
ukes Rd TN1............159 C5
ukes Wlk 7 ME15 ....100 A4
ulverton Prim Sch SE9..29 D6
ulverton Rd SE9..........29 D6
ulwich Prep Sch TN7..180 A4
umbourne La TN30 ...193 D2
umbreck Rd SE9........12 A4
unbar Ct BR2.............42 A5
unblane Rd SE9...........11 E5
uncan Ho 2 SE7 ....11 B8
uncannon Place 2 DA9..17 C3
uncan Rd ME7.............89 D1
uncroft SE18...............12 E7
undale Rd TN12, TN3...161 A3
undonald Cl 7..............1 E7
unedin Ho
9 Maidstone ME15 ...116 E5
Newham E16 ....1 F5
2 Tilbury RM18 ....19 A5
unkeld Ho 6 ME15 ....100 A7
unkeld Rd SE9............28 E5
unkin Rd DA1............16 A3
unkirk Cl DA12..........36 C3
unkirk Dr ME5...........67 F6
unkley Villas TN15......79 F1
UNK'S GREEN.............111 A6
unk's Green Rd TN11...111 A5
unlin Dr ME4.............40 C2
unlop Ct 7 TN18......109 A2
unlop Rd RM18.........18 F6
unning's La ME1.........53 C4
unnings The ME16......99 A2
unn Lodge TN2..........159 D2
unnock Rd E6...............1 E7
unnose Ct RM19.........16 B8
UNN STREET..............85 A8
un Street Rd ME7.......85 A8
unoon Cotts BR6........73 A5
unorlan Farm ME2....159 E4
unorlan Farm Cotts
TN2.......................159 E4
unstable Ct 3 SE3.....11 A7
unstall Welling Est
DA16.....................13 B5
unstan Glade BR5......43 D3
unstan Gr TN4..........159 B6
unstan Rd TN4..........159 B6
unstan Ct 10 DA2......16 B1
unster Terr 3 ME15..116 E8
UNTON GREEN..........91 E8
unton Green Prim Sch
TN13.....................91 E7
unton Green Sta TN13.91 E7
unvegan Rd SE9.........11 F3
unwich Rd DA7..........13 F6
upree Rd SE7..............1 B1
urant Rd BR8.............32 A2
urban Ho 7 ME15.....116 E5
URGATES.................184 E5
urham Cl ME15.........100 C1
urham Rd
Bromley BR2.............42 A5
Gillingham ME8.........69 C7
Sidcup DA14............30 B3
urham Rise SE18.........2 D1
uriun Way DA8..........15 B7
urley Gdns ME4.........53 D2
urlings Orch TN15......94 D6
urndale La DA11........35 A8
URRANT GREEN.......183 B6
urrant Way
Orpington BR6..........57 D8
Swanscombe DA10....35 D5
urrell Gdns ME5........54 C1
ursley Cl SE3.............11 C5
ursley Gdns SE3........11 D6
ursley Rd SE3 ....11 C5
urval Dr ME1.............67 E8
uvard's Pl ME9..........71 F1
uxberry Cl BR2..........42 E4
ux Court Rd ME23.....23 D2
uxford Ho 12 SE2.......3 D4
ux Hill TN15............110 F8
ux La TN15...............94 F1
welly La TN8............121 D3
yke Dr BR5...............44 C2
ykewood Cl DA5.........31 E5
ylan Rd DA17.............4 A3
ymchurch Cl BR6......57 E6
yneley Rd SE12.........28 C5
ynes Rd TN15............76 E2
ynevor Rd TN4.........159 C7

Eaglestone Cl TN15 .....95 A8
Eagle Way DA11.........18 A2
Ealdham Prim Sch SE9...11 C3
Ealdham Sq SE9.........11 C3
Ealing Cl ME5.............68 C4
Eardemont Cl DA1......14 F3
Eardley Point 7 SE18...2 B2
Eardley Rd
Erith DA17.................4 A1
Sevenoaks TN13.........92 B3
Earl Cl ME5................68 B4
Earl Rd DA11.............35 E6
Earl Rise SE18..............2 D2
Earlshall Rd SE9.........12 A3
Earl's Rd TN4...........158 F4
Earl St ME14.............99 F4
Eason Villas TN12....148 D6
EAST BARMING 98 F1
East Beckton District Ctr
E6.........................2 A7
East Borough Prim Sch
ME14....................100 B5
Eastbrook Rd SE3......11 B6
Eastbury Rd
Newham E6 ....2 A8
Orpington BR5..........43 D3
East Cliff Rd TN4.....159 A6
Eastcombe Ave SE7...11 B8
Eastcote Rd DA16.....12 D5
Eastcote BR6..............43 F1
Eastcote Rd DA16, DA16...12 D4
Eastcourt La
Gillingham, Lower Twydal ME7,
ME8......................55 C5
Gillingham ME8.........55 C5
East Crescent Rd DA12..19 C1
East Cross TN30.......193 B7
East Ct 6 ME15 ....100 A1
East Dr BR5...............44 B3
EAST END
Benenden................181 C3
Headcorn................152 B4
East End Rd ME4, ME7...54 F6
Easterfields ME19......98 C5
Eastern Ave RM20......16 F8
Eastern Rd ME7.........54 F6
Eastern Way
Erith SE28..................3 D5
1 Grays RM17..........18 A8
EAST FARLEIGH........115 B7
East Farleigh Prim Sch
ME15....................115 B6
East Farleigh Sta ME16..115 B8
Eastfield Gdns TN10...127 E5
Eastfield Ho ME16 .....99 B2
Eastgate ME1............53 C5
Eastgate Cl SE28........3 D7
Eastgate St ME1.........53 C5
Eastgate Rd TN30....193 C8
Eastgate Terr ME1......53 C5
East Hall Hill ME17...133 E7
East Hall Rd BR5........44 F2
EAST HILL 61 B1
East Hill
Biggin Hill TN16........72 B1
Dartford DA1............32 F8
Sutton at Hone DA4...47 D7
Tenterden TN30.......193 B8
East Hill Dr DA1.........32 F8
East Hill Farm Pk TN15..61 B1
East Hill Rd TN15......77 B7
East Ho DA1..............15 F4
East Holme DA8..........14 C6
East Kent Ave DA11...18 C1
East La DA4...............47 D7
Eastland Cl 3 TN4.....42 C7
Eastlands Rd TN4.....158 E1
Eastleigh Rd DA7......14 C4
Eastling Cl ME8..........55 D3
Easting Ho 8 BR5......44 D1
EAST MALLING..........98 A7
EAST MALLING HEATH...97 E4
East Malling Research
ME19....................98 C6
East Malling Sta ME19.98 A6
East Mascalls 17 SE7...11 C8
Eastmead Cl BR1......42 E7
East Mill DA11............18 F1
East Milton Rd DA12...36 D8
East Row ME1...........53 C5
Eastry Cl ME15...........99 C7
Eastry Rd DA8...........14 A7
East St
Addington ME19........80 D3
Bexley DA7...............14 A3
Bromley BR1.............42 A7
Chatham ME4............54 A3
Gillingham ME7.........54 D6
Grays RM20.............17 E8

East St continued
Harrietsham ME17........119 E5
Hunton ME15.............131 F7
Snodland ME6 ....82 B8
Tonbridge TN9 ....127 C2
EAST STREET 80 E3
East Street N TN19 ....80 D3
East Sutton Park (HM Young
Offender Inst & Prison)
ME17....................135 B7
East Sutton Rd ME17,
TN27.....................135 C4
East Ter
Gravesend DA12 ....19 C1
Sidcup DA15............29 E7
East Thamesmead Bsns Pk
DA18......................3 F4
East Thurrock Rd RM17..18 C8
EAST TILBURY..........20 C7
Eastview ME4.............40 B2
Eastview Ave SE18 ....12 E7
Eastway BR2.............42 A2
East Weald Dr TN30..183 B1
Eastwell 5 TN30.......193 A7
Eastwell Barn Mews
TN30.....................193 A8
Eastwell Cl
Maidstone ME14 ......100 A5
Sidcup DA15............29 E7
EASTWOOD..............136 C6
Eastwood Rd ME17...136 C5
East Woodside DA5....30 E7
Eaton Cl BR7.............29 C2
Eaton Rd DA14...........30 C6
Eaton Sq DA3............48 D6
Ebbsfleet Ind Est DA11..18 A2
Ebbsfleet Int Domestic Sta
DA11.....................18 B1
Ebbsfleet Wlk DA11....18 B1
Ebdon Way S13 ....11 B4
Ebony Wlk ME16 ....99 B3
Ebury Rd BR2............56 E7
Ebury Sq ME12 ....36 C6
Eclipse Rd E13............1 B8
Edam Ct 11 DA14......30 A5
Eddington Cl ME15....116 B6
Edelin Rd ME14.........101 A5
Eden Ave ME5............68 A7
EDENBRIDGE
122 D1
138 D8
Edenbridge Cl BR5.....44 D5
Paddock Wood TN12 ..145 E6
Edenbridge Hospl
TN8......................122 D1
Edenbridge L Ctr TN8..122 C2
Edenbridge Prim Sch
TN8......................122 D1
Edenbridge Sta TN8...122 C3
Edenbridge Town Sta
TN8......................122 D2
Edenbridge Trad Ctr
TN8......................138 D8
Edenbridge War Meml Hospl
TN8......................138 D7
Eden Cl DA5..............31 D4
Eden Ct
1 Hawkhurst TN18....188 F2
10 Orpington BR5......44 D1
Tonbridge TN10.......127 C5
Edendale Rd DA7......14 D5
Eden Farm La ME19....97 D8
Edenhurst TN13.........92 A2
Eden Pl DA12............36 B8
Eden Rd
High Halstow ME23....23 E4
Joyden's Wood DA5...31 D4
Royal Tunbridge Wells
TN1......................159 A2
Edensmuir Ct SE3.......11 A7
Eden Valley Mus* TN8..122 C1
Eden Villas TN8.........138 D7
Eden Wlk ME19..........97 D3
Eden Wlk 8 TN1.......159 A2
Edgar Cl
Kings Hill ME19 ....97 B3
Swanley BR8.............45 F6
Edgar Rd
Kemsing TN15...........76 E2
Tatsfield TN16 ....88 D6
Edgeborough Way BR1..42 D8
Edgebury BR7, SE9.....29 B4
Edgebury Prim Sch BR7..29 C4
Edgefield Cl DA1.........33 B7
Edge Hill SE18...........12 B8
Edge Hill Ct DA14......29 F4
Edgehill Gdns DA13...49 F8
Edgehill Rd BR7..........29 C4
Edgeler Ct ME6...........81 F7
Edger Pl 5 ME15......100 A4
Edgeway ME4............40 B2
Edgewood Dr BR6......58 A5
Edgeworth Rd SE9 ....11 D3
Edgington Way DA14...30 D1
Edinburgh Ct DA8.......14 D7
Edinburgh Mews RM18..19 B5

Edinburgh Rd
Chatham ME4............54 C2
Gillingham ME7 ....54 D5
Grain ME3................27 B5
Edinburgh Sq ME15 ...116 C7
Edington Rd SE2.........3 B3
Edisbury Wlk ME8......69 D5
Edison Gr SE18 ....12 F7
Edison Rd
Bexley DA16.............12 F6
2 Bromley BR2........42 A7
Edith Cavell Way SE18..11 E6
Edith Ct BR1.............42 D6
Edith Pond Ct SE9.....29 B6
Edith Rd BR6............58 A5
Ediva Rd DA13...........50 A4
Edmund Cl
Maidstone ME16 ......99 A3
Meopham Station DA13..50 A4
Edmund Hurst Dr E6 ...2 B8
Edmund Rd
Bexley DA16.............13 A4
Orpington BR5..........44 C3
Edmunds Ave BR5......44 D6
Edna Rd ME14...........99 F8
Edward Alderton Theatre*
DA7......................13 D4
Edward Ct
Chatham ME5............54 C1
2 Newham E16 ....1 A8
Edward Harvey Ct DA17..3 F1
Edward Rd
Biggin Hill TN16........72 E1
Bromley BR1.............28 C1
Chislehurst BR7.........29 B3
Edwards Cl ME8.........69 C5
Edwards Ct DA4.........60 E7
Edwards Gdns BR8.....45 D5
Edwards Rd DA17.........4 A2
Edward St
Chatham ME4............54 A3
Rochester ME2...........53 B7
Royal Tunbridge Wells
TN4......................158 F8
Edward Tyler Rd SE12..28 C6
Edward Wlk ME17......97 F8
Edwin Arnold Ct DA15..29 F8
Edwin Cl DA7.............13 F8
Edwin Petty Pl DA2....33 C8
Edwin Rd
Dartford DA2............32 C5
Gillingham ME8.........69 C8
Edwins Pl ME9...........71 C7
Edwin St
Gravesend DA12 ....36 B8
Newham E16 ....1 A8
Egdean Wlk TN13.......92 C4
EGERTON................137 F4
Egerton Ave BR8........45 F8
Egerton CE Prim Sch
TN27....................137 F3
Egerton Cl DA1...........32 B7
EGERTON FORSTAL...137 D1
Egerton House Rd TN27..137 E4
Egerton Rd ME14.........99 E4
Eggpie La TN11, TN14...125 E7
Egham Rd E13............1 B8
Eglantine La DA4........47 B3
Eglinton Hill SE18......12 B7
Eglinton Prim Sch SE18..12 A8
Eglinton Rd
Swanscombe DA10....17 F1
Woolwich SE18 ....12 B8
Egremont Rd ME15...100 F2
Egret Ct ME4.............40 B2
Eileen Ct BR7............29 A3
Eisenhower Dr E6 ....1 E8
Elaine Ave SE2...........52 E7
Elaine Ct ME2............52 E6
Elaine Prim Sch ME2...52 E6
Elbourne Trad Est DA17..4 B3
Elbury Dr E16.............1 A7
Elder Cl
Kingswood ME17......118 D2
Sidcup DA15............29 F7
Elder Ct ME8.............69 B6
Elderslie Rd SE9........12 A2
Eldon St ME4.............54 A4
Eldon Way TN12.......145 F7
Eldred Dr BR5...........58 D8
Eleanor Cl ME8..........69 C3
Eleanor Wlk 10 SE18...11 F2
Elford Cl SE3.............11 C3
Elford Rd ME4............22 B5
Elgal Cl BR6..............57 B5
Elgar Cl TN10...........127 E6
Elgar Gdns RM18.......19 B6
Elgin Gdns ME2..........52 D5
Elham Cl
Bromley BR1.............28 D1
Gillingham ME8.........55 B3
Elibank Rd SE9...........12 A3
Eling Ct ME15...........116 A8
Eliot Rd DA1..............16 B2
Elizabeth Cl RM18.....19 B5
Elizabeth Cotts DA4...60 E8
Elizabeth Ct
Chatham ME5............68 A7
Dartford DA2............33 D3
Erith DA8.................14 D7
Gillingham ME8.........55 C1
6 Gravesend DA11 ....19 A1
Elizabeth Fry Pl SE18...11 E6
Elizabeth Garlick Ct 1
TN1......................159 B4

Elizabeth Garrett Anderson
Ho 9 DA17...............4 A3
Elizabeth Ho
Maidstone ME14 ......100 A6
Rochester ME1...........53 C4
Elizabeth Huggins Cotts
DA11.....................36 B6
Elizabeth Pl DA4..........46 E3
Elizabeth Smith's Ct ME19..97 F7
Elizabeth St DA9........16 E2
Elizabeth Terr SE9......11 F1
Elizabeth Way BR5.....44 C6
Eliza Cook Cl DA9.......17 B3
Ellard Ct DA16............13 C4
Ellenborough Rd DA14..30 E3
Ellen Cl BR1..............42 D6
Ellen's Pl ME9...........71 C6
Ellenswood Cl ME15...101 A1
Ellen Wilkinson Prim Sch
E6..........................1 E8
Ellerman Rd RM18.......18 F5
Ellerslie DA12............36 D8
Ellerslie Ct 3 DA12...36 D8
Ellesmere Ct SE12......28 A7
Ellingham Leas ME15..116 C2
Elliott Rd BR2............42 D5
Elliotts La TN16..........90 C3
Elliott St DA12..........36 D8
Ellis Cl
Eltham SE9...............29 C6
Five Oak Green TN12...145 B7
Swanley BR8.............45 D5
Elliscombe Mount SE7..11 C8
Elliscombe Rd SE7.....11 C8
Ellis Cl DA1...............33 B7
Ellis Ho 8 ME14........100 B4
Ellison Rd DA15.........29 D7
Elliston Ho 8 SE18 ......2 A2
Ellis Way DA1............32 F6
Elm Ave
Chatham ME4............53 E1
Chattenden ME3........40 A4
Elmbank Dr BR1.........42 D7
Elmbourne Dr DA17 .....4 B2
Elmbrook Gdns SE9....11 E3
Elm Cl
Dartford DA1............32 C7
Egerton TN27...........137 F3
Higham ME3............38 C3
Elm Cotts BR8 ....46 B8
Elm Court Ind Est ME7..68 E3
Elm Cres ME19...........97 F8
Elmcroft Ave DA15.....13 A1
Elmcroft Rd BR6........44 A2
Elmdene Rd SE18 ....2 B1
Elm Dr BR8...............45 D7
Elmfield
Gillingham ME8.........55 A3
Tenterden TN30.......193 B8
Elmfield Cl
Gravesend DA11 ....36 B7
Sevenoaks Weald TN14..108 B2
Elmfield Ct
Bexley DA16.............13 B6
Coxheath ME17.........115 C3
Tenterden TN30.......193 B8
Elmfield Pk BR1.........42 A6
Elmfield Rd BR1.........42 A6
Elm Gr
Erith DA8.................14 D7
Maidstone ME15 ......100 B3
Orpington BR6..........43 F1
Tonbridge TN11.......126 F5
Elmhurst
Bexley DA17.............13 E8
Swanscombe DA9......17 B1
Elmhurst Ave TN2.....160 D8
Elmhurst Gdns ME4....53 E3
Elmhurst Rd SE9........28 E5
Elmington Cl DA5.......14 B1
Elm La TN10.............127 C3
Elmlea Dr BR7...........28 F2
Elmley Cl 10 E6 ....1 E8
Elmley St SE18............2 D2
Elm Par 10 DA14........30 A4
Elm Rd
Dartford DA1............32 D2
Erith DA8.................15 A6
Gillingham ME7.........54 E6
Gravesend DA12 ....36 C5
Grays RM17.............18 C8
Hoo St Werburgh ME3..40 E3
Orpington BR6..........58 A3
Royal Tunbridge Wells
TN4......................142 F1
Sidcup DA14............30 A4
Stone DA7...............16 E1
Westerham TN16.......89 E2
Elmshurst Gdns TN10..127 C7
Elmslie Ct SE12.........12 A1
ELMSTEAD...............28 D2
Elmstead Ave BR7......28 F3
Elmstead Cl TN13......91 E5
Elmstead Glade BR7....28 F2
Elmstead La BR7........28 F3
Elmstead Rd DA8.......14 E6
Elmstead Woods Sta BR7..28 E2
Elmsted Cres DA16.....13 C8
Elmstone Cl ME16......99 B2
ELMSTONE HOLE.......136 E8
Elmstone Hole Rd
Fairbourne Heath ME17..119 D1
Platt's Heath ME17 ....136 D8
Elmstone La ME16......99 B2
Elmstone Rd ME8........69 D7

Elmstone Terr 🖫 BR5 . . . 44 C5
Elm Terr
　🖫 Eltham SE9 . . . . 12 A1
　West Thurrock RM20 . . . . 17 B8
Elmtree Cotts TN14 . . . . 74 D4
Elm Tree Cotts ME3 . . . . 25 A3
Elm Tree Ct 🖫 SE7 . . . . 11 C8
Elm Tree Dr ME1 . . . . . . 53 A2
Elm Wlk
　Aylesford ME20 . . . . 82 E1
　Orpington BR6 . . . . 56 F7
Elmwood Dr DA5 . . . . . . 30 E8
Elmwood Rd ME3 . . . . . 39 F6
ELPHICKS 177 A8
Elphick's Pl TN2 . . . . . . 173 B8
Elrick Cl DA8 . . . . 14 E8
Elsa Rd DA16 . . . . 13 C5
Elsinore Ho 🖫 SE18 . . . . . 1 E2
Elster Pl ME19 . . . . 97 B3
Elstow Cl SE9 . . . . 12 B1
Elstree Gdns DA17 . . . . . 3 E2
Elswyn Ho 🖫 DA14 . . . . 30 A5
Elwyn Gdns SE12 . . . . . . 28 A8
Ely Cl
　Erith DA8 . . . . 14 F5
　Gillingham ME8 . . . . 55 E2
Ely Ct TN1 . . . . 159 B4
Ely Gdns TN10 . . . . 127 D4
Elysian Ave BR5 . . . . 43 F3
Embassy Cl ME7 . . . . 54 F1
Embassy Ct
　Bexley DA16 . . . . 13 B4
　Sidcup DA14 . . . . 30 B5
Ember Cl BR5 . . . . 43 C2
Emblin Ct 🖫 DA14 . . . . . 30 A4
Emerald Cl
　Newham E16 . . . . 1 E7
　Rochester ME1 . . . . 67 D7
Emersons Ave BR8 . . . . . 31 F1
Emerton Cl DA6 . . . . 13 E3
Emes Rd DA8 . . . . 8 C7
EM Forster Theatre★
　TN9 . . . . 127 C2
Emily Jackson Cl TN13 . . 92 B3
Emily Jackson Ho TN13 . . 92 B3
Emily Rd ME5 . . . . 61 E1
Emmanuel Ho 🖫 SE18 . . . 2 D1
Emmet Hill La ME18 . . . 130 F5
Emmetts Garden★ TN14 106 D5
Emmetts La TN14, TN16 . 106 D6
Emmetts Rd TN16 . . . . . 106 C5
Empire Rd ME2 . . . . 52 F5
Empire Walk DA17 . . . . . 4 B2
Empress Dr BR7 . . . . 29 B2
Empress Rd DA12 . . . . . . 36 E8
Emsworth Gr ME14 . . . . 100 D6
Endeavour Foyer The 🖫
　ME4 . . . . 48 A7
Enderfield Ct BR7 . . . . . . 43 A8
Engineer Cl SE18 . . . . . . 12 A8
Englefield Cl BR5 . . . . . . 43 F5
Englefield Cres
　Cliffe Woods ME3 . . . . . . 39 B7
　Orpington BR5 . . . . 44 A5
English Martyrs RC Prim Sch
　🖫 ME2 . . . . 53 B8
Ennerdale Ho ME15 . . . 116 F7
Ennerdale Rd DA7 . . . . . 14 A6
Ennis Rd SE18 . . . . 12 C8
Enfield Rd
　Leigh TN11 . . . . 125 E1
　Tonbridge TN11 . . . . . . 142 A6
Ensign Ho RM17 . . . . 7 B8
Enslin Rd SE9 . . . . 29 A8
Enterprise Bsns Est ME2 . 53 D7
Enterprise Cl ME2 . . . . . 53 D8
Enterprise Ctr The ME5 . . 84 C8
Enterprise Rd ME15 . . . 100 A1
Enterprise Way TN8 . . . 122 C3
Epaul La ME1 . . . . 53 C6
Eppe Cl 🖫 ME2 . . . . 53 B8
Epsom Cl
　Bexley DA7 . . . . 14 B4
　Maidstone ME15 . . . . . 116 F6
　West Malling ME19 . . . . 97 B8
Epstein Rd SE28 . . . . 3 B5
Erebus Dr SE28 . . . . 9 C8
Erica Cl TN2 . . . . 158 F1
Eridge Ct TN2 . . . . 158 F1
ERIDGE GREEN 172 B3
Eridge Green Cl BR5 . . . . 44 C1
Eridge Rd
　Groombridge TN3 . . . . . 171 D5
　Royal Tunbridge Wells TN2,
　TN4 . . . . 158 E1

Eridge Sta TN3 . . . . 171 E2
Erindale SE18 . . . . 12 D8
Erindale Terr SE18 . . . . . 12 D8
ERITH 4 C1
Erith & District Hospl
　DA8 . . . . 14 D8
Erith High St DA8 . . . . . . 4 E1
Erith Mus★ DA8 . . . . 4 E1
Erith Playhouse★ DA8 . . . 4 F1
Erith Rd
　Bexley DA7 . . . . 14 B4
　Erith DA8, DA17 . . . . 4 B1
　Erith Sch DA8 . . . . 14 D7
Erith Small Bsns Ctr 🖫
　DA8 . . . . 14 F8
Erith Sta DA8 . . . . 4 E1
Ermington Rd SE9 . . . . . 29 C6
Ernest Dr ME16 . . . . 99 B5
Ernest Rd ME4 . . . . 54 A3
Erskine Ho 🖫 SE7 . . . . . 11 C8
Erskine Park Rd TN4 . . . 158 C4
Erskine Rd DA13 . . . . . . 80 B8
Erwood Rd SE7 . . . . 1 E1
Escott Gdns SE9 . . . . 28 E4
Escreet Gr SE18 . . . . 2 A2
Eschol Rd ME3 . . . . 41 C6
Esher Cl DA5 . . . . 30 E7
Eskdale Cl DA2 . . . . 33 C7
Eskdale Rd DA7 . . . . 14 A6
Esmonde Ho 🖫 ME7 . . . . 54 A6
Esplanade ME1 . . . . 53 B5
Essenden Rd DA17 . . . . . . 4 A1
Essex Cl TN2 . . . . 172 F8
Essex Rd
　🖫 Dartford DA1 . . . . . . 15 D1
　Gravesend DA11 . . . . . . 36 A7
　Halling ME2 . . . . 66 A6
　Longfield DA3 . . . . 48 D7
　Maidstone ME15 . . . . . 116 E6
　West Thurrock RM20 . . . 17 A8
Estelle Ho ME1 . . . . 67 D7
Estridge Way TN10 . . . . 127 F5
Estuary Cotts RM18 . . . . 20 D7
Estuary Reach ME4 . . . . . 53 F6
Etfield Gr DA14 . . . . 30 B3
Ethelbert Rd
　Bromley BR1 . . . . 42 A6
　Erith DA8 . . . . 14 B4
　Hawley DA2 . . . . 33 D6
　Orpington BR5 . . . . 44 D6
　Rochester ME1 . . . . 53 C4
Ethel Brooks Ho SE18 . . . 12 B8
Ethel-Maud Ct ME7 . . . . 54 D7
Ethel Rd E16 . . . . 1 B7
Ethel Terr BR6 . . . . 58 C2
Etherington Hill TN3 . . . 158 C8
Ethnam La TN18 . . . . . . 196 E4
Ethronvi Rd DA7 . . . . . . 13 E4
Eton Cl ME5 . . . . 67 F4
Eton Ct TN13 . . . . 92 B4
Eton Pl TN18 . . . . 194 F8
Eton Rd BR6 . . . . 58 B6
Eton Way DA1 . . . . 15 C3
Eugenie Mews BR7 . . . . . 43 B8
Europa Pk RM20 . . . . . . 17 C8
Europa Trad Est DA8 . . . . 4 D1
Europe Rd SE18 . . . . 1 F1
Euroway ME20 . . . . 98 E8
Eustace Pl 🖫 SE18 . . . . . 1 F2
Evanlode Ho 🖫 SE2 . . . . . 3 C4
Evans Cl DA9 . . . . 17 A2
Evans Ct SE9 . . . . 28 E6
Eva Rd ME7 . . . . 54 D3
Evelyn Cl ME2 . . . . 53 C8
Evelyn Denington Rd E6 . . 1 F8
Evelyn Ho 🖫 ME2 . . . . . . 53 C8
Evelyn Rd
　Maidstone ME15 . . . . . . 99 E3
　Newham E16 . . . . 1 B5
　Otford TN14 . . . . 76 C2
Evenden Ho TN17 . . . . . 179 D5
Evenden Rd DA13 . . . . . . 50 A2
Everard Ave BR2 . . . . . . 42 A1
Everest Cl 🖫 DA11 . . . . . 35 E5
Everest Ct SE9 . . . . 28 C8
Everest Dr ME3 . . . . 40 E4
Everest La ME2 . . . . 39 B1
Everest Mews ME3 . . . . . 40 E4
Everest Pl BR8 . . . . 40 D5
Everest Rd SE9 . . . . 11 F2
Everett Wlk DA17 . . . . . . 3 F1
Everglade TN16 . . . . 72 D1
Everglade Cl DA3 . . . . . . 48 F5
Everglades The ME7 . . . . 68 F6
Evergreen Cl
　Gillingham ME7 . . . . 69 A5
　Higham ME3 . . . . 38 B3
　Leybourne ME19 . . . . . . 81 E2
Eversfield Ct SE12 . . . . . 28 B6
Eversley Ave DA7, DA8 . . . 14 E5
Eversley Cl ME16 . . . . . . 99 C6
Eversley Cross DA7 . . . . 14 E5
Eversley Rd SE7 . . . . 11 B8
Evesham Rd DA12 . . . . . . 36 D6
Evorg Ho 🖫 ME4 . . . . . . 54 B2
Evry Rd DA14 . . . . 30 C2
Ewart Rd ME4 . . . . 53 E1
Ewehurst La TN3 . . . . . . 157 F6
Ewe & Lamb Mews TN30 199 E3
Ewell Ave ME19 . . . . 97 A8
Ewell La ME15 . . . . 114 D5
Ewins Cl TN12 . . . . 146 A6
ExCeL London★ E16 . . . . 1 B6
Excel Waterfront E16 . . . . 1 B6
Exchange Mews 🖫 TN4 . 159 A5
Exedown Rd TN15 . . . . . 78 C4

Exeter Cl
　Newham E6 . . . . 1 F7
　Tonbridge TN10 . . . . . . 127 D4
Exeter Rd
　Bexley DA16 . . . . 12 F5
　Gravesend DA12 . . . . . . 36 D5
　Newham E16 . . . . 1 A8
Exeter Wlk ME1 . . . . 67 C7
Exford Gdns SE12 . . . . . 28 B7
Exford Rd SE12 . . . . 28 B7
Exmouth Rd
　Bexley DA16 . . . . 13 C7
　Gillingham ME7 . . . . 54 C7
　Grays RM17 . . . . 18 B8
Exton Gdns ME14 . . . . . 68 C2
Exton Rd ME14 . . . . 100 F5
Eye The ME4 . . . . 53 F5
Eyhorne St ME17 . . . . . 102 D2
EYHORNE STREET 102 C2
Eylesden Ct ME14 . . . . . 101 C4
EYNSFORD 60 D7
Eynsford Castle★ DA4 . . . 60 D8
Eynsford Cl BR5 . . . . 43 C3
Eynsford Cres DA5 . . . . . 30 D7
Eynsford Rd
　Crockenhill BR8 . . . . 45 E3
　Eynsford DA4 . . . . 46 F1
　Maidstone ME16 . . . . . . 99 D7
Eynsford Sta DA4 . . . . . . 60 D6
Eynsham Dr SE2 . . . . 3 B3
Eynswood Dr DA14 . . . . . 30 C3

F

Fackenden La TN14 . . . . 76 C7
Factory Rd
　Newham E16 . . . . 1 E5
　Northfleet DA11 . . . . . . 18 C1
Faesten Way DA5 . . . . . . 31 E5
Fagus Cl ME5 . . . . 68 B1
Faircare Pl DA3 . . . . 48 E8
Fair Acres ME2 . . . . 42 A4
Fairbank Ave BR6 . . . . . . 57 B8
FAIRBOURNE HEATH . . 119 B1
Fairbourne Heath Cotts
　ME17 . . . . 119 B1
Fairbourne La ME17 . . . . 119 C4
Fairby La DA3 . . . . 48 E3
Fairby Rd SE12 . . . . 11 D1
Faircrouch La TN5 . . . . . 184 B5
Fairfax Bsns Ctr ME15 . . 116 F4
Fairfax Cl ME8 . . . . 49 C5
Fairfax Gdns SE3 . . . . . . 11 C6
Fairfax Ho ME15 . . . . . . 116 F4
Fairfax Mews E16 . . . . . . 1 B5
Fairfax Rd
　Dartford DA1 . . . . 16 A1
　Tilbury RM18 . . . . 18 F6
Fairfield Ave TN2 . . . . . . 159 C5
Fairfield Cl
　Kemsing TN15 . . . . 77 A1
　Sidcup DA15 . . . . 12 F1
Fairfield Gr SE7 . . . . 11 D8
Fairfield Rd
　Bexley DA7 . . . . 13 F5
　Borough Green TN15 . . . 94 F8
　Bromley BR1 . . . . 28 A1
　Orpington BR5 . . . . 43 D3
Fairfields DA12 . . . . 36 E3
Fairfield Way TN11 . . . . 126 F5
Fairford Ave DA7 . . . . . . 14 D6
Fairglen Cotts TN5 . . . . 184 B4
Fairglen Rd TN5 . . . . . . 184 B4
Fairhurst Dr ME15 . . . . . 115 B4
Fairings The TN30 . . . . . 193 B8
Fairland Ho BR2 . . . . 42 B5
Fairlands Ct 🖫 SE9 . . . . . 12 A1
Fairlawn
　St Paul's Cray BR5 . . . . . 11 C8
Fairlawn Ave DA7 . . . . . . 13 D5
Fairlawn Cl ME18 . . . . . 114 A8
Fairlawn Ct SE7 . . . . 11 C7
Fairlead Rd ME1 . . . . 53 D1
Fairlight Cl TN4 . . . . . . 143 A2
Fairlight Cross DA1 . . . . 49 C6
Fairlight Ct TN10 . . . . . . 127 B4
Fairman's La TN12 . . . . . 162 B6
Fairmead BR1 . . . . 42 F5
Fairmeadow ME14 . . . . . 99 F4
Fairmead Rd TN8 . . . . . 122 C5
Fairmile Ho BR5 . . . . 44 A7
Fairmile Rd TN2 . . . . . . 159 E5
Fairmont Cl DA17 . . . . . . 3 F1
Fairoak Cl BR5 . . . . 43 B2
Fairoak Dr SE9 . . . . 12 D2
FAIRSEAT 79 C7
Fairseat La
　Fairseat TN15 . . . . 79 B5
　Stansted TN15 . . . . 63 A1
Fairthorn Rd SE7 . . . . . . 1 A1
Fairtrough Rd BR6 . . . . . 74 B7
Fairview
　Erith DA8 . . . . 14 F7
　Hawkhurst TN18 . . . . . . 188 F2
　New Ash Green DA3 . . . . 62 B7
Fairview Ave ME8 . . . . . . 69 B5
Fairview Cl TN9 . . . . . . 143 B7
Fairview Com Prim Sch
　ME8 . . . . 69 C5
Fairview Cotts ME15 . . . 115 F5
Fair View Cotts TN5 . . . 185 A6
Fairview Dr
　Higham ME3 . . . . 38 B4
　Orpington BR6 . . . . 57 D6

Fairview Gdns DA13 . . . . 50 A4
Fairview Ind Pk RM13 . . . 4 D8
Fairview Rd DA13 . . . . . . 35 E1
Fairview Trad Est RH8 . . 104 A2
Fairwater Ave DA16 . . . . 13 A3
Fairway
　Bexley DA6 . . . . 13 E2
　Orpington BR5 . . . . 43 D4
Fairway Cl ME1 . . . . 53 C1
Fairway Ct 🖫 SE9 . . . . . . 12 A1
Fairway Dr
　Dartford DA2 . . . . 33 B8
　Erith SE28 . . . . 3 E7
Fairways Ct 🖫 DA11 . . . . 36 B8
Fairways The ME14 . . . . 159 A7
Fairway The
　Bromley, Southborough
　BR1 . . . . 42 F4
　🖫 Bromley, Sundridge BR1 . 28 B1
　Gravesend DA11 . . . . . . 36 B6
　Rochester ME1 . . . . 53 C1
Falcon Ave
　Bromley BR1 . . . . 42 A5
　Grays RM17 . . . . 18 C2
Falcon Cl DA1 . . . . 16 F8
Falcon Gn ME20 . . . . 81 F1
Falcon Mews DA11 . . . . . 35 E7
Falcons Cl TN16 . . . . 72 D2
FALCONWOOD 12 E3
Falconwood Ave DA16 . . . 12 E5
Falconwood Par DA16 . . . 12 F3
Falconwood Sta SE9 . . . . 12 D3
Falkland Pl ME5 . . . . 67 E1
Fallowfield
　Bean DA2 . . . . 34 B5
　Chatham ME5 . . . . 68 B8
Fallowfield Cl ME14 . . . . 100 E4
Falmouth Pl TN12 . . . . . 145 C7
Falstaff Cl DA1 . . . . 31 E8
Fanconi Rd ME5 . . . . 68 B3
Fancy Row ME4 . . . . 101 C5
Fane Way ME8 . . . . 69 D4
Fantail Ct SE28 . . . . 3 C7
Fant La ME16 . . . . 99 B2
Faraday Ave DA14 . . . . . . 30 B6
Faraday Dr
　Dartford DA2 . . . . 33 B8
Faraday Ho
　Erith DA8 . . . . 4 A3
　Rochester ME1 . . . . 53 D5
Faraday Lodge TN2 . . . . 159 E5
Faraday Rd
　Bexley DA16 . . . . 13 A4
　Maidstone ME14 . . . . . 100 C7
Faraday Ride TN10 . . . . . 127 D7
Faraday Way
　Greenwich SE10 . . . . 1 D3
　Orpington BR5 . . . . 44 B5
Fareham Wlk 🖫 ME15 . . . 116 F6
Faringdon Ave BR2 . . . . . 43 A3
Farington Cl ME16 . . . . . 99 B4
Farjeon Rd SE3 . . . . 11 D6
Farleigh Ave BR2 . . . . . . 42 A2
Farleigh Gill ME14 . . . . . 99 A2
Farleigh Hill ME15 . . . . . 99 E1
Farleigh Hill Ret Pk ME15 99 E1
Farleigh La ME15 . . . . . . 99 A1
Farleigh Trad Est ME15 . . 99 E1
Farley Cl ME5 . . . . 68 D2
Farleycroft TN16 . . . . 89 C1
Farley La TN16 . . . . 105 B8
Farley Nursery TN16 . . . 105 C8
Farley Rd DA12 . . . . 36 F7
Farlow Cl DA11 . . . . 35 F5
Farm Ave ME8 . . . . 45 C6
Farmcombe Cl TN2 . . . . 159 B2
Farmcombe La TN2 . . . . 159 B2
Farmcombe Rd TN2 . . . . 159 C2
Farmcote Rd SE12 . . . . . 28 A7
Farmcroft DA11 . . . . 36 A6
Farmdale Ave ME1 . . . . . 52 F2
Farmdale Rd SE10 . . . . . 1 A1
Farmer Cl ME17 . . . . . . 118 A6
Farm Ground Cl TN9 . . . 143 E8
Farm Hill Ave ME2 . . . . . 33 A1
Farm Holt DA3 . . . . 48 F1
Farm La TN10 . . . . 127 A4
Farmland Wlk BR7 . . . . . 29 B3
Farm Pl DA1 . . . . 15 A3
Farm Place TN15 . . . . . . 92 F8
Farm Rd
　Chatham ME5 . . . . 67 E3
　Sevenoaks TN14 . . . . . . 92 C7
Farmstead Dr TN8 . . . . . 122 D3
Farm Vale DA5 . . . . 14 B1
Farnaby Dr TN13 . . . . . . 92 A1
Farnaby Rd SE9 . . . . 11 C3
FARNBOROUGH 57 D5
Farnborough ME16 . . . . . 99 C2
Farnborough Comm BR6 . 57 C5
Farnborough Ct 🖫 BR6 . . 57 C5
Farnborough Hill BR6 . . . 57 C5
Farnborough Prim Sch
　BR6 . . . . 57 C5
Farnborough Way BR6 . . . 57 D5
Farne Cl ME15 . . . . 116 A6
Farnham Beeches TN3 . . 158 A4
Farnham Cl TN3 . . . . . . 158 A3
Farnham La TN3 . . . . . . 158 A4
Farnham Pl TN3 . . . . . . 158 A3
Farnham Rd DA16 . . . . . 13 C5
FARNINGHAM 46 F2
Farningham Rd ME14 . . . 100 C6
Farningham Hill Rd DA4 . . 46 A3
Farningham Road Sta
　DA4 . . . . 47 B7
Farningham Wood★ BR8,
　DA4 . . . . 46 D5
Farnol Rd DA1 . . . . 16 A3
Faro Cl BR1 . . . . 43 A7

Farraday Cl ME1 . . . . 67 D8
Farrance Ct TN1 . . . . . . 159 B4
Farrant Cl BR6 . . . . 58 A3
Farrants Ct BR1 . . . . 42 F7
Farrell Ct DA2 . . . . 32 C5
Farrier Cl
　Bromley BR1 . . . . 42 D6
　Maidstone ME14 . . . . . 100 E5
Farriers Cl 🖫 DA12 . . . . . 36 F7
Farriers End ME8 . . . . . . 70 C8
Farriers The TN8 . . . . . . 122 B3
Farrington Ave BR5 . . . . . 44 B6
Farrington Pl BR7 . . . . . . 29 D1
Farringtons Sch BR7 . . . . 29 C1
Fartherwell Ave ME19 . . . 97 A8
Fartherwell Rd ME19 . . . 97 A8
Farthing Cl DA1 . . . . 16 F3
Farthing Cnr ME9 . . . . . . 69 F3
Farthingfield TN5 . . . . . . 79 A3
FARTHING GREEN 134 C1
Farthing Hill TN5 . . . . . . 186 E1
Farthings Cotts ME14 . . . 83 F1
Farthing St BR6 . . . . 56 F2
FARTHING STREET 56 F2
Farwell Rd DA14 . . . . . . 30 C4
Farwig La BR1 . . . . 42 A8
Fashoda Rd BR2 . . . . 42 F5
Fauchon's Cl ME14 . . . . 100 F3
Fauchon's La ME14 . . . . 100 F4
F Ave SE18 . . . . 2 B3
Faversham Rd ME17 . . . . 120 E4
Fawkes Ave DA1 . . . . 32 F6
Fawkham Ave DA3 . . . . . 49 C6
Fawkham CE Prim Sch
　DA3 . . . . 48 B8
FAWKHAM GREEN 62 B8
Fawkham Green Rd DA3 . . 62 B7
Fawkham Ho 🖫 BR5 . . . . 44 D3
Fawkham House Sch
　TN15 . . . . 62 D3
Fawkham Manor Hospl
　DA3 . . . . 48 C3
Fawkham Rd
　Longfield DA3 . . . . 48 D6
　West Kingsdown TN15 . . . 62 A4
Fawley Cl ME14 . . . . 99 E2
Fay Cl ME1 . . . . 53 B3
Faygate Cres DA6 . . . . . . 14 A2
Fazan Ct TN5 . . . . 184 F4
Fearon St SE10 . . . . 1 A1
Featherby Cotts ME7 . . . . 54 F4
Featherby Inf Sch ME8 . . . 55 A3
Featherby Jun Sch ME8 . . 55 A3
Featherby Rd ME8 . . . . . 55 A3
Federation Rd SE2 . . . . . . 3 C2
Feenan Highway RM18 . . 19 B6
Felderland Cl ME17 . . . . 116 E5
Felderland Dr ME17 . . . . 116 E5
Felderland Rd ME17 . . . . 116 E5
Feldspar Cl ME5 . . . . 62 B8
Felhampton Rd SE9 . . . . 29 B8
Felix Manor BR7 . . . . 29 E2
Felixstowe Ct E16 . . . . . . 2 C2
Felixstowe Rd SE2 . . . . . . 3 B1
Fell Mead TN12 . . . . . . 129 F6
Fellowes Way TN11 . . . . 126 E5
Fellows Cl ME8 . . . . 69 B8
Feltram Way SE7 . . . . 1 A1
Felma Ho 🖫 SE2 . . . . 11 C1
Felspar Cl SE18 . . . . 2 F1
Felstead Rd BR6 . . . . 58 B8
Felsted Rd E16 . . . . 1 D2
Felton Cl BR5 . . . . 43 B5
Felton Ho SE3 . . . . 11 C3
Felton Lea DA14 . . . . 29 F5
Fendyke Rd DA17 . . . . . . 3 D3
Fen Gr DA15 . . . . 12 F1
Fen Mdw TN15 . . . . 78 C7
Fenn Cl BR1 . . . . 28 A1
Fennel Cl ME16 . . . . 99 B1
Fennell Cl ME1 . . . . 53 B1
Fennell St SE18 . . . . 12 A1
Fenners Marsh DA12 . . . . 36 F7
Fenn St ME3 . . . . 24 B7
FENN STREET 24 B7
Fen Pond Rd
　Ightham TN15 . . . . 94 C1
　Ightham TN15 . . . . 94 D1
Fens Way BR8 . . . . 32 A4
Fenton Cl BR7 . . . . 29 A2
Fenwick Cl 🖫 SE18 . . . . . 12 A1
Feoffe Cotts TN7 . . . . . . 190 E1
Ferbies TN3 . . . . 158 A4
Ferbies Cl TN3 . . . . 158 A4
Ferby Ct 🖫 DA15 . . . . . . 29 F7
Ferdinand Terr TN3 . . . . 171 C2
Ferguson Ave DA12 . . . . 36 C1
Fern Bank DA4 . . . . 60 E1
Fernbank Cl ME5 . . . . . . 67 F5
Fern Cl DA8 . . . . 15 A4
Fern Ct DA7 . . . . 14 A1
FERNDALE 159 D4
Ferndale
　Bromley BR1 . . . . 42 C1
　Royal Tunbridge Wells
　TN2 . . . . 159 D1
　Sevenoaks TN13 . . . . . . 92 C7
Ferndale Ct
　Bexley DA7 . . . . 13 E1
　Royal Tunbridge Wells
　TN2 . . . . 159 C2
Ferndale Point TN2 . . . . 159 C2
Ferndale Rd
　Gillingham ME7 . . . . 54 E6
　Gravesend DA12 . . . . . . 36 B7
Ferndale St E6 . . . . 2 C2
Ferndale Way BR6 . . . . . 57 D6
Ferndell Ave DA5 . . . . . . 31 C5

Ferndene DA3 ... 49 D6
Fern Down DA13 ... 80 B8
Ferndown Ave BR1 ... 43 D1
Ferndown Cl ME7 ... 69 A5
Ferndown Rd SE9 ... 28 D8
Fernheath Way DA2 ... 31 D3
Fern Hill Rd ME16 ... 99 A2
Fernhill St E16 ... 1 F5
Fernholt TN10 ... 127 C7
Fernhurst Cres TN4 ... 143 A2
Fernleigh Rd ME2 ... 82 B2
Fernside La TN13 ... 108 D6

Ferns The
Larkfield ME20 ... 82 B1
Platt TN15 ... 95 C7
Royal Tunbridge Wells
  TN1 ... 159 C4
Fernwood Cl BR1 ... 42 C7
Ferranti Cl SE18 ... 1 D3
Ferrier Cl ME8 ... 69 E4
Ferrier Point 8 E16 ... 1 A8
Ferringham TN4 ... 158 F4

Ferry La
Rainham RM13 ... 4 E7
Wouldham ME1 ... 66 C4
Ferry La Ind Est RM13 ... 4 F8
Ferry Pl SE18 ... 2 A3

Ferry Rd
Halling ME2 ... 66 B4
Tilbury RM18 ... 19 A4
Festival Ave DA3 ... 49 D6

Festival Cl
Erith DA8 ... 14 F7
Sidcup DA14 ... 30 D7
Festoon Way E16 ... 1 D6
Ffinch Cl ME20 ... 98 D8
Fiddlers Cl DA9 ... 17 B3
Fiddlers Cl BR1 ... 43 A6

Field Cl
Bromley BR1 ... 42 C7
Chatham ME5 ... 67 E6
Field Ct DA11 ... 35 F6
Field Dr TN8 ... 122 D3
Fieldfare Rd SE28 ... 3 C6
FIELD GREEN ... 195 E8
Fielding Ave RM18 ... 19 B6
Fielding Dr ME20 ... 82 A3
Fielding La ME2 ... 42 C5
Field Rd DA13, TN15 ... 63 E6
Fieldside Cl BR6 ... 57 C6
Fields La ME18 ... 113 E7
Fieldway BR5 ... 43 D3
Fieldworks Rd ME7 ... 54 A7
Fiennes Way TN13 ... 108 C8
Fiesta Dr RM9 ... 4 C8
Fife Rd E16 ... 1 A8
Fifteenpenny Fields SE9 ... 12 A2
Fifth Ave RM20 ... 17 A8
FIG STREET ... 108 A7
Fiji Terr ME14 ... 100 A7
Filborough Way DA12 ... 37 B6
Filey Cl TN16 ... 88 B8
Filmer La TN14 ... 92 E6
Filston Cl TN15 ... 75 E5
Filston Rd DA8 ...
Finchale Rd SE2 ... 3 A3
Finchams Musical Mus*
  TN17 ... 177 A5

Finch Ct
Maidstone ME14 ... 99 E7
Sidcup DA14 ... 30 B5
Finchley Cl DA1 ... 10 A1
Finchley Rd RM17 ... 18 B8
Finch's Cross RH8 ... 121 A8
Findlay Cl ME8 ... 69 D6
Finglesham Ct BR5 ... 44 D1
Finglesham Ct ME15 ... 116 C8
Finsbury Way DA5 ... 13 F1
Fintonagh Dr ME4 ... 100 B6
Finucane Dr BR5 ... 44 C2
Firbank Cl E16 ...
Fircroft Way TN8 ... 122 C3
Fir Dene BR6 ... 57 A7
Fircrest Cl DA3 ... 49 B6
Firepower:The Royal
Artillery Mus & Greenwich
Heritage Ctr* SE18 ... 2 B3
Firethorn Cl ME7 ... 54 E6
Fir Ave ME17 ... 116 D5
Firmingers Rd BR6 ... 59 C5
Firmin Rd DA1 ... 15 C2
Firs Cl ME20 ... 82 E1
Firs Ct TN4 ... 158 F6
Firside Gr DA15 ... 29 F7

Firs The
Bexley DA7 ... 13 C4
Chatham ME5 ... 54 C2
Gillingham ME7 ... 54 E3
Northfleet DA11 ... 35 E7
West Thurrock RM20 ... 17 A8

Firs The
Coldblow DA5 ... 31 D7
Sidcup SE9 ... 29 F5
First La ME17 ... 101 E2
First St TN3 ... 157 F3

Fir Tree Cl
Grays RM17 ... 18 D8
5 Orpington BR6 ... 57 F5
Staplehurst TN12 ... 149 F3
Tonbridge TN11 ... 126 E5

Fir Tree Gr
Bredhurst ME7 ... 69 B1
Chatham ME5 ... 68 D1
Fir Tree Rd TN4 ... 158 F3
Fishermans Wlk SE28 ... 2 E4
Fishermen's Hill DA11 ... 18 B2

Fisher Rd ME5 ... 68 B7
Fishers Cl TN12 ... 149 F5
Fisher's Gate Cotts TN17 ... 170 A1
Fishers Rd TN12 ... 149 F5

Fisher St
Maidstone ME14 ... 100 A6
Newham E16 ... 1 A8
Fisher's Way DA17 ... 4 C5
Fishguard Way E16 ... 2 B5
FISHINGHURST ... 178 F7
Fishponds Rd BR2 ... 56 D5
Fitzgilbert Cl ME7 ... 55 A5
Fitzroy Ct DA1 ... 33 B7
Fitzthorold Ho ME7 ... 54 E7
Fitzwilliam Mews E16 ... 1 A5
Fitzwilliam Rd ME14 ... 100 F5
Five Acre Wood Sch
  ME15 ... 116 B7
Five Arches Bsns Est
  DA14 ... 30 D3
Fiveash Rd DA11 ... 35 F8
Five Bells La 5 ME1 ... 53 D4
Five Elms Rd BR2 ... 56 C7
Five Fields La TN8 ... 123 B4
FIVE OAK GREEN ... 144 D6

Five Oak Green Rd
Capel TN11, TN12 ... 144 D6
Tonbridge TN11 ... 143 F7
Five Oak La TN12 ... 144 B1
Five Oaks Mews BR1 ... 28 A5
Five Ways TN1 ... 159 B3
Five Ways Ct ME4 ... 54 A4
FIVE WENTS ... 117 D2
Five Wents BR8 ... 46 A7
Flack Gdns ME3 ... 40 A6
Flamborough Cl TN16 ... 88 B8
Flamingo Cl ME5 ... 68 A7
Flamsteed Rd SE7 ... 1 E1

Flats The
Gravesend DA12 ... 36 E8
Swanscombe DA9 ... 17 C7

Flaxman Ct
5 Chatham ME7 ... 54 A6
Erith DA17 ... 4 A1
Flaxman Dr ME16 ... 99 C6
Flaxmore Ct DA7 ... 14 B4
Flaxmore Pl TN4 ... 143 A2
Flaxton Rd SE18 ... 12 E2
Fleet Ave DA2 ... 33 C7
Fleet Dale Par DA2 ... 33 C7
Fleetdown Inf Sch DA2 ... 33 C6
Fleetdown Jun Sch DA2 ... 33 C6
FLEET-DOWNS ... 33 D7
Fleet Ho DA13 ... 35 B2

Fleet Rd
Dartford DA2 ... 33 C7
Northfleet DA11 ... 35 C6
Rochester ME1 ... 53 D1
Fleet Terr DA11 ... 35 D7
Fleetwood Cl E16 ... 1 D8

Fleetwood Ct
1 Newham E16 ... 1 F8
Orpington BR6 ... 57 A6
Fleming Cl DA11 ... 35 C7
Fleming Gdns RM18 ... 19 C6
Fleming Ho SE1 ... 3 C1

Fleming Way
Erith SE28 ... 3 D6
Tonbridge TN10 ... 127 E7
Fletcher Cl E6 ... 2 B6
Fletcher Gardens ME6 ... 81 F8
Fletcher Rd TN12 ... 149 E3
Fletchers Cl BR1 ... 4 A1
Fletching Rd SE7 ... 11 D8
FLIMWELL ... 187 C3
Flimwell Cl TN5 ... 187 D4
Flint Cl 8 BR6 ... 57 F4
Flint Down Cl BR5 ... 44 A8
Flint Gn ME5 ... 68 C3
Flint La ME17 ... 120 C8
Flint St RM20 ... 17 B8
Flintmill Cres SE3, SE9 ... 11 E5
Floathaven Cl SE28 ... 3 A5
Floats The TN3 ... 91 E6
Flood Hatch ME15 ... 99 D2
Florance La TN3 ... 171 B6
Flora St DA17 ... 3 F1
Florence Cl RM17, RM20 ... 17 E8
Florence Cotts 5 TN8 ... 122 C1
Florence Farm Mobile Home
  Pk TN15 ... 62 A1
Florence Ho SE18 ... 11 F6

Florence Rd
4 Bromley BR1 ... 42 A8
Erith DA17, SE2 ... 3 C2
Maidstone ME16 ... 99 E3
Florence St 3 ME2 ... 53 B8
Floyd Cl ME1 ... 53 B4
Floyd Rd SE7 ... 1 C1
Flume End ME15 ... 99 D2
Flyers Way The TN16 ... 89 D1
Foalhurst Cl TN10 ... 127 E4
Foley Cl DA1 ... 33 B7
Foley Rd TN16 ... 72 D1
Foley St ME14 ... 100 A5
Folkestone Ho 4 ME15 ... 116 F6
Fontana ME5 ... 68 A3
Fontwell Cl ME15 ... 116 F6
Fontwell Dr BR2 ... 43 A4
Foord Cl DA2 ... 33 E6
Foord Rd ME17 ... 120 D5
Foord St ME1 ... 53 D4
Footbury Hill Rd BR6 ... 44 A2

FOOTS CRAY ... 30 B2
Foots Cray High St DA14 ... 30 D2
Foots Cray La DA14 ... 30 C7
Foots Cray Meadows*
  DA14 ... 30 D3
Footscray Rd SE9 ... 29 C7
FORCE GREEN ... 89 D4
Force Green Farm Cotts
  TN16 ... 89 E4
Force Green La TN16 ... 89 E4
FORDCOMBE ... 157 B5
Fordcombe CE Prim Sch
  TN3 ... 157 B5
Fordcombe Cl ME15 ... 116 F7

Fordcombe Rd
Fordcombe TN3 ... 157 C4
Penshurst TN11 ... 141 A3
Fordcroft Rd BR5 ... 44 B4
Forde Ave BR1 ... 42 C6
Fordgate Bsns Pk DA7 ... 4 C4
Ford Rd 8 SE18 ... 2 B1
Fordingbridge Cl RM19 ... 9 B5

Ford La
Trottiscliffe ME19 ... 80 A4
Wrotham Heath TN15, ME19 ... 79 F2
Ford Rd DA11 ... 18 B2
Fords Park Rd E16 ... 1 A7

Fordwich Cl
Maidstone ME16 ... 99 B7
Orpington BR6 ... 43 F2
Fordwich Dr ME2 ... 39 A2
Fordwich Gn ME8 ... 55 C3
Foreland St SE18 ... 2 D2
Foreman Ctr TN27 ... 151 D5
Foremans Barn Rd ME15 ... 114 F3
Foreman's Wlk TN27 ... 151 D5
Forest Cl BR7 ... 43 A8
Forestdale Rd ME5 ... 84 A8
Forest Dene TN2 ... 159 C1

Forest Dr
Chatham ME5 ... 67 F2
Orpington BR2 ... 56 E6
Forest Gr TN10 ... 127 C5
Forest Hill ME5 ... 99 F1
Forest Lawns BR1 ... 42 C8

Forest Rd
Erith DA8 ... 15 A4
Paddock Wood TN12 ... 146 A6
Royal Tunbridge Wells
  TN2 ... 159 C1
Forest Ridge BR2 ... 56 F6

Forest Way
Eltham DA15 ... 29 D8
Kings Hill ME19 ... 97 A3
Orpington BR5 ... 43 F4
Pembury TN2 ... 160 D8
Royal Tunbridge Wells
  TN2 ... 159 D1

Forstal Rd
Egerton Forstal TN27 ... 137 C1
Forstal ME20 ... 83 C2

Forstal The
Cobham TN3 ... 171 F3
Hadlow TN11 ... 128 F8
Pembury TN2 ... 160 E8
Forsters ME17 ... 117 E4
Forsyth Cl ME4 ... 54 A1
Forsyth Ct 7 ME7 ... 54 C7
Fort Amherst* ME4 ... 53 F5
Fortis Cl E16 ... 1 C7
Fort Luton* ME4 ... 54 A1
Fort Pitt Gram Sch ME4 ... 53 E4
Fort Pitt Hill ME1, ME4 ... 53 E4
Fort Pitt St ME4 ... 53 E3

Fort Rd
Badgers Mount TN14 ... 75 C4
Tilbury RM18 ... 19 C5
Fortrye Cl DA11 ... 35 E6

Fort St
Newham E16 ... 1 B5
Rochester ME1 ... 53 D4
Fortuna Cl DA3 ... 48 F5
Fortune Way ME19 ... 97 B3
Fortune Wlk 7 SE28 ... 2 D3
Forty Acre La E16 ... 1 A8
Forward Way ME1 ... 67 C6
Fossdene Prim Sch SE7 ... 1 B1
Fossdene Rd SE7 ... 1 B1
Fosse Bank Cl TN9 ... 143 A7
Fosse Bank Sch TN11 ... 126 C6
Fosse Rd TN9 ... 127 B2
Fossett Lodge DA7 ... 14 C6
Fossington Rd DA17 ... 3 D2
FOSTEN GREEN ... 181 D6
Fosten La TN27 ... 181 D6
Foster Clarke Dr ME17 ... 116 D5
Foster Clark Est ME15 ... 100 B2
Fosters Cl BR7 ... 28 F3
Fosters Mews DA3 ... 48 E7
Fosters Old School La TN3 ... 13 B5
Fosters Prim Sch DA16 ... 13 A4
Foster St ME15 ... 100 A3
Fostington Way ME5 ... 67 F1
Foulds Cl ME8 ... 69 A3
Founder Cl E6 ... 2 B7
Foundry Cl TN1 ... 194 A3
Foundry Wharf ME1 ... 53 E4

Fountain Ct
Eynsford DA4 ... 60 E8
Sidcup DA15 ... 13 B2
Fountain La ME16 ... 99 A2
Fountain Rd ME2 ... 38 E1
Fountain Wlk DA11 ... 18 F1
Fouracre Cotts ME9 ... 70 E6
Four Acres ME19 ... 98 B5
FOUR ELMS ... 123 A5
Four Elms Hill ME3 ... 39 E4
Four Elms Prim Sch TN8 ... 123 B5
Four Elms Rd TN8 ... 122 D4
Four Elms Rdbt ME3 ... 39 E3
Four Oaks Rd TN12, TN27 ... 150 E1

Fourth Ave
Gillingham ME7 ... 54 E4
West Thurrock RM20 ... 17 A8
FOUR THROWS ... 195 C6
Four Trees TN8 ... 122 C3
FOUR WENTS ... 189 B6

Four Wents
Langley Heath ME17 ... 117 E3
Maidstone ME17 ... 116 F2
Four Wents Cl 6 TN5 ... 94 F7
Fourwents Rd ME3 ... 40 D7
Fowey Cl ME5 ... 68 C5

Fowler Cl
Gillingham ME8 ... 69 C3
Sidcup DA14 ... 30 E3
Foxborough Cl ME8 ... 69 D5
Foxbury DA3 ... 62 E7
Foxbury Ave BR7 ... 29 C2

Foxbury Cl
Bromley BR1 ... 28 B2
Orpington BR6 ... 58 A5
Foxbury Rd BR1 ... 28 B2
Foxbury Wlk DA11 ... 35 D4
Foxbush TN11 ... 126 C6

Fox Cl
Newham E16 ... 1 A8
Orpington BR6 ... 58 A5
Foxcroft Rd SE18 ... 12 B6
Foxden Dr ME15 ... 100 F1
Foxearth Cl TN16 ... 72 E1
FOXENDOWN ... 64 C8
Foxendown La DA13 ... 50 B1
Foxes Dale SE3 ... 11 A4
Foxfield Prim Sch SE18 ... 2 C1
Foxfield Rd BR6 ... 57 D8

Foxglove Cl
3 Marlpit Hill TN8 ... 122 D3
Sidcup DA15 ... 13 A1
Foxglove Cres ME5 ... 67 E4
Foxglove Rise ME14 ... 69 E7
Foxgloves The TN12 ... 146 B5
Foxgrove Path SE28 ... 2 E5
Fox Hill ME2 ... 56 C5

Foxhole La
Four Throws TN18 ... 195 D8
Hawkhurst TN18 ... 189 E1
Matfield TN12 ... 161 C8
Wadhurst TN5 ... 185 B4
Foxhole Rd SE9 ... 11 E2
Fox Hollow Cl 2 SE18 ... 2 E1
Fox Hollow Dr DA7 ... 13 D4
Foxhome Cl BR7 ... 29 A2
Fox House Rd DA17 ... 4 B1
Fox in the Wood TN5 ... 184 C6

Fox La BR2 ... 56 C5
Fox Lea 5 TN15 ... 94 F7
Fox Manor Way RM20 ... 17 B8
Fox St ME7 ... 54 C6
Foxtail Cl ME4 ... 40 E2
Foxton Ho E16 ... 2 A4
Foxton Rd RM20 ... 17 D8

Foxwood Gr
Northfleet DA11 ... 35 E7
Pratt's Bottom BR6 ... 58 C1
Foxwood Rd DA2 ... 34 B5
Foxwood Way DA2 ... 49 D7
Framley Rd TN10 ... 127 F5
Framlingham Cres SE9 ... 28 F4
Frances St SE18 ... 1 F2
Francis Ave DA7 ... 14 A5
Francis Ct 7 DA8 ... 4 A3
Francis Dr ME5 ... 68 A2

Francis La
Kings Hill ME19 ... 97 D3
Maidstone ME15 ... 116 F5

Francis Rd
Dartford DA1 ... 15 D2
Orpington BR5 ... 44 D6
Tonbridge TN11 ... 126 D6
Frankapps Cl ME9 ... 71 B6
Frank Burton Cl 5 SE7 ... 1 B1
Frankfield Rise TN2 ... 159 A1
Frank Godley Cl DA14 ... 30 B3
Franklin Dr ME14 ... 100 D4
Franklin Pas SE9 ... 11 E4

Franklin Rd
Bexley DA7 ... 13 E6
Gillingham ME7 ... 54 D5
Gravesend DA12 ... 36 D3
Maypole DA2 ... 31 E6
Franklins Cotts ME15 ... 115 C5
Franks Ct ME8 ... 55 B2
Frank's Hollow Rd TN3 ... 142 C2
Franks La DA4 ... 47 A4
Frankswood Ave BR5 ... 43 E4
Frank Woolley Rd TN10 ... 127 C5
FRANT ... 173 F3
Frant CE Prim Sch TN3 ... 173 B4
Frant Cotts TN5 ... 186 E1
Frant Field TN8 ... 122 C1
Frant Green Rd TN3 ... 173 B3
Frant Rd TN2, TN3 ... 173 A7
Frant Sta TN3 ... 173 F5

Fraser Cl
Coldblow DA5 ... 31 C7
4 Newham E6 ... 1 E7
Fraser Ho 3 SE18 ... 2 A2
Fraser Rd ... 4 D1
Frederick Andrews Ct
  RM17 ... 18 D8
Frederick Ho 4 SE18 ... 1 E2
Frederick Pl SE18 ... 2 B1
Frederick Rd ME7 ... 54 C4
FREE HEATH ... 175 C1
Free Heath Rd TN3, TN5 ... 175 C3

Freehold The
East Peckham TN12 ... 129 F6
Hadlow TN11 ... 111 D1
Freeland Ct 20 DA14 ... 30 A5
Freelands Gr BR1 ... 42 B8

Freelands Rd
Bromley BR1 ... 42 B8
Snodland ME6 ... 81 F8
Freeland Way DA8 ... 15 A6
Freeman Gdns ME4 ... 53 F2
Freeman Rd DA12 ... 36 E5
Freeman Way ME15 ... 116 E7
Freemasons Rd E16 ... 1 B7

Freesia Cl
Gillingham ME7 ... 54 F6
Orpington BR6 ... 57 F5
Freight La TN17 ... 179 C3
Fremantle Ho RM18 ... 18 F6
Fremantle Rd DA17 ... 4 A2
Fremlin Cl TN4 ... 158 B4
Fremlins Rd ME14 ... 101 C4
Fremlin Walk Sh Ctr
  ME14 ... 99 F4
FRENCH STREET ... 105 F6

Frensham Rd
Rolvenden TN17 ... 192 A1
Sidcup SE9 ... 29 D6
Frensham Wlk ME5 ... 67 F1
Freshland Rd ME16 ... 99 B4
Freshwater Rd ME5 ... 68 B7
Freta Rd DA6 ... 13 F2
Frewing Ct ME7 ... 29 A3
Friar Rd BR5 ... 44 A4
Friars Ave ME5 ... 67 F2
Friars Mews SE9 ... 12 A2
Friars Pk SE9 ... 82 E2
Friars The* ME20 ... 82 C2
Friars Way TN2 ... 159 D6
Friars Wlk SE2 ... 3 D1
Friary Pl 3 ME2 ... 53 B7
Friary Prec ME2 ... 53 B7
Friday Rd DA8 ... 4 D1
Friday St ME17 ... 135 B6
Friezland Rd TN4 ... 158 D1
Frinsley La TN17 ... 165 C1
Frimley Cl DA14 ... 30 C2
FRINDSBURY ... 53 C8
Frindsbury Hill ME2 ... 39 C1
Frindsbury Rd ME2 ... 53 B8
Frinstead Gr BR5 ... 44 D5
Frinstead Wlk ME16 ... 99 B7
Frinsted Cl ME8 ... 55 C3
Frinsted Rd DA8 ... 14 D7

Frinton Rd DA14 . . . . 30 E6
Friston Way ME1 . . . . 67 D8
Friswell Pl 🔢 DA6 . . . . 14 A3
Frithwood Cl ME15 . . . . . . 100 F1
FRITTENDEN 166 F7
Frittenden CE Prim Sch
  TN17 . . . . 166 E6
Frittenden Rd
  Rochester ME2 . . . . 39 D2
  Staplehurst TN12 . . . . . . 150 B2
Frobisher Ct 🔢 DA1 . . . . . 15 D1
Frobisher Gdns ME1 . . . . . 53 C2
Frobisher Rd
  Erith DA8 . . . . 15 A7
  Newham E6 . . . . 2 A7
Frobisher Way
  Gravesend DA12 . . . . 36 E3
  Swanscombe DA9 . . . . . . 17 B3
FROGHOLE 105 D2
Frog Hole La TN8, TN16 . . 105 D2
Frog La
  Ranham ME13 . . . . 4 D8
  Royal Tunbridge Wells
    TN1 . . . . 159 A2
  West Malling ME19 . . . . . 97 C8
Frogmore Wlk ME17 . . . . 120 C5
Frognal Ave DA14 . . . . 30 A2
Frognal Cnr BR7 . . . . 29 F2
Frognal Pl DA14 . . . . 30 A3
Frognal Place La TN17,
  TN27 . . . . 181 E3
Frog's La TN17 . . . . 191 E1
Froissart Rd SE9 . . . . 11 E2
Fromandez Dr TN12 . . . . 162 F5
Frome Ct TN10 . . . . 127 B5
Frost Cres ME5 . . . . 68 A7
Froyle Cl ME16 . . . . 99 F6
Fruitfields TN5 . . . . 187 C3
Fry Cl ME3 . . . . 27 A6
Fry's Cotts ME3 . . . . 25 C4
Frythe Cl TN17 . . . . 179 D4
Frythe Cres TN17 . . . . . . 179 D4
Frythe Rd TN17 . . . . 179 D4
Frythe Wlk TN17 . . . . 179 D4
Fuchsia St SE2 . . . . 3 B1
Fuggles Cl TN12 . . . . 145 E6
Fuggles Ct TN17 . . . . 190 D6
Fulbert Dr ME14 . . . . 100 F5
Fuller Cl
  Durgates TN5 . . . . 184 E5
  Orpington BR6 . . . . 57 F5
Fullers Cl ME14 . . . . 101 A4
Fullers Hill 🔢 TN16 . . . . . 89 D1
Fulmar Rd ME2 . . . . 52 D6
Fulmer Rd E16 . . . . 1 D8
Fulthorp St SE3 . . . . 11 A5
Fulwich Rd DA1 . . . . 15 F1
Furfield Chase ME15 . . . . 116 E4
Furfield Cl ME15 . . . . 116 E5
FURFIELD HOOK 116 D4
Furnace Ave TN3 . . . . 176 A3
Furnace La
  Hook Green TN3 . . . . 175 E4
  Horsmonden TN12 . . . . . 162 F4
Furner Cl DA1 . . . . 14 F4
Furness Dch BR8 . . . . 31 F2
Furnival Ct TN2 . . . . 172 F8
Furrell's Rd ME1 . . . . 53 D5
Further Field TN12 . . . . . 149 E5
FURTHER QUARTER 169 C3
Furze Bank TN8 . . . . 123 B5
Furzefield Ave TN3 . . . . . 158 A8
Furzefield Cl BR7 . . . . 29 B2
Furzefield Rd SE3 . . . . 11 B7
Furzehill Sq BR5 . . . . 44 B5
Fyfe Way BR1 . . . . 42 A7

G

Gable Cl DA1 . . . . 15 A2
Gables Cl SE12 . . . . 28 A7
Gables The
  🔢 Bromley BR1 . . . . 28 B1
  New Barn DA3 . . . . 49 C6
Gabriel Gdns DA12 . . . . . 36 E3
Gabriel's Hill ME15 . . . . . 100 A4
Gabrielspring Rd DA3 . . . 61 D8
Gabriel Spring Rd (East)
  DA3 . . . . 61 F8
Gadsby La TN26 . . . . 169 F3
Gads Hill ME7 . . . . 54 F6
Gads Hill Sch ME3 . . . . . . 38 C2
Gadwall Cl E16 . . . . 1 B7
Gadwall Way SE28 . . . . 2 D4
Gafford's Bridge Cotts
  TN12 . . . . 147 C4
Gagetown Terr 🔢 ME4 . . . 99 F7
Gainsborough Ave
  Dartford DA1 . . . . 15 C2
  Tilbury RM18 . . . . 19 B6
Gainsborough Cl ME8 . . . 69 D6
Gainsborough Ct 🔢 BR2 . . 42 C5
Gainsborough Dr
  Maidstone ME14 . . . . . . 99 B4
  Northfleet DA11 . . . . 35 D5
Gainsborough Gdns
  TN10 . . . . 127 E5
Gainsborough Ho ME1 . . . 53 D5
Gainsborough Sq DA7 . . . 13 D4
Gaitskell Rd SE9 . . . . 29 C7
Galahad Ave ME2 . . . . 52 E6
Galahad Rd BR1 . . . . 28 A4
Galena Cl ME5 . . . . 68 A1
Galena Ho 🔢 SE18 . . . . 2 F1

Gallants La
  Coxheath ME15 . . . . 115 A2
  East Farleigh ME15 . . . . 114 F6
Galleon Bvd DA2 . . . . 16 D3
Galleon Cl
  Erith DA8 . . . . 4 D2
  Rochester ME1 . . . . 67 C8
Galleon Mews 🔢 DA11 . . . 35 E8
Galleon Way ME2 . . . . 39 F3
Galley Hill Rd DA11, DA10 . 17 F2
Galley Hill Trad Est DA10 . 17 E2
Gallions Mount Prim Sch
  SE18 . . . . 2 F1
Gallions Prim Sch E6 . . . . . 2 A7
Gallions Rd SE7 . . . . 1 B2
Gallions Reach Sh Pk E6 . . 2 C8
Gallions Reach Sta SE6 . . . 2 B6
Gallions View Rd SE28 . . . . 2 E4
Gallon Cl SE7 . . . . 1 C2
Gallops The DA13 . . . . 79 F7
Gallosson Rd SE18 . . . . 2 E2
Galloway Dr DA1 . . . . 31 E8
Gallows Wood DA3 . . . . . . 62 A6
Gallus Sq SE3 . . . . 11 B4
Galsworthy Cl SE28 . . . . . . 3 B5
Galsworthy Cres SE3 . . . . 11 C6
Galsworthy Rd RM18 . . . . 19 C6
Galton Ho SE18 . . . . 11 F6
Games Ho 🔢 SE7 . . . . 11 C8
Gandy's La ME17 . . . . 116 C2
Garden Ave DA7 . . . . 14 A4
Garden Cl
  Lewisham SE12 . . . . 28 B5
  Maidstone ME15 . . . . . . 116 E4
  Staplehurst TN12 . . . . . 149 F1
  Toy's Hill TN16 . . . . 106 C3
Garden Cotts
  Leigh TN11 . . . . 126 A2
  Orpington BR5 . . . . 44 C7
Garden Ct
  🔢 Eltham SE9 . . . . 12 A1
  Sevenoaks TN13 . . . . . . 92 D5
  Wouldham ME1 . . . . 66 C5
Gardeners Cl SE28 . . . . . . 28 E5
Garden Ho 🔢 TN1 . . . . . . 159 B4
Gardenia Cl SE9 . . . . 39 B2
Gardenia Rd BR1 . . . . 43 B5
Garden La BR1 . . . . 28 B2
Garden of England Pk
  (Mobile Home Pk)
  ME17 . . . . 119 B7
Garden Pl DA2 . . . . 32 D5
Garden Rd
  Bromley BR1 . . . . 28 B2
  Royal Tunbridge Wells
    TN1 . . . . 159 B4
  Sevenoaks TN13 . . . . . . 92 D5
  Tonbridge TN9 . . . . 127 C8
Garden Row 🔢 DA11 . . . . 35 F5
Garden St
  Chatham ME7 . . . . 54 A6
  Royal Tunbridge Wells
    TN1 . . . . 159 B4
Gardens The ME17 . . . . . . 115 C3
Garden Terr ME15 . . . . . . 93 A6
Garden Way ME19 . . . . . . 96 F2
Gardiner Cl BR5 . . . . 44 C7
Gardiner Ho SE18 . . . . 11 E7
Gardiner St ME7 . . . . 54 C6
Gardyne Mews 🔢 TN9 . . 143 B8
Gareth Dr BR1 . . . . 28 A6
Garfield Rd ME7 . . . . 54 D6
Garganey Wlk SE28 . . . . . . 3 D6
Gargery Cl 🔢 DA12 . . . . . 36 F7
Garibaldi St SE18 . . . . 2 E2
Garland Rd SE18 . . . . 12 D7
Garlands TN11 . . . . 126 D8
Garlinge Rd TN4 . . . . 143 A1
Garner Ct RM18 . . . . 18 F5
Garner Dr ME1 . . . . 62 A1
Garnett Cl SE9 . . . . 11 F4
Garnet Wlk 🔢 E6 . . . . 1 E8
Garrard Cr
  Bexley DA7 . . . . 14 A4
  Chislehurst BR7 . . . . 29 B3
Garrick Cl TN10 . . . . 127 E7
Garrick Dr SE28 . . . . 2 D3
Garrick St 🔢 DA1 . . . . . . 26 E1
Garrington Cl ME14 . . . . 100 C6
Garrison Cl SE18 . . . . 12 A7
Garrison Rd ME12 . . . . . . 27 F3
Garrolds Cl BR8 . . . . 45 D7
Garrow DA3 . . . . 49 B6
Garside Rd SE28 . . . . 2 D3
Garth Rd TN13 . . . . 108 C7
Gartly Cotts DA1 . . . . 15 C2
Garvary Rd E16 . . . . 1 B7
Garvock Dr TN13 . . . . 92 A1
Gascoyne Rd ME15 . . . . . 101 B2
Gascoyne Dr DA1 . . . . 14 F4
Gas House Rd ME1 . . . . . . 53 C6
Gasoline Alley TN15 . . . . . 79 D2
Gasson Rd DA10 . . . . 17 E1
Gassons Rd ME6 . . . . 81 E8
Gatcombe Cl
  Chatham ME5 . . . . 68 A5
  Maidstone ME16 . . . . . . 99 B5
Gatcombe Rd E16 . . . . 1 A5
Gateacre Ct 🔢 DA14 . . . . 30 B4
Gate Farm Rd TN3, TN11 . 142 C4
Gatefield Cotts TN17 . . . 191 F4
Gate House Cotts SE12 . . 28 B6
Gatehouse Farm Cotts
  TN3 . . . . 142 C4
Gatekeeper Chase ME8 . . 69 F8
Gates Green Rd BR2, BR4 . 56 A6
Gateway Acad The RM16 . 19 A8
Gateway Bsns Ctr 🔢 SE28 . 2 D3

Gateway Par DA12 . . . . . . 36 F4
Gateway Prim Sch The
  DA2 . . . . 16 B1
Gatland La ME16 . . . . 99 B2
Gatling Rd SE2 . . . . 3 A1
Gatton Way DA11 . . . . 30 F4
Gatwick Farm Cotts
  RH19 . . . . 154 A4
Gatwick Rd DA12 . . . . 36 B6
Gault Cl ME15 . . . . 101 A2
Gautrey Sq 🔢 E6 . . . . 1 F7
Gavestone Cres SE12 . . . . 28 B8
Gavestone Rd SE12 . . . . . 28 B8
Gavestone Terr SE12 . . . . 28 B8
Gavin Ho SE18 . . . . 2 E2
Gayhurst Cl ME8 . . . . 69 D6
Gaylor Rd RM18 . . . . 18 F6
Gazza Trad Est TN11 . . . . 125 D7
Gazelle Glade DA12 . . . . . 36 F3
Gean Cl ME5 . . . . 84 A8
Geddes Pl 🔢 DA6 . . . . 14 A3
Gedge's Hill TN12 . . . . . . 145 F3
Gefferty's Ct SE9 . . . . 28 E5
General Gordon Pl 🔢 SE18 . 2 B2
Genesta Glade DA12 . . . . . 37 A3
Genesta Rd SE18 . . . . 12 C8
Geneva Ave ME8 . . . . 55 A2
Gentian Cl
  🔢 Chatham ME5 . . . . 67 E4
  Maidstone ME14 . . . . . . 100 C5
Geoffrey Whitworth
  Theatre * DA1 . . . . 15 A3
George Akass Ho 🔢 SE18 . . 2 C1
George Crooks Ho 🔢
  RM17 . . . . 18 B8
George La
  Hayes BR2 . . . . 42 B1
  Leeds ME17 . . . . 118 B7
  Rochester ME1 . . . . 53 C6
George Marsham Ho
  ME15 . . . . 115 F3
Georges Cl BR5 . . . . 44 C6
George's Rd TN16 . . . . 88 D7
George St
  Chainhurst ME15 . . . . . 132 A7
  Grays RM17 . . . . 18 A8
  Maidstone ME15 . . . . . . 100 A3
  Royal Tunbridge Wells
    TN2 . . . . 159 C3
  Sparrow's Green TN5 . . . 184 F5
  Staplehurst TN12 . . . . . 149 E6
  Tonbridge TN9 . . . . 143 B8
George Summers Cl ME2 . 53 E8
Georgian Cl DA12 . . . . 42 B1
Georgian Ct BR2 . . . . 115 D3
Georgian Way ME8 . . . . . . 69 C4
Georgia Pl TN2 . . . . 159 C4
Geraint Rd BR1 . . . . 28 A4
Gerald Ave ME4 . . . . 53 F2
Gerald Rd DA12 . . . . 36 E8
Gerda Rd SE9 . . . . 29 C6
Gerdview Dr DA2 . . . . 32 C4
Gerrard Ave ME1 . . . . 67 E8
Gerrard Ho 🔢 BR2 . . . . . . 42 C5
Gertrude Rd DA17 . . . . 4 A2
Gibbet La TN12 . . . . 162 F6
Gibbetts BR7 . . . . 157 F3
Gibbons La DA1 . . . . 15 D1
Gibbs Field TN11 . . . . . . 126 A2
Gibbs Hill
  Headcorn TN27 . . . . 151 E5
  Nettlestead ME18 . . . . . 113 B5
Gibraltar Ave ME7 . . . . . . 54 B7
Gibraltar Hill ME4 . . . . . . 53 F4
Gibraltar La ME14 . . . . . . 99 F8
Gibson Cl DA11 . . . . 35 F5
Gibson Dr ME19 . . . . 96 A6
Gibson Ho ME1 . . . . 39 F6
Gidd's Pond Cotts ME14 . 100 E6
Giddyhorn La ME16 . . . . . 99 C5
Gideon Cl DA17 . . . . 4 B2
Gifford Cl ME8 . . . . 55 C3
Giggs Hill BR5 . . . . 44 A8
Gighill Rd ME20 . . . . 81 F4
Gilbert Cl
  Gillingham ME7 . . . . 69 A5
  Swanscombe DA10 . . . . 17 D1
  Woolwich SE18 . . . . 11 F6
Gilbert Rd
  Bromley BR1 . . . . 28 A1
  Erith DA17 . . . . 4 A3
Gilbert Terr 🔢 ME14 . . . . 99 F7
Gilbourne Rd SE18 . . . . . . 12 F8
Gilchrist Cotts TN14 . . . . 108 C2
Gildenhill Rd BR8 . . . . 32 C1
Gildersome St SE18 . . . . . 12 A8
Giles Field DA12 . . . . 37 F7
Gillan Ct 🔢 SE12 . . . . 28 B5
Gill Ave
  Newham E16 . . . . 1 A7
  Rochester ME2 . . . . 39 D2
Gill Cres DA11 . . . . 35 F5
Gill Cl DA1 . . . . 2 C2
Gilletts La ME19 . . . . 98 A6
Gillies Ct DA14 . . . . 29 E4
Gillies Rd TN15 . . . . 61 E5
GILLINGHAM 54 D3
Gillingham Gate ME7 . . . . 54 C8
Gillingham Gate Rd ME7 . 54 C8
Gillingham Rd ME7 . . . . . 54 C6
Gillingham Sta ME7 . . . . . 54 D5
Gillingham Rd BR5 . . . . . . 44 B1
GILL'S GREEN 188 F5
Gill's Rd
  Green Street Green DA2 . . 34 B1
  Sutton at Hone DA4 . . . . 47 F8

Gill The TN2 . . . . 160 E8
Gilroy Way 🔢 BR5 . . . . . . 44 B2
Gimble Way TN2 . . . . 144 D1
Gingerbread La TN18 . . . 187 F2
Ginsbury Cl ME2 . . . . 53 E6
Gipsy Cross La TN3 . . . . 157 F3
Gipsy La RM17 . . . . 18 C8
Gipsy Rd DA16 . . . . 13 D5
Giralda Cl E16 . . . . 1 D8
Glade Bsns Ctr The MR20 . 16 F8
Glades Sh Ctr BR1 . . . . . . 42 A7
Glades The DA12 . . . . 36 D2
Gladeswood Rd DA17 . . . . 4 B2
Glade The
  Bromley BR1 . . . . 42 D7
  Chatham ME5 . . . . 68 A2
  Greenwich SE7 . . . . 11 C7
  Sevenoaks TN13 . . . . . . 92 B4
  Tonbridge TN10 . . . . . . 127 E7
Gladstone Rd
  Chatham ME4 . . . . 53 E2
  Dartford DA1 . . . . 15 F1
  Maidstone ME14 . . . . . . 100 A6
  Orpington BR6 . . . . 57 C5
  🔢 Rusthall TN4 . . . . . . 158 B4
  Tonbridge TN9 . . . . 127 B1
Gladwell Rd BR1 . . . . 28 A2
Gladwyn Cl ME8 . . . . 69 D4
Glamford Rd ME2 . . . . 52 D5
Glamis Cl ME5 . . . . 68 A5
Glanfield Ct TN1 . . . . 159 C5
Glanville Rd
  Bromley BR2 . . . . 42 B6
  Gillingham ME7 . . . . 54 D5
  Rochester ME2 . . . . 53 A8
Glasbrook St SE9 . . . . 28 D8
Glasgow Ho 🔢 ME15 . . . 116 E7
Glassenbury Dr ME5 . . . . 67 F2
Glassenbury Rd TN17 . . . 178 E4
Glassmill La BR2 . . . . 42 A7
Glass Yd SE18 . . . . 2 A3
Glastonbury Cl BR5 . . . . . 44 C1
Glayton Gdns ME5 . . . . . . 67 F4
Gleaming Wood Dr ME5 . . 84 D8
Gleaners Cl ME14 . . . . . . 100 E4
Gleanings Mews ME1 . . . . 53 C5
Glebe Cl TN12 . . . . 153 B2
Glebe Cotts TN16 . . . . 90 B4
Glebe Gdns ME17 . . . . . . 120 E5
Glebe Ho 🔢 BR2 . . . . 2 A2
Glebe House Dr BR2 . . . . . 42 B1
Glebe La
  Maidstone ME16 . . . . 99 A1
  Sevenoaks TN13 . . . . . . 92 B1
Glebeland TN27 . . . . 137 F4
Glebelands
  Bidborough TN3 . . . . . . 142 C3
  Biddenden TN27 . . . . . . 167 F1
  Crayford DA1 . . . . 14 F3
  Penshurst TN11 . . . . . . 141 A3
Glebe Mdw ME18 . . . . . . 113 E7
Glebe Pl DA4 . . . . 47 C5
Glebe Rd
  Bromley BR1 . . . . 42 A8
  Gillingham ME7 . . . . 54 E3
  Northfleet DA11 . . . . 35 F7
  Sevenoaks Weald TN14 . 108 B3
Glebe The
  Bidborough TN3 . . . . . . 142 D3
  Chislehurst BR7 . . . . 43 C8
  Cuxton ME2 . . . . 52 C2
  Pembury TN2 . . . . 160 D8
  Penshurst TN11 . . . . . . 141 A3
Glebe Way DA8 . . . . 14 E8
Gleeson Dr BR6 . . . . 57 F6
Glenalvon Way 🔢 SE18 . . 1 E2
Glenbarr Cl SE9 . . . . 12 B8
Glencairne Cl E16 . . . . 1 D8
Glencoe Jun Sch ME4 . . . 54 A2
Glencoe Rd ME4 . . . . 54 A2
Glen Ct
  Lewisham SE12 . . . . 28 A8
  Sidcup DA14 . . . . 30 A4
Glendale BR8 . . . . 45 F4
Glendale Cl SE9 . . . . 12 A4
Glendale Ct TN2 . . . . 159 D6
Glendale Rd
  Erith DA8 . . . . 4 C2
  Northfleet DA11 . . . . 35 E5
Glendale Way SE28 . . . . . . 3 C6
Glendower Cres BR6 . . . . 44 A3
Glendown Rd SE2 . . . . 3 A1
Glen Dunlop Ho The
  TN13 . . . . 92 C5
Gleneagles Cl 🔢 BR6 . . . . 43 D1
Gleneagles Ct ME5 . . . . . 67 F2
Gleneagles Gn 🔢 BR6 . . . 43 D1
Glenesk Rd SE9 . . . . 12 B3
Glengall Rd DA7 . . . . 13 E4
Glenhead Cl SE9 . . . . 12 B4
Glenhouse Rd SE9 . . . . . . 12 A5
Glenhurst Ave DA5 . . . . . 30 F7
Glenister St SE18 . . . . 2 A4
Glenlea Rd SE9 . . . . 12 A5
Glenleigh Rd ME18 . . . . . 113 D6
Glenluce Rd SE3 . . . . 11 A8
Glenlyon Rd SE9 . . . . 12 B6
Glenmere Row SE12 . . . . 11 A1
Glenmore Pk TN2 . . . . . . 172 F8
Glenmore Rd DA16 . . . . . 12 F6
Glenmount Path 🔢 SE18 . . 2 C1
Glenrose Cl SE14 . . . . 30 B3
Glenshiel Rd SE9 . . . . 12 A2
Glen The BR6 . . . . 57 A7
Glentrammon Ave BR6 . . 57 F4

Glentrammon Cl BR6 . . . . 57 F5
Glentrammon Gdns BR6 . 57 F4
Glentrammon Rd BR6 . . . 57 F4
Glenure Rd SE9 . . . . 12 A2
Glenview SE2 . . . . 13 D8
Glen View Rd DA1 . . . . . . 36 C7
Glen View Rd BR1 . . . . . . 42 D7
Glenwood TN30 . . . . 183 B3
Glenwood Cl
  Chatham ME5 . . . . 54 C3
  Gillingham ME7 . . . . 69 A7
  Maidstone ME16 . . . . . . 99 C5
Glenwood Ct 🔢 DA14 . . . 30 A4
Glimpsing Gn DA18 . . . . . . 3 E5
Glistening Glade ME8 . . . 69 E6
Gload Cres BR5 . . . . 58 D8
Globe Ct SE18 . . . . 12 C8
Globe La ME4 . . . . 53 F5
Globe Yd 🔢 DA11 . . . . . . 19 B1
Gloucester Ave
  Bexley DA16 . . . . 12 F3
  Sidcup DA15 . . . . 29 E6
Gloucester Cl ME8 . . . . . . 70 A8
Gloucester Ct RM18 . . . . 18 F5
Gloucester Par DA15 . . . . 13 A2
Gloucester Rd
  Dartford DA1 . . . . 32 B8
  Erith DA17 . . . . 4 A2
  Gravesend DA12 . . . . . . 36 C7
  Maidstone ME15 . . . . . . 116 D8
  Turner's Green TN5 . . . . 184 F6
Glover Cl SE2 . . . . 3 C2
Glovers Cl TN16 . . . . 72 B3
Glovers Mill Me4 . . . . 53 D5
Gloxinia Rd DA13 . . . . 35 B2
Glyn Davies Cl TN13 . . . . 83 E6
Glyndebourne Pk BR6 . . . 57 B8
Glynde Rd DA7 . . . . 13 E6
Glyndon Rd SE18 . . . . 2 C2
Glyn Dr DA14 . . . . 30 B4
Glynne Cl ME8 . . . . 69 D6
Goad Ave ME5 . . . . 68 B3
GOATHURST COMMON . . 107 B5
Goatsfield Rd TN16 . . . . . 88 C2
Goddards Cl TN17 . . . . . 179 B4
GODDARD'S GREEN 180 F2
Goddard's Green Cotts
  TN17 . . . . 180 F1
GODDEN GREEN 93 B3
Godden Rd ME6 . . . . 81 F7
Godden Way ME8 . . . . . . 55 A4
Goddings Dr ME1 . . . . 53 A3
Goddings Dr ME1 . . . . 58 C4
GODDINGTON 58 C2
Goddington Chase BR6 . . 58 B6
Goddington Ho BR6 . . . . . 58 C7
Goddington La
  Harrietsham ME17 . . . . 119 B6
  Orpington BR6 . . . . 58 A2
Godfrey Cl ME2 . . . . 38 F7
Godfrey Evans Cl TN10 . . 127 F4
Godfrey Hill SE18 . . . . . . 1 F2
Godfrey Rd SE18 . . . . 1 F2
Godstow Rd SE2 . . . . 3 C6
Godwin Ho SE18 . . . . 11 F6
Godwin Rd BR2 . . . . 42 C6
Goldace RM17 . . . . 17 F7
Goldcrest Cl
  Newham E16 . . . . 1 D0
  Woolwich SE28 . . . . 3 C7
Goldcrest Dr ME4 . . . . . . 40 C2
GOLDEN GREEN 128 F1
Golden Plover Cl E16 . . . . 1 A2
Golden Sq TN30 . . . . 193 B6
Golden Wood Cl ME5 . . . . 84 D7
Goldfinch Cl
  Larkfield ME20 . . . . 82 A3
  Orpington BR6 . . . . 58 A7
  Paddock Wood TN12 . . 146 A7
Goldfinch Rd SE28 . . . . . . 2 D1
Goldie Leigh Hospl SE2 . . 13 C1
Golding Cl
  Ditton ME20 . . . . 82 C1
  Rochester ME1 . . . . 53 E3
Golding Gdns TN12 . . . . 130 A7
Golding Rd TN13 . . . . 84 C5
Goldings TN12 . . . . 145 E5
Goldings Cl ME19 . . . . . . 97 A4
Goldings The ME8 . . . . . . 69 C7
Goldmark No SE3 . . . . 11 B8
Goldsel Rd BR8 . . . . 45 E1
Goldsmid Rd TN9 . . . . . . 143 C6
Goldsmith St 🔢 SE18 . . . . 2 B1
Goldsmith RM17 . . . . 17 F
Goldsmith Cl TN30 . . . . . 183 B
Goldsmith Rd ME8 . . . . . 69 E
Gold St DA12, DA13 . . . . 50 E
Goldstone Wlk ME5 . . . . . 68 A
GOLD STREET . . . . 50 E
Goldsworth Dr ME2 . . . . . 39 A
Goldwell La ME14 . . . . . . 100 C
Goldwing Cl E16 . . . . 1 A
Golf Links Ave DA11 . . . . 36 F6
GOLFORD . . . . 180 B
Golford Rd TN17 . . . . 179 F
Golf Rd BR1 . . . . 43 A
Gollogly Terr 🔢 SE7 . . . . 1 C
Gooch Cl ME16 . . . . 99 D
Goodall Cl ME8 . . . . 69 E
Goodbury Rd TN15 . . . . . 72 B
Goodensfield TN15 . . . . . 184 E
Gooding Ho SE7 . . . . 1 C
Goodley Stock Rd TN8,
  TN16 . . . . 105 B
Goodmead Rd BR6 . . . . . 44 A
Good Shepherd Prim Sch
  The ME4 . . . . 53 E

Goods Hill TN30 192 D8
Goods Station Rd TN1 159 B4
Goodtrees La TN8 155 B2
Goodwin Cl TN8 122 B2
Goodwin Dr
Maidstone ME14 100 B8
Sidcup DA14 30 D6
Goodwin Rd ME3 39 B7
Goodwins The TN2 158 F1
Goodwood Cl
High Halstow ME23 23 E4
Maidstone ME15 116 F6
Goodwood Cres DA12 36 C2
Goodworth Rd TN15 78 F3
Goosander Way SE28 2 D3
Goose Cl ME5 68 A7
GOOSE GREEN
Biddenden 181 E8
Hadlow 112 B2
Goose Green Cl BR5 44 A7
Gooseneck La TN27 151 C5
Goose Sq 8 E6 1 F7
Gordon Cl RM18 20 D7
Gordon Ct ME17 115 E3
Gordon Ho SE12 28 A8
Gordon Inf Sch ME2 53 A8
Gordon Jun Sch ME2 53 A8
Gordon Pl DA12 19 C1
Gordon Prim Sch SE9 11 F3
Gordon Promenade DA12 19 C1
Gordon Promenade E
DA12 19 D1
Gordon Rd
Chatham, Luton ME4 54 B2
Chatham ME4 54 A7
Dartford DA1 32 D8
Erith DA17 4 C2
Gillingham ME7 54 E5
Hoo St Werburgh ME3 40 D5
Northfleet DA11 35 E8
Rochester ME2 53 A8
Royal Tunbridge Wells
TN4 159 C7
Sevenoaks TN13 92 B2
Sidcup DA15 12 E2
Gordon Terr ME1 53 C4
Gordon Way BR1 42 A8
Gore Cotts DA2 33 C4
Gore Court Rd ME15 116 F5
Gore Farm Cotts DA2 33 C5
Gore Green Rd ME3 38 E7
Gore La TN17 163 E4
Gore Rd
Dartford DA2 33 C6
Silver Street ME9 87 F5
Gorham Cl ME6 81 F7
Gorham Dr
Maidstone ME15 101 A1
Tonbridge TN9 143 E8
Gorman Rd SE18 1 F2
Gorringe Ave DA4 47 D7
Gorse Ave ME5 67 F5
Gorse Cl E16 1 A7
Gorse Cres ME20 98 D8
Gorse Rd
Orpington BR5 59 A8
Rochester ME2 52 F8
Royal Tunbridge Wells
TN2 159 E5
Gorse Way DA3 49 A4
Gorse Wood Rd
Hartley DA3 49 A5
New Barn DA3 49 A6
Gorst St ME7 54 C5
Gossage Rd SE18 2 D1
Goss Hill BR8, DA2 32 C2
Gosshill Rd BR7 43 A7
Gossington Cl BR7 29 B4
Gothic Cl DA1 32 D5
GOUDHURST 177 F8
Goudhurst Cl ME16 99 E4
Goudhurst & Kilndown CE
Prim Sch TN17 177 F8
Goudhurst Rd
Cranbrook TN17 179 D8
Gillingham ME8 55 B3
Horsmonden TN12 163 B5
Knox Bridge TN12, TN17 165 C6
Marden TN12 148 B5
Gouge Ave DA11 35 E7
Gould Rd ME5 68 B3
Gourock Rd SE9 12 A2
Gover Hill TN11, ME18 111 E6
Gover View TN11 111 E7
Gower Ho ME14 100 A6
Grace Ave
Bexley DA7 13 F5
Maidstone ME16 99 D6
Grace Cl SE9 28 D5
Gracious La TN13 108 B5
Gracious Lane Bridge
TN13 108 A6
Gracious Lane End TN14 107 F5
Grafton Ave ME1 67 E8
GRAFTY GREEN 136 F7
Graham Cl ME4 53 F6
Graham Ct 12 BR1 28 B1
Graham Ho SE18 12 B7
Graham Rd DA7 14 A3
GRAIN 27 B6
Grainey Field ME9 70 E4
Grainger Wlk TN10 127 E6
Grain Rd
Gillingham ME8 69 C3
Grain ME3 26 D3
Grampian Cl
Orpington BR6 43 F3
Grampian Cl *continued*
Royal Tunbridge Wells
TN2 159 D5
Grampian Way ME15 101 A1
Gram Sch for Girls
Wilmington The DA2 32 B5
Granada Ho 8 ME15 100 A4
Granada St 9 ME15 100 A4
Granary TN12 146 B6
Granary Cl
Gillingham ME8 55 F1
Maidstone ME14 100 E5
Granary Cotts TN16 90 C3
Granby Ho 8 SE18 1 F2
Granby Rd
Eltham SE9 11 F4
Northfleet DA11 18 D1
Woolwich SE18 2 B3
Grand Ct 7 ME7 54 C6
Grand Depot Rd SE18 2 A1
Grandshore La TN17 166 B5
Grandsire Gdns ME3 40 E6
Grand View Ave TN16 72 C3
GRANGE 55 B6
Grange Cl
Edenbridge TN8 122 C1
Leybourne ME19 81 C2
Sidcup DA15 30 A5
Westerham TN16 89 C1
Grange Cres
6 Dartford DA2 16 B1
Erith SE28 3 C7
Tenterden TN30 183 A3
Grange Dr
Bromley BR7 28 F2
Pratt's Bottom BR6 58 C2
Grange Gdns TN4 158 D4
Grange Hill
Chatham ME5 54 B3
Plaxtol TN15 110 E8
Grangehill Pl SE9 11 F4
Grangehill Rd SE9 11 F3
Grange Ho
Erith DA8 15 A5
Gravesend DA11 36 A8
Maidstone ME16 99 A2
Grange La
Boxley ME14 84 A1
Hartley DA3 49 B2
Grange Park Coll ME19 81 B3
Grange Rd
Gillingham ME7 55 A6
Gravesend DA11 36 A8
Grays RM17 18 B8
Orpington BR6 57 C8
Platt TN15 95 C7
Rochester ME2 53 B7
Rusthall TN4 158 D4
Sevenoaks TN13 108 A8
Tenterden TN30 182 F3
Grange Rdbt ME7 55 A6
Grange The
East Malling ME19 98 A7
Langton Green TN3 157 F3
Sutton at Hone DA4 47 D8
Westerham TN16 89 C1
West Kingsdown TN15 61 F2
Grange Way
Erith DA8 15 B7
Hartley DA3 48 F3
Rochester ME1 53 C3
Grangeways Cl DA11 35 F4
Grangewood DA5 30 F7
Granite St SE18 2 F1
Grant Dr ME15 116 D6
Granton Rd DA14 30 C2
Grant Rd ME3 39 C3
Grant's Cotts ME17 120 B5
Grants La TN8, RH8 121 C6
Granville Ct
Erith SE2 3 D1
Maidstone ME14 100 A6
Sevenoaks TN13 92 A3
Granville Mews DA14 30 A4
Granville Rd
Bexley DA16 13 C4
Gillingham ME7 54 E5
Limpsfield RH8 104 A7
Maidstone ME14 100 A6
Northfleet DA11 35 F7
Royal Tunbridge Wells
TN1 159 C5
Sevenoaks TN13 92 A3
Sidcup DA14 30 B4
Westerham TN16 89 C1
Granville Sch The TN13 92 A4
Grapple Rd ME14 100 A7
Grasdene Rd SE18 13 A7
Grasmere Ave BR6 57 B7
Grasmere Gdns BR6 57 B7
Grasmere Gr ME2 39 C2
Grasmere Rd
Bexley DA7 14 C5
Orpington BR6 57 B7
Grass Banks DA1 32 F7
Grasshaven Way SE28 2 F5
Grassington Rd 11 DA14 30 A4
Grasslands ME17 117 E4
Grassmere ME19 81 F2
Grassy Glade ME7 69 B6
Grassy La TN13 108 B8
Grave La TN12 149 C8
Gravel Hill DA6 14 B2
Gravel Hill Cl DA6 14 B1
Gravel Hill Prim Sch DA6 14 B3
Gravelly Bottom Rd
ME17 118 B2
Gravelly Ways TN12 130 D5
Gravel Pit Way BR6 44 A1
Gravel Rd
Orpington BR2 56 E8
Sutton at Hone DA4 33 B1
Gravel Wlk ME1 53 D5
Gravelwood Cl BR7 29 C5
Graveney Cl ME3 39 C7
Graveney Rd ME15 116 F7
GRAVESEND 19 B2
Gravesend Gram Sch
DA12 36 D8
Gravesend Gram Sch for
Girls DA11 36 A7
Gravesend Rd
Higham ME2, ME3, DA12 38 C2
Rochester ME2 52 F8
Shorne DA12 37 D5
Vigo Village TN15 79 D6
Gravesend Rd Education Ctr
DA11 19 A1
Gravesend Sta DA11 19 B1
Graves Est DA16 13 B5
Gravesham Com Hospl
DA11 19 A1
Gravesham Ct 8 DA12 36 B8
Gray Ho SE2 3 D1
Grayland Cl BR1 42 D8
Graylands RM17 17 E8
Graylings The ME1 53 B3
Grayne Ave ME3 27 B5
GRAYS 18 A7
Grays Farm Prim Sch BR5 44 B8
Grays Farm Rd BR5 44 B8
Grays Rd TN16 89 D7
Grays Sh Ctr RM17 18 A8
Grays Sta RM17 18 A8
Grazeley Cl DA6 14 C2
Great Ash BR7 29 A1
Great Basin Rd ME12 27 F2
Great Bounds Dr TN4 142 E3
Great Brooms Rd TN4 159 C8
GREAT BUCKLAND 64 F4
Great Comp Garden*
TN15 95 E6
Great Courtlands TN3 158 A3
Great Durgates TN5 184 E5
Great Elms TN11 111 E1
Great Elms Rd BR2 42 C5
Great Footway TN3 157 F3
Great Hall Arc 3 TN1 159 B3
Great Hall Arcade 9
TN1 159 B3
Great Harry Dr SE9 29 A5
Great Ivy Mill Cotts
ME15 115 F7
Great Lines ME7 54 B5
Great Lodge Ret Pk TN2 143 E1
Great Mead TN8 122 C3
GREATNESS 92 D6
Greatness La TN14 92 C6
Greatness Rd TN14 92 C6
Great Oak
Hurst Green TN19 194 A3
Royal Tunbridge Wells
TN2 159 D6
Great Queen St DA1 15 F1
Great South Ave ME4 54 A1
Great Thrift BR5 43 C5
Great Till Cl TN14 75 E3
Greatwood BR7 29 A1
Grebe Apartments 15
ME15 116 E5
Grebe Cl ME3 25 C4
Grebe Ct ME20 81 F1
Grecian Rd TN1 159 B2
Grecian St ME14 100 A6
Greenacre DA1 32 D6
Greenacre Cl
Chatham ME5 68 A5
Swanley BR8 45 E5
Greenacres SE9 12 A1
Green Acres 5 DA14 29 F4
Greenacre Sch ME5 67 F5
Greenacres Cl BR6 57 C6
Greenacres Prim Sch SE9 29 A6
Greenbank ME5 68 B8
Green Bank Cl ME7 69 A5
Greenbank Lodge 2 BR7 43 A8
Greenbanks DA1 32 E6
Greenbay Rd SE7 11 D7
Greenborough Cl ME15 116 E6
Green Cl ME1 53 D2
Greencourt Rd BR5 43 E4
Green Court Rd BR8 45 D3
Greencroft Cl E6 1 D8
Greendale Wlk 4 DA11 35 E5
Green Farm Cl BR6 57 F5
Green Farm La DA12 37 E5
Greenfield TN8 122 D1
Greenfield Cl
Eccles ME20 83 A6
Rusthall TN4 158 C5
Greenfield Cotts ME14 84 C3
Greenfield Ct SE9 28 E5
Greenfield Dr BR1 42 C7
Greenfield Gdns BR5 43 D2
Greenfield Rd
Gillingham ME7 54 D6
Joyden's Wood DA2 31 D3
Greenfields ME15 116 E8
Greenfields Cl ME3 39 D3
Greenfields Com Prim Sch
ME15 116 E8
Greenfields Sch TN27 182 C6
Greenfinches
Gillingham ME7 68 F6
New Barn DA3 49 B6
Greenfrith Dr TN10 127 B6
Green Gdns BR6 57 C5
Greenhaven Dr SE28 3 B7
Green Hedges TN30 193 B8
GREEN HILL 72 F7
Greenhill TN12 149 E5
Green Hill
Biggin Hill BR6 72 F7
Maidstone ME15 101 B1
Woolwich SE18 1 F1
Greenhill Cts SE18 1 F1
Greenhill La TN27 153 F7
Green Hill La ME17 119 D1
Greenhill Rd
Northfleet DA11 35 F6
Otford TN14 76 C4
Otford TN14 76 C5
Greenhill Terr SE18 1 F1
GREENHITHE 17 B2
Greenhithe 3 ME15 100 A3
Greenhithe Cl DA15 29 E8
Greenhithe for Bluewater Sta
DA9 17 A2
Greenholm Rd SE9 12 B2
GREENHURST 104 B3
Greenhurst La
Limpsfield RH8 104 A4
Oxted RH8 104 A3
Greening St SE2 3 C2
Green La
Cliffe ME3 22 B6
Collier Street TN12 147 E8
East End TN17 181 C2
Eltham BR7, SE9 29 B5
Four Elms TN8 123 C7
Grain ME3 27 B5
High Halden TN26 169 F3
Lamberhurst TN12 162 B3
Langley Heath ME17 117 E3
Maidstone ME17 116 C3
Meopham Station DA13 50 B2
Paddock Wood TN12 146 A5
Platt's Heath ME17 119 F2
Smarden TN27 153 A1
Sutton Valence ME17 134 B4
Trottiscliffe ME19 80 A5
Greenlands
Platt TN15 95 C7
Sole Street DA12 50 D4
Greenlands Rd TN15 93 B8
Green Lane Bsns Pk SE9 29 A6
Green Lane Cotts
Collier Street TN12 131 D1
Langley Heath ME17 117 E3
Green La The TN11 125 F1
Green Lawns 10 SE18 2 B2
Greenlaw St SE18 2 A3
Greenleas TN2 160 C6
Greenleigh Ave BR5 44 B5
Greenoak Rise TN16 72 C1
Green Pl DA1 14 E2
Green Rd TN12 163 A6
Greensand Rd ME15 101 A2
Greensand Ridge ME17 118 E2
Green Sands ME5 84 C8
Green's Cotts ME15 115 A4
Greens End SE18 2 B2
Greenshields Ind Est E16 1 A4
Greenside
High Halden TN26 183 E7
Maidstone ME15 100 B3
Sidcup DA5 30 E7
Swanley BR8 45 D7
Greenside Wlk TN16 72 B1
Greenslade Prim Sch
SE18 12 D8
Greensleeves Way ME19 97 C3
Green Sq TN5 184 F5
Green St ME7 54 C5
GREEN STREET GREEN
Hartley 34 A2
Orpington 57 E4
Green Street Green Prim Sch
BR6 57 F4
Green Street Green Rd DA1,
DA2 33 D4
Green The
Bexley, Bexleyheath DA7 14 A6
Bexley, Falconwood DA16 12 E3
Biddenden TN27 182 D6
Dartford DA2 33 D6
East Farleigh ME15 115 B7
Frant TN3 173 C3
Hayes BR2 42 A2
Langton Green TN3 157 E3
Leigh TN11 125 F1
Lewisham BR1 28 A5
Orpington BR5 30 B1
Sevenoaks TN13 92 D5
Sidcup DA14 30 A4
Westerham TN16 89 D1
West Tilbury RM18 19 E8
Greentrees Ave TN10 127 F5
Green Vale DA6 13 D2
Greenvale Gdns ME8 55 B2
Greenvale Inf Sch ME4 54 A2
Greenvale Rd SE9 12 A3
Green View Ave TN11 126 A1
Greenview Cres TN11 126 E4
Greenview Wlk ME8 55 A4
Greenway
Chatham ME5 67 D6
Chislehurst BR7 29 B3
Cranbrook TN17 179 B4
Tatsfield TN16 88 C7
Green Way
Bromley BR2 42 E3
Eltham SE9 11 D2
Hartley DA3 48 E4
Green Way *continued*
Maidstone ME16 99 B3
Royal Tunbridge Wells
TN2 159 E8
Greenway Court Farm Cotts
ME17 103 A1
Greenway Court Rd
ME17 103 A1
Greenway La ME17 119 A7
Greenways
Addington ME19 80 E2
Maidstone ME14 100 F5
New Barn DA3 49 D6
Greenways The TN12 145 F5
Greenway The
Orpington BR5 44 B3
Oxted RH8 104 B2
GREENWICH 1 A3
Greenwich Cl
Chatham ME5 68 B4
Maidstone ME16 99 D4
Greenwich Com Coll 1
SE18 2 C2
Greenwich Cres E6 1 E8
Greenwich Hts SE18 11 E7
Greenwich Sh Pk SE7 1 B2
Green Wlk DA1 14 F3
Greenwood Cl
Orpington BR5 43 E3
Sidcup DA15 30 A6
Greenwood Gdns RH8 104 A1
Greenwood Ho 8 RM17 18 B8
Greenwood Pl TN15 79 A2
Greenwood Rd DA5 31 D4
Greenwood Way TN13 91 F2
Greggs Wood Rd TN2 159 E7
Gregor Mews SE3 11 A7
Gregory Cl ME8 69 E4
Gregory Cres SE9 28 D8
Gregory Ho SE3 11 B5
Grenada Rd SE7 11 C7
Grenadier Cl ME15 100 F2
Grenadier St E16 2 A5
Grenfell Cl TN16 72 C7
Grenville Cl DA13 64 A8
Gresham Ave DA3 48 F4
Gresham Cl
3 Gillingham ME8 55 F1
Sidcup DA5 13 F1
Tonbridge TN10 127 E7
Gresham Rd
Coxheath ME17 115 D3
Newham E16 1 B7
Greshams Way TN8 122 A2
Gresswell Cl DA14 30 A5
Greybury La TN8 138 B3
Greyfriars Cl ME16 99 D5
Greyhound Way DA1 14 E1
Grey Ladies Oasts TN15 95 B3
Greys Park Cl BR2 56 D5
Greystone Pk TN14 90 E2
Greystones Cl TN15 76 E2
Greystones Rd ME15 101 A2
Grey Wethers ME14 83 E4
Gribble Bridge La TN27 182 B5
Grice Ave TN16 72 C6
Grieveson Ho ME4 54 A4
Grieves Rd DA11 35 F5
Griffin Manor Way SE28 2 D3
Griffin Rd SE18 2 D2
Griffin Way SE28 2 E3
Griffin Wlk DA9 16 F2
Griffiths Ho 2 SE18 12 B8
Grigg La TN27 152 C7
Grigg's Cross BR5 44 D3
Griggs Way TN15 95 A7
Grimsby Gr E16 2 B4
Grinling Ho 6 SE18 2 A2
Grizedale Cl ME1 67 D8
Gromenfield TN3 171 C7
GROOMBRIDGE 171 C7
Groombridge Cl DA16 13 A2
Groombridge Hill TN3 157 D1
Groombridge Pl* TN3 171 C8
Groombridge Place Gdns*
TN3 171 C8
Groombridge Rd TN3 157 A1
Groombridge St Thomas' CE
Aided Prim Sch TN3 171 C6
Groombridge Sq 13
ME15 116 F6
Groombridge Station*
TN3 171 C7
Groom Cl BR2 42 B5
Groom Way ME17 120 E6
Grosmont Rd SE18 2 F1
Grosvenor Ave ME4 53 E3
Grosvenor Bridge TN1 159 B5
Grosvenor Cres DA1 15 D2
Grosvenor Ho 5 ME15 116 F5
Grosvenor Manor DA5 31 D6
Grosvenor Pk TN1 159 A4
Grosvenor Rd
Bexley DA6 13 E2
Erith DA17 14 A8
Gillingham ME7 55 A1
Orpington BR5 43 E3
Royal Tunbridge Wells
TN1 159 A4
Grosvenor Sq DA3 48 E6
Grosvenor Wlk TN1 159 A4
Grove Ave TN1 159 A2
Grovebury Cl DA8 14 D8
Grovebury Ct DA6 14 B2
Grovebury Rd SE2 3 B4

Grove Cl
Goose Green TN11 . . . . .112 C3
Hayes BR2 . . . . 56 A8
Grove Cotts TN30 . . . . 193 B6
Grove Ct
Greenwich SE3 . . . . 11 A6
8 Rochester ME1 . . . . . . 53 B7
GROVE GREEN 100 E5
Grove Green La ME14 . . . . 100 E5
Grove Green Rd ME14 . . . . 100 F5
Groveherst Rd DA1 . . . . 15 F4
Grove Hill Gdns TN1 . . . . . 159 B2
Grove Hill Ho TN1 . . . . 159 B3
Grove Hill Rd TN1 . . . . 159 B3
Grovehurst La TN12 . . . . . . 163 C5
Grove La ME15 . . . . 131 D7
Grovelands ME17 . . . . 120 E5
Grovelands Rd BR5 . . . . . . 30 A1
Grovelands Way RM17 . . . . 17 F8
Grove Market Pl SE9 . . . . . . 11 C7
GROVE PARK 28 B5
Grove Park Rd SE9 . . . . . . 28 D6
Grove Park Sta SE12 . . . . . 28 B5
Grove Rd
Bexley, Bexleyheath DA7 . . 14 C3
8 Bexley, West Heath
DA17 . . . . 13 F8
Chatham ME4 . . . . 54 B2
Gillingham ME7 . . . . 55 A6
Grays RM17 . . . . 18 C8
Maidstone ME15 . . . . . . 116 C7
Northfleet DA11 . . . . 18 B2
Penshurst TN11, TN8 . . . 140 E2
Rochester ME2 . . . . 53 B8
Seal TN15 . . . . 93 B5
Sevenoaks TN14 . . . . 92 C6
Tatsfield TN16 . . . . 88 C7
Upper Halling ME2 . . . . . . 65 E5
Grover St **3** TN1 . . . . . . 159 B4
Groves The ME6 . . . . 81 F7
Grove The
Bexley DA6 . . . . 13 D3
Biggin Hill TN16 . . . . 72 E1
Fawkham Green DA3 . . . . . 48 A2
Gravesend DA12 . . . . 36 B8
Maidstone ME14 . . . . 101 A3
Pembury TN2 . . . . 160 D8
Sidcup DA14 . . . . 30 E4
Swanley BR8 . . . . 45 F6
Swanscombe DA10 . . . . . . 17 F2
West Kingsdown TN15 . . . 61 F1
Grove Vale BR7 . . . . 29 A2
Grove Wood Ct BR1 . . . . . . 43 A6
Grove Wood Cotts TN11 . . 109 A1
Grovewood Ct ME14 . . . . . 100 E4
Grovewood Dr ME14 . . . . . 100 E4
GRUBB STREET 48 B8
Grub St RH8 . . . . 104 C6
Guardian Ct ME8 . . . . 55 C1
Guardian Ind Est TN12 . . 148 C7
Guards Ct TN10 . . . . 127 E7
Guestwick TN10 . . . . 127 F5
Guibal Rd SE12 . . . . 28 B7
Guildables La RH8, TN8 . . 121 E7
Guildford Gdns ME2 . . . . . . 52 C6
Guildford Rd
Newham E6 . . . . 1 F7
7 Royal Tunbridge Wells
TN1 . . . . 159 B3
Guildhall Mus* ME1 . . . . . . 53 C6
Guild Rd
Erith DA8 . . . . 14 F7
Greenwich SE7 . . . . 11 D8
Guiness Dr ME2 . . . . 39 B2
Gulland Ho **4** ME14 . . . 100 B4
Gullands ME17 . . . . 117 E4
Gulliver Rd DA15 . . . . 29 E6
Gumley Rd RM20 . . . . 17 E8
Gumping Rd BR5, BR6 . . . . 57 C8
Gun Back La TN12 . . . . . . 163 A5
Gundulph Ho TN10 . . . . . . 127 C3
Gundulph Rd
Bromley BR2 . . . . 42 C6
Rochester ME1 . . . . 53 E4
Gundulph Sq ME1 . . . . 53 C6
Gunfleet Cl DA12 . . . . 36 E8
GUN GREEN 189 C2
Gun Hill ME18 . . . . 19 D8
Gun La ME7 . . . . 53 B7
Gun Lane Bsns Est **5**
ME2 . . . . 53 B7
Gunner La SE18 . . . . 2 A1
Gunnery Terr SE18 . . . . 2 C3
Gunning St SE18 . . . . 2 E2
Gunnis Cl ME8 . . . . 69 D4
Gunn Rd DA10 . . . . 17 E1
Gun Tower Mews ME1 . . . . 53 B4
Gurdon Rd SE7 . . . . 1 B1
Guston Rd ME14 . . . . 100 C6
Guy Barnett Gr SE3 . . . . . . 11 A4
Gwillim Cl DA15 . . . . 13 A2
Gwynn Rd DA11 . . . . 35 C6
Gybbon Rise TN12 . . . . . . 149 E3
Gybbons Rd TN17 . . . . 191 F3
Gypsy Way ME23 . . . . 23 E3

H

Haberdashers Askes Knights
Acad BR1 . . . . 28 A4
Hackney Rd ME16 . . . . 99 C2
Hadden Rd SE28 . . . . 2 E3
Haddon Gr DA15 . . . . 30 A8

Haddon Rd BR5 . . . . 44 C4
Hadleigh Ct ME7 . . . . 69 A3
Hadleigh Wlk **1** E6 . . . . . . 1 E7
Hadley Cl DA13 . . . . 64 B8
Hadley Ct TN4 . . . . 158 F6
Hadley Gdns ME7 . . . . . . 102 E2
Hadley House ME5 . . . . 43 F7
Hadley Rd DA17 . . . . 3 F2
HADLOW 111 E1
Hadlow Coll TN11 . . . . . . 128 D8
Hadlow Coll Mottingham Ctr
SE12 . . . . 28 C7
Hadlow Ct TN9 . . . . 127 C2
Hadlow Pk TN11 . . . . 111 E1
Hadlow Rd
Bexley DA16 . . . . 13 C7
Maidstone ME14 . . . . . . 100 C5
Sidcup DA14 . . . . 30 A4
Tonbridge TN9 . . . . 127 D3
Hadlow Road E TN10,
TN11 . . . . 128 A5
Hadlow Sch TN11 . . . . . . 128 E8
HADLOW STAIR 127 F4
Hadlow Stair Rd TN10 . . . 127 F4
Hadlow Way DA13 . . . . 35 E1
Haffenden Ct TN12 . . . . . 148 D6
HAFFENDEN QUARTER . . 169 A7
Haffenden Rd TN30 . . . . . 183 B1
Ha-Ha Rd SE18 . . . . 11 F8
Haig Ave
Chatham, Luton ME4 . . . . 54 A2
Chatham ME1 . . . . 53 D1
Gillingham ME7 . . . . 54 E4
Haig Ct BR7 . . . . 29 B3
Haig Gdns DA12 . . . . 36 C8
Haig Rd TN16 . . . . 72 E2
Haig Villas ME3 . . . . 40 A5
Haileybury Rd BR6 . . . . . . 58 A6
Hailey Rd Bsns Pk DA18 . . . 4 A4
Hailey Rd DA18 . . . . 4 A4
Hailing Mews BR2 . . . . 42 B6
Hailstone Cl TN11 . . . . . . 128 E8
Haimo Prim Sch SE9 . . . . . 11 D2
Haimo Rd SE9 . . . . 11 D2
Hainault St SE9 . . . . 29 B7
Halcot Ave DA6 . . . . 14 C2
Haldane Gdns DA11 . . . . . . 35 C7
Haldane Rd SE28 . . . . 3 B6
Halden Cl ME15 . . . . 116 F6
Halden La TN17 . . . . 191 F6
HALE 68 D8
Hale Cl DA16 . . . . 57 C6
Hale Cotts DA9 . . . . 17 C2
Hale Ct TN12 . . . . 130 A7
Hale La TN14 . . . . 75 F2
Hale Oak Rd
Hall's Green TN8, TN14 . . 124 E4
Sevenoaks Weald TN14 . . 108 B1
Hale Rd ME3 . . . . 39 C7
Hales Cl TN30 . . . . 193 B8
Hales Ct TN30 . . . . 193 B8
Hale St TN12 . . . . 130 A7
Haleys **7** ME1 . . . . 83 A8
Half Moon La TN11 . . . . . 126 D6
Halfpence La DA12 . . . . 51 B7
Halfpenny St SE18 . . . . 99 A2
Halfway St DA15 . . . . 29 E7
Halifax St ME5 . . . . 68 B6
Halifield Dr DA17 . . . . 3 E3
Hallam Cl BR7 . . . . 28 E3
Halford Way DA1 . . . . 15 C2
Hallgate SE3 . . . . 11 A4
Hall Hill TN15 . . . . 93 C4
HALLING 66 B5
Halling Prim Sch ME2 . . . . 66 B3
Halling Sta ME2 . . . . 66 A3
Hall Place Cres DA1, DA5 . 14 D2
Hall Place & Gdns* DA1 . . 14 C1
Hall Rd
Aylesford ME20 . . . . 82 F1
Chatham ME5 . . . . 68 C3
Dartford DA1 . . . . 15 F3
High Halstow ME3 . . . . . . 24 C6
Northfleet, Pepper Hill
DA11 . . . . 35 C5
Wouldham SE1 . . . . 66 C3
Halls Cotts TN5 . . . . 184 F5
Hallsfield Rd ME5 . . . . 67 D2
HALL'S GREEN 125 A7
Hall's Hole Rd TN2 . . . . . 159 E4
Hallsville Prim Sch E16 . . . . 1 A7
Hall The SE3 . . . . 11 A4
Hall View SE9 . . . . 28 D6
Hallwards TN12 . . . . 149 E2
Hallwood Cl ME8 . . . . 69 D5
Hallwood Ho ME5 . . . . 68 C2
Hallywell Cres E6 . . . . 1 F8
Halons Rd SE9 . . . . 23 F4
Halsbrook Rd SE3 . . . . 11 D4
HALSTEAD 57 A1
Halstead La TN14 . . . . 74 E5
Halstead Prim Sch TN14 . . 74 F7
Halstead Rd DA8 . . . . 14 E6
Halstead Wlk ME16 . . . . . . 99 C7
Halstow CI ME15 . . . . 106 B6
Halstow Prim Sch **9** SE10 . 1 A1
Halstow Rd SE10, SE3 . . . . . 1 A1
Halt Robin Rd DA17 . . . . . . 4 B2
Hambledon Ct ME16 . . . . . 99 B3
Hambledown Rd DA15 . . . . 29 E8
Hamble Rd TN10 . . . . 127 B5
Hambro Ave BR2 . . . . 42 A1
Hamelin Rd ME7 . . . . 68 F8
Hamerton Rd DA11 . . . . . . 18 B2
HAM GREEN 199 C1
Hamilton Cl ME6 . . . . 81 F7

Hamilton Ct
Maidstone ME5 . . . . 54 C1
Rochester ME1 . . . . 53 B4
Royal Tunbridge Wells
TN4 . . . . 159 A5
Hamilton Ho
Coxheath ME17 . . . . 115 C3
Maidstone ME15 . . . . . . 116 F5
1 Royal Tunbridge Wells
TN4 . . . . 159 A5
Hamilton Rd
Bexley DA7 . . . . 13 E5
Gillingham ME7 . . . . 54 D7
Sidcup DA15 . . . . 30 A4
Hamilton Wlk DA8 . . . . 14 F7
Ham La
Gillingham ME7 . . . . 68 E3
Lenham ME17 . . . . 120 C5
Hamlea Cl SE12 . . . . 11 A2
Hamlet Est DA8 . . . . 4 D1
Hamlet Ho
Eltham SE9 . . . . 12 A2
8 Erith DA8 . . . . 14 E7
Hamlin Rd TN13 . . . . 91 E6
Hamlyn Ct TN13 . . . . 91 E6
Hammelton Rd **2** BR1 . . . 42 A8
Hammerton Ct DA5 . . . . . . 31 E5
HAMMERWOOD 154 B3
Hammerwood Pk*
RH19 . . . . 154 C2
Hammonds **9** TN18 . . . 189 A2
Hammonds Sq ME6 . . . . . . 82 A8
Hammond Way **2** SE28 . . 3 B6
Hamond Hill **6** ME4 . . . . 53 E4
Hampden Ave ME19 . . . . . . 96 F3
Hampshire CI ME5 . . . . 68 C7
Hampshire Dr ME15 . . . . . 116 C8
Hampshires The ME17 . . . 119 C6
Hampson Way ME14 . . . . . 101 A4
Hampstead Cl SE28 . . . . 3 B5
Hampstead La ME18 . . . . . 113 C1
Hampton Cl ME5 . . . . 68 A5
Hampton Cotts TN14 . . . . . 74 F4
Hampton Cres DA12 . . . . . 36 E6
Hampton Ct DA8 . . . . 14 D7
Hampton Ho DA7 . . . . 14 B3
Hampton Rd ME14 . . . . . . 100 C6
Hamptons Rd TN11 . . . . . 111 B5
Ham River Hill ME14 . . . . . 39 A6
Ham Shades Cl **1** DA15 . . 30 A5
Hamwick Gn ME5 . . . . 68 C1
Hanameel St E16 . . . . 1 B5
Hanbury Cl ME18 . . . . 113 E7
Hanbury Dr TN16 . . . . 72 B6
Hanbury Wlk DA5 . . . . 31 E5
Hancock Cl ME3 . . . . 39 B1
Handel Cres RM18 . . . . 19 A7
Handel Wlk TN10 . . . . 127 E6
Hands Wlk E16 . . . . 1 A7
Hanes Dene ME5 . . . . 65 F5
Hang Grove Hill BR6 . . . . . 73 B6
Hanging Bank TN14 . . . . . 104 B2
Hangmans Cnr BR7 . . . . . . 43 B8
Hanley Ct TN13 . . . . 92 B4
Hanmer Way TN12 . . . . . . 149 E2
Hannah Cl ME4 . . . . 54 A3
Hanover Ave E16 . . . . 1 A5
Hanover Ct
10 Bromley BR2 . . . . . . 42 A6
Maidstone ME14 . . . . . . 100 B5
Hanover Dr
Chislehurst BR7 . . . . 29 C4
Gillingham ME8 . . . . 69 C4
Hanover Gn ME20 . . . . 81 F3
Hanover PI DA3 . . . . 62 F8
Hanover Rd
Coxheath ME17 . . . . 115 C3
Royal Tunbridge Wells
TN1 . . . . 159 A4
Hanover Way DA7 . . . . 13 D4
Hansol Rd DA6 . . . . 13 E2
Hansom Terr **1** BR1 . . . . 42 B8
Hanson Dr ME15 . . . . 115 F3
Hanway ME4 . . . . 55 A2
Harbex Cl DA5 . . . . 31 E5
Harbledown Ho ME16 . . . . 99 B2
Harbledown Manor ME8 . . 55 B3
Harbledown Pl **7** BR5 . . . 44 C5
Harborough Ave DA15 . . . . 29 F8
HARBOURLAND 100 B8
Harbourland Cl ME14 . . . 100 B8
Harbourne La TN26, TN30 183 D5
Harbour The ME17 . . . . . . 134 E5
Harcourt Ave DA15 . . . . . . 30 C8
Harcourt Gdns ME8 . . . . . . 63 C4
Harcourt Rd DA6 . . . . 13 E3
Harden Cl **1** SE18 . . . . 1 E2
Harden Rd DA11 . . . . 35 F6
Hardie Cl ME19 . . . . 81 F1
Hardinge Ave TN4 . . . . . . 142 E3
Hardinge Cl ME8 . . . . 69 D4
Hardinge Cres SE18 . . . . . . 2 C3
Hardinge St SE18 . . . . 2 B3
Harding Ho **9** SE18 . . . . . . 1 F2
Harding Rd DA7 . . . . 13 F5
Hardman Rd SE7 . . . . 1 B1
Hardres Terr BR5 . . . . 58 D8
Hardstown ME4 . . . . 54 A4
Hardwick Cres **2** DA2 . . . 16 B1
Hardwick Ct DA8 . . . . 14 D4
Hardwick Ho ME15 . . . . . 116 E8
Hardwick Rd TN1 . . . . 126 E6
Hardy Ave
Newham E16 . . . . 1 A5
Northfleet DA11 . . . . 35 E6
Hardy Cl DA1 . . . . 26 B6
Hardy Gr DA1 . . . . 16 A3
Hardy Lodge ME1 . . . . 53 B4

Hardy Rd **2** SE3 . . . . 11 A8
Hardy St ME14 . . . . 100 A6
Harebell Cl
3 Chatham ME5 . . . . . . 67 F4
Maidstone ME14 . . . . . . 100 E5
Harebell Dr E6 . . . . 2 A8
Haredale Cl ME1 . . . . 67 D7
Harefield Rd DA14 . . . . 30 D5
Harenc Sch DA14 . . . . 30 C3
HAREPLAIN 167 C4
Harescroft TN2 . . . . 172 F7
Hare St
2 Chatham ME4 . . . . . . 54 B3
Woolwich SE18 . . . . 2 A2
Harewood Lincoln Ho **4**
DA11 . . . . 18 D1
Harfst Way BR8 . . . . 45 C8
Hargate Ct TN2 . . . . 172 F8
Hargood Rd SE3 . . . . 11 C6
Harland Ave DA15 . . . . 29 E6
Harland Rd SE12 . . . . 28 A7
Harlands Gr BR6 . . . . 57 B6
Harland Way TN4 . . . . 142 F4
Harlech Cl ME2 . . . . 38 F1
Harlequin Ho **1** DA18 . . . . 3 E3
Harley **5** BR7 . . . . 43 D8
Harleyford BR1 . . . . 42 C8
Harley Gdns BR6 . . . . 57 E6
Harlington ME17 . . . . 116 C5
Harlinger St **1** SE18 . . . . . 1 E3
Harlington Rd DA7 . . . . 13 E4
Harman Ave DA11 . . . . 36 B3
Harman Cl ME5 . . . . 68 B3
Harman Dr DA15 . . . . 12 F1
Harmer Ct
Royal Tunbridge Wells
TN4 . . . . 143 A2
Swanscombe DA10 . . . . . 17 F1
Harmer Rd DA10 . . . . 17 F1
Harmer St DA12 . . . . 19 C1
Harmers Way TN27 . . . . . 137 F3
Harmony St TN4 . . . . 158 D4
Harmony Way **1** BR1, BR2 42 A7
Harmsworth St TN17 . . . . 190 E6
Harness Rd SE28 . . . . 3 A4
Harnetts Cl BR8 . . . . 45 D2
Harold Ave
Erith DA17 . . . . 3 F1
Gillingham ME7 . . . . 54 E4
Harold Campbell Ct DA1 . . 32 D8
Harold Gibbons Ct SE7 . . . 11 C8
Harold Ho **2** TN2 . . . . . . 159 C7
Harold Rd
Cuxton ME2 . . . . 52 C3
Hawley DA2 . . . . 32 F4
Harper Rd E6 . . . . 1 F7
Harp Farm Rd ME14 . . . . . 84 C4
Harple La ME14 . . . . 84 F1
Harpswood ME17 . . . . 102 F1
Harptree Dr ME5 . . . . 67 F5
Harraden Rd SE3 . . . . 11 C6
Harrier Mews SE28 . . . . 2 D4
Harrier Way E6 . . . . 1 F8
Harries Rd TN12 . . . . 149 E2
Harrietsham Sta ME17 . . . 119 D6
Harriet Dr ME1 . . . . 53 B3
Harriet Mews DA15 . . . . . . 13 B5
Harriet Way BR2 . . . . 42 A6
Harrietsham CE Prim Sch
ME17 . . . . 119 C6
Harrington Ho **2** BR1 . . . 42 A8
Harrington Way SE18 . . . . . 1 D3
Harris Acad DA16 . . . . 12 E3
Harris Cl SE3 . . . . 35 F5
Harris Ho ME2 . . . . 66 B4
Harrison Ct **4** ME8 . . . . . 55 F1
Harrison Dr
Bromley BR1 . . . . 43 B5
Harrietsham ME17 . . . . . . 23 E4
High Halstow ME23 . . . . . 23 E4
Harrison Rd TN15 . . . . 94 F7
Harrison Way TN13 . . . . . . 92 A5
Harris PI ME15 . . . . 99 F5
Harris Rd DA7 . . . . 13 F6
Harrogate Ct **8** SE12 . . . . 28 A8
Harrowby Gdns DA11 . . . . 35 E6
Harrow Cl TN8 . . . . 122 D3
Harrow Ct
Chatham ME5 . . . . 68 C4
Stockbury ME9 . . . . 86 D8
Harrow Gdns BR6 . . . . 58 B6
Harrow Manor Way SE2 . . . 3 C3
Harrow Rd
Gillingham ME7 . . . . 68 F6
Halstead TN14 . . . . 74 E4
Harrow Way ME14 . . . . . . 100 E5
Hart Dyke Cres BR8 . . . . . . 45 D6
Hart Dyke Rd
Orpington BR5 . . . . 44 C1
Swanley BR8 . . . . 45 D6
Hartfield Cl TN10 . . . . 127 E5
Hartfield Cres BR4 . . . . 56 A7
Hartfield PI DA11 . . . . 35 D8
Hartfield Rd
Cowden TN8 . . . . 155 C6
Hayes BR4 . . . . 56 A7
Stick Hill TN8 . . . . 139 A2
Hartford Rd DA5 . . . . 14 A1
Hartford Wlk **8** DA17 . . . . 4 A1
Hart Ho BR6 . . . . 44 A2
Harting Rd SE9 . . . . 28 E5
Hartington Cl BR6 . . . . 57 C5
Hartington Rd E16 . . . . 1 B7
Hartington St ME4 . . . . 54 A3
Hartlake Rd TN11 . . . . . . 128 D3
Hartlands Cl DA5 . . . . 13 F1
Hart Lane DA13 . . . . 64 C3

Hartlepool Ct E16 . . . . 2 B4
HARTLEY
Cranbrook 178 F1
New Barn 48 F3
Hartley Bottom Rd DA3 . . 49 C2
Hartley Cl
Bromley BR1 . . . . 42 F7
Maidstone ME15 . . . . . . 116 F6
Hartley Court Gdns
TN17 . . . . 179 A3
HARTLEY GREEN 48 E4
Hartley Hill DA3 . . . . 49 A1
Hartley Mews ME8 . . . . . . 55 B3
Hartley Prim Sch DA3 . . . . 48 E3
Hartley Rd
Bexley DA16 . . . . 13 C2
Hartley TN17 . . . . 179 A3
Longfield DA3 . . . . 48 E7
Westerham TN16 . . . . 89 D2
HARTLIP 70 F7
Hartlip Endowed CE Prim
Sch ME9 . . . . 70 D5
Hartlip Hill ME9 . . . . 70 F7
Hartmann Rd E16 . . . . 1 E5
Hartnokes TN18 . . . . 189 A2
Hartnup St ME16 . . . . 99 C2
Hartop Cl ME7 . . . . 48 D8
Harpiece **1** ME8 . . . . 55 F2
Hartridge Farm ME15 . . . 115 A7
Hart Shaw DA3 . . . . 49 B7
Hartshill Rd ME15 . . . . 35 F6
Hartslands Rd TN13 . . . . . 92 C4
Hartslock DA18, SE2 . . . . . . 3 D4
Hartsmead Rd SE9 . . . . 28 F6
Hart St ME16 . . . . 99 F3
Hart Street Commercial Ctr
ME16 . . . . 99 F3
Hartville Rd SE18 . . . . 2 E2
Hartwell Ho **2** SE7 . . . . . . 1 B1
Harty Ave ME8 . . . . 69 B3
Harvard Ct **9** SE9 . . . . . . 12 A1
HARVEL 64 C3
Harvel Ave ME2 . . . . 52 F7
Harvel Ct BR5, BR7 . . . . . . 44 A6
Harvel Cres SE2 . . . . 3 D1
Harvel La DA13 . . . . 64 B2
Harvel Rd DA13 . . . . 80 A8
Harvel St DA13 . . . . 64 C3
Harvest Bank Rd BR4 . . . . 56 A7
Harvesters Cl ME8 . . . . . . 69 E7
Harvesters Way ME14 . . . 100 D4
Harvest Ho TN10 . . . . 127 D6
Harvest Ridge ME19 . . . . . 81 D2
Harvest Way BR8 . . . . 45 D2
Harvey Gdns SE7 . . . . 1 C1
Harvey Point **9** E16 . . . . . 1 A8
Harvey Rd ME8 . . . . 69 E8
Harvill Rd DA14 . . . . 30 E3
Harwood Ave BR1 . . . . 42 B7
Harwood Ct **3** ME7 . . . . . 18 C8
Haslemere Rd DA7 . . . . 14 A5
Haslemere Trad & Ind Est
ME15 . . . . 116 F5
Hasler Cl SE28 . . . . 3 C6
Hasletts Cl TN1 . . . . 159 B6
Haslewood Rd TN27 . . . . . 153 B2
Hassendean Rd SE3 . . . . . . 11 B7
Hassock Wood BR2 . . . . . . 56 E6
Hassop Wlk SE9 . . . . 22 E1
Hasted Cl DA9 . . . . 17 C1
Hasted Rd
Greenwich SE7 . . . . 1 D1
Higham ME3 . . . . 38 D2
Newington ME9 . . . . 71 B7
Hasteds ME17 . . . . 102 D2
Haste Hill Cl ME17 . . . . . . 116 B3
Haste Hill Rd ME17 . . . . . 116 B3
Hast Hill Ho BR2 . . . . 56 B6
Hastings Cl
Maidstone ME15 . . . . . . 100 B3
Newenden TN17, TN18 . . 197 C6
Orpington BR2 . . . . 56 B8
Pembury, Kipping's Cross
TN2 . . . . 160 F5
Pembury TN2 . . . . 160 D6
The Moor TN18 . . . . 194 F6
Hastings St SE18 . . . . 2 C3
Hatches La TN11, TN12 . . 129 D6
Hatch Rd ME17 . . . . 120 C5
Hatfield Ct SE3 . . . . 11 A7
Hatfield Rd ME2 . . . . 53 A8
Hatham Green La TN15 . . . 62 D1
Hathaway Cl BR2 . . . . 42 F1
Hathaway Ct
Gillingham ME8 . . . . 69 D8
Rochester ME1 . . . . 53 B5
Hatherall Rd ME14 . . . . . . 100 B6
Hatherley Cres DA14 . . . . . 30 A6
Hatherley Rd DA14 . . . . . . 30 A6
Hathern Gdns SE9 . . . . 29 A4
Hatmill La TN12 . . . . 162 A7
Hattersfield Cl DA17 . . . . . . 3 F2
Hatton Cl
Northfleet DA11 . . . . 35 E5
Woolwich SE18 . . . . 12 E1
Hatton Ct BR7 . . . . 23 B8
Hatton Mews **4** DA9 . . . . 17 C3
Hatton Rd ME5 . . . . 68 C3
Havant Wlk **8** ME15 . . . . 116 F6
Havelock
Bromley BR2 . . . . 42 C6
Dartford DA1 . . . . 15 B1
Erith DA17 . . . . 3 F2
Northfleet DA11 . . . . 35 F7
Tonbridge TN9 . . . . 127 B2

Eltham SE9. . . . . 28 F5
Istead Rise DA13. . . . . 49 F8
Rochester ME1 . . . . 53 C2
Sidcup DA14 . . . . 30 C2
Swanleye BR8 . . . . 45 F7
Haven Cl
Haven Hill TN15. . . . . 63 A3
Haven Lodge **9** SE18 . . . . . 2 B2
Haven St ME8. . . . . 39 C5
Haven Way ME4. . . . . 40 B1
Havering Cl TN17 . . . . 159 F6
Haverstock Ct **2** BR5 . . . . 44 B7
Haverthwaite Rd BR6 . . . . . 57 D7
HAVIKER STREET 131 E1
Havisham Cl ME1 . . . . 53 D2
Havisham Rd DA12. . . . . 37 A7
Hawbeck Rd ME8 . . . . 69 C3
Hawden Cl TN11 . . . . 126 F4
Hawden La TN11 . . . . 126 F4
Hawden Rd TN9 . . . . 127 B2
Hawes Rd BR1. . . . . 42 B8
Hawfield Bank BR6 . . . . 58 D7
HAWKENBURY
Headcorn. 150 D7
Royal Tunbridge Wells 159 D2
Hawkenbury Cl TN2. . . . . . 159 D2
Hawkenbury Mead TN2. . . . 159 D1
Hawkenbury Rd
Hawkenbury TN12. . . . . . . 150 D6
Royal Tunbridge Wells,
TN3 . . . . 159 D1
Hawkenbury Rise ME2 . . . . . 39 B2
Hawkes Cl **11** RM17 . . . . . 18 B8
Hawkes Pl TN13 . . . . 108 A8
Hawkes Rd ME20. . . . . 82 F5
Hawkridge Gr ME18. . . . . . . 97 A3
Hawksmoor Cl
3 Newham E6 . . . . 1 E7
Woolwich SE18 . . . . 2 E1
Hawksmoor Sch SE28 . . . . . 3 B6
Hawkwell Bsns Ctr TN2. . 144 F2
Hawkwell Cotts TN2 . . . . 144 F2
Hawkwood 99 B5
Hawkwood Cl ME1 . . . . 53 D5
Hawkwood La BR7. . . . . 43 C8
HAWLEY 32 F3
Hawley Ct ME16. . . . . 99 E4
Hawley Rd DA1, DA2, DA4. . 33 A4
Hawley Terr DA2 . . . . 33 A4
Hawley Vale DA2. . . . . 33 A4
Hawser Rd ME1. . . . . 53 C6
Hawstead La BR6 . . . . 58 F5
Hawthorn Cl
Edenbridge TN8 . . . . 122 C2
Gravesend DA12 . . . . 36 C4
Orpington BR5. . . . . 43 D3
Hawthorn Cotts **2** DA16. . 13 A4
Hawthorn Cl ME19. . . . . 97 C2
Hawthorndene Cl BR2. . . . . 56 A8
Hawthorndene Rd BR2. . . . . 56 A8
Hawthorn Ave
Biggin Hill TN16. . . . . 72 D4
Gillingham ME8 . . . . 55 C2
Hawthorne Cl ME4. . . . . 42 F6
Hawthorne Rd **4** ME16. . . . 99 A3
Hawthorne Rd BR1. . . . . 42 B6
Hawthorn Ho **6** ME5. . . . . . 67 F5
Hawthorn La TN13 . . . . 91 F5
Hawthorn Pk BR8 . . . . 46 A7
Hawthorn Pl DA8 . . . . 4 C1
Hawthorn Rd
Bexley DA6 . . . . 13 F3
Dartford DA1. . . . . 32 D7
Rochester ME2 . . . . 52 E6
Hawthorns
Chatham ME5. . . . . 67 F1
Hartley DA3. . . . . 48 F5
Hawthorns The
Aylesford ME20 . . . . 82 E1
Chatham ME5. . . . . 67 F6
Oxted RH8 . . . . 104 A2
The Moor TN18 . . . . 194 F8
Hawthorn Terr DA15 . . . . . . 12 F2
Hawthorn Wlk
Royal Tunbridge Wells
TN2 . . . . 159 E8
Tonbridge TN10 . . . . 127 C7
Haxted Pl TN8 . . . . 122 C4
Haxted Rd BR1. . . . . 42 B8
Hayday Rd E16. . . . . 1 A8
Haydens Cl BR5 . . . . 44 C3
Haydens Mews TN9 . . . . . 127 C3
Haydens The TN9 . . . . 127 C3
Haydon Cl ME16 . . . . 99 B4
HAYES 42 A2
Hayesbrook Sch The **2**
TN9. . . . . 143 A8
Hayes Cl
Hayes BR2. . . . . 56 A8
Higham ME3 . . . . 38 C3
West Thurrock RM20 . . . . . 17 C8
Hayes Cotts ME19. . . . . 96 D7
Hayesden La TN11, TN3 . . . 142 B5
Hayesford Park Dr BR2. . . . 42 A4
Hayes Gdn BR2 . . . . 42 A1

Hayes La
Hayes BR2. . . . . 42 A4
Stockbury ME9. . . . . 86 F6
Hayes Prim Sch BR2 . . . . . . 42 B1
Hayes Rd
Bromley BR2. . . . . 42 A5
Stone DA9 . . . . 33 E8
Hayes Sch BR2 . . . . 56 B8
Hayes St BR2 . . . . 42 B1
Hayes Sta BR2. . . . . 42 A1
Hayes Terr DA12 . . . . 37 E3
Hayes Wlk ME19 . . . . 97 A2
Hayes Wood Ave BR2 . . . . . 42 B1
Hayfield Pl ME19 . . . . 81 E2
Hayfield BR5 . . . . 44 A4
Hayfields ME5. . . . . 62 A8
Haygate Ho ME1 . . . . 53 C4
Hayle Mill Cotts ME15 . . . 115 F8
Hayle Mill Rd ME15 . . . . . 115 F8
Hayle Rd ME15. . . . . 100 A3
Hayley Cl ME2 . . . . 52 C2
Hayley Ho ME17 . . . . 14 A8
Haymans Hill TN12. . . . . . 163 C7
Hayman Wlk ME20 . . . . 74 C7
Haymen St ME4. . . . . 53 E3
Haynes Ho 3 ME4 . . . . . 100 B4
Haynes Rd
Gravesend DA11 . . . . 36 A6
Northfleet DA11. . . . . 35 F5
Hayrick Cl ME14 . . . . 100 E5
Haysden Ctry Pk* TN11 . 142 D8
Hay's Mead DA13 . . . . 50 F3
Hays Rd ME6 . . . . 81 F6
Haywain Cl
Maidstone ME14 . . . . 100 F4
Paddock Wood TN12 . . . . 146 A5
Hayward Ave ME2. . . . . 53 B8
Hayward Cl DA1 . . . . 14 D2
Hayward Dr DA1 . . . . 32 F6
Hayward's Ho ME1. . . . . 53 C4
Haywood Rd BR2 . . . . 42 D5
Haywood Rise BR6 . . . . 57 E5
Hazard Ho **4** DA11. . . . . . . 19 A1
Hazel Ave
Hoo St Werburgh ME3 . . . . . 40 E3
Maidstone ME14 . . . . 99 C5
Hazelbank TN3 . . . . 157 F3
Hazel Cotts TN14. . . . . 75 A6
Hazelden Cl TN15 . . . . 62 A2
Hazelden Cotts ME2 . . . . . . 38 C6
Hazel Dr
Chatham ME5. . . . . 66 B8
Orpington BR6. . . . . 57 B8
Hazel Dr DA8 . . . . 15 B6
Hazel End BR8. . . . . 45 E4
Hazel Gr
Chatham ME5. . . . . 66 B8
Orpington BR5. . . . . 57 B8
Hazelmere **8** DA14 . . . . . . 30 A4
Hazelmere Rd BR5 . . . . 43 D5
Hazelmere Way BR2 . . . . . . 42 A3
Hazel Rd
Dartford DA1. . . . . 32 D6
Erith DA8 . . . . 15 A6
Hazel Shaw TN10 . . . . 127 D7
Hazels The ME8. . . . . 69 B5
HAZEL STREET 85 A3
Bicknor. 87 A3
Horsmonden. 162 F4
Hazel Street Rd ME9 . . . . . 86 E4
Hazelview ME19 . . . . 80 E3
Hazel Wlk BR2 . . . . 43 A3
HAZELWOOD 73 D8
Hazelwood Cl TN2 . . . . . . 159 D8
Hazelwood Cotts TN5 . . . 186 D1
Hazelwood Dr ME16. . . . . . 99 B4
Hazelwood Hts RH8 . . . . . 104 A4
Hazelwood Rd
Downe TN14 . . . . 73 D8
Oxted RH8 . . . . 104 A4
Hazelwood Sch RH8 . . . . . 104 A4
Hazen Rd
Kings Hill ME19 . . . . 97 B3
Kings Hill ME19 . . . . 97 B3
Hazlemere Dr ME7 . . . . 55 A5
Hazlitt Ct **4** SE28 . . . . 3 C5
Hazlitt Dr ME14 . . . . 99 D5
Hazlitt Pl ME15 . . . . 116 B8
HEADCORN 151 D4
Headcorn Prim Sch
TN27 . . . . 151 C5
Headcorn Rd
Bromley BR1. . . . . 28 A3
Gillingham ME8 . . . . 55 B4
Lashenden TN27 . . . . 168 A5
Platt's Heath ME17 . . . . . . 119 F1
Smarden Bell TN27 . . . . . . 152 C3
Staplehurst TN12. . . . . 158 B4
Sutton Valence ME17. . . . . 134 E4
Ulcombe ME17. . . . . 135 F5
Headcorn Sta TN27 . . . . . . 151 D4
Headingley Rd ME16 . . . . . . 99 B6
Headley Cl TN8 . . . . 122 C2
Headley Ho 5 BR5. . . . . . . 44 B7
Head Race The ME15. . . . . . 99 D2
Headstock Rise ME3 . . . . . . 40 B7
Headway Ctr TN4. . . . . 158 B4
Healy Dr **1** BR6 . . . . 57 F6
Heansill La TN18 . . . . 194 E8
HEARNDEN GREEN 135 B1
Hearns Rd BR5 . . . . 44 C5
Heartenoak Rd TN18 . . . . 189 B3
Heath Ave DA7 . . . . 13 D8
Heath Cl
Orpington BR5. . . . . 44 C3
Swanley BR8 . . . . 45 E7
Heathclose Ave DA1 . . . . . . 32 B8
Heathclose Rd DA1 . . . . 32 B7
Heathcote Cl ME20. . . . . . . 82 F2
Heath Ct TN12 . . . . 162 F6

Heathdene Dr DA17 . . . . . . 4 B2
Heathend Rd DA5 . . . . 31 E7
Heatherbank
Chislehurst BR7 . . . . 43 A7
Eltham SE9. . . . . 11 F5
Heather Bank ME14 . . . . . 146 B6
Heatherbank Cl DA1 . . . . . . 14 E1
Heather Cl
Chatham ME5. . . . . 67 F4
Newham E16 . . . . 2 A7
Heather Dr
Dartford DA1. . . . . 32 A8
Maidstone ME15 . . . . 100 B2
Tenterden ME30 . . . . 183 B3
Heather End BR8 . . . . 45 D5
Heather Rd SE12 . . . . 28 A7
Heatherside Rd DA14. . . . . . 30 C5
Heathers The TN17. . . . . . . 179 A3
Heather Wlk TN10 . . . . 127 B6
Heatherwood Cl ME17. . . . 118 E2
Heathfield
Chislehurst BR7 . . . . 29 C2
Langley Heath ME17 . . . . . 117 E4
Heathfield Ave ME14 . . . . . 100 C1
Heathfield Cl
Chatham ME5. . . . . 68 B7
Maidstone ME14 . . . . 100 B7
Orpington BR2. . . . . 56 C5
Heathfield Ct DA14. . . . . . . 30 B3
Heathfield La BR7. . . . . 29 C2
Heathfields TN2 . . . . 159 D4
Heathfield Terr
Bexley SE18 . . . . 12 F8
Swanley BR8 . . . . 45 D7
Heath Gdns DA1 . . . . 32 C7
Heath Gr ME16. . . . . 99 A2
Heath House 1 DA15 . . . . 29 F4
Heath La DA1. . . . . 32 B7
Heathlands Rise DA1. . . . . 15 B1
Heathlee Rd DA1. . . . . 14 E1
Heathley End ME7 . . . . 29 C2
Heath Mead SE14 . . . . 100 B5
Heath Park Dr BR1. . . . . . . 42 E6
Heath Rd
Coldblow DA5 . . . . 31 C7
Coxheath ME17 . . . . 115 C3
Crayford DA1. . . . . 14 F1
East Farleigh ME15. . . . . . . 114 E4
Langley Heath ME17 . . . . . 117 E4
Maidstone, Cock Street
ME17. . . . . 116 C2
Maidstone, East Barming
ME16. . . . . 98 F3
Heath Rise BR2. . . . . 42 A3
HEATH SIDE 31 F5
Heath Side BR5 . . . . 43 C2
Heathside Ave
Bexley DA7 . . . . 13 E5
Coxheath ME17 . . . . 115 C4
Heath St DA1. . . . . 32 D8
Heath Terr TN12 . . . . 163 A6
Heath The ME19 . . . . 97 F5
Heathview TN4 . . . . 142 F2
Heathview Ave DA1 . . . . 14 E1
Heathview Cres DA1 . . . . . . 32 B7
Heath View Dr SE2. . . . . 13 D8
Heath Villas SE18 . . . . 2 F1
Heathway E3 . . . . 11 A7
Heath Way DA7, DA8 . . . . . . 14 D6
Heathwood Gdns
Swanley BR8 . . . . 45 C7
Woolwich SE7 . . . . 1 E1
Heathwood Wlk DA5 . . . . . . 31 E7
HEAVERHAM. 77 E2
Heaverham Rd TN15 . . . . . . 77 C2
Heavitree Cl **3** SE18 . . . . . . 2 D1
Heavitree Rd SE18 . . . . 2 D1
Hectorage Rd TN9 . . . . 143 D8
Hector St SE18 . . . . 2 E2
Hedge Barton Trailer Pk
TN3 . . . . 156 F5
Hedge Place Rd DA9 . . . . . . 17 A1
Hedgerows The DA11 . . . . . 35 E6
Hedgerow The ME14 . . . . . 100 E5
Hedges The ME14 . . . . 100 A7
Hedley Ave RM20 . . . . 17 C8
Hedley St ME14 . . . . 100 A5
Hegarty Ct ME6 . . . . 65 F1
Heights The SE7 . . . . 1 C1
Helegan Cl BR6. . . . . 57 F6
Helen Allison Sch DA12 . . . 50 A2
Helen Cl DA1 . . . . 32 B8
Helen Keller Cl TN18 . . . . 127 D4
Helen St SE18 . . . . 2 B2
Hellegan Cl BR6 . . . . 57 F6
Hellyar Ct ME1. . . . . 53 C4
Hemmings Cl DA14. . . . . . . 30 B6
HEMPSTEAD 69 A5
Hempstead Ind Sch ME7. . 69 A5
Hempstead Jun Sch ME7. . 69 A5
Hempstead Rd ME7, ME8. . 69 A5
Hempstead Valley Dr
ME7. . . . . 69 A4
Hempstead Valley Sh Ctr
ME7. . . . . 69 A3
Hemsted Forest Walks*
TN17 . . . . 180 E2
Hemsted Rd DA8. . . . . 14 E7
Henbane Cl ME14 . . . . 100 E5
Henderson Dr DA1. . . . . 16 A3
Henderson Rd TN16. . . . . . . 72 C7

Hendley Dr TN17. . . . . 179 C5
Hendry Ho ME3 . . . . 39 F6
Hendy Rd ME6 . . . . 82 B8
Henfield Cl DA5. . . . . 14 A1
Hengist Rd
Eltham SE12. . . . . 28 B8
Erith DA8 . . . . 14 C7
Hengrove Ct DA5 . . . . 30 E7
Henham Gdns TN12 . . . . . 130 A6
HENHURST 50 E8
Henhurst Hill DA12. . . . . . . 50 D8
Henhurst Rd
Gravesend DA13 . . . . 36 E1
Henhurst DA12 . . . . 50 E8
Heniker La ME17 . . . . 135 A4
Henley Bsns Pk ME2 . . . . . 53 D7
Henley Cl
Chatham ME5. . . . . 68 A6
Gillingham ME8 . . . . 69 D8
Royal Tunbridge Wells
TN2. . . . . 159 C4
Henley Ct DA5 . . . . 30 F8
Henley Deane DA11 . . . . . . 35 E4
Henley Fields
Maidstone ME14 . . . . 100 E6
Tenterden TN30 . . . . 183 B2
Henley Mdws TN30. . . . . . 183 A2
Henley Rd
Newham E16 . . . . 1 F4
Paddock Wood TN12 . . . . 146 A2
Henley St TN3 . . . . 50 F3
HENLEY STREET. 50 F3
Henley View TN30. . . . . . . 183 B2
Henniker Cotts TN17 . . . . 179 A3
Henrietta Chase ME4. . . . . . 40 B2
Henry Addlington Cl E6 . . . 2 B8
Henry Cooper Way SE9. . . . 28 C4
Henrys Cl ME18 . . . . 113 D6
Henry St
Bromley BR1. . . . . 42 B8
Chatham ME4. . . . . 54 B3
10 Grays RM17 . . . . 18 C8
Henson Cl BR6. . . . . 57 B8
Henville Rd BR1. . . . . 42 B8
Henwick Prim Sch **11** SE9 11 E4
Henwick Rd SE9 . . . . 11 E4
HENWOOD GREEN 160 E6
Henwood Green Rd TN2. 160 E6
Henwoods Cres TN2 . . . . . 160 D6
Henwoods Mount TN2. . . 160 E6
Herald Wlk **2** DA1. . . . . . . 15 F2
Herbert Pl SE18. . . . . 12 B8
Herbert Rd
Bexley DA7 . . . . 13 E5
Bromley BR2. . . . . 42 E4
Chatham ME4. . . . . 54 A3
Gillingham ME8 . . . . 49 F8
Hextable BR8. . . . . 32 B2
Swanscombe DA10 . . . . 17 F1
Woolwich SE18 . . . . 12 B8
Herdsdown ME3 . . . . 40 D5
Hereford Cl ME8 . . . . 55 D2
Hereford Rd ME15 . . . . 116 D7
Heritage Dr ME7 . . . . 54 F1
Heritage Quay DA12. . . . . . 19 C1
Heritage Rd ME5. . . . . 68 A6
Heritage The BR6. . . . . 44 A2
Herlun Way ME19. . . . . 55 A6
Herman Terr ME4. . . . . 54 A3
Hermitage Cl SE2. . . . . 3 C3
Hermitage Cnr ME17 . . . . 133 F6
Hermitage Ct
Maidstone ME16 . . . . 98 F5
Tonbridge TN9 . . . . 127 C2
Hermitage Farm ME19 . . . . 97 C8
Hermitage La
Boxley ME14 . . . . 84 F2
Detling ME14 . . . . 85 A4
Rabbit's Cross ME17 . . . . . 133 E6
Hermitage Rd ME3 . . . . 34 A6
Hermitage The ME19 . . . . . 97 D8
HERNE POUND 96 D2
Herne Rd ME8 . . . . 55 C2
Herne The TN15. . . . . 95 C5
Heron Apartments 3
ME15 . . . . 116 F5
Heron Cl TN8 . . . . 122 C3
Heron Cotts TN18 . . . . 197 D3
Heron Cres DA14 . . . . 29 E4
Heron Ct BR2. . . . . 42 C5
Heronden Rd ME15. . . . . . . 116 F4
Herongate Rd BR8 . . . . 31 E2
Heron Hill DA17 . . . . 3 F2
Heron Ho DA14 . . . . 30 B5
Heron Rd ME20 . . . . 81 F2
Heronsbank ME3. . . . . 23 E4
Heronscourt Prim Sch SE28 2 D3
Herons Way TN7 . . . . 160 E8
Heron Way
Chatham ME5. . . . . 68 B7
Lower Stoke ME3. . . . . 25 C4
Hero Wlk ME1 . . . . 53 C4
Herringham Rd SE7 . . . . 1 C3
Herts Cres ME15 . . . . 115 F3
Hertsfield Ave ME2. . . . . . . 39 A2
Hertsfield Farm Cotts
TN12 . . . . 133 D4
Hervey Rd SE3 . . . . 11 B6
Herying Cl ME2 . . . . 66 B4
Hesketh Ave SE3. . . . . 11 A4
Hesketh Pk TN2 . . . . 160 E6
HEVER 139 D6
Hever Ave TN15. . . . . 61 E4
Hever Castle & Gdns*
TN8. . . . . 139 D7

Hever CE Prim Sch TN8 . . 139 D6
Hever Cl ME15 . . . . 116 F6
Hever Court Rd DA12 . . . . . 36 D2
Hever Croft
Eltham SE9. . . . . 29 A4
Rochester ME2 . . . . 52 F5
Hever Gdns
Bromley BR1 . . . . 43 A7
Maidstone ME16 . . . . 99 E3
Heverham Rd SE18. . . . . 2 E2
Hever Ho ME2 . . . . 39 C1
Hever La TN8 . . . . 139 A4
Hever Mews ME1 . . . . 53 C3
Hever Rd
Bough Beech TN8. . . . . 123 D2
Hever TN8 . . . . 139 B7
West Kingsdown TN15. . . . . 61 E4
Hever Road Cotts TN8. . . . 123 E2
Heversham Rd DA7 . . . . 14 A6
Hever Sta TN8 . . . . 139 A6
Heverswood TN14. . . . . 59 A2
Hever Wood Rd TN15. . . . . . 61 E4
Hewett Ho **7** SE18 . . . . . . 2 B8
Hewett Pl BR8 . . . . 45 D5
Hewitt Cl
Gillingham ME7 . . . . 54 F6
Maidstone ME16 . . . . 99 D7
Hewitts Rd BR6, TN14. . . . . 58 F3
HEXTABLE 31 E1
Hextable Cl ME14 . . . . 99 D7
Hextable Com Prim Sch
BR8. . . . . 31 F2
Hextable Sch BR8 . . . . 45 F8
Hibbs Cl BR8 . . . . 45 D7
Hibernia Dr DA12 . . . . 36 F5
Hibernia Point **11** SE2 . . . . . 3 D4
Hickin Cl SE7 . . . . 1 D2
Hickman Cl E16 . . . . 1 D8
Hickory Dell ME7 . . . . 69 A5
Hide E6 . . . . 2 A7
Higgins' La ME4 . . . . 53 F5
HIGHAM 38 B4
Higham Cl ME15 . . . . 99 E2
Higham Gdns TN10. . . . . . 127 F5
Higham La TN10, TN11, . . 127 F6
Higham Prim Sch ME3 . . . . 38 C5
Higham Rd
Cliffe ME3 . . . . 22 A4
Rochester ME3 . . . . 39 C3
Tonbridge TN11 . . . . 127 F7
Higham School Rd TN10. . 127 E6
Higham Sta ME3. . . . . 38 D6
Higham View ME14 . . . . . . 83 E4
HIGHAM WOOD 127 F6
High Bank ME1 . . . . 53 D2
Highbanks Cl DA16 . . . . 13 B7
High Beeches
Orpington BR6. . . . . 58 A4
Royal Tunbridge Wells
TN2. . . . . 159 D6
Highberry M15. . . . . 30 E3
Highberry Rd SE3 . . . . 81 E2
Highbrook Rd SE3 . . . . 11 D4
HIGH HALDEN 159 C8
High Brooms Ind Pk
TN2 . . . . 159 C8
High Brooms Rd TN4. . . . . 159 C8
High Brooms Sta TN2 . . . . 159 C7
Highbury La TN30 . . . . 193 A7
Highbury Pl TN5. . . . . 184 F5
Highclose Rd ME19 . . . . . . 96 D7
Highcombe SE7 . . . . 11 B8
Highcombe Cl SE9 . . . . 28 E7
High Croft Cotts BR8 . . . . . 46 A5
Highcroft Gn ME15 . . . . . . 116 F4
Highcroft Hall BR8 . . . . 45 D1
Highcross Rd DA13 . . . . 34 D2
High Cross Rd TN15. . . . . . 94 B1
High Dewar Rd ME8 . . . . . . 70 A8
Highdown Cotts TN17 . . . 176 F3
High Elms ME8 . . . . 55 E1
High Elms Ctry Pk* BR6. . 57 D3
High Elms Rd BR6. . . . . 57 C2
Highfield Ave
Erith DA8 . . . . 14 B8
Orpington BR6. . . . . 57 F5
Highfield Cl
Gillingham ME8 . . . . 69 D7
Hawkhurst TN18 . . . . 189 A1
Pembury TN2 . . . . 160 D6
Highfield Cotts DA2. . . . . . 32 B2
Highfield Ct DA2 . . . . 32 B8
Highfield Rd
Bexley DA6 . . . . 13 F2
Biggin Hill TN16. . . . . 72 C3
Bromley BR1. . . . . 42 F5
Dartford DA1. . . . . 32 D8
Gillingham ME8 . . . . 69 D7
Kemsing TN15 . . . . 76 F3
Royal Tunbridge Wells
TN4. . . . . 159 C7
St Paul's Cray BR7. . . . . 43 F6
Highfield Road N DA1. . . . . 15 D1
Highfield Road S DA1 . . . . . 32 D7
Highfields Rd TN8 . . . . 122 C4
High Firs BR8. . . . . 45 E5
High Firs Prim Sch BR8 . . . 45 F5
Highgate Ct **8** TN18 . . . . 188 F2
Highgate Hill TN18 . . . . . . 188 F1
High Gr
Bromley BR1. . . . . 42 B8
Woolwich SE18 . . . . 12 C6
Highgrove TN2 . . . . 173 A8
Highgrove Cl BR7. . . . . 42 E8
Highgrove Rd ME5 . . . . 68 A5

HIGH HALDEN. 183 D7
High Halden CE Prim Sch
TN26. .183 E7
High Halden Rd TN26,
TN27 .168 C2
HIGH HALSTOW 23 F3
High Halstow National
Nature Reserve★ ME3. . .23 E5
High Halstow Prim Sch
ME23. .23 E3
High Hilden Cl TN10. . . . . . .127 A4
High House La TN11. . . . . . .111 C2
Highland Rd
Badgers Mount TN14. . . . . .75 B8
Bexley DA6 . . . . .14 A3
Maidstone ME15 . . . . .116 E6
Highlands
Dartford DA1. . . . . .32 C8
Royal Tunbridge Wells
TN2. .159 D7
Highlands Cl ME12. . . . . .52 D5
Highlands Hill BR8. . . . . .46 A8
Highlands Pk TN15. . . . . .92 E6
Highlands Rd BR5. . . . . .44 C2
Highmead SE18. . . . . .12 F7
High Meads Rd E16. . . . . .1 D7
High Oak Hill ME9 . . . . .71 D8
High Point SE9 . . . . .29 B5
High Rd DA2. . . . . .32 C5
Highridge ME7. . . . . .54 F1
High Ridge TN17. . . . . .177 E8
Highridge Cl ME14. . . . . .100 F5
High Rocks★ TN3 . . . . .158 A1
High Rocks La TN3, TN4. .158 C1
High Rocks Sta★ TN3 . . . .158 B1
High St
Aylesford ME20 . . . . .82 F3
Bean DA2. . . . . .34 B5
Bidborough TN3. . . . . .142 C3
Biddenden TN27. . . . . .167 F1
Borough Green TN15. . . . . . .94 F7
Brasted TN14, TN16. . . . . . .90 C3
Brenchley TN12. . . . . .162 B8
Bromley BR1 . . . . .42 A6
Chatham, Brompton ME7. . .54 A6
Chatham ME4. . . . . .54 A4
Cowden TN8. . . . . .155 B5
Cranbrook TN17. . . . . .179 C4
Dartford DA1. . . . . .1 E1
Downe BR6 . . . . .73 A8
East Malling ME19. . . . . .98 A6
Edenbridge TN8 . . . . .122 C1
Eynsford DA4. . . . . .60 E8
Farningham DA4. . . . . .46 F2
Flimwell TN5. . . . . .187 C3
Forstal ME20. . . . . .83 A3
Frant TN3. . . . . .177 C3
Gillingham, Rainham ME8 . .69 FB
Goudhurst TN17. . . . . .177 E8
Grain ME3 . . . . .27 B6
Gravesend DA11 . . . . .19 B1
2 Grays RM17. . . . . .18 A8
Hadlow TN11. . . . . .128 E8
Halling ME2. . . . . .66 A4
Hawkhurst TN18 . . . . .188 B2
Headcorn TN27. . . . . .151 C5
Kemsing TN15 . . . . .77 B2
Lamberhurst TN3. . . . . .176 B5
Leigh TN11. . . . . .125 F1
Lenham ME17 . . . . .120 D5
Limpsfield RH8. . . . . .104 B7
Lower Stoke ME3. . . . . .25 C4
Maidstone ME14 . . . . .3 C6
Marden TN12. . . . . .148 D6
Newington ME9 . . . . .71 C6
Northfleet DA11. . . . . .18 C1
Orpington, Broom Hill BR6 . .64 A1
Orpington, Farnborough
BR6. . . . . .57 C5
Orpington, Green Street Green
BR6. . . . . .57 F4
Orpington, St Mary Cray
BR5. . . . . .44 C4
Otford TN14. . . . . .76 A3
Pembury TN2. . . . . .160 C6
Penshurst TN11. . . . . .141 B4
Rochester ME1 . . . . .53 C6
Rochester, Strood ME2 . . . .53 B7
Rochester, Upper Upnor
ME2. .39 F1
Rolvenden TN17. . . . . .191 E4
Royal Tunbridge Wells
TN1. .159 A2
Rusthall TN4. . . . . .158 C4
Seal TN15. . . . . .92 F6
Sevenoaks, Chipstead TN13 .91 C5
Sevenoaks TN13 . . . . .91 C2
Shoreham TN14. . . . . .59 F1
Sidcup DA14. . . . . .30 A4
Snodland ME6 . . . . .82 A8
Staplehurst TN12. . . . . .149 F3
Sutton Valence ME17. . . . . .134 E7
Swanley BR8. . . . . .45 F5
Swanscombe DA10 . . . . .12 F2
Swanscombe, Greenhithe
DA9. .17 B3
Tenterden TN30. . . . . .193 A7
Ticehurst TN5. . . . . .186 C1
Tonbridge TN9 . . . . .127 C2
Wadhurst TN5. . . . . .184 F4
Westerham TN16. . . . . .105 C8
West Malling ME19. . . . . . . .97 C8
Wouldham ME1. . . . . .66 C5
Wrotham TN15. . . . . .79 A3

High St continued
Yalding ME18. . . . . .113 F1
Highstead Cres DA8. . . . . . . .14 E7
HIGH STREET 188 D2
High Street ME3 . . . . .25 C4
High Tor Cl BR1. . . . . .28 B1
High Tor View SE28 . . . . .2 E5
High Trees DA2 . . . . .16 B1
Highview
Vigo Village DA13 . . . . .80 B8
Woolwich SE18 . . . . .12 B7
High View ME3. . . . . .38 C4
Highview ME15. . . . . .116 A8
Highview Dr ME5 . . . . .67 D5
Highview Rd DA14 . . . . .30 B4
Highway Prim Sch The
BR6. . . . . .58 C5
Highway The BR6. . . . . .58 C5
Highwood BR6. . . . . .57 C8
Highwood Dr BR6. . . . . .57 C8
Highwoods Cl ME3. . . . . .38 C4
High Woods La TN3. . . . . . .160 B3
Hilary Cl DA8 . . . . .14 C6
Hilary Gdns ME1. . . . . .52 F1
Hilbert Cl TN2 . . . . .159 C5
Hilbert Rd TN2. . . . . .159 C5
Hilborough Way BR6. . . . . . .57 D5
Hilda May Ave BR8. . . . . .47 F2
Hilda Rd ME4. . . . . .54 A3
Hilda Vale Cl BR6. . . . . .57 A6
Hilda Vale Rd BR6. . . . . .57 B6
Hilden Ave TN11. . . . . .126 F4
HILDENBOROUGH 126 E6
Hildenborough CE Prim Sch
TN11. . . . . .126 D6
Hildenborough Cres
ME16 .99 C7
Hildenborough Rd
Leigh TN11. . . . . .126 A3
Shipbourne TN11. . . . . .109 E4
Hildenborough Sta TN11 .109 E6
Hildenbrook Farm TN11. .109 E2
Hilden Dr DA8 . . . . .15 B7
Hildenfields TN10 . . . . .127 A4
Hilden Grange Sch TN10 .127 B3
Hilden Oaks Sch TN10. . . .127 B3
HILDEN PARK. 126 F4
Hilden Park Rd TN11 . . . . .126 F4
Hilders Cl TN8 . . . . .122 B4
Hilders La TN8 . . . . .122 A4
Hillary Ave DA11 . . . . .35 E5
Hillary Ct SE9. . . . . .28 E6
Hillary Rd ME14. . . . . .100 A7
Hillborough Ave TN13 . . . . .92 D5
Hillborough Gr ME5. . . . . . . .68 A3
Hill Brow
Bromley BR1 . . . . .42 D8
Crayford DA1. . . . . .14 F1
Maidstone ME14 . . . . .101 A5
Hillbrow Cl DA5. . . . . .31 D4
Hillbury Gdns TN5 . . . . .186 D1
Hill Chase ME5 . . . . .67 E3
Hill Cl
Chislehurst BR7. . . . . .29 B3
Istead Rise DA13. . . . . .35 E1
Hill Cres
Coldblow DA5 . . . . .31 C7
Lenham ME17 . . . . .120 D5
Hillcrest TN8 . . . . .123 B5
Hill Crest
Royal Tunbridge Wells
TN4. .159 B8
Sevenoaks TN13 . . . . .92 A5
Sidcup DA15 . . . . .30 B8
Hillcrest Ave RM20. . . . . . . .17 A8
Hillcrest Dr
Cuxton ME2 . . . . .52 C2
Royal Tunbridge Wells
TN2. .159 D7
Stone DA9 . . . . .17 A2
Hillcrest Rd
Biggin Hill TN16. . . . . .72 D3
Bromley BR1 . . . . .28 A4
Chatham ME4. . . . . .53 F2
Dartford DA1. . . . . .31 F8
Marplit Hill TN8. . . . . .122 C4
Orpington BR6. . . . . .58 A8
Hillcroft DA4 . . . . .60 D7
Hillcroft Rd E6. . . . . .2 B8
Hill Ct ME3 . . . . .39 F4
Hilden Shaw ME15. . . . . . . .116 A8
Hillindown Lodge BR6 . . . .58 B8
Hilldrop Rd BR1 . . . . .28 B2
Hill End
Orpington BR6. . . . . .57 F8
Woolwich SE18 . . . . .12 A6
Hill Farm Cl ME23. . . . . .23 E3
Hillfield Pl TN13. . . . . .91 E7
Hillfield Rd TN13. . . . . .91 E7
Hillfield Villas TN20. . . . . . .183 F8
Hillgarth TN4 . . . . .159 A8
HILL GREEN 70 C1
Hill Green Rd ME9 . . . . .86 D8
HILL HOATH 140 C6
Hill House Rd DA2. . . . . .33 C8
Hillingdale TN16 . . . . .72 B1
Hillingdon Ave TN13 . . . . . . .92 D6
Hillingdon Rd
Bexley DA7 . . . . .14 C4
Gravesend DA11 . . . . .36 B6
Hillingdon Rise TN13. . . . . .92 E6
HILL PARK 89 B4
Hill Rd
Burham ME5. . . . . .67 A3
Dartford DA2. . . . . .32 E6
Rochester ME1 . . . . .53 A2
Wouldham ME1. . . . . .66 F5
Hillreach SE18. . . . . .1 F1

Hill Rise DA2 . . . . .33 E3
Hillsgrove Cl DA16 . . . . .13 C7
Hills Grove Prim Sch
DA16. .13 C7
Hill Shaw DA3 . . . . .48 F3
Hillshaw Cres ME2 . . . . .52 D5
Hillside
Dartford DA2. . . . . .33 E3
Erith DA17. . . . . .4 C2
Farningham DA4 . . . . .46 F2
Rochester ME1 . . . . .53 A2
Tonbridge TN9 . . . . .143 A7
Hillside Ave
Gravesend DA12 . . . . .36 D6
Rochester ME2 . . . . .53 B8
Hillside Cotts TN5. . . . . . . .185 B8
Hillside Ct
2 Rochester ME2. . . . . .53 A7
Swanley BR8 . . . . .46 A5
Wateringbury ME18. . . . . . .113 E7
Hillside Dr DA12 . . . . .36 D6
Hillside La BR2 . . . . .56 A8
Hillside Prim Sch BR5. . . . .44 C2
Hillside Rd
Chatham ME5. . . . . .54 A4
Dartford DA1. . . . . .15 A1
Kemsing TN15 . . . . .76 F2
Oxted RH8. . . . . .104 A1
Tatsfield TN16 . . . . .88 E8
Hillside Terr DA12 . . . . .36 B7
Hillside The BR6. . . . . .58 B2
Hills La TN15 . . . . .77 C7
Hillsley Ct **13** DA14 . . . . .30 A4
Hill St TN1. . . . . .159 B5
Hill Terr ME4 . . . . .53 F3
Hill The
Cranbrook TN17. . . . . .179 D4
Northfleet DA11. . . . . .18 C1
HILL TOP 146 B1
Hilltop
Tonbridge TN9 . . . . .143 B7
West Farleigh ME15 . . . . . .114 D3
Hill Top TN17. . . . . .164 E5
Hill Top Cotts ME17. . . . . .115 E2
Hilltop Gdns
Dartford DA1. . . . . .15 F2
Orpington BR6. . . . . .57 E8
Hilltop Prim Sch ME2 . . . . .39 C1
Hilltop Rd
Rochester ME2 . . . . .39 C1
West Thurrock RM20. . . . . . .17 B8
Hill View
Basted TN15. . . . . .94 F4
Borough Green TN15. . . . . . .95 A7
Hill View Cl TN15 . . . . .95 A7
Hill View Ct BR6. . . . . .43 F1
Hillview Cres BR6. . . . . .43 F1
Hill View Dr
Bexley DA16 . . . . .2 E5
Woolwich SE28 . . . . .2 F5
Hillview Ho DA12 . . . . .36 C7
Hillview Rd BR7 . . . . .29 A4
Hill View Rd
New Barn DA3. . . . . .49 B6
Orpington BR6. . . . . .57 F8
Rusthall TN4. . . . . .158 C4
Tonbridge TN11. . . . . .126 F5
Hillview Sch for Girls
TN9. .143 D8
Hill View Way ME5 . . . . .67 E5
Hillydale Dr BR2 . . . . .56 F7
Hillyfield Cl ME14 . . . . .38 F1
Hilton Rd ME3 . . . . .39 B7
Hind Cres DA8 . . . . .14 D7
Hines Terr ME5 . . . . .54 C1
Hinksden Rd TN17, TN18 .189 F3
Hinksey Path SE2 . . . . .3 C3
Hinstock Rd SE18 . . . . .12 C7
Hinton Cl SE9. . . . . .28 E7
Hinton Cres ME7. . . . . .48 E5
Historic Dockyard The★
ME4. .54 A8
Hitchen Hatch La TN13. . . .92 B4
Hither Chantlers TN3. . . . .158 A2
Hither Farm Rd SE3 . . . . . . .11 C4
Hive The DA1 . . . . .18 B1
Hoath Cl ME8. . . . . .69 B7
Hoath La ME8. . . . . .69 B7
Hoath Mdw TN12 . . . . .163 A6
Hoath Way ME7, ME8 . . . . .69 B5
Hobart Rd RM18 . . . . .19 B4
Hoblands End BR7 . . . . .29 E2
HOCKENDEN. 45 B6
Hockenden La BR8. . . . . .45 B7
HOCKER EDGE 165 D2
Hockers Cl ME14. . . . . .101 A8
Hockers La ME14 . . . . .101 A8
Hoddesdon Rd DA17. . . . . . .4 A1
Hodgkins Cl SE28 . . . . .3 C6
Hodgson Cres ME6. . . . . . . .66 A1
Hodsoll Ct BR5. . . . . .44 D4
Hodsoll St TN15. . . . . .63 D1
HODSOLL STREET 63 D2
Hodson Cres BR5. . . . . .44 D3
Hogarth Cl E16 . . . . .1 D8
Hog Hill ME14 . . . . .101 B5
Hoghole La TN3 . . . . .175 F2
Hog La DA11. . . . . .35 F5
Hogs Orch RH8 . . . . .46 B8
Hogtrough Hill TN16. . . . . . .90 A5
Holbeach Gdns DA15. . . . . .12 F1
Holborn Coll SE7 . . . . .1 D2
Holborn Rd E13. . . . . .1 B8
HOLBOROUGH 66 A2
Holborough Rd ME6. . . . . . .66 A1
Holborn Ho BR7 . . . . .33 D8
Holbrook Cl BR7. . . . . .29 D1

Holbrook Way BR2. . . . . .42 F4
Holburne Cl SE3. . . . . .11 C6
Holburne Gdns SE3 . . . . . . .11 D6
Holburne Rd SE3. . . . . .11 D6
Holcombe Cl TN16. . . . . .89 D1
Holcombe Rd
Chatham ME4. . . . . .53 F2
Rochester ME1 . . . . .53 C3
Holcote Cl DA17 . . . . .3 E3
Holden Cnr TN4. . . . . .142 F1
Holden Park Rd TN4 . . . . . .159 A8
Holden Rd TN4 . . . . .142 F1
Holder Cl ME5 . . . . .68 C6
Holding St ME8 . . . . .55 F1
Hole La TN8 . . . . .122 A6
Hole Park★ TN17 . . . . .191 C6
Holford St **1** TN9 . . . . .127 B1
Holgate St SE7. . . . . .1 D3
HOLLAND 104 A1
Hollandbury Pk ME19 . . . . .97 C2
Holland Cres RH8. . . . . .104 A2
Holland Ho ME1 . . . . .53 D5
Holland Jun Sch RH8. . . . .104 A1
Holland La RH8. . . . . .104 A2
Holland Rd
Chatham ME5. . . . . .67 C8
Maidstone ME14 . . . . .100 E5
Oxted RH8. . . . . .104 A1
Hollands Cl DA12 . . . . .37 E3
Hollies Ave DA15. . . . . .29 F7
Hollies The
Gravesend DA12 . . . . .36 D2
Hurst Green RH8 . . . . .104 B2
New Barn DA3. . . . . .49 C6
Sidcup DA15 . . . . .30 A8
Holligrave Rd BR1. . . . . .42 A8
Hollin Cl TN4 . . . . .158 F4
Hollingbourne Ave DA7 . . . .13 F6
Hollingbourne Hill ME17 .102 F4
Hollingbourne Prim Sch
ME17. . . . . .102 E2
Hollingbourne Rd ME8 . . . .55 C2
Hollingbourne Sta ME17 .102 C3
Hollingbourne Tower **4**
BR5. . . . . .44 D1
Hollington Ct BR7. . . . . .29 B2
Hollingworth Ct ME14. . . .100 C3
Hollingworth Rd
Maidstone ME14 . . . . .116 F5
Orpington BR2, BR5. . . . . . .43 B2
Hollingworth Way TN16 . . .89 D1
Hollow La
Hartlip ME9. . . . . .70 E5
Snodland ME6 . . . . .81 F6
Hollow Trees Dr TN11. . . .126 A1
Holly Bank TN12 . . . . .162 B8
Hollybrake Cl BR7 . . . . .29 D1
Hollybush Ct TN13 . . . . .92 C3
Hollybush Ct TN13 . . . . .92 C3
Hollybush La BR6. . . . . .59 A4
Holly Bush La TN13 . . . . . . .92 C3
Hollybush Rd DA12. . . . . . . .36 C6
Holly Cl
Chatham ME5. . . . . .68 C8
Gillingham ME7 . . . . .54 E6
Holly Cotts TN8. . . . . .122 B2
Hollycroft ME2 . . . . .52 C2
Holly Ct **1** DA14. . . . . .30 B4
Hollydale Dr BR2 . . . . .56 F7
Hollydene Rd TN5. . . . . . . .184 F6
Holly Farm Rd ME15. . . . . .117 C6
Holly Gdns
Bexley DA7 . . . . .14 C3
Maidstone ME14 . . . . .100 B7
Holly Hill DA13 . . . . .64 F3
Holly Hill Rd DA8, DA17. . .4 B1
Holly Rd
Dartford DA1. . . . . .32 D7
Orpington BR6. . . . . .58 A3
Rochester ME2 . . . . .39 D7
Rochester, Strood ME2 . . . .52 E5
Hollytree Ave BR8 . . . . .45 E7
Holly Tree Cl ME17 . . . . . . .118 E2
Hollytree Dr ME3 . . . . .38 B3
Hollytree Par DA14. . . . . . . .30 C2
Hollywood La
Knockmill TN15 . . . . .77 F8
Rochester ME2 . . . . .39 C2
Hollywood Way DA8 . . . . . .15 B6
Holmbury Manor **21** DA14 .30 A4
Holmbury Pk BR7. . . . . .29 E1
Holmcroft Way BR2. . . . . . . .42 F4
Holm Ct **5** SE12 . . . . .28 B5
Holmdale Rd BR7. . . . . .29 C3
Holmden Ct **2** TN8 . . . . . . .122 C1
Holmdene Cl **1** BR1 . . . . . . .42 E6
Holmes Cl ME23 . . . . .23 E3
Holmes Ct ME19 . . . . .80 F4
Holmesdale Cl
Durgates TN5. . . . . .184 E5
Maidstone ME15 . . . . .115 F3
Holmesdale Hill DA4 . . . . . .47 D8
Holmesdale Rd
Bexley DA7 . . . . .13 D5
Sevenoaks TN13 . . . . .92 A5
Sutton at Hone DA4. . . . . . .47 C8
Holmesdale Tech Coll
ME6. .81 F7
Holmewood House Sch
TN3. .158 A2
Holmewood Rd TN4. . . . . .159 C2
Holmewood Ridge TN3. . .157 F3
Holmhurst Ct TN4. . . . . . . .158 F4
Holmhurst Rd DA17. . . . . . . .4 B1
Holmleigh Ave DA1 . . . . .15 C2

Holm Mill La ME17 . . . . . .119 B6
Holmoaks
Gillingham ME8 . . . . .55 E2
Maidstone ME14 . . . . .100 C5
Holmsdale Gr DA1, DA7. . .14 E4
Holmside ME7 . . . . .54 E3
Holm Wlk SE3 . . . . .11 A5
Holmwood Cotts BR6 . . . . .58 C1
Holmwood Ct DA14 . . . . . . .29 F3
Holmwood Villas **6** SE7. . . .1 A1
Holstein Way **6** DA18. . . . . . .3 E3
Holt Cl
Sidcup DA14 . . . . .30 E4
Woolwich SE28 . . . . .3 C6
Holt Rd E16 . . . . .1 E5
Holt Wood Ave ME20 . . . . . .98 E8
Holtwood Cl ME8 . . . . .69 D6
HOLTYE. 154 F7
Holtye Cres ME15. . . . . .100 B2
Holtye Rd RH19. . . . . .154 A4
Holwood Park Ave BR2,
BR4. . . . . .56 F6
Holy Family RC Prim Sch
SE3. . . . . .11 C3
Holy Family RC Prim Sch
ME15. . . . . .116 F4
Holyhead Cl **3** E6 . . . . .1 F8
Holy Innocents RC Prim Sch
BR6. . . . . .57 F7
Holyoake Terr TN13. . . . . . .92 A3
Holyrood Mews E16. . . . . . . .1 A5
Holy Trinity CE Prim Sch
Dartford DA1. . . . . .15 C2
Gravesend DA12 . . . . .36 C8
Holy Trinity Coll Prep Sch
BR1. . . . . .42 C8
Holy Trinity Lamorbey CE
Prim Sch DA15 . . . . .30 A7
Holywell Cl
Greenwich SE3 . . . . .11 A8
Orpington BR6. . . . . .58 A6
Homedean Rd TN13 . . . . . . .91 C4
Home Farm BR6 . . . . .59 A5
Home Farm Cl TN11. . . . . .126 A3
Home Farm Cotts BR5. . . . .44 D8
Home Farm Rd TN3. . . . . . .173 C4
Homefarm Est ME20 . . . . . .82 F1
Home Farm La TN2 . . . . . . .159 E8
Homefield Cl
Orpington BR5. . . . . .44 B5
Swanley BR8. . . . . .45 F6
Homefield Rd
Bromley BR1 . . . . .42 C8
Sevenoaks TN13 . . . . .91 E5
Homefield Rise BR6. . . . . . .44 A1
Home Gdns DA1 . . . . .15 E1
Home Hill BR8. . . . . .31 F1
Home Lea BR6. . . . . .57 F5
Homemead
7 Gravesend DA12 . . . . . . .36 B8
Swanscombe DA9 . . . . .17 B1
Home Mead Cl **6** DA12. . . .36 B8
Homemead Rd BR2 . . . . . . .42 F4
Home Pk RH8. . . . . .104 A4
Homer Cl DA7 . . . . .14 C6
Homesdale Bsns Ctr BR1 .42 D6
Homesdale Rd
Bromley BR1, BR2. . . . . .42 C6
Orpington BR5. . . . . .43 E2
Homestead Rd
Marplit Hill TN8 . . . . .122 B5
Orpington BR6. . . . . .58 B4
Homestead The
Crayford DA1. . . . . .14 E2
Dartford DA1. . . . . .15 C1
Groombridge TN3 . . . . .171 C7
Homevale Cotts TN14 . . . . .74 E4
Homewards Rd ME3. . . . . . . .9 B2
Homewood Cotts DA12 . . . .37 E1
Homewood Cres BR7. . . . . .29 E2
Homewood Rd
Langton Green TN3 . . . . . . .157 F3
Tenterden TN30. . . . . .183 B1
Homewood Sch TN30 . . . .183 B1
Homlesdale Bsns Ctr
TN15. .95 C8
Honduras Terr **8** ME4. . . .100 A7
Hone St ME2. . . . . .53 B8
Honey Bee Glade ME8 . . . .69 E6
Honeybourne Way BR5 . . . .43 D1
Honeycombe Lodge **7**
DA11. .18 D1
Honeycrest Ind Pk TN12. .149 E5
Honeycrock Hill ME9 . . . . . .86 F8
Honeyden Rd DA14. . . . . . . .30 E2
Honey La ME15 . . . . .117 B6
Honeypot Cl ME2 . . . . .53 B8
Honeysuckle Cl
3 Chatham ME5. . . . . .67 E4
Gillingham ME7 . . . . .68 F4
Honeysuckle Ct **4** SE28 . .28 A8
Honiton Rd DA16. . . . . .12 F5
Honywood Rd ME17. . . . . . .120 C4
Hoo Comm ME3 . . . . .40 A4
Hood Ave BR5. . . . . .44 B4
Hook Cl ME5. . . . . .67 E5
Hook Farm Rd BR2. . . . . . . .42 D4
Hookfields DA11. . . . . .35 E5
HOOK GREEN
Dartford. 32 A4
Lamberhurst 175 C4
Meopham Station. 50 A3
Northfleet 35 A2

Hook Green Ct DA13 . . . . . 50 A4
Hook Green La DA2 . . . . . . 31 F5
Hook Green Rd DA13 . . . . . 34 F1
Hook Hill TN5 . . . . 186 A6
Hook La
  Bexley DA16 . . . . 13 A4
  Harrietsham ME17 . . . . . . 119 C6
Hook Lane Prim Sch
  DA16 . . . . 13 A4
Hook Place Cotts DA13 . . . 35 A2
Hook Rd ME6 . . . . 81 F8
Hookstead TN26 . . . . 183 C7
Hookwood Bglws RH8 . . . . 104 B7
Hookwood Cnr RH8 . . . . . . 104 B7
Hookwood Cotts TN14 . . . . 74 C8
Hookwood Rd BR6, TN14 . . 74 C7
Hooper Rd E16 . . . . 1 A7
Hoopers La ME3 . . . . 24 F5
Hooper's Pl ME1 . . . . 53 C4
Hooper's Rd ME1 . . . . 53 C4
Hoopers Yd TN13 . . . . 92 C1
Hoo Rd ME2, ME3 . . . . 39 D3
HOO ST WERBURGH 40 B5
Hoo St Werburgh Prim Sch
  ME3 . . . . 40 D5
Hop Bine Cl TN12 . . . . 130 A7
Hope CI TN11 . . . . 111 E1
Hope CI SE12 . . . . 28 B5
Hope Cotts DA2 . . . . 34 B6
Hopedale Rd SE7 . . . . 11 B8
Hopehouse La TN17,
  TN18 . . . . 196 E7
Hope Rd DA10 . . . . 17 F1
Hopes Gr TN26 . . . . 183 D7
Hope St
  Chatham ME4 . . . . 54 A3
  Maidstone ME14 . . . . 99 F6
Hope Terr ME3 . . . . 38 D7
Hopewell Bsns Ctr ME5 . . . 68 C8
Hopewell Dr
  Chatham ME5 . . . . 68 C8
  Gravesend DA12 . . . . 36 F3
Hop Farm Family Pk*
  TN12 . . . . 130 A3
Hopgarden Cl
  Lamberhurst TN3 . . . . . . 176 A5
  [12] Marlpit Hill TN8 . . . . 122 D3
Hopgarden La TN13 . . . . . . 108 A8
Hopgarden Oast ME18 . . . . 113 F1
Hopgarden Rd TN10 . . . . . 127 D6
Hoppers Cnr ME15 . . . . . . 114 D7
Hop Pocket Cl TN12 . . . . . 180 A8
Hop Pocket La TN12 . . . . . 145 F7
Hopton Ct BR2 . . . . 42 A1
Hopton Rd SE18 . . . . 2 C3
Hopwood Gdns TN4 . . . . . 159 A6
Horace Rd ME2 . . . . 52 E5
Horatio Pl ME1 . . . . 53 B4
Horizon Cl TN4 . . . . 159 B8
Horizon Prim Sch BR8 . . . . 45 E7
Horley Cl DA6 . . . . 14 A2
Horley Rd SE9 . . . . 28 E4
Hornbeam Ave
  Chatham ME5 . . . . 68 B2
  Royal Tunbridge Wells
  TN4 . . . . 143 D1
Hornbeam Cl
  Larkfield ME20 . . . . 82 B2
  Paddock Wood TN12 . . . . 145 F5
Hornbeam Ho [6] DA15 . . . 30 A5
Hornbeam La DA13 . . . . . . 14 C5
Hornbeam Rd ME18 . . . . . . 88 A8
Hornbeam Way BR2 . . . . . . 43 A3
Horncastle Cl SE12 . . . . . . 28 A8
Horncastle Rd SE12 . . . . . . 28 A8
Horne Ho SE16 . . . . 11 E6
Hornfair Rd SE7 . . . . 11 D7
Hornfield Cotts DA13 . . . . . 64 C3
Horning Cl SE9 . . . . 28 E4
Horn La SE10 . . . . 1 A2
Horn Link Way SE10 . . . . . . 1 A2
Horn Park Cl SE12 . . . . 11 B2
Horn Park La SE12 . . . . 11 B1
Horn Park Prim Sch SE12 . 28 B8
HORNS GREEN 73 E2
Horns La ME18 . . . . 106 C1
Horns Lodge Farm TN11 . . 127 C8
Horns Lodge La TN11 . . . . 127 A8
Horn's Oak Rd DA13 . . . . . 64 B6
Horn Rd TN18 . . . . 194 B8
HORN STREET 81 D6
Horn Yd [7] DA11 . . . . 19 B1
Horsa Rd
  Eltham SE12 . . . . 28 C8
  Erith DA8 . . . . 14 C7
Horsecroft Cl BR6 . . . . 64 H1
Horsegrove Ave TN5 . . . . . 186 F1
Horse Leaze E6 . . . . 2 A7
Horsell Rd BR5 . . . . 44 B8
*Horseshoe Cl
  Gillingham ME7 . . . . 68 F5
  Maidstone ME14 . . . . 100 E5
HORSESHOE GREEN 139 C1
Horseshoes La ME17 . . . . . 117 E4
Horse Wash La ME1 . . . . . . 53 C6
Horsfeld Gdns SE9 . . . . . . 11 E2
Horsfeld Rd SE9 . . . . 11 D2
Horsfield Cl DA2 . . . . 33 C8
Horsham Rd DA6 . . . . 14 A2
Horsley Ho SE18 . . . . 12 A7
Horsley Rd
  Bromley BR1 . . . . 42 B8
  Rochester ME1 . . . . 53 B4
HORSMONDEN 163 A5
Horsmonden Cl BR6 . . . . . 43 F2
Horsmonden Prim Sch
  TN12 . . . . 163 A6
Horsmonden Rd TN12 . . . . 162 D6

Horsted Ave ME4 . . . . 53 E1
Horsted Inf Sch ME4 . . . . . 67 D5
Horsted Jun Sch ME4 . . . . 67 D5
Horsted Ret Pk ME5 . . . . . . 67 D5
Horsted Way ME4 . . . . 67 D7
Horton Downs ME15 . . . . . 100 F1
HORTON KIRBY 47 D5
Horton Kirby CE Prim Sch
  DA4 . . . . 47 C6
Horton Pl TN16 . . . . 89 D1
Horton Rd DA4 . . . . 47 C6
Hortons Cl TN17 . . . . 190 D7
Hortons Way [1] TN16 . . . . 89 D1
Horton Tower [2] BR5 . . . . 44 C5
Horton Way DA4 . . . . 46 F2
Horwood CI ME1 . . . . 61 E4
Hoselands View DA3 . . . . . 48 E5
Hoser Ave SE12 . . . . 28 A6
Hosey Common La TN16 . . 105 F5
Hosey Common Rd TN8,
  TN16 . . . . 105 D5
Hosey Hill TN16 . . . . 105 E8
Hoskin's CI E16 . . . . 1 C7
Hospital La [3] ME1 . . . . . . 53 E4
Hospital Rd
  Hollingbourne ME17 . . . . 118 B8
  Sevenoaks TN13 . . . . 92 C6
Hostier CI ME2 . . . . 66 B4
Hotel Rd ME8 . . . . 55 A2
Hotham CI
  Sutton at Hone DA4 . . . . 33 B1
  Swanley Village BR8 . . . . 46 B8
Hothfield Rd ME8 . . . . 55 F1
Hottsfield DA3 . . . . 48 E6
Hougham Ho [11] BR5 . . . . 44 D1
Houghton Ave ME7 . . . . . . 69 B3
Houselands CI TN9 . . . . . . 127 B2
Hove CI RM17 . . . . 18 A8
Hovendens TN17 . . . . 180 A8
Hoveton Rd SE28 . . . . 3 C7
Howard Ave
  Rochester ME1 . . . . 53 D3
  Sidcup DA5 . . . . 30 C8
Howard Dr ME16 . . . . 99 B5
Howard Gdns TN2 . . . . 149 A1
Howard Rd
  Bromley BR1 . . . . 28 A1
  Dartford DA1 . . . . 16 A1
  East Malling ME19 . . . . . . 97 F8
  Howard Sch The ME8 . . . . 69 D8
Howarth Rd SE2 . . . . 3 A2
Howbury Ctr PRU The
  DA8 . . . . 15 A7
Howbury La DA8 . . . . 15 A5
Howbury Wlk ME8 . . . . 69 D4
Howden CI SE28 . . . . 3 D6
Howells CI TN15 . . . . 61 E4
Howerd Way SE18 . . . . 11 E6
Howes Cotts TN18 . . . . . . 194 F6
HOW GREEN 123 C1
How Green La TN8 . . . . . . 123 C2
Howick CI TN12 . . . . 148 E6
Howick Mans SE18 . . . . 1 E3
Howland Cotts TN12 . . . . . 148 E6
Howland Rd TN12 . . . . 148 E6
Howlands TN15 . . . . 78 F4
Howlands Ct TN15 . . . . 78 F4
Howlsmere CI ME2 . . . . . . 66 B3
Hubbard's Hill TN13,
  TN14 . . . . 108 B4
Hubbard's La ME15 . . . . . . 116 A3
Hubble Dr ME15 . . . . 116 E7
HUCKING 86 E1
Huckleberry CI ME5 . . . . . 68 B3
Hudson CI ME15 . . . . 55 C1
Hudson Ho DA4 . . . . 47 D7
Hudson Pl SE18 . . . . 2 C1
Hudson Rd DA7 . . . . 13 F6
Huggen's College
  Almshouses DA11 . . . . . . 18 B2
Hugh Christie Tech Coll
  TN10 . . . . 127 D6
Hughes Dr ME2 . . . . 39 D2
Hulberry Farm DA4 . . . . . . 60 B8
Hulkes La ME1 . . . . 53 E4
Hull Pl E16 . . . . 2 C5
Hulsewood CI DA2 . . . . 32 B5
Humber CI [1] TN18 . . . . . 189 A2
Humber Cres ME2 . . . . 52 F7
Humber Rd
  Dartford DA1 . . . . 26 C7
  Greenwich SE3 . . . . 11 A8
Humboldt Rd SE6 . . . . 159 D5
Hume Ave RM18 . . . . 19 B5
Hume CI RM18 . . . . 19 A4
Hume Terr E16 . . . . 1 B7
Humphreys TN12 . . . . 161 F6
Hundred of Hoo Sch The
  ME3 . . . . 40 C5
HUNGERSHALL PARK . . . 158 E2
Hungershall Park Cl TN4 . 158 E1
Hungershall Pk TN4 . . . . . 158 E2
Hunsdon Dr TN13 . . . . 92 B4
Hunstanton CI ME8 . . . . . . 69 F3
Hunters CI DA5 . . . . 31 E5
Hunters Ct [5] ME7 . . . . . . 54 C7
Hunter Seal TN11 . . . . 126 E2
Huntersfield CI ME5 . . . . . 68 C1
Hunter's Gr BR6 . . . . 57 C6
Hunters Lodge [10] DA15 . . 30 A5
Hunters Way
  Gillingham ME7 . . . . 54 E1
  Marlpit Hill TN8 . . . . 122 B2
  Royal Tunbridge Wells
  TN2 . . . . 158 F1
Hunters Way W ME5 . . . . . 54 E1
Hunters Wlk TN14 . . . . 74 E5

Huntingdon Wlk [2]
  ME15 . . . . 116 E7
Huntingfield Rd DA13 . . . . 50 A2
Huntington CI TN17 . . . . . 179 D4
Huntington Rd ME17 . . . . 115 B3
Huntley Ave DA11 . . . . 18 C1
Huntley Mill Rd TN5 . . . . 186 E3
Huntleys Pk TN4 . . . . 158 F5
HUNTON 131 D7
Hunton CE Prim Sch
  ME15 . . . . 131 D7
Hunton Hill
  Coxheath ME15 . . . . 115 A2
  Hunton ME15 . . . . 114 F1
Hunton Ho [4] BR5 . . . . . . 44 C4
Hunton Rd TN12 . . . . 132 A3
Hunt Rd
  Northfleet DA11 . . . . 35 F5
  Tonbridge TN10 . . . . 127 E6
Hunts CI SE3 . . . . 11 A5
Hunts Farm CI TN15 . . . . . 95 A7
Hunts La TN17 . . . . 177 F8
Huntsman Ho [2] DA11 . . . 35 F8
Huntsman La
  Maidstone ME14 . . . . 100 B4
  Wrotham Heath TN15 . . . 79 E1
Huntsmans CI ME1 . . . . . . 61 E5
Huntsman's Cnr ME4 . . . . . 67 E8
Hunts Mede CI ME9 . . . . . 80 A5
Huntsmoor House BR5 . . . 44 B5
Hunt St
  Chatham ME5 . . . . 67 E6
  Staplehurst TN12 . . . . . . 149 F4
  Tenterden TN30 . . . . 192 F7
Hurst CI
  Newham E6 . . . . 1 D8
  Sidcup DA15 . . . . 30 A6
Hurst Farm Rd TN14 . . . . 108 B3
Hurstfield BR2 . . . . 42 A4
HURST GREEN 194 B3
Hurst Green CE Prim Sch
  TN19 . . . . 194 A2
Hurst Green CI RH8 . . . . . 104 A3
Hurst Green Rd RH8 . . . . . 104 A3
Hurst Green Sch RH8 . . . . 104 A3
Hurst Hill ME5 . . . . 67 E2
Hurst La ME15 . . . . 97 A2
Hurst PI SE2 . . . . 3 D1
Hurstings The ME15 . . . . . 99 D2
Hurst La
  Erith DA8 . . . . 8 E1
  Sevenoaks Weald TN14 . . 108 B2
Hurslands RH8 . . . . 104 A3
Hurstmere Foundation Sch
  DA15 . . . . 30 C7
Hurst PI
  Gillingham ME8 . . . . 69 FB
  Woolwich SE2 . . . . 3 C1
Hurst Prim Sch DA5 . . . . . 30 D7
Hurst Rd
  Erith DA8 . . . . 14 C7
  Sidcup DA5 . . . . 30 D7
Hurst Springs DA5 . . . . . . 30 E7
Hurst Way
  Maidstone ME16 . . . . 98 F2
  Sevenoaks TN13 . . . . 108 C8
Hurstwood ME5 . . . . 67 E4
Hurstwood Ave
  Bexley DA7, DA8 . . . . 14 E6
  Sidcup DA5 . . . . 30 E7
Hurstwood Dr BR1 . . . . . . 42 F6
Hurstwood La TN4 . . . . . . 158 F3
Hurstwood Pk TN4 . . . . . . 158 F3
Hurstwood Rd ME7 . . . . . . 69 B1
Husheath Hill TN17 . . . . . 164 F6
Hussar Ho ME1 . . . . 53 C3
Husseywell Cres BR2 . . . . 42 A1
Hutchins Rd SE28 . . . . 3 A5
Hutsford CI ME8 . . . . 69 D5
Hutson Terr RM19 . . . . 16 D8
Huxley CI [3] ME1 . . . . 53 D4
Huxley Ho SE1 . . . . 2 C3
Huxley Rd DA16 . . . . 12 F2
Hyacinth Rd ME2 . . . . 52 E6
Hybrid CI ME1 . . . . 53 D1
Hyde Dr BR5 . . . . 44 B5
Hyde Ho ME1 . . . . 16 A5
Hyde Rd
  Bexley DA7 . . . . 13 F5
  Maidstone ME16 . . . . 99 D6
Hyders Forge TN15 . . . . . . 111 A8
Hyde's Orch TN27 . . . . . . 153 F1
Hylton St SE18 . . . . 2 F2
Hyndford Cres DA9 . . . . . . 17 C2
Hyperion Dr ME2 . . . . 38 F1
Hythe Ave DA7 . . . . 13 F7
Hythe CI
  Orpington BR5 . . . . 44 C5
  Royal Tunbridge Wells
  TN4 . . . . 143 A1
Hythe St DA1 . . . . 15 E1

I

Ice Bowl The* ME8 . . . . . . 55 A1
Ickleton Rd SE9 . . . . 28 E4
Icough Ct SE3 . . . . 11 B7
Iddenden Cotts TN18 . . . . 188 D2
IDE HILL 106 F4
Ide Hill CE Prim Sch
  TN14 . . . . 106 F4
Ide Hill Rd
  Bough Beech TN8, TN14 . 123 F5
  Ide Hill TN14 . . . . 106 F2
Iden Cres TN12 . . . . 149 F2
Iden Croft Herbs* TN12 . . 150 A1
IDEN GREEN
  Goudhurst 178 C8
  Hawkhurst 190 D4
Iden Green Cotts TN17 . . . 178 C8
Iden Rd ME2 . . . . 39 C1
Idenwood CI ME8 . . . . 69 D6
Idleigh Court Rd DA3,
  DA13 . . . . 63 C8
Idleigh Court Rd ME15 . . . 116 A4
Ifield Sch The DA12 . . . . . 36 C3
Ifield Way DA12 . . . . 36 D2
IGHTHAM 94 D6
Ightham By-Pass TN15 . . . 94 C7
Ightham Cotts DA2 . . . . . . 34 B6
Ightham Mote* TN15 . . . . 110 A7
Ightham Prim Sch TN15 . . 94 B6
Ightham Rd
  Bexley DA8 . . . . 14 A7
  Shipbourne TN11, TN15 . 110 C5
Ikona Ct SE9 . . . . 6 A1
Ilex Ho ME16 . . . . 97 A4
Ilkley Rd E16 . . . . 1 C8
Illustrious CI ME5 . . . . 68 A6
Imber Ct [4] SE9 . . . . 12 A1
Impala Gdns TN4 . . . . 159 B6
Imperial Bsns Pk DA11 . . . 18 F1
Imperial CI ME10 . . . . 97 B3
Imperial Ct BR7 . . . . 29 B2
Imperial Dr DA12 . . . . 36 F3
Imperial PI BR7 . . . . 43 A8
Imperial Rd ME4 . . . . 54 C3
Imperial Ret Pk DA11 . . . . 19 A1
Imperial Way BR7 . . . . 29 C5
Inca Dr SE9 . . . . 29 B8
Indus Rd SE7 . . . . 11 C7
Industrial Est The TN8 . . . 122 B3
Ingleborough La TN15 . . . . 95 C8
Ingleby Way BR7 . . . . 29 A3
Ingleden Park Rd TN30 . . . 183 C1
Ingledew Rd SE18 . . . . 2 D1
Ingle PI ME18 . . . . 97 A2
Ingle Rd ME4 . . . . 53 F2
Ingleside Gr [3] SE3 . . . . . 11 A8
Ingleton Ave DA16 . . . . . . 13 A2
Inglewood
  Chislehurst BR7 . . . . 29 D2
  Swanley BR8 . . . . 45 E7
Inglewood Copse BR1 . . . . 42 F7
Inglewood Rd DA12 . . . . . . 14 D3
Ingoldsby Rd DA12 . . . . . . 36 F7
Ingram Ct ME20 . . . . 82 B4
Ingram Rd
  Dartford DA1 . . . . 32 E7
  Gillingham ME7 . . . . 54 E6
Ingress Gdns DA9 . . . . 17 D2
Ingress Park Ave DA9 . . . . 17 C3
Ingress Terr DA13 . . . . 34 E4
Inigo Jones Rd SE7 . . . . . . 11 E7
Inner Lines ME7 . . . . 54 A6
Institute Rd ME4 . . . . 54 A4
Instone Rd DA1 . . . . 32 D8
International University of
  Americas (London Campus)
  [12] SE18 . . . . 12 C8
Inverary PI SE18 . . . . 12 C8
Inveray Rd SE7 . . . . 1 B1
Invermore PI SE18 . . . . 2 C2
Inverness Ho [7] ME15 . . . 116 E7
Inverness Mews E16 . . . . . . 2 C5
Invicta CI BR7 . . . . 29 A3
Invicta Gram Sch for Girls
  ME14 . . . . 100 C4
Invicta Par [3] DA14 . . . . . 30 A4
Invicta Prim Sch SE3 . . . . 11 A7
Invicta Rd
  Dartford DA2 . . . . 16 B1
  Greenwich SE3 . . . . 11 A8
Invicta Villas ME14 . . . . . . 101 C4
IO Ctr SE18 . . . . 2 C3
Iona CI ME15 . . . . 68 D1
Iona Rd ME15 . . . . 116 A7
Ionia Wlk DA12 . . . . 36 F5
Ireland CI E6 . . . . 1 F8
Irene Rd BR6 . . . . 43 F2
Iris Ave DA5 . . . . 13 E1
Iris CI ME5 . . . . 84 A8
Iris Cres DA7 . . . . 13 F8
Iron Mill La DA1 . . . . 14 F3
Iron Mill Pl DA1 . . . . 14 F3
Ironside CI ME5 . . . . 68 A8
Ironstones TN1 . . . . 158 B3
Irvine CI ME3 . . . . 38 B3
Irvine Way BR6 . . . . 44 A3
Irving Ho TN1 . . . . 159 B5
Irving Way BR8 . . . . 45 D7
Irving Wlk DA10 . . . . 34 E8
Isabella Dr BR6 . . . . 57 C6
Island Way E ME4 . . . . 40 C1
Island Way W ME4 . . . . 40 B2
Isla Rd SE18 . . . . 12 C8
Islehurst CI BR7 . . . . 43 A8

Hoo-Jen 221

Islingham Farm Rd ME3 . . 39 D4
Ismays Rd TN15 . . . . 94 C3
ISTEAD RISE 49 E8
Istead Rise DA13 . . . . 35 F1
Istead Rise Prim Sch
  DA13 . . . . 49 E8
Itchingwood Common Rd
  RH8 . . . . 104 E2
Ito Way ME8 . . . . 55 A3
Ivans Field ME17 . . . . 117 B1
Ivedon Rd DA16 . . . . 13 C5
Ivens Way ME17 . . . . 119 D6
Iverhurst CI DA6 . . . . 13 D2
Iversgate CI ME8 . . . . 55 F2
Ives Rd TN9 . . . . 126 F1
Ivor Gr SE9 . . . . 29 B7
Ivor Ho DA14 . . . . 30 C3
Ivorydown BR1 . . . . 28 A4
Ivy Bower CI DA9 . . . . 17 B2
Ivybridge Ct [1] BR7 . . . . . 43 A8
Ivy CI
  Dartford DA1 . . . . 33 A8
  Gravesend DA12 . . . . 36 D5
  Maidstone ME17 . . . . 118 D2
IVY HATCH 94 A1
Ivy House La TN13, TN14 . 75 E2
Ivy La
  Bells Yew Green TN3 . . . 174 A5
  Knockholt TN14 . . . . 74 E3
  New Mews ME17 . . . . 118 E2
Ivy PI ME1 . . . . 53 A2
Ivy Rd E16 . . . . 1 A7
Ivy St ME8 . . . . 69 F8
Ivy Villas DA9 . . . . 17 A2
Izane Rd DA6 . . . . 13 F3

J

Jackass La BR2 . . . . 56 C4
Jacklin CI ME5 . . . . 67 F2
Jackson Ave ME1 . . . . 67 E8
Jackson CI
  Gillingham ME8 . . . . 55 C1
  [1] Stone DA9 . . . . 17 A2
Jackson Ho [6] SE7 . . . . . . 11 B8
Jackson Rd BR2 . . . . 56 F8
Jackson's Cnr ME3 . . . . . . 24 A3
Jackson St SE18 . . . . 12 A8
Jackson Way TN17 . . . . . . 181 C3
Jacob Ho [5] DA8 . . . . 3 D4
Jacob's La ME3 . . . . 41 B6
Jade CI E16 . . . . 1 D7
Jade Hill ME2 . . . . 66 A6
Jaffray Rd BR2 . . . . 42 D5
Jaggard Way TN12 . . . . . . 149 E3
Jagger CI DA2 . . . . 33 C8
Jago CI SE18 . . . . 12 C8
Jail La
  Biggin Hill TN16 . . . . 72 E3
  Cudham TN16 . . . . 73 A3
Jamaica Terr ME14 . . . . . . 100 A7
James Ave TN15 . . . . 61 D3
James CI TN11 . . . . 111 F1
James Newman Ct SE9 . . . 29 A5
James Rd
  Cuxton ME2 . . . . 52 C2
  Dartford DA1 . . . . 15 A1
James St
  [8] Chatham ME4 . . . . . . 53 F4
  Gillingham ME7 . . . . 54 C6
  Maidstone ME14 . . . . 100 A5
  Rochester ME1 . . . . 53 C4
James Watt Way DA8 . . . . 14 F8
James Whatman Way
  ME14 . . . . 99 F5
Jane Seymour Ct DA15 . . . 29 D8
Janet Ct DA7 . . . . 14 A3
Janson Ct [1] DA14 . . . . . . 30 B4
Japonica CI ME5 . . . . 68 C2
Jaquets Ct DA5 . . . . 31 A6
Jarrah Cotts RM19 . . . . . . 16 D8
Jarrett Ave ME2 . . . . 39 C2
Jarvis La TN17 . . . . 164 B3
Jarvis PI TN30 . . . . 183 B3
Jasmine CI
  [2] Chatham ME5 . . . . . . 67 F4
  [4] East Malling ME19 . . . 97 F8
  Orpington BR6 . . . . 57 B8
Jasmine Gdns
  Borough Green TN15 . . . . 94 F7
  Groombridge TN3 . . . . . . 171 C7
Jasmine Ct SE12 . . . . 11 A1
Jasmine Rd ME19 . . . . 97 F8
Jason Wlk SE9 . . . . 29 A4
Jasper Ave ME1 . . . . 53 D2
Jasper Rd E16 . . . . 1 D7
Javelin Rd ME19 . . . . 96 F3
Jay Gdns BR7 . . . . 28 F4
Jefferson Dr ME8 . . . . 55 C1
Jefferson Wlk [13] SE18 . . 12 A8
Jeffery St ME7 . . . . 54 C6
Jeffrey Ct TN12 . . . . 149 E4
Jeffrey Ct DA8 . . . . 14 C7
Jeffrey Row SE12 . . . . 11 B2
Jeffrey St ME14 . . . . 100 A5
Jeken Rd SE9 . . . . 11 C3
Jellicoe Ave DA12 . . . . 36 C5
Jellicoe Avenue W DA12 . . 36 C5
Jenkins CI [3] DA11 . . . . . . 35 F5
Jenkins' Dale ME4 . . . . . . 53 F3
Jenkins Dr ME15 . . . . 116 E5
Jenner CI DA14 . . . . 30 A4
Jenner Ho [4] DA17 . . . . . . 4 A3
Jenner Rd ME1 . . . . 53 C4

Jenner Way ME20 . . . . 82 F6
Jennifer Ct ME3 . . . . 40 F5
Jenningtree Rd DA8 . . . . 15 B7
Jenningtree Way DA17 . . . . . 4 C4
Jenton Ave DA7 . . . . 13 E5
Jerome Rd ME20 . . . . 81 F4
Jersey Dr BR5 . . . . 43 D3
Jersey Rd
  Newham E16 . . . . 1 C8
  Rochester ME2 . . . . 53 A8
Jeskyns Ctry Pk★ DA12 . . 50 E8
Jeskyns Rd DA12 . . . . 50 E6
Jessamine PI DA2 . . . . 33 C8
Jessamine Terr BR8 . . . . 45 C8
Jessett CI DA8 . . . . 4 D2
Jessup CI SE18 . . . . 2 C2
Jetty Rd
  Kingsnorth ME3 . . . . 41 D7
  Sheerness ME12 . . . . 27 F3
Jetty Wlk **3** RM17 . . . . 18 A8
Jevington Way SE12 . . . . 28 B7
Jewell Gr TN12 . . . . 148 D5
Jewels Hill TN16 . . . . 72 A6
Jeyes Rd ME7 . . . . 54 C4
Jezreels Rd ME1 . . . . 54 D3
Jim Bradley CI **10** SE18 . . . 2 A2
Jiniwin Rd ME1 . . . . 67 D7
Joan Cres SE9 . . . . 28 D8
Jockey La TN17 . . . . 179 D5
Johannesburg Ho **2**
  ME15 . . . . 116 F5
John Brunt Ct TN12 . . . . . . 146 A7
John Burns Cotts RH8 . . . . 104 E5
John Coopper Ho ME3 . . . . 25 C5
John F Kennedy Sch E16 . . 1 D8
John Hunt Ct SE9 . . . . 28 E6
John Mayne CE Prim Sch
  The TN27 . . . . 167 F1
John Newton Ct DA16 . . . . . 13 B4
Johns CI DA3 . . . . 48 F4
Johnson Ave ME7 . . . . 54 C7
Johnson CI DA11 . . . . 35 D5
Johnson Rd BR2 . . . . 42 D4
Johnsons Ave TN14 . . . . 59 B1
Johnsons Ct TN15 . . . . 92 F6
Johnsons Way DA9 . . . . 17 C1
John Spare Ct TN4 . . . . 159 A6
Johns Rd TN16 . . . . 73 B3
John's Rd
  Meopham Station DA13 . . . 49 F4
  Tatsfield TN16 . . . . 88 D7
John St
  Grays RM17 . . . . 18 C8
  Maidstone ME14 . . . . 100 A6
  Rochester ME1 . . . . 53 C4
  Royal Tunbridge Wells
  TN4 . . . . 159 A5
John Wesley Ct SE9 . . . . 12 A3
John Wilson St SE18 . . . . 2 A2
Joiners Ct ME4 . . . . 54 B2
Jonas Dr TN5 . . . . 184 E5
Jonas La TN5 . . . . 184 E5
Jordan CI ME15 . . . . 116 E5
Josling CI RM17 . . . . 17 F8
Joyce CI TN17 . . . . 179 C5
Joyce Dawson Way SE28 . . 3 A6
Joyce Green Ho DA1 . . . . . . 15 F4
Joyce Green La DA1 . . . . 15 F4
Joyce Green Wlk DA1 . . . . . 15 F3
Joyce Page CI SE7 . . . . 11 D8
JOYDEN'S WOOD 31 F4
Joydens Wood Cty Inf Sch
  DA5 . . . . 31 E4
Joyden's Wood Jun Sch
  DA2 . . . . 31 E4
Joyden's Wood Rd DA5 . . . 31 E5
Joy Rd DA12 . . . . 36 C7
Joy Wood ME17 . . . . 116 D5
Jubilee CI DA1 . . . . 17 C1
Jubilee Cnr ME17 . . . . 135 E3
Jubilee Cotts
  Sevenoaks TN14 . . . . 92 B7
  Sutton Valence ME17 . . . 134 E7
Jubilee Cres
  Gravesend DA12 . . . . 36 E6
  Ightham TN15 . . . . 94 C6
Jubilee Ct DA1 . . . . 32 B3
Jubilee Ctry Pk★ BR1,
  BR5 . . . . 43 B5
Jubilee Field TN30 . . . . 179 E6
Jubilee Prim Sch SE28 . . . . 3 C6
Jubilee Rd
  Chelsfield BR6 . . . . 59 A4
  West Thurrock RM20 . . . . . 17 B8
Jubilee Rise TN15 . . . . 92 F6
Jubilee St
  Gillingham ME7 . . . . 54 C6
  Knockholt TN14 . . . . 74 E4
Jubilee Way DA14 . . . . 30 A6
Judd Rd TN9 . . . . 143 B7
Judd Sch The TN9 . . . . 143 A8
Judeth Gdns DA12 . . . . 36 E3
Judkins CI ME5 . . . . 62 B5
Jugkans Rd BR6 . . . . 44 A1
Julia Garfield Mews E16 . . . 1 C7
Julian Ct **3** DA14 . . . . 30 A4
Julian Rd BR6 . . . . 58 A4
Julians Ct TN13 . . . . 108 A8
Julians Way TN13 . . . . 108 A8
Junction Rd
  Bodiam TN18, TN32 . . . . . 195 A3
  Dartford DA1 . . . . 15 D1
  Gillingham ME7 . . . . 54 D4
Juniper CI
  Biggin Hill TN16 . . . . 72 E2

Juniper CI continued
  Chatham ME5 . . . . 68 A4
  Hurst Green RH8 . . . . 104 B2
  Maidstone ME16 . . . . 99 B6
  Royal Tunbridge Wells
  TN4 . . . . 143 D1
Juniper La E6 . . . . 1 E8
Jupp CI ME3 . . . . 38 C6
Jupp St **3** DA11 . . . . 19 B1
Jutland CI ME3 . . . . 9 D1
Jutland Ho SE18 . . . . 1 E2

K

K9 Est RM13 . . . . 4 E7
Kale Rd DA18 . . . . 3 E4
Karloff Way ME2 . . . . 39 B2
Kashgar Rd SE18 . . . . 2 F2
Kashmir Rd SE7 . . . . 11 D7
Katherine Ct ME4 . . . . 54 B3
Katherine Gdns SE9 . . . . . . 11 D3
Katherine Rd TN4 . . . . 138 C8
Katherine Villas TN8 . . . . . 138 C8
Kaysland Park TN15 . . . . . . 61 E3
Keary Rd DA10 . . . . 34 F8
Keating CI ME1 . . . . 53 A3
Keats Ave E16 . . . . 1 B8
Keats Gdns RM18 . . . . 19 B5
Keats Ho DA1 . . . . 14 E2
Keats Rd
  Bexley DA16 . . . . 12 F6
  Erith DA17 . . . . 4 C3
  Lunsford ME20 . . . . 81 F3
Kechill Gdns BR2 . . . . 42 A2
Kedleston Dr BR5 . . . . 38 A1
Keeble CI SE18 . . . . 12 B8
Keedonwood Rd BR1 . . . . . 28 A3
Keefe CI ME5 . . . . 67 D1
Keel Ct ME2 . . . . 53 D8
Keeley Mews ME7 . . . . 54 E3
Keel Gdns TN4 . . . . 158 E8
Keeling Rd SE9 . . . . 11 D2
Keemor CI SE18 . . . . 12 A7
Keep The SE3 . . . . 11 A5
Keightley Dr SE9 . . . . 29 C7
Keir Hardie Prim Sch E16 . 1 A8
Keir Hardie Ho **7** DA17 . . 4 A3
Keith Ave DA4 . . . . 33 B2
Keith Park Cres TN16 . . . . . 72 C7
Keith Sutton House SE9 . . . 29 C6
Kelbrook Rd SE3 . . . . 11 E4
Kelchers La TN11 . . . . 128 F5
Kelham Ho **10** SE18 . . . . . 12 B8
Kellaway Rd
  Chatham ME5 . . . . 68 A2
  Greenwich SE3 . . . . 11 D5
Kellner Rd SE28 . . . . 2 F3
Kelly Dr ME7 . . . . 54 C7
Kelly Ho
  15 Greenwich SE7 . . . . . . 11 C8
  Rochester ME1 . . . . 67 C7
Kelsall CI SE3 . . . . 11 B5
Kelsey Rd BR5 . . . . 44 B7
Kelso Dr DA12 . . . . 36 F4
Kelvin CI TN10 . . . . 127 D7
Kelvin Ho **3** DA17 . . . . 4 A3
Kelvin Par BR6 . . . . 43 E1
Kelvin Rd
  Bexley DA16 . . . . 13 A4
  Tilbury RM18 . . . . 19 A5
Kemble CI TN2 . . . . 159 E7
Kemble Dr BR2 . . . . 56 E7
Kembleside Rd TN16 . . . . . 72 C1
Kemnal Rd BR7 . . . . 29 D3
Kemnal Tech Coll BR5 . . . . 30 B1
Kemnal Warren BR7 . . . . . . 29 D2
Kemp CI ME5 . . . . 62 C5
Kempley Ct **2** RM17 . . . . 18 D8
Kempton CI
  Chatham ME5 . . . . 68 C2
  Erith DA8 . . . . 14 C8
Kempt St SE18 . . . . 12 A8
KEMSING 77 B2
Kemsing CI DA5 . . . . 24 E7
Kemsing Prim Sch TN15 . . 77 A2
Kemsing Rd
  Greenwich SE10 . . . . 1 A1
  Wrotham TN15 . . . . 78 C3
Kemsing Sta TN15 . . . . 93 D8
Kemsley CI
  Northfleet DA11 . . . . 35 F4
  Swanscombe DA9 . . . . 17 B1
Kemsley Ct BR5 . . . . 44 B8
Kemsley Rd TN16 . . . . 88 D8
KEMSLEY STREET 69 C1
Kemsley Street Rd ME7 . . . 69 C1
Kencot CI DA18 . . . . 3 E4
Kendal CI TN9 . . . . 127 C2
Kendal Dr TN9 . . . . 127 C2
Kendall Ave ME19 . . . . 97 C3
Kendall Ct DA16 . . . . 30 A5
Kendall Gdns DA11 . . . . 35 F8
Kendall PI **4** ME15 . . . . . 116 C6
Kendall Rd SE18 . . . . 11 E6
Kendal Pk TN4 . . . . 158 E5
Kendal Way ME8 . . . . 69 D8
Kendon Bsns Pk ME2 . . . . . 53 D8
Kenia Wlk ME18 . . . . 97 D2
Ketridge La ME18 . . . . 97 D2
Kettle La ME15 . . . . 114 E6
Kettlewell Ct BR8 . . . . 45 F7
Kevington CI BR5 . . . . 43 F5
Kevington Dr BR7 . . . . 43 F5
KEVINGTOWN 44 E3
Kewlands ME14 . . . . 100 C6
KEYCOL 71 E6

Kenley CI
  Sidcup DA5 . . . . 31 A8
  St Paul's Cray BR7 . . . . 43 E6
Kenley Ho **6** BR5 . . . . 44 B7
Kenmere Rd DA16 . . . . 13 C5
Kennacraig CI E16 . . . . 1 A5
Kennard CI ME1 . . . . 52 F2
Kennard St E16 . . . . 2 A5
Kennedy CI BR5 . . . . 43 D1
Kennedy Gdns TN13 . . . . . . 92 D5
Kennedy Ho
  Benenden TN17 . . . . 190 E6
  Northfleet DA11 . . . . 35 D5
Kennel Barn Rd ME9 . . . . . . 87 C5
Kennet Ct **2** BR8 . . . . 45 E6
Kennet Rd
  Crayford DA1 . . . . 15 A4
  Tonbridge TN10 . . . . 127 C5
Kennett Ct **15** BR5 . . . . . 44 D1
Kennington CI
  Gillingham ME8 . . . . 55 B4
  Maidstone ME15 . . . . 116 F7
Kensington Ct **5** ME7 . . . 18 C8
Kensington Ho ME16 . . . . . 99 A2
Kent Ave
  Bexley DA16 . . . . 12 F2
  Maidstone ME15 . . . . 100 C1
Kent CI
  Orpington BR6 . . . . 57 E4
  Paddock Wood TN12 . . . . 146 A6
  Rochester ME2 . . . . 53 A3
Kent Coll TN2 . . . . 144 D3
Kent & East Sussex Rly★
  Rolvenden TN30 . . . . 192 D5
  Tenterden TN30 . . . . 193 A8
KENT HATCH 105 B3
Kent Hatch Rd
  Crockham Hill RH8, TN8 . 105 B4
  The Chart RH8, TN8 . . . . 104 D4
Kent Ho
  10 Hawkhurst TN18 . . . 189 A2
  Royal Tunbridge Wells
  TN1 . . . . 159 C6
  Sutton at Hone DA4 . . . . . . 47 D7
Kentish Ct **8** ME16 . . . . . 99 E4
Kentish Gdns TN2 . . . . 172 E8
Kentish Mans **15** TN1 . . 159 A2
Kentish Rd DA17 . . . . 4 A2
Kent Kraft Ind Est DA11 . . 17 F2
Kentlea Rd SE28 . . . . 2 E4
Kent Life★ ME14 . . . . 83 D1
Kentmere Rd SE18 . . . . 2 E2
Kent Rd
  Dartford DA1 . . . . 15 E1
  Gravesend DA11 . . . . 36 A7
  4 Grays RM17 . . . . 18 D8
  Halling ME2 . . . . 60 A6
  Longfield DA3 . . . . 48 D7
  Orpington BR5 . . . . 44 B3
  Royal Tunbridge Wells
  TN4 . . . . 159 A6
  Snodland ME6 . . . . 82 A6
Kent Showground ME14 . . 85 C3
Kent St TN18 . . . . 189 B1
KENT STREET 96 E2
Kent & Sussex Hospl
  TN4 . . . . 159 A4
Kent Terr
  Lower Higham ME3 . . . . . . 38 D7
  Meopham DA13 . . . . 64 A7
Kenward Ct TN11 . . . . 128 E8
Kenward Rd
  Eltham SE9 . . . . 11 D2
  Maidstone ME15 . . . . 99 C5
  Yalding ME18 . . . . 113 E2
Kenwood Ave
  Chatham ME5 . . . . 68 A4
  New Barn DA3 . . . . 49 C6
Kenwyn Rd DA1 . . . . 15 F6
Kenya Rd SE7 . . . . 11 D7
Kenya Terr **7** ME14 . . . . 100 A7
Kenyon Wlk ME8 . . . . 69 B3
Kerry CI E16 . . . . 1 B7
Kerry Hill Way ME14 . . . . . 99 E6
Kersey Gdns SE9 . . . . 28 E4
Kesteven CI ME2 . . . . 66 B5
Kestlake Rd DA5 . . . . 13 C1
KESTON 56 D6
Keston CI DA16 . . . . 13 C7
Keston Ct
  Gillingham ME8 . . . . 55 A2
  Sidcup DA5 . . . . 30 F8
Keston Gdns BR2 . . . . 56 C6
Keston CE Prim Sch BR2 . . 56 C5
Keston Park CI BR2 . . . . 56 F7
Kestrel Ave E6 . . . . 1 E8
Kestrel CI TN8 . . . . 122 D3
Kestrel Ho ME7 . . . . 54 B6
Kestrel Rd ME5 . . . . 62 C2
Keswick CI TN9 . . . . 127 C2
Keswick Dr ME16 . . . . 99 B5
Keswick Gdns RM19 . . . . . . 16 C8
Keswick Rd
  Bexley DA7 . . . . 14 A6
  Orpington BR6 . . . . 44 A2
Ketridge La ME18 . . . . 97 D2
Kettle La ME15 . . . . 114 E6
Kettlewell Ct BR8 . . . . 45 F7
Kevington CI BR5 . . . . 43 F5
Kevington Dr BR7 . . . . 43 F5
KEVINGTOWN 44 E3
Kewlands ME14 . . . . 100 C6
KEYCOL 71 E6

Keycol Hill ME9 . . . . 71 F5
Keyes Ave ME4 . . . . 53 F2
Keyes Gdns TN9 . . . . 142 F2
Keyes Rd DA1 . . . . 16 A3
Keymer CI TN16 . . . . 72 D3
Keynes Ct **9** SE28 . . . . 3 B6
Keynsham Gdns SE9 . . . . . 11 E2
Keynsham Rd SE9 . . . . 11 E2
KEY'S GREEN 161 C4
Keyworth CI TN12 . . . . 145 F6
Khalsa Ave DA12 . . . . 36 C8
Khartoum PI DA12 . . . . 19 C1
Khartoum Rd ME7 . . . . 54 A6
Khyber Rd ME4, ME7 . . . . . 54 B7
Kibbles La TN4 . . . . 158 E8
KIDBROOKE 11 C6
Kidbrooke Gdns SE3 . . . . . 11 A6
Kidbrooke Gr SE3 . . . . 11 B6
Kidbrooke La SE3 . . . . 11 E3
Kidbrooke Park CI SE3 . . . . 11 B6
Kidbrooke Park Prim Sch
  SE3 . . . . 11 C6
Kidbrooke Park Rd SE12,
  SE3 . . . . 11 B4
Kidbrooke Sch SE3 . . . . 11 D5
Kidbrooke Sta SE3 . . . . 11 B4
Kidbrooke Way SE3 . . . . . . 11 B5
Kiddens BR8 . . . . 45 B7
Kidd PI SE7 . . . . 1 E8
Kidds Cotts BR8 . . . . 45 D3
Kierbeck Bsns Complex
  E16 . . . . 1 B4
Kilburn Ho **6** ME14 . . . . 100 A5
Kildare Rd E16 . . . . 1 A8
Killewarren Way BR5 . . . . . 44 C3
Killick CI TN13 . . . . 91 D7
Killick Rd ME3 . . . . 40 D5
Killicks Cotts ME18 . . . . . . 130 F8
Killigarth Ct **22** DA14 . . 30 A4
Kiln Barn Rd ME19, ME 20 . 98 C7
Kilnbridge CI ME15 . . . . . . 115 B7
Kilnbridge Wks ME15 . . . . 115 B7
KILNDOWN 176 F3
Kilndown CI DA12 . . . . 36 D2
Kilndown CI ME16 . . . . 99 C7
Kiln Field TN30 . . . . 193 C7
Kilnfields BR6 . . . . 59 A4
Kiln La TN13 . . . . 125 F1
Kiln Way TN12 . . . . 146 A5
Kilnwood TN14 . . . . 74 F6
Kimbell PI SE3 . . . . 11 C3
Kimber Ho **11** SE18 . . . . 12 B8
Kimberley Dr DA14 . . . . 30 D6
Kimberley Rd ME7 . . . . 54 D3
Kimberly CI DA17 . . . . 3 F2
Kimmeridge Gdns SE9 . . . 28 E4
Kimmeridge Rd SE9 . . . . . . 28 E4
Kincraig BR7 . . . . 43 A8
Kincraig Dr TN13 . . . . 92 B4
Kinder CI SE28 . . . . 3 D6
King Arthur's Dr ME2 . . . . . 39 A1
King Edward Ave DA1 . . . . . 15 D1
King Edward Rd
  Chatham ME4 . . . . 53 F2
  Gillingham ME7 . . . . 54 F6
  Maidstone ME15 . . . . 99 F2
  Rochester ME1 . . . . 53 C5
  Stone DA9 . . . . 17 A2
Kingfisher Apartments **13**
  ME15 . . . . 116 E5
Kingfisher CI
  Erith SE28 . . . . 3 C6
  Orpington BR5 . . . . 44 D5
Kingfisher Ct
  11 Maidstone ME15 . . . 100 B4
  West Kingsdown TN15 . . . . 61 E3
Kingfisher Dr
  Chatham ME5 . . . . 68 C7
  Swanscombe DA9 . . . . 17 A1
Kingfisher Mdw ME16 . . . . 99 F3
Kingfisher PI DA4 . . . . 47 C7
Kingfisher Prim Sch ME5 . 68 B7
Kingfisher Rd ME20 . . . . . . 82 A2
Kingfisher St E6 . . . . 1 E8
King George Ave E16 . . . . . . 1 D7
King George Rd ME5 . . . . . . 67 E4
King George V Hill TN1 . . 159 C5
King George VI Ave TN16 . 72 D3
King George V Meml Houses
  ME8 . . . . 55 C2
King Harolds Way DA7 . . . . 13 E7
King Henry Mews **7** BR6 . 57 F5
King Hill ME19 . . . . 97 A5
King & John's Wlk SE9 . . . 11 E1
King & Queen CI SE9 . . . . . 28 E4
Kings Acre ME15 . . . . 101 A1
Kingsand Rd SE12 . . . . 28 A6
Kings Ave BR1 . . . . 28 A2
King's Ave ME1 . . . . 53 C3
King's Bastion ME7 . . . . 54 A5
Kings CI DA1 . . . . 14 E3
Kings Cotts
  Cranbrook TN17 . . . . 179 D6
  Leeds ME17 . . . . 117 F6
King's Cotts
  Wateringbury ME18 . . . . . 113 B8
  Yalding ME18 . . . . 114 A1
Kings Ct
  Horsmonden TN12 . . . . . . 163 A6
  13 Maidstone ME14 . . . 100 A6
Kingsdale Rd SE18 . . . . 12 F8

Kingsdown CI
  Gillingham ME7 . . . . 69 B4
  5 Gravesend DA12 . . . . 36 F7
  Maidstone ME16 . . . . 99 E4
Kingsdown Ind Est ME20 . 98 B8
Kingsdown Way BR2 . . . . . . 42 A3
Kings Dr DA12 . . . . 36 B5
Kings FARM 36 C5
Kings Farm Prim Sch
  DA11 . . . . 36 C4
Kingsfield Ho ME9 . . . . 28 D5
Kingsford Com Sch E6 . . . . 1 F7
Kingsford Cotts TN17 . . . . 190 D6
Kingsford Way E6 . . . . 1 F8
Kingsgate CI
  Bexley DA7 . . . . 13 E6
  Maidstone ME16 . . . . 99 C4
  Orpington BR5 . . . . 44 C6
Kingsgate La TN30 . . . . . . 199 C5
Kings Highway SE18, SE2 . 12 F8
KINGS HILL 97 A2
Kings Hill Ave ME19 . . . . . . 97 A4
Kingshill Dr ME3 . . . . 40 D6
Kings Hill Prim Sch ME19 97 A3
Kingsholm Gdns SE9 . . . . . 11 E3
Kingshurst Rd SE12 . . . . . . 28 A8
Kingsingfield CI TN15 . . . . 61 E3
Kingsingfield Rd TN15 . . . . 61 E2
Kings La TN12 . . . . 147 C7
Kingsland Gr TN27 . . . . 151 D5
Kingsland Rd TN27 . . . . . . 137 E1
Kingsley Ave DA1 . . . . 16 A2
Kingsley Ct
  Bexley DA6 . . . . 14 A3
  Wadhurst TN5 . . . . 185 A4
  1 Woolwich SE28 . . . . . . 3 C5
Kingsley Mews BR7 . . . . . . 29 B2
Kingsley Rd
  Maidstone ME15 . . . . 100 A3
  Orpington BR6 . . . . 57 F3
Kingsley Wood Dr SE9 . . . . 28 E5
Kingsman Par SE18 . . . . 1 F3
Kingsman St SE18 . . . . 1 F2
Kingsmead TN16 . . . . 72 D3
Kingsmead CI DA15 . . . . . . 30 A6
Kingsmead Cotts BR2 . . . . 42 E1
Kingsmead Pk
  Allhallows-on-Sea ME3 . . . . 9 E3
  Paddock Wood TN12 . . . . 146 A6
Kingsmere BR7 . . . . 42 E8
KINGSNORTH 41 D5
Kingsnorth CI ME3 . . . . 40 E6
Kingsnorth Ct BR8 . . . . 45 C3
Kingsnorth Ind Est ME2 . . 41 D7
Kingsnorth Rd ME8 . . . . 55 C4
Kings Oak Mews ME5 . . . . . 67 F4
King's Orch
  Eltham SE9 . . . . 11 E1
  Rochester ME1 . . . . 53 C5
Kings Pk TN2 . . . . 159 D3
Kings Prep Sch ME1 . . . . . . 53 C5
Kings Rd
  Biggin Hill TN16 . . . . 72 C2
  Headcorn TN27 . . . . 151 C5
  Orpington BR6 . . . . 57 F6
King's Rd
  Chatham ME5 . . . . 54 D1
  Tonbridge TN9 . . . . 143 D1
Kings Reach ME15 . . . . 116 D8
Kingsridge Gdns DA1 . . . . . 15 D1
Kings Row
  1 Maidstone ME15 . . . . 100 A1
  Rochester ME1 . . . . 53 B4
King's Sch ME1 . . . . 53 C5
King's Standing Ind Est
  TN2 . . . . 143 F2
Kings Standing Way TN2 143 F1
King St
  Chatham ME4 . . . . 54 A4
  Gillingham ME7 . . . . 54 C6
  Gravesend DA12 . . . . 19 B1
  Maidstone ME14 . . . . 100 A4
  Rochester ME1 . . . . 53 C4
  West Malling ME19 . . . . 97 C3
Kings Toll Rd TN3 . . . . 161 A6
Kingston Cres ME5 . . . . 68 C4
Kingston Ct DA11 . . . . 18 B1
Kingston Dr ME15 . . . . 116 A8
Kingsway
  Chatham ME5 . . . . 54 D1
  Gillingham ME7 . . . . 54 E1
  Orpington BR5 . . . . 43 D4
Kingswear Gdns ME2 . . . . . 53 C7
Kings Wlk
  Grays RM17 . . . . 18 A8
  Maidstone ME14 . . . . 100 B5
KINGSWOOD 118 E3
Kingswood Ave
  Chatham ME4 . . . . 53 F2
  Erith DA8 . . . . 3 C2
  Swanley BR8 . . . . 45 F6
Kingswood CI
  Dartford DA1 . . . . 15 C1
  Orpington BR6 . . . . 43 D2
  Royal Tunbridge Wells
  TN2 . . . . 159 C3
Kingswood Ho
  12 Maidstone ME14 . . . 99 A3
  1 Sidcup DA14 . . . . 30 B4
Kingswood Prim Sch
  ME7 . . . . 118 C2
Kingswood Rd
  Gillingham ME7 . . . . 54 D6
  Kit's Coty ME20 . . . . 83 D8
  Royal Tunbridge Wells
  TN2 . . . . 159 C3
  Sevenoaks TN13 . . . . 91 E7

King William Rd **6** ME7 . . 54 C7
Kinlet Rd SE18 . . . . 12 C6
Kinnell Cl **13** DA14 . . . . 30 B4
Kinnings Row TN9 . . . . 127 C2
Kinross Cl ME5 . . . . 68 B7
Kinveachy Gdns SE7 . . . . 1 E1
Kipling Ave RM18 . . . . 19 C6
Kipling Dr ME20 . . . . 81 F4
Kipling Rd
  Bexley DA7 . . . . 13 E6
  Dartford DA1 . . . . 16 B2
KIPPING'S CROSS 161 B5
KIPPINGTON 92 A1
Kippington Cl TN13 . . . . 91 F3
Kippington Dr SE9 . . . . 28 D7
Kippington Rd TN13 . . . . . . 92 A2
Kirby Cl TN17 . . . . 179 D4
Kirby Rd
  Chattenden ME3 . . . . 39 F5
  Dartford DA2 . . . . 33 D8
Kirkcourt TN13 . . . . 92 A4
Kirkdale SE26 . . . . 115 F5
Kirkdale Cl ME5 . . . . 68 D1
Kirkdale Cotts ME5 . . . . . . 115 F5
Kirkdale Rd
  Maidstone ME15 . . . . 115 F6
  Royal Tunbridge Wells
    TN1 . . . . 159 B4
Kirkham St SE6 . . . . 1 E1
Kirkham St SE18 . . . . 12 E8
Kirk La SE18 . . . . 12 E8
Kirkland Cl DA15 . . . . 23 E1
Kirkman St TN12 . . . . 149 E3
Kirkside Rd SE3 . . . . 11 A8
Kitchener Ave
  Chatham ME4 . . . . 54 A1
  Gravesend DA12 . . . . 36 C5
Kitchener Cotts ME3 . . . . . . 25 C4
Kitchener Rd
  Chattenden ME3 . . . . 39 F4
  Rochester ME2 . . . . 53 A8
Kite La TN12 . . . . 162 A6
Kit Hill Ave ME5 . . . . 67 E3
KIT'S COTY 83 C7
Kit's Coty Ho★ ME20 . . . . . . 83 C6
Knatts La TN15 . . . . 93 F6
KNATTS VALLEY 93 A1
Knaves Acre TN27 . . . . 151 D5
Knaves Acre ME8 . . . . 69 D5
Knave Wood Rd TN15 . . . . . 76 E2
Knee Hill SE2 . . . . 3 C1
Knee Hill Cres SE2 . . . . 3 C2
Knight Ave ME7 . . . . 54 D7
Knighton Rd TN14 . . . . 75 F2
Knight Rd
  Rochester ME2 . . . . 53 A6
  Tonbridge TN10 . . . . 127 C6
Knightrider Ct ME15 . . . . . . 100 A3
Knightrider St ME15 . . . . . . 100 A3
Knightsbridge Ct TN14 . . . . 158 F5
Knightsbridge Ct TN15 . . . . . 159 B6
Knightsbridge Mews BR7 . . 28 F1
Knights Ct
  Hoo St Werburgh ME3 . . . . 40 E5
  Pembury TN2 . . . . 160 D1
Knights Croft TN3 . . . . 62 F7
Knight's Ct **7** DA8 . . . . 14 F7
Knights Field ME4 . . . . 60 E7
Knights Manor Way ME1 . . . 15 F1
Knights Park Ind Est ME2 . . 53 A6
Knights Pk TN11 . . . . 143 F1
Knights Rd
  Hoo St Werburgh ME3 . . . . 40 D5
  Newham E16 . . . . 1 A4
Knights Ridge BR6 . . . . 58 B5
Knight's Ridge TN2 . . . . . . 160 D7
Knight's Way TN2, TN11 . . . 143 F1
Knight's Way TN27 . . . . 151 F6
KNOCKHALL 17 C1
Knockhall Chase DA9 . . . . . 17 C2
Knockhall Com Prim Sch
  DA9 . . . . 17 C2
Knockhall Rd DA9 . . . . 17 C2
KNOCKHOLT 74 B2
KNOCKHOLT POUND 74 D4
Knockholt Rd
  Eltham SE9 . . . . 11 D2
  Halstead TN14 . . . . 74 F6
Knockholt Sta TN14 . . . . . . 58 E2
Knockhurst Ct TN30 . . . . . . 183 C1
KNOCKMILL 77 E7
Knock Mill La TN15 . . . . 78 A5
Knockwood Rd TN30 . . . . . 183 C1
Knole★ TN15 . . . . 108 B2
Knole Cl TN14 . . . . 108 B2
Knole Gate SE9 . . . . 29 E5
Knole La TN13, TN15 . . . . . 92 C1
Knole Paddock & Raleys Ctr
  TN13 . . . . 92 C3
Knole Rd
  Chatham ME5 . . . . 68 C3
  Dartford DA1 . . . . 32 B8
  Sevenoaks TN13 . . . . 92 D4
Knole The
  Eltham SE9 . . . . 29 A4
  Istead Rise DA13 . . . . 35 E1
Knole Way TN13 . . . . 92 C2
Knoll Rd
  Sidcup DA14 . . . . 24 A4
  Sidcup, Old Bexley DA5 . . . 14 A1
Knoll Rise BR6 . . . . 43 F1
Knoll The BR2 . . . . 42 A1
Knotley Hall Cotts TN11 . 125 A2
Knott Ct ME14 . . . . 99 F6
Knotts Pl TN13 . . . . 92 A3

Knowle Ave DA7 . . . . 13 F7
Knowle Rd TN3 . . . . 157 F3
Knowle Cott TN3 . . . . 173 E1
Knowle Cotts TN3 . . . . 173 E1
Knowle La TN12 . . . . 146 C3
Knowle Lodge BR7 . . . . 28 F2
Knowle Rd
  Maidstone ME14 . . . . 100 B6
  Orpington BR2 . . . . 56 E8
  Paddock Wood TN12 . . . . 146 D3
  Wouldham ME1 . . . . 66 D4
Knowles Gdns TN27 . . . . . 151 D5
Knowles Wlk ME12 . . . . . . 149 F4
Knowlton Gdns ME16 . . . . . 99 B2
Knowlton Gn BR5 . . . . 42 A4
Knowsley Way TN11 . . . . . . 126 D6
KNOX BRIDGE 165 F6
Knox Ct TN15 . . . . 92 F6
Koonocla Cl TN16 . . . . 72 D4
Kydbrook Cl BR5 . . . . 43 A2
Kyetop Wlk ME8 . . . . 69 D6
Kynaston Rd
  Bromley BR1 . . . . 28 A3
  Orpington BR5 . . . . 44 B2

L

LABOUR-IN-VAIN 78 F5
Labour-in-Vain Rd TN15 . . . 78 E5
Laburnum Ave
  Dartford DA1 . . . . 32 D7
  Swanley BR8 . . . . 45 D6
Laburnum Ct TN2 . . . . 159 D7
Laburnum Dr ME20 . . . . 82 A2
Laburnum Gr DA11 . . . . 35 D8
Laburnum Way BR2 . . . . 43 B2
Lacebark Cl DA15 . . . . 29 F8
Lacey Cl ME17 . . . . 117 E4
Laceys La ME17 . . . . 132 C7
Lacknut Cotts DA13 . . . . . . 63 E2
Lacock Gdns
  Loose ME15 . . . . 116 A8
  Maidstone ME15 . . . . 100 A1
Lacy Cl ME16 . . . . 99 D7
Ladbrooke Cres DA14 . . . . . 30 D5
Ladbrooke Rd **7** ME4 . . . 100 A5
LADDINGFORD 130 E5
Laddingford Farm Ind Est
  ME18 . . . . 130 D4
Laddingford St Mary's CE
  Prim Sch ME18 . . . . 130 E4
Ladds Cnr ME7 . . . . 55 B5
Ladds La ME6 . . . . 66 A2
Ladds Way BR8 . . . . 45 D5
Ladham Rd TN17 . . . . 164 A2
Ladies Mile TN6, TN7 . . . . 170 D4
Lady Boswell's CE Prim Sch
  TN13 . . . . 92 C2
Ladyclose Ave ME3 . . . . 39 A7
Ladycroft Gdns **6** BR6 . . . 57 C5
Ladycroft Way BR6 . . . . 57 C5
Ladyfern Ct TN2 . . . . 159 C4
Ladyfields
  Chatham ME5 . . . . 68 D2
  Northfleet DA11 . . . . 35 F4
Ladyfields Cl ME9 . . . . 71 F5
Lady Oak La TN5, TN17 . . 187 C7
Lady Shaw **18** ME16 . . . . . 154 F8
Ladysmith Rd SE9 . . . . 12 A1
Lady Vane Cl TN11 . . . . . . 110 C5
Ladywell Ho **7** BR5 . . . . . . 44 B7
Ladywood Ave BR5 . . . . 43 E4
Ladywood Rd
  Cuxton ME2 . . . . 52 B2
  Dartford DA2 . . . . 33 E3
Lagonda Way DA1 . . . . 15 C3
Lagoon Rd BR5 . . . . 44 B4
Lake Ave BR5 . . . . 28 A2
Lakedale Rd SE18 . . . . 2 E1
Lake Dr ME3 . . . . 38 C6
Lakelands
  Harrietsham ME17 . . . . . . 110 F5
  Loose ME15 . . . . 116 A7
Lakeman Way TN4 . . . . 159 B7
Lake Rd
  Ditton ME20 . . . . 98 E8
  Royal Tunbridge Wells
    TN4 . . . . 158 E4
Laker Ho ME14 . . . . 100 A6
Laker Rd ME1 . . . . 67 C6
Lakeside
  Royal Tunbridge Wells
    TN2 . . . . 159 E6
  Snodland ME6 . . . . 81 F6
Lakeside Ave SE28 . . . . 3 A5
Lakeside Cl
  Bexley DA5, DA15 . . . . 13 C2
  Bough Beech TN8 . . . . 123 F4
Lakeside Dr BR2 . . . . 56 E7
Lakeside Pk ME2 . . . . 53 E7
Lakes Rd BR2 . . . . 56 C5
Lakes The ME20 . . . . 82 A4
Lakeswood Rd BR5 . . . . 43 C3
Lakeview Cl ME6 . . . . 82 A6
Lakeview Rd DA16 . . . . 13 B3
Lake View Rd TN13 . . . . 92 A4
Lake Wlk ME20 . . . . 82 A4
Lakewood Dr ME8 . . . . 69 C6
Lambarde Ave SE9 . . . . 29 A4
Lambarde Cl ME2 . . . . 66 A4
Lambarde Dr TN13 . . . . 92 A4
Lambarde Rd TN13 . . . . 92 A4
Lambardes DA3 . . . . 62 F7
Lambardes Cl TN14 . . . . 74 C8

Lambard Ho **8** ME14 . . . . 100 A5
Lamb Cl RM18 . . . . 19 C5
Lambe Ct ME4 . . . . 66 A2
LAMBERHURST 176 B5
Lamberhurst Cl **19** BR5 . . . 44 D1
Lamberhurst Gn ME8 . . . . . 55 B3
LAMBERHURST
  QUARTER 161 D1
Lamberhurst Rd
  Horsmonden TN12, TN3 . . 162 E3
  Lamberhurst TN3, TN12 . . 176 C4
  Maidstone ME16 . . . . 99 B7
Lamberhurst St Mary's CE
  Prim Sch TN3 . . . . 176 B6
Lamberhurst Vineyard★
  TN3 . . . . 176 A4
Lambert Ct TN16 . . . . 72 D3
Lambert Ct DA8 . . . . 14 C8
Lambert Mews **4** ME6 . . . 82 A8
Lambert Rd E16 . . . . 1 B7
Lamberts Pl TN12 . . . . 163 B5
Lamberts Rd TN2 . . . . 159 D8
Lambert's Yd TN9 . . . . 127 B1
Lambes Ct ME8 . . . . 69 D5
Lambeth Cl ME5 . . . . 68 B4
Lambourn Dr ME20 . . . . 97 A2
Lambourne Pl SE3 . . . . 11 B6
Lambourne Rd ME15 . . . . . 100 F2
Lambourn Ho BR1 . . . . 28 E1
Lambourn Way
  Chatham ME5 . . . . 68 C2
  Royal Tunbridge Wells
    TN2 . . . . 159 D1
Lambs Bank TN9 . . . . 143 B7
Lambscroft Ave SE9 . . . . . . 28 D5
Lamb's Cross ME17 . . . . . . 134 A5
Lambsfrith Gr ME7 . . . . 66 C5
Lamb's Mobile Home Pk
  TN12 . . . . 146 A7
Lamorbey Cl DA15 . . . . 29 F6
Lamorna Ave DA12 . . . . 36 D6
Lamorna Cl BR6 . . . . 44 A2
Lampington Row TN3 . . . . 157 E3
Lamplighters Cl
  2 Dartford DA1 . . . . 15 F1
  Gillingham ME7 . . . . 48 F5
Lamport Cl SE18 . . . . 1 F2
Lamson Rd RM13 . . . . 4 F8
Lancashire Rd ME15 . . . . . 116 E7
Lancaster Ct
  Gillingham ME8 . . . . 69 C7
  Gravesend DA12 . . . . 36 C5
Lancaster Gdns BR1 . . . . . . 42 E4
Lancaster Way ME19 . . . . . . 96 F3
Lance Croft DA3 . . . . 42 F8
Lancelot Ave ME2 . . . . 52 E7
Lancelot Cl ME2 . . . . 52 E6
Lancelot Ct BR6 . . . . 58 B8
Lancelot Rd DA16 . . . . 13 A4
Lancer Ho ME1 . . . . 53 C3
Lances Cl DA13 . . . . 50 A2
Lancet La ME15 . . . . 116 A6
Lancey Cl SE7 . . . . 1 D2
Lancing Rd BR6 . . . . 58 B8
Landale Gdns DA1 . . . . 32 C8
Landor Ct ME7 . . . . 69 A3
Landseer Ave DA11 . . . . 35 D5
Landseer Cl TN10 . . . . 127 C6
Landstead Rd SE18 . . . . 12 D7
Landway TN15 . . . . 92 F7
Land Way ME13 . . . . 38 D5
Landway The
  Borough Green TN15 . . . . . 94 F7
  Kemsing TN15 . . . . 77 A2
  Maidstone ME14 . . . . 101 A4
  Orpington BR5 . . . . 44 C6
Lane Ave DA9 . . . . 17 C1
LANE END 33 D3
Lane End DA7 . . . . 14 B4
Lanes Ave DA11 . . . . 36 A5
Laneside BR7 . . . . 29 C3
Lane The
  Fordcombe TN3 . . . . 157 C5
  Greenwich SE3 . . . . 11 A4
Langafel CE Prim Sch
  DA3 . . . . 49 A6
Langafel Cl DA3 . . . . 48 E7
Langbrook Rd SE3 . . . . 11 D5
Langdale Cl
  Gillingham ME8 . . . . 55 D1
  Orpington BR6 . . . . 57 B7
Langdale Cres DA7 . . . . 14 A6
Langdale Rise ME16 . . . . . . 99 C5
Langdale Wlk **5** DA11 . . . 35 E5
Langdon Rd
  Bromley BR2 . . . . 42 B6
  Rochester ME1 . . . . 53 C4
Langdon Shaw DA14 . . . . . . 29 F3
Langford Pl DA14 . . . . 30 A5
Langham Gr ME16 . . . . 99 C4
Langholm Rd TN3 . . . . 157 E3
Langhorne Rd **6** SE7 . . . . . 11 C8
LANGHURST 121 E7
Langlands Dr DA2 . . . . 33 E3
LANGLEY 117 C4
Langley Ct **1** SE9 . . . . 12 A1
Langley Gdns
  2 Bromley BR2 . . . . 42 C5
  Orpington BR5 . . . . 43 B3
Langley Rd DA16 . . . . 13 C8
LANGLEY HEATH 117 F4
Langley Ho
  11 Bromley BR1 . . . . 28 B1
  11 Maidstone ME16 . . . . . 99 A3
Langley Rd DA16 . . . . 13 C8
Langmore Ct DA7 . . . . 13 D4
Langton Dr ME14 . . . . 100 C4
LANGTON GREEN 157 E3

Langton Green Prim Sch
  TN3 . . . . 157 E4
Langton Rd
  Rusthall TN3, TN4 . . . . . . 158 C3
  Speldhurst TN3 . . . . 158 A7
Langton Ridge TN3 . . . . . . 158 B3
Langton Way
  Greenwich SE3 . . . . 11 B7
  Maidstone ME15 . . . . 99 F2
Langworth Cl DA2 . . . . 32 D5
Lankester Parker Rd ME1 . . 67 C6
Lannoy Rd SE9 . . . . 29 C7
Lanridge Rd SE2 . . . . 3 D3
Lansbury Cres DA1 . . . . 16 A2
Lansbury Ct **4** SE28 . . . . . . 3 B6
Lansbury Gdns RM18 . . . . . 19 A6
Lansbury Ho **5** DA17 . . . . . 3 F1
Lansdowne Ave
  Bexley DA7 . . . . 13 D7
  Maidstone ME15 . . . . 116 C6
  Orpington BR6 . . . . 43 B1
Lansdowne Ct **9** ME4 . . . 53 F4
Lansdowne La SE7 . . . . 1 D1
Lansdowne Mews SE7 . . . . . 1 D1
Lansdowne Prim Sch
  RM18 . . . . 18 F5
Lansdowne Rd
  Bromley BR1 . . . . 28 B1
  Chatham ME4 . . . . 54 A3
  Royal Tunbridge Wells
    TN1 . . . . 159 B4
  Sevenoaks TN13 . . . . 92 D5
  Tonbridge TN9 . . . . 127 B2
Lansdowne Sq
  Northfleet DA11 . . . . 18 F1
  8 Royal Tunbridge Wells
    TN1 . . . . 159 B4
Lansdown Pl DA11 . . . . 35 F7
Lansdown Rd
  Sidcup DA14 . . . . 30 B5
  Tilbury RM18 . . . . 18 F5
Lantern Cl BR6 . . . . 57 B6
Lantern Ho SE18 . . . . 2 A1
Lanthorne Mews
  Royal Tunbridge Wells,
  Calverley Park TN1 . . . . . 159 B3
  Royal Tunbridge Wells
    TN1 . . . . 159 B5
Lapins La ME19 . . . . 96 F2
Lapis Cl DA12 . . . . 37 B7
Lapwing Cl DA8 . . . . 15 B7
Lapwing Rd ME3 . . . . 27 B5
Lapwings DA3 . . . . 49 B6
Lapwings The DA12 . . . . . . 36 D6
Lapworth Cl BR6 . . . . 58 C8
Larch Cl ME20 . . . . 82 B2
Larch Cres
  Hoo St Werburgh ME3 . . . . 40 E3
  Tonbridge TN10 . . . . 127 C6
Larch Dene BR6 . . . . 57 A8
Larches The ME3 . . . . 38 C3
Larch Gr
  Paddock Wood TN12 . . . . 145 E6
  Sidcup DA15 . . . . 29 F7
Larch Rd DA1 . . . . 32 D7
Larch Way BR2 . . . . 43 A2
Larch Wlk BR8 . . . . 45 D7
Larch Wood Cl ME5 . . . . . . 68 D1
Larchwood Rd SE9 . . . . 29 B6
Largo Wlk DA8 . . . . 15 A1
LARKFIELD 82 A2
Larkfield TN12 . . . . 145 A7
Larkfield Ave ME7 . . . . 54 E4
Larkfield Cl
  Hayes BR2 . . . . 56 A8
Larkfield ME20 . . . . 82 A1
Larkfield L Ctr ME20 . . . . . . 82 A3
Larkfield Rd
  Larkfield ME20 . . . . 82 B1
  Sevenoaks TN13 . . . . 91 C4
  Sidcup DA14 . . . . 29 F5
Larkfields DA11 . . . . 35 E5
Larkin Cl ME2 . . . . 39 B2
Larks Field DA3 . . . . 48 F5
Larkspur Cl
  4 Newham E6 . . . . 1 E8
  Orpington BR6 . . . . 58 C7
Larkspur Lodge DA14 . . . . . 30 B5
Larkspur Rd
  Chatham ME5 . . . . 67 E4
  West Malling ME19 . . . . . . 81 F1
Larkstore Pk TN12 . . . . 149 E5
Larkwood Cl DA8 . . . . 15 A6
Larner Rd DA8 . . . . 14 E7
Laser Quay ME2 . . . . 53 D6
LASHENDEN 167 F6
Lashenden Air Warfare
  Mus★ TN27 . . . . 152 A2
Lassa Rd SE9 . . . . 11 F2
Latham Cl
  Biggin Hill TN16 . . . . 72 C3
  Dartford DA2 . . . . 33 E6
  Newham E6 . . . . 1 E7
Latham Rd DA6 . . . . 14 A2
Latimer Pl **4** ME7 . . . . . . 54 C7
Latona Dr DA12 . . . . 51 C3
La Tourne Gdns BR6 . . . . . . 57 C7
Latymers TN11 . . . . 141 B4
Launcelot Prim Sch BR1 . . 28 A4
Launcelot Rd BR1 . . . . 28 A4
Launder Way ME15 . . . . 99 E2
Launton Dr DA6 . . . . 13 D3
Laura Dr BR8 . . . . 32 A1

Laura Pl ME1 . . . . 53 A2
Laurel Ave DA12 . . . . 36 C6
Laurel Bank
  Royal Tunbridge Wells
    TN4 . . . . 159 B8
  Wadhurst TN5 . . . . 185 A4
Laurel Cl
  Dartford DA1 . . . . 32 C7
  Sidcup DA14 . . . . 30 A5
Laurel Gdns BR1 . . . . 42 E5
Laurel Gr ME17 . . . . 118 C2
Laurel Ho SE7 . . . . 11 C8
Laurel Rd
  Gillingham ME7 . . . . 54 C7
  Royal Tunbridge Wells
    TN2 . . . . 159 D7
Laurels The
  12 Bromley BR1 . . . . 42 B8
  Bromley BR2 . . . . 42 A5
  13 Erith DA17 . . . . 4 A1
  Maidstone ME16 . . . . 99 C2
  New Barn DA3 . . . . 49 D6
  Wilmington DA2 . . . . 32 C5
Laurel Way TN2 . . . . 159 D7
Laurie Gray Ave ME5 . . . . . 67 D1
Lavenda Cl ME7 . . . . 69 A4
Lavender Cl
  Bromley BR2 . . . . 42 E3
  1 Chatham ME5 . . . . 67 E4
  East Malling ME19 . . . . 97 F8
Lavender Gdns TN5 . . . . . . 186 C1
Lavender Hill
  Swanley BR8 . . . . 45 D6
  Tonbridge TN9 . . . . 143 C8
Lavender Ho **3** ME4 . . . . 116 D8
Lavender Rd ME19 . . . . 97 F8
Lavender Sq **3** TN18 . . . . 189 A2
Lavenders Rd ME19 . . . . . . 97 C6
Lavender Wlk **6** ME19 . . . 97 F8
Lavernock Rd DA7 . . . . 14 A5
Laverstoke Rd ME16 . . . . . . 99 C8
Lavidge Rd SE9 . . . . 29 F6
Lavinia Rd **1** DA1 . . . . 15 F1
Lavisham Ho BR1 . . . . 28 B3
Lawford Gdns DA1 . . . . 15 C2
Lawn Cl
  Bromley BR1 . . . . 28 B1
  Chatham ME4 . . . . 54 B2
  Swanley BR8 . . . . 45 C7
  Tenterden TN30 . . . . 192 F7
Lawn Pk TN13 . . . . 108 B8
Lawn Prim Sch DA11 . . . . . 18 C1
Lawn Rd
  Northfleet DA11 . . . . 18 C1
  Tonbridge TN9 . . . . 143 B8
Lawns Cres RM17 . . . . 18 D8
Lawns The
  Brenchley TN12 . . . . 162 B8
  Sidcup DA14 . . . . 30 B4
  Sidcup SE3 . . . . 33 F5
Lawrance Sq **1** DA11 . . . . 35 F4
Lawrence Cl ME15 . . . . 116 A7
Lawrence Dr DA12 . . . . 51 A5
Lawrence Gdns RM18 . . . . . 19 B7
Lawrence Hill Gdns DA1 . . 15 C1
Lawrence Hill Rd DA1 . . . . 15 C1
Lawrence Rd
  Erith DA8 . . . . 14 B7
  Hayes BR4 . . . . 56 A6
  Tonbridge TN10 . . . . 127 E6
Lawrence St ME7 . . . . 54 C5
Lawrence Trad Est RM17 . . 17 E8
Lawson Cl E16 . . . . 1 C8
Lawson Gdns DA1 . . . . 15 D3
Lawson Ho **1** SE18 . . . . . . 12 A8
Lawson Rd DA1 . . . . 15 D3
Laxtons Mews TN9 . . . . . . 127 C2
Laxey Rd BR6 . . . . 57 F4
Laxey The ME15 . . . . 99 E1
Laxton Cl ME15 . . . . 100 F3
Laxton Dr ME17 . . . . 117 A1
Laxton Gdns TN12 . . . . 145 E7
Laxton Wk ME19 . . . . 97 B3
Layfield Ho **4** SE10 . . . . . . 1 A1
Layfield Rd ME7 . . . . 54 F7
Layhams Rd BR2 . . . . 56 A3
Laymarsh Cl DA17 . . . . 3 F3
Layzell Wlk SE9 . . . . 28 D7
Lea Ct ME4 . . . . 53 E1
LEADINGCROSS GREEN . . 120 C3
Leafield La DA14 . . . . 30 F5
Leafy Glade ME8 . . . . 69 B6
Leafy Gr BR2 . . . . 56 C5
Leafy La
  Culverstone Green DA13 . . 64 A3
  Maidstone ME16 . . . . 99 B5
Leafy Oak Rd SE12 . . . . 28 C5
Leake Ho ME1 . . . . 53 C1
Lealands Ave TN11 . . . . . . 126 A1
Lealands Cl TN3 . . . . 171 C6
Leaman Ct ME2 . . . . 23 E4
Leamington Ave
  Bromley BR1 . . . . 28 C3
  Orpington BR6 . . . . 57 E6
Leamington Cl BR1 . . . . 28 C3
Leamington Dr ME16 . . . . . 99 B4
Leamouth Rd E6 . . . . 1 E8
Leander Dr DA12 . . . . 36 F4
Leander Rd ME1 . . . . 67 C7
Lea Rd TN11 . . . . 108 C8
Learoyd Gdns E6 . . . . 2 A6
Leas Dale SE9 . . . . 29 A5
Leas Gn BR7 . . . . 29 F2
Leas The
  Turner's Green TN5 . . . . . 185 A6

Leas The continued
Woolwich SE18 . . . . 12 B6
Leatherbottle Gn DA18 . . . . . 3 F3
Leather Cl TN8 . . . . 138 C8
Lea Vale DA1 . . . . 14 D3
Leaves Gn SR2 . . . . 72 D8
LEAVES GREEN 72 D8
Leaves Green Cres BR2 . . . . 72 C8
Leaves Green Rd
Biggin Hill BR2 . . . . 72 D8
Keston BR2 . . . . 56 D1
Lebanon Gdns TN16 . . . . . . 72 D2
Lebrun Sq SE3 . . . . 5 B4
Leckwith Ave DA7 . . . . 13 E8
Leclair Ho SE3 . . . . 5 B4
Leconfield Cl TN9 . . . . 142 F7
Leda Ho SE18 . . . . 1 F3
Leechcroft Ave
Sidcup DA15 . . . . 23 F1
Swanley BR8 . . . . 45 F6
Leech Ct ME15 . . . . 118 A7
LEEDS 118 A7
Leeds & Broomfield CE Prim
Sch ME17 . . . . 118 D7
Leeds Castle ★ ME17 . . . . . 118 D7
Leeds Cl BR6 . . . . 58 D8
Leeds Ho ME2 . . . . 39 C1
Leeds Rd ME17 . . . . 117 E3
Leeds Sq ME8 . . . . 55 B3
Lee Gn BR5 . . . . 44 A4
LEE GREEN 39 A6
Lee Green Rd ME3 . . . . 39 B6
Lee Rd ME6 . . . . 82 A8
Leesons Hill BR5, BR7 . . . . 44 A6
Leesons Prim Sch BR5 . . . . 44 A6
Leesons Way BR5 . . . . 43 F7
Lees Rd ME18 . . . . 130 E7
Lee Sta SE12 . . . . 11 A1
Leet Cl ME7 . . . . 54 E6
Leeward Rd ME1 . . . . 53 C1
Leewood Cl SE12 . . . . 11 A1
Leewood Pl BR8 . . . . 45 D5
Legatt Rd SE9 . . . . 11 D2
Legge La ME19 . . . . 81 D6
Leggs' La TN3 . . . . 157 E5
Leicester Dr TN2 . . . . 172 F8
Leicester Rd
Maidstone ME15 . . . . 116 D7
Tilbury RM18 . . . . 18 F6
Leicester Sq TN11 . . . . 141 B4
LEIGH 125 E1
Leigh Ave ME15 . . . . 116 B6
LEIGH GREEN 193 F6
Leigh Green Ind Est
TN30 . . . . 193 E6
Leigh Pl DA16 . . . . 13 A5
Leigh Prim Sch TN11 . . . . . 125 F1
Leigh Rd
Gravesend DA11 . . . . 36 B6
Rochester ME3 . . . . 39 C3
Tonbridge TN11 . . . . 126 D3
Leigh Sta TN11 . . . . 125 F1
Leigh Tech Acad DA1 . . . . . 33 A7
Leigh Terr
2 Orpington BR5 . . . . . . 44 B6
Teston ME18 . . . . 98 A1
Leighton Cl TN4 . . . . 159 A7
Leighton Gdns RM18 . . . . . 19 A7
Leila Parrell Pl 22 SE7 . . . . 11 C8
Leitch Row ME7 . . . . 54 A7
Leith Hill BR5 . . . . 44 A8
Leith Hill Gn BR5 . . . . 44 A8
Leith Park Rd DA12 . . . . . . 36 B7
Le May Ave SE12 . . . . 28 B5
Lemonwell Ct SE9 . . . . 12 C2
Lemonwell Dr SE9 . . . . 12 C2
Le Corbusier 25 SE18 . . . . . 1 F2
Lenborough Rd TN15 . . . . . 94 F6
Lendrim Cl 111 ME7 . . . . . . 54 A6
Leneda Dr TN2 . . . . 172 E8
Leney Rd ME18 . . . . 113 E7
Lenfield Ave ME14 . . . . 100 B4
LENHAM 120 C8
Lenham Cl 111 ME15 . . . . . 100 B4
Lenham Heath Rd ME17 . . . 120 C2
Lenham Ho ME17 . . . . 120 E5
Lenham Prim Sch ME17 . . . 120 C5
Lenham Rd
Bexley DA7 . . . . 13 F8
Broadstone TN27, ME17 . . 136 D3
Fairbourne Heath ME17 . . 119 C1
Headcorn TN27 . . . . 151 E6
Lenham Sta ME17 . . . . . . 120 C4
Lenham Way ME8 . . . . 55 A3
Lenmead ME17 . . . . 119 C6
Lennard Rd
Bexley DA7 . . . . 13 F8
Orpington BR2 . . . . 42 F1
Sevenoaks TN13 . . . . 91 E7
Lennox Ave DA11 . . . . 19 A1
Lennox Ho 6 DA7 . . . . 4 A3
Lennox Rd
Gravesend DA11 . . . . 36 A8
Northfleet DA11 . . . . 35 F8
Lennox Road E DA11 . . . . . 36 A8
Lenor Cl DA6 . . . . 13 E3
Lensbury Way SE2 . . . . 3 D3
Lenside Dr ME15 . . . . 101 A2
Lenton St SE18 . . . . 2 D2
Len Valley Wlk ME15 . . . . . 100 F1
Leonard Ave
Otford TN14 . . . . 76 B3
Swanscombe DA10 . . . . . 34 E8
Leonard Cl ME16 . . . . 99 B6

Leonard Ct DA14 . . . . 30 B5
Leonard Judge Ho DA2 . . . . 33 F3
Leonard Pl BR2 . . . . 56 E7
Leonard Rd 4 ME4 . . . . . . 54 B3
Leonard Robbins Path 3
SE28 . . . . 3 B6
Leonard St E16 . . . . 1 E5
Leopold Rd 4 ME4 . . . . 54 A3
Lesley Cl
Istead Rise DA13 . . . . 49 F8
Sidcup DA15 . . . . 31 B8
Swanley BR8 . . . . 45 D6
Lesley Pl ME16 . . . . 99 E5
Lesley Tew Ct TN10 . . . . . . 127 C5
Leslie Cres TN30 . . . . 183 B2
Leslie Rd
Gillingham ME7 . . . . 54 D7
Newham E16 . . . . 1 A8
Leslie Smith Sq 7 SE18 . . . 12 A8
Lesnes Abbey (remains of) ★
SE2 . . . . 3 D2
Lesney Park Rd DA8 . . . . . . 14 D8
Lesney Pk DA8 . . . . 14 D8
Lessness Ave DA7 . . . . 13 D7
LESSNESS HEATH 4 C1
Lessness Heath Prim Sch 17
DA17 . . . . 4 A1
Lessness Pk DA17 . . . . 4 A1
Lessness Rd 12 DA17 . . . . . 4 A1
Lested La ME17 . . . . 117 B1
Lester Rd ME4 . . . . 54 A3
Lestock Ho SE3 . . . . 11 D6
Letchworth Ave ME4 . . . . . 53 F1
Letchworth Cl BR2 . . . . 42 A4
Letchworth Dr BR2 . . . . 42 A4
Le Temple Rd TN12 . . . . . . 146 B6
Letter Box La TN13 . . . . . . 108 C6
LETTS GREEN 72 A8
Leverholme Gdns SE9 . . . . . 29 A4
Levett Cl ME1 . . . . 31 A8
Levetts La TN32 . . . . 195 D1
Leviathan Way
Chatham ME4 . . . . 54 A8
St Mary's Island ME4 . . . . 40 A1
Lewd La TN27 . . . . 153 A3
Lewes Cl RM17 . . . . 18 A8
Lewes Rd BR1 . . . . 42 D7
Lewin Cl SE18 . . . . 2 E2
Lewing Cl BR6 . . . . 43 E1
Lewin Rd DA6 . . . . 13 E3
Lewis Ave ME8 . . . . 55 B2
Lewis Court Dr ME17 . . . . . 116 C3
Lewis Ct DA11 . . . . 35 F6
LEWISHAM 2 B7
Lewis King Ho 7 BR1 . . . . . 28 B1
Lewis Mews ME6 . . . . 81 F6
Lewis Rd
Bexley DA16 . . . . 13 C4
Istead Rise DA13 . . . . 49 F8
Sidcup DA14 . . . . 30 C5
Swanscombe DA10 . . . . . 17 E1
Lewis Row ME17 . . . . 133 E6
Leybank TN11 . . . . 126 F4
LEYBOURNE 81 D2
Leybourne Castle ★ ME19 . 80 D2
Leybourne Cl
Chatham ME5 . . . . 68 A2
Hayes BR2 . . . . 42 A4
Leybourne Dell TN17 . . . . 190 E6
Leybourne Lakes Ctry Pk ★
ME20 . . . . 82 A5
Leybourne Rd ME2 . . . . 52 F8
Leybourne Ss Peter & Paul
CE Prim Sch ME19 . . . . . 81 E2
Leybourne Way ME20 . . . . 81 F4
Leybridge Ct SE12 . . . . 11 A2
Leyburn Ct TN9 . . . . 127 C3
Leyburn Ho SE18 . . . . 11 E7
Leycroft Gdns DA8 . . . . 15 B6
Leydenhatch La BR8 . . . . . . 45 D8
Leyes Rd E16 . . . . 1 D7
Leyhill Cl BR8 . . . . 45 E4
Leyland Rd SE12 . . . . 11 A2
Leysdown Ave DA7 . . . . 14 C3
Leysdown Rd SE9 . . . . 28 F6
Leyton Ave ME7 . . . . 54 E1
Leyton Cross DA2 . . . . 32 A6
Leyton Cross Rd DA2 . . . . . 54 A3
Leywood Rd DA13 . . . . 64 D3
Lezayre Rd BR6 . . . . 57 F4
Liberty Mews ME8 . . . . 63 D7
Libya Terr 6 ME14 . . . . . . 100 A7
Lichdale Cl 8 BR6 . . . . 57 F6
Lichfield Cl ME5 . . . . 55 D2
Lichfield Ho 12 ME15 . . . . 116 F7
Liddon Rd BR1 . . . . 42 D6
LIDSING 68 F1
Lidsing Rd ME14 . . . . 84 E6
Lidwells La TN17 . . . . 163 E1
Lieth Park Rd DA12 . . . . . . 36 C7
Liffler Rd SE18 . . . . 2 E1
Lighterman's Mews 2
DA11 . . . . 35 E8
Lightermans Way 6 DA9 . . 17 C3
Lightfoot Gn TN18 . . . . . . 188 E3
Lilac Cres ME2 . . . . 52 E6
Lilac Gdns BR8 . . . . 45 F7
Lilac Gn 4 ME19 . . . . 82 A1
Lilac Pl DA13 . . . . 50 B2
Lilac Rd ME2 . . . . 52 E6
Lila Pl BR8 . . . . 45 E5
Lilburne Gdns SE9 . . . . 11 C2
Lilestone Rd SE9 . . . . 11 E2
Lilian Barker Cl SE12 . . . . . 11 A3
Lilk Hill ME14 . . . . 101 C3
Lillechurch Rd ME3 . . . . . . 38 F7
Lillieburn ME19 . . . . 81 D2
Lillie Rd TN16 . . . . 72 D1

Lily Nichols Ho E16 . . . . . . 1 E5
Limavady Ho SE18 . . . . 2 A2
Lime Ave
Benenden TN17 . . . . 180 D6
Northfleet DA11 . . . . 35 D8
Lime Cl
Bromley BR1 . . . . 44 A4
Frant TN3 . . . . 173 B3
Marden TN12 . . . . 148 C6
Lime Cotts TN12 . . . . 149 F3
Lime Cres ME19 . . . . 98 A7
Lime Ct
Eltham SE9 . . . . 29 B6
Gillingham ME8 . . . . 69 C3
Lime Gr
Biddenden TN17 . . . . . . 182 D7
Orpington BR6 . . . . 57 B8
Sidcup DA15 . . . . 23 F1
Lime Hill Rd TN1 . . . . 159 A4
Lime Kiln Dr SE7 . . . . 11 B8
Lime Pit La TN13, TN14 . . . 75 C2
Limepits Cross ME9 . . . . . . 71 F3
Lime Rd BR8 . . . . 45 D6
Lime Row DA18 . . . . 4 F3
Limes Cl TN30 . . . . 193 C8
Limes Gr TN18 . . . . 188 F5
Limes Row BR6 . . . . 57 B5
Limes The
Edenbridge TN8 . . . . . . 122 C1
Frittenden TN17 . . . . . . 166 E6
Lenham ME17 . . . . 120 D5
Orpington BR6 . . . . 58 E8
Lime Tree Ave DA9 . . . . 34 A7
Limetree Cl ME5 . . . . 68 B8
Lime Tree Cl TN9 . . . . 127 C2
Limetree Mews TN16 . . . . . 88 D7
Lime Trees TN12 . . . . 149 E4
Limetree Terr
8 Bexley DA16 . . . . 13 A4
Eltham SE9 . . . . 12 E6
Lime Tree Wlk TN13 . . . . . . 92 B2
Limewood Rd DA8 . . . . 14 C7
LIMPSFIELD 104 A6
Limpsfield CE Inf Sch
RH8 . . . . 104 C6
Limpsfield Grange Sch
RH8 . . . . 104 A8
Linchmere Rd 7 SE12 . . . . 28 A8
Lincoln Cl
Erith DA8 . . . . 14 F5
Rochester ME2 . . . . 52 D6
Lincoln Ct 3 SE1 . . . . 28 C5
Lincoln Green Rd BR5 . . . . 43 F4
Lincoln Rd
Erith DA8 . . . . 14 F5
Gillingham ME7 . . . . 54 D7
Maidstone ME15 . . . . . . 116 D8
Sidcup DA14 . . . . 30 B3
Lincolnshire Terr DA2 . . . . 33 D4
Lincolnshott DA13 . . . . 35 B3
Lindel Ct ME18 . . . . 97 B3
Linden Ave DA1 . . . . 32 C7
Linden Chase TN13 . . . . . . 92 B5
Linden Cl
Orpington BR6 . . . . 58 A5
Paddock Wood TN12 . . . 146 A6
Purfleet RM19 . . . . 16 C8
Royal Tunbridge Wells
TN4 . . . . 159 A2
Linden Ct
Sidcup DA14 . . . . 29 E4
Tonbridge TN10 . . . . . . 127 B7
Lindenfield BR7 . . . . 43 B7
Linden Fields TN2 . . . . . . 159 A1
Lindisfarne Gdns ME16 . . . 99 E3
Lindridge La TN12 . . . . . . 149 C5
Lindridge Sq TN13 . . . . 91 E5
Lindsey Cl BR1 . . . . 42 E6
Lindwood Cl 6 E6 . . . . 1 F8
Lineacre Cl ME8 . . . . 69 D6
Lines Terr ME4 . . . . 54 A4
Lingey Cl DA15 . . . . 29 F6
Lingfield Ave DA2 . . . . 33 B8
Lingfield Cres SE9 . . . . 12 D3
Lingfield Mews 4 TN8 . . . 122 C1
Lingfield Rd
Borough Green TN15 . . . . 95 B7
Edenbridge TN8 . . . . . . 138 A8
Gravesend DA12 . . . . 36 B6
Lingley Dr ME2 . . . . 39 C2
Ling Rd
Erith DA8 . . . . 14 C8
Newham E16 . . . . 1 A8
Lingwood DA7 . . . . 14 C4
LINK 20 Bsns Pk ME20 . . . . 82 B3
Linkden Cotts TN18 . . . . . 196 E5
Link Field BR2 . . . . 42 A3
LINKHILL 196 E4
Link Hill La TN27 . . . . 137 D3
Links Cl SE9 . . . . 29 B7
Links The
Addington ME19 . . . . 80 E2
Chatham ME5 . . . . 68 B8
Links View
Dartford DA1 . . . . 32 C7

Links View continued
Woolwich SE18 . . . . 12 B6
Link The
Eltham SE9 . . . . 29 A5
New Ash Green DA3 . . . . . 62 F8
Linkway ME20 . . . . 82 C1
Link Way
Bromley BR2 . . . . 42 E2
Royal Tunbridge Wells
TN2 . . . . 159 E8
Linley Cl RM18 . . . . 20 D7
Linnet Ave TN12 . . . . 146 A5
Linnet Cl SE28 . . . . 3 C6
Linsdale Rd BR6 . . . . 58 A4
Linsted Ct SE9 . . . . 12 E1
LINTON 115 F1
Linton Cl
Bexley DA16 . . . . 13 B6
2 Greenwich SE7 . . . . . 1 C1
Linton Dann Cl ME3 . . . . . . 40 D6
Linton Gore ME17 . . . . . . 115 D3
Linton Hill TN12 . . . . 132 F6
Linton Mead Prim Sch
SE28 . . . . 3 B5
Linton Park Sch ME17 . . . 116 A2
Linton Rd ME15 . . . . 115 F4
Lintorn Symonds Rd ME3 . 39 F5
Linwood Ave ME2 . . . . 52 E8
Lionel Gdns SE9 . . . . 11 D2
Lionel Oxley Ho 5 RM17 . . 18 B8
Lionel Rd
Eltham SE9 . . . . 11 D2
Tonbridge TN9 . . . . 143 A8
Lion Rd
Bexley DA6 . . . . 13 F3
Newham E6 . . . . 1 F8
Lions Cl SE9 . . . . 28 D5
Liphook Way ME16 . . . . 99 C8
Lipscombe Rd TN2 . . . . . . 159 D6
Lipton Cl SE28 . . . . 3 C6
Liptraps La TN2 . . . . 159 D7
Lipwell Hill ME23 . . . . 23 B4
Liskeard Cl BR7 . . . . 29 C2
Liskeard Gdns SE3 . . . . 11 A6
Lismore Cl ME15 . . . . 116 A7
Lismore Ct ME14 . . . . 93 F4
Lister Cl ME19 . . . . 97 F8
Lister Dr DA11 . . . . 35 C7
Lister Ho SE2 . . . . 3 B4
Lister Rd RM18 . . . . 19 A5
Lister Wlk SE28 . . . . 3 D6
Listmas Rd ME4 . . . . 54 B3
Little Acorns Sch TN30 . . . 183 A5
Little Alley TN8 . . . . 138 E5
Little Oak La TN9 . . . . 143 D8
LITTLE BAYHAM 174 F4
Little Bayham Cotts TN3 . . 174 F4
Little Birches DA15 . . . . . . 29 E6
Little Boundes CI TN4 . . . . 142 F3
Littlebourne Ave ME8 . . . . 55 B4
Littlebourne Rd ME14 . . . . 100 C6
Little Brook Hospl DA2 . . . 16 C1
Littlebrook Manor Way
DA1 . . . . 16 E1
Little Browns La TN8 . . . . 121 F4
Little Buckland Ave ME16 . 99 D6
Littlecombe SE7 . . . . 11 B8
Littlecourt Rd TN13 . . . . . . 92 A3
Littlecroft
Eltham SE9 . . . . 12 A4
Istead Rise DA13 . . . . 35 B1
Little Ct ME16 . . . . 99 D2
Littledale
Dartford DA2 . . . . 33 C5
Woolwich SE2 . . . . 13 A8
Littlefield TN11 . . . . 128 E8
Little Field TN12 . . . . 149 E5
Little Footway TN3 . . . . . . 157 F3
Little Mallett TN3 . . . . 1 E1
Little Heath Rd DA7 . . . . . . 13 F7
Little Hill TN30 . . . . 183 B2
LITTLE HOUSES 137 D2
Little John Ave BR5 . . . . . . 44 B4
Little John's Cross TN17 . . 191 F1
Littlejohn Rd BR5 . . . . 44 B4
Little Julians Hill TN13 . . . 108 A8
Little Kit's Coty Ho ★
ME20 . . . . 83 C5
Little Mallett TN3 . . . . 157 F3
Little Market Row ME19 . . . 81 E2
Littlemede SE9 . . . . 28 F5
LITTLE MILL 129 D5
Little Mill Farm Cotts
TN12 . . . . 148 C8
Littlemore Rd SE2 . . . . 3 A4
Little Mount Sion TN1 . . . 159 A2
Little Oakham Ct ME3 . . . . 25 C4
Little Orch ME17 . . . . 115 D3
Little Oxley ME19 . . . . 81 E2
Little Pk TN5 . . . . 184 E5
Little Queen St DA1 . . . . . . 32 F8
Little Redlands BR1 . . . . . . 42 E7
Little Robhurst TN26 . . . . 183 D8
Little Sheephurst Cotts
TN12 . . . . 147 E5
Little Thrift BR5 . . . . 43 C5
Little Victory Mount ME4 . 40 B2
Little Wood TN13 . . . . 92 D5
Little Wood Cl BR5 . . . . 24 A1
Little York Mdws ME7 . . . . 55 C4
LIVERTON STREET 119 F1
Liveryman Wlk 12 DA9 . . . 17 C3
Livesey Cl SE28 . . . . 2 C3
Livesey St ME18 . . . . 98 A1
Livingstone Bldgs ME7 . . . 54 D5
Livingstone Circ ME7 . . . . . 54 D5
Livingstone Gdns DA12 . . . 36 D3
Livingstone Hospl 3 DA1 . 32 F8

Livingstone Rd
Gillingham ME7 . . . . 54 E5
Gravesend DA12 . . . . 36 D3
Livingstone Wlk 6 ME15 . 116 F5
Lizban St SE3 . . . . 11 B2
Llanover Rd SE18 . . . . 12 A7
Lloyd Ho BR1 . . . . 28 B3
Lloyds Gn TN30 . . . . 199 D4
Loam Ct DA1 . . . . 32 E7
Loampits Cl TN9 . . . . 127 D3
Lobelia Cl
Gillingham ME7 . . . . 54 E6
8 Newham E6 . . . . 1 E8
Locarno Ave ME8 . . . . 55 A2
Lochat Rd ME3 . . . . 39 E6
Lochmere Cl DA8 . . . . 14 B8
Lockesley Dr BR5 . . . . 44 A3
Lockham Farm Ave
ME17 . . . . 116 D5
Lockington Cl TN9 . . . . . . 142 F7
Lockington Gr ME1 . . . . . . 53 C5
Lock La ME14 . . . . 83 D1
Lockmeadow Entertainment
Ctr ME16 . . . . 99 F3
LOCKSBOTTOM 57 B7
Lockside TN9 . . . . 127 C2
Locksley Cl ME5 . . . . 67 E2
Lock's Yd TN13 . . . . 84 S7
Lockswood ME16 . . . . 90 D7
Lockyer Rd RM19 . . . . 16 C8
Lockyers Hill DA13 . . . . . . 64 F5
Lodden Ct 14 BR5 . . . . 44 D1
Loddington La
Linton ME17 . . . . 133 A8
Maidstone, Boughton
Monchelsea ME17 . . . . 116 A1
Loder Cl ME17 . . . . 120 B5
Lodge Cl 15 C1
Lodge Cl
Orpington BR6 . . . . 44 B1
Wateringbury ME18 . . . . 113 D8
Lodge Cres BR6 . . . . 44 B1
Lodge Farmhouse ME20 . . 82 E3
Lodge Gdns ME17 . . . . 135 F6
Lodge Hill DA16 . . . . 13 B7
Lodge Hill La ME3 . . . . 39 F7
Lodge La
Cobham DA12 . . . . 51 B5
Royal Tunbridge Wells
TN3 . . . . 172 A8
Sidcup DA5 . . . . 13 D1
Westerham TN16 . . . . . . 105 C8
Lodge Oak La TN9 . . . . . . 143 D8
Lodge Rd
Bromley BR1 . . . . 28 C1
Maidstone ME14 . . . . . . 100 D5
Staplehurst TN12 . . . . . . 149 E5
Tonbridge TN9 . . . . 127 B2
Lodgewood Cotts TN8 . . . 123 D2
Logs Hill BR1, BR2 . . . . 42 E8
Logs Hill Cl BR7 . . . . 42 E8
Lolland Ho 6 SE18 . . . . 1 E2
Lomaria Ct TN2 . . . . 159 C4
Lomas La TN5 . . . . 196 F5
Lombard St DA4 . . . . 47 C5
Lombard Trad Est SE7 . . . . 1 B2
Lombard Wall SE7 . . . . 1 B2
Lombardy Ct ME7 . . . . 69 A6
Lombardy Dr ME14 . . . . . . 100 C5
Lomer Farm DA13 . . . . 64 A8
LONDON BEACH 183 B5
London City Airport E16 . . . 1 E5
London City Airport Sta
E16 . . . . 1 E5
Londonderry Ho 19
ME15 . . . . 116 F7
Londonderry Par DA1 . . . . . 14 D7
London Ind Pk E6 . . . . 2 B8
London La
Bromley BR1 . . . . 28 A1
Sissinghurst TN17 . . . . . 166 A2
London Rd
Addington ME19 . . . . 80 D2
Badgers Mount TN14 . . . . 75 C6
Bidborough TN4 . . . . 142 F3
Bromley BR1 . . . . 42 A8
Chelsfield TN14 . . . . 58 F2
Crayford DA1 . . . . 14 D2
Ditton ME20 . . . . 82 C1
Farningham BR8, DA4 . . . 46 D3
Flimwell TN5 . . . . 187 D3
Gillingham ME8 . . . . 63 D3
Grays RM17, RM20 . . . . . 17 E8
Hartlip ME8, ME9 . . . . . . 70 D7
Hildenborough TN11, TN15,
TN15 . . . . 126 B7
Hurst Green TN19 . . . . . 194 A3
Maidstone ME16 . . . . 99 C6
Newington ME9 . . . . 71 A6
Northfleet DA11 . . . . 18 D1
Otford TN13 . . . . 75 D1
Rochester ME2 . . . . 53 A7
3 Royal Tunbridge Wells
TN4 . . . . 159 A4
Royal Tunbridge Wells
TN4 . . . . 159 A8
Sevenoaks, Dunton Green
TN13 . . . . 91 E7
Sevenoaks TN13 . . . . 92 B2
Stone DA2, DA9 . . . . 16 E1
Swanley BR8 . . . . 45 D7
Swanscombe DA9 . . . . . . 17 C2
Tilbury RM18 . . . . 19 B5
Tonbridge TN10, TN11 . . 127 B3
West Kingsdown TN15 . . . 62 A1
Wrotham Heath TN15, ME19 79 F1

London Rd continued
Wrotham TN15 . . . . 79 B3
London Road E ME20 . . . . 98 F8
London Road Purfleet
RM19 . . . . 16 C8
London Road Ret Pk
ME16 . . . . 99 E5
London Road West Thurrock
RM20 . . . . 17 A8
Lonewood Way TN11 . . . . 111 F2
Long Barn Rd TN14 . . . . 108 B2
Longbury CI BR5 . . . . 44 B6
Longbury Dr BR5 . . . . 44 B6
Long Catlis Rd ME8 . . . . . 69 D4
Longcroft SE9 . . . . 29 A5
Longdon Wood BR2 . . . . . 56 E6
Longdown Ho ME5 . . . . . . 67 F6
Longfellow Rd ME7 . . . . . 54 C3
LONGFIELD 48 E7
Longfield TN30 . . . . 193 A6
Longfield Acad DA3, DA13 . 48 F6
Longfield Rd
High Halstow ME23 . . . . 23 E4
New Barn DA3, DA13 . . . 49 D7
LONGFIELD HILL 49 D5
Longfield Pl ME15 . . . . . 116 C8
Longfield Rd
Meopham Station DA3,
DA13, ... 49 E3
Royal Tunbridge Wells TN1, TN2,
TN11 . . . . 143 E1
Longfields Dr ME14 . . . . 101 A5
Longfield Sta DA3 . . . . . . 48 E6
LONGFORD 91 D6
Longford CI ME8 . . . . 70 A8
Longford CI ME8 . . . . 70 A8
Longham Copse ME15 . . 100 F1
Longhill Ave ME5 . . . . . . 54 B3
Longhurst Dr ME14 . . . . . 67 F2
Long La
Bexley DA7 . . . . 13 E6
Rabbit's Cross ME17 . . . 133 D5
LONGLANDS 29 D5
Longlands Ct DA15 . . . . . 29 F5
Longlands Park Cres
DA15 . . . . 29 E6
Longlands Prim Sch DA15 29 E5
Longlands Rd DA15 . . . . . 29 F5
Longleat Ct 3 DA6 . . . . . . 13 E3
Longleigh La SE2, DA17 . . 13 C8
Longley Rd
Gillingham ME8 . . . . 55 F1
Newham E16 . . . . 1 E5
Long Mark Rd 3 E16 . . . . . 1 D8
Longmarsh La SE28 . . . . . . 2 E5
Longmarsh View DA4 . . . . 47 B8
Longmead BR7 . . . . 43 A7
Longmead Dr DA14 . . . . . 30 D6
Longmeade DA12 . . . . . . 36 F7
Longmeadow TN13 . . . . . 91 D6
Longmeadow Rd DA15 . . . 29 E2
Long Mead Prim Sch
TN10 . . . . 127 B5
Long Meads TN3 . . . . . . 158 B4
Long Mead Way TN10 . . . 127 B4
Long Mill La
Crouch TN15 . . . . 93 B3
Platt TN15 . . . . 95 C7
Longparish CI ME15 . . . . 116 F6
Longreach Rd DA8 . . . . . . 15 B7
Long Rede La ME15 . . . . . 98 F3
Long Shaw CI ME17 . . . . 116 D4
Longshaw Rd ME15 . . . . 116 F5
Long Slip TN3 . . . . 158 A3
Longten's Cotts DA12 . . . 37 E6
Longtown St TN2 . . . . 16 B1
Longview Way TN1 . . . . . 159 D7
Longwalk DA13 . . . . 49 F7
Long Wlk SE18 . . . . 12 B8
Longwood ME5 . . . . 68 B1
Longworth CI SE28 . . . . . . 3 D7
Lonsdale CI SE9 . . . . 28 C5
Lonsdale Cres DA2 . . . . . 33 C7
Lonsdale Dr ME8 . . . . 69 E7
Lonsdale Gdns TN1 . . . . 159 A3
Lonsdale Rd DA7 . . . . 15 E8
Loop Rd BR7 . . . . 29 C2
LOOSE 115 F4
LOOSE HILL 115 F5
Loose Inf & Jun Sch
ME15 . . . . 116 A6
Loose Rd ME15 . . . . 116 A7
Loraine Ct BR7 . . . . 29 B3
Lord Chatham's Ride
TN14 . . . . 74 A1
Lord Roberts Terr SE18 . . . 2 A1
Lord Romney's Hill ME14 100 F3
Lord St
Gravesend DA12 . . . . . . 36 B8
Newham E16 . . . . 1 E5
LORDS WOOD 68 C1
Lordswood CI DA2 . . . . . . 33 E4
Lords Wood CI ME5 . . . . . 68 B2
Lordswood Ind Est ME5 . . 84 C8
Lordswood Inf & Jun Sch
ME5 . . . . 68 B3
Lords Wood La ME5 . . . . . 68 B3
Lordswood L Ctr ME5 . . . 68 C3
Lord Warwick St SE18 . . . . 1 F3
Lorenden PI TN18 . . . . . . 188 F1
Lorimar Bsns Ctr RM13 . . . 4 E8
Lorraine Ct DA9 . . . . 17 B1
Lorton CI DA12 . . . . 36 E6
Lossenham La TN18 . . . . 197 D3
Lotus Rd TN16 . . . . 72 F1
Louise Ct 8 DA6 . . . . 13 E3
Louis Gdns BR7 . . . . 28 F4

Louisville Ave ME7 . . . . . 54 D4
Louvain St ME7 . . . . 33 E8
Lovage App E6 . . . . 1 E8
Love La
East Tilbury RM18 . . . . . 20 C8
Rochester ME1 . . . . 53 C5
Sidcup DA14 . . . . 14 A1
Swift's Green TN27 . . . . 152 B5
Wateringbury ME18 . . . 113 D7
Woolwich SE18 . . . . 2 B2
Lovelace Ave BR2 . . . . . . 63 A3
Lovelace CI
Gillingham ME8 . . . . 69 D4
West Kingsdown TN15 . . . 61 E4
Lovelace Gn SE9 . . . . 11 F4
Lovel Ave DA16 . . . . 13 A5
Lovers La TN17 . . . . 163 F1
Lover's La DA4 . . . . 17 D3
Lovibonds Ave BR6 . . . . . 51 C7
Low CI DA9 . . . . 11 A2
Lowe Ave E16 . . . . 1 A8
Lower Bell La ME20 . . . . . 82 B2
LOWER BITCHET 93 C1
Lower Bloors La ME8 . . . . 55 E3
Lower Boxley Rd 10
ME14 . . . . 100 A5
LOWER BUSH 50 F5
Lower Buttermere CI ME7 55 A5
Lower Camden BR7 . . . . . 42 F8
Lower Church Hill DA9 . . . 16 E2
LOWER COULSEY
WOOD 185 E8
LOWER COX STREET 85 D6
Lower Croft BR8 . . . . 45 F5
Lower Fant Rd ME16 . . . . 99 D3
Lower Farm Rd ME17 . . . 133 D5
Lower Featherby Rd ME7 . 55 B5
Lower Gn TN11 . . . . 125 F1
Lower Gravel Rd BR2 . . . . 50 F1
LOWER GREEN
Pembury 160 D8
Rusthall 158 C5
Lower Green Rd
Pembury 160 D8
Rusthall TN3, TN4 . . . . 158 C5
LOWER HARTLIP 70 E4
Lower Hartlip Rd ME9 . . . 70 E5
LOWER HAYSDEN 142 D8
Lower Haysden La TN11,
TN9 . . . . 142 D8
Lower Hazelhurst TN5 . . 186 A4
LOWER HIGHAM 38 D6
Lower Higham Rd DA12 . . 37 B7
Lower High St TN5 . . . . . 185 A4
LOWER LUDDESDOWN . . . 51 A2
Lower Park Rd DA17 . . . . . 4 A2
Lower Platts TN5 . . . . . . 186 F1
Lower Rainham Rd ME7 . . 55 D5
Lower Range Rd DA12 . . . 36 E8
Lower Rd
East Farleigh ME15 . . . . 115 B7
Erith DA8 . . . . 4 D2
Erith DA17 . . . . 4 B3
Hextable BR8 . . . . 32 B1
Higham DA12, ME3 . . . . 38 B6
Maidstone ME15 . . . . . 100 B3
Northfleet DA11 . . . . 18 A3
Orpington BR5 . . . . 44 B3
Shorne DA12 . . . . 37 E6
Sutton Valence ME17 . . 124 F1
West Farleigh ME15 . . . 114 D7
Lower Rochester Rd ME3 . 38 E6
Lower St
Leeds ME17 . . . . 118 A7
Tonbridge TN11 . . . . . . 125 F5
LOWER STOKE 25 C5
Lower Stone St ME15 . . . 100 A3
LOWER TOVIL ME15 . . . . 99 E2
LOWER TWYDALL 55 C5
Lower Twydall La ME7,
ME8 . . . . 55 A6
LOWER UPNOR 40 A3
Lower Warren Rd ME20 . . 83 E6
Lower Woodlands Rd
ME7 . . . . 55 A6
Lowestoft Mews E16 . . . . . 2 B4
Lowfield St DA1 . . . . 32 E8
Low Meadow ME2 . . . . . . 66 B5
Lownds Ct BR1 . . . . 22 A1
Lowry CI DA8 . . . . 4 B1
Lowry The 7 TN9 . . . . . . 143 B8
LOW STREET 19 E8
Low Street La RM18 . . . . 19 F8
Loxwood CI BR5, BR6 . . . . 52 D8
Lubbock CI ME2 . . . . 53 C1
Lubbock Ct BR7 . . . . 28 E1
Lubbock Ho BR7 . . . . 28 E1
Lubbock Rd BR7 . . . . 28 E1
Lubbock Wlk ME8 . . . . . . 69 D5
Lucas CI TN2, TN4 . . . . . 159 C7
Lucas Cres 9 DA7 . . . . . . 17 C3
Lucas Rd ME6 . . . . 81 E7
Lucerne Ct 5 DA18 . . . . . . 3 E3
Lucerne Rd BR6 . . . . 43 F1
Lucerne St ME14 . . . . . . 100 A4
Lucilina Dr TN8 . . . . 138 C8
Lucknow Rd TN12 . . . . . 146 A8
Lucknow St SE18 . . . . 12 E7
Lucks Hill ME19 . . . . 97 D8
Lucks La
Paddock Wood TN12 . . 146 B8
Rabbit's Cross ME17 . . . 133 F4
Lucks Way TN12 . . . . . . 148 B8
Luddenham CI ME14 . . . 100 C6
Luddesdon Rd DA8 . . . . . 14 A7

LUDDESDOWN 50 F1
Luddesdown Ct★ DA13 . . 50 F1
Luddesdown Ho 5 BR5 . . 44 C4
Luddesdown Rd DA13 . . . 51 A2
Ludham CI SE28 . . . . 3 C7
Ludlow CI BR2 . . . . 42 A6
Ludwell Rd SE2 . . . . 3 B3
Luffman Rd SE12 . . . . 28 B5
Lughorse La ME15, ME18 . 114 C1
Lullarook CI TN16 . . . . . . 72 C3
Lullingstone Ave 8 . . . . . 45 F6
Lullingstone Castle★ DA4 60 B5
Lullingstone CI
Gillingham ME7 . . . . 69 B3
Orpington BR5 . . . . 30 B1
Lullingstone Cres BR5 . . . 30 B1
Lullingstone La DA4 . . . . . 60 C8
Lullingstone Pk DA4 . . . . 60 C8
Lullingstone Pk Visitor Ctr★
DA4 . . . . 60 B4
Lullingstone Rd
3 Bexley DA17 . . . . 13 F8
Maidstone ME15 . . . . . . 99 C7
Lullingstone Roman Villa
(rems of)★ DA4 . . . . . . 60 B7
Lulworth Rd
Bexley DA16 . . . . 12 F5
Bromley SE9 . . . . 28 E6
Lumley CI SE28 . . . . 4 A1
Lumsden Terr 8 ME4 . . . . 53 E4
Lunar CI TN16 . . . . 72 D3
Lunedale Rd DA2 . . . . 33 C7
LUNSFORD 81 E4
Lunsford District Ctr
ME20 . . . . 82 A4
Lunsford La ME20 . . . . . . 81 F2
Lunsford Prim Sch ME20 . 82 A2
Lunsford CI SE12 . . . . 28 B4
Lurkins Rise TN17 . . . . . 177 D7
Lushington Rd ME14 . . . . 99 E7
Lusted Hall La TN16 . . . . 88 C7
Lusted Rd TN13 . . . . 91 E7
LUTON 54 B2
Luton High St ME5 . . . . . 54 C2
Luton Inf Sch ME5 . . . . . . 54 C2
Luton Jun Sch ME4 . . . . . 54 C2
Luton Rd
Chatham ME4, ME5 . . . . 54 B2
Sidcup DA14 . . . . 30 C5
Luxfield Rd SE9 . . . . 28 E7
Luxon Rd DA13 . . . . 64 E4
LUXTED 73 A5
Luxted Rd BR6 . . . . 73 A6
Lyall Way ME8 . . . . 49 F5
Lychfield Dr ME2 . . . . 53 A8
Lych Gate Rd BR6 . . . . . . 44 A1
Lydd CI DA14 . . . . 29 E5
Lydden Ct SE9 . . . . 12 E1
Lydd Rd
Bexley DA7 . . . . 13 F7
Camden ME4 . . . . 68 B5
Lydens La TN8 . . . . 138 F6
Lydford Ct 3 DA2 . . . . . . 36 B3
Lydia Cotts 2 DA11 . . . . . 36 B8
Lydia Rd DA8 . . . . 14 F8
Lydstep Rd BR7 . . . . 29 A4
Lyford St SE18 . . . . 1 E2
Lyle CI ME2 . . . . 53 B8
Lyle Pk TN13 . . . . 92 B4
Lyme Farm Rd SE12 . . . . 11 B3
Lyme Rd DA16 . . . . 13 B6
Lyminge CI
Gillingham ME8 . . . . 55 C2
Sidcup DA14 . . . . 29 F4
Lymington CI 2 E6 . . . . . . 1 E8
Lymington Rd ME15 . . . . 116 F4
Lyndale Est RM20 . . . . . . 17 B8
Lyndean Ind Est SE2 . . . . . 3 C3
Lynden Way BR8 . . . . 45 D6
Lyndhurst Ave ME8 . . . . . 69 C7
Lyndhurst CI
Bexley DA7 . . . . 14 B4
Orpington BR6 . . . . 57 B6
Lyndhurst Dr TN13 . . . . . 91 E3
Lyndhurst Rd
Bexley DA7 . . . . 14 B4
Maidstone ME15 . . . . . 116 C8
Lyndhurst Way DA13 . . . . 49 F8
Lyndon Ave DA15 . . . . . . 12 F2
Lyndon Rd DA17 . . . . 4 A2
Lynette Ave ME2 . . . . 33 A3
Lyngs CI ME18 . . . . 130 F8
Lynley CI ME15 . . . . 116 D6
Lynmead CI TN8 . . . . . . 122 B4
Lynmere Rd DA16 . . . . . . 13 B5
Lynmouth Rise BR5 . . . . . 44 B5
Lynors Ave ME2 . . . . 39 A1
Lynstead CI BR1 . . . . 42 C7
Lynstead Ho ME16 . . . . . . 99 A1
Lynsted CI DA6 . . . . 14 B2
Lynsted Gdns SE9 . . . . . . 11 D4
Lynsted Rd ME8 . . . . 55 B3
Lynton Ave BR5 . . . . 44 B5
Lynton Dr ME5 . . . . 68 B3
Lynton Rd DA11 . . . . 36 A7
Lynton Road S DA11 . . . . 36 A7
Danaway ME9 . . . . 71 D4
Five Wents ME17 . . . . . 117 E2
Gillingham ME8 . . . . 69 C6
Goose Green ME18, TN11 . 112 C3
Grays RM17 . . . . 18 A8
Headcorn TN27 . . . . . . 151 B7
Horsmonden, Claygate
TN12 . . . . 147 C3

Lytchet Rd BR1 . . . . 28 B1
Lytham CI SE28 . . . . 3 E7
Lytton Strachey Path 3
SE28. . . . . 3 B6
Lyveden Rd SE3 . . . . 11 B7

M

Mabbett Ho 2 SE18 . . . . . 12 A8
Mabel Cotts DA3 . . . . 49 A6
Mabel Rd BR8 . . . . 32 A2
Mabledon Rd TN9 . . . . . . 143 A8
MacAllister Ho SE18 . . . . 12 B8
McAlpine Cres ME15 . . . 115 F3
McArthur Dr ME19 . . . . . . 97 D3
MacAulay CI ME20 . . . . . . 82 A4
MacAulay Way 2 SE28 . . . 3 B5
McAuley CI SE9 . . . . 12 A2
Macbean St SE18 . . . . 2 B3
McCabe Ct TN12 . . . . . . 149 E2
McCall Cres SE7 . . . . 1 E1
McCudden Rd DA1 . . . . . . 15 F4
McCudden Row 8 ME7 . . . 54 A6
McDermott Rd TN15 . . . . . 94 F7
McDonald Ct TN12 . . . . . 146 A6
McDonald Rd ME7 . . . . . . 54 D6
McDowall CI 11 E16 . . . . . . 1 A8
Mace Ct RM17 . . . . 18 E8
Mace Farm Cotts TN14 . . 73 E6
Mace La TN14 . . . . 73 D6
MacGregor Rd E16 . . . . . . 1 C8
McIntyre Ct 6 SE18 . . . . . . 1 E2
Mackenders CI ME20 . . . . 83 A6
Mackenders Gn ME20 . . . 83 A6
Mackenders La ME20 . . . 83 A6
McKenzie CI ME20 . . . . . . 98 F8
McKenzie Rd ME5 . . . . . . 62 C5
McKenzie Rd ME5 . . . . . . 68 A3
Mackenzie Way DA12 . . . 36 D2
McKillop Way DA14 . . . . . 30 C1
McKinlay Ct DA16 . . . . . . 13 C4
Mackintosh St ME23 . . . . 23 F3
MacLeod Ho SE18 . . . . . . 11 E6
McLeod Rd SE2 . . . . 3 B2
McMichaels Way TN19 . . 194 A3
McMillan CI DA12 . . . . . . 36 C4
Macmillan Gdns 2 DA1 . . 16 A3
Macoma Rd SE18 . . . . . . 12 D8
Macoma Terr SE18 . . . . . 12 D8
Madan CI TN16 . . . . 89 E2
Madan Rd TN16 . . . . 89 E2
Mada Rd BR6 . . . . 57 B7
Madden CI DA14 . . . . 29 F5
Madden CI DA10 . . . . 17 E1
Maddocks CI DA14 . . . . . 30 E3
MADEIRA PARK 159 B2
Madeira Pk TN2 . . . . 159 B2
Madginford CI ME15 . . . . 101 A2
Madginford Park Inf Sch
ME15 . . . . 101 A2
Madginford Park Jun Sch
ME15. . . . . 101 A2
Madginford Rd ME15 . . . 100 F2
Madhuran Ct ME2 . . . . . . 53 A7
Madison Cres DA7 . . . . . . 13 C7
Madison Gdns DA7 . . . . . 13 C7
Madison Way TN13 . . . . . 91 F4
Madras Ho 2 ME15 . . . . . 116 C5
Maesmaur Rd TN16 . . . . . 88 D6
Mafeking Rd ME5 . . . . . . 67 F3
Magdalen CI ME7 . . . . . . 69 A4
Magdalen Gr BR6 . . . . . . 58 B6
Magellan Boulevard E6 . . . 2 C6
Magnet Rd RM20 . . . . 17 C8
Magnolia Ave ME8 . . . . . . 69 B5
Magnolia CI TN9 . . . . . . 143 C7
Magnolia Dr TN16 . . . . . . 72 E3
Magnolia Ho 8 ME16 . . . . 99 A3
Magnolia Bottom TN15 . . 76 E6
Magpie CI ME20 . . . . 82 A1
Magpie Gn 3 TN9 . . . . . 122 D3
Magpie Hall CI BR2 . . . . . 42 E3
Magpie Hall La BR2 . . . . . 42 E3
Magpie Hall Rd ME4 . . . . 54 A2
Magwitch CI ME9 . . . . . . 69 F1
Magwitch CI ME14 . . . . . . 53 B4
Maida Rd
Chatham ME4 . . . . 54 B2
Erith DA17 . . . . 4 A3
Maida Vale Rd DA1 . . . . . 15 A2
Maiden Erlegh Ave DA5 . . 36 D7
Maiden La DA1 . . . . 15 A3
MAIDSTONE 100 C3
Maidstone Barracks Sta
ME16. . . . . 99 E5
Maidstone East Sta ME16. 99 F5
Maidstone Gram Sch
ME15. . . . . 100 B3
Maidstone Gram Sch for
Girls ME16. . . . . 99 E5
Maidstone Hospl ME16 . . . 99 E5
Maidstone L Ctr ME15 . . . 99 E7
Maidstone Mus & Gallery★
1 ME14 . . . . 99 F5
Maidstone Rd
Bredhurst ME7, ME8 . . . 69 B2
Chatham ME5 . . . . 53 F2
Chatham, Walderslade ME5. 67 D4
Colt's Hill TN12, TN2 . . 145 B4
Danaway ME9 . . . . 71 D4
Five Wents ME17 . . . . . 117 E2
Gillingham ME8 . . . . 69 C6
Goose Green ME18, TN11 . 112 C3
Grays RM17 . . . . 18 A8
Headcorn TN27 . . . . . . 151 B7
Horsmonden, Claygate
TN12 . . . . 147 C3

Maidstone Rd continued
Horsmonden TN12 . . . . 163 A7
Lenham ME17 . . . . 120 D5
Matfield TN12 . . . . 161 C6
Nettlestead Green ME18. 113 C3
Pembury TN2 . . . . 144 E1
Platt TN15 . . . . 95 C7
Rochester ME1 . . . . 53 C3
Seal TN15. . . . . 93 C5
Sevenoaks TN13 . . . . . . 91 E5
Sidcup DA14 . . . . 30 F1
Staplehurst TN12 . . . . . 149 E7
Swanley DA14, BR8 . . . . 45 B8
Underling Green TN12 . . 132 F2
Maidstone West Sta ME16 99 F3
Mailyns The ME8. . . . . . . 69 D7
Main Gate Rd ME4 . . . . . . 53 F7
Main Rd
Biggin Hill TN16 . . . . . . 72 C5
Chattenden ME3 . . . . . . 39 F4
Cooling ME3 . . . . 22 F4
Crockenhill BR8 . . . . 45 D3
Crockham Hill TN8 . . . . 105 C1
Cudham TN16 . . . . 89 A7
Farningham DA4 . . . . . . 46 F3
Halstead TN14 . . . . 74 C3
Hoo St Werburgh ME3 . . 41 D5
Kingsnorth ME3 . . . . 41 D7
Longfield DA3 . . . . 48 E7
Marlpit Hill TN8 . . . . . . 122 B6
Orpington BR5 . . . . 44 C7
Sidcup DA14, DA15 . . . . 29 E5
Sundridge TN14 . . . . . . 90 E3
Sutton at Hone DA4. . . . 33 B1
Swanley BR8 . . . . 45 F8
Mainridge Rd BR7 . . . . . . 29 A4
Main Road Gorse Hill
DA4 . . . . 61 D7
Maison Des Fleurs ME16 . 99 C2
Majendie Rd SE18. . . . . . . 2 D1
Major Clark Ho TN17 . . . 179 C5
Major York's Rd TN4 . . . 159 A1
Malabar Rd TN11 . . . . 72 E2
Malden Dr ME14 . . . . . . 100 A8
Mallard Apartments 14
ME15 . . . . 116 E5
Mallard CI DA1 . . . . 15 F2
Mallard Path 6 SE28. . . . . 2 D3
Mallards Way ME15 . . . . 101 A1
Mallard Way
Lower Stoke ME3 . . . . . . 25 C4
Marlpit Hill TN8 . . . . . . 122 C3
Mallard Wlk
Larkfield ME20 . . . . 81 F2
Sidcup DA14 . . . . 30 C2
Malling Ct ME19 . . . . 97 F7
Mallingdene CI ME13. . . . 39 88
Malling Rd
Kings Hill M18, ME19 . . . 96 F3
Lunsford ME6, ME20 . . . 81 F5
Snodland ME6 . . . . 82 A7
Teston ME18 . . . . 98 A1
Malling Sch The ME19 . . . 97 F7
Mallings Dr ME14 . . . . . 101 C4
Mallings La ME14 . . . . . 101 C4
Malling Terr ME16 . . . . . . 99 C4
Mallow CI DA11 . . . . 18 D8
Mallows The ME14 . . . . . . 99 E7
Mallow Way 1 ME5 . . . . . 67 F4
Mall Sh Ctr The 5 DA6. . . 14 A3
Mall The
6 Bexley DA6 . . . . 14 A3
2 Bromley BR1. . . . . . . 42 A6
Malpas PI DA4 . . . . 47 C8
Malmaynes Hall Rd ME3 . 24 D3
Malta Ave ME5 . . . . 68 A7
Malta Rd RM18 . . . . 18 F5
Malta Terr 5 ME14 . . . . . 100 A4
Maltby CI BR6 . . . . 44 A1
Malthouse CI ME17. . . . . 120 D5
Malthouse Hill ME15. . . . 115 F4
Malthouse La DA12 . . . . . 37 E3
Malt House La TN30. . . . . 193 A7
Malthouse Rd TN15 . . . . . 62 F2
Malthouse The ME15 . . . 115 A8
Malthus Path 7 SE28 . . . . 3 C5
Maltings Ent Ctr The
DA12 . . . . 36 F7
Maltings The
Gillingham ME8 . . . . 70 A8
3 Gravesend DA11 . . . . 19 A1
Hadlow TN11 . . . . 128 E8
Loose ME17 . . . . 116 B4
Maidstone, Grove Green
ME14. . . . . 100 E5
Orpington BR6 . . . . 43 F3
Westerham TN16 . . . . . 105 C8
MALTMAN'S HILL 153 F3
Malt Mews ME1 . . . . 53 C5
Malton Mews SE18 . . . . . 12 E8
Malton St SE18 . . . . 12 E8
Malton Way TN2 . . . . 159 F7
Malt Shovel Cotts DA4 . . . 60 D7
Malus CI ME5 . . . . 68 B1
Malvern Ave DA7 . . . . 13 E7
Malvern Ho 6 DA7 . . . . . . 18 D1
Malvern Rd
Gillingham ME7 . . . . 54 E3
Orpington BR6 . . . . 58 B6
Malvina Ave DA12 . . . . . . 36 C6
Malyons Rd BR8 . . . . 31 F1
Mamignot CI ME14 . . . . . 101 A5

Manchester Cl ME5 . . . . 68 C6
Manchester Ct E16. . . . . 1 B7
Mandela Ho SE18 . . . . 12 D8
Mandela Rd E16 . . . . 1 A7
Mandeville Cl **1** SE3. . . . . . . 11 B7
Mandeville Ct **1** ME14 . . 100 A5
Manford Ind Est DA8 . . . . 15 B8
Mangold Way **4** DA18. . . . 3 E3
Mangravet Ave ME15. . . . 116 C7
Manister Rd SE2 . . . . 3 A3
Manitoba Gdns **6** BR6 . . . 57 F4
Manley Boulevard ME6. . . . 66 A2
Manning Ct **3** SE28. . . . . . . 3 B5
Manningham Ho ME19 . . . 98 A6
Manning Rd BR5. . . . . 44 D4
Mannock Rd DA1. . . . . 15 F4
Mann Sq TN3 . . . . 143 D7
Manorbrook SE3. . . . . 11 A3
Manor Cl
Chalk DA12 . . . . 37 B6
Crayford DA1. . . . . 14 E3
Dartford DA2. . . . . 32 A5
Erith SE28 . . . . 3 C2
Maidstone ME14 . . . . 101 B3
Royal Tunbridge Wells
TN4 . . . . 158 E3
Manor Com Prim Sch The
DA10. . . . . 34 F8
Manor Cotts
Lamberhurst TN3. . . . . . . 176 B5
Langley ME17 . . . . 117 C5
Manor Ct
Gillingham ME7 . . . . 55 C4
Maidstone ME14 . . . . 101 B3
Sole Street DA13. . . . . 50 D4
Manordene Rd SE28. . . . . . . 3 D7
Manor Dr DA3 . . . . 49 A3
Manor Farm Cotts TN15 . . 94 A6
Manor Field DA3. . . . . 37 E3
Manor Fields TN4. . . . . 142 F3
Manorfields Cl BR7. . . . . 43 F6
Manor Forstal DA3. . . . . 62 F7
Manor Gdns ME5 . . . . 67 F4
Manor Gr TN10 . . . . 127 C3
Manor Ho
14 Chatham ME7. . . . . . . 54 A6
Chislehurst BR7. . . . . 43 D8
Manor Ho The
Limpsfield RH8. . . . . 104 B7
Sidcup DA15 . . . . 30 A7
Sidcup, Old Bexley DA5. . 31 B7
Manor House Dr ME16 . . 99 D3
Manor House Gdns TN8 . 122 C1
Manor La
Fawkham Green DA3. . . . . 48 C2
Hartley DA3. . . . . 49 A3
Rochester ME1. . . . . 52 F3
Manor Mews ME4 . . . . 54 A5
Manor Oak Prim Sch BR5 44 D4
Manor Park Ctry Pk★
ME19. . . . . 97 B7
Manor Park Rd BR7 . . . . 43 D8
Manor Pk
Chislehurst BR7. . . . . 43 D8
Erith DA8. . . . . 15 A8
Royal Tunbridge Wells
TN4 . . . . 158 E3
Manor Pl
Bromley BR1 . . . . 42 E8
Chislehurst BR7. . . . . 43 D7
Manor Rd
Chatham ME4. . . . . 53 F4
Crayford DA1. . . . . 14 E3
Edenbridge TN8 . . . . 122 B1
Erith DA8. . . . . 15 B8
22 Gravesend DA12 . . . . 19 B1
Grays RM17. . . . . 18 C8
Knockmill TN15 . . . . 77 F8
New Barn DA3. . . . . 49 C4
Royal Tunbridge Wells
TN4 . . . . 142 E1
Rusthall TN4. . . . . 158 C4
Sidcup DA15 . . . . 30 A5
Sidcup, Old Bexley DA5. . 31 B7
Sole Street DA13. . . . . 50 D4
Sundridge TN14. . . . . 82 E3
Swanscombe DA10 . . . . . . 34 E8
Tatsfield TN16. . . . . 88 E7
Tilbury RM18 . . . . 19 A5
West Thurrock RM20. . . . 17 C8
Manor Rise ME14 . . . . 101 B3
Manorside Cl SE2. . . . . 3 D2
Manor St ME7. . . . . 54 A6
Manor The TN2 . . . . 159 E5
Manor Way
Bexley DA7 . . . . 14 D4
Bromley BR2 . . . . 42 E3
Eltham SE3. . . . . 11 A3
Grays RM17. . . . . 18 B7
Northfleet DA11. . . . . 18 A3
Orpington BR5. . . . . 43 C5
Sidcup DA5 . . . . 31 A7
Royal Tunbridge Wells
TN4 . . . . 142 E1
Manor Way Bsns Ctr RM13 4 D8
Manor Way Business Park
DA11. . . . . 18 A3
Manse Ct DA14. . . . . 30 C3
Mansel Dr ME1 . . . . 53 A2
Manse Par BR8 . . . . 46 A5
Mansergh Ct SE18. . . . . 11 F7
Manse Way BR8. . . . . 46 A5
Mansfield Cl BR5. . . . . 44 D2
Mansfield Rd BR8. . . . . 31 F2
Mansfield Wlk ME16. . . . . . 99 E2
Mansion House Cl TN27 . 168 A2

Mansion Row ME7 . . . . 54 A6
Manthorpe Rd SE18. . . . . . . 2 C1
Manton Rd SE2 . . . . 3 A2
Manwarings The TN12 . 163 A6
Manwood St E16. . . . . 1 F5
Maple Ave
Gillingham ME7 . . . . 54 E6
Maidstone ME16 . . . . 99 C6
Maple Cl
Larkfield ME20. . . . . 82 A2
Orpington BR5. . . . . 43 D4
Royal Tunbridge Wells
TN2. . . . . 159 A1
Swanley BR8 . . . . 45 E1
Maple Cres DA15 . . . . 13 A1
Maplecroft Cl E6. . . . . 1 E7
Maple Ct
Erith DA8 . . . . 14 F7
Newham E6 . . . . 2 A8
Royal Tunbridge Wells
TN4. . . . . 158 E4
Sidcup DA14 . . . . 30 B3
Stone DA9 . . . . 33 E8
Mapledene ME14 . . . . 93 A7
Maple Gardens TN2. . . . 173 B8
Maplehurst Cl DA2 . . . . 31 E6
Maple Leaf Cl TN16 . . . . . . 72 D3
Maple Leaf Dr DA15. . . . . . 29 F7
Maple Rd
Dartford DA1. . . . . 32 C7
Gravesend DA12 . . . . 36 C4
Grays RM17. . . . . 18 C8
Hoo St Werburgh ME3. . . . 40 E3
Rochester ME2. . . . . 52 F6
MAPLESCOMBE 61 B5
Maplescombe Farm Cotts
DA4 . . . . 61 B5
Maplescombe La DA4. . . . 61 B6
Maplesden TN12. . . . . . . 148 D5
Maplesden Cl ME16 . . . . . 98 F3
Maplesden Noakes Sch
ME16. . . . . 99 E6
Maples The DA3 . . . . 49 B6
Mapleton Cl BR2 . . . . 123 A7
Mapleton Dl BR2 . . . . 42 A3
Mapleton Rd
Four Elms TN8 . . . . 123 A8
Westerham TN8, TN16. . 105 E3
Maple Tree PI SE3 . . . . 11 E6
Maplin Ho **3** SE2 . . . . 3 D4
Maplin Rd E16. . . . . 1 B7
Maplins Cl **5** ME8 . . . . . . 5 F1
Mara Ct ME4. . . . . 53 F1
Maran Way DA18. . . . . 3 D3
Marathon Paddock ME7. . 54 C4
Marathon Way SE28. . . . . . . 2 F4
Marble Cl ME7. . . . . 54 F6
Marble Ho **3** SE18. . . . . . . 2 F1
Marbrook Ct SE12. . . . . 28 C5
Marc Brunel Way ME4. . . . 54 A7
Marcellina Way BR6 . . . . . . 57 F7
Marcet Rd DA1 . . . . 15 C2
Marconi Ho SE2 . . . . 3 C1
Marconi Rd DA11. . . . . 35 D5
Marconi Way ME1. . . . . . . 67 D7
Marcus Rd DA1 . . . . 32 A8
MARDEN 148 C5
Marden Ave BR2. . . . . 42 A3
MARDEN BEECH. 148 B3
Marden Cres DA5 . . . . 14 C2
Marden Prim Sch TN12. . 148 B5
Marden Rd
Colliers' Green TN17. . . . 165 A1
Rochester ME2. . . . . 39 C1
Staplehurst TN12. . . . . . . 149 C5
Marden Sta TN12 . . . . 148 C6
MARDEN THORN 148 B3
Marechal Niel Ave DA15. . 29 D5
Marechal Niel Par DA15 . 29 D5
Margaret Barr Row DA10. 34 E8
Margaret Gardner Dr SE9 28 F6
Margaret Rd DA5. . . . . 13 D1
Margate Ct ME7. . . . . 54 E6
Margetts La ME1. . . . . 66 D1
Margetts Pl ME2. . . . . 40 A3
Mar Ho **5** SE7. . . . . 11 C8
Marigold Way ME16. . . . . . 99 A3
Marina Ct **1** BR2 . . . . 42 A6
Marina Dr
Bexley DA16 . . . . 12 E5
Dartford DA1. . . . . 33 A7
Northfleet DA11. . . . . 18 F1
Marine Dr
Hoo St Werburgh ME3. . . . 40 E3
Hoo St Werburgh ME3. . . . 40 E3
Woolwich SE18 . . . . 1 F2
Mariners Dr
Northfleet DA11. . . . . 17 B3
Mariners The ME4 . . . . 53 B4
Mariners View ME7 . . . . . . 54 F7
Mariners Way **5** DA11 . 35 E8
Mariners Wlk DA8 . . . . 14 F8
Marine View ME4 . . . . 40 B1
Marion Cl ME5. . . . . 68 A2
Marion Cotts TN15 . . . . . . 95 E8
Marion Cres
Maidstone ME15 . . . . 116 B8
Orpington BR5. . . . . 44 B4
Maritime Cl
Rochester ME2 . . . . 53 D8
Swanscombe DA9 . . . . 17 B2
Maritime Est ME2. . . . . 53 C8
Maritime Gate DA11. . . . . 35 E8
Maritime Ind Est ME1. . . . . 1 B2
Maritime Way ME4 . . . . . . 54 B8
Marjorie McClure Sch
BR7. . . . . 43 C8

Marjory Pease Cotts
RH8 . . . . 104 E5
MARKBEECH. 139 D2
Mark Cl
Bexley DA7. . . . . 13 E6
Orpington BR5. . . . . 56 E6
Markers Lodge DA12 . . . . . 36 E8
Market Alley **9** DA11 . . . 19 B1
Market Bldgs **8** ME14. . . 99 F4
Market Colonnade 1
ME14. . . . . 99 F4
Market Mdw BR5 . . . . 44 C5
Market Par
Bromley BR1 . . . . 42 A8
5 Sidcup DA14. . . . . 30 B4
Market Pl
2 Bexley DA6. . . . . 14 A3
Dartford DA1. . . . . 32 E8
10 Royal Tunbridge Wells
TN2. . . . . 159 A2
1 Tilbury RM18 . . . . 19 A5
Market Sq
Bromley BR1 . . . . 42 A7
Royal Tunbridge Wells
TN1. . . . . 159 B4
Westerham TN16. . . . . 89 D1
Market St
Dartford DA1. . . . . 32 E8
17 Royal Tunbridge Wells
TN2. . . . . 159 A2
Staplehurst TN12. . . . . . . 149 F5
Woolwich SE18 . . . . 2 A2
Market Way **8** TN16 . . . . 89 D1
Mark La DA12 . . . . 37 C5
Marks Sq DA11 . . . . 35 F4
Mark St ME4. . . . . 54 A2
Mark Way BR8 . . . . 46 A4
Marlborough Cl
Orpington BR6. . . . . 43 F3
Royal Tunbridge Wells
TN4. . . . . 158 D6
Marlborough Cres TN13 . . 91 E3
Marlborough Ct TN16 . . . 89 C1
Marlborough Ctr ME3. . . . 40 D5
Marlborough Ho **4** ME8. . 69 F8
Marlborough House Sch
TN18. . . . . 188 E2
Marlborough La SE7 . . . . . 11 C7
Marlborough Par ME16. . . 91 A3
Marlborough Park Ave
DA15 . . . . 30 A7
Marlborough Rd
Bexley DA7. . . . . 13 D4
Bromley BR2 . . . . 42 C5
Dartford DA1. . . . . 15 C1
Gillingham ME7 . . . . 54 B5
Woolwich SE18 . . . . 2 C3
Marlborough Sch DA15. . . 30 A8
Marle Place Gdns★
TN12. . . . . 162 C4
Marle Place Rd TN12. . . . 162 C4
Marler Ho DA8. . . . . 14 F5
Marley Ave DA7. . . . . 13 D8
Marley La TN27 . . . . 152 C3
Marley Rd
Harrietsham ME17. . . . . . 119 F6
Hoo St Werburgh ME3. . . . 40 D6
Marley Way ME1. . . . . 53 C2
Marlfield TN12. . . . . 149 E4
Marlhurst TN8 . . . . 122 B4
Marlin Ct **12** DA14. . . . . . 30 A4
Marling Cross DA12 . . . . . . 36 E1
Marlings Cl BR7 . . . . 43 E5
Marlings Park Ave BR7 . . 43 E5
Marling Way DA12 . . . . 36 E3
Marlow Copse ME5 . . . . . . 67 F1
Marlow Ct TN13. . . . . 92 B4
Marlowe Cl BR7 . . . . 29 D2
Marlowe Gdns SE9 . . . . . . 12 A1
Marlowe Rd ME20. . . . . . . 82 A3
Marlowes The DA1 . . . . . . 14 D3
MARLPIT. 116 E2
Marlpit Cl TN8. . . . . 122 C4
Marlpit Cotts ME17. . . . . . 116 E2
Marlpit Gdns TN5. . . . . . . 186 E1
Marlpit Hill
Marlpit The TN5 . . . . 184 E5
Marlwood Cl DA15 . . . . . . 29 E6
Marmadon Rd SE18 . . . . . . 2 F2
Marne Ave DA16 . . . . 13 A4
Marquis Dr ME7 . . . . 69 B3
Marrabon Cl DA15 . . . . . . 30 A7
Marram Ct ME14 . . . . 92 E4
Marrians View **1** ME5. . . 54 C2
Marriott Rd DA1 . . . . 33 A8
Marriotts Wharf **2** DA11 19 B1
Marsala Ho SE6 . . . . 57 F6
Marshall Gdns TN11. . . . . 111 E1
Marshall Path **8** SE28 . . . 3 C5
Marshall Rd ME8 . . . . 69 C8
Marshalls Gr SE18. . . . . 1 E2
Marshalls Land TN30. . . . 183 A3
Marsham La TN11, ME18. 111 F4
Marsham St ME14. . . . . . . 92 A5
Marsham Cres ME17. . . . . 117 B1
Marsham St ME14. . . . . . . 100 A4
Marsh Brook CI SE3 . . . . . 11 D4
Marsh Cres ME23 . . . . 23 E4
MARSH GREEN. 138 B5
Marsh Green Rd TN8. . . . 138 C5
Marsh La ME3. . . . . 22 B6
Marshland View ME3. . . . . 25 C5
Marsh Quarter La TN18. . 196 C3
Marsh Rd ME1 . . . . 66 B5
Marsh St
Dartford DA1 . . . . 15 F6
Rochester ME2 . . . . 53 B7
Marsh View DA12 . . . . 36 F7

Marsh Way
New Hythe ME20. . . . . 82 A4
Rainham RM13. . . . . 4 D8
Marston Cl ME5. . . . . 67 E3
Marston Ct DA14. . . . . 29 F4
Marston Dr ME14 . . . . . . 100 C5
Marston Ho RM17. . . . . . . 18 A8
Marston Wlk ME5. . . . . 67 E3
Martens Ave DA7. . . . . 14 C3
Martens Cl DA7. . . . . 14 C3
Martham Ct SE28 . . . . 3 D6
Martin Bowes Rd SE9 . . . 11 F4
Martin Ct ME7. . . . . 69 A3
Martindale Ave
Newham E16 . . . . 1 A6
Orpington BR6. . . . . 58 A5
Martin Dene DA6. . . . . 13 F2
Martin Dr DA2 . . . . 16 C1
Martin Hardie Way TN10 127 E5
Martin Ho
Dartford DA2. . . . . 33 C8
Gravesend DA11 . . . . 36 A5
Martin House DA11 . . . . . 35 F6
Martin Rd
Dartford DA2. . . . . 32 C5
Rochester ME2. . . . . 53 B8
Martin Rise DA6 . . . . 13 F2
Martins Cl
Lower Higham ME3. . . . . . 38 D6
Orpington BR5. . . . . 44 D6
Tenterden TN30. . . . . 193 C8
Martins La TN12 . . . . 112 E2
Martins Pl SE28. . . . . 2 E5
Martin Sq ME20. . . . . 82 A2
Martin's Shaw TN13. . . . . . 91 C5
Martin St SE28. . . . . 2 E5
Martins Wlk SE28 . . . . 2 E5
Martyn Ho SE2. . . . . 13 D8
Marvels Cl SE12 . . . . 28 B6
Marvels La SE12 . . . . 28 C5
Marvels Lane Prim Sch
SE12 . . . . 28 C4
Marvillion Ct TN12 . . . . . 129 F6
Marvin Ho **9** SE18 . . . . . 12 B8
Marwell TN16. . . . . 89 B1
Marwood Cl DA16. . . . . . . 13 B4
Marybank SE18 . . . . 1 F2
Mary Burrows Gdns TN15. 77 B2
Mary Cl ME4. . . . . 54 A2
Mary Day's TN17. . . . . . . 177 E7
Maryfield Cl DA5. . . . . 31 E5
Maryland Ct ME8 . . . . 69 E5
Maryland Dr ME16 . . . . . . 98 F2
Maryland Rd TN2. . . . . . . 159 D1
Mary Last Cl ME6. . . . . 81 E7
Mary Lawrenson Pl 2
SE3. . . . . 11 A7
Mary Macarthur Ho **5**
DA17. . . . . 4 A3
Mary Magdalene Ho 8
TN9 . . . . 143 B8
Maryon Ct BR5. . . . . 44 B5
Maryon Gr SE7. . . . . 1 E2
Maryon Rd SE7, SE18 . . . . 1 E2
Mary Rose Mall E6. . . . . 1 F7
Mary Slessor Ho **14** DA17. . 4 A3
Maryville DA16 . . . . 12 F5
Mascall's Court La TN12. 146 B4
Mascall's Court Rd TN12 146 A4
Mascalls Ct **23** SE7 . . . . . 11 C8
Mascalls Pk TN12 . . . . 145 F5
Mascalls Rd SE7 . . . . 11 C8
Mascalls Sch TN12 . . . . . 146 A4
Masefield Cl DA8 . . . . 14 F6
Masefield Dr ME3. . . . . 39 B8
Masefield Rd
Dartford DA1. . . . . 16 B2
Lunsford ME20 . . . . 81 F4
Northfleet DA11. . . . . 35 D5
Masefield View BR6. . . . . . 57 C7
Masham Way TN9 . . . . . . 142 F7
Masham Ho **6** DA18 . . . . . 3 D4
Mason Cl
Bexley DA7. . . . . 14 B4
Newham E16 . . . . 1 A6
Masons Hill
Bromley BR2 . . . . 42 B5
Woolwich SE18 . . . . 2 B2
Mason Way ME2 . . . . 39 B2
Master Gunner Pl SE18. . 11 E6
Masters La ME19 . . . . 81 B5
Masterson Ho DA4 . . . . . . 47 D7
Masthead Cl DA2 . . . . 16 C3
Matchless Dr SE18 . . . . . . 12 A7
MATFIELD 161 D8
Matfield Cl BR2. . . . . 42 A5
Matfield Cres ME14 . . . . . 100 C5
Matfield Rd DA17 . . . . 14 A8
Matilda Cl ME8 . . . . 69 B8
Matrix Bsns Ctr DA1 . . . . 15 E2
Matterdale Gdns ME16 . . 98 E2
Matthews Ho **5** ME7 . . . 11 C8
Matthews La TN11, ME18. 111 F4
Mattison Pl ME9 . . . . 103 F7
Matts Hill Rd ME9 . . . . 69 F2
Maud Cashmore Way SE18 1 F3
Maude Rd BR8 . . . . 32 A2
Maudslay Rd SE9 . . . . 11 F4
Maundene Prim Sch ME5. 68 B5
Maunders Cl ME5. . . . . 68 C8
Mavelstone Cl BR1. . . . . . . 42 E8
Mavelstone Rd BR1. . . . . . 42 E8
Mavis Wlk **5** E6 . . . . 1 E8
Maxey Rd SE18 . . . . 2 C2
Maximfeldt Rd DA8 . . . . . . 4 E1
Maximilian Dr ME2. . . . . . 66 B4
Maxim Rd
Crayford DA1. . . . . 14 E2

Maxim Rd continued
Erith DA8. . . . . 4 E2
Maxted Ct TN12. . . . . 149 E4
Maxton Cl ME14. . . . . 100 F5
Maxwell Dr ME16 . . . . 99 B6
Maxwell Gdns BR6 . . . . . . 57 F7
Maxwell Ho **12** SE18. . . . 12 B8
Maxwell House BR7 . . . . . 29 B1
Maxwell Rd
Bexley DA16 . . . . 13 A4
Chatham ME7. . . . . 54 A6
May Ave
Northfleet DA11. . . . . 35 F7
Orpington BR5. . . . . 44 B4
May Avenue Ind Est **1**
DA11. . . . . 35 F7
Maybury Ave DA2. . . . . 33 C7
Maybury Ct BR5. . . . . 43 B4
Maycotts La TN12. . . . . . . 145 D1
May Ct RM17 . . . . 18 E8
Mayday Gdns SE3 . . . . 11 E5
Mayerne Rd SE9 . . . . 11 D2
Mayes Cl BR8 . . . . 46 A5
Mayeswood Rd SE12 . . . . 28 C4
Mayfair **3** ME4 . . . . 53 C8
Mayfair Ave
Bexley DA7. . . . . 13 D6
Loose ME15. . . . . 116 A8
Mayfair Rd DA1 . . . . 15 D2
Mayfield
Bexley DA7. . . . . 13 F4
Sevenoaks TN13 . . . . 91 E7
Swanscombe DA10 . . . . . . 17 E1
Mayfield Ave BR6. . . . . 43 F2
Mayfield Cl
Chatham ME5. . . . . 68 A1
Gillingham ME8 . . . . 55 E2
Mayfield Ct DA14 . . . . 30 B3
Mayfield La TN5 . . . . 184 D4
Mayfield Pk TN5 . . . . 184 E5
Mayfield Rd
Bromley BR1 . . . . 42 E4
Erith DA17. . . . . 4 C2
Northfleet DA11. . . . . 35 F8
Royal Tunbridge Wells
TN4 . . . . 158 F4
Mayfield Villas DA14 . . . . 30 C2
Mayflower Ho ME1 . . . . . . 53 B4
Mayfly Cl BR5. . . . . 44 D5
Mayford Rd ME5. . . . . 68 D2
Mayhill Rd SE7 . . . . 11 B8
Maylam Ct TN10 . . . . 127 C4
Maylands Dr DA14 . . . . . . 30 D5
Maynard Cl DA8. . . . . 14 F7
Maynard Ho SE18. . . . . 2 C2
Maynard Pl ME5. . . . . 54 C2
Maynards TN12 . . . . 148 C5
Mayor's La DA2 . . . . 32 C3
Mayor's Pl **10** TN30. . . . 193 A7
May Pl DA12. . . . . 50 D4
Mayplace Ave DA1 . . . . . . 15 A3
Mayplace Cl DA7. . . . . 14 B4
Mayplace La SE18 . . . . 12 B7
Mayplace Prim Sch DA7. 14 D3
Mayplace Road E DA7 . . . 14 A3
Mayplace Road W DA7 . . 14 A3
MAYPOLE
Dartford. 31 E7
Orpington. 58 F4
Maypole Cotts BR6. . . . . . 59 A4
Maypole Cres DA8 . . . . . . 15 D8
Maypole Dr ME19 . . . . 97 C3
Maypole La TN17 . . . . 177 F8
Maypole Prim Sch DA5. . 31 E5
Maypole Rd
Chelsfield BR6. . . . . 58 F4
Gravesend DA12 . . . . 36 F7
May Rd
Gillingham ME7 . . . . 54 C4
Hawley DA2. . . . . 32 F4
Rochester ME1. . . . . 53 C3
May St
Cuxton ME2 . . . . 52 B2
Snodland ME6 . . . . 74 F7
May Terr ME1. . . . . 54 A7
Maytham Bglws TN17 . . 192 A1
Maytham Rd TN17 . . . . . 198 C7
Mayview DA1. . . . . 32 E7
Mayweed Ave ME5. . . . . . 67 E4
May Wynne Ho E16 . . . . . . 1 B7
Mead Cl BR8. . . . . 46 A4
Mead Cres DA1 . . . . 32 D7
Meades Cl TN12 . . . . 148 D6
Meadfield Rd DA13. . . . . . 64 A8
Mead Gn ME5. . . . . 68 C3
Mead Rd TN16. . . . . 72 D3
Meadow Bank
Leigh TN11 . . . . 125 F1
West Malling ME19 . . . . . 97 C8
Meadow Bank Cl TN15 . . 61 F2
Meadowbank Ct ME19. . . 97 C8
Meadow Bank Mews
ME19 . . . . 97 C8
Meadowbank Rd ME4 . . . 54 A4
Meadow Cl
Bexley DA6. . . . . 13 F2
Chatham ME5. . . . . 67 F5
Chislehurst BR7. . . . . 29 B3
Sevenoaks TN13 . . . . 92 A4
Upper Halling ME2. . . . . . 65 E4
Meadow Cres ME2. . . . . . . 65 E4
Meadow Croft BR1. . . . . . . 42 E6
Meadowdown ME14 . . . . 100 E4
Meadowdown Cl ME7 . . . 69 A4
Meadowford Cl SE28 . . . . . 3 A6
Meadow Hill Rd **6** TN1. 159 B3

Meadow La
Culverstone Green DA13... 64 A1
Lewisham SE12 .... 28 B5
Marlpit Hill TN8 .... 122 B4
Meadowlands
Oxted RH8 .... 104 A1
Seal TN15 .... 92 F7
Meadow Rd
Gravesend DA11 .... 36 A6
Groombridge TN3 .... 171 C7
Northfleet DA11 .... 35 C7
Royal Tunbridge Wells,
  Southborough TN4 ..... 142 F1
Royal Tunbridge Wells
  TN1 .... 159 A4
Rusthall TN4 .... 158 C4
Tonbridge TN9 .... 143 B8
Meadows TN7 .... 180 D1
Meadows Ct DA14 .... 30 B2
Meadowside
Dartford DA1 .... 32 E7
Eltham SE3, SE9 .... 11 C3
Meadowside Cotts TN5.. 186 F1
Meadows Sch TN4 .... 142 F2
Meadows The
Biddenden TN27 .... 167 F2
8 Maidstone ME15 .... 74 F6
3 Maidstone ME15 ...... 99 E2
Orpington BR6 .... 58 C4
Wittersham TN30 .... 199 D4
Meadowsweet Cl 3 E16... 1 D8
Meadowsweet View ME4.. 40 B2
Meadow The
Chislehurst BR7 .... 29 C2
Tonbridge TN9 .... 160 E8
Meadow View
Flimwell TN5 .... 187 A3
Orpington BR5 .... 44 C6
Sidcup DA15 .... 30 B8
Meadow View Cotts
Hurst Green TN19 .... 194 A3
Laddingford ME18 .... 130 E5
Meadowview Rd DA5..... 13 F1
Meadow View Rd ME17.. 116 B3
Meadow Way
Dartford DA2 .... 33 C8
Marden TN12 .... 148 C6
Orpington BR6 .... 57 A7
Wouldham ME1 .... 66 C5
Meadow Wlk
Dartford DA2 .... 32 C4
Maidstone ME15 .... 100 B3
Snodland ME6 .... 81 F7
Mead Rd
Chislehurst BR7 .... 29 C2
Dartford DA1 .... 32 D7
Edenbridge TN8 .... 138 D7
Gravesend DA11 .... 36 B6
Mead Rd Ind Sch BR7 .. 29 C2
Mead Sch The TN2 ...... 159 A1
Meadside Wlk ME5 .... 67 F6
Meads The
Hartley TN17 .... 178 F1
Royal Tunbridge Wells
  TN2 .... 159 C2
Mead The
Leybourne ME19 .... 81 E2
Ash Green DA3 .... 62 E8
Mead Wall ME3 .... 5 F2
Meadway
Halstead TN14 .... 74 F6
Tonbridge TN11 .... 126 E5
Mead Way BR2 .... 42 A3
Meadway The
Orpington BR6 .... 58 B4
Sevenoaks TN13 .... 91 F5
Meath Cl BR5 .... 44 B4
Medbury Rd DA12 .... 36 F7
Medburn Cl ME7 .... 28 B3
Medhurst Cres DA12 .... 36 F6
Medhurst Gdns DA12... 36 F5
MEDHURST ROW 123 A2
Medick Ct RM17 .... 18 E8
Medina Ho 6 DA8 ..... 14 E7
Medina Rd
Ditton ME20 .... 82 C1
Tonbridge TN10 .... 127 C6
Medlar Gr ME7 .... 69 A4
Medlar Ho 8 DA5....... 30 A5
Medlar Rd RM17 .... 18 E8
Medlars The
Maidstone ME14 .... 100 D6
Meopham Station DA13.. 50 A3
Medway Ave
High Halstow ME23 ..... 23 E4
Yalding ME18 .... 113 F1
Medway City Est ME2 .. 53 D7
Medway Com Coll ME4.. 54 A1
Medway Cotts
Iden Green TN17 .... 190 D3
Marden TN12 .... 148 C6
Medway Ct
Aylesford ME20 .... 82 F2
Forstal ME20 .... 83 A2
19 Orpington BR5 ...... 44 D1
Medway Ent Ctr ME2 ... 53 D8
Medway Ho 5 ME14 .... 92 A5
Medway Hts 6 ME4 ..... 53 E4
Medway Maritime Hospl
ME7.................... 54 B4
Medway Rd
Crayford DA1 .... 15 A4
Gillingham ME7 .... 54 C7
Royal Tunbridge Wells
  TN1 .... 159 B5

Medway St
Chatham ME4 .... 53 F5
Maidstone ME14 .... 99 F4
Medway Trad Est ME6.. 99 F2
Medway View
Barnes Street TN11 ..... 129 A5
Middle Stoke ME3 .... 25 C3
Medway Villas ME15 .... 115 B7
Medway Wharf Rd TN9 127 C1
Meerbrook Rd SE3 .... 11 C4
Meeson's La RM17 .... 17 F8
Meeting House La 2 ME4 53 F4
Megby Cl ME8 .... 11 C6
Megrims Hill TN18 ...... 196 A6
Meirs Court Rd ME8..... 69 E6
Melanda Cl BR7 .... 28 F3
Melanie Cl DA7 .... 13 E6
Melba Cl ME19 .... 97 D4
Melba Gdns RM18 .... 19 A7
Melbourne Cl BR6 .... 63 E2
Melbourne Ct RM18 ..... 18 E6
Melbourne Quay 4 DA11. 19 B1
Melbourne Rd
Chatham ME4 .... 54 A3
Tilbury RM18 .... 18 E6
Melbury Cl BR7 .... 28 F2
Melbury Grange BR1 .... 42 E8
Meldrum Cl
Orpington BR5 .... 44 C3
Oxted RH8 .... 104 A3
Melford Dr ME16 .... 99 C4
Melliker La DA13 .... 50 A3
Melling St SE18 .... 12 E8
Mellish Ind Est SE18 .... 1 D3
Mells Cres SE9 .... 28 F4
Melody Cl ME8 .... 69 C4
Melody Rd TN16 .... 72 C1
Melrose Ave
Dartford DA1 .... 31 E8
Kings Hill ME19 .... 97 C3
Melrose Cl
Lewisham SE12 .... 28 B7
Loose ME15 .... 116 A7
Melrose Cres BR6........ 57 D5
Melrose Gdns SE3 .... 11 E6
Melthorpe Gdns SE3 .... 11 E6
Melville Ct ME4 .... 53 F6
Melville Rd
Maidstone ME15 .... 100 A3
Sidcup DA14 .... 30 C6
Memess Path 4 SE18.. 12 A8
Memorial Hospl SE18 .. 12 A5
Mendip Ho 1 DA11 .... 18 D1
Mendip Rd DA7 .... 14 E6
Mendip Wlk TN2 .... 159 D5
Mennie Ho SE18 .... 11 F6
Meon Ct 20 BR5........ 44 D1
MEOPHAM 64 B8
MEOPHAM GREEN 64 A8
Meopham L Ctr DA13 ... 64 A8
Meopham Prim Sch DA13 50 A2
Meopham Sch DA13 ..... 64 A8
Meopham Sta DA13 ..... 50 A4
MEOPHAM STATION .. 50 B4
Mera Dr DA7 .... 14 A3
Merbury Cl SE28 .... 2 D5
Merbury Rd SE28 .... 2 E4
Mercer Cl ME20 .... 82 B4
Mercer Ct ME15 .... 67 E1
Mercer Dr ME17 .... 119 F6
Mercers
Hawkhurst TN18 .... 189 A1
Langton Green TN3 .... 158 A3
Mercers TN12 .... 145 E6
Mercers ME19 .... 97 F2
Mercer St TN1 .... 159 B5
Mercer Way ME17 ...... 117 B1
Merchant Pl TN12 ..... 148 C5
Merchland Rd SE9 .... 29 C7
Mercury Cl ME1 .... 53 A3
Mere Cl BR6 .... 57 B8
Meredith Cl ME17 ...... 117 F7
MERESBOROUGH 70 A5
Meresborough Cotts ME8 69 F5
Meresborough La ME8,
  ME9 .... 70 B5
Meresborough Rd ME8.. 70 A7
Mereside BR6 .... 57 A8
Merevale Ho 3 TN1 .. 159 A3
Merewood Cl 1 BR1.... 43 A7
Merewood Rd DA7 ...... 42 F8
MEREWORTH 112 D8
Mereworth Cl BR2 ...... 36 A3
Mereworth Com Prim Sch
ME18 .... 112 D8
Mereworth Dr SE18 .... 12 C7
Mereworth Ho ME7 ..... 39 C1
Mereworth Rd
Royal Tunbridge Wells
  TN4 .... 159 A6
West Peckham ME18 .. 112 C7
Merganser Gdns SE28 .. 2 D3
Meriden Cl BR1 .... 28 D1
Meridian Cl ME16 ...... 99 E4
Meridian Pk ME2 .... 53 C6
Meridian Rd SE7 .... 11 D7
Meridian Trad Est SE7 .. 1 B2
Meriel Wlk DA9 .... 17 B3
Merifield Rd SE9 .... 11 A2
Merioys Cl DA3 .... 49 C6
Merino Pl DA15 .... 13 A2
Merivale Gr ME5 .... 62 B4
Merle Common Rd RH8 . 121 B7
Merlewood Rd TN13 ..... 92 B4
Merlewood Dr BR7....... 42 F8
Merlin Ave ME20 .... 81 F2
Merlin Cl TN10 .... 127 E4
Merlin Gdns BR1 .... 28 A5

Merlin Ho ME4 .... 54 B8
Merlin Prim Sch BR1 ... 28 A5
Merlin Rd DA16 .... 13 A3
Merlin Road N DA16 .... 13 A3
Merlin Way ME7 .... 54 C5
Mermaid Cl
Chatham ME5 .... 68 A6
Northfleet DA11 .... 35 D8
Mermerus Gdns DA12 .. 36 F4
Merrals Wood Rd ME2 . 52 D5
Merrilees Rd DA15 ...... 29 E8
Merriman Ho ME3 .... 39 F6
Merriman Rd SE3 .... 11 C6
Merriments Gdns*
TN19 .... 194 B5
Merriments La TN19 ... 194 A5
Merrion Cl TN4 .... 159 B7
Merrion Way TN4 .... 159 B7
Merry Boys Rd ME3 ..... 39 B8
Merrydown Way BR7.... 42 F8
Merryfield Cl SE9 .... 11 A5
Merryfield Ct 6 TN9 .. 143 B8
Merryfields ME2 .... 39 A1
Merryfields Cl DA3 ..... 48 F5
Merryhills Ct TN16 ..... 72 D3
Merryweather Cl DA1 .. 15 F1
Mersey Rd TN10 .... 127 B5
Merton Ave DA3 .... 48 F5
Merton Cl ME5 .... 68 C5
Merton Court Prep Sch
DA14 .... 30 C4
Merton Ct DA16 .... 13 B5
Merton Gdns BR5 .... 43 B4
Merton Rd ME15 .... 100 F2
Mervyn Ave SE9 .... 29 C6
Mervyn Stockwood House
SE9 .... 29 C6
Mesne Way TN14 .... 75 F7
Messent Rd SE9 .... 11 D2
Messeter Pl SE9 .... 12 A1
Meteor Rd ME19 .... 96 F3
Methuen Rd
Bexley DA6 .... 13 F3
Maidstone ME16 .... 99 D5
Metro Ctr The BR5 ...... 44 B3
Mewsend TN16 .... 72 D1
Mews The
Gravesend DA12 .... 36 D7
Headcorn TN27 .... 151 C6
Longfield DA3 .... 48 E6
1 Pembury TN2 ...... 150 C6
Pembury TN2 .... 160 C6
Rochester ME2 .... 47 C8
8 Royal Tunbridge Wells
  TN1 .... 159 B3
7 Sidcup DA14 .... 30 A4
Meyer Rd DA8 .... 14 D8
Micawber Cl ME5 .... 68 A1
Michael Gdns DA12 .... 36 F4
Michael Marshall House
SE9 .... 29 C6
Michaels La DA3, TN15.. 62 D8
Michele Cotts ME3 ...... 38 C6
Mickleham Cl BR5 ...... 44 A7
Mickleham Rd BR5 ..... 44 A7
Mid Comp Cotts TN15 .. 95 E6
Middle Field TN2 ...... 160 E8
Middleham Ct 23 ME4 21 B1
Middle La TN15 .... 92 F6
Middle Mill Rd ME19 ... 97 F7
Middle Park Prim Sch
SE9 .... 28 D8
Middle Rd ME1 .... 47 E2
Middlesex Rd ME15 ... 116 D7
Middle St 4 ME7 ...... 54 A6
MIDDLE STOKE 25 B4
Middleton Ave DA14 ... 30 C3
Middleton Cl ME8 .... 69 E4
Middleton Ct 3 ME8 .. 28 B1
Middle Wlk TN2 .... 159 E8
Middlings Rise TN13 ... 91 F2
Middlings The TN13 .... 91 F2
Middlings Wood TN13 .. 92 A2
Midfield Ave
Bexley DA7 .... 14 C4
Hextable BR8 .... 32 B2
Midfield Prim Sch BR5.. 30 A1
Midfield Way BR5 .... 30 A1
Midhurst Cl ME15 ..... 100 A3
Midhurst Hill DA6 ...... 14 A2
Mid Kent Bsns Pk ME6 . 82 B7
**MidKent Coll (Chatham
Maritime)** ME4 .... 54 B8
MidKent Coll (City Way Ctr)
ME1.................... 53 E4
MidKent Coll (Horsted Ctr)
ME5.................... 67 F4
**MidKent Coll (Oakwood Park
Ctr)** ME16 .... 99 C3
Mid Kent Sh Ctr The
ME16 .... 99 C7
Midley Cl ME16 .... 99 C7
Midsummer Cl SE12 .... 11 A3
Midsummer Rd ME6 .... 81 E8
Midway The TN4 .... 158 D2
Midwinter Cl 3 DA16.. 13 A4
Mierscourt Cl ME8 ...... 70 A8
Miers Court Prim Sch
ME8.................... 69 F7
Miers Court Rd ME8 .... 69 E6
Mike Spring Ct DA12 .. 36 D4
Milburn Rd ME7 .... 48 C7

Mildmay Pl TN14 .... 75 F8
Mildred Cl DA1 .... 16 A1
Mildred Rd DA8 .... 4 E1
MILEHOUSE 148 E8
Milebush La TN12 ...... 132 E1
MILE END GREEN 48 C8
Mile End Green Cotts
DA3.................... 48 D7
Mile La TN17 .... 178 B8
MILE OAK 146 C4
Mile Oak Rd TN12 ..... 146 C3
Miles Dr SE28............. 2 E5
Miles Pl ME1 .... 53 D3
Milestone Bldgs TN12 149 F3
Mile Stone Rd DA2 ...... 16 B1
Milestone Sch DA3 ...... 48 F1
Milford Cl
Bexley DA6 .... 13 E8
Maidstone ME16 .... 99 D5
Military Rd ME4 .... 53 F5
Milk House Cotts TN17 . 180 A8
Milking La
Biggin Hill, Downe BR6 .. 72 E7
Biggin Hill, Leaves Green
  BR2.................... 72 D8
Milk St
Bromley BR1 .... 28 B2
Newham E16 .... 2 B5
Millais Pl RM18 .... 19 A7
Millais Mdw SE12 .... 11 A3
MILLBANK
Mill Bank
Headcorn TN27 .... 151 C6
Tonbridge TN9 .... 127 C2
Millbank Way SE12..... 11 A2
Millbro BR8 .... 46 A8
Millbrook ME19 .... 81 D1
Millbrook Cl ME16 ..... 12 D3
Millbrook Cl ME15 ...... 99 F1
Mill Brook Rd BR5 ...... 44 C5
Mill Cl
Lenham ME17 .... 120 C4
Rochester ME2 .... 39 B1
Mill Cotts ME15 .... 114 B6
Mill Cres TN9 .... 127 C2
Millcroft Rd ME3 .... 22 B4
Mill Ct
Bidborough TN3 .... 142 C3
Sutton at Hone DA4 .... 47 C7
14 Woolwich SE28 ...... 3 B6
Millen Ct DA4 .... 47 C5
Millennium Cl E16 .... 1 B7
Miller Cl BR1 .... 28 B3
Miller Ct DA7 .... 14 B4
Miller Rd DA12 .... 37 A6
Millers Cl DA1 .... 32 D8
Millers Cotts TN11 .... 144 C6
Millersthumb TN17.... 165 C4
Millers Wharf 1 ME15 . 99 E2
Millers Wlk DA13 .... 64 A7
Miller Way ME2 .... 39 D2
Millfield
High Halden TN26 ..... 183 D7
New Ash Green DA3 .... 62 B8
Millfield Dr DA11 .... 35 E6
Millfield La TN15 .... 62 B8
Millfield Rd TN15 .... 61 D4
Millfields ME5 .... 68 C2
Millfields Cl BR5 .... 44 B5
Millfields Rd ME2 .... 52 C7
Millhall ME20 .... 82 E2
Mill Hall Bsns Est ME20 82 D2
Mill Hall Rd ME20 ...... 82 C3
Mill Hill TN8 .... 138 D7
Mill Hill La DA12 .... 37 D3
Mill House Cl DA4 ...... 46 E1
Millhouse La ME19 ..... 80 D3
Mill La
Benover ME18 .... 131 A7
Chatham, Bluebell Hill ME5. 67 D1
Chatham, Luton ME5 .... 54 C1
Coxheath ME17 .... 115 D4
Eynsford DA4 .... 46 E1
Farthing Street BR6..... 57 B1
Frittenden TN17 .... 166 D8
Hartlip ME9 .... 70 E6
Hildenborough TN11,
  TN15 .... 109 C2
Horsmonden TN12 .... 147 B1
Ightham TN15 .... 86 F1
Maidstone ME14 .... 99 F6
Oxted RH8 .... 104 A1
Sevenoaks TN14 .... 92 D6
Shoreham TN14 .... 75 F3
Sissinghurst TN17 .... 179 F8
Smarden TN27 .... 153 A2
Snodland ME6 .... 82 B8
Tenterden TN30 .... 183 B1
The Chart RH8 .... 104 A4
Tonbridge TN9 .... 127 C2
Wateringbury ME18 .. 113 C5
Westerham TN16 ...... 105 C8
West Thurrock RM20 ... 17 D8
Woolwich SE18 .... 2 A1
Millman Ct SE3 .... 11 B7
Mill Pl
Chislehurst BR7 .... 43 B8
Crayford DA1 .... 15 A3
Millpond Cl ME2 .... 53 B8
Mill Pond Ct TN14..... 92 D6
Millpond La TN30 ..... 182 D2
Mill Pond Rd DA1 .... 15 E1
Mill Rd
Erith DA8 .... 14 C7
Gillingham ME7 .... 48 C7
Hawley DA2 .... 32 F4
Newham E16 .... 1 B5

Mill Rd *continued*
Northfleet DA11 .... 35 E8
Rochester ME2 .... 53 B8
Sevenoaks TN13 .... 91 E6
Mill Row DA5 .... 31 B8
Mills Cres TN15 .... 92 F8
Millside Ind Est DA1 ... 15 D3
Mills Rd ME20 .... 98 E7
Mill St
East Malling ME19 ...... 97 F7
Iden Green TN17, TN18.. 190 C3
Maidstone, Loose ME15 . 115 F5
Maidstone ME15 .... 99 F4
Snodland ME6 .... 82 B8
Westerham TN16 ...... 105 D8
Mills Terr ME4 .... 54 A3
Millstock Terr 2 ME15.. 99 E2
Mill Stone Cl DA4 .... 47 C7
Millstone Mews DA4 .... 47 C8
Millstream ME13 ...... 156 D2
Mill Stream Pl TN9 .... 127 D3
MILL STREET 97 E7
Mill Vale BR2 .... 42 A7
Mill View TN11 .... 111 D1
Mill Wlk ME16 .... 99 A3
Millwood Cl 8 ME4 .... 53 F4
Millwood Ho 1 SE28... 2 D3
Millwood Rd BR5 .... 44 C6
Milne Gdns SE9 .... 11 E2
Milne Ho 8 SE18 .... 1 F2
Milner Rd ME7 .... 54 D7
Milners ME17 .... 117 F6
Milner Wlk SE9 .... 29 D7
Milroy Ave DA11 .... 35 E6
Milstead Cl ME14 ..... 100 C5
Milsted Rd ME8 .... 55 C3
MILTON 19 D1
Milton Ave
Badgers Mount TN14 ... 59 A3
Cliffe Woods ME3 .... 39 B8
Gravesend DA12 .... 36 C7
Milton Ct
Gravesend DA12 .... 36 C6
Kings Hill ME19 .... 97 A3
Milton Dr TN2 .... 159 D7
Milton Gdns
Tilbury RM18 .... 19 B6
Tonbridge TN9 .... 142 F7
Milton Hall Rd DA12 ... 36 D7
Milton Ho ME1 .... 14 E2
Milton Ho ME20 .... 97 B3
Milton Lodge 9 DA14 . 30 A4
Milton Pl DA12 .... 19 C1
Milton Rd
Bexley DA16 .... 12 F5
Erith DA17 .... 4 A2
Gillingham ME7 .... 54 C3
Gravesend DA12 .... 36 C8
Sevenoaks TN13 .... 91 E6
Swanscombe DA10 ..... 11 D8
Milton Rd Bsns Pk 4
DA12 .... 36 C8
Milton St
Maidstone ME16 .... 99 C2
Swanscombe DA10 ..... 17 D1
Milverton Way SE9 ..... 29 A4
Milward Wlk 14 SE18 . 12 A8
Mimosa Cl DA6 .... 58 C8
Mincers Cl ME5 .... 68 C2
Mineral St SE18 .... 2 E3
Minerva Cl DA14 .... 29 E4
Minerva Rd ME2 .... 53 A8
Ministry Way SE9 .... 28 F6
Minster Rd
Bromley BR1 .... 28 B1
Gillingham ME8 .... 55 C3
Minstrels Cl TN8 .... 122 C2
Mint Bsns Pk E16 .... 1 A8
Minters Orch TN15 ..... 95 B7
Miranda Ho 6 DA17 .... 4 A1
Mirfield St SE7 .... 1 D1
Miriam Ct DA14 .... 30 B4
Miriam Rd SE18 .... 2 E1
Mirror Path SE9 .... 28 C5
Miskin Cotts ME3 .... 22 B6
Miskin Rd
Dartford DA1 .... 32 D8
Hoo St Werburgh ME3 .. 40 E5
Miskin Way DA12 .... 36 D2
Mitchell Ave
Chatham ME4 .... 53 F2
Northfleet DA11 .... 35 D6
Mitchell Cl
Dartford DA1 .... 32 E6
Erith DA17 .... 4 C3
Lenham ME17 .... 120 C5
Woolwich SE2 .... 3 C2
Mitchell Rd
Kings Hill ME19 .... 96 F2
Orpington BR6 .... 57 F6
Mitchell Way 5 BR1 .. 42 A8
Mitchell Wlk
Newham E6 .... 1 F8
Swanscombe DA10 ..... 34 E8
Mitchem Ct TN15 .... 61 E3
Mitre Ct
9 Erith DA17 .... 4 A2
Tonbridge TN9 .... 127 C2
Mitre Rd ME1 .... 53 B4
Moatbridge Sch SE9 ... 11 D1
Moat Cl
Orpington BR6 .... 57 F4
Sevenoaks TN13 .... 91 D5
Moat Croft DA16 .... 13 C4

Moat Ct
  Eltham SE9. . . . . 11 F1
  Sidcup DA15 . . . . 29 F5
Moat Farm TN2 . . . . 173 A7
Moat Farm Rd ME3 . . . . . . 24 D6
Moat La
  Cowden TN8 . . . . 155 E7
  Erith DA8 . . . . 15 A6
Moat Rd TN27 . . . . 151 B5
Mockbeggar La TN17,
  TN27 . . . . 181 C4
Model Farm Cl SE9 . . . . . . 28 E5
Modest Cnr TN4 . . . . 142 E1
MODEST CORNER 142 E1
Moira Rd SE9 . . . . 11 F3
Molash Rd BR5 . . . . 38 C5
Molehill Copse Prim Sch
  ME15 . . . . 116 D7
Molescroft SE9 . . . . 29 C5
Molescroft Way TN9 . . . . 142 F7
Moles Mead TN8 . . . . 122 C2
Mollison Rise DA12 . . . . . . 36 E3
Molyneux Almshouses 1
  TN4 . . . . 158 B4
Molyneux Cl TN4 . . . . 158 F4
Molyneux Park Gdns
  TN4 . . . . 158 F4
Molyneux Park Rd TN4 . . 158 F4
Monarch Cl
  Chatham ME5 . . . . 68 A6
  Tilbury RM18 . . . . 19 B5
Monarch Dr E16 . . . . 1 D8
Monarch Rd 3 DA17 . . . . . . 4 A3
Monarch Terr TN9 . . . . 97 C3
Monckton's Ave ME14 . . . 99 F7
Monckton's Dr ME14 . . . . 99 E7
Monckton's La ME14 . . . . . 99 F7
Moncrieff Cl 5 E6 . . . . 1 E7
Moncrief ME14 . . . . 101 B4
Monds Cotts TN14 . . . . 90 E3
Monica James Ho 2
  DA14 . . . . 30 A5
Monkdown ME15 . . . . 101 A1
Monk Dr E16 . . . . 1 A6
Monkreed Villas DA3 . . . . 49 D4
Monks Cl SE2 . . . . 3 D2
MONK'S HILL 168 C7
Monks La
  Limpsfield TN8 . . . . 121 E6
  Newbury's TN5 . . . . 185 B8
Monks Orch DA1 . . . . 32 D6
Monks Way BR5 . . . . 43 D1
Monk's Well 13 DA9 . . . . . 17 C3
Monks Wlk
  Northfleet DA13 . . . . 35 A2
  6 Tonbridge TN9 . . . . . . 143 B8
Monkton Rd
  Bexley DA16 . . . . 12 F5
  Borough Green TN15 . . . . . 94 F7
Monkwood Cl ME1 . . . . 67 B8
Monmouth Cl
  Bexley DA16 . . . . 13 A3
  Gillingham ME8 . . . . 55 D2
Monroe Way ME19 . . . . . . 97 D3
Monson Rd TN1 . . . . 159 B4
Monson Way 5 TN1 . . . . 159 B4
Montacute Gdns TN2 . . . 158 F2
Montacute Rd TN2 . . . . . 159 A1
Montague Ct 13 DA15 . . . 30 A5
Montague Pl BR8 . . . . 45 F5
Montague Terr 1 BR2 . . . 42 A5
Montbelle Prim Sch SE9 . 29 A4
Montbelle Rd SE9 . . . . 29 B5
Montbretia Cl BR5 . . . . 44 C5
Montcalm Cl BR2 . . . . 42 A3
Montcalm Rd SE7 . . . . 11 D7
Monteith Cl TN3 . . . . 158 A3
Monterey Cl DA5 . . . . 31 C6
Montfort Dr ME19 . . . . 97 A2
Montfort Rd
  Chatham ME5 . . . . 67 F2
  Kemsing TN15 . . . . 76 E2
  Rochester ME2 . . . . 53 A8
Montgomery Ave ME5 . . 68 A7
Montgomery Cl
  2 Gravesend DA12 . . . . . 36 D4
  Sidcup DA15 . . . . 12 F1
Montgomery Rd
  Gillingham ME7 . . . . 54 C3
  Royal Tunbridge Wells
  TN4 . . . . 159 B7
  Sutton at Hone DA4 . . . . . . 47 D8
Montpelier Ave DA5 . . . . . 30 D8
Montpelier Gate ME16 . . . 90 F5
Montreal Rd
  Sevenoaks TN13 . . . . 91 E4
  Tilbury RM18 . . . . 19 A5
Montrose Ave
  Bexley DA16 . . . . 12 E4
  Gillingham ME5 . . . . 54 E2
  Sidcup DA15 . . . . 30 A6
Montrose Cl DA16 . . . . 12 F4
Mont St Aignan Way 6
  TN8 . . . . 122 C1
Mont St Aignan Way
  TN8 . . . . 138 C8
Monypenny TN17 . . . . 191 F3
Monypenny Cl TN11 . . . . 128 D8
Moon Ct SE12 . . . . 11 A1
MOON'S GREEN 199 A3
Moon's La FN7 . . . . 138 A1
Moonstone Dr ME5 . . . . . . 68 B2
Moorcroft Gdns BR2 . . . . 42 E4

Moorden La TN11 . . . . 125 A1
Moordown SE18 . . . . 12 B6
Moore Ave
  Grays RM20 . . . . 17 E8
  Tilbury RM18 . . . . 19 B5
Moore Cl DA2 . . . . 33 D6
Moorelan Rd 1 BR1 . . . . . 42 A8
Moore Rd DA10 . . . . 17 E1
Moore St ME2 . . . . 53 A8
Moorfield Rd BR6 . . . . 44 A2
Moorhead Way SE3 . . . . . . 11 B4
Moorhen Cl DA8 . . . . 15 B7
Moor Hill TN18 . . . . 194 F8
Moorhouse Cotts TN16 . 105 A7
Moorhouse Rd RH8,
  TN16 . . . . 105 A6
Mooring Rd ME1 . . . . 53 D1
Moorings The E16 . . . . 1 C8
Moor La TN8 . . . . 138 A4
Moorlands BR7 . . . . 29 B1
Moor Park Cl ME8 . . . . 70 A8
Moor Rd The TN14 . . . . 92 C7
Moorside Rd BR1 . . . . 28 A4
Moor St ME8 . . . . 70 B8
MOOR STREET 70 B7
Moor The TN18 . . . . 194 F8
Morants Court Cross
  TN14 . . . . 75 C1
Morants Court Rd TN13 . 91 C8
Morden Cl SE3 . . . . 11 A5
Morden Road Mews SE3 . 11 A5
Morden St ME1 . . . . 53 C4
Morebreddis Cotts TN17. 164 A1
Morel Cl TN13 . . . . 92 B5
Morella Wlk ME17 . . . . . . 120 C5
Morello Cl BR8 . . . . 45 D5
Morement Rd ME3 . . . . 40 D6
More Park RC Prim Sch
  ME19 . . . . 97 D8
Moreton Cl DA1 . . . . 14 E4
Moreton Ind Est BR8 . . . . 46 A4
Morewood Cl TN13 . . . . . . 91 F4
Morgan Dr DA9 . . . . 33 E8
Morgan Rd
  Bromley BR1 . . . . 28 A1
  Rochester ME2 . . . . 53 A8
Morgan St E16 . . . . 1 A8
Morhen Cl ME6 . . . . 81 E7
Moriarty Cl BR1 . . . . 43 B5
Morland Ave DA1 . . . . 15 B2
Morland Dr
  Lamberhurst TN3 . . . . 176 B5
  Rochester ME2 . . . . 53 A8
Morland Ho 4 BR7 . . . . . . 43 A8
Morley Bsns Ctr TN9 . . . 127 D1
Morley Cl BR6 . . . . 57 B8
Morley Dr TN12 . . . . 163 A6
Morley Rd
  Chislehurst BR7 . . . . 43 C8
  Tonbridge TN9 . . . . 127 D1
Morne Cotts TN14 . . . . 75 F8
Morning Cross Cotts ME3 22 B4
Mornington Ave BR1 . . . . 42 C6
Mornington Cl TN16 . . . . 72 D2
Mornington Ct DA5 . . . . . . 31 D7
Morris Cl
  Maidstone ME17 . . . . 116 D5
  Orpington BR6 . . . . 57 E7
  West Malling ME19 . . . . . . 81 F1
Morris Gdns DA1 . . . . 16 A2
Morry La
  Chartway Street ME17 . . . 118 D1
  Ulcombe ME17 . . . . 135 D7
Morston Gdns SE9 . . . . 28 F4
Mortgramit Sq SE18. . . . . . 2 A3
Mortimer Rd
  Biggin Hill TN16 . . . . 72 C7
  Erith DA8 . . . . 14 D8
  Orpington BR6 . . . . 44 A1
Mortimers Ave ME3 . . . . . 39 A8
Mortlake Rd E16 . . . . 1 B7
Mortley Cl TN9 . . . . 127 C2
Morton Cl
  Maidstone ME15 . . . . 116 D6
  Swanley BR8 . . . . 45 E7
Morvale Cl DA17 . . . . 3 F2
Moselle Rd TN16 . . . . 72 F1
Mosquito Rd ME19 . . . . . . 96 F3
Mossbank ME5 . . . . 68 A3
Mosslea Rd
  Bromley BR2 . . . . 42 D4
  Orpington BR6 . . . . 57 C7
Moss Way DA2 . . . . 33 D4
Mossy Glade ME8 . . . . 69 E6
Mostyn Rd ME14 . . . . 100 C4
Mosul Way BR2 . . . . 42 E3
Mosyer Dr BR5 . . . . 58 D8
Mote Ave ME15 . . . . 100 B3
Mote Cotts TN15 . . . . 110 A7
Mote Hall Villas ME14 . . 101 C4
Mote Pk ME15 . . . . 100 D2
Mote Rd
  Maidstone ME15 . . . . 100 A3
  Shipbourne TN15, TN11 . 110 A7
Mote The DA3 . . . . 62 F8
Motherwell Way RM20 . . 17 A8
Motorway Ind Est ME20 . 83 C2
MOTTINGHAM 28 D6
Mottingham Gdns SE9 . . 28 E7
Mottingham La
  Bromley SE12, SE9 . . . . . . 28 C7
  Eltham SE12 . . . . 28 C8

Mottingham Prim Sch
  SE9. 28 F5
Mottingham Rd SE9 . . . . . 28 F5
Mottingham Sta SE9 . . . . 28 F7
Mottisfont Rd SE2 . . . . 3 B2
MOTT'S HILL 171 A3
Mouat Ct ME5 . . . . 68 A3
Mouchotte Cl TN16 . . . . . 72 C7
Moultain Hill BR8 . . . . 46 A5
Mound The SE9 . . . . 11 A1
Mountain Cl 6 TN15 . . . . 78 F3
Mount Ave ME18 . . . . 114 A1
Mountbatten Ave
  Chatham ME5 . . . . 68 A7
  Higham ME3 . . . . 38 C4
Mountbatten Cl SE18 . . . . 12 E8
Mount Castle La ME17 . . 120 F1
Mount Cl
  Bromley BR1 . . . . 42 E8
  Sevenoaks TN13 . . . . 91 F4
Mount Culver Ave DA. . . . 30 D2
Mount Dr
  Bexley DA16 . . . . 13 E2
  Maidstone ME14 . . . . 101 B4
Mount Edgcumbe Rd
  TN4 . . . . 159 A3
MOUNT EPHRAIM 158 F4
Mount Ephraim TN4 . . . . 159 A4
Mount Ephraim Ct TN4 . 159 A4
Mount Ephraim Rd TN1 . 159 A4
Mountfield TN15 . . . . 95 A7
Mountfield Cl DA13 . . . . . . 63 F2
Mountfield Ct 4 TN1 . . . 159 B3
Mountfield Gdns TN1 . . . 159 B3
Mountfield Pk TN9 . . . . . 143 C8
Mountfield Rd TN1 . . . . . 159 B3
Mountfield Way 1 BR5 . . 44 C5
Mount Harry Rd TN13 . . . 92 B4
Mounthurst Rd BR2 . . . . . 42 A2
Mountjoy Cl SE2 . . . . 3 B4
Mouts La
  Hartlip ME9 . . . . 70 D4
  Maidstone ME14 . . . . 101 B4
Mount Lodge ME1 . . . . . . 53 B2
Mount Pleasant
  Biggin Hill TN16 . . . . 72 D2
  Chatham ME5 . . . . 54 B3
  Durgates TN5 . . . . 184 E5
  Forstal ME20 . . . . 83 A3
  Ide Hill TN14 . . . . 106 F4
  Lamberhurst TN3 . . . . 175 E6
  Paddock Wood TN12 . . . . 145 F7
  Tenterden TN30 . . . . 193 C8
  The Moor TN18 . . . . 194 F8
  Tonbridge TN11 . . . . 126 D6
Mount Pleasant Ave 2
  ME14 . . . . 101 A5
Mount Pleasant La TN3 . 176 A6
Mount Pleasant Pl SE18 . . 2 A2
Mount Pleasant Rd
  Dartford DA1 . . . . 15 F1
  Royal Tunbridge Wells
  TN1 . . . . 159 A3
  Sevenoaks Weald TN14 . . 108 B2
Mount Pleasant Terr
  ME17 . . . . 119 E2
Mount Pleasant Wlk DA5 14 C2
Mount Rd
  Bexley DA6 . . . . 13 E2
  Chatham ME4 . . . . 53 D7
  Crayford DA1 . . . . 14 F1
  Rochester ME1 . . . . 53 B2
Mountsfield Cl ME16 . . . . . 99 D5
Mounts Hill TN17 . . . . 190 B7
MOUNT SION 159 A2
Mount Sion TN1 . . . . 159 A2
Mounts La TN17 . . . . 192 A3
Mounts Rd DA9 . . . . 17 B1
Mount The
  Bexley DA6 . . . . 14 B2
  3 Chislehurst BR7 . . . . . . 43 A8
Mount View Ct 3 ME4 . . 53 F3
Mountview Rd BR6 . . . . 44 A2
MOWSHURST 122 E3
Moyle Cl ME8 . . . . 69 D4
Mozart Ct ME4 . . . . 53 E3
Muir Rd ME16 . . . . 100 A2
Muir St E16 . . . . 1 E5
Mulbarton Ct BR7 . . . . 29 D2
Mulberry Cl
  Gillingham ME7 . . . . 69 A4
  Greenwich SE7 . . . . 11 D8
  Meopham Station DA13. . . 50 B3
  Royal Tunbridge Wells
  TN4 . . . . 143 D1
Mulberry Ct
  Bexley DA16 . . . . 12 F5
  Maidstone ME14 . . . . 100 B5
Mulberry Gdns TN30 . . . 193 B8
Mulberry Rd DA11 . . . . . . 35 E4
Mulberry Way DA17 . . . . . . 4 C4
Mulgrave Rd 13 SE18 . . . . 1 F2
Mulgrave Prim Sch 10
  SE18 . . . . 2 A2
Mulgrave Rd SE18 . . . . 2 A2
Mullein Ct 7 RM17 . . . . . . 18 D8
Mullender Ct DA12 . . . . . . 37 A7
Muller Ho SE18 . . . . 2 A1
Multon Rd TN15 . . . . 61 E4
MUNDAY BOIS 153 F8
Munday Bois Cotts TN27. 153 F8
Munday Bois Rd TN27 . . 137 E1
Munday La TN9 . . . . 127 D1
Munday Rd E16 . . . . 1 A7
Munday Works Est TN9 . 127 C1

Munford Dr DA10 . . . . 34 E8
Mungeam Ho ME1 . . . . 53 C4
Mungo Park Rd DA12 . . . . 36 D3
Mungo Park Way BR5 . . . 44 D2
Munnery Way ME7 . . . . . . 57 B8
Munnings Ho E16 . . . . 1 B5
Munn's La ME9 . . . . 70 E6
Munsgore La ME9 . . . . 71 A3
Murchison Ave DA5 . . . . . 30 E7
Murrain Dr ME15 . . . . 101 A1
Murray Ave BR1 . . . . 42 B7
Murray Bsns Ctr BR5 . . . . 44 B6
Murray Cl E28 . . . . 2 E5
Murray Ho 15 SE18 . . . . 1 F2
Murray Lodge TN2 . . . . . 159 D2
Murray Rd
  Orpington BR5 . . . . 44 B6
  Rochester ME2 . . . . 53 C8
Murray Sq E16 . . . . 1 B6
Murton-Neale Cl 3
  TN18 . . . . 189 A2
Muscovy Ho DA18. . . . . 3 E4
Muskerry Ct TN4 . . . . 158 B4
Musket La
  Eyhorne Street ME17. . . . 102 C2
  Leeds ME17 . . . . 102 A2
Mussenden La DA3, DA4 . 47 E3
Mustang Rd ME19 . . . . . . 96 F3
Mycenae Rd SE3 . . . . 11 A8
Mynn Cres ME14 . . . . 101 A4
Myra St SE2 . . . . 3 A2
Myrtle Alley SE18 . . . . 2 A3
Myrtle Cl DA8 . . . . 14 E6
Myrtle Cres ME5 . . . . 67 F5
Myrtledene Rd SE2. . . . . . . 3 A1
Myrtle Pl DA2 . . . . 33 D8
Myrtle Rd DA1 . . . . 32 D6

N

Nadine St SE7 . . . . 1 C1
Nagpur Ho 4 ME15 . . . . . 116 E5
Nag's Head La
  Bexley DA16 . . . . 13 B4
  Rochester ME1 . . . . 53 B4
Nairn Ct RM18 . . . . 18 F5
Nansen Rd DA12 . . . . 36 D4
Napier Cl
  6 Lewisham SE12 . . . . . . 28 B5
  Maidstone ME14 . . . . 99 F7
Napier Prim Sch ME7 . . . 54 D4
Napier Rd
  Bromley BR2 . . . . 42 B5
  Erith DA17 . . . . 3 F2
  Gillingham ME7 . . . . 54 D4
  Northfleet DA11 . . . . 35 F7
  Royal Tunbridge Wells
  TN2 . . . . 159 D2
Napoleon Dr TN2 . . . . 148 D5
Napoleon Wlk ME17. . . . . 120 C5
Napwood Cl ME8 . . . . 69 D6
Nares Rd ME8 . . . . 69 D4
Narrow Boat Cl SE28 . . . . . 2 E3
Narrow Way BR2 . . . . 42 E3
Naseby Ct DA14 . . . . 29 F4
NASH 56 A4
Nash Bank DA13 . . . . 49 F7
Nash Cl ME5 . . . . 68 C2
Nash Cotts 16 DA14 . . . . . 30 A5
Nash Croft DA1 . . . . 35 E4
Nashenden Farm La ME1 . 67 A8
Nashenden La ME1. . . . . . 52 F1
Nash Gn BR1 . . . . 28 A2
Nash La BR2 . . . . 56 A4
Nash St DA13 . . . . 50 A7
NASH STREET 50 A7
Nassau Path 8 SE28 . . . . . 3 C5
Natal Rd ME4 . . . . 54 A3
Nathan Way SE28, SE18 . . 2 E3
Naylor's Cotts ME7 . . . . . . 69 B1
Neale St ME4 . . . . 53 F2
Neal Rd TN15 . . . . 61 E5
Neatscourt Rd E6 . . . . 1 D8
Neills Rd TN3 . . . . 175 D2
Nellington Ct TN4 . . . . . . 158 B4
Nellington Rd TN3, TN4 . 158 B4
Nelson Ave ME19 . . . . 127 A1
Nelson Cl TN16 . . . . 72 E2
Nelson Ct ME5 . . . . 54 C1
Nelson Ho
  8 Maidstone ME15 . . . . 116 F5
  Swanscombe DA9 . . . . 17 D2
Nelson Mandela Rd SE3 . 11 C4
Nelson Rd
  Bromley BR2 . . . . 42 C5
  Dartford DA1 . . . . 15 C1
  Erith DA17 . . . . 3 F1
  Gillingham ME7 . . . . 54 D4
  Northfleet DA11 . . . . 35 F6
  Royal Tunbridge Wells
  TN2 . . . . 159 D2
  Sidcup DA14 . . . . 30 A4
  Wouldham ME1 . . . . 66 C5
Nelson St E6 . . . . 1 F7
Nepicar Farm ∗ TN15 . . . 79 D1
Nepicar La TN15 . . . . 79 D3
Neptune Bsns Pk ME2 . . . 53 E7
Neptune Cl ME2 . . . . 53 E7
Neptune Way 3 E6 . . . . . . 1 E7
Neptune Wlk DA8 . . . . 4 A2
Nesbit Rd SE9 . . . . 11 D3
Nesbitt Ho DA6 . . . . 14 B2
Ness Rd DA8 . . . . 15 D8
Nestor Ct ME18 . . . . 114 A8
Nethercombe Ho 3 SE3 . 11 A8
Nethewode Ct DA17. . . . . . 4 B3
Netley Cl ME14 . . . . 100 D4

NETTLESTEAD 113 D6
Nettlestead Cl TN12 . . . . 146 A7
Nettlestead Ct
  Nettlestead ME18 . . . . 113 C5
  Paddock Wood TN12 . . . . 146 A8
NETTLESTEAD GREEN . . 113 B2
Nettlestead La ME18 . . . . 113 A6
Nettlestead Oast TN12 . . 146 A8
Nevill Cl ME19 . . . . 81 C1
Neville Cl
  Maidstone ME14 . . . . 100 B8
  Sidcup DA15 . . . . 29 F4
Neville Rd ME4 . . . . 53 E2
Nevill Gate TN2 . . . . 159 B1
Nevill Ground The
  (Tunbridge Wells CC)
  TN1 . . . . 159 B1
Nevill Lodge TN2 . . . . 159 C4
Nevill Pk TN4 . . . . 158 E3
Nevill Pl ME6 . . . . 82 A7
Nevill Rd ME6 . . . . 82 A7
Nevill Ridge TN4 . . . . 158 D3
Nevill St TN2 . . . . 159 A2
Nevill Terr TN2 . . . . 158 F2
New Acres Rd SE28 . . . . . . 2 F4
Newark Cl 1 ME2 . . . . 53 B7
Newark Knok 2 E6 . . . . 2 A7
Newark Rd ME2 . . . . 53 B7
NEW ASH GREEN 62 F8
New Ash Green Prim Sch
  DA3 . . . . 62 F8
NEW BARN 49 A7
Newbarn La TN14, TN16 . . 73 C2
New Barn Pk BR5 . . . . 45 E8
New Barn Rd
  Northfleet DA13. . . . . 35 C3
  Sutton Valence ME17,
  TN12 . . . . 134 C2
  Swanley BR8 . . . . 45 F8
New Barns Rd ME14 . . . . 100 A8
New Barn St E13 . . . . 1 B8
New Bassetts Cotts
  TN12 . . . . 163 B5
New Beacon Sch TN14 . . 107 F8
Newbery Rd DA8 . . . . 14 F6
Newborough Ct TN10 . . . 127 C6
Newbridge Pk TN12 . . . . 130 A1
New Brompton Coll ME7 . 54 B4
Newbury Ave ME16 . . . . . . 99 C6
Newbury Cl
  Cliffe Woods ME3 . . . . 39 B8
  Dartford DA1 . . . . 33 B8
Newbury Cotts TN5 . . . . . 185 B8
Newbury Ct DA14 . . . . 29 F4
Newbury La TN5 . . . . 185 C8
Newbury Rd BR2 . . . . 42 A2
NEWBURY'S 185 B8
NEW CHARLTON 1 C2
Newchurch Rd ME15 . . . . 100 A1
New College of Cobham
  DA12 . . . . 51 A5
Newcomen Rd TN4 . . . . . 159 A5
New Cotts
  Bean DA2 . . . . 34 B5
  Shipbourne TN11 . . . . 110 D5
  The Moor TN18 . . . . 194 B7
  Tilbury RM18 . . . . 19 B8
New Covenant Pl 4 ME1 . 53 D4
New Ct 3 TN9 . . . . 127 C2
New Cut ME15 . . . . 115 D7
New Cut Rd ME14 . . . . . . 100 D5
New Delhi Ho 4 ME15 . . 116 E5
NEW ELTHAM 29 C6
New Eltham Sta SE9 . . . . 29 C7
New Farm Ave BR2 . . . . . . 42 A5
New Ferry App SE18 . . . . . . 2 A3
New Hall Farm La ME3 . . 25 B6
NEWHAM 1 F8
Newham College of FE
  E16. . . . . 1 C1
Newham L Ctr E16 . . . . 1 C8
Newhaven Gdns SE9 . . . . 11 D3
Newhaven La 4 E16 . . . . . . 1 A8
NEW HOUSE 35 F6
New House La DA11 . . . . . 36 A6
Newhouse Terr TN8 . . . . . 122 C3
NEW HYTHE 82 B4
New Hythe Bsns Pk ME20 82 B3
New Hythe La ME20 . . . . . 82 B3
New Hythe Sta ME20 . . . . 82 C4
Newick Cl DA5 . . . . 31 E8
Newing Gn BR1 . . . . 28 D1
NEWINGTON 71 A6
Newington CE Prim Sch
  ME9. 71 B7
Newington Ct TN5 . . . . . . 186 E1
Newington Ent Ctr ME9 . 71 B8
Newington Ho 9 BR5 . . . . 44 D1
Newington Ind Est ME9 . 70 F6
Newington Sta ME9 . . . . . 71 A6
Newington Wlk ME14 . . 100 C6
New Inn Cotts TN15 . . . . 115 C7
Newitt Rd ME3 . . . . 40 E5
NEWLAND GREEN 153 D8
Newland Green La TN27 153 D8
Newlands TN3 . . . . 158 D1
Newlands Cl SE9 . . . . 12 A1
Newlands Farm Rd ME3 . 24 B4
Newlands La DA13 . . . . . . 63 F1
Newlands Lodge DA8 . . . . 14 D8
Newlands Rd TN4 . . . . 159 B7
Newlands Rise TN4 . . . . . 159 A6

Newland St E16 1 F5
Newlands Way TN4 159 B7
New Line Learning Academy ME15 116 B6
Newling Cl E6 1 F7
New Lydenburg Commercial Est SE7 1 C3
New Lydenburg St SE7 1 C3
Newlyn Cl BR6 58 A6
Newlyn Ct 1 ME14 100 A4
Newlyn Dr TN12 149 F5
Newlyn Rd DA16 12 F5
Newman Ct 1 BR1 42 A8
Newman Ho SE18 12 A7
Newman Rd BR1 42 A8
Newman's Rd DA11 35 F6
Newmarket Gn SE9 28 D8
Newmarsh Rd SE28 2 F5
New Mill Rd BR5 44 C8
Newnham Cl ME8 55 C2
Newnham Lodge DA17 4 A1
Newnhams Cl BR1 42 F6
Newnham St ME4 54 B3
New Pond Rd TN17 190 D6
Newports BR8 45 D2
New Pound La ME18 96 C1
New Rd
Bexley DA16 13 B5
Burham ME1 66 F1
Chatham ME4 53 F4
Cliffe ME3 22 A4
Cranbrook TN17 179 B4
Ditton ME20 82 C1
East Malling ME19 98 A8
Egerton TN27 137 F3
Erith SE2 3 D1
Fordcombe TN11 141 A1
Gravesend DA11 19 B1
Grays RM17 18 B8
Headcorn TN27 151 D5
Hextable BR8 31 F1
Langley ME17 117 C5
Limpsfield RH8 104 B5
Meopham Station DA13 49 F4
Orpington BR6 44 A2
Paddock Wood TN12 146 A6
Rochester ME1 53 D4
Sundridge TN14 90 E2
Sutton at Hone DA4 47 D7
Swanley BR8 45 F6
New Road Ave ME4 53 E4
New Road Bsns Est ME20 98 B8
New Road Hill BR2, BR4 56 F2
New Road Prim Sch 4 ME4 54 A3
Newry Rd ME3 40 B8
New Sch at West Heath The TN13 108 B6
New St
Chatham ME4 53 E3
New Street TN15 63 D4
Westerham TN16 105 C8
New Stairs ME4 53 F6
Newstead Ave BR6 57 E8
Newstead Wood Sch for Girls BR6 57 D7
NEW STREET 63 D5
New Street Hill BR1 28 C3
New Street Rd DA13, TN15 63 C6
New Swan Yd 8 DA12 19 B1
New Tavern Fort★ DA12 19 C1
Newton Abbot Rd DA11 35 F6
Newton Ave TN10 127 E7
Newton Cl
Chatham ME5 68 C2
1 Maidstone ME16 99 E3
Newton Ct 4 BR1 42 E6
Newton Gdns TN12 145 F7
Newton Ho
Swanscombe DA9 17 D2
Woolwich SE2 3 C1
Newton Rd
Bexley DA16 13 A4
Royal Tunbridge Wells TN1 159 B4
Tilbury RM18 19 A5
Newton's Ct DA9 16 D3
Newton Terr BR2 42 D3
Newton Willows TN3 171 C7
NEWTOWN 139 D4
NEW TOWN
Dartford 16 A1
Halling 66 A6
West Malling 97 A8
Newtown Cotts TN12 149 E6
New Town Cotts TN11 125 A3
New Villas ME15 115 C7
New Wharf Rd TN9 127 B1
New Wlk 4 TN15 78 F3
New Years La BR6, TN14 74 A5
Niagara Cl ME19 97 B3
Nicholas Cl ME16 99 A3
Nicholas Ct SE12 28 A7
Nicholas Stacey Ho 4 SE7 1 B1
Nichol La BR1 28 A1
Nicholson Ho SE18 11 E7
Nickelby Cl SE28 3 C7
Nicklaus Dr ME5 67 F3
Nickleby Cl ME1 53 C2
Nickleby Rd DA12 37 A7
Nicola Terr DA7 13 E6
Nicolson Rd BR5 44 D2
Nicolson Way TN13 92 D5
Nigeria Rd SE7 11 D7
Nightingale Cl
Biggin Hill TN16 72 C4
Gillingham ME8 69 E6
Nightingale Cl *continued*
Larkfield ME20 81 F2
Northfleet DA11 35 E4
Nightingale Cnr BR5 44 D5
Nightingale Ct ME2 52 C6
Nightingale Gr 3 DA1 16 A3
Nightingale Ho SE18 2 A1
Nightingale La
Bromley BR1 42 D7
Goathurst Common TN14 107 B5
Nightingale Pl SE18 12 B8
Nightingale Prim Sch SE18 2 B1
Nightingale Rd
Kemsing TN15 76 E2
Orpington BR5 43 C3
Nightingales The
Royal Tunbridge Wells TN4 159 A5
Sissinghurst TN27 180 F8
Nightingale Vale SE18 12 A8
Nightingale Way
Newham E6 1 E8
Swanley BR8 45 E6
Nile Path 6 SE18 12 A8
Nile Rd ME7 54 C4
Nimrod Ho E16 1 B8
Nine Acres Rd ME2 52 B3
Nine Elms Gr DA11 36 A8
Nine Hams Rd TN16 88 D6
Nineveh La TN17, TN18 189 E6
Ninhams Wood BR6 57 A6
Nita Ct SE12 28 A7
Nithdale Rd SE18 12 C7
Niven Cl ME3 39 C3
Nizels La TN11 125 F8
No 1 St SE18 2 B3
NOAH'S ARK 93 A8
Noah's Ark TN15 77 B1
Noble Tree Cross TN11 126 B6
Noble Tree Rd TN11 126 B6
Noel Terr 15 DA14 30 B4
NOKE STREET 39 B4
Nook The ME18 113 F2
Norah La ME3 38 B3
Nore Cl ME7 54 E1
Norfield Rd DA2 31 D3
Norfolk Cl
Chatham ME5 68 C3
Dartford DA1 16 A2
Gillingham ME8 55 D2
Norfolk Cres DA15 29 E8
Norfolk Gdns DA7 13 F6
Norfolk Pl DA16 13 A5
Norfolk Rd
Gravesend DA12 36 D8
Maidstone ME15 116 C8
Royal Tunbridge Wells TN1 159 B2
Tonbridge TN9 127 A1
Norham Ct 25 DA2 16 B1
Norheads La TN16 72 B2
Norlands Cres BR7 43 B8
Norlands Gate BR7 43 B8
Norman Cl
Gillingham ME8 69 B5
Kemsing TN15 76 D2
Maidstone ME14 100 B6
Orpington BR6 57 C7
Rochester ME2 52 F4
Norman Ct TN8 122 B2
Normandy Prim Sch DA7 14 D6
Normandy Terr E16 1 B7
Normandy Way DA8 14 E6
Normanhurst Ave DA7, DA16 13 D6
Normanhurst Rd
Borough Green TN15 95 A7
Orpington BR5 44 B7
Norman Par DA14 30 D6
Norman Rd
Dartford DA1 32 E7
Erith DA17 4 B3
Royal Tunbridge Wells TN1 159 B5
Snodland ME6 82 A6
West Malling ME19 97 B8
Norman Rise TN17 179 D4
Normans Cl DA11 36 A8
Norman St TN14 106 F5
Norman Villas 4 TN18 188 F2
Norreys Rd ME8 69 E7
Norrington Rd ME15 116 B6
Norris Cl 15 TN18 189 A2
Norris Ho 14 SE7 11 C8
Norris Way DA1 14 F4
Norstead Gdns TN4 159 B8
Norsted La BR6 74 B8
Northall Rd DA7 14 C5
North Ash Rd DA3 62 F7
North Bank Cl ME2 52 F5
North Beckton Prim Sch E6 1 F8
North Borough Jun Sch ME14 100 A6
Northbourne BR2 42 A2
Northbourne Rd ME8 55 B4
North Cl DA6 13 D3
Northcote Rd
Northfleet DA11 35 F7
Rochester ME2 53 A7
Sidcup DA14 29 E4
2 Tonbridge TN9 127 B1
NORTH CRAY 30 F5
North Cray Rd DA14 30 E4
North Cres ME17 115 D4
North Ct 4 BR1 42 B8
North Ct 2 ME15 100 A1
North Dane Way ME5 68 C4
Northdown ME9 86 D8
North Down TN12 149 E4
Northdown Bsns Pk ME17 120 F6
Northdown Cl
Lenham ME17 120 F6
Maidstone ME14 100 B7
Paddock Wood TN12 145 F6
Northdown Rd
Bexley DA16 13 C5
Kemsing TN15 76 E2
Longfield DA3 48 E7
North Downs Bsns Pk TN13 75 C3
North Downs Terr ME19 80 A5
North Down View ME17 119 F6
North Dr BR6 57 E6
NORTH END 14 F6
North End Farm DA13 34 F4
North End La BR6 57 B2
Northend Prim Sch DA8 14 F6
Northend Rd DA8 14 F6
North End Trad Est DA8 14 E6
North Farm La TN2 143 E2
North Farm Rd TN2 159 C8
Northfield DA3 48 F6
Northfield Ave BR5 44 C3
Northfield Cl BR1 42 E8
Northfields
Maidstone ME16 98 F2
Speldhurst TN3 158 A8
NORTHFLEET 18 D1
Northfleet Cl ME14 100 C5
NORTHFLEET GREEN 35 C3
Northfleet Ind Est DA11 17 F3
Northfleet Sch for Girls DA11 35 D6
Northfleet Sta DA11 18 B1
Northfleet Tech Coll DA11 35 D7
North Folly Rd ME15 114 F3
North Frith Pk TN11 110 F1
Northgate ME1 53 C6
North Glade The DA5 30 F7
Northgrove Rd 9 TN18 188 F2
NORTH HALLING 66 A8
North Hill Rd TN18 188 C1
NORTHIAM 197 C1
Northiam Sta★ TN31 197 C2
North Kent Ave DA11 18 C1
Northlands 5 BR1 42 C7
Northlands Ave BR6 57 E6
Northlands Cotts TN32 195 C1
Northleigh Cl ME15 116 A6
North Lockside Rd ME4 54 D8
North Meadow ME19 96 D7
North Meadow Cotts ME19 96 D7
Northolme Rise BR6 57 E8
Northover BR1 28 A4
North Pk SE9 12 A1
Northpoint 12 BR1 42 A8
Northpoint Bsns Est ME2 53 D8
North Pole La BR2 56 A4
North Pole Rd ME16, ME18 98 C2
North Pondside Rd ME4 54 A8
North Rd
Bromley BR1 42 B8
Chatham, Brompton ME4, ME7 54 A7
Chatham ME4 54 B8
Cliffe ME3 22 B6
Dartford DA1 15 A1
Erith DA17 4 B4
Goudhurst TN17 163 E1
Woolwich SE18 2 E2
Northridge Rd DA12 36 C5
North Riding DA3 49 D6
Northside Rd BR1 42 A8
North Side Three Rd ME4 54 C8
North St
Bexley DA7 14 A3
Biddenden TN27 168 A2
Bromley BR1 42 A8
Cowden TN8 155 A6
Dartford DA1 32 D8
Gravesend DA12 36 B8
Headcorn TN27 151 C5
Maidstone ME16 98 F2
Rochester ME2 53 B7
Royal Tunbridge Wells TN2 159 C3
Sutton Valence ME17 134 E8
Warmlake ME17 117 E1
NORTH STREET 24 E1
North Street Cotts ME17 134 E8
North Terr ME3 39 F6
Northumberland Ave
Bexley DA16 12 E4
Gillingham ME8 55 E1
Northumberland Cl DA8 14 C7
Northumberland Ct
Bexley DA8 14 C6
Maidstone ME15 116 D7
Northumberland Gdns BR1 43 A5
NORTHUMBERLAND HEATH 14 C7
Northumberland Heath Prim Sch DA8 14 B7
Northumberland Pk DA8 14 C7
Northumberland Rd
Istead Rise DA13 35 F1
Maidstone ME15 116 D8
Newham E6 1 E7
Northumberland Way DA8 14 D6
Northview BR8 45 E7
North View ME15 100 B1
Northview Ave RM18 19 A6
North View Cotts ME15 115 C7
North View Rd TN13, TN14 92 C6
Northward Hill Nature Reserve★ ME3 7 B2
North Way ME14 100 B7
North West Kent Coll (Dartford Campus) DA1 32 C6
North West Kent Coll (Gravesend Campus) DA12 36 F7
North West Kent Coll (Thameside Campus) DA12 19 F1
Northwood Ave ME23 23 E4
Northwood Dr 2 DA9 17 A1
Northwood Pl DA18 3 F3
Northwood Prim Sch DA18 3 F3
Northwood Rd TN10 127 C6
NORTH WOOLWICH 2 B4
North Woolwich Old Sta Mus★ E16 2 A4
North Woolwich Rd E16 1 A5
North Woolwich Rdbt E16 1 D5
Norton Cres TN10 127 B7
Norton Gr ME5 67 E3
Norton Rd
Five Wents ME17 117 D1
Royal Tunbridge Wells TN4 143 A1
Nortons La TN30 182 E5
Nortons Way TN12 145 B7
Norvic Ho DA8 14 F7
Norway Terr 4 ME14 100 A7
Norwich Ave TN10 127 D5
Norwich Cl ME2 52 D6
Norwood Cl ME3 22 B4
Norwood Ct 5 DA1 16 A3
Norwood La DA13 50 B3
Notre Dame RC Prim Sch SE18 12 B8
Nottidge Rd TN4 158 D1
Nottingham Ave
Maidstone ME15 116 D7
Newham E16 1 C7
Nottingham Wlk ME2 52 D6
Novar Cl BR6 43 F2
Novar Rd SE9 29 C7
Nower The TN14, TN16 89 F8
Nuffield Rd BR8 32 A2
Nugent Ind Pk BR5 44 C5
Nunappleton Way RH8 104 A3
Nunnery La TN11 156 F8
Nunnington Cl SE9 28 E5
Nuralite Ind Ctr ME3 38 A8
Nursery Ave
Bexley DA7 13 F4
Maidstone, Bearsted ME14 101 B3
Maidstone ME16 99 B6
Nursery Cl
Dartford DA2 33 C8
Flimwell TN5 187 B3
Orpington BR6 44 A2
Sevenoaks TN13 92 C5
Swanley BR8 45 C7
Tonbridge TN10 127 E4
Nursery Gdns
Chislehurst BR7 29 B2
Hoo St Werburgh ME3 40 E5
Nursery Gr DA11/DA12 36 B3
Nursery Ho DA4 47 C5
Nursery Pl TN13 91 D4
Nursery Rd
Ditton ME20 82 C1
Gillingham ME8 69 D8
Meopham Station DA13 50 A4
Paddock Wood TN12 145 F8
Royal Tunbridge Wells TN4 159 B8
Nursery The DA8 14 F7
Nurstead Ave DA3 49 D6
Nurstead Church La DA13 50 A5
Nurstead La DA3, DA13 49 D5
Nurstead Rd DA8 14 A7
Nutfield Cl ME5 68 B8
Nutfield Ct 7 BR1 42 A6
Nutfields TN15 94 B4
Nutfield Way BR6 57 B8
Nuthatch DA3 49 B7
Nuthatch Gdns SE28 2 D4
Nutley Cl BR8 45 F8
Nutmead Cl DA5 31 C7
Nuttall Ct BR5 44 B6
Nut Tree Cl BR6 58 D7
Nutwood Cl ME14 100 E4
Nuxley Rd DA17 4 A1
Nyanza St SE18 12 D8

O

OAD STREET 71 E1
Oak Apple Ct SE12 28 A7
Oakapple Ho 10 ME16 99 A3
Oakapple La ME16 99 A3
Oak Ave
Biddenden TN27 182 D7
Gillingham ME7 54 E6
Sevenoaks TN13 108 B7
Oakbrook Cl BR1 28 B4
Oak Cl
Crayford DA1 14 F3
Hoo St Werburgh ME3 40 E3
Oak Cotts TN8 123 B6
Oakcroft 3 SE12 28 B5
Oak Croft ME14 101 B4
Oak Ct BR1 42 F7
Oakdale La TN8 105 C2
Oakdale Rd TN4 158 F4
Oakdene Ave
Chislehurst BR7 29 A3
Erith DA8 14 C8
Oakdene Rd
Orpington BR5 44 A3
Sevenoaks TN13 92 A5
Oak Dr
Higham ME3 38 B4
Larkfield ME20 82 B2
Oak End Cl TN4 143 A2
Oakenden La TN8 140 C2
Oakenden Rd DA13 50 E1
Oakenholt Ho 1 SE2 3 D4
Oakes Cl E6 1 F7
Oak Farm Gdns TN27 151 D6
Oak Farm La TN15 63 E1
Oakfield
Hawkhurst TN18 188 F2
Rolvenden TN17 192 A1
Oakfield Cotts TN17 190 D4
Oakfield Court Rd TN2 159 C3
Oakfield La
Dartford DA1, DA2 32 B6
Orpington BR2 56 D6
Oakfield Park Rd DA1 32 D6
Oakfield Pl DA1 32 D6
Oakfield Prim Sch DA1 32 D6
Oakfield Rd
Marlpit Hill TN8 122 B5
Matfield TN12 161 D8
Oakfields TN13 92 B1
Oakham Dr BR2 42 A5
Oakhill House BR5 44 A8
Oakhill Rd BR6 57 F8
Oak Hill Rd TN13 92 A2
Oak Ho
6 Chatham ME5 67 F4
3 Royal Tunbridge Wells TN2 159 C7
13 Sidcup DA15 30 A5
Oakhouse Rd DA6 14 A2
Oakhurst Ave DA7 13 E7
Oakhurst Cl
Bromley BR7 42 F8
Chatham ME5 67 F3
Oakhurst Gdns DA7 13 E7
Oak La
Headcorn TN27 151 D5
Sevenoaks TN13 108 A8
Oakland Cl ME5 67 F3
Oaklands
Chislehurst BR7 29 D2
Cranbrook TN17 179 D4
Loose ME15 116 A8
Oaklands Ave DA15 29 F8
Oaklands Cl
Bexley DA6 13 F2
Orpington BR5 43 E3
West Kingsdown TN15 61 E4
Oaklands Ct BR6 57 C8
Oaklands Inf & Jun Sch ME5 67 F4
Oaklands Inf Sch TN16 72 C3
Oaklands Jun Sch TN16 72 C3
Oaklands La TN16 72 C5
Oaklands Rd
Bexley DA6 13 F2
Dartford DA2 33 C7
Groombridge TN3 171 B6
Hawkhurst TN18 189 A1
Northfleet DA11 35 F4
Oaklands Way TN11 126 F4
Oakland Villas TN3 171 B7
Oaklea Rd TN12 145 F6
Oakleigh Cl
Chatham ME5 67 E2
Swanley BR8 45 E6
Oakleigh Ct TN12 162 F6
Oakleigh Gdns BR6 57 E6
Oakleigh Park Ave BR7 43 A8
Oakley Cl
8 Newham E6 1 E7
West Thurrock RM20 17 C8
Oakley Ct DA1 33 B7
Oakley Dr
Orpington BR2 56 E7
Sidcup SE9 29 D7
Oakley Lodge SE12 28 A8
Oakley Pk DA5 30 C8
Oakley Rd BR2 56 E8
Oakley Sch
Pembury TN2 160 D5
Tonbridge TN10 127 B5
Oak Lodge
Royal Tunbridge Wells TN2 159 D2
Sevenoaks TN13 92 A3
Oak Lodge La TN16 89 D2
Oakmead
Meopham DA13 64 A8
Tonbridge TN10 127 C6
Oakmead Ave BR2 42 A3
Oakmere Rd SE2 13 A8
Oakmont Pl 6 BR6 43 D1
Oak Rd
Erith DA8 15 A5
Erith, Northumberland Heath DA8 14 C7
Five Oak Green TN12 145 B7
Gravesend DA12 36 C4
Grays RM17 18 C8
Hoo St Werburgh ME3 40 E3

Oak Rd *continued*
Orpington BR6 .... 58 A3
Rochester ME2 .... 52 E6
Royal Tunbridge Wells
TN2 .... 159 D7
Stone DA9 .... 16 E1
Westerham TN16 .... 89 D2
Oaks Bsns Village The
ME5 .... 68 C1
Oaks Dene ME5 .... 67 F1
Oaks Forstal TN18 ..... 196 C5
Oaks Rd TN30 .... 193 B8
Oaks The
Aylesford ME20 .... 82 E1
Dartford DA2 .... 16 B1
Smarden TN27 .... 152 F2
Swanley BR8 .... 45 E7
Woolwich SE18 .... 2 C1
Oak Tern **3** TN18 ... 188 F2
Oak Tree Ave
Maidstone ME16 .... 116 C7
Stone DA9 .... 33 F8
Oak Tree Cl
Marden TN12 .... 148 D5
Royal Tunbridge Wells
TN2 .... 159 A1
Oak Tree Gdns BR1 .... 28 B3
Oak Trees **10** TN18 ... 116 E5
Oak Trees Com Sch
ME15 .... 116 C7
Oakum Ct ME4 .... 54 B2
Oak View TN8 .... 122 B2
Oak Warren TN13 ...... 108 A6
Oakway Cl DA5 .... 13 E1
Oakways SE9 .... 12 B1
Oakwood Ave BR2 ..... 42 B6
Oakwood Cl
Chislehurst BR7 ...... 29 A2
Dartford DA1 .... 33 B7
Oakwood Ct
Maidstone ME16 .... 99 D3
Swanley BR8 .... 45 C7
Oakwood Dr
Bexley DA7 .... 14 C3
Sevenoaks TN13 .... 92 B4
Oakwood Gdns BR6 .... 57 C8
Oakwood Ind Est DA11 .. 18 A2
Oakwood Park Gram Sch
ME16 .... 99 C3
Oakwood Rise
Longfield DA3 .... 48 E6
Royal Tunbridge Wells
TN2 .... 159 E2
Oakwood Sch DA7 ..... 14 E3
Oasis The **3** BR1 .. 42 C7
Oast Cl ME18 .... 159 D7
Oast Cl ME18 .... 113 F1
Oastfield Cl ME3 .... 22 E1
Oastfield Ct TN15 ... 92 C2
Oast Ho The **9** ME8 .. 69 F8
Oast House Way BR5 .. 84 B5
Oast La TN10 .... 127 A4
Oasts The ME14 .... 101 C4
Oastview ME8 .... 70 A8
Oast View TN12 .... 163 A6
Oast Way DA3 .... 48 E3
Oatfield Cl TN17 .... 179 C5
Oatfield Dr TN17 .... 179 C5
Oatfield Rd BR6 ..... 85 A5
Occupation La SE18 .. 12 B6
Ocelot Ct **6** ME4 .. 54 B3
Ockham Dr BR5 .... 30 A1
OCKLEY 189 A3
Ockley Ct DA14 ...... 29 E5
Ockley La TN18 ...... 189 A3
Ockley Rd TN18 ...... 189 A2
Octavia Cl ME5 ...... 68 B3
Octavia Way **12** SE28 .. 3 B6
Odd Rise ME7 .... 55 A5
Odeon Ct **1** E16 .. 1 A8
Odeon Par SE9 .... 11 E3
Odiham Dr ME16 ...... 99 C7
Offenham Rd SE9 ..... 28 F4
Offen's Dr TN12 ..... 149 E3
OFFHAM 96 D8
Offham Prim Sch ME19 .. 96 D8
Offham Rd ME19 ...... 97 A7
Officers' Rd ME4 .... 54 B8
Officers Terr ME4 ... 53 F7
Ogilby St SE18 ...... 1 F2
Okehampton Cres DA16 .. 13 C6
Okemore Gdns BR5 .... 44 C5
Old Ashford Rd ME17 .. 120 E5
Old Bailey The ME17 .. 119 E6
Old Barn Cl
Gillingham ME7 .... 68 F6
Kemsing TN15 .... 77 A2
Tonbridge TN9 .... 142 F8
Old Barn Rd ME19 .... 81 E2
Old Barn Way DA7 .... 14 D4
OLD BEXLEY 14 A1
Old Bexley Bsns Pk DA5 .. 31 B8
Old Bexley CE Prim Sch
DA5 .... 30 F7
Old Bexley La DA5 ... 31 E6
OLDBURY 94 B6
Oldbury Cl
Oldbury TN15 .... 94 B5
Orpington BR5 .... 44 D5
Oldbury Cotts TN15 .. 94 B6
Oldbury La TN15 ..... 189 A4

Old Carriageway The
Gillingham ME7 .... 68 F4
Sevenoaks TN13 .... 91 C5
Old Chapel Rd BR8 ... 45 C2
Old Chatham Rd
Kit's Coty ME20 ...... 83 D6
Sandling ME14 .... 83 F1
Old Church Cl BR6 ... 44 B1
Oldchurch Ct **3** ME16 .. 99 E1
Old Church La TN12 .. 112 E4
Old Church Rd
Burham ME1 .... 66 C1
Mereworth ME18, TN12 .. 112 D5
Pembury TN2 .... 144 D2
Old Clem Sq **12** SE18 .. 12 A8
Old Coach Rd TN15 ... 78 E5
Old Corn Stores The
ME14 .... 101 C4
Old Court Ho The TN13 .. 92 C3
Old Courtyard The BR1 .. 42 B8
Old Dairy The TN12 .. 129 E6
Old Dartford Rd DA4 .. 46 F3
Old Dover Rd SE3 .... 11 B7
Old Downs DA3 .... 48 E4
Old Downs The DA3 ... 48 E4
Old Dr ME15 .... 115 F6
Old Farm Ave DA15 .. 29 E6
Old Farm Gdns DA15 .. 85 F6
Old Farmhouse The BR8 .. 31 E1
Old Farm Road E DA15 .. 30 A6
Old Farm Road W DA15 .. 29 F6
Oldfield Cl
Bromley BR1 .... 42 F5
Gillingham ME8 .... 69 D8
Maidstone ME15 .... 100 E1
Oldfield Dr ME1 ..... 66 C5
Oldfield Rd
Bexley DA7 .... 13 E5
Bromley BR1 .... 42 F5
Old Fire Sta The SE18 .. 2 A1
Old Forge La ME9 .... 86 F3
Old Forge Way DA14 .. 30 B4
Old Gardens Cl TN2 .. 173 B8
Old Gdn The TN13 .... 91 D4
Old George Ct ME3 ... 39 F4
Old Hadlow Rd TN10 .. 127 F4
Old Ham La ME17 ..... 120 A4
Old Hill
Chislehurst BR7 ...... 43 A8
Orpington BR6 .... 57 E4
Old Homesdale Rd BR2 .. 42 C5
Old Ho The BR7 ...... 43 D8
Old House La
Hartlip ME9 .... 70 E4
Langton Green TN3 ... 157 D4
Old Kent Rd TN12 ... 146 A6
Old La
Ightham TN15 .... 94 C4
Tatsfield TN16 ...... 88 D6
Old London Rd
Badgers Mount TN14 .. 59 A1
Halstead TN14 .... 74 E4
Tonbridge TN10 ...... 127 C3
Wrotham TN15 .... 78 F4
Old Loose Cl ME15 .. 115 F5
Old Loose Hill ME15 .. 115 F4
Old Maidstone Rd
Keycol ME8 .... 71 F5
Sidcup DA14 .... 30 F1
Oldman Ct SE12 ..... 28 B6
Old Manor Dr DA12 .. 36 C7
Old Manor Way
Bexley DA7 .... 14 D5
Bromley BR7 .... 43 D8
Old Market The TN12 .. 148 D6
Old Mill Cl DA4 .... 46 E1
Old Mill La TN27 .... 168 A1
Old Mill Rd ME20 ... 83 C3
Old Mill Rd
Maidstone ME17 ...... 101 F1
Woolwich SE18 .... 12 D8
Old Oast Bsns Ctr The
ME20 .... 83 A1
Old Orch TN11 .... 125 A3
Old Orchard TN18 ... 196 B5
Old Orchard La ME19 .. 81 D1
Old Orchard The ME8 .. 70 A8
Old Otford Rd TN14 .. 76 A1
Old Park Rd SE2 .... 3 A1
Old Parsonage Ct ME19 .. 97 C7
Old Pattens La ME4 .. 53 D2
Old Perry St
Chislehurst BR7 ...... 29 E1
Northfleet DA11 ...... 29 E1
Old Polhill TN14 .... 75 D4
Old Post Office La SE3 .. 11 B4
Old Rd
Chatham ME4 .... 53 F4
Crayford DA1, DA7 ... 14 D3
East Peckham TN12 ... 130 A6
Wateringbury ME18 ... 113 C7
Old Regent Dr TN17 .. 191 D3
Old Riding School The
TN3 .... 171 B2
Old Road E DA12 ..... 36 D7
Old Road W DA11 ..... 36 A7
Old Saw Mill The TN15 .. 95 D5
Old School Cl ME17 .. 120 D4
Old School Ct
Chattenden ME3 ...... 39 F4
Egerton TN27 .... 137 F3
Old School Ho The **3**
TN8 .... 122 C1
Old School La ME19 .. 80 F4
Old School Pl ME15 .. 100 A5

Old School The
Goudhurst TN17 ...... 177 E8
Maidstone ME16 ...... 98 E1
Orpington BR6 .... 57 B5
Old School Yd DA12 .. 36 E8
Old Soar Manor★ TN15 .. 95 B1
Old Soar Rd TN15 ... 95 C1
Old Station Rd TN5 .. 184 E6
Old Tannery Cl TN30 .. 192 F7
Old Terry's Lodge Rd
TN15 .... 78 A4
Old Timber Top Cotts The
TN13 .... 92 C4
Old Tovil Rd ME15 .. 100 A2
Old Trafford Cl ME16 .. 99 B6
Old Tramyard **1** SE18 .. 2 C2
Old Tree La ME17 ... 116 D3
Old Tye Ave TN16 ... 72 E3
Old Vicarage Sch The
TN12 .... 148 E2
Old Vicarage The DA13 .. 50 A1
Old Wardsdown TN5 .. 187 B3
Old Watling St
Gravesend DA11 ...... 36 A3
Rochester ME2 .... 52 B8
Old Weavers Cotts TN17 .. 190 D5
Old White Hart Cotts
TN16 .... 90 C3
Old Wlk The TN14 ... 76 C2
Old Yard The TN16 .. 90 C3
Old Yews The DA3 ... 49 B6
Oleander Cl BR6 .... 57 D5
Oliver Cl
Chatham ME4 .... 54 B2
West Thurrock RM20 .. 16 F7
Oliver Cres DA4 .... 46 F2
Oliver Ct SE18 ..... 2 C2
Olive Rd DA1 .... 32 D7
Oliver Gdns E6 ..... 1 E8
Oliver North Ho ME15 .. 114 E7
Oliver Rd
Staplehurst TN12 .... 149 E4
Swanley BR8 .... 45 D6
West Thurrock RM20 .. 16 F7
Olivers Mill DA3 ... 62 E8
Olivers Row ME14 ... 101 C4
Oliver Twist Cl ME1 .. 53 B8
Olivier Dr ME2 ..... 39 B2
Olivier Rd ME5 ..... 84 A8
Olliffe Cl ME5 ..... 67 F2
Olron Cres DA6 ..... 13 E2
Olven Rd SE18 ...... 12 C8
Olyffe Ave DA16 ... 13 A5
O'Neill Path **7** SE18 .. 12 A8
Onslow Cres BR7 ... 43 B8
Onslow Dr DA14 .... 30 D6
Onslow Rd ME1 ..... 53 D3
Opal Cl E16 .... 1 D7
Opal Gn ME4 .... 68 B2
Openshaw Rd SE2 ... 3 B2
Orache Dr ME14 .... 100 E5
Orange Court La BR6 .. 57 A2
Orangery La SE9 ... 11 F2
Orange Terr ME1 ... 47 C5
Orbital One DA1 ... 33 B6
Orbit Cl ME5 ...... 84 A8
Orchard Ave
Aylesford ME20 ...... 82 E1
Bexley DA17 .... 13 F8
Dartford DA2 .... 32 B7
Gravesend DA11 ...... 36 B3
Rochester ME2 .... 38 F1
Orchard Bank ME17 .. 117 B1
Orchard Bsns Ctr
Maidstone ME16 ...... 99 C8
Paddock Wood TN12 ... 146 A8
Royal Tunbridge Wells
TN2 .... 159 D8
Tonbridge TN9 .... 127 E1
Orchard Cl
Bexley DA7 .... 13 E6
Coxheath ME17 .... 115 C3
Edenbridge TN8 ...... 122 B2
Horsmonden TN12 ..... 162 F6
Langley Heath ME17 .. 117 E4
New Barn DA3 .... 49 B7
Royal Tunbridge Wells
TN9 .... 159 D6
Sevenoaks TN14 ...... 92 C7
Orchard Cotts
Chislehurst BR7 ...... 29 E2
East Farleigh ME15 .. 106 B8
Nettlestead Green ME18 .. 113 C1
Orchard Cres
Horsmonden TN12 ..... 163 A6
Wateringbury ME18 ... 113 D6
Orchard Ct
Benenden TN17 .... 190 D6
Sidcup DA15 .... 12 F2
Orchard Dr
Edenbridge TN8 ...... 122 B2
Maidstone ME14 ...... 100 E4
Meopham Station DA13 .. 49 F4
Tonbridge TN10 ...... 127 E5
Tonbridge TN11 ...... 127 E5
Orchard Gdn TN27 ... 151 E5
Orchard Gn
Bromley BR1 .... 42 C8
Orpington BR6 .... 57 E8
Orchard Gr
Larkfield ME20 .... 82 B2
Orpington BR6 .... 43 F1
Royal Tunbridge Wells
TN1 .... 159 B5
Orchard Hill DA11 .. 14 E2
Orchard Ho DA8 .... 14 F6
Orchard Ind Est ME15 .. 116 F3

Orchardlea DA13 .... 34 F3
Orchard Lea TN11 .. 126 F5
Orchard Pl
Coxheath ME17 .... 115 C3
Keston BR2 .... 56 D2
2 Maidstone ME16 .. 99 E3
Orpington BR5 .... 44 C6
Sundridge TN14 ...... 90 D3
Orchard Prim Sch DA14 .. 30 B3
Orchard Rd
Bexley DA16 .... 13 B4
Bromley BR1 .... 42 C8
East Peckham TN12 ... 130 A6
Erith DA17 .... 4 C2
Northfleet DA11 ...... 35 C6
Orpington BR6 .... 57 B5
Otford TN14 .... 75 F3
Pratt's Bottom BR6 .. 58 C1
Sevenoaks TN13 ...... 91 E5
Sidcup DA14 .... 29 E4
Swanscombe DA10 .... 17 E2
Tenterden TN30 ...... 183 C8
Orchard Rise TN3 ... 171 B7
Orchard Rise E DA15 .. 12 F2
Orchard Rise W DA15 .. 12 E2
Orchard Sh Ctr **5** DA1 .. 15 E1
Orchard St
Dartford DA1 .... 15 E1
Gillingham ME8 .... 69 E8
Maidstone ME15 .... 100 A3
Orchard Terr DA9 ... 16 E2
Orchard The
Maidstone ME14 ...... 101 B4
Sevenoaks TN13 ...... 91 E6
Swanley BR8 .... 45 D7
Orchard View
Detling ME14 .... 101 A8
Tenterden TN30 ...... 193 C8
Orchard Villas
Chainhurst TN12 ..... 132 A4
1 Chatham ME4 ... 53 F3
Chislehurst BR7 ...... 29 E2
Sidcup DA14 .... 30 C2
Orchard Way
Cranbrook TN17 ...... 179 B4
Dartford DA2 .... 32 D5
Horsmonden TN12 ..... 163 A6
Kemsing TN15 .... 77 A2
Oxted R48 .... 104 A2
Snodland ME6 .... 81 F7
Orchid Cl
1 Newham E6 .... 1 E8
Rochester ME2 .... 52 C6
Orchidhurst TN2 .... 159 D7
Ordnance Rd
Gravesend DA12 ...... 19 C1
Woolwich SE18 .... 12 A8
Ordnance St ME4 ... 53 E3
Ordnance Terr **9** ME4 .. 53 E3
Oregon Sq BR6 ..... 43 D1
Orford Ct **7** DA2 .. 16 B1
Oriental Rd E16 .... 1 D5
Orient Ct ME19 .... 97 B7
Oriole Way
Larkfield ME20 .... 81 F2
Woolwich SE28 .... 3 C5
Orion Rd ME1 ...... 67 C7
Orissa Rd SE18 .... 2 D2
Orlestone Gdns BR6 .. 58 E5
Orlick Rd DA12 .... 37 B7
Ormesby Cl SE28 ... 3 D6
Ormiston Rd SE10 .. 1 A1
Ormonde Ave BR6 .. 57 F5
Ormsby Gn ME8 .... 69 E3
Ormsby Point **8** SE18 .. 2 B2
Orpines The ME18 .. 113 F7
ORPINGTON 59 A2
Orpington By-Pass TN14 .. 59 A2
Orpington Coll of FE BR6 .. 44 A1
Orpington Hospl BR6 .. 57 F6
Orpington Rd BR7 .. 43 C6
Orpington Sta BR6 .. 57 E8
Orpington Trad Est **10**
BR5 .... 44 C5
Orwell Cl ME20 .... 81 F2
Orwell Ct RM13 .... 4 D8
Orwell Spike ME19 .. 97 A5
Osberton Rd SE12 .. 11 A2
Osborne Rd
Bexley DA17 .... 13 F8
Gillingham ME7 ...... 54 C5
Osbourne Rd DA2 .. 16 B1
Osgood Ave BR6 ... 57 F5
Osgood Gdns **1** BR6 .. 57 F5
Oslin Wlk ME19 ... 97 C2
OSMERS HILL 184 F7
Osmers Hill TN5 .. 184 F7
Osmunda Ct TN2 ... 159 C4
Osney Ho **6** SE2 .. 3 D4
Osney Way DA12 ... 36 F6
Osprey Ave ME5 ... 54 E2
Osprey Cl
Newham E6 .... 1 E8
Orpington BR2 .... 42 E1
Osprey Wlk ME20 .. 81 F1
Ospringe Ct SE9 .. 12 D1
Ospringe Pl TN2 .. 159 F6
Osterberg Rd DA1 .. 15 F3
Osterley Ct BR5 .. 44 A8
Ostlers Cl **2** ME6 .. 82 A8
Oswald Dr ME2 .... 52 E5
OTFORD 76 A3
Otford Cl
Bromley BR1 .... 43 A6
Sidcup DA15 .... 14 B1
Otford La TN14 .... 75 B6
Otford Prim Sch TN14 .. 76 B3
Otford Rd TN14 .... 92 B7

Otford Sta TN14 ... 76 C3
OTHAM 117 B7
OTHAM HOLE 117 B6
Otham La ME15 ..... 101 C2
Otham St
Maidstone ME15 ...... 101 C2
Otham ME15 .... 117 B7
Otley Rd E16 ...... 1 C7
Otlinge Rd BR5 ... 44 D5
Ottawa Rd RM18 ... 19 A5
Otterbourne Pl ME15 .. 100 E1
Otterden Cl BR6 .. 57 E6
Otteridge Rd ME14 .. 101 A3
Otters Cl BR5 .... 44 D5
Ottershaw Ho BR5 .. 44 B8
Otway St
Chatham ME4 .... 54 A3
Gillingham ME7 ...... 54 D6
Otway Terr **1** ME4 .. 54 A3
Oulton Cl SE28 ... 3 C5
Our Lady of Grace RC Prim
ME7, SE7 .... 11 B8
Our Lady of Hartley RC Prim
Sch DA3 .... 48 F4
Our Lady of the Rosary RC
Prim Sch DA15 .... 12 E1
Our Lady's RC Prim Sch **11**
DA1 .... 15 D1
Oval The
New Barn DA3 .... 49 C6
Sidcup DA15 .... 30 A8
Ovenden Rd
Sevenoaks TN14 ...... 90 F6
Sundridge TN14 ...... 90 D6
Overcliffe DA11 ... 19 A1
Overcourt Cl DA15 .. 13 B1
Overdale TN14 ..... 108 B2
Overmead
Eltham DA15 .... 29 D8
Swanley BR8 .... 45 E4
Over Minnis DA3 .. 62 F7
Overton Rd SE2 ... 3 D3
Overy Liberty DA1 .. 32 E8
Overy St DA1 ..... 15 E1
Owen Cl
2 East Malling ME19 .. 97 F8
Woolwich SE28 .... 3 C5
Owenite St SE2 ... 3 B2
Owens Way ME7 .... 55 A6
Owletts★ DA12 .... 50 F6
Owletts Cl ME15 .. 116 D8
Owl House Gdns★ TN3 .. 175 C7
Oxenden Wood Rd BR6 .. 58 C4
Oxenhill Rd TN15 .. 76 E2
Oxenhoath Rd TN11 .. 111 D4
Oxfield TN8 .... 122 D3
Oxford Cl DA12 ... 36 F6
Oxford Ct **6** DA14 .. 29 F4
Oxford Mews DA5 .. 31 A8
Oxford Rd
Gillingham ME7 ...... 54 D3
Maidstone ME15 ...... 116 D8
Sidcup DA14 .... 30 B3
Oxford St ME15 ... 82 A8
Oxhawth Cres BR2 .. 43 B3
Ox La TN30 .... 183 B2
Ox Lea TN3 .... 158 A3
Oxleas Cl 2 B7
Oxleas Cl DA16 ... 12 D5
Oxleas Wood Nature
Reserve★ SE18 ...... 12 C4
Oxley Shaw La ME19 .. 81 E2
Oyster Catchers Cl E16 .. 1 B7
Ozolins Way E16 .. 1 A7

P

Pacific Cl DA10 ... 17 E2
Pacific Rd E16 ... 1 A7
Packer Pl ME5 .... 68 A8
Packham Cl BR6 ... 58 C7
Packham Rd DA11 .. 35 F5
Packhorse Rd SE9 .. 91 C4
Packmores Rd SE9 .. 12 E2
Padbrook RH8 ..... 104 A6
Padbrook Cl RH8 .. 104 B6
Paddlesworth Rd ME6 .. 65 F3
Paddock Cl
Fordcombe TN3 .... 157 B5
Greenwich SE3 .... 11 A5
Limpsfield RH8 ...... 104 A4
Marlpit Hill TN8 .... 122 C3
Orpington BR6 .... 57 F5
Platt TN15 .... 95 C4
Sutton at Hone DA4 .. 47 C6
Paddock Rd DA6 ... 13 E3
Paddocks Cl BR5 .. 58 D8
Paddocks The
Addington ME19 ...... 80 D4
Cowden TN8 .... 155 B7
Gillingham ME7 ...... 69 A5
Sevenoaks TN13 ...... 92 D3
Paddock The
Ashurst TN3 .... 156 F5
Chatham ME4 .... 53 F4
Dartford DA2 .... 32 D5
Farthing Street BR2 .. 56 E2
Hadlow TN11 .... 111 E8
Pembury TN2 .... 160 C6
Vigo Village TN15 ... 69 A3
Westerham TN16 ...... 89 C3
Paddock Way BR7 .. 29 D7
PADDOCK WOOD 145 F6
Paddock Wood Bsns Ctr
TN12 .... 146 A2
Paddock Wood Prim Sch
TN12 .... 146 A6

Paddock Wood Sta TN12 146 A7
Pad's Hill ME15 100 A4
Padsole La ME15 100 A4
Padstow Cl 3 BR6 57 F6
Padstow Manor 1 ME7 54 C6
Pageant Cl RM18 19 C6
Page Cl DA2 34 C5
Page Cres DA8 14 F7
Page Heath La BR1 42 D6
Page Heath Villas BR1 42 D6
Pagehurst Rd TN12 149 B3
Paget Gdns BR7 43 B8
Paget Rise SE18 12 A7
Paget Row ME7 54 C5
Paget St ME7 54 C5
Paget Terr SE18 12 B8
Pagitt St ME4 53 E3
Paiges Farm Cl TN14 108 C2
Pains Hill RH8 104 C4
Painters Ash La DA11 35 D5
Painters Ash Prim Sch DA11 35 D5
Palace Ave ME15 100 A4
Palace Ct
  5 Bromley BR1 42 B8
  Eltham SE9 11 F1
  Gillingham ME5 54 D2
Palace Gr BR1 42 B8
Palace Ind Est ME15 116 F4
Palace Rd
  Bromley BR1 42 B8
  Hill Park TN16 89 A6
Palace View
  Bromley BR1 42 B6
  Lewisham SE12 28 A6
Palace Wood Prim Sch ME16 99 C6
Pale Park La DA12 51 E8
Palewell Cl BR5 44 B7
Palladian Circus 1 DA9 17 C3
Pallant Way BR6 57 A7
Pallet Way SE18 11 E6
Palmar Cres DA7 14 A5
Palmar Rd
  Bexley DA7 14 A5
  Maidstone ME16 99 D6
Palmarsh Rd BR5 44 D5
Palm Ave DA14 30 D2
Palmeira Rd DA7 13 D4
Palmer Ave DA12 36 D4
Palmers Brook TN11 111 F2
PALMER'S GREEN 162 D8
Palmers Green La TN12 146 D1
Palmers Orch TN14 75 F8
Palmerston Cres SE18 12 C8
Palmerston Rd
  Chatham ME4 53 F1
  Grays RM20 17 D8
  Orpington BR6 57 C5
Palmers Yd TN27 151 E5
Pamela Ct ME7 54 D5
Panbro Ho SE18 11 F6
Panfield Rd SE2 3 A3
Pankhurst Ave E16 1 B5
Pankhurst Ho SE18 12 A7
Pankhurst Rd ME3 40 D6
Pannell Rd ME3 27 A6
Panter's BR8 31 F1
Pantiles Sh Ctr The TN1 159 A2
Pantiles The
  Bexley DA7 13 F7
  Bromley BR1 42 E6
  20 Royal Tunbridge Wells TN2 159 A2
Panton Cl ME5 68 C4
Pantyles The TN14 107 B5
Papermill La DA1 15 D3
Papillons Wlk SE3 11 A4
Papion Gr ME5 67 E2
Parade The
  Crayford DA1 14 F2
  Gravesend DA12 36 D6
  Kemsing TN15 76 E2
  Meopham Station DA13 50 A2
  Rochester ME2 52 E8
  Staplehurst TN12 149 F3
  Swanscombe DA10 17 F2
Paradise Cotts ME9 70 E5
Paradise Path SE28 3 A5
Paradise Pl 14 SE18 1 E2
Paragon Cl E16 1 A7
Paragon The SE3 11 A5
Parbrook Rd ME3 24 B2
Parham Rd ME4 53 F2
Parish CE Prim Sch BR1 28 A1
Parish Gate Dr DA15 12 E1
Parish Wharf 5 SE18 1 E2
Park App DA16 13 B3
Park Ave
  Bromley BR1 28 A2
  Edenbridge TN8 122 B2
  Gillingham ME7 54 D3
  Gravesend DA12 36 C7
  Maidstone ME17 115 E2
  Maidstone, Penenden Heath ME14 100 B6
  Northfleet DA11 35 E7
  Orpington BR6 57 A8
  Tonbridge TN11 126 F5
  West Thurrock RM20 17 B8
Park Barn Rd ME17 118 C5
Park Cliff Rd DA9 17 C3
Park Corner Rd DA13 34 F4
Park Cotts
  8 Hawkhurst TN18 189 A2
  Sevenoaks TN13 92 C2
Park Cres
  Chatham ME4 67 F8
  Erith DA8 14 D8
Park Crescent Rd DA8 14 D8
Parkdale Rd SE18 2 E1
Park Dr
  Longfield DA3 48 E6
  Woolwich SE7 11 E8
Parker Ave RM18 19 C6
Parker Cl
  Gillingham ME8 69 E5
  Newham E16 1 E5
Parker Ho 4 SE18 2 B1
Parker Ind Ctr DA1 33 C7
Parker Rd RM17 17 F8
Parker's Cnr ME3 9 C2
Parker St E16 1 E5
Park Farm Houses ME20 98 B8
Park Farm Rd
  Bromley BR1 42 D8
  Ryarsh ME19 80 F6
Parkfield
  Hartley DA3 48 E5
  Sevenoaks TN15 92 F4
Parkfield Rd ME8 55 F1
Parkfields ME2 52 C7
Parkfield Way BR2 42 F4
PARKGATE 182 B2
Parkgate Cotts BR6 59 C6
Parkgate Rd BR6 59 C6
Park Gdns DA8 4 D2
Park Gr
  Bexley DA7 14 C3
  Bromley BR1 42 B8
Park Hill
  Bromley BR1 42 F5
  Meopham Station DA13 49 F5
Parkhill Rd
  Sidcup DA15 29 E5
  Sidcup, Old Bexley DA5 30 F8
Park Hill Rd TN14 76 E2
Park Ho
  Maidstone ME14 100 B6
  Sevenoaks TN13 92 C5
  Sidcup DA14 30 A3
Park House Cotts DA4 60 F5
Park House Gdns TN4 143 A2
Parkhurst Gdns 2 DA5 31 A8
Parkhurst Rd DA5 31 A8
Park La
  Gill's Green TN17, TN18 188 D7
  Godden Green TN15 93 A4
  Kemsing TN15 77 A1
  Maidstone, Cock Stone ME17 116 D2
  Maidstone, Ringlestone ME14 99 F7
  Sevenoaks TN13 92 C3
  Swanley Village BR8 46 C7
Parkland Cl TN13 108 D6
Parkland Mead BR1 43 B6
Parklands TN4 158 E8
Park Lane TN17 177 D1
Park Manor ME7 54 B5
Park Mead DA15 13 B1
Park Mews BR7 29 B2
Parkmore BR7 29 B1
Park Pl
  8 Bromley BR1 42 B8
  Gravesend DA12 36 C8
  Hever TN8 139 D4
  Sevenoaks TN13 91 D4
Park Rd
  Addington ME19 80 C3
  Chislehurst BR7 29 B2
  Dartford DA1 33 A8
  Dunk's Green TN11 111 C5
  Gravesend DA11 36 B7
  Leybourne ME19 81 D3
  Limpsfield RH8 104 A8
  Maidstone ME15 100 C1
  Marden Thorn TN12 149 A4
  Mereworth TN12 112 F5
  Orpington BR5 44 C4
  Royal Tunbridge Wells, Southborough TN4 143 A2
  Royal Tunbridge Wells TN4 159 B5
  Swanley BR8 45 F5
  Swanscombe DA10 17 E1
Park Road Ind Est BR8 45 F6
Parkside
  Cliffe Woods ME3 39 B7
  Halstead TN14 74 F6
  Sidcup DA14 30 B6
Parkside Ave
  Bexley DA1, DA7 14 E5
  Bromley BR1 42 E5
  Tilbury RM18 19 B5
Parkside Cotts TN16 88 E6
Parkside Cross DA7 14 E5
Parkside Ct TN30 192 F7
Parkside Lodge DA17 4 C1
Parkside Par DA1 14 F5
Parkside Rd DA17 4 C2
Park St TN2 159 C3
Park Terr
  Sundridge TN14 90 D3
  Swanscombe DA9 17 B2
Park The DA14 30 A3
Parkview TN2 159 D4
Park View
  Hodsoll Street TN15 63 C2
  Sevenoaks TN13 92 C3
Park View Cl TN8 122 B2
Parkview Ct DA11 36 A6
Park View Ct
  2 Lewisham SE12 28 C5
Park View Ct *continued*
  Maidstone ME15 100 E1
Parkview Rd SE9 29 B6
Park View Rd DA16 13 C4
Park View Terr 2 TN30 193 A7
Park Villas ME14 100 E4
Parkway
  Erith DA18 3 E3
  Tonbridge TN10 127 D5
Park Way
  Coxheath ME17 115 D3
  Joyden's Wood DA5 31 E5
  Maidstone ME15 100 B1
Parkway Prim Sch DA18 3 E3
Park Way Prim Sch ME15 100 B1
PARK WOOD
  Gillingham 69 D4
  Maidstone 116 E4
Parkwood Cl TN2 159 C6
Park Wood Gn ME8 69 D5
Parkwood Hall Sch BR8 46 B6
Park Wood Ind Est ME15 117 A4
Parkwood Inf Sch ME8 69 E5
Parkwood Jun Sch ME8 69 E5
Park Wood La TN12 150 C1
Park Wood Par 13 ME15 116 F5
Parkwood Rd
  Biggin Hill TN16 88 F6
  Sidcup DA5 30 F8
Park Wood Sh Ctr ME8 69 D5
Park Wood Trad Est ME15 117 A4
Parnham Cl BR1 43 B6
Paroma Rd DA17 4 A3
Parr Ave ME7 54 D6
Parr Ct DA10 34 E8
Parrock Ave DA12 36 C7
PARROCK FARM 36 D4
Parrock Rd DA12 36 C7
Parrock St DA12 36 B8
Parrock The DA12 36 C7
Parrs Head Mews ME1 53 C6
Parry Ave E6 1 F7
Parry Pl SE18 2 B2
Parsley Way ME16 99 A3
Parsonage Bank DA4 60 E8
Parsonage Cl TN4 158 B5
Parsonage La
  Lamberhurst TN3 176 B6
  Rochester ME2 53 C8
  Sidcup DA14 30 F4
  Sutton at Hone DA4 33 B2
Parsonage Manorway DA17 14 A8
Parsonage Rd
  Rusthall TN4 158 B5
  West Thurrock RM20 17 C8
Parson's Croft TN8 139 C5
Parsons La
  Dartford DA2 32 B5
  Stansted TN15 62 E1
Partridge Ave ME20 81 F3
Partridge Cl 1 E16 1 D8
Partridge Dr
  Orpington BR6 57 C7
  St Mary's Island ME4 40 B1
Partridge Gn SE9 29 A5
Partridge Rd DA14 29 E4
Partridge Sq 3 E6 1 E8
Pasadena Cvn Pk TN15 61 B1
Pasley Rd ME4, ME7 54 A7
Pasley Road E ME7 54 B7
Pasley Road N ME4 54 B7
Pasley Road W ME7 54 A7
Passey Pl SE9 11 F1
Passfield Ho SE18 2 D2
Passfield Path 13 SE28 3 B6
Passmore Way ME15 99 E1
Pastens Rd RH8 104 C4
Paston Cres SE12 28 B8
Patagonia Ho TN2 159 C3
Pat Bassant Row DA10 34 E8
Patch The TN13 91 E5
Pat Drew Ho BR1 42 C8
Patience Cotts TN14 108 B2
Patricia Ct
  Bexley SE2 13 B7
  Chislehurst BR7 43 D8
Patrixbourne Ave ME8 55 C2
Pattenden Gdns TN12 130 A7
Pattenden La TN12 148 C7
Pattens Gdns ME1 53 E2
Pattens La ME1, ME4 53 E1
Pattens Pl ME1 53 D2
Patterdale Rd DA2 33 D7
Patterson Ct DA1 16 A2
Pattinson Point 14 E16 1 A8
Pattison Wlk SE18 2 C1
Paulinus Cl BR5 44 C6
Pavement The TN30 183 B3
Pavilion Gdns TN13 92 C3
Pavilion La ME18 113 A8
Pavilion L Ctr The BR1 42 A7
Pavilion Shop Ctr The 7 TN9 127 B1
Pavilion The 5 TN9 127 B1
Pavings The ME17 102 C2
Paxton Ct 5 SE12 28 C5
Paxton Rd BR1 28 A1
Paynes Cotts TN13 75 D1
Paynesfield Rd TN16 88 D7
Payne's La ME15 116 B7
Peace Cotts ME15 131 D7
Peace St SE18 12 A8
Peach Croft DA11 35 E4
Peach Hall TN10 127 C6
Peacock Mews 7 ME16 99 E4
Peacock Rise ME5 68 A4
Peacock St DA12 36 C8
Peacock Wlk E16 1 B7
Peal Cl ME3 40 E5
Peareswood Rd DA8 14 F6
Pearl Cl E6 2 A7
Pearl Way ME18 97 C3
Pearse Pl TN3 176 B5
PEARSON'S GREEN 146 F3
Pearson's Green Rd
  Paddock Wood, Mile Oak TN12 146 D5
  Paddock Wood, Pearson's Green TN12 146 F3
Pearson Way DA1 32 F6
Pear Tree Ave ME20 82 C1
Peartree Cl
  Bexley DA8 14 D6
  Bromley BR2 42 D4
Pear Tree Cl
  Cranbrook TN17 179 D3
  Swanley BR8 45 D7
Peartree Cotts ME8 70 B8
Peartree La DA12 38 A2
Pear Tree La
  Gillingham ME7 68 E7
  Loose ME15 116 B6
Pear Tree Pl ME3 38 B3
Pear Tree Row ME17 117 B5
Peartree Way SE10 1 A2
Pear Tree Wlk ME9 71 A5
Pease Hill TN15 62 F4
Peasley La TN17 177 D6
Peatfield Cl DA15 29 E5
Peat Way ME3 10 D1
Pebble Hill Cotts RH8 104 B6
PECKHAM BUSH 129 E8
Peckham Cl ME2 53 C8
Peckham Ct TN12 129 F6
Peckham Ho 6 BR5 44 D1
Peckham Hurst Rd TN11 111 E7
Pedham Place Est BR8 46 A4
Peel Rd BR6 57 C5
Peel St ME14 100 A6
Peel Yates Ho 12 SE18 1 E2
PEENING QUARTER 199 B6
Peens La ME17 133 C7
Pegasus Ct DA12 36 C5
Peggoty Cl ME3 38 B3
Pegley Gdns SE12 28 A6
Pegwell St SE18 12 E7
Pelham Cotts DA5 31 B7
Pelham Ct 19 DA14 30 A5
Pelham Prim Sch DA7 14 A4
Pelham Rd
  Bexley DA7 14 A4
  Gravesend DA11 36 A8
Pelham Road S DA11 35 F7
Pelham Terr 4 DA11 35 F8
Pelican Cl ME2 52 C6
Pelican Ct ME18 113 E7
PELL BRIDGE 185 A5
Pell Cl TN5 185 A6
PELL GREEN 185 A7
Pellipar Gdns SE18 1 F1
Pellipar Rd SE18 1 F1
Pells La TN15 78 A7
Pemberton Gdns BR8 45 E7
Pemberton Sq 4 ME2 53 C8
Pemble Cl TN12 145 A7
Pembroke ME4 54 B8
Pembroke Cl DA8 4 D2
Pembroke Ct ME4 54 A4
Pembroke Gdns ME8 69 E4
Pembroke Par DA8 4 C1
Pembroke Pl DA4 47 B8
Pembroke Rd
  Bromley BR1 42 D7
  Coxheath ME17 115 C3
  Erith DA8 4 D2
  Newham E6 1 F8
  Sevenoaks TN13 92 B2
  Tonbridge TN9 127 A1
Pembroke Rise ME4 54 A7
PEMBURY 160 C6
Pembury Cl TN2 160 D7
Pembury Cres DA14 30 E6
Pembury Gdns ME16 99 D3
Pembury Gr TN9 143 C8
Pembury Grange TN2 160 A6
Pembury Hall Rd TN11, TN2 144 C3
Pembury Hospl TN2 160 B7
Pembury Rd
  Bexley DA7 13 E8
  Pembury TN11 144 A2
  Royal Tunbridge Wells TN2 159 E4
  Tonbridge TN11, TN9 143 D7
Pembury Sch TN2 160 D8
Pembury Way ME8 55 E2
Pembury Wlks TN11, TN2 144 C2
Pencroft Dr DA1 32 C8
Pendant Ct BR6 58 A5
Penda Rd DA8 14 B7
Pendennis Rd
  Orpington BR6 58 C8
  Sevenoaks TN13 92 B4
Penderel Mews TN30 193 B8
Pendlebury Gn SE18 11 E6
Pendragon Rd BR1, SE12 28 A5
Pendragon Sch BR1 28 A5
Pendrell St SE18 12 D8
Pendrill Pl TN5 184 F5
Penenden DA3 62 F8
Penenden Ct ME14 100 B7
PENENDEN HEATH 100 B7
Penenden Heath Rd ME14 100 C7
Penenden St ME14 100 A6
Penfold Cl
  Chatham ME5 68 B7
  Maidstone ME15 116 E5
Penfold Gdns ME15 116 E4
Penfold Hill ME17 118 B8
Penfold Ho 14 SE18 12 B8
Penfold La DA5 30 D7
Penfolds Cl TN10 127 C5
Penfold Way ME15 115 F6
Penford Gdns SE9 11 D4
Pengarth Rd DA5 13 D1
Penguin Cl ME2 52 D6
Penhale Cl BR6 58 A6
Penhall Rd SE7 1 D2
Penhill Rd DA5 30 C8
Penhurst Cl ME14 100 F5
Peninsular Park Rd SE7 1 A2
Penlee Cl TN8 122 C2
Penmon Rd SE2 3 A3
Pennant Rd ME1 67 C7
Penney Cl DA1 32 D8
Penn Gdns BR7 43 B7
Pennine Way
  Bexley DA7 14 E6
  Maidstone ME15 101 A1
  Northfleet DA11 35 E5
Pennine Wlk TN2 159 D5
Pennington Manor 1 TN4 142 F2
Pennington Pl TN4 143 B1
Pennington Rd TN4 143 A2
Pennington Way SE12 28 B6
Penn La
  Bexley DA5 13 D1
  Ide Hill TN14 106 E8
Penns Yd TN2 160 C6
Penny Cress Gdns ME16 99 C3
Penn Yd TN2 160 C6
Pennyfields TN17 179 D4
Pennyroyal Ave E6 2 A7
Penpool La DA16 13 B4
Penrith Ct ME7 55 A5
Penryn Manor 4 ME7 54 C6
PENSHURST 141 B4
Penshurst Ave DA15 13 A1
Penshurst CE Prim Sch TN11 141 A4
Penshurst Cl
  Gillingham ME8 55 E2
  New Barn DA3 49 D7
  West Kingsdown TN15 61 E4
Penshurst Enterprise Ctr TN11 141 C4
Penshurst Place & Gdns* TN11 141 B4
Penshurst Rd
  Bexley DA7 13 F6
  Penshurst TN3, TN11 141 A5
  Poundsbridge TN11, TN3 157 E8
Penshurst Sta TN11 124 F1
Penshurst Way BR5 44 C5
Penstocks The ME15 99 D2
Pentagon Sh Ctr ME4 53 F4
Penton Ho 3 SE2 3 D4
Pentstemon Dr DA10 17 E2
Penventon Ct 3 RM18 19 A5
Pen Way TN10 127 E5
Pepingstraw Cl ME19 96 D7
Pepper Cl E6 1 F8
PEPPER HILL 35 C5
Pepper Hill DA11 35 C5
Pepperhill La DA11 35 C5
Pepys Cl
  4 Dartford DA1 16 A3
  Northfleet DA11 35 D5
  Tilbury RM18 19 C6
Pepys Cres E16 1 A5
Pepys Rise BR6 43 F1
Pepy's Way ME2 52 F8
Perch Cl ME20 82 A4
Perch La TN3 161 D1
Percival Rd BR6 57 B8
Percy Rd DA7 13 E5
Percy St 13 RM17 18 C8
Percy Terr
  Bromley BR1 43 B6
  Royal Tunbridge Wells TN4 159 A6
Peregrine Ct DA16 12 F6
Peregrine Rd ME19 97 A2
Peridot Ct ME15 116 E5
Peridot St E6 1 E8
Perie Row 9 ME7 54 A6
Perimeter Rd ME20 82 C3
Periton Rd SE9 11 D3
Perkins Cl DA9 16 F2
Perpins Rd SE9 12 E1
Perran Cl DA3 48 F5
Perryfield St ME14 99 F6
Perry Gr DA1 16 A3
Perry Hall Cl BR6 44 A2
Perry Hall Prim Sch BR6 43 F3
Perry Hall Rd BR6 44 A2
Perry Hill ME3 22 C1
Perry Ho DA14 30 A3
Perrys La BR6, TN14 74 C6
Perry St
  Chatham ME4 53 E3
  Chislehurst BR7 29 E2
  Crayford DA1 14 E4
  Maidstone ME14 99 F6
  Northfleet DA11 35 F7

PERRY STREET....... 35 F8
Perry Street Gdns BR7.. 29 E2
Perth Ho 4 RM18...... 19 A5
Pescot Ave DA3....... 49 B6
Pested Bars Rd ME17... 116 D5
Petchart CI ME2....... 52 C3
Peterborough Gdns ME2 52 C6
Peters CI DA16........ 12 E5
Petersfield TN2....... 160 E7
Petersfield Dr BR5..... 63 F1
Petersham Dr BR5..... 44 A6
Petersham Gdns BR5... 43 F7
Peter St 5 DA12...... 36 B8
Peterstone Rd SE2..... 3 B4
Petham Court Cotts BR8. 64 C1
Petham Gn ME8....... 55 C2
Petlands ME17........ 116 D5
Petrie Ho 3 SE18..... 12 A1
Pettacre CI SE28...... 2 C3
Petten CI BR5......... 44 D1
Petten Gr BR5........ 44 D1
PETTERIDGE......... 161 F6
Petteridge La TN12.... 161 F7
PETTINGS.......... 63 B3
Pettits Row TN17..... 147 D8
Pett La ME9......... 87 B7
Pettman Cres SE28, SE18. 2 D3
Pett St SE18......... 1 E2
PETTS WOOD........ 43 D5
Petts Wood Rd BR5.... 43 D4
Petts Wood Sta BR5.... 43 C4
Petworth Rd DA6...... 14 A2
Pevensea CI ME16..... 99 F4
Peveral E6........... 2 A7
Peveral Dr ME14...... 101 A5
Peveral Gn ME8....... 69 D4
Peveril CI 15 DA2..... 16 B1
Phalarope Way ME4.... 40 C2
Pharaoh Way ME4..... 40 C2
Pheasant CI E16...... 1 B7
Pheasant La ME15..... 116 B8
Pheasant Rd ME4...... 54 C2
Phelps CI TN15....... 61 E4
Philimore CI SE18...... 2 E1
Philip Ave BR8....... 45 D5
Philpot Almshouse SE9.. 11 F1
Philpot Path 2 SE9.... 11 F1
Philippa Gdns SE9..... 11 D2
Phillippines CI TN6.... 138 D8
Phillips CI DA1....... 15 B1
Phillips Ct ME8....... 55 B2
Philpots TN11........ 125 E6
Philpott's Cross TN18.. 188 E2
Phineas Pett Rd SE9... 11 E4
Phipps Ho 1 SE7...... 1 B1
Phoenix Cotts 11 ME7.. 113 D6
Phoenix Ct 11 ME7.... 54 C6
Phoenix Dr
  Orpington BR2...... 56 D7
  Wateringbury ME18.. 113 D7
Phoenix Ind Est ME1... 53 D7
Phoenix Pk ME15..... 116 F4
Phoenix PI DA1....... 32 D8
Phoenix Rd ME15..... 68 B2
Phoenix Yard Cotts ME18. 97 F1
Picardy Manorway DA17. 4 B3
Picardy Rd DA17...... 4 A2
Picardy St DA17...... 4 A3
Piccadilly Apartments 4
  ME5............... 54 B3
Pickering Ct 12 DA2... 16 B1
Pickering Ho 6 SE18... 2 A2
Pickering St ME15..... 116 B6
Pickford CI DA7...... 13 E5
Pickforde La TN5..... 186 D1
Pickford La DA7...... 13 E5
Pickford Rd DA7...... 13 E5
Pickhill Oast TN30.... 193 B4
Pickhurst La BR2..... 42 A1
Pickle's Way ME3..... 22 A6
Pickmoss La TN14.... 76 A3
Pickwick Cres ME1.... 53 C3
Pickwick Ct SE9...... 28 F7
Pickwick Gdns DA11... 35 D5
Pickwick House DA11.. 35 D5
Pickwick Way BR7.... 29 C2
Piedmont Rd SE18.... 2 D1
Pier Approach Rd ME7. 54 D7
Pierce Mill La TN11... 129 C6
Piermont PI 1 ME7... 42 E7
Pier Par 3 E16...... 2 A5
Pier PI ME2......... 40 A3
Pier Rd
  Gillingham ME7..... 54 E7
  Newham E16........ 2 A4
  Northfleet DA11.... 18 F1
  Swanscombe DA9.... 17 B3
Pier Road Ind Est ME7. 54 D7
Pier Way SE28....... 2 D3
Pigdown La TN8....... 139 D4
Piggott's Cross TN8... 123 D7
Pigsdean Rd DA13..... 51 B2
Pike CI
  Bromley ME1....... 28 B3
  New Hythe ME20.... 82 A4
Pikefields ME8....... 55 C2
PIKEFISH.......... 130 F3
Pikefish La TN12, ME18. 130 F2
Pikey La ME19....... 97 C5
Pile La TN12........ 150 A5
Pilgrim Sch The ME1... 52 F2
Pilgrims Ct
  Dartford DA1....... 16 A2
  Greenwich SE3...... 11 A6
Pilgrims La RH8...... 88 D3

Pilgrims Lakes ME17.... 119 E6
Pilgrims Rd
  Upper Halling ME2.... 65 F6
  Wouldham ME1...... 66 C5
Pilgrims' Rd DA10..... 17 E2
Pilgrims View
  Sandling ME14....... 83 E3
  Swanscombe DA9..... 17 C1
Pilgrims Way
  Boxley ME14........ 84 E3
  Broad Street ME14, ME17 102 C6
  Cuxton ME2......... 53 C6
  Dartford DA1........ 33 B8
  Detling ME14........ 85 B1
  Eccles ME20......... 83 B6
  Hollingbourne ME17... 102 F3
  Lenham ME17........ 119 A1
  Thurnham ME14...... 101 E8
Upper Halling ME2, ME6,
  ME19.............. 65 D3
Vigo Village ME19..... 80 B7
Wrotham TN15....... 79 A3
Pilgrims' Way
  Hill Park TN16...... 89 B4
  Kemsing TN14, TN15... 77 C3
Pilgrims Way Cotts TN15. 77 A2
Pilgrims Way E TN14... 76 D3
Pilgrims Way W TN14... 75 E3
Pilkington Rd BR6..... 57 C8
Pillar Box La
  Crouch TN11........ 111 D5
  Oldbury TN15........ 93 E5
Pilot Rd ME1......... 67 C8
Pilots PI DA12........ 19 C1
Pimpernel CI ME14.... 101 B4
Pimpernel Way ME5.... 67 A7
Pimp's Court Cotts ME15 116 E5
Pinchbeck Rd BR6..... 57 F4
Pincott Rd DA6....... 14 A3
Pincroft Wood DA3.... 49 C6
PINDEN............ 48 C7
Pine Ave ME14........ 36 D7
Pine CI
  Larkfield ME20...... 82 A2
  Swanley BR8........ 45 F5
Pine Cotts ME14...... 99 E8
Pinecrest Gdns BR6.... 56 E4
Pinecroft DA16....... 13 A7
Pine Glade BR6....... 56 F6
Pine Gr
  Edenbridge TN8...... 122 B2
  Gillingham ME7...... 69 A5
  Maidstone ME14..... 100 B6
Pine Ho
  3 Chatham ME5..... 67 F5
  5 Maidstone ME14... 100 B4
Pinehurst
  Chislehurst BR7..... 29 E2
  Sevenoaks TN14..... 92 E6
Pinehurst Wlk 4 BR6... 43 D1
Pine Lodge ME16...... 99 C3
Pineneedle La TN13.... 92 B4
Pine PI ME15......... 99 E1
Pine Rd ME2......... 52 F6
Pine Ridge TN10...... 127 B6
Pine Rise DA13....... 50 A3
Pinesfield La ME19.... 80 B6
Pines Rd BR1........ 42 E7
Pine Tree La TN5..... 94 A2
Pine View TN15....... 99 C7
Pinewood BR7........ 29 A2
Pinewood Ave
  Sevenoaks TN13..... 92 D6
  Sidcup DA15........ 29 D7
Pinewood CI
  Orpington BR6...... 43 D1
  Paddock Wood TN12... 145 F6
Pinewood Ct TN4..... 143 A1
Pinewood Dr
  Chatham ME5....... 84 D8
  Orpington BR6...... 57 E5
Pinewood Gdns TN14... 143 A1
Pinewood Rd DA2..... 31 E6
Pinewood Rd
  Bexley SE2......... 13 D8
  Bromley BR2........ 42 A5
Royal Tunbridge Wells
  TN2................ 159 D5
Pinkham TN12........ 130 A5
Pinkham Gdns TN12.... 130 A5
Pinks Hill BR8....... 45 E4
Pinnacle Hill TN4.... 149 B5
Pinnacle Hill N DA7... 14 B3
Pinnacles The ME4.... 40 C1
Pinnell Rd SE9....... 11 D3
Pinnock La TN12...... 149 E1
Pinnock's Ave DA11.... 36 B7
Pintail CI
  Grain ME3......... 27 B6
  Newham E6......... 1 E8
Pintails The ME4..... 40 B1
Pinton Hill TN5...... 186 B3
Pinto Way SE3....... 11 B3
Pioneer Cotts TN11.... 141 A1
Pioneer Ct 5 ME1.... 53 A5
Pioneer Way ME4..... 45 C6
Pipers CI TN5........ 185 A4
Piper's Green Rd TN16.. 106 B7
Pipers La TN16....... 106 A8
Pippenhall SE9....... 12 B1
Pippin CI ME17....... 115 B2
Pippin Croft ME17.... 69 A6
Pippin Rd TN12....... 129 F6
Pippins The DA13..... 50 A3
Pippin Way ME19..... 97 A2
PIPSDEN........... 189 D1
Pip's View ME3....... 22 F5

Pirbright CI ME5...... 68 D2
Pirie St E16......... 1 B5
Pirrip CI DA12....... 36 F6
Pitchfont La RH8..... 104 B8
Pitfield DA3......... 48 F5
Pitfield Cres SE28.... 3 A5
Pitfield Dr DA13..... 63 F7
Pitfold CI SE12...... 11 B1
Pitfold Rd SE12...... 11 A1
Pit La TN8.......... 122 C4
Pittlesden TN30...... 193 A7
Pittlesden PI 1 TN30.. 193 A7
Pitt Rd
  Chartway Street ME17. 118 A2
  Maidstone ME16..... 99 B1
  Orpington BR6...... 57 C7
Pittsmead Ave BR2.... 42 A2
PITTSWOOD........ 128 B8
Pittswood Cotts TN11.. 128 A8
Pixot Hill TN12...... 146 B2
Pix's La TN17........ 192 A3
Pizien Well Rd ME18.. 113 B7
Place Farm Ave BR6... 43 D1
Place La ME9........ 70 D4
Plain Rd TN12....... 148 C4
Plains Ave ME15..... 100 C1
Plain The TN17...... 177 E8
PLAISTOW......... 28 A2
Plaistow Gr BR1..... 28 B1
Plaistow La BR1..... 42 C8
Plaistow Sq ME14.... 100 C6
Plane Ave DA11..... 35 D8
Plane Tree Ho SE7.... 1 D1
Plane Wlk TN10..... 127 C7
Plantagenet Ho SE18... 1 F3
Plantation CI DA2.... 16 F1
Plantation Dr BR5... 44 D1
Plantation La ME14... 101 A3
Plantation Rd
  Erith DA8.......... 15 A6
  Gillingham ME7..... 55 A6
  Hextable BR8....... 32 A2
Plantation The SE3... 11 A5
PLATT............ 95 C7
Platt CE Prim Sch TN15. 95 C7
Platt Comm TN15.... 95 C7
Platters The ME8.... 69 C7
Platt The TN8...... 122 D1
Platt House La TN15.. 79 C6
Platt Ind Est TN15... 95 B7
Platt Mill CI TN15... 95 B7
Platt Mill Terr TN15.. 95 B7
PLATT'S HEATH..... 119 E1
Platts Heath Prim Sch
  ME17.............. 119 F2
Platt The
  Plaxtol TN15....... 173 B1
  Sutton Valence ME17.. 134 E7
Plaxdale Green Rd TN15. 78 D7
PLAXTOL.......... 110 E8
Plaxtol CI BR1...... 42 C8
Plaxtol La TN15, TN11.. 110 D8
Plaxtol Prim Sch TN15.. 110 E7
Plaxtol Rd DA8..... 14 A7
PLAXTOL SPOUTE... 111 A8
Playstool CI ME9.... 71 B6
Playstool Rd ME9.... 71 A6
Pleasance Rd BR5.... 44 B6
Pleasant Row 10 ME7.. 54 A6
Pleasant Valley La ME15. 116 A8
Pleasant View
  15 Erith DA8....... 4 E1
  Orpington BR6...... 57 C5
Pleasaunce CI SE9.... 11 F3
Pleasure House La ME17 135 A8
Plewis Ho ME7....... 54 E7
Plomley CI ME8...... 69 D4
Plough Cotts ME17... 117 D2
Plough Wents Rd ME17. 117 B2
Plough Wlk TN8..... 122 C3
Plover CI
  Chatham ME5....... 68 D1
  Marlpit Hill TN8.... 122 C3
Plover Rd ME20..... 81 F2
Plowenders CI ME19... 80 D2
Pluckley CI ME8..... 55 C3
Pluckley Rd TN27.... 153 D2
Plug La DA13....... 64 D5
Plumcroft Prim Sch SE18. 12 C8
Plumey Feather Cotts
  TN6.............. 170 E3
Plum La SE18....... 12 C7
Plummer La TN30.... 192 F6
Plummers Croft TN13.. 91 E6
Plumpton Wlk 8 ME15. 116 F6
PLUMSTEAD........ 2 F2
Plumstead Common 12 F8
Plumstead Common Rd
  SE18.............. 12 C8
Plumstead High St SE18,
  SE2................ 2 E2
Plumstead Manor Sch
  SE18.............. 2 C2
Plumstead Rd SE18.... 2 C2
Plumstead Sta SE18... 2 C2
Plum Tree Cotts TN18.. 194 E8
Plumtree Gr ME7..... 69 A4
PLUMTREE GREEN.... 151 A8
Plum Tree La ME9..... 86 B8
Plumtree Rd ME17.... 150 F7
Plumtrees ME16...... 99 A2
Plymouth Dr TN13.... 92 C3
Plymouth Pk TN13.... 92 C3

Plymouth Rd
  Bromley BR1....... 42 B8
  Newham E16....... 1 A8
Plympton CI 8 DA17.. 3 E3
Plymstock Rd DA16... 13 C7
Poachers CI ME5..... 68 C5
Pochard CI ME4..... 40 B1
Pocket Hill TN13.... 108 A7
Pococks Bank TN6... 123 C3
Podkin Wood ME5.... 83 F8
Pointer CI SE28..... 3 D7
Pointer Sch The SE3.. 11 A7
Polebrook Rd SE3.... 11 C4
Polegate Cotts RM17.. 17 E8
Polesden Rd TN2.... 159 D2
Polesteeple Hill TN16. 72 D2
Polhill TN13, TN14.... 75 C8
Polhill Bank Nature
  Reserve* TN14..... 75 D6
Polhill Dr ME5...... 67 F2
Police Station Rd ME19. 97 C8
Pollard CI E16...... 1 A6
Pollard Ct ME7..... 54 C5
Pollards Oak Cres RH8. 104 A3
Pollards Oak Rd RH8.. 104 A3
Pollards Wood Hill RH8. 104 B5
Pollards Wood Rd RH8. 104 B4
Pollard Wlk DA14.... 30 C2
Polley CI TN12...... 160 D7
Pollyhaugh DA4..... 50 E7
Polperro CI BR6..... 43 F3
Polthorne Gr SE18... 2 D2
Polytechnic St 14 SE18. 2 A2
Pond CI SE3........ 11 A5
Pond Farm Rd
  Hucking ME17...... 86 D1
  Oad Street ME9.... 71 F1
Pondfield La DA12... 37 E1
Pondfield Rd BR6.... 57 B7
Pond Hill ME3...... 22 B6
Pond La TN15....... 93 E2
Pond Path ME7..... 29 B2
Pondwood Rise ME4.. 43 E2
Pontefract Rd BR1... 28 A3
Pontoise CI TN13.... 91 F5
Pontoon Dock Sta E16. 1 C5
Pook La TN27....... 168 D3
Poona Rd TN1...... 159 B2
Poonah Rd ME15.... 122 E7
Pope CI TN12....... 149 E4
Pope House La TN30.. 183 B4
Pope Rd BR2....... 42 D4
Popes La ME8....... 121 A8
Popes Row Cotts TN17. 176 F2
Pope St ME16....... 99 C2
Pope Street Cotts SE9.. 28 F7
Popes Wood ME14.... 36 C4
Poplar Ave
  Gravesend DA12.... 36 C4
  Orpington BR6..... 57 B8
Poplar CI
  Hoo St Werburgh ME3. 40 E3
  Rochester ME2..... 52 F5
Poplar Hill TN30.... 199 D4
Poplar Gr ME16..... 99 C5
Poplar Mount DA17.. 4 C2
Poplar PI SE28...... 3 C6
Poplar Rd
  Rochester ME2..... 52 E5
  Wittersham TN30... 199 D4
Poplars CI DA3...... 49 C6
Poplars The DA12.... 36 B8
Poplar Wlk DA13.... 50 B3
Poplicans Rd ME2... 52 B3
Poppy CI
  Erith DA17........ 4 B4
  Gillingham ME7.... 54 E5
Maidstone ME15..... 99 D3
Porchester CI
  Hartley DA3....... 48 F5
  Loose ME15........ 116 A6
Porchfield CI DA12... 36 C5
Porcupine CI SE9.... 28 E6
Porrington CI BR7... 43 A8
Port Ave DA9...... 17 B1
Port CI
  Chatham ME5...... 68 B3
  Maidstone ME14.... 101 A5
Porter CI RM20..... 17 C8
Porter Rd E6....... 1 F7
Porter CI TN12..... 161 F6
Porters Wlk ME1.... 117 E4
Porters Wood TN12.. 161 E6
Porteus CI DA1..... 32 D6
Porthallow CI 11 BR6. 57 F6
Port Hill BR6...... 74 B7
Porthkerry Ave DA16. 13 A3
Portland Ave
  Gravesend DA12.... 36 B6
  Sidcup DA15....... 13 A1
Portland CI TN10.... 127 D7
Portland Cres SE9... 28 E6
Portland PI
  1 Snodland ME6.... 82 A8
  Swanscombe DA9.... 17 C3
Portland Rd
  Bromley, Mottingham SE9. 28 E6
  Bromley, Sundridge BR1. 28 C3
  Gillingham ME7..... 54 E6
  Gravesend DA12.... 36 B7
  Northfleet DA11.... 18 D1
  Wouldham ME1..... 66 C4
Portland St 11 ME4.. 54 B2
Portland Villas DA12.. 36 B7
Portman CI
  Bexley DA5........ 13 E4
  Maypole DA5....... 31 E7

Portman Pk TN9...... 127 C3
Portmeadow Wlk SE2... 3 B4
Portobello Par TN15... 62 A2
Portree Mews ME7.... 54 E3
Port Rise ME4....... 53 F3
Portsdown CI ME1.... 99 B2
Portsea Rd RM18..... 52 C6
Portsmouth Ave ME2... 52 D6
Portsmouth Mews E16.. 1 B5
Port Victoria Rd ME3... 27 C4
Portway Gdns SE18.... 11 D7
Portway Rd ME3..... 39 B7
Post Barn Rd ME4..... 53 F2
Postern Ind Est TN9... 127 D1
Postern La TN9, TN11... 127 E1
Postley Ind Ctr ME15... 100 A2
Postley Rd ME15...... 100 A1
Postmill Dr ME15..... 99 F1
Post Office Rd 12 TN18. 188 F2
Post Office Sq TN1.... 159 A3
Potash La TN15...... 95 C6
Pot Kiln La TN26..... 169 E4
POTMAN'S HEATH.... 198 E4
POTTER'S FORSTAL... 137 B2
Potter's La TN18..... 189 A6
Pottery Rd
  Coldblow DA5...... 31 C6
  Hoo St Werburgh ME3.. 40 D5
Potyn Ho ME1...... 53 C4
Poulters Wood BR2... 56 D5
Pound Bank CI TN15... 61 F2
Pound Ct BR8....... 57 D8
Pound Court Dr BR6... 57 D8
Poundfield Rd TN18... 196 B5
Pound Green Ct 4 DA5. 31 A8
Pound Ho TN11...... 128 D8
Pound La
  Halstead TN14...... 74 D4
  Sevenoaks TN13.... 92 C3
Pound Park Rd SE7... 1 D2
Pound Pl SE9....... 12 A1
Pound Rd TN12...... 129 F6
POUNDSBRIDGE..... 157 D7
Poundsbridge Hill TN11,
  TN3.............. 157 D7
Poundsbridge La TN11.. 141 D2
Pounsley Rd TN13.... 91 E6
Pout Rd ME6........ 81 F7
POVEREST......... 44 A4
Poverest Prim Sch BR5.. 44 A4
Poverest Rd BR5..... 44 A4
Povey Ave ME2..... 39 C2
Powdermill CI TN4... 159 C6
Powder Mill La
  Dartford DA1...... 32 F6
  Leigh TN11........ 126 B3
Royal Tunbridge Wells
  TN4.............. 159 B6
  Tonbridge TN11.... 126 E2
POWDER MILLS..... 126 E2
Powell Ave DA2..... 33 E6
Powell CI ME20..... 83 A3
Powerhub Bsns Ctr ME16. 99 F5
Power Ind Est DA8... 15 A6
Powercroft Rd DA14.. 30 C2
Power Station Rd ME3.. 27 B4
Powis St SE18...... 2 A3
Powlett Rd ME2..... 39 C1
Powster Rd BR1..... 28 B3
Powys CI DA7....... 13 D8
Poynder Dr ME6.... 66 A2
Poynder Rd ME18... 19 B6
Poynings CI BR6.... 58 C8
Poyntell Cres BR7... 43 D8
Poyntell Rd TN12... 149 F4
Pragnell Rd SE12... 28 B6
Prail's La TN12..... 145 E2
Pratling St ME20.... 83 C4
PRATLING STREET.... 83 C3
PRATT'S BOTTOM.... 58 D7
Pratts Bottom Prim Sch
  TN14.............. 74 C1
Premier Bsns Ctr ME4.. 54 C6
Premier Par ME20.... 82 E1
Prentiss Ct SE7..... 1 D2
Prescott Ave BR5.... 43 B3
Presentation Ho 9 DA12. 36 B8
Preston Av Sq SE7.... 28 F4
Preston Ave ME7.... 54 E3
Preston Ct DA14.... 29 F4
Preston Dr DA7..... 13 D6
Preston Hall Hospl ME20. 82 F7
Preston Ho
  Sutton at Hone DA4.... 47 D3
  1 Woolwich SE18.... 2 A2
Preston Rd
  Northfleet DA11.... 35 E7
  Tonbridge TN9..... 127 A4
Prestons Rd BR2.... 56 A8
Preston Way ME8.... 55 B2
Prestwood CI SE18... 13 A8
Pretoria Ho
  4 Erith DA8........ 14 E2
  6 Maidstone ME15.. 116 E5
Pretoria Rd
  Chatham ME4...... 53 F2
  Gillingham ME7.... 54 D3
Prettymans La TN8... 122 F4
Pridmore Rd ME6... 81 F6
Priestdale Ct ME4... 53 E1
Priestfield Rd ME7... 54 E1
Priestfields ME1.... 53 B3
Priestfield Stad (Gillingham
  FC) ME7........... 54 E1
Priest Hill RH8..... 104 B6
Priestlands Park Rd DA15 29 F1
Priestley Dr
  Lunsford ME20..... 81 F7

Priestley Dr *continued*
Tonbridge TN10 127 E7
Priest's Wlk DA12 37 A6
PRIESTWOOD 64 B5
PRIESTWOOD GREEN 64 C5
Priestwood Rd DA13 64 C5
PRIMMER'S GREEN 184 F5
Primmett Cl TN15 61 E4
Primrose Ave ME8 69 B5
Primrose Cl ME4 67 E7
Primrose Dr ME20 82 D1
Primrose Ho 10 ME15 116 E7
Primrose Rd ME2 65 E5
Primrose Terr DA12 36 C7
Primrose Wlk TN12 146 A5
Prince Arthur Rd ME7 54 B6
Prince Charles Ave
Chatham ME5 68 B4
Sutton at Hone DA4 47 D7
Prince Consort Dr BR7 43 D8
Prince Henry Rd SE7 11 D7
Prince Imperial Rd
Chislehurst BR7 29 B1
Woolwich SE18 11 F6
Prince John Rd SE9 11 E2
Prince Michael of Kent Ct
DA1 15 A5
Prince of Wales Rd SE3 11 A6
Prince Phillip Lodge The
ME20 82 F1
Prince Regent La E16 1 C7
Prince Regent Sta E16 1 C6
Prince Rupert Rd SE9 11 F3
Princes Ave
Chatham ME5 68 B5
Dartford DA2 33 B7
Orpington BR5 43 E4
Princes Cl DA14 30 D5
PRINCES PARK 68 B6
Prince's Plain BR2 42 E1
Princes Plain Prim Sch
BR2 42 E2
Princes Rd
Dartford DA1 32 D7
Dartford, Fleet-Downs DA1 33 C7
Gravesend DA12 36 C5
Hextable BR8 32 A2
Princess Alice Way SE28 2 D4
Princess Cl SE28 3 D7
Princess Margaret Rd
RM18 20 D7
Princess Mary Ave ME4 54 B7
Princess Par BR6 57 A7
Princess Royal University
Hospl BR6 57 A6
Princess St DA7 13 F4
Princes St
Gravesend DA11 19 B1
Maidstone ME14 100 A5
Prince's St
Rochester ME1 53 C4
Royal Tunbridge Wells
TN2 159 C3
Princes View DA1 33 A7
Princes Way ME14 85 A1
PRINTSTILE 142 A3
Prinys Dr ME8 69 C4
Priolo Rd SE7 1 C1
Prioress Cres 11 DA9 17 C3
Prior Pl ME1 53 B1
Priorsdean Cl ME16 98 E1
Priorsford Ave BR5 44 B5
Priors Heath TN17 177 C2
Prior's Way TN8 155 A6
Priory Ave BR5 43 D3
Priory Cl
Bromley BR7 42 F8
Dartford DA1 15 D2
East Farleigh ME15 115 B8
Priory Ct
5 Dartford DA1 15 D1
Gillingham ME8 55 A2
Rochester ME1 53 D5
Priory Dr SE2 3 D1
Priory Fields DA4 60 F8
Priory Gate 4 ME14 100 A5
Priory Gdns DA1 15 D2
Priory Gdns★ BR6 44 B2
Priory Gr
Aylesford ME20 82 D1
Tonbridge TN9 143 B8
Priory Hill DA1 15 D1
Priory Ho 4 SE7 11 C8
Priory Hospl Hayes Grove
The BR2 56 A8
Priory La DA4 46 F1
Priory Leas SE9 28 E7
Priory Mews DA2 33 C8
Priory Pl DA1 15 D1
Priory Rd
Dartford DA1 15 D1
Gillingham ME8 55 A2
Maidstone ME15 100 A3
Rochester ME2 53 A6
Tonbridge TN9 143 C8
Priory Retail Pk DA1 15 D2
Priory Sch The BR5 44 C1
Priory Sh Ctr The DA1 32 E8
Priory Sports Ctr BR6 44 C1
Priory St TN9 143 B8
Priory Way TN30 193 C7
Priory Wlk TN9 143 B8
Pristling La TN12 165 B8
Pritchard Ct ME7 54 C3
Progress Est The ME15 117 A4
Prospect Ave 8 ME2 53 B8
Prospect Cl DA17 4 A2
Prospect Cotts
Lamberhurst TN3 176 A3
Pratt's Bottom BR6 58 C2
Prospect Gr DA12 36 D8
Prospect Pk TN4 142 F1
Prospect Pl
Bromley BR2 42 B6
Collier Street TN12 131 C2
Prospect Pl DA1 15 F1
Prospect Pl
Gravesend DA12 36 D8
Grays RM17 18 B8
Maidstone ME16 99 E3
Prospect Rd
Royal Tunbridge Wells, Camden
Park TN2 159 C3
Royal Tunbridge Wells
TN4 158 F8
Sevenoaks TN13 92 C4
Prospect Row
Chatham, Brompton ME7 54 A6
Chatham ME4 54 A3
Prospect Vale SE18 1 E2
Prospero Ho 7 DA17 4 A1
Provender Way ME14 100 E5
Providence Chapel TN12 148 C6
Providence Cotts
Groombridge TN3 171 C7
Higham ME3 38 B2
Providence Pl TN27 151 A7
Providence St DA9 17 A2
Prudhoe Ct 27 DA2 16 B1
Pucknells Cl BR8 45 C8
Puddingcake La TN17 192 C5
Pudding La
Maidstone ME14 99 F4
Seal TN15 92 F6
Pudding Rd ME8 69 F8
PUDDLEDOCK 31 E2
Puddledock La
Hextable BR8, DA2 31 F2
Toy's Hill TN16 106 A3
Puffin Rd ME3 27 B5
Pullington Cotts TN17 190 E6
Pullman Mews SE12 28 B5
Pullman Pl SE9 11 E2
Pump Cl ME19 81 D1
Pump La
Chelsfield BR6 59 B5
Gillingham ME7, ME8 55 D3
Pump Terr TN1 159 B4
Punch Croft DA3 62 E7
Purbeck Rd ME4 53 E2
Purcell Ave TN10 127 F6
PURFLEET 16 A8
Purfleet By-Pass RM19 16 D8
Purland Rd SE28 2 F4
Purneys Rd SE9 11 D3
Purrett Rd SE18 2 F1
Purser Way ME7 54 C7
Pursey Cl TN15 61 E4
PUTLANDS 145 F5
Putlands Sp & L Ctr
TN12 146 A5
Puttenden Rd TN11 110 F3
PYE CORNER 136 A6
Pym Orch TN16 90 C3
Pympes Court Farm Ctr★
ME15 115 E6
Pynham Cl SE2 3 B3
Pyrus Cl ME5 84 A8

Q

Quadrant The DA7 13 D7
Quaggy Wlk SE3 11 A3
Quaker Cl TN13 92 D4
Quaker Dr TN17 179 D6
Quaker La TN17 179 D6
Quakers Cl DA3 48 E6
Quaker's Hall La TN13 92 C5
Quantock Cl TN2 159 D5
Quantock Rd DA1 14 E5
Quarries The ME17 116 C4
Quarry Bank TN9 143 A7
Quarry Cotts
Rockrobin TN5 184 D7
Sevenoaks TN13 92 A4
Quarry Hill TN15 92 D4
Quarry Hill Par 3 TN9 143 B8
Quarry Hill Rd
Borough Green TN15 94 F6
Tonbridge TN9 143 B8
Quarry Rd
Maidstone ME15 100 A2
Royal Tunbridge Wells
TN1 159 B5
Quarry Rise TN9 143 A7
Quarry Sq ME14 100 A5
Quarry Wood Ind Est
ME20 98 E8
Quay La DA9 17 B3
Quayside ME4 54 B8
Quebec Ave TN16 89 D1
Quebec Cotts 9 TN16 89 D1
Quebec Ho★ TN16 89 D1
Quebec Rd RM18 19 A5
Quebec Sq 10 TN16 89 D1
Queen Anne Ave BR2 42 A6
Queen Anne Gate DA7 13 D4
Queen Anne Rd ME14 100 B4
Queen Borough Gdns
BR7 29 D2
Queenbridge Ind Pk
RM20 17 A8
Queendown Ave ME8 69 D5
Queendown Warren Nature
Reserve★ ME9 70 B3
Queen Elizabeth Sq
ME15 116 D6
Queen Elizabeth The
SE18 11 E7
Queen Mary's Hospl DA14 30 A2
Queen Mother Ct The
ME1 53 B4
Queen's Ave
Maidstone ME16 99 D5
Snodland ME6 82 A8
Queens Cotts TN5 184 E6
Queenscroft Rd SE9 11 D1
Queens Ct
Edenbridge TN8 122 D1
Gillingham ME8 70 A8
11 Hawkhurst TN18 189 A2
Paddock Wood TN12 146 C8
1 Sidcup DA14 30 A4
Queen's Dr TN14 92 C7
Queen's Farm Rd DA12 37 E7
Queensgate ME16 99 D5
Queens Gate Gdns BR7 43 D8
Queens Gdns DA2 33 B7
Queen's Gdns TN4 159 B6
Queens Ho ME16 99 B3
Queensland Ct RM18 18 F5
Queensland Ho 2 E16 2 A5
Queen's Mews 12 TN18 189 A2
Queen's Pas BR7 29 B2
Queens Rd
Erith DA8 14 E8
Gravesend DA12 36 C5
Queen's Rd
Bexley DA16 13 B5
Bromley BR1 42 A7
Chatham ME5 54 D1
Chislehurst BR7 29 B2
Gillingham ME7 54 C4
Hawkhurst TN18 189 A2
Maidstone ME16 99 C4
Royal Tunbridge Wells
TN4 159 B6
Snodland ME6 82 A8
Queens St ME3 40 B8
Queen St
Bexley DA7 13 F4
Chatham ME4 54 A4
Erith DA8 14 E8
Gravesend DA12 19 B1
Kings Hill ME19 97 B3
Paddock Wood TN12 146 D7
Rochester ME1 53 C4
Sandhurst TN18 196 B5
QUEEN STREET 146 D7
Queensway
Allhallows-on-Sea ME3 9 D3
Hayes BR2, BR4 56 A6
Orpington BR5 43 C3
Queens Way ME14 85 A1
Queenswood Rd
Kit's Coty ME20 83 D7
Sidcup DA15 12 F1
Quentins Rd TN16 73 B3
Quernmore Cl BR1 28 A2
Quernmore Rd BR1 28 A2
Quern The ME15 99 E1
Quested Way ME17 119 C6
Questor DA1 32 F6
Quickrells Ave ME3 22 B5
Quickthorn Cres ME5 67 E5
Quiet Nook BR2 56 D7
Quilter Rd BR5 44 D1
Quilters Place SE9 29 C7
Quilter St SE18 2 F1
Quincewood Gdns TN10 127 B7
Quindell Place ME19 97 C3
Quinion Cl ME5 84 A8
Quinnell Cl SE18 2 F1
Quinnell St ME8 55 E1
Quixote Cres ME2 39 B1

R

RABBIT'S CROSS 133 E3
Rabbits Rd DA4 47 E7
Rablus Pl DA4 46 F3
Racefield Cl DA12 37 E1
Rackham Cl DA16 13 B5
Radburn Pl DA10 17 E2
Radfield Dr 3 DA2 33 C8
Radfield Way DA15 29 D8
Radland Rd E16 1 A7
Radleigh Gdns ME1 53 E1
Radley Ho 13 SE2 3 D4
Radnor Ave DA16 13 B2
Radnor Cl
Chislehurst BR7 29 E2
Maidstone ME14 99 E7
Radnor Cres SE18 13 A7
Radzan Cl DA2 31 E6
Raeburn Ave DA1 15 B2
Raeburn Cl TN10 127 E6
Raeburn Rd DA15 12 E1
Rafford Way BR1 42 B6
Raggatt Pl ME15 100 B2
Ragge Way TN15 92 F7
Raggleswood BR7 43 A8
Rag Hill TN16 88 E6
Rag Hill Cl TN16 88 E6
Rag Hill Rd TN16 88 E6
Raglan Ct SE12 11 A2
Raglan Prim Sch BR2 42 D5
Raglan Rd
Bromley BR2 42 C5
Erith DA17 3 F2
Raglan Rd *continued*
Woolwich SE18 2 C1
Ragstone Ct ME20 98 C8
Ragstone Fields ME15 116 E4
Ragstone Rd ME15 101 A2
Ragstones TN15 92 F7
Railway Cotts
Cowden TN8 155 D8
Marden TN12 148 D6
Railway Pl
Erith DA17 4 A3
21 Gravesend DA12 19 B1
Railway Sidings The
DA13 50 A4
Railway St
Chatham ME4 53 F4
Gillingham ME7 54 D6
Northfleet DA11 18 A2
Railway Street Ind Pk
ME7 54 D6
Railway Terr TN16 89 D1
RAINHAM
Essex 4 F8
Gillingham 69 E8
Rainham Cl
Maidstone ME15 100 A1
Sidcup SE9 12 E1
Rainham Mark Gram Sch
ME8 55 D2
Rainham Rd ME5 54 C3
Rainham Sch for Girls
ME8 69 C8
Rainham Sh Ctr 2 ME8 55 F1
Rainham Sta ME8 55 F1
Rainton Rd SE7 1 A1
Raleigh Cl
Chatham ME5 68 A6
Erith DA8 14 F8
Raleigh Mews 6 BR6 57 F5
Ramac Ind Est SE7 1 B1
Ramac Way SE7 1 B1
Ramillies Cl ME5 68 A6
Ramillies Rd DA15 13 B1
Rammell Mews TN17 179 D4
Rampion Cl ME14 100 E5
RAMSDEN 44 C1
Ramsden Cl BR5 44 C1
Ramsden La TN17 190 F4
Ramsden Rd
Erith DA8 14 D7
Orpington BR5 44 B1
Ramsey Cl ME15 100 A2
Ramsgate Cl E16 1 B5
RAMSLYE 158 D1
Ramslye Rd TN4 172 E8
Ramus Wood Ave BR6 57 E5
Rance Ho 11 SE18 1 E2
Rancliffe Gdns SE9 11 E3
Randall Cl DA8 14 C8
Randall Hill Rd TN15 78 F3
Randall Rd ME4 53 E1
Randalls Row ME15 115 F5
Randall St ME14 99 F6
Randle's La TN14 74 D5
Randolph App E16 1 C7
Randolph Cl DA7 14 C4
Randolph Cotts ME2 39 B1
Randolph Ho ME7 54 C5
Randolph Rd
Gillingham ME7 54 C5
Orpington BR2 42 F1
Ranelagh Gdns DA11 35 F8
Rangefield Rd BR1 28 A3
Range Rd DA12 36 E8
Rangeworth Pl DA15 29 F5
Rankine Rd TN2 159 D7
Ranleigh Gdns DA7 13 F7
Ranmore Path BR5 44 A5
Ranscombe Cl ME2 52 D5
Ranscombe Farm Cotts
ME2 52 C4
Ransom Rd 1 SE7 1 C1
Ranters La TN17 177 C7
Ranworth Cl DA7, DA8 14 E5
Raphael Ave RM18 19 B7
Raphael Ct TN11 126 E7
Raphael Rd DA12 36 D8
Rashleigh Way DA4 47 C5
Ratcliffe Cl SE12 28 A8
Ratcliffe Highway
High Halstow ME3 24 D5
Hoo St Werburgh ME3 40 C6
Rathmore Rd
Gravesend DA11 36 B8
Greenwich SE7 1 B1
Raven Cl ME20 82 A1
Ravensbourne Coll of Design
& Communication BR7 28 F3
Ravensbourne Ct 22 BR5 44 D1
Ravensbourne Rd
Bromley BR1 42 A6
Crayford DA1 15 A4
Ravensbourne Sch The
BR2 42 B5
Ravensbury Rd BR5 44 A5
Ravenscourt Rd BR5 44 B7
Ravenscroft Cl 5 E16 1 A8
Ravenscroft Cres SE9 28 F5
Ravenscroft Rd E16 1 A8
Ravens Dane Cl ME15 101 A1
Ravenshill BR7 43 B8
Raven's Hoe DA14 30 A3
Ravens Knowle ME1 66 D4
Ravensleigh Gdns BR1 28 B3
Ravensquay Bsns Ctr BR5 44 B4
Ravens Way SE12 11 A2
Ravenswood DA5 30 E7
Ravenswood Ave
Rochester ME2 39 B1
7 Rochester ME2 53 B8
Royal Tunbridge Wells
TN2 159 D6
Ravens Wood Sch BR2 56 D7
Ravensworth Rd SE9 28 F4
Ravine Gr SE18 12 E8
Rawdon Rd ME15 100 A3
Rawlings Cl 3 BR6 57 F5
Rawsthorne Cl E16 1 F5
Rayfield Cl BR2 42 E3
Rayfield Ct ME6 66 B1
Rayford Cl DA1 15 C2
Ray Lamb Way DA8 15 B7
Rayleas Cl SE18 12 B6
Rayleigh Cl ME16 99 D7
Rayleigh Ho 2 ME15 116 D8
Rayleigh Rd E16 1 B5
Raymere Gdns SE18 12 E7
Raymer Rd ME14 100 B8
Raymond Postgate Ct 5
SE28 3 B6
Raynehurst Com Prim Sch
DA12 36 F5
Rayners Ct DA11 18 B1
Raynham Villas TN12 132 A4
Rays Hill DA4 47 C4
Reader's Bridge Rd
TN30 182 E4
Readers Ct ME18 114 A8
Reading Ho 4 ME15 116 F5
Readscroft Rd ME8 69 D5
Read Way DA12 36 E3
Rebecca Ct DA14 30 B4
Recreation Ave ME6 82 A8
Recreation Cl ME14 100 B6
Recreation Ground Rd
TN30 193 B7
Rectory Bsns Ctr 2 DA14 30 B4
Rectory Cl
Crayford DA1 14 E3
Sidcup DA14 30 B4
Snodland ME6 82 A8
Wouldham ME1 66 C5
Rectory Ct 3 RM17 18 D8
Rectory Dr TN3 142 D3
Rectory Field Cres SE7 11 C7
Rectory Fields TN17 179 D5
Rectory Grange ME1 53 C2
Rectory La
Brasted TN16 90 C3
Harrietsham ME17 119 E5
Ightham TN15 94 C5
Maidstone ME16 99 A1
Sevenoaks TN13 92 C1
Sidcup DA14 30 C4
Sutton Valence ME17 134 C6
Titsey TN16 88 E4
Rectory Lane N ME19 81 E2
Rectory Lane S ME19 81 E1
Rectory Mdw DA13 35 A2
Rectory Park Rd TN12 163 A2
Rectory Pl SE18 2 A2
Rectory Rd
Cliffe ME3 22 A3
4 Grays RM17 18 D8
New Ash Green TN15 63 C5
Orpington BR2 56 D3
Swanscombe DA10 34 E8
West Tilbury RM18 19 D8
Reculver Wlk ME15 116 F7
Redbank ME19 81 E2
Red Barracks Rd 4 SE18 1 F2
Redbourne Dr SE28 3 D7
Redbridge Cl ME5 68 C4
Red Cedars Rd BR6 43 E2
Redcliffe La ME14 100 B7
Redding Cl DA2 33 E6
Redding Ho SE18 1 E3
Reddy Rd DA8 14 F8
Rede Court Rd ME2 52 E8
Rede Wood Rd ME16 98 F3
Redfern Ave ME7 54 E5
Redfern Ho ME2 65 F5
Redgate Dr BR2 56 B8
RED HILL 97 F1
Red Hill
Chislehurst BR7 29 B3
Red Hill ME18 97 F1
Red Hill Prim Sch BR7 29 B3
Redhill Rd DA3 62 F6
Redhill Wood DA3 63 A7
Redhill Wood Sch DA3 48 F3
Red Ho The RH8 104 C5
Red House★ DA6 13 E3
Red House Gdns ME18 113 C7
Red House La DA6 13 E3
Redhouse Rd TN16 88 C6
Red La
Limpsfield RH8 121 B7
Oxted RH8 104 B2
Redland Shaw ME4 53 E1
Redlands Rd TN13 91 F3
Redlane Cotts RH8 104 B2
Redleaf Cl
Erith DA17 14 A8
Royal Tunbridge Wells
TN2 159 D6
Red Leaf Cl TN11 124 F2
Red Lion Cl BR5 44 C3
Red Lion La SE18 12 A6
Red Lion Pl SE18 12 A6
Red Lion Sq TN15 110 E8
Red Lodge Cres DA5 31 E5

Red Lodge Rd DA5 . . . . 31 D5
Redmans Ind Est RM18. . . 20 A8
Redmans La BR6, TN4. . . . 59 E4
Red Oak TN18 . . . . 194 E8
Red Oak Cl BR4 . . . . 57 B8
Redpoll Way DA18 . . . . 3 D5
Redpoll Wlk TN12 . . . . . . 146 A5
Red Robin Cotts ME9 . . . . . 71 B6
Redroses Cl TN12 . . . . . . 129 F6
Redruth Manor **3** ME4 . . . 54 C6
Redsells Cl ME15. . . . . . . 101 A1
Redshank Rd ME4. . . . . 40 B1
Red St DA13 . . . . 35 B2
Redstart Cl E6 . . . . 1 E8
REDSTREET. 35 B2
Redvers Rd ME4 . . . . 54 A2
Redwall La
   Bogden TN12 . . . . 133 C4
   Linton ME15, ME17 . . . . 132 C6
Redwell Gr ME19 . . . . 97 C2
Redwell La TN15 . . . . 94 B4
Redwing Cl ME20 . . . . 82 A2
Redwing Path SE28 . . . . 2 D4
Redwing Rd ME5 . . . . 68 B7
Redwings La TN2 . . . . 144 E2
Redwood Cl
   Chatham ME5 . . . . 68 B2
   Sidcup DA15 . . . . 30 A7
Redwood Ct DA1 . . . . 16 A1
Redwood Pk TN12 . . . . . . 145 A5
Reed Ave BR6 . . . . 57 E7
Reed Cl
   Eltham SE12 . . . . 11 A2
   Newham E16 . . . . 1 A8
   New Hythe ME20 . . . . 82 A5
Reed Court Cotts TN12 . . 132 A5
Reed Court Farm* TN12 132 A5
Reed Ct DA9 . . . . 17 C3
Reedham Cres ME3 . . . . . . 34 B7
Reeds La TN11 . . . . 110 E5
Reed St ME3 . . . . 22 B6
Reeves Cl TN12 . . . . 149 E4
Reeves Cres BR8 . . . . 45 D6
Reeves Ct
   Ditton ME19 . . . . 82 A1
   Fordcombe TN3 . . . . 157 B5
Reeves Rd SE18 . . . . 12 B8
Reeves Terr TN5 . . . . 186 E1
Reflection The E16 . . . . 2 B4
Reform Rd ME4 . . . . 54 B2
Regency Cl
   Gillingham ME8 . . . . 69 C3
   West Kingsdown TN15 . . . 61 E4
Regency Hall **31** TN2 . . . 159 A2
Regency Ho TN2 . . . . 159 A2
Regency Way DA6 . . . . 13 E4
Regent Dr ME15 . . . . 116 A8
Regent Pl TN2 . . . . 159 D3
Regent Rd ME7 . . . . 54 C4
Regents Ct **3** DA11 . . . . . 19 B1
Regents Dr BR2 . . . . 56 D5
Regent's Pl SE13 . . . . 11 A5
Regent Sq DA17 . . . . 4 B2
Regent St TN17 . . . . 191 E4
Regent Way ME15 . . . . 97 C3
Regina Ct TN4 . . . . 158 F4
Reginald Ave ME2 . . . . 52 C3
Reginald Rd ME16. . . . . . . 99 E3
Reidhaven Rd SE18 . . . . 2 E2
Reigate Rd BR1, SE12 . . . . 28 A5
Reinckendorf Ave SE9 . . . 12 D1
Reinden Gr ME15 . . . . 100 F1
Rembrandt Cl ME10 . . . . . 127 E6
Rembrandt Dr DA11 . . . . . . 35 E5
Remington Rd E6 . . . . 1 F7
Rendlebury Ho **12** SE18. . . . 1 F2
Renfrew Cl E6 . . . . 2 A6
Rennets Cl SE9 . . . . 12 E2
Rennets Wood Ho SE9 . . . 12 D2
Rennets Wood Rd SE9 . . . 12 D2
Renovation The E16 . . . . 2 B4
Renown Rd ME5 . . . . 68 C2
Renshaw Cl **7** DA17 . . . . . 13 F8
Renton Dr BR5 . . . . 44 D2
Repository Rd SE18 . . . . 1 F1
Repton Rd BR6 . . . . 58 A6
Repton Way ME5. . . . . 67 F4
Reservoir Cl DA9 . . . . 17 C1
Resolution Cl ME5 . . . . 68 A6
Resolution Wlk SE18 . . . . . . 1 F3
Restavon Pk TN16. . . . . . . 73 B3
Restharrow Rd ME14 . . . . 100 E4
Restharrow Way ME4 . . . . 40 C1
Restmore Cl ME3 . . . . 22 A4
Restons Cres SE9 . . . . 12 E1
Retreat The
   Grays RM17 . . . . 18 B8
   Orpington BR6 . . . . 58 B4
   Platt TN15 . . . . 95 D8
Revell Rise SE18 . . . . 12 F8
Revenge Rd ME5 . . . . 84 C8
Reventlow Rd SE9 . . . . 29 C7
Reynard Cl BR1 . . . . 43 A6
Reynolds Gdns **3** SE7. . . . . 1 B1
Reynolds Cl TN10 . . . . 127 E6
Reynolds Fields ME3 . . . . . 38 C6
Reynolds La TN4 . . . . 158 F7
Reynolds Performing Arts
   Academy DA5 . . . . 31 E6
Reynolds Pl SE3 . . . . 11 B7
Rhodes Ho **5** ME5 . . . . 54 C2
Rhode St ME4 . . . . 54 A4
Rhodewood Cl ME15 . . . . 101 A1
Rhododendron Ave DA13. 64 A6

Ribblesdale Rd DA2 . . . . . . 33 C7
Ribston Cl BR2. . . . . 42 F1
Ribston Gdns TN12. . . . . . 145 F7
Ricardo Path **5** SE28 . . . . . 3 C5
Rice Par BR5 . . . . 43 D4
Richard Beau Nash
   Apartments **4** TN1 . . . 159 B4
Richard Cl SE18 . . . . 1 E2
Richard House Dr E16. . . . . 1 F7
Richard Neve Ho **6** SE18 . . 2 C2
Richard's Cl TN11 . . . . 124 F2
Richardson Cl **7** DA9 . . . . . 17 A2
Richardson Rd TN4 . . . . . 159 A5
Richard St
   Chatham ME4 . . . . 53 F4
   Rochester ME1 . . . . 53 C3
Richborough Ct ME13 . . . . 44 D5
Richborough Dr ME2 . . . . . 39 A1
Richings House BR5 . . . . . . 44 A8
Richmer Rd DA8 . . . . 15 A7
Richmond Ave ME19 . . . . . 97 B3
Richmond Cl
   Biggin Hill TN16 . . . . 88 B8
   Chatham ME5 . . . . 68 B4
   Rochester ME2 . . . . 39 F1
Richmond Ct
   Bromley BR1 . . . . 28 B1
   Sevenoaks TN13 . . . . 92 B4
Richmond Dr DA12 . . . . . . 36 E6
Richmond Pl
   Royal Tunbridge Wells
     TN2. . . . . 159 B3
   Woolwich SE18 . . . . 2 C2
Richmond Rd
   Gillingham ME7 . . . . 54 C7
   1 Grays RM17 . . . . 18 C8
Richmond Way ME15. . . . 116 A8
Richmount Gdns SE13. . . . 11 A4
Ricketts Hill Rd TN16. . . . . 88 E7
Rickyard Path SE9 . . . . 11 E3
Riddlesdale Ave TN4 . . . . 159 A6
Riddons Rd SE12 . . . . 28 C4
Rideout St SE18 . . . . 1 F2
Rider Cl DA15 . . . . 12 E1
Ridge Ave DA1 . . . . 14 F1
Ridgebrook Rd SE3 . . . . . . 11 D4
Ridge Cl SE28 . . . . 24 C7
Ridgecroft Cl DA5. . . . . . . 31 C7
Ridge La DA13 . . . . 64 A2
Ridgelands TN3 . . . . 142 C4
Ridge Meadow Prim Sch
   ME5 . . . . 67 F6
Ridge The
   Groombridge TN3 . . . . . . 171 A6
   Orpington BR6 . . . . 57 D8
   Sidcup DA5 . . . . 30 F8
Ridge View Sch TN10 . . . 127 D5
Ridgeway
   Dartford DA2 . . . . 33 E1
   Hayes BR2 . . . . 36 A3
   Hurst Green TN19 . . . . . 194 A3
   Pembury TN2 . . . . 160 D3
   The Moor TN18 . . . . 194 E8
Ridge Way
   Crayford DA1 . . . . 14 F1
   Marlpit Hill TN8 . . . . 122 D4
Ridgeway Ave DA12. . . . . . 36 B5
Ridgeway Bglws DA12. . . . 37 F1
Ridgeway Cres
   Orpington BR6 . . . . 57 E7
   Tonbridge TN10 . . . . 127 D4
Ridgeway Crescent Gdns
   BR6 . . . . 57 E7
Ridgeway Dr BR1 . . . . 28 B4
Ridgeway Cl DA15 . . . . 12 F2
Ridgeway The TN4 . . . . . . 143 B1
Ridgeway The
   Chatham ME4 . . . . 54 A6
   Gillingham ME7 . . . . 54 C7
   Shorne DA12 . . . . 31 E1
   Tonbridge TN10 . . . . 127 D4
Ridgeway W DA15. . . . . . . 12 E2
Ridgewood Dr DA3 . . . . . . 49 C7
Ridgway ME16 . . . . 99 B2
Ridgwell Rd E16 . . . . 1 C8
Ridgy Field Cl TN15 . . . . . 79 A2
Riding La TN11 . . . . 109 D2
Riding Pk TN11 . . . . 126 D7
Ridings The
   Biggin Hill TN16 . . . . 72 E2
   Paddock Wood TN12 . . . 146 A7
   Royal Tunbridge Wells
     TN2 . . . . 159 F6
Ridlands Gr RH8 . . . . 104 E5
Ridlands La RH8 . . . . 104 E5
Ridlands Rise RH8 . . . . . . 104 E4
RIDLEY. 63 B4
Ridley Ct BR6. . . . . 57 C6
Ridley Rd
   Bexley DA6 . . . . 13 B6
   Bromley BR2 . . . . 42 A6
   Rochester ME1 . . . . 53 B4
Riefield Rd SE9 . . . . 12 C2
Riggall Ct ME2 . . . . 52 A3
Riggs Way **6** TN15 . . . . . . 78 F3
Ring Cl BR1 . . . . 28 B1
Ringden Ave TN12 . . . . . . 145 F6
Ringer's Ct **8** BR1 . . . . . . 42 A6
Ringer's Rd BR1 . . . . 42 A6
Ringle Gn TN18 . . . . 196 C5
RINGLESTONE
   Harrietsham 103 B1
   Maidstone 99 F7
Ringlestone Cres ME14 . . . 99 F8
Ringlestone Rd ME17. . . . 103 D4
Ringlet Cl E16 . . . . 1 B8
Ringlet Rd ME4 . . . . 40 B2
Ringmer Way BR1. . . . . . . 42 F4

Ringshall Rd BR5 . . . . 44 A6
Rings Hill TN11 . . . . 126 B4
Ringside TN8 . . . . 122 C2
Ringwood Ave BR6. . . . . . . 58 C1
Ringwood Rd ME15 . . . . . 116 C8
Ringwood Rd ME15 . . . . . . 69 D8
Ripley Arts Ctr* BR1. . . . . 42 DB
Ripley Cl BR1 . . . . 42 F4
Ripley Rd
   Erith DA17 . . . . 4 A2
   Newham E16 . . . . 1 C7
Ripleys Market DA1 . . . . . . 32 E8
Ripon Cl ME8 . . . . 55 D3
Ripon Rd SE18 . . . . 12 B8
Rippersley Rd DA16 . . . . . 13 A6
Rippolson Rd SE18 . . . . 2 F1
Risden La TN18 . . . . 195 D7
Risedale Rd DA7 . . . . 14 C4
RISEDEN
   Durgates 184 B1
   Kilndown 177 A5
Riseden Rd TN5. . . . . 184 C1
Rise The
   Chatham ME4. . . . . 54 A7
   Crayford DA1. . . . . 14 F3
   Gillingham ME7 . . . . 69 A3
   Gravesend DA12 . . . . 36 E4
   Rochester ME1. . . . . 53 D3
   Sevenoaks TN13 . . . . . . 108 C7
   Sidcup DA5 . . . . 30 C8
   Swanscombe DA9 . . . . . . 17 A1
Ritch Rd ME6 . . . . 81 E8
Ritter St SE18. . . . . 12 A8
Ritz Bigs TN1 . . . . 159 A3
Rivendell Cl ME3. . . . . 27 B5
Rivenhall Way ME3 . . . . . . 40 F6
River Bank Cl **8** ME15. . . 100 B4
Riverbank Rd BR1. . . . . 28 A5
River Cl ME15. . . . . 115 A7
River Cotts ME4 . . . . 44 C7
River Ct TN13 . . . . 91 E5
Riverdale Est TN9 . . . . . . 143 D8
Riverdale Rd
   Erith DA8 . . . . 4 C1
   Sidcup DA5 . . . . 13 F1
   Woolwich SE18 . . . . 2 F1
River Dr ME2 . . . . 52 E7
Riverhead Cl ME16 . . . . . . 99 D6
Riverhead Ho TN13 . . . . . . 91 E5
Riverhead Inf Sch TN13 . . 91 E4
Riverhead Mews TN13 . . . 91 E4
Riverhill TN15 . . . . 108 E4
Riverhill Cotts TN15 . . . . 108 E4
Riverhill House Gdns*
   TN15 . . . . 108 E5
Riverhope Mans SE18 . . . . . 1 E3
River Lawn Rd TN9. . . . . . 127 B1
Riverleigh Ct TN13 . . . . . . 83 F2
Rivermead ME4. . . . . 40 C2
Rivermead Sch ME7. . . . . . 54 E6
River Park View BR6 . . . . . 44 B2
River Rd IG11. . . . . 3 A3
Rivers Cl ME18. . . . . 113 E7
Rivers Wlk ME17 . . . . 120 C5
Riverside DA1 . . . . 16 A3
River View
   Edenbridge TN8 . . . . 122 C1
   Eynsford DA4 . . . . 60 D8
   Greenwich SE7 . . . . 1 B3
Riverside Business Park
   ME20. . . . . 82 C5
Riverside Cl BR5 . . . . 44 C4
Riverside Cotts TN14 . . . . 59 F1
Riverside Ct
   2 Orpington BR5 . . . . . 44 C4
   2 Tonbridge TN9 . . . . 127 C1
Riverside East Rd ME4 . . . 40 C1
Riverside Ind Est DA1 . . . . 15 E2
Riverside Pk ME16 . . . . . . 115 A8
Riverside Rd DA14 . . . . . . 30 E6
Riverside Ret Pk TN14. . . . 92 C8
Riverside Sch BR5 . . . . 44 C7
Riverside Way DA1 . . . . . . 15 E2
River St **6** ME7. . . . . 54 A6
Riverston Sch SE12 . . . . . . 11 A2
Riverview **6** ME4 . . . . 53 F3
Riverview Ct
   18 Erith DA17 . . . . 4 A1
   Stone DA9 . . . . 16 F1
Riverview Cty Inf Sch
   DA12. . . . . 12 B7
Riverview Hts SE18 . . . . . . 12 E8
Riverview Jun Sch DA12. . 36 E4
RIVERVIEW PARK. 36 E4
Riverview Rd DA9 . . . . 17 A2
River Way ME20. . . . . 82 B4
River Wlk TN9 . . . . 127 B1
Riverwood La BR7 . . . . 43 D8
Rixon Ho SE18 . . . . 12 A8
Roach St ME7 . . . . 35 A7
Roan Ct ME2 . . . . 52 F8
Robert Napier Sch The
   ME7. . . . . 54 E3
Roberton Dr BR1. . . . . 42 C8
Roberts Cl
   Eltham SE9 . . . . 29 D7
   8 Orpington BR5 . . . . . 44 C4
Roberts Ho SE18 . . . . 11 E6
Roberts Mews BR6 . . . . . . 41 A5
Robertson Ho SE18 . . . . . . 11 F6
Roberts Orchard Rd ME16 98 F3

Roberts Rd
   Erith DA17 . . . . 4 A1
   Gillingham ME8 . . . . 69 EB
   Snodland ME6 . . . . 81 F8
Robert St
   Newham E16 . . . . 2 B5
   Woolwich SE18 . . . . 2 D2
Robina Cl DA6 . . . . 13 D3
Robina Ct BR8 . . . . 46 A5
Robin Cres E6 . . . . 1 D8
Robin Ct **6** ME1 . . . . 53 D4
Robin Hill Dr BR7 . . . . 28 E2
Robin Ho **5** ME15 . . . . . . 98 E6
Robin Hood Gn BR5. . . . . . 44 A4
Robin Hood La
   Bexley DA6 . . . . 13 E2
Robin Hood La (Lower)
   ME5 . . . . 67 F2
Robin Hood La (Upper)
   ME5 . . . . 67 E1
Robinia Ave DA11 . . . . 35 D8
Robins Ave ME17 . . . . 120 C5
Robins Cl ME17 . . . . 120 C4
Robins Ct ME14 . . . . 100 B7
Robins Gr BR4 . . . . 56 A7
Robin Way BR5 . . . . 44 B6
Robinwood Dr TN15 . . . . . 92 F8
Robson Cl E6 . . . . 1 E7
Robson Dr
   Aylesford ME20 . . . . 82 D2
   Hoo St Werburgh ME3 . . 40 D6
Robson Ho SE18 . . . . 12 A7
Robyns Cotts TN26 . . . . . 183 E8
Robyns Croft **6** DA11 . . . 35 E5
Robyns Way
   Edenbridge TN8 . . . . 138 D8
   Sevenoaks TN13 . . . . 91 F5
Rocfort Rd ME6. . . . . 82 A8
Rochdale Ho TN1 . . . . 159 C5
Rochdale Rd
   Royal Tunbridge Wells
     TN1. . . . . 159 C6
   Woolwich SE2 . . . . 3 B2
ROCHESTER 53 B6
Rochester Ave
   Bromley BR1 . . . . 42 B7
   Rochester ME1 . . . . 53 C4
Rochester Castle* ME1. . . 53 C6
Rochester Cath* ME1. . . . 53 C6
Rochester Cl
   Rochester ME3 . . . . 00 D6
   Sidcup DA14 . . . . 30 A6
Rochester Cres ME1 . . . . . 00 C6
Rochester Ct DA5. . . . . . . 14 A1
Rochester Dr DA5. . . . . . . 14 A1
Rochester Gate ME1 . . . . . 53 D5
Rochester Gram Sch for Girls
   ME1 . . . . 53 C2
Rochester Ho **1** ME15 . . 116 D7
Rochester Ind Coll ME1 . . 53 D4
Rochester Rd
   Burham ME1 . . . . 66 E2
   Chalk DA12 . . . . 37 B6
   Dartford DA1 . . . . 33 A8
   Pratling Street ME20. . . . 83 B4
   Rochester ME2 . . . . 52 D4
   Tonbridge TN10 . . . . 127 D4
Rochester Sch ME1 . . . . . . 53 E3
Rochester Sta ME1. . . . . . 53 D5
Rochester Way
   Dartford DA1. . . . . 31 F8
   Eltham, Kidbrooke SE3, SE9 11 A4
   Eltham SE9 . . . . 12 B4
Rock Ave ME7 . . . . 54 C3
Rock Cotts TN3 . . . . 173 B1
Rockdale TN13 . . . . 92 B2
Rockdale Rd TN13 . . . . . . 92 C2
Rock Farm Oasthouse
   ME18. . . . . 113 C6
Rock Hill BR6. . . . . 59 B4
Rock Hill Ho TN27 . . . . . . 137 E2
Rockliffe Manor Prim Sch
   SE18 . . . . 12 F8
Rockmount Rd SE18. . . . . . 2 F1
Rock Rd
   Borough Green TN15 . . . . 94 F7
   Maidstone ME14 . . . . . . 100 A6
ROCKROBIN 184 D6
Rocks Cl ME19 . . . . 98 A6
Rocks Hill TN17. . . . . 166 A4
Rocks Rd The ME19 . . . . . 98 B6
Rock Villa Rd TN1. . . . . . . 159 B4
Rockwell St ME15. . . . . . . 99 E1
Rocky Hill ME16 . . . . 99 E4
Rocky Hill Terr **2** ME16. . 99 E4
Rodeo Cl DA8. . . . . 15 B6
Roding Rd E6. . . . . 2 B8
Rodmell Rd TN2 . . . . 159 A2
Rodney Ave TN10 . . . . . . 127 E4
Rodney Gdns BR4 . . . . 56 A6
Rodway Rd BR1 . . . . 42 B1
Roebourne Way E16 . . . . . . 2 A5
Roebuck Bsns Pk ME17. 119 D5
Roebuck Ho SE11 . . . . 53 E5
Roebuck Rd ME11 . . . . 53 C5
Roedean Cl BR6. . . . . 58 B6
Roedean Rd TN2 . . . . 159 A1
Roehampton Cl DA12. . . . . 36 E8
Roehampton Dr BR7 . . . . . 23 D2
Roethorne Gdns TN30. . . 193 B8
Roffen Rd ME1 . . . . 53 C2
Rogers Ct BR8 . . . . 46 A5
Rogersmead **14** TN30. . . 193 A7
Rogers Rough Rd TN17. . . 177 B2

Rogers Wood La DA3. . . . . 62 B6
Rogley Hill TN27 . . . . 181 B6
Rogues Hill TN11 . . . . 141 C3
Rokeby Cl DA16 . . . . 12 D5
Rokesby Rd ME8 . . . . 56 D6
Rollesby Way SE28 . . . . 3 C7
Rolleston Ave BR5 . . . . 43 B3
Rolleston Cl BR5. . . . . 43 B2
Rollo Rd BR8 . . . . 31 F1
ROLVENDEN 191 E4
Rolvenden Ave ME8 . . . . . 55 C3
Rolvenden Gdns BR1 . . . . 28 D1
Rolvenden Hill TN17 . . . . 192 C5
ROLVENDEN LAYNE. . . . 192 B1
Rolvenden Prim Sch
   TN17. . . . . 191 E3
Rolvenden Rd
   Rochester ME1 . . . . 39 C2
   Tenterden TN30 . . . . 192 F4
Rolvenden Sta* TN17 . . . 192 D6
Roman Cl ME14 . . . . 67 D1
Roman Hts ME14. . . . . . . 100 C6
Roman Rd
   Edenbridge TN8 . . . . 138 D5
   Northfleet DA11. . . . . 35 C5
   Snodland ME6 . . . . 81 F8
Roman Sq SE28 . . . . 3 C5
Roman Villa Rd DA2, DA4 . 33 C2
Roman Way
   Crayford DA1. . . . . 14 E2
   Maidstone ME15 . . . . . . 116 E4
   Rochester ME2. . . . . 52 F4
Romany Cl ME5. . . . . 54 D1
Romany Rd ME8 . . . . 55 C2
Romany Rise BR5 . . . . 43 C1
ROMDEN 153 C1
Romden Rd
   Smarden, Haffenden Quarter
     TN27 . . . . 169 B8
   Smarden, Romden TN27 153 C1
Romero Sq SE3 . . . . 11 C3
Rome Terr ME4 . . . . 53 F4
ROMFORD 160 F7
Romford Rd TN2. . . . . 160 F7
Romney Cl ME14 . . . . 101 A3
Romney Dr BR1 . . . . 28 D1
Romney Gdns DA7 . . . . . . 13 F6
Romney Ho ME15 . . . . . . 100 A4
Romney Rd
   Chatham ME5 . . . . 68 B5
   Northfleet DA11 . . . . 35 E5
   Woolwich SE18 . . . . 2 C3
Romney St TN15 . . . . 77 A7
Romney Way TN10 . . . . . 127 E5
Romsey Cl
   Orpington BR6 . . . . 57 C7
   Rochester ME2 . . . . 52 EB
Ronald Ho SE3 . . . . 11 C3
Ronalds Rd BR1. . . . . 42 A8
Ronaldstone Rd DA15 . . . 12 E1
Ronfearn Ave BR5 . . . . 44 D4
Ron Green Ct TN8 . . . . 14 D8
Ronver Rd SE12 . . . . 28 A7
Roodlands La TN8 . . . . . . 123 D6
Rookdean TN13. . . . . 91 C5
Rookery Cres ME3 . . . . 22 B6
Rookery Dr BR7 . . . . 43 A8
Rookery Dr BR7. . . . . 43 A8
Rookery Gdns BR5 . . . . . . 44 C4
Rookery Hill ME6 . . . . 81 F8
Rookery La BR2. . . . . 42 D3
Rookery Lodge ME3 . . . . . 22 C5
Rookery Rd BR6 . . . . 57 A8
Rookery The RM20 . . . . . . 17 A8
Rookery View RM17 . . . . . 18 D8
Rookesley Rd BR5 . . . . 44 D2
Rook La ME9 . . . . 71 F6
Rookley Ct TN2 . . . . 159 D2
Rooks Hill TN15. . . . . 109 D6
Rooks View ME9 . . . . 71 E6
Rook Wlk **8** E6 . . . . 1 E8
Roopers TN3 . . . . 158 A2
Roosevelt Ave ME5. . . . . . 68 A8
Ropemakers Ct ME4 . . . . . 54 A3
Roper Cl ME8 . . . . 69 C3
Roper's Gate TN2 . . . . . . 158 E1
Roper's Green La ME3 . . . . 18 B2
Roper's La ME3 . . . . 40 B1
Roper St SE9 . . . . 12 A1
Ropery Bsns Pk SE7. . . . . . 1 C2
Rope Wlk
   Chatham ME4 . . . . 53 F4
   Cranbrook TN17. . . . . . . 179 C5
Rope Wlk The TN18 . . . . . 196 B5
Rope Yard Rails SE18 . . . . 2 B3
ROSACRE 104 A1
Roseacre RH8 . . . . 104 A1
Roseacre Gdns ME14. . . . 101 A1
Roseacre La ME14 . . . . . . 101 A1
Roseacre Jun Sch ME14 . 101 A1
Roseacre La ME14 . . . . . . 101 A1
Roseacre Rd DA16 . . . . 13 B6
Rose Ave DA12 . . . . 37 A5
Rosebank Gdns DA11. . . . 35 E5
Rosebank Wlk **3** SE18 . . . 1 E7
Rosebery Gdns
   Dartford DA1 . . . . 32 C1
   Orpington BR6 . . . . 57 E7
Rosebery Ave DA15 . . . . . 29 E6
Rosebery Ct DA11. . . . . . . 35 E8
Rosebery Rd
   Chatham ME4 . . . . 53 E1
   Gillingham ME7 . . . . 54 C2
   Grays RM17 . . . . 12 C8
Rose Bruford Coll DA15 . . 30 B8
Rose Cotts
   Lamberhurst TN3 . . . . . . 176 A6
   Rochester ME2 . . . . 52 B6
   St Mary Hoo ME3. . . . . . . 24 E7

Rosecroft Cl
Biggin Hill TN16 . . . . 72 F1
Orpington BR5 . . . . 44 C3
Rose Ct ME17 . . . . 115 D1
Rose Dale BR6 . . . . 57 B8
Rosedale Cl
Dartford DA2 . . . . 33 B8
Woolwich SE2 . . . . 3 B3
Rosedale Cnr BR7 . . . . . . 42 F8
Rosedene Cl DA1 . . . . . . 32 C8
Rosefield
Sevenoaks TN13 . . . . 92 A3
15 Sidcup DA14 . . . . 30 A4
Rosegarth DA13 . . . . 49 E8
Rosehill Rd TN16 . . . . . . 72 C2
Rose Hill Sch TN4 . . . . . 158 E5
Rosehill Wlk TN1 . . . . . . 159 A3
Roseholme ME16 . . . . 99 D2
Roselare Cl TN16 . . . . . . 89 D1
Roseleigh Ave ME16 . . . . 99 C5
Rosemary Cl
1 Chatham ME5 . . . . . . 67 F4
Oxted RH8 . . . . 104 A2
Rosemary La 1 ME1 . . . . 53 D4
Rosemary La
Flimwell TN5 . . . . 187 A5
Hodsoll Street TN15 . . . . . 63 D3
Swift's Green TN27 . . . . 152 F5
Rosemary Rd
Bexley DA16 . . . . 12 F6
Maidstone ME15 . . . . . . 101 A3
West Malling ME19 . . . . . 81 F1
Rosemount Gdns TN27 . 151 B7
Rosemount Cl ME15 . . . 115 F4
Rosemount Ct ME2 . . . . . 39 A1
Rosemount Dr BR1 . . . . . 42 F5
Roseneath BR6 . . . . 58 C3
Rose St
Northfleet DA11 . . . . 18 B1
Rochester ME1 . . . . 53 D3
Tonbridge TN9 . . . . 143 C8
Rose Terr ME19 . . . . 96 D7
Rosetta Prim Sch E16 . . . . 1 B8
Roseveare Rd SE12 . . . . . 28 C4
Rosewood Cl DA2 . . . . . . 11 A2
Rosewood DA2 . . . . 31 E4
Rosewood Ct DA14 . . . . . 30 C5
Rose Yd ME14 . . . . 100 A4
Rosher Ho DA11 . . . . 18 F1
ROSHERVILLE 18 D4
Rosherville CE Prim Sch
DA11 . . . . 18 E1
Rosherville Way DA11 . . . 18 E1
Roslin Way BR1 . . . . 28 A3
Ross Ct SE9 . . . . 28 F1
Ross Ct Wlk? 27 E7
Rossdale TN2 . . . . 159 D5
Rose Mews SE18 . . . . . . 11 B6
Ross House SE18 . . . . . . 11 E6
Rossland Cl DA6 . . . . 14 B2
Rosslyn Gn ME16 . . . . . . 99 B5
Rossmore DA14 . . . . 30 A3
Ross Rd DA1 . . . . 15 A1
Ross St ME1 . . . . 53 D4
Ross Way SE9 . . . . 11 A4
Rotary Gdns ME7 . . . . . . 54 F2
Rother Ct 28 BR5 . . . . . . 44 D1
Rothermere Ct TN17 . . . 190 E6
Rother Rd TN10 . . . . . . 127 C5
Rother Vale 68 C3
Rothesay Ct 6 SE12 . . . . 28 B5
Rothley Cl TN30 . . . . . . 193 B8
Rouge La DA12 . . . . 36 B7
Rougemont Rd ME19 . . . . 97 C2
Roughetts Rd ME19 . . . . 80 F3
Roughway La TN11 . . . . 111 C7
Round Ash Way DA3 . . . . 48 E3
Round Green Cotts TN17 164 F4
Roundhay ME19 . . . . 88 E1
Roundhill Rd TN2 . . . . . 159 D1
Roundlyn Gdns BR5 . . . . 44 B5
Round St DA12, DA13 . . . 50 D5
ROUND STREET 50 D5
Roundtable Rd BR1 . . . . . 28 A5
Roundway TN16 . . . . 72 D4
Roundwell ME14 . . . . . . 101 D3
Roundwood BR7 . . . . 43 B7
Round Wood Cl ME5 . . . . 68 A1
Routh St SE28 . . . . 1 E8
Rover Rd ME5 . . . . 68 B2
Rowan Cl
Aylesford ME20 . . . . 82 E1
Meopham Station DA13 . . 50 B3
Paddock Wood TN12 . . . 145 F5
Rowan Cres DA1 . . . . 32 C7
Rowan Ct 2 SE12 . . . . . 28 A8
Rowan Ho
7 Chatham ME5 . . . . . . 67 F5
7 Maidstone ME16 . . . . 99 B4
Royal Tunbridge Wells
TN4 . . . . 158 E4
Rowan House DA14 . . . . . 29 F5
Rowan Lea ME5 . . . . 52 C1
Rowan Mews TN9, TN10 . 127 C4
Rowan Rd
Bexley DA16 . . . . 13 E4
Swanley BR8 . . . . 45 D6
Rowans Cl DA3 . . . . 48 D7
Rowan Shaw TN12 . . . . 127 D6
Rowan Tree Rd TN2 . . . . 158 E1
Rowan Wlk
Chatham ME5 . . . . 53 E3
Orpington BR2 . . . . 56 F7
Rowanwood Ave DA15 . . 30 A7
Rowbrocke Cl ME8 . . . . . 69 D3
Rowdow La TN14, TN15 . 76 E5

Rowenden Vineyard★
TN17 . . . . 191 B2
Rowe Pl ME20 . . . . 82 F6
Rowfield 6 TN8 . . . . . . 122 D3
Rowhill Cotts DA2 . . . . . 31 E2
Rowhill Rd DA2 . . . . 32 A3
Rowhill Sch DA2 . . . . . . 32 C4
Rowland Ave ME14 . . . . . 54 E2
Rowland Cl
Gillingham ME7 . . . . 54 E1
Maidstone ME16 . . . . . . 99 E4
Rowlands Manor BR5 . . . 44 C3
Rowlatt Cl DA2 . . . . 32 C4
Rowlatt Rd DA2 . . . . 32 C5
Rowley Ave ME15 . . . . . . 30 B8
Rowley Hill TN2 . . . . . . 144 D1
Rowmarsh Cl DA11 . . . . . 19 E3
Rowntree Path 1 SE28 . . 3 B5
Row The DA3 . . . . 62 F8
Rowton Rd SE18 . . . . . . 12 C7
Rowzill Rd BR8 . . . . 31 F2
Royal Albert Sta E16 . . . . 1 A6
Royal Albert Way
Newham, Cyprus E6. . . . . 2 A6
Newham E16 . . . . 1 C6
Royal Ave TN9 . . . . 143 D8
Royal Chase TN4 . . . . . 158 F4
Royal Cl BR6 . . . . 57 B6
Royal Connaught Apartments
E16 . . . . 1 D5
Royal Ct SE9 . . . . 28 F7
Royal Docks Com Sch The
E16 . . . . 1 E7
Royal Docks Heritage Rly★
E16 . . . . 1 E5
Royal Eagle Cl ME2 . . . . 53 E7
Royal Engineers Mus★
ME7. . . . . 54 B6
Royal Engineers' Rd ME14 54 F7
Royal Oak Cotts TN8 . . . 105 C2
Royal Oak Rd DA6 . . . . . 15 C2
Royal Oak Terr DA12 . . . 36 C7
Royal Par BR7 . . . . 29 C1
Royal Parade Mews BR7. . 29 C1
RUSTHALL 158 C4
Royal Pier Rd DA12 . . . . 19 C1
Royal Park Prim Sch
DA14 . . . . 30 E5
Royal Rise TN9 . . . . 143 C8
Royal Sovereign Ave ME4 94 F7
Royal Star Arc 3 ME14 . . 99 F4
ROYAL TUNBRIDGE
WELLS 159 A2
Royal Tunbridge Wells Bsns
Pk TN2 . . . . 143 D1
Royal Victoria Pl E16 . . . . 1 B6
Royal Victoria Place Sh Ctr
TN1 . . . . 159 A2
Royal Victoria Sq E16 . . . 1 B6
Royal Victoria Sta E16 . . . 1 A6
Royal Wells Coll 4 TN4 . 159 A4
Royal West Kent Ave
TN10 . . . . 127 D4
Roydene Rd SE18 . . . . . . 2 E1
Roydon Hall Rd TN12 . . 112 F4
Royston Rd
Crayford DA1. . . . . 14 F1
Maidstone ME15 . . . . . . 101 A3
Roystons Cl ME8 . . . . . . 55 F2
Royton Ave SE17 . . . . . 120 D5
RSPCA Leybourne Animal
Ctr★ ME19 . . . . 81 E5
Rubin Pl ME19 . . . . 97 B3
Ruby Walk ME19 . . . . . . 97 C3
Ruckinge Way ME8 . . . . . 55 C3
Ruck La TN12 . . . . 162 E3
Ruddstreet Cl SE18 . . . . . 2 C2
Rudge Cl ME5 . . . . 66 B8
Rudland Rd DA2 . . . . 14 B4
Ruegg Ho 6 SE18. . . . . . 12 A8
Ruffet Ct TN2 . . . . 158 E1
Ruffets Wood DA12 . . . . 36 C2
Rugby Cl ME5 . . . . 67 F4
Ruggles ME2 . . . . 23 E3
Rumania Wlk DA12 . . . . . 36 F5
Rumstead La ME17, ME9 . 86 C4
Rumstead Rd ME9 . . . . . 86 E4
Rumwood Ct ME17 . . . . 117 B5
Runciman Ct BR6 . . . . . . 58 C1
Runham La ME17 . . . . . . 119 E3
Running Horse Rdbt The
ME14 . . . . 83 E1
Runnymede Ct DA2 . . . . . 33 C7
Runnymede Gdns ME15 . 116 A8
Rural Vale DA11 . . . . 35 E8
Ruscombe Ct TN4 . . . . . 142 F2
Rushbrook Rd SE9 . . . . . 29 C6
Rush Cl ME5 . . . . 68 A3
Rushdean Rd ME2 . . . . . . 52 D5
Rushdene SE2 . . . . 3 D3
Rushdene Wlk TN16 . . . . 72 D2
Rushes The ME20 . . . . . . 82 B4
Rushet Rd BR5 . . . . 44 A7
Rushetts Rd ME17 . . . . . 157 F4
Rushetts Rd TN16 . . . . . . 81 B3
Rusheymead Ho 5 SE18 . 2 F1
Rushford Cl TN27 . . . . . 151 D5
Rushgrove St SE18 . . . . . 1 F2
Rushley Cl BR2 . . . . 56 E6
Rushlye Cl TN3 . . . . 173 F5
Rushmead Dr ME15 . . . . 116 A7
Rushmere Ct TN15 . . . . . 94 D7
Rushmore Cl BR1 . . . . . . 42 E6
Rushmore Hill BR6, TN14. 74 D6

Rymers Cl TN2 . . . . 159 D7
Rymill St E16 . . . . 2 A5
Rysted La TN16 . . . . 89 D1

S

Sabre Ct ME7 . . . . 55 A1
Sackville Ave BR2 . . . . . . 42 A1
Sackville Cl TN13 . . . . . . 92 B5
Sackville Rd DA2 . . . . . . 32 E6
Sackville Sch TN11 . . . . 126 C6
Sacred Heart Sch TN5 . . 184 C5
Saddington St DA12 . . . . 36 C8
Saddlers Cl ME14 . . . . . 100 E5
Saddler's Pk DA4 . . . . . . 60 D7
Sadlers Cl ME5 . . . . 67 D2
Saffron Cl ME14 . . . . 99 B3
Saffron Way 1 ME5 . . . . 67 F5
Sage Cl 8 E6. . . . . 1 F8
Sage Rd ME1 . . . . 53 B3
Saigasso Cl E16 . . . . 1 D7
Sailfield Ct ME4 . . . . 53 F7
Sailmakers Ct 5 ME4 . . . 54 B2
St Aidan's Way DA12 . . . 36 E5
St Albans Cl ME7 . . . . . . 54 E1
St Alban's Cl DA12 . . . . . 36 D5
St Alban's Gdns DA12 . . . 36 D5
St Alban's Rd DA1 . . . . . 26 D6
St Alban's Road Inf Sch
DA1 . . . . 15 F1
St Alfege Rd SE7 . . . . . . 11 D8
St Andrew's Art Ctr★
DA11 . . . . 19 B1
St Andrews Cl
Erith SE28 . . . . 3 D7
Paddock Wood TN12 . . . 146 A6
St Andrew's Cl ME16 . . . 99 A2
St Andrews Ct
28 Gravesend DA12 . . . 19 B1
Royal Tunbridge Wells
TN4 . . . . 143 A1
St Andrew's Ct 4 BR8 . . 45 E6
St Andrews Dr BR5 . . . . . 44 B2
St Andrews Ho BR1 . . . . . 28 B2
St Andrews Mews SE3 . . . 11 A7
St Andrews Park Rd TN14 143 A1
St Andrews Pk ME16 . . . . 99 A3
St Andrews Rd
Gillingham ME7 . . . . 54 D7
Paddock Wood TN12 . . . 146 A6
Sidcup DA14 . . . . 30 D5
St Andrew's Rd
10 Gravesend DA12 . . . 36 B8
Maidstone ME16 . . . . . . 99 A3
Tilbury RM18 . . . . 18 E5
St Andrews Wlk RH8. . . . 104 F4
St Andrew's Wlk ME1 . . . 9 D2
St Annes Ct ME16 . . . . . 99 E4
St ANN'S GREEN 148 F8
St Ann's Green La TN12 . 148 F8
St Anns Way TN16 . . . . . 73 B3
St Anselm's RC Prim Sch
DA1 . . . . 16 A2
St Anthony's Ct ME4 . . . . 57 B8
St Aubyns Cl BR6 . . . . . . 57 F7
St Aubyns Gdns BR6 . . . . 57 F8
St Audrey Ave DA7 . . . . . 14 A5
St Augustine Ho 1 TN9 . 143 B8
St Augustine of Canterbury
RC Prim Sch ME8. . . . . . 69 D3
St Augustine's Ave BR2 . . 42 E4
St Augustine's RC Prim Sch
DA7. . . . . 3 F2
St Augustine's RC Prim Sch
TN4 . . . . 159 A7
St Barnabas CE Prim Sch 1
TN1 . . . . 159 B5
St Barnabas Cl
Gillingham ME7 . . . . 54 D3
Maidstone ME16 . . . . . . 99 C8
St Barnabas' Cl 1 TN1 . 159 B5
St Bartholomew's Hospl
ME1 . . . . 53 E4
St Bartholomew's La 4
ME1 . . . . 53 E4
St Bartholomews RC Prim
Sch 3 BR8 . . . . 45 E6
St Bartholomew's Terr 2
ME1 . . . . 53 E4
St Benedict Rd ME6 . . . . 81 E8
St Benedict's Rd DA2. . . . 36 E6
St Benedicts Prim Sch
ME5. . . . . 68 C2
St Benets CE Prim Sch TN30 193 B8
St Benets Way TN30 . . . 193 B8
St Benjamins Dr BR6 . . . 58 C2
St Bernards Rd TN10 . . . 127 C6
St Blaise Ave BR1 . . . . . . 42 B7
St Boltophs CE Prim Sch
TN13 . . . . 92 B3
St Botolph Rd DA11 . . . . 35 D6
St Botolph's Ave TN13 . . . 92 A3
St Botolph's RC Prim Sch
DA11 . . . . 35 D8
St Botolph's Rd TN13 . . . 92 B3
St Brelade's CE Prim Sch 1
TN18 . . . . 122 A3
St Brides Cl DA18 . . . . . . 3 D4
St Catherines Cl ME5 . . . 68 C6
St Catherine's RC Sch for
Girls DA6 . . . . 14 C2
St Chad's Dr DA12 . . . . . 36 E5
St Chad's Rd RM18 . . . . . 19 A7
St Clement's Ave RM20. . 17 B8
St Clements Ct DA11 . . . 35 F5
St Clements Ct RM17 . . . 17 F8

St Clement's Ho ME1 . . . 53 D5
St Clements Rd DA9 . . . . 17 C3
St Clement's Rd RM20 . . 17 C7
St Clement's Way RM20 . 16 F8
St Clere Hill Rd TN15 . . . 77 F7
St Columba's Cl DA12 . . . 36 E5
St Columba's RC Boys Sch
DA6. . . . . 14 B2
St David's Bridge TN17 . 179 D4
St David's Cres DA12 . . . 36 D4
St Davids Gate ME16 . . . 99 A2
St David's Rd
Allhallows ME3 . . . . 9 D2
Hextable BR8. . . . . 31 F1
Royal Tunbridge Wells
TN4 . . . . 159 B6
St Domingo Ho SE18 . . . . 1 F2
St Dunstan's Dr DA12 . . . 36 E5
St Dunstans Wlk TN17 . 179 D4
St Eanswythe's Ct TN9 . 143 C8
St Edith's Rd TN15 . . . . . 77 A2
St Edmund Ho SE2 . . . . . 13 D8
St Edmunds Cl DA18 . . . . 3 D4
St Edmund's Cotts TN15 . 62 A2
St Edmund's Ct TN15 . . . 62 A2
St Edmunds Rd DA1 . . . . 16 A3
St Faiths Ct ME14 . . . . . 101 B4
St Faith's La ME14 . . . . 101 B4
St Faith St ME14 . . . . . . 99 F4
St Fidelis RC Prim Sch
DA8. . . . . 14 C8
St Fidelis' Rd DA8 . . . . . . 4 D1
St Francis Ave DA12 . . . . 36 E4
St Francis Cl
Maidstone ME14 . . . . . . 100 B7
Orpington BR6 . . . . 43 E3
Rochester ME2 . . . . 52 E6
St Francis' RC Prim Sch
ME15. . . . . 99 C4
St Francis Rd DA8 . . . . . . 64 B3
St Francis' Rd DA8 . . . . . . 4 D2
St George's Bickley CE Prim
Sch BR1 . . . . 42 D7
St George's CE Prim Sch 7
TN15. . . . . 78 F3
St George's CE Sch DA11. 36 A6
St George's Cl SE28. . . . . 3 D7
St Georges Cres DA12 . . . 36 D4
St George's Ct 4 TN14 . 159 A5
St George's Ct TN15 . . . . 78 F3
St Georges Mews 11
TN9 . . . . 143 B8
St George's Pk TN2 . . . . 172 F8
St George's RAF Chapel of
Remembrance★ TN16 . . 72 C6
St Georges Rd
Orpington BR5 . . . . 43 D3
Swanley BR8 . . . . 45 F5
St George's Rd
Bromley BR1 . . . . 42 F6
Gillingham ME7 . . . . 54 C6
Sevenoaks TN13 . . . . . . 92 B5
Sidcup DA14 . . . . 30 D2
St George's Rd W BR1. . . 42 E7
St George's Sh Ctr DA11 . 36 A6
St Georges Sq DA3. . . . . 48 E6
St George's Sq ME15 . . . 99 E3
St George's Wlk ME3 . . . . 9 D2
St German's Pl SE3 . . . . . 11 A6
St Giles Cl BR6 . . . . 57 D5
St Gregory's Cres DA12. . 36 E6
St Gregory's Ct DA12 . . . 36 E6
St Gregory's RC Comp Sch
TN4 . . . . 159 A7
St Helens DA14 . . . . 30 B5
St Helens CE Prim Sch
ME3. . . . . 22 B5
St Helens Cotts ME15 . . 114 E8
St Helens La ME15 . . . . 114 E8
St Helens Rd
Cliffe ME3 . . . . 22 B5
7 Erith DA18 . . . . 3 D4
St Helier's Cl ME16. . . . . 99 B2
St Hilary Ho SE12 . . . . . . 13 D8
St Hildas TN15 . . . . 110 F8
St Hilda's Way DA12 . . . . 36 E5
St James' CE Inf Sch
TN2 . . . . 159 C4
St James' CE Jun Sch
TN2 . . . . 159 C4
St James' CE Prim Sch
ME3. . . . . 27 B6
St James Cl
6 East Malling ME19 . . . 97 F8
Grain ME3 . . . . 27 B6
Tonbridge TN10 . . . . . . 127 D7
St James Ct
5 Bromley BR2 . . . . 42 A7
Greenwich SE3 . . . . 11 B6
Stone DA9 . . . . 16 F1
St James' La DA9 . . . . . . 33 E8
St James Oaks TN15 . . . . 36 A8
St James' Pk TN1 . . . . . 159 C5
St James Pl DA11 . . . . . . 15 D1
St James' Rd
BR5. . . . . 43 B4
St James Rd ME3 . . . . . . 27 B5
St James' Rd TN1 . . . . . 159 C5
St James's Ave DA11 . . . . 36 A8
St James's Ct SE18 . . . . . 2 C1
St James's Ct TN1 . . . . . 159 B4
St James Sq SA3 . . . . . . 48 E6
St James's Rd
Gravesend DA12 . . . . . . 19 A1
Sevenoaks TN13 . . . . . . 92 B5

St James's St DA11 ...... 19 A1
St James the Great Prim Sch
ME19 .... 97 F8
St James Way DA14 ...... 30 E3
St Joachim's RC Prim Sch
E16 .... 1 C6
St John Fisher RC Prim Sch
DA18 .... 3 E3
St John Fisher RC Sch (Main
Site) ME8 .... 53 E3
St John Fisher RC Sch (Sixth
Form Site) ME4 .... 53 F2
ST JOHN'S
Royal Tunbridge Wells ...159 A5
Sevenoaks 92 B5
St John's CE Inf Sch ME4. 53 E3
St John's CE Prim Sch
Maidstone ME14 ....100 E4
Royal Tunbridge Wells
Sevenoaks TN13 ....159 B7
TN4 ....159 B7
St John's CI ME3 ....38 C4
St Johns Ct DA8 ....4 D1
St John's Ct TN13 ....92 C5
St John's Hill TN3, TN14 . 92 C5
St John's Jerusalem★
DA4 ....33 B1
St John's La DA13 ....48 F3
St John's Par 4 DA4 .....30 B4
St John's Pk
Greenwich SE3 ....11 A7
Royal Tunbridge Wells
TN4 ....159 A8
St John's Prim Sch DA12. 36 E7
St John's RC Comp Sch
DA12 ....36 D7
St Johns Rd ME3 ....40 E6
St John's Rd
Bexley DA16 ....13 B4
Dartford DA2 ....33 C8
Erith DA8 ....4 D1
Gillingham ME7 ....54 C3
Gravesend DA12 ....36 D8
Higham ME3 ....38 C4
Newham E16 ....1 A7
Orpington BR5 ....43 E3
Royal Tunbridge Wells
TN4 ....159 A6
Sevenoaks TN13 ....92 C5
Sidcup DA14 ....30 B4
St John's Terr SE18 ......12 D8
St Johns Way
Edenbridge TN8 ....122 C3
Rochester ME1 ....53 A2
St Josephs CI BR6 ....57 F6
St Josephs Convent Prep Sch
DA12 ....36 C6
St Joseph's Ct 8 SE12 .. 28 B5
St Joseph's RC Prim Sch
Bromley BR1 ....28 C1
Crayford DA1 ....14 D3
Northfleet DA11 ....35 D8
St Justin CI BR5 ....44 D6
St Katharine's Knockholt CE
Prim Sch TN14 ....74 B2
St Katherines Cotts DA12. 37 E4
St Katherine's La ME6... 81 F7
St Katherines Rd DA18 .. 3 D4
St Katherine's Sch ME6 . 81 F7
St Keverne Rd
Bromley SE9 ....28 E4
Eltham SE9 ....28 F8
St Kilda Rd BR6 ....43 F1
St Laurence Ave ME16... 99 C8
St Laurence CI BR5 ......44 D6
St Lawrence Ave TN4 ...142 D3
St Lawrence CE Prim Sch
TN15 ....159 B5
St Leonards Ave ME4... 53 F2
St Leonards
4 Bexley DA16 ....13 A4
Grays RM17 ....17 F8
St Leonards Rd ME16... 99 C8
St Leonards Rise BR6 ... 57 E6
St Leonard's St ME19 ... 97 B7
ST LEONARD'S STREET .. 97 B6
St Leonard's Tower★
ME19 ....97 A7
St Luke's Ave ME14 .....100 E4
St Lukes CI
Dartford DA2 ....33 E3
Swanley BR8 ....45 D7
St Lukes Cotts BR8 ......45 D7
St Lukes Ct ME14 ....100 E4
St Lukes CE Sixth Form Coll
DA14 ....30 A3
St Luke's Rd
Maidstone ME14 ....100 E4
Royal Tunbridge Wells
TN4 ....159 B6
St Luke's Way ME1 ......9 D2
St Margaret Clitherow RC
Prim Sch
Tonbridge TN10 ....127 B6
Woolwich SE28 ....3 B5
ST MARGARETS 33 D1
St Margarets at Troy Town
Prim Sch ME1 ....53 B4
St Margarets Ave DA15. 29 C5
St Margaret's Banks ME1. 53 D5
St Margaret's CE Prim Sch
SE18 ....2 D2
St Margarets CI
Maidstone ME16 ....99 B2
Orpington BR6 ....58 B6

St Margaret's CI DA2.... 33 D6
St Margarets Collier Street
CE Prim Sch TN12 ....131 D1
St Margaret's Cres DA12 . 36 E5
St Margaret's Ct
6 Gillingham ME8 ....69 F8
High Halstow ME23 ......23 E3
St Margarets Dr ME8 ... 69 C5
St Margaret's Gr SE18... 12 C8
St Margaret's Inf Sch ME8 69 E8
St Margaret's Jun Sch
ME8 ....69 E8
St Margaret's Mews ME1. 53 C5
St Margaret's Rd
Dartford DA2, DA4 ...... 33 E7
Northfleet DA11 ....35 E7
St Margaret's St ME1... 53 C5
St Margaret's Terr SE18 . 2 C1
St Margarets Villas
TN12 ....147 D8
St Mark's Ave DA11 .....35 F8
St Marks CE Prim Sch
ME20 ....82 F6
St Mark's CE Prim Sch
Bromley BR2 ....42 A6
Royal Tunbridge Wells
TN4 ....158 D1
St Marks Ho ME7 ....54 C5
St Marks Ind Est E16.... 1 D5
St Mark's Rd
Bromley BR2 ....42 B6
Royal Tunbridge Wells
TN2 ....172 F7
St Martins CI
Erith DA18 ....3 D4
Newington ME9 ....71 C7
St Martin's CI ME4 ......85 A1
St Martin's Dr DA4 ......60 D7
St Martins Mdw TN1 ... 90 C4
St Martin's Rd DA1 ......15 F1
ST MARY CRAY 44 B4
St Mary Cray Prim Sch
BR5 ....44 C3
St Mary Cray Sta BR5 .. 44 B5
ST MARY HOO 24 D6
St Mary Magdalene CE Prim
Sch 15 SE18 ....2 A2
St Mary's ME3 ....24 D5
St Mary's Abbey ME19...97 C8
St Mary's CE Prim Sch
BR8 ....45 F2
St Mary's Church Rd TN14 90 F2
St Mary's CI
Gravesend DA12 ....36 C6
Grays RM17 ....18 D8
Laddingford ME18 ....130 E4
Orpington BR5 ....57 E7
Platt TN15 ....95 C7
Ticehurst TN5 ....186 D1
St Marys Ct ME5 ....11 D7
St Mary's Ct
Erith DA17 ....3 D2
5 Westerham TN16 .....89 D1
St Mary's Dr TN13 ....91 E4
St Mary's Gdns ME4 ....54 B7
St Mary's Ho TN18 ......72 C1
St Mary's Sr TN16 ....72 C1
ST MARY'S ISLAND 40 C1
St Mary's Island CE Prim Sch
ME4 ....40 B2
St Mary's La
Speldhurst TN3 ....158 A8
Ticehurst TN5 ....186 D1
St Mary's Pl
Eltham SE9 ....12 A1
Newington ME9 ....71 C7
St Mary's RC Prim Sch
Eltham SE9 ....12 A2
Gillingham ME7 ....54 D6
Tilbury RM18 ....18 F5
St Mary's Rd
Coldblow DA5 ....31 C7
Gillingham ME7 ....54 C6
Rochester ME2 ....53 B7
Stone DA9 ....16 E2
Swanley BR8 ....45 E5
Tonbridge TN9 ....143 B7
Wrotham TN15 ....79 A2
St Mary St SE18 ....2 A2
St Mary's View ME9 ....71 C7
St Mary's Wik ME1 ......66 F1
St Matthew's CI ME9 ...71 C7
St Matthews Dr
Bromley BR1 ....42 F6
Rochester ME1 ....53 A2
St Matthew's High Brooms
CE Prim Sch TN4 ....159 B8
St Matthew's Way ME3 . 9 D2
St Mellion CI SE28 ....3 D7
St Merryn CI SE18 ....12 D7
ST MICHAELS 183 B4
St Michaels Ho RH8 ..... 104 A5
St Michael's CE Inf Sch
ME16 ....99 E3
St Michael's CE Jun Sch
ME16 ....99 E3
St Michael's CE Prim Sch
Bexley DA16 ....13 C6
Tenterden TN30 ....183 A3
St Michaels CI
Bromley BR1 ....42 E6
4 Newham E16 ....1 D8
Pratling Street ME20.... 83 C3
St Michael's CI
Chatham ME5...............53 F3
Erith DA8 ....3 D4

St Michaels Ct TN11.....126 E7
St Michael's Ct 6 ME2... 53 B8
St Michaels Dr TN14 ....76 E3
St Michael's Prim Sch
TN7 ....170 B5
St Michael's RC Prim Sch 8
ME4 ....53 F3
St Michael's Rd
Bexley DA16 ....13 B4
Maidstone ME16 ....99 D3
Royal Tunbridge Wells
TN4 ....159 B7
St Michael's Rise DA16 . 13 B5
St Michael's Terr TN14.. 76 E4
St Michael's Terr TN30.. 183 A3
St Mildred's CI 4 TN30. 193 A7
St Mildreds Rd 5 SE12.. 28 A8
St Nicholas CE Inf Sch
ME2 ....53 A7
St Nicholas CI DA16.....92 B2
St Nicholas Dr TN13.....92 C1
St Nicholas Gdns ME2... 52 F7
St Nicholas Rd SE18.....2 F2
St Nicolas La BR7 ....42 E8
St Olaves Prep Sch SE9 . 29 B6
St Olave's & St Saviour's
Gram Sch BR6 ....44 B8
St Patrick's Gdns DA12. 36 D5
St Patrick's RC Prim Sch
SE18 ....2 D2
St Paulinus CE Prim Sch
DA1 ....14 E3
St Paulinus CI DA1 ......14 E3
St Paul's Acad SE2 ......13 A8
St Pauls CE Prim Sch
TN4 ....158 B4
BR8 ....46 B8
St Pauls CI TN10 ....127 D5
St Paul's CI
Greenwich SE7 ....1 D1
Rochester ME2 ....52 D5
Swanscombe DA10 ......34 E8
ST PAUL'S CRAY 44 A7
St Paul's Cray CE Prim Sch
BR5 ....44 D6
St Paul's Cray Rd BR5,
BR7 ....44 C1
St Paul's Ct TN14 ....158 C4
St Pauls Inf Sch ME14.. 100 A7
St Paul's Rd DA8 ....14 C7
St Paul's St TN14 ....158 C4
St Paul's Sq BR2 ....42 A7
St Paul's Wood Hill BR5. 43 F7
St Peter Rd TN16.........73 B3
St Peter Chanel RC Prim Sch
DA14 ....30 C3
St Peter & Paul RC Prim Sch
BR5 ....43 E7
St Peter's Bridge ME14. 99 F4
St Peters CE Prim Sch
ME20 ....83 A3
St Peter's CE Prim Sch
TN2 ....159 C3
St Peters CI
Chislehurst BR7 ....29 D1
Ditton ME20 ....82 B1
St Peter's CI DA10 ......34 F8
St Peter's Ct ME20 ......82 C1
St Peters Inf Sch ME1 .. 53 C5
St Peters La BR5 ....44 A7
St Peter's Path ME1 .....53 C5
St Peters Pl ME20 ....82 F6
St Peters RC Prim Sch
SE18 ....2 B2
St Peters RC Prim Sch
ME20 ....82 B2
St Peters Row TN3 ......157 B5
St Peter's
Maidstone ME16 ....99 F4
Royal Tunbridge Wells
TN1 ....53 D4
St Peters Wharf Ret Pk
ME16 ....99 F4
St Philip's Ave ME15 ... 100 B2
St Philips Ct TN10 ....53 C5
St Philomena's RC Prim Sch
BR5 ....44 C2
St Quentin Rd DA16 .... 12 F4
St Ronan's CI ME15 .....116 C7
St Ronan's Sch TN18 ...189 D2
St Rowans View 2 DA11. 32 F8
St Saviours Rd ME15 ... 116 D6
SAINT'S HILL 157 A8
Saints Hill TN11 ....157 A8
St Simon Stock RC Sch
ME16 ....99 C4
St Stephen's CI 7 ME19. 71 C7
St Stephen's Cotts TN1.. 159 B5
St Stephen's Ct TN1.....159 B5
St Stephens Mews ME1.. 53 B7
St Stephen's Prim Sch
TN9 ....143 D8
St Stephen's RC Prim Sch
DA16 ....13 A5
St Stephen's Sq ME15 .. 99 E2
St Stephen's St TN1 ....143 B8
St Thomas-a-Becket RC
Prim Sch SE2 ....31 A8
St Thomas CI DA5 ....31 A8
St Thomas' Dr BR5 ......43 C1
St Thomas More RC Prim
Sch
Bexley DA7 ....13 F5
Chatham ME5...............68 A5
2 Eltham SE9 ....11 E4
St Thomas More RC Sch 14
SE9 ....12 A1

St Thomas of Canterbury RC
Prim Sch ME8 ....55 B2
St Thomas' RC Prim Sch
Grays RM17 ....18 C8
Sevenoaks TN13 ....92 B2
St Thomas Rd
Erith DA17 ....4 C4
Newham E16 ....1 A7
Northfleet DA11 ....35 E6
St Thomas's Almshouses
DA11 ....36 B7
St Thomas's Ave DA11.. 36 B7
St Thomas's Pl 15 RM17. 18 C8
St Timothy's Mews 3
BR1 ....42 B8
St Vincents Ave ME14.. 16 A2
St Vincents La ME19 .... 80 A2
St Vincents RC Prim Sch
SE9 ....28 E4
St Vincents Rd DA1 ..... 16 A1
St Welcume's Way ME17 119 E6
St Werburgh Cres ME3.. 40 D5
St Werburgh St ME3 .... 40 D5
St William of Perth Prim Sch
ME1 ....53 B2
St William's Way ME1 .. 53 D2
St Winifred's Rd TN16... 72 F1
Sala Ho SE3 ....11 B3
Salamons Way RM13 ... 4 E7
Salcote Rd DA12 ....36 E3
Salem Pl DA11 ....35 D8
Salem St ME15 ....100 A3
Salisbury CI SE28 .... 3 C7
Salisbury Ave
Gillingham ME8 ....69 D8
Swanley BR8 ....46 A5
Salisbury CI TN10 ....127 D5
Salisbury Ho 4 ME15 ... 116 D7
Salisbury Mews BR2 .... 42 E4
Salisbury Rd
Bromley BR2 ....42 E4
Chatham ME4 ....54 A3
Dartford DA2 ....33 C7
Kit's Coty ME20 ....83 D7
Langton Green TN3 ...... 157 F3
Maidstone ME14 ....100 A6
Northfleet DA11 ....35 F7
Royal Tunbridge Wells
TN4 ....159 C8
Sidcup DA5 ....31 A7
Tonbridge TN10 ....127 D4
Salix Rd RM17 ....18 D8
Sallow CI ME4 ....40 C1
Sallows Shaw DA13 .....50 C4
Sally Port ME7 ....54 A6
Sally Port Gdns ME7 ... 54 B6
Salmon Rd
Dartford DA1 ....15 F4
Erith DA17 ....4 A1
Salomons Mus★ TN3... 158 D8
Salomons Rd
Newham E13 ....1 C8
Rusthall TN4 ....158 C4
Saltash Rd DA16 ....13 C6
Saltbox Hill TN16 ....76 A8
Saltcote CI DA1 ....14 E1
Salter's Cross ME18 ....114 A1
Saltford CI 2 DA8 ....4 E1
Saltings Rd ME6 ....82 A7
Saltings The 5 DA9......17 C3
Salt La ME3 ....21 F4
Salt's Ave ME15 ....115 F3
Salts La ME15 ....116 A4
Saltwood CI BR6 ....58 C6
Saltwood Rd ME15 ......99 F1
Salvadori Ct TN2 ....160 D6
Samara CI ME5 ....68 A1
Sam Bartram CI SE7 .... 1 C1
Samphire CI ME14 ....100 E4
Samphire Ct ME17 ...... 18 E8
Samphire Way ME4 .....40 A2
Sampson CI DA17 ....3 D3
Samson Ho SE18 ....2 C2
Samuel CI SE18 ....1 F2
Samuels Twr ME4 ....54 B4
Sanctuary CI DA1 .... 16 A2
Sanctuary Rd ME8 ......55 A3
Sanctuary The DA5 ..... 13 D1
Sanctus Ct ME1 ....46 A2
Sandalwood House DA15. 29 F5
Sandbach Pl SE18 ....2 C1
Sandbanks Hill DA2 ....34 B2
Sandbourne Dr ME14... 83 F1
Sandby Gn SE9 ....11 E4
Sandcliff Rd DA8 ....4 D1
Sandcroft Way ME15 ...100 A2
Sandeman Way TN27 ... 167 F2
Sanderling CI SE28 ..... 3 C6
Sanderling Way DA9 ... 17 A1
Sandersons Ave TN14... 59 B1
Sanderson So BR1 ....43 A6
Sanderson Way TN9.....127 E1
Sanderstead Rd BR5 ...44 B3
Sandfield Rd TN11 ......157 A7
Sandford Rd
Bexley DA7, DA6 ....13 C4
Bromley BR2 ....42 A5
Sandgate Ct ME8 ....69 F4
Sandgate Rd DA16 ......13 C7
Sandham Point SE18 ... 2 B2
Sandhill La ME3 ....38 D6
Sandhole Cotts TN12 ...161 C4
SANDHURST 196 C6
Sandhurst Ave TN2......160 E5

Sandhurst CI
Gillingham ME8 ....55 C3
Royal Tunbridge Wells
TN2 ....159 C6
Sandhurst Cross TN18.. 196 A6
SANDHURST CROSS 150 F1
Sandhurst Cross TN12.. 150 F7
Sandhurst La ME17 .....159 D5
Sandhurst La TN17 ......191 B3
Sandhurst Pk TN2........159 C6
Sandhurst Prim Sch
TN18 ....196 C5
Sandhurst Rd
Bexley DA5 ....13 D3
Orpington BR6 ....58 A6
Royal Tunbridge Wells
TN2 ....159 D6
Sidcup DA15 ....30 A5
Tilbury RM18 ....19 C5
Sandhurst Vineyards★
TN18 ....196 E5
Sandilands TN13 ....91 D5
Sand La TN17 ....166 F4
SANDLING 82 C4
Sandling CI ME14 ....100 E1
Sandling La ME14 ....100 AH
Sandling Prim Sch ME14 100 D8
Sandling Rd ME14 ....99 F1
Sandling Rise SE9 ....29 A1
Sandling Way ME4 ......40 B
Sandown Ct TN2 ....159 Fe
Sandown Gr TN2 ....159 C6
Sandown Gr TN2 ....159 Fe
Sandown Pk TN2 ....159 Fe
Sandown Rd
Gravesend DA12 ....36 C
West Malling ME19 ......97 B
Sandow TN13 ....99 D
Sandpiper CI DA9 ....17 F
Sandpiper Dr DA8 ....15 B
Sandpiper Rd ME5 ......68 D
Sandpipers The DA12... 36 C5
Sandpiper Way BR5 ....44 D
Sandpit Pl SE7 ....1 E
Sandpit Rd DA1 ....15 C
Sandra Ct 5 ME2 ....53 B
Sand Rd TN3 ....179 A
Sandringham Ct ME19... 97 A
Sandringham Dr
Bexley DA16 ....12 E
Maypole DA2 ....31 E
Sandringham Ho ME1 .. 53 B
Sandringham Mews TN4 159 A
Sandringham Rd
Bromley BR1 ....28 A
Gillingham ME8 ....69 E
Sandrock Ho TN2 ....159 C
Sandrock Rd TN2 ....159 C
Sandrook Villas TN18 .. 188 F
Sandshaw Ct DA3 ....48 E
Sandstone La E16.........1 E
Sandstone Rd SE12 .....28 E
Sandstone Rise ME5 ... 84 C
Sandtoft Rd SE7 ....11 E
SANDWAY ....120 A
Sandway Path 6 BR5 ...44 C
Sandway Rd
Harrietsham ME17.......119 E
Orpington BR5 ....44 C
Sandy Bank Rd DA12... 36 E
Sandy Bury BR6 ....57 D
Sandycroft SE2 ....13 A
Sandycroft Rd ME2 ..... 38 F
Sandy Dell ME7 ....69 A
Sandy Hill Ave SE18 .... 2 B
Sandy Hill La SE18 ......2 B
Sandy Hill Rd SE18 .....2 B
Sandy La
Bean DA13, DA11 ....34 D
Ightham TN15 ....94 F
Limpsfield RH8 ....104 A
Maidstone, Harbourland
ME14 ....100 C
Maidstone, Ware Street
ME14 ....101 A
New Town ME19 ....81 A
Orpington BR6 ....44 A
Ruxley BR5 ....44 A
Sevenoaks TN13 ....92 C
Tenterden TN30 ....193 I
Tilbury RM16 ....19 I
Westerham TN16.........89 C
West Thurrock RM20.... 17 A
Wrotham Heath TN15, ME19 79 F
Sandy Mount ME14 .....101 A
Sandy Ridge
Borough Green TN15 ... 95 A
Chislehurst BR7 ....29 A
Santana Ho SE18 ....12 C
Santer Ho TN18 ....194 I
Santers Ct TN18 ....188 I
Sapho Pk DA12 36
Saphora CI BR6 57
Sappers Wlk ME7 54
Sapphire CI E6 2
Saracen CI ME7 55
Saracen Fields ME5 84
Sara Cres DA9 17
Sarafand Ho ME1 53
Sarah Ct 2 DA4 13
Sara Ho 6 DA8 13
Sara Turnbull Ho 8 SE18.. 1
Sark Wlk E16...............1
Sarre Rd 9 BR5 44
Sarsen Hts ME5 67
Sarsens CI DA12 50

Sassoon CI ME20. . . . . 82 A4
Satanita CI 1 D7
Saunders CI DA11. . . . . . 35 E6
Saunder's Cross TN14 . . 59 B2
Saunders Rd
  Royal Tunbridge Wells
  TN4 . . . . 158 E1
  Woolwich SE18 . . . . .2 F1
Saunders St
  ☑ Chatham ME4. . . . . . 53 F3
  Gillingham ME7 . . . . . . 54 C6
Saunders Way
  Dartford DA1. . . . . 32 F6
  Woolwich SE28 . . . . 3 B6
Savage Gdns E6 . . . . 1 F7
Savage Rd ME5 . . . . 68 B3
Saville CI TN10. . . . . . . 127 D7
Saville Ho E16. . . . . 2 B5
Saville Rd E16 . . . . 1 E5
Savoy Rd DA1. . . . . 15 D2
Sawyers Ct ME4. . . . . . . 54 B2
Saxby Rd ME15 . . . . 93 D5
Saxby Wood TN11. . . . . 125 F1
Saxon CI
  Kings Hill ME19 . . . . . . 96 F2
  Northfleet DA11. . . . . . 35 C5
  Otford TN14. . . . . 75 F2
  Rochester ME2. . . . . . . 38 F1
Saxon Rd
  Bromley BR1 . . . . 28 A1
  Hawley DA2. . . . . 32 E4
Saxons Dr ME14 . . . . . . 100 B7
Saxon Way Prim Sch ME7 54 E6
Saxon Wlk DA14 . . . . . . 30 C2
Saxton St ME7. . . . . 54 C5
Saxville Rd BR5 . . . . 44 B6
Sayer Ct DA9 . . . . 17 A2
Sayers La ☑ TN30. . . . . . 193 A7
Sayes Court Rd BR5. . . . . 44 A7
Scabbarbour Rd TN14. . 108 C1
Scadbury Gdns BR5. . . . . 44 A7
Scadbury Pk★ BR7. . . . . 29 F2
Scads Hill CI BR6. . . . . . 43 F3
Scarborough CI TN16 . . 72 C1
Scarborough La ME1. . . . 66 D2
Scarlet CI BR5 . . . . 44 B5
Scarlet CI ME5. . . . . 68 C5
Scarsbrook Rd SE3. . . . . 44 A1
Schofield Wlk SE3 . . . . . 11 A7
Scholars Rise ME2 . . . . . 52 D7
Scholey CI ME2. . . . . . . 66 B4
School App ☑ TN15. . . . . 94 F7
School Ave ME7 . . . . 54 E4
School CI DA13 . . . . 50 A2
School Cotts
  Bromley BR1 . . . . 28 A1
  Crockenhill BR8 . . . . . . 45 D2
  Seal TN15. . . . . 92 F6
  Sidcup DA14 . . . . 30 C3
School Cres DA1. . . . . . 14 F3
School Field TN8 . . . . . 122 C2
Schoolfield Rd RM20. . . 17 A8
School Hill TN3 . . . . . . 176 B6
School House La TN12 . 163 E7
School La
  Bean DA2. . . . . 34 C5
  Bexley DA5. . . . . 13 B4
  Borden ME9. . . . . 71 F4
  Culverstone Green DA13 . 64 A2
  Hadlow TN11. . . . . . . 128 E8
  Hextable BR8. . . . . . . 32 B1
  Higham ME3 . . . . 28 D5
  Horton Kirby DA3, DA4 . 47 E4
  Knockmill TN15 . . . . . . 77 F8
  Maidstone ME15 . . . . . 100 E1
  Newington ME9 . . . . . . 71 B7
  Platt's Heath ME17 . . . 119 F2
  Plaxtol TN11, TN15. . . 110 E6
  Seal TN15. . . . . 92 F6
  Sutton Valence ME17 . . 124 E7
  Trottiscliffe ME19 . . . . 80 A5
  Wouldham ME1 . . . . . . 66 D5
School Rd
  Chislehurst BR7 . . . . . . 29 C1
  Gravesend DA12 . . . . . . 36 C5
School Rise TN2 . . . . . . 158 F1
Schools at Somerhill The
  TN11. . . . . 143 F7
School Terr ☑ TN18 . . . 188 F2
School Villas ME18. . . . . 113 D5
Schooner CI DA2 . . . . . . 16 C3
Schooner Ho ☑ ME4 . . . . . 4 E1
Schooner Wlk ME2. . . . . 39 F3
Schrieber Mews ME7. . . . 54 C5
Scilla Ct ☑ RM17 . . . . . . 18 D8
Scimitar CI ME7 . . . . . . 55 A1
Scords La TN16. . . . . . . 106 C4
Scotby Ave ME5. . . . . . . 68 B4
Scotland La DA12 . . . . . . 50 F6
Scotney Castle Gdns★
  TN3. . . . . 176 D3
Scotney Castle (remains)★
  TN3. . . . . 176 D3
Scotney CI BR6. . . . . . . 57 A6
Scotney Ho ME2 . . . . . . 39 C1
Scotsdale CI BR5 . . . . . . 43 E5
Scotsdale Rd SE12 . . . . 11 B2
Scott CI ME20. . . . . 98 C8
Scott Cres DA8 . . . . 14 F6
Scott Ho ☑ DA17 . . . . 3 F1
Scott Rd
  Gravesend DA12 . . . . . . 36 D3
  Tonbridge TN9 . . . . . . 142 F7
Scotts Ho DA16 . . . . 13 C6

Scotts Park Prim Sch
  BR1. . . . . 42 C8
Scotts Passage ☑ SE18 . . 2 B2
Scotts Rd BR1. . . . . 28 A1
Scott St ME14. . . . . 99 F6
Scotts Terr SE9 . . . . 28 E6
Scott's Terr ME4. . . . . . . 53 F3
Scotts Way
  Royal Tunbridge Wells
  TN2. . . . . 172 E8
  Sevenoaks TN13 . . . . . . 91 E5
Scott Wilkie Prim Sch E16 1 C7
Scoulding Rd E16. . . . . . 1 A7
Scragged Oak Rd
  Detling ME17. . . . . 85 C5
  Hucking ME17 . . . . 86 C1
Scratchers La DA3 . . . . . 61 E7
Scratton Fields DA12. . . . 50 E4
Scrubs La ME16. . . . . . . 99 D4
Scudders Hill DA3 . . . . . 48 C3
Seabrooke Rise RM17. . . 18 B8
Seabrook Rd TN10 . . . . 127 A3
Seacourt Rd SE2. . . . . . . 3 D4
Seaford Ct ME1. . . . . . . 53 B5
Seagull La E16. . . . . 1 A6
Seagull Rd ME2. . . . . . . 52 D6
SEAL 93 A6
Sealand Ct ME1. . . . . . . 53 B5
Seal CE Prim Sch TN15. . 92 F7
Seal Dr TN15 . . . . 92 F6
Seal Ho TN15 . . . . 92 F6
Seal Hollow Rd TN13. . . 92 D4
Seal Rd TN13, TN14, TN15 . 92 D6
Seamew CI ME2 . . . . 52 C7
Searchlight Heights ME3 . 40 A4
Searles Dr E6. . . . . 2 B8
Seaton Rd
  Chatham ME4. . . . . 54 C1
  Gillingham ME7 . . . . . . 54 E3
  West Thurrock RM20. . . 17 A8
Second Ave
  Chatham ME4. . . . . 54 C1
  Gillingham ME7 . . . . . . 54 E3
Secretan Rd ME1 . . . . . . 53 B1
Sedcombe CI DA14. . . . . 30 C4
Sedgebrook Rd SE3. . . . 11 D4
Sedge Cres ME5 . . . . . . 67 E4
Sedge Ct RM17 . . . . 18 E7
Sedgemere Rd SE2 . . . . . 3 C3
Sedgemoor Ho ME1. . . . . 5 B5
Sedley DA13. . . . . 35 A2
Sedley CI
  Aylesford ME20 . . . . . . 82 F2
  Cliffe Woods ME3 . . . . . 39 C7
  Gillingham ME8 . . . . . . 69 C3
Sedley's CE Prim Sch
  DA13. . . . . 35 A3
Sefton CI BR5. . . . . 43 F5
Sefton Rd BR5 . . . . 43 F5
Sejant Ho ☑ RM17 . . . . . 18 B8
Selah Dr BR8 . . . . 45 C8
Selborne Ave DA5. . . . . 30 E7
Selborne Rd DA14. . . . . 30 B4
Selborne CI DA3. . . . . . 49 D6
Selborne Rd ME7 . . . . . . 54 D7
Selborne Wlk ME15 . . . 116 F6
Selby CI
  Chislehurst BR7 . . . . . . 29 A2
  ☑ Newham E6 . . . . 1 E8
Selby Rd
  Maidstone ME15 . . . . . 116 F4
  Newham E13 . . . . 1 B8
Select Bsns Ctr TN12. . . 149 E5
Selkirk Dr DA8. . . . . . . 14 E5
Sellbourne Rd ME15 . . . 173 C4
Selling Gn ME8 . . . . 55 C3
Sellwood Ct ME1. . . . . . 33 B7
Selsey Cres DA16 . . . . . 13 C6
Selstead CI ME8 . . . . . . 55 C2
Selwood Ho ME7 . . . . . . 29 C2
Selwyn Cres DA16 . . . . . 13 B3
Selwyn PI ☑ BR5 . . . . . . 44 B6
Selwyn Rd RM18 . . . . . . 18 F5
Semple Gdns ME4 . . . . . 54 B3
Senacre La ME15 . . . . . 116 E6
Senacre Sq ME15 . . . . . 116 E6
Senacre Wood Prim Sch
  ME15. . . . . 116 F7
Senator Wlk ☑ SE28 . . . . 2 D3
Sencler Ho
  Bexley SE2 . . . . 13 D8
  Erith SE2 . . . . 3 D1
Senlac PI TN3 . . . . 171 C7
Senlac Rd SE12 . . . . 28 B7
Sennen Wlk SE9 . . . . . . 28 E5
Sennocke Ct TN13. . . . . 92 B2
Senonoaks L Ctr TN13. . 92 C2
Senonoaks Mus & Gall
  TN13. . . . . 92 C2
SEPHAM HEATH. 75 B6
Sequoia Gdns BR6. . . . . 43 F2
Sermon Dr BR8 . . . . 45 C6
Serpentine Ct TN13 . . . . 92 A4
Serpentine Rd TN13. . . . 92 D4
Serviden Dr BR1. . . . . . 22 A6
Sessions House Sq ME14 . 99 F5
Setford Rd ME5. . . . . . . 68 C6
Settington Ave ME5 . . . . 54 C1
Seven Acres
  Crockenhill BR8 . . . . . . 45 D3
  New Ash Green DA3 . . . . 62 E7
Seven Mile La
  Kings Hill TN15. . . . . . 96 A3
  Mereworth TN11, TN12 . 112 E3

Seven Mile La continued
  Wrotham Heath TN15 . . . 95 F7
SEVENOAKS 92 D2
Sevenoaks Bsns Ctr TN14. 92 C6
Sevenoaks By-Pass TN13,
  TN14 . . . . 107 F7
Sevenoaks CI DA7. . . . . . 14 B3
SEVENOAKS COMMON . . 108 B6
Sevenoaks Hospl TN13 . . 92 C6
Sevenoaks Mus★ TN13 . . 92 C2
Sevenoaks Prep Sch
  TN15. . . . . 93 A1
Sevenoaks Prim Sch
  TN13. . . . . 92 B5
Sevenoaks Rd
  Borough Green TN15 . . . 94 F7
  Ightham TN15 . . . . 94 A4
  Orpington BR6. . . . . . . 57 F6
  Otford TN14. . . . . 76 B3
  Pratt's Bottom BR6, TN14 . 58 C2
Sevenoaks Sch
  Sevenoaks TN13 . . . . . . 92 B1
  Sevenoaks TN13 . . . . . . 92 C1
  Sevenoaks TN13. . . . . . 92 A3
Sevenoaks Way BR5. . . . 44 C7
Sevenoaks Way Ind Est ☑
  BR5. . . . . 44 C6
SEVENOAKS WEALD . . . 108 B2
Sevenoaks Wildfowl
  Reserve★ TN14 . . . . . . 92 A7
Seven Wents TN15 . . . . . 94 A4
Severn CI TN10 . . . . . . 127 C5
Severn Rd ME5 . . . . 68 C5
Sevington Pk ME15 . . . . 115 F6
Sewell Rd SE2 . . . . 3 B4
Sexton Rd RM18 . . . . . . 18 B8
Sexton St ME14 . . . . . . 53 E6
Seymour Dr BR2 . . . . . . 42 F1
Seymour Rd
  ☑ Chatham ME5. . . . . . 54 B3
  Northfleet DA11. . . . . . 35 F6
  Tilbury RM18 . . . . 18 F6
Seymour Wlk DA10. . . . . 34 E8
Shacklands Rd TN14 . . . 59 D1
Shackleton CI ME5 . . . . 68 B6
Shades The ME2 . . . . . . 52 C7
Shaftesbury CI ME19 . . . 81 F1
Shaftesbury Ct
  Erith DA8. . . . . 14 F6
  ☑ Woolwich SE28 . . . . . . 3 C5
Shaftesbury Dr ME16 . . . 91 D6
Shaftesbury La DA1. . . . 16 B3
Shaftesbury Rd TN4. . . . 159 A5
Shaftesbury Ct E6. . . . . . 2 A7
Shakespeare Ave RM18. . 19 B6
Shakespeare Farm Rd
  ME3. . . . . 24 F7
Shakespeare Rd
  Bexley DA7 . . . . 13 E6
  Dartford DA1. . . . . 16 A3
  Gillingham ME7 . . . . . . 54 C3
  Tonbridge TN9 . . . . . . 142 F8
Shalder Ho ME7 . . . . . . 54 D7
Shalfleet CI ☑ ME5 . . . . 68 A7
Shalford CI BR6. . . . . . . 57 C6
Shallons Rd SE9 . . . . . . 23 B4
Shambles The TN13. . . . 92 C2
Shamel Bsns Ctr ME2. . . 53 C7
Shamley Rd ME8 . . . . . . 68 D2
Shamrock CI DA12 . . . . 36 F8
Shandon CI TN12 . . . . . 159 C4
Shanklin CI ME5 . . . . . . 68 C8
Shannon Ct BR6. . . . . . . 44 A2
Sharland Ct ME7 . . . . . . 54 D4
Sharland Rd DA12. . . . . 36 C6
Sharman Ct DA14 . . . . . 30 A4
Sharnal La ME3 . . . . 24 A2
Sharnal St ME3 . . . . 24 A1
SHARNAL STREET. 24 A1
Sharnbrooke CI DA16 . . 13 C4
Sharon Ct ME5 . . . . 67 F4
Sharon CI ☑ DA14 . . . . . 30 B4
Sharp's Field TN27 . . . . 151 E5
Sharps Gn ME8 . . . . 55 D5
Sharp Way DA1 . . . . . . 15 F4
Sharsted Way
  Gillingham ME7 . . . . . . 69 A3
  Maidstone ME14 . . . . . 101 B5
Shawbrooke Rd SE9 . . . . 11 D3
Shaw CI
  Cliffe Woods ME3 . . . . . 39 B8
  Maidstone ME14 . . . . . 100 C7
  Woolwich SE28 . . . . 3 B5
Shaw Cres RM18. . . . . . 19 B6
Shawfield Pk BR1 . . . . . 42 D7
Shawhill Ho ME19 . . . . . 80 B1
Shaw Ho
  ☑ Erith DA17 . . . . 3 F1
  ☑ Newham E16 . . . . . . 2 A5
Shaw Rd TN16 . . . . 88 C7
Shawstead Rd ME7, ME7 . 68 C3
Shaws Way ME1 . . . . 61 C1
Shaw The TN2 . . . . 159 C2
Sheafe Dr TN17 . . . . . . 179 C5
Sheal's Cres ME15 . . . . 100 A2
Sheals Ct ME15 . . . . . . 100 A2
Shearers CI ME14 . . . . . 100 E4
Shears CI DA2 . . . . 32 C6
Shears Green Ct DA11 . . 35 F5
Shears Green Jun & Inf Schs
  ☑ DA11 . . . . 35 F5
Shearwater
  Maidstone ME16 . . . . . . 99 B5
  New Barn DA3 . . . . 49 B6
Shearwater CI ME2. . . . . 52 C7
Shearwood Cres DA1. . . 15 A4

Sheen Rd BR5 . . . . 43 F5
Sheepcote La BR5, BR8 . . 44 F4
Sheephurst La TN12. . . 147 E5
SHEERNESS 27 F3
Sheerness Harbour Est
  ME12. . . . . 27 F3
Sheerness Mews E16. . . . 2 B4
Sheerwater Rd E16 . . . . 1 F8
Sheet Hill TN15. . . . . . . 94 D2
Sheffield Rd ☑ TN4. . . . 142 F2
Sheilings The TN15 . . . . 92 F7
Shelbury CI DA14 . . . . . 30 A5
Sheldon Dr ME8 . . . . . . 69 F8
Sheldon Bsns Ctr ME2 . . 53 D8
Sheldon CI SE12 . . . . . . 11 B2
Sheldon Rd DA7 . . . . . . 13 F6
Sheldon Way ME20. . . . . 82 B3
Sheldrake CI E16 . . . . . . 1 F5
Sheldwich Terr BR2. . . . 42 E3
Shelduck La DA2 . . . . . . 34 B4
Shell CI BR2 . . . . 42 E3
Shelldrake CI ME3 . . . . . 27 B5
Shelley CI BR6. . . . . 57 E7
Shelley Dr DA1. . . . . . . 14 E2
Shelley PI RM18 . . . . . . 19 B6
Shelley Rd ME16 . . . . . . 99 C2
Shelley Rise ME1 . . . . . . 53 A3
Shelleys La TN14 . . . . . . 74 A3
Shelton CI TN10 . . . . . . 127 C5
Shenden CI TN13 . . . . . 108 C7
Shenden Way TN13 . . . . 108 C7
Shenfield Ho SE18 . . . . . 11 D7
Shenley Gr ME14. . . . . . 83 F2
Shenley Rd DA1. . . . . . . 33 A8
Shenstone CI DA1. . . . . 14 D3
Shenstone Sch DA1 . . . . 14 D3
Shepherds CI BR6. . . . . . 57 F7
Shepherds Gate ME7. . . 68 F5
Shepherds Gate Dr
  ME14. . . . . 100 E6
Shepherds Gn BR7 . . . . 23 B1
Shepherdsgrove La
  RH19 . . . . 154 A4
Shepherds La
  Dartford DA1. . . . . 32 B8
  Woolwich SE28 . . . . 3 E7
Shepherds Leas SE9 . . . 12 D3
Shepherd St DA11 . . . . . 35 D8
Shepherds Way
  Langley Heath ME17 . . . 117 C4
  Lower Stoke ME3. . . . . . 25 C4
Shepherds Wlk TN2 . . . 159 D4
Sheppards Coll ☑ BR1 . . 42 A8
Shepperton CI ME5 . . . . 68 C4
Shepperton Rd BR5 . . . . 43 C3
Sheppey CI DA8. . . . . . . 15 B7
Sheppey Rd ME15. . . . . 106 A7
Sheppey PI ☑ ME1 . . . . . 28 B1
Sheppy PI DA12. . . . . . . 36 B8
SHEPWAY 116 D8
Shepway CI ME15 . . . . . 106 C8
Sherard Mans SE9 . . . . . 11 F2
Sherard Rd SE9 . . . . 11 E2
Sheraton Ct ME5 . . . . . . 67 F1
Sherborne Gr TN15 . . . . 77 A2
Sherborne Rd BR5 . . . . . 43 F4
Sherbourne CI
  Royal Tunbridge Wells
  TN2. . . . . 159 D2
  West Kingsdown TN15. . 61 E4
Sherbourne Dr
  Maidstone ME14 . . . . . . 99 B2
  Rochester ME2. . . . . . . 39 A1
Sherbrooke CI DA7. . . . . 14 A3
Sherenden La TN12. . . . 164 D8
Sherenden Pk TN11 . . . 129 A5
Sherenden Rd TN11 . . . 144 D7
Sherfield Rd RM17 . . . . 18 B8
Sheridale Bsns Ctr ME2 . 53 A6
Sheridan CI
  Chatham ME5. . . . . 68 C7
  Maidstone ME14 . . . . . . 99 E8
  Swanley BR8 . . . . 45 F6
Sheridan Cres BR7. . . . . 43 B7
Sheridan Ct
  Dartford DA1. . . . . 16 A3
  Rochester ME1. . . . . . . 53 A2
Sheridan Lodge ☑ BR2. . 42 C5
Sheridan PI BR1 . . . . . . 42 D7
Sheridan Rd
  Bexley DA7 . . . . 13 E4
  Erith DA17. . . . . 4 A2
Sheriff Dr ME5 . . . . 68 A2
Sheringham CI ME5 . . . . 68 C7
Sheringham Rd ☑ ME15 116 E8
Sherington Prim Sch ☑
  SE7. . . . . 11 B8
Sherington Rd SE7. . . . . 11 B8
Sherlies Ave BR6 . . . . . . 57 E8
Sherman Ct ME7 . . . . . . 55 B1
Sherman Rd BR1. . . . . . 42 A8
Shernden La TN8 . . . . . 138 C4
Shernolds ME15 . . . . . . 116 B7
Shernold Sch ME16 . . . . 99 D5
Sherway CI TN17 . . . . . 151 E5
Sherway Rd TN27 . . . . . 152 D6
Sherwin Knight Inf Sch
  ME2. . . . . 52 E5
Sherwin Knight Jun Sch
  ME2. . . . . 52 E5
SHERWOOD 159 E6
Sherwood Ave
  Chatham ME5. . . . . 68 A2
  New Hythe ME20 . . . . . . 82 B4
Sherwood Ct DA1 . . . . . 33 C1
Sherwood Ho
  Chatham ME5. . . . . 68 A3

Sherwood Ho continued
  Erith DA8. . . . . 14 E8
Sherwood Park Ave DA15 13 B1
Sherwood Park Prim Sch
  Royal Tunbridge Wells
  TN2. . . . . 159 D6
  Sidcup DA15 . . . . 13 B1
Sherwood PI TN3 . . . . . 157 E3
Sherwood Rd
  Bexley DA16 . . . . 12 E4
  Royal Tunbridge Wells
  TN2. . . . . 159 E5
Sherwood Way TN2 . . . 159 D6
Shieldhall St SE2 . . . . . . 3 C2
Shillingheld CI ME14 . . . 100 F5
Shinecroft TN14 . . . . . . 76 A3
Shingle Barn La ME15 . . 114 C3
Shinglewell Rd DA8 . . . . 14 A7
SHIPBOURNE 110 C5
Shipbourne Prim Sch
  TN11. . . . . 110 C4
Shipbourne Rd
  Shipbourne TN11 . . . . . 110 D6
  Tonbridge TN10 . . . . . . 127 C5
Ship Field CI TN16 . . . . 88 C6
Ship Hill TN16 . . . . 88 D6
Ship La
  Rochester ME1 . . . . 53 E4
  Sutton at Hone BR8, DA4 . 46 E8
Shipley Ct ME14 . . . . . . 100 A4
Shipman Rd E16 . . . . 1 C7
Shipwrights Ave ME4. . . 54 B2
Shirebrook Rd SE3 . . . . 11 D4
Shire Ct DA18. . . . . 3 E3
Shirehall Rd DA2 . . . . . . 32 E4
Shire La
  Farthing Street BR6. . . . 57 C3
  Orpington BR6. . . . . . . 57 E5
Shires The TN12 . . . . . . 146 A7
Shirley Ave
  Chatham ME5. . . . . 67 D5
  Sidcup DA15 . . . . 30 D7
Shirley CI
  Chalk DA12 . . . . 37 B6
  Dartford DA1. . . . . 15 C3
Shirley Ct ME15 . . . . . . 116 E5
Shirley Gdns TN4 . . . . . 158 C5
Shirley Gr TN4 . . . . 158 C5
Shirley House Dr SE7 . . . 11 C7
Shirley Hts ☑ DA6 . . . . . 13 E3
Shirley Rd DA15 . . . . . . 29 E5
Shirley Way ME15. . . . . 101 A3
Shoesmith Lane ME19 . . 97 D3
Sholden Gdns BR5 . . . . . 44 C4
Sholden Rd ME2 . . . . . . 39 C1
SHOOTERS HILL. 12 C6
Shooters Hill SE18 . . . . 12 A6
Shooters Hill Post 16
  Campus SE18 . . . . 12 A6
Shooters Hill Rd SE18,
  SE3. . . . . 11 D6
SHOREHAM 75 F8
Shoreham Aircraft Mus★
  TN14. . . . . 75 F8
Shoreham Ho DA15 . . . . 30 C7
Shoreham Ho TN14 . . . . 76 A8
Shoreham La
  Badgers Mount TN14 . . . 75 A7
  Chelsfield BR6 . . . . 59 A3
  Sevenoaks TN13 . . . . . . 91 F4
  Tenterden TN30 . . . . . . 183 A3
Shoreham Prim Sch TN14 75 F8
Shoreham Rd
  Orpington BR5. . . . . . . 44 B7
  Otford TN14. . . . . 76 B5
Shoreham Sta TN14 . . . . 76 B8
Shoreham Way BR2 . . . . 42 A3
Shoreham Wlk ME15 . . . 116 F7
Shorehill CI TN15 . . . . . 76 F2
Shorehill La TN15. . . . . . 76 F4
Shore The
  Northfleet DA11. . . . . . 18 C2
  Northfleet, Rosherville DA11 18 F1
Shorland Ct ME1. . . . . . 53 B5
SHORNE. 37 E3
Shorne CE Prim Sch
  DA12. . . . . 37 E3
Shorne CI
  Orpington BR5. . . . . . . 44 D5
  ☑ Sidcup DA15. . . . . . . 13 B1
Shornefield CI BR1. . . . . 43 A6
Shorne Ifield Rd DA12. . 37 C2
Shornells Way SE2. . . . . 3 C1
Shorne Marshes Nature
  Reserve★ ME3. . . . . . . 21 B4
SHORNE RIDGEWAY 37 E2
Shorne Woods Ctry Pk★
  DA12. . . . . 37 C1
Short La RH8 . . . . 104 B3
Shortlands CI DA17 . . . . . 3 F3
Shortlands Gn ME15 . . . 116 F5
Short Path SE18 . . . . . . 12 B8
Shorts St ☑ ME4 . . . . . . 54 B3
Shorts St ☑ ME1 . . . . . . 53 A3
Shortway ME15 . . . . . . 11 E4
Shottenden Rd ME7 . . . . 54 D7
Shottery CI SE9 . . . . . . 28 E5
SHOVER'S GREEN 185 C1
Showfields Rd TN2 . . . . 158 F1
Shrapnel CI SE18 . . . . . 11 E7
Shrapnel Rd SE9 . . . . . . 11 F4
Shrewsbury La SE18 . . . 12 B6
Shroffold Rd BR1 . . . . . 28 A5

Shropshire Terr **1** ME15 116 E7
Shrubbery Rd
 Gravesend DA12 . . . . 36 C7
 Sutton at Hone DA4 . . . . 47 D8
Shrubcote TN30 . . . . 193 C7
Shrublands Ct
 Royal Tunbridge Wells
 TN2 . . . . 159 C4
 1 Tonbridge TN9 . . . . 127 C2
Shrubsall Cl SE9 . . . . 28 E7
Shrubshall Mdw TN15 . . . . . 111 A8
Shrubsole Dr ME14 . . . . 83 F3
Shurlock Ave BR8 . . . . 45 D7
Shurlock Dr BR6 . . . . 57 C6
Shuttle Cl
 Biddenden TN27 . . . . 168 A2
 Sidcup DA15 . . . . 29 F8
Shuttlemead DA5 . . . . 30 F8
Shuttle Rd DA1 . . . . 15 A4
Sibley Cl
 Bexley DA6 . . . . 13 E2
 Bromley BR1 . . . . 42 E4
Sibthorpe Rd SE12 . . . . 28 C8
SIDCUP 30 A3
Sidcup By Pass Rd DA14 . . . 29 E4
Sidcup Hill DA14 . . . . 30 C3
Sidcup Hill Gdns DA14 . . . . 30 C3
Sidcup Pl DA14 . . . . 30 A3
Sidcup Rd SE12, SE9 . . . . . . 28 D7
Sidcup Sta DA15 . . . . 30 A4
Sidcup Tech Ctr DA14 . . . . . 30 D2
Sidewood Rd SE9 . . . . 29 D7
Sidings The TN13 . . . . 91 E7
Sidmouth Ct DA1 . . . . 33 B7
Sidmouth Rd
 Bexley DA16 . . . . 13 C7
 Orpington BR5 . . . . 44 B5
Sidney Cl TN2 . . . . 172 F8
Sidney Gdns TN14 . . . . 76 C2
Sidney Ho SE18 . . . . 11 F6
Sidney Rd
 Gillingham ME7 . . . . 54 C7
 Rochester ME1 . . . . 53 A2
Sidney St ME16 . . . . 99 C2
Siebert Rd SE3 . . . . 11 A8
Siedle Ho **9** SE18 . . . . . . 12 A8
Siemens Rd SE18 . . . . 1 D3
Signal Ct **6** ME8 . . . . 55 F1
Silchester Ct ME14 . . . . 100 C7
Silecroft Rd DA7 . . . . 14 A4
Silk Cl SE12 . . . . 11 A1
Silk Mills Cl TN13 . . . . 92 C6
Silver Bank ME5 . . . . 43 C5
Silver Birch Ave DA13 . . . . . 63 F1
Silver Birch Cl
 Joyden's Wood DA2 . . . . . . 31 E4
 Woolwich SE28 . . . . 3 A5
Silver Birches ME5 . . . . 68 A3
Silver Birch Wlk ME18 . . . . . 113 D6
Silver Cl TN9 . . . . 143 B6
Silverdale
 Hartley DA3 . . . . 48 F5
 Maidstone ME16 . . . . 99 A2
Silverdale Dr
 Bromley SE9 . . . . 28 E6
 Gillingham ME8 . . . . 69 F7
Silverdale La
 Royal Tunbridge Wells
 TN4 . . . . 159 B6
 Sandhurst Cross TN18 . . . . 195 F5
Silverdale Rd
 Bexley DA7 . . . . 14 B5
 Orpington, Petts Wood BR5 . 43 C5
 Orpington, St Paul's Cray
 BR5 . . . . 44 A6
 Royal Tunbridge Wells
 TN4 . . . . 159 B6
Silverden Cotts TN18 . . . . . . 195 F4
Silver Hill
 Chatham ME4 . . . . 53 F3
 Hurst Green TN19 . . . . 194 B1
 Rochester ME1 . . . . 52 F2
Silver Hill Gdns **4** ME4 . . 53 F3
Silverhurst Dr TN10 . . . . 127 C7
Silverland St E16 . . . . 1 C8
Silverlocke Rd RM17 . . . . . . 18 D8
Silver Rd DA12 . . . . 36 E6
Silverspot Ct ME8 . . . . 69 F7
Silver Spring Cl DA8 . . . . . . 14 B8
Silver St ME9 . . . . 87 F5
Silverstone La TN16 . . . . 89 C6
Silverstone Ct **10** BR1 . . . 42 C7
Silver Streak Way ME2 . . . . . 52 E5
SILVER STREET 87 F5
SILVERTOWN 1 C4
Silvertown Way E16 . . . . 1 A5
Silver Tree ME5 . . . . 68 B1
Silverweed Rd ME5 . . . . 67 F4
Silwood Cl TN2 . . . . 159 C7
Simmonds Ct **2** TN4 . . . . 158 B4
Simmonds Dr DA3 . . . . 49 A4
Simmonds La ME15 . . . . 117 B6
Simmons Rd SE18 . . . . 2 B1
Simnel Rd SE12 . . . . 28 B8
Simon Ct **6** SE28 . . . . . . 3 B5
Simone Cl BR1 . . . . 42 D8
Simpson Rd ME6 . . . . 82 A6
Simpson's Cotts BR2 . . . . . . 56 C7
Simpsons Pl **6** BR1 . . . . . 42 A6
Simpson's Rd BR1, BR2 . . . . 42 A6
Sinclair Cl ME8 . . . . 69 E5
Sinclair Way DA2 . . . . 33 D4
Sindal Shaw Ho ME5 . . . . . . 67 E4
Singapore Dr ME7 . . . . 54 B5

Single's Cross TN14 . . . . 74 D4
Single's Cross La TN14 . . . . . 74 C5
Single St TN16 . . . . 73 B4
SINGLE STREET 73 B4
SINGLEWELL 36 D2
Singlewell Prim Sch
 DA12 . . . . 36 D2
Singlewell Rd DA11 . . . . 36 B4
Sinkerweazel TN17 . . . . 179 E2
SINKHURST GREEN 150 E2
Sion Wlk **8** TN1 . . . . 159 A2
Sirdar Strand DA12 . . . . 36 F3
Sir David's Pk TN4 . . . . 142 E1
Sir Evelyn Rd ME1 . . . . 53 B1
Sir John Hawkins Hospl
 ME4 . . . . 53 E4
Sir John Hawkins Way
 ME4 . . . . 53 F4
Sir Joseph Williamson's
 Mathematical Sch ME1 . . . 53 C1
Sir Martin Bowes Ho **11**
 . . . . 2 A2
Sir Thomas Longley Rd
 ME2 . . . . 53 E6
Siscup Rd SE9 . . . . 29 B6
Siskin Gdns TN12 . . . . 146 A5
Siskin Wlk ME20 . . . . 81 F2
SISSINGHURST 180 B7
Sissinghurst Castle Gdn*
 TN17 . . . . 166 D1
Sissinghurst CE Prim Sch
 TN17 . . . . 180 B8
Sissinghurst Dr ME16 . . . . . 99 B4
Sissinghurst Rd
 Biddenden TN27 . . . . 167 C2
 Sissinghurst TN17, TN27 . . 180 D8
Sittingbourne Rd
 Maidstone, Detling ME14 . . 100 E8
 Maidstone, Penenden Heath
 ME14 . . . . 100 B6
Siward Rd BR2 . . . . 42 C6
Six Bells La TN13 . . . . 92 C1
Six Fields Path TN30 . . . . . . 193 A7
Six Penny Cl TN8 . . . . 138 C8
Skeet Hill La BR5, BR6 . . . . 58 E8
Skeffington St SE18 . . . . . . 2 C3
Skeynes Rd TN8 . . . . 122 B1
Skibbs La BR5, BR6 . . . . . . 58 E7
Skinner Gdns TN17 . . . . 180 A8
Skinners La TN18 . . . . 122 D2
Skinners' Sch The TN4 . . . . 159 A6
Skinner St
 Chatham ME4 . . . . 53 F3
 Gillingham ME7 . . . . 54 C5
Skinner's Terr **15** TN9 . . . 143 B8
Skinner Street Prim Sch **12**
 ME7 . . . . 54 C6
Skinner's Way ME17 . . . . . . 117 E4
Skinney La DA4 . . . . 47 D6
Skippers Cl DA9 . . . . 11 B2
Skua Ct ME2 . . . . 52 C7
Skye Ct ME15 . . . . 116 A7
Sky Studios E16 . . . . 2 A4
Sladebrook Rd SE3 . . . . 11 D4
Slade Cl ME5 . . . . 68 B2
Sladedale Rd SE18 . . . . 2 E1
Slade Gdns DA8 . . . . 14 F6
SLADE GREEN 15 A1
Slade Green Inf Sch DA8 . . . 15 A7
Slade Green Jun Sch DA8 . . 15 A7
Slade Green Rd DA8 . . . . . . 15 B7
Slade Green Sta DA8 . . . . . 15 A6
Slade Prim Sch TN9 . . . . . . 127 B2
Slades Dr BR7 . . . . 29 C4
Slade The
 Lamberhurst TN3 . . . . 176 A3
 Tonbridge TN9 . . . . 127 B2
 Woolwich SE18 . . . . 12 E8
Slaney Rd TN12 . . . . 149 F4
Slater Cl **9** SE18 . . . . 2 A2
Slaters TN8 . . . . 123 F2
Slatin Rd ME2 . . . . 53 B8
Sleeches Cross TN3 . . . . . . 173 B2
Sleepers Stile Rd TN5 . . . . . 175 B1
Sicketts Hill ME4 . . . . 54 A4
Slip Mill Rd TN18 . . . . 188 E4
Slip The TN16 . . . . 89 C1
Slipway Rd ME12 . . . . 27 F3
Sloane Gdns BR6 . . . . 57 C7
Sloane Sq DA3 . . . . 48 E6
Slocum Cl SE28 . . . . 3 C6
Small Bridge Cotts TN17 . . . 163 B2
Small Bridge Rd TN12,
 TN17 . . . . 163 B2
Small Grains DA3 . . . . 62 B7
SMALL HYTHE 193 C1
Small Hythe Cl ME15 . . . . . . 101 B2
Smallhythe Place (Mus)*
 TN30 . . . . 193 C1
Small Hythe Rd TN30 . . . . . 193 B4
Small Profits ME15, ME18 . . 114 A4
SMARDEN 153 A1
SMARDEN BELL 152 D2
Smarden Bsns Est TN27 . . . 168 D7
Smarden Cl **8** DA17 . . . . . 4 A1
Smarden Gr SE9 . . . . 28 F4
Smarden Prim Sch TN27 . . . 153 A1
Smarden Rd
 Standen TN27 . . . . 168 B6
 Swift's Green TN27 . . . . . . 152 B4
Smarts Cotts ME14 . . . . 101 C4
Smarts Hill TN11 . . . . 141 A1
Smart's Rd DA12 . . . . 36 C6
Smetham Gdns ME2 . . . . . . 39 B1
Smithers Cl TN11 . . . . 111 E1
Smithers Ct TN12 . . . . 130 A7
Smithers La TN12 . . . . 130 E3

Smithfield Rd ME3 . . . . 27 C5
Smithies Rd SE2 . . . . 3 B2
Smith Rd ME1 . . . . 53 A2
Smith's Hill ME15 . . . . 114 C5
Smith's La TN8 . . . . 105 C2
Smiths Orch ME9 . . . . 87 F5
Smith St ME2 . . . . 53 A6
Smithy Field **7** TN8 . . . . . 122 D3
Smithy The TN5 . . . . 184 A3
Smugglers TN18 . . . . 189 A1
Smugglers Wlk DA9 . . . . 17 B2
Smythe Cl TN4 . . . . 142 E3
Smythe Rd DA4 . . . . 19 B6
Snag La TN14 . . . . 73 D7
Snape La TN5 . . . . 184 D1
Snape View TN5 . . . . 184 F4
Snelling Ave DA11 . . . . 35 F6
Snipe Cl
 Erith DA8 . . . . 15 B7
 Pembury TN2 . . . . 160 E8
Snipe Ct ME2 . . . . 52 C7
Snoad La TN12 . . . . 165 A8
Snodhurst Ave ME5 . . . . 67 E5
Snodhurst Ho **2** ME5 . . . . 68 A7
SNODLAND 82 B7
Snodland CE Prim Sch
 ME6 . . . . 81 F8
Snodland Rd ME10 . . . . 81 D7
Snodlands Cl BR6 . . . . 57 A1
Snodland Sta ME6 . . . . 82 B8
SNOLL HATCH 129 E5
Snoll Hatch Rd TN12 . . . . . . 129 F5
Snowdon Ave ME14 . . . . . . 100 B5
Snowdon Cl ME5 . . . . 68 B7
Snowdon Par ME14 . . . . . . 100 C5
Snow Ho ME2 . . . . 54 E7
Snughorne La TN27 . . . . . . 168 D8
Sobraon Villas TN15 . . . . . . 95 C7
Solefield Sch TN13 . . . . 108 C3
Solefields Rd TN13 . . . . 108 C8
Solent Gdns ME5 . . . . 68 B8
Soleoak Dr TN13 . . . . 108 B8
Sole St DA12, DA13 . . . . . . 50 A4
SOLE STREET 50 C4
Sole Street Farm ME3 . . . . . 39 B3
Sole Street Sta DA13 . . . . . 50 D4
Solomons Rd ME4 . . . . 53 F4
Somerden Rd BR5 . . . . 44 D2
Somerfield Cl ME16 . . . . 99 D5
Somerfield Hospl The
 ME16 . . . . 99 E5
Somerfield La ME16 . . . . . . 99 D4
Somerfield Rd ME16 . . . . . . 99 D4
Somerhill Ave DA15 . . . . . . 30 B8
Somerhill Rd
 Bexley DA16 . . . . 13 B5
 Tonbridge TN9 . . . . 143 D8
Somerset Ave DA16 . . . . . . 12 F3
Somerset Cl ME5 . . . . 68 C8
Somerset Rd
 Dartford DA1 . . . . 32 B8
 Maidstone ME15 . . . . 116 C8
 Orpington BR6 . . . . 44 A2
 Royal Tunbridge Wells
 TN4 . . . . 159 A6
Somerset Villas TN3 . . . . . . 171 C2
Somersham Rd DA7 . . . . . . 13 E5
Somertrees Ave SE12 . . . . . 28 B6
Somerville Gdns TN4 . . . . . . 158 F4
Somerville Rd DA1 . . . . 15 F1
Somner Wlk ME15 . . . . 116 F4
Sonnet Wlk TN16 . . . . 72 C1
Soper's La TN18 . . . . 188 D4
Sophia Rd E16 . . . . 1 B7
Sophurst La TN12 . . . . 161 C5
Sopurst Wood TN12 . . . . . . 161 D5
Sopwith Cl TN16 . . . . 72 D3
Sorrel Cl SE28 . . . . 3 A5
Sorrel Ct **8** RM17 . . . . . . 18 D8
Sorrel Gdns E6 . . . . 1 E8
Sorrell Cl **4** TN8 . . . . 122 D3
Sorrell Rd ME5 . . . . 67 F4
Sorrell Way DA11 . . . . 35 E4
Sortmill Rd ME6 . . . . 82 B7
Sounds Lodge BR8 . . . . 45 C3
Southampton Mews E16 . . . 1 B5
South Ash Rd TN15 . . . . 62 E4
South Ave ME8 . . . . 55 B2
Southbank
 Cliffe ME3 . . . . 22 B2
 Staplehurst TN12 . . . . 149 E2
 Sutton Valence ME17 . . . . 124 E7
 Westerham TN16 . . . . 89 D1
SOUTHBOROUGH
 Bromley 42 F3
 Royal Tunbridge Wells 143 B1
Southborough CE Prim Sch
 TN4 . . . . 158 F8
Southborough Ct TN4 . . . . . 143 A2
Southborough La BR2 . . . . . 42 F4
Southborough Prim Sch
 BR2 . . . . 43 A4
South Borough Prim Sch
 ME15 . . . . 100 A2
Southborough Rd BR1 . . . . . 42 E5
Southbourne BR2 . . . . 42 A2
Southbourne Gdns SE12 . . . 11 B2
Southbourne Gr ME5 . . . . . . 68 A4
South Brook La TN8 . . . . . . 123 C7
South Bush La ME8 . . . . 70 B6
South Cl DA6 . . . . 13 D3
South Cres ME17 . . . . 115 C4
Southcroft Ave DA16 . . . . . . 12 E4
Southcroft Rd BR6 . . . . 57 E7
South Ct TN14 . . . . 159 A6

SOUTH DARENTH 47 D8
Southdene TN14 . . . . 74 F6
SOUTHDOWNS 47 D7
South Dr BR6 . . . . 57 E5
South Eastern Rd ME2 . . . . 53 C7
Southend Cl SE9 . . . . 12 B1
Southend Cres SE9 . . . . 12 B1
SOUTHENDEN 152 C8
Southenden Rd TN27 . . . . . 136 E1
Southern Pl BR8 . . . . 45 D5
Southey Mews E16 . . . . 1 A5
Southey Way **1** ME20 . . . 81 F4
Southey Wlk RM18 . . . . 19 B6
Southfield Cl DA1 . . . . 15 F4
Southfield Rd
 Orpington BR7 . . . . 44 A6
 Royal Tunbridge Wells
 TN4 . . . . 159 A6
Southfields
 Hextable BR8 . . . . 31 F1
 Rochester ME1 . . . . 53 C3
 Speldhurst TN3 . . . . 158 A7
 Turner's Green TN5 . . . . . . 184 F6
Southfields Cl TN15 . . . . . . 61 F2
Southfields Shaw DA13 . . . . 64 B1
Southfields Way TN4 . . . . . . 159 B8
SOUTHFLEET 35 A3
Southfleet Ave DA3 . . . . 49 B7
Southfleet Rd
 Bean DA2 . . . . 34 C4
 6 Northfleet DA11 . . . . . 35 F7
 Orpington BR6 . . . . 57 E6
 Swanscombe DA10 . . . . . . 35 A7
South Frith TN4 . . . . 143 A8
Southgate TN4 . . . . 158 F3
Southgate Rd TN30 . . . . . . 193 C7
South Gipsy Rd DA16 . . . . . 13 D4
South Glade The DA5 . . . . . 30 F7
South Gr TN1 . . . . 159 A2
Southhill Rd
 Bromley BR7 . . . . 28 F1
 Chatham ME4 . . . . 53 F3
South Kent Ave DA11 . . . . . 18 C1
South La ME17 . . . . 134 E6
Southland Rd SE18 . . . . 12 F7
Southlands Ave BR6 . . . . . . 57 E5
Southlands Ct BR2 . . . . 42 D5
Southlands Gr BR1 . . . . 42 E6
Southlands Rd BR1, BR2 . . . 42 E6
Southlees La ME9 . . . . 86 F3
South Molton Rd E16 . . . . . . 1 A7
Southold Rise SE9 . . . . 28 F5
Southover BR1 . . . . 28 A3
South Park Bsns Village
 ME15 . . . . 100 A1
South Pk TN13 . . . . 92 B2
South Pondside Rd ME4 . . . 54 A8
Southport Rd SE18 . . . . 2 D2
South Rd
 Chatham, Brompton ME4,
 ME7 . . . . 54 A7
 Chatham ME4 . . . . 54 A5
 Erith DA8 . . . . 14 F7
 Marden TN12 . . . . 148 E5
South Ridge BR2 . . . . 42 C5
South Rise Prim Sch SE18 . . 2 D1
South Rise Way SE18 . . . . . 2 D1
South Row
 Greenwich SE3 . . . . 11 A5
 Penshurst TN8 . . . . 140 D5
South Side Three Rd ME4 . . 54 C8
Southspring DA15 . . . . 29 D8
South St
 Bromley BR1 . . . . 42 A7
 Culverstone Green DA13 . . 63 F4
 Gravesend DA12 . . . . 36 B8
 Maidstone ME16 . . . . 98 E1
SOUTH STREET
 Biggen Hill 89 A8
 Meopham 63 F4
 Stockbury 86 C7
South Street Rd ME9 . . . . . 86 C7
South Terr
 Chattenden ME3 . . . . 39 F6
 Farningham DA4 . . . . 46 F2
South View
 Bromley BR1 . . . . 42 C7
 Oxted RH8 . . . . 104 A2
Southview Ave RM18 . . . . . . 19 A6
South View Cl DA5 . . . . 46 A5
South View Cl DA5 . . . . 13 F1
South View Ct **11** BR1 . . . 42 C7
Southview Hts RM20 . . . . . . 17 C8
South View Rd
 Dartford DA2 . . . . 32 D5
 Royal Tunbridge Wells
 TN4 . . . . 159 D8
 Turner's Green TN5 . . . . . . 184 F6
 West Thurrock RM20 . . . . . 17 C8
South View Terr TN17 . . . . . 177 E8
Southwark Pl BR1 . . . . 42 F6
Southwark Rd ME2 . . . . 52 D6
Southwark Rd ME2 . . . . 42 A2
Southways BR2 . . . . 42 A2
Southways ME17 . . . . 134 E7
Southwell Rd ME2 . . . . 52 D6
Southwold Rd DA5 . . . . 14 B1
Southwood ME16 . . . . 98 F2
Southwood Ave TN4 . . . . . . 159 A6
Southwood Bldgs **5**
 TN4 . . . . 158 B4
Southwood Ct **5** BR1 . . . . 42 F5
Southwood Ho SE9 . . . . 29 B6

Southwood Rd
 Eltham SE9 . . . . 29 B6
 Rusthall TN4 . . . . 158 B5
 Woolwich SE28 . . . . 3 D5
Sovereign Bvd ME7, ME8 . . 54 F2
Sovereign Cl
 Bromley BR2 . . . . 42 F3
 Sutton at Hone DA4 . . . . . 47 B6
Sovereign Ho SE18 . . . . 1 F3
Sovereigns The ME16 . . . . . 99 D4
Sovereigns Way TN12 . . . . . 148 C6
Sovereign Way TN9 . . . . . . 127 C5
Soverign Ho BR7 . . . . 29 D3
Sowerby Cl SE9 . . . . 11 F7
Spade La ME9 . . . . 70 C6
Spa Ind Pk TN2 . . . . 159 E8
Spar Ct TN11 . . . . 111 F7
Sparepenny La DA4 . . . . . . 46 E3
Sparkes Cl BR2 . . . . 42 B5
Sparkeswood Ave TN17 . . . 191 F3
Sparkeswood Cl TN17 . . . . . 191 F3
Sparrow Dr BR5 . . . . 43 D3
SPARROW'S GREEN 184 F5
Sparrows Green Rd TN5 . . . 184 F5
Sparrows La SE9 . . . . 29 C2
Spa Valley Rly* TN3 . . . . . . 171 A2
Spearhead Rd ME14 . . . . . . 99 F2
Spearman St **3** SE18 . . . . 12 A4
Spectrum Bsns Ctr ME2 . . . 53 E6
Spectrum Bsns Est ME15 . . 116 F4
SPEED GATE 61 F6
Speedgate Farm DA3 . . . . . 61 F6
Speedgate Hill DA3 . . . . 62 A6
Speedwell Ave ME5 . . . . . . 67 F4
Speedwell Cl
 Gillingham ME7 . . . . 54 E5
 Maidstone ME14 . . . . 100 E
 5 Marpit Hill TN8 . . . . . . 122 D
Speedwell Ct RM17 . . . . . . 18 E
Spekehill SE9 . . . . 28 F
Spekes Rd ME7 . . . . 69 Be
SPELDHURST . . . . 158 A
Speldhurst CE Prim Sch
 TN3 . . . . 158 A
Speldhurst St ME11 . . . . . . 158 D
Speldhurst Hill TN3 . . . . 158 B
Speldhurst Rd
 Langton Green TN3 . . . . . . 157 F
 Royal Tunbridge Wells TN3,
 TN4 . . . . 158 E
Spelmonden Rd TN12 . . . . . 162 F
Spembley Ct ME4 . . . . 53 F
Spencer Cl
 Chatham ME5 . . . . 68 A
 Orpington BR6 . . . . 57 F
Spencer Ct **5** BR6 . . . . . . 57 C
Spencer Flats ME5 . . . . 68 B
Spencer Gdns SE9 . . . . 11 F
Spencer Mews
 6 Royal Tunbridge Wells,
 Mount Sion TN1 . . . . 159 A
 10 Royal Tunbridge Wells
 TN1 . . . . 159 B
Spencer St DA11 . . . . 36 A
Spencer Way ME15 . . . . . . 116 E
Spencer Wlk RM18 . . . . 19 B
Spenlow Dr ME5 . . . . 84 A
Spenny La TN12 . . . . 147 E
Speranza St SE18 . . . . 2 F
Speyside TN10 . . . . 127 B
Spielman Rd DA1 . . . . 15 B
Spiers The ME7 . . . . 55 C
Spillway The ME15 . . . . 99 D
Spindle Cl SE18 . . . . 1 E
Spindle Glade ME14 . . . . . . 100 C
Spindle Ho **8** DA15 . . . . . 30 A
Spindles RM18 . . . . 19 A
Spindlewood Cl ME5 . . . . . . 68 B
Spinel Cl SE18 . . . . 3 F
Spinnaker Ct **4** ME1 . . . . 53 C
Spinnens Acre Jun Sch
 ME5 . . . . 68 C
Spinners Cl TN27 . . . . 168 A
Spinners Wents TN11 . . . . . 111 C
Spinney Oak BR1 . . . . 42 F
Spinneys The BR1 . . . . 42 F
Spinney The
 Chatham ME5 . . . . 68 B
 Maidstone ME15 . . . . 100 B
 Sidcup DA14 . . . . 30 B
 Swanley BR8 . . . . 45 A
 Tonbridge TN9 . . . . 143 A
Spinney Way TN14 . . . . 73 A
Spire Alexandra Hospl
 ME5 . . . . 84 A
Spire Cl DA12 . . . . 36 F
Spires The
 Dartford DA1 . . . . 32 B
 Maidstone ME16 . . . . 99 A
 Rochester ME2 . . . . 52 F
Spire Chambridge Wells Hospl
 TN3 . . . . 157 F
Spital St DA1 . . . . 26 C
Spitfire Cl ME5 . . . . 98 F
Spitfire Rd ME19 . . . . 96 B
Splashes L Ctr ME8 . . . . . . 55 F
Spode La TN8 . . . . 138 E
Sponden La TN18 . . . . 196 A
Spongs La TN17 . . . . 166 A
Sportsfield ME14 . . . . 100 D
Sportsmans Cotts ME19 . . . 97 F
Spot La ME15 . . . . 101 C
Spout La
 Brenchley TN12 . . . . 162 B
 Crockham Hill TN8 . . . . . . 105 F
Spray Hill TN3 . . . . 179 A
Spray St SE18 . . . . 2 B
Sprig The ME14 . . . . 101 B

Spring Cott DA1 .... 32 D8
Springcroft DA3 .... 49 A4
Spring Cross DA3 .... 63 A7
Spring Ct 17 DA15 .... 30 A5
Springdale Cotts ME3 .... 39 A3
Springett Almshouses
TN18 .... 194 E8
Springett Cl ME20 .... 82 F6
Springett Way ME17 .... 115 D3
Springfield Ave
Maidstone ME14 .... 99 F7
Swanley BR8 .... 45 F5
Tenterden TN30 .... 183 C2
Springfield Cotts TN12 .. 162 F5
Springfield Gdns BR1 .... 42 F5
Springfield Gr SE7 .... 11 C8
Springfield Ind Est TN18. 188 F3
Springfield Rd
Bexley, Bexleyheath DA7 ... 14 B3
Bexley, Welling DA16 .... 13 B4
Bromley BR1 .... 42 F5
Edenbridge TN8 .... 122 B1
Gillingham ME7 .... 54 E6
Groombridge TN3 .... 171 C7
Lunsford ME20 .... 81 F4
Royal Tunbridge Wells
TN4 .... 142 F1
Springfields TN5 .... 186 E1
Springfield Terr 7 ME4 ... 53 F4
Springfield Wlk 3 BR6 ... 43 D1
Spring Gdns
Biggin Hill TN16 .... 72 C1
Orpington BR6 .... 58 B4
4 Rusthall TN4 .... 158 B4
Spring Gr DA12 .... 36 B7
Springhead TN2 .... 159 D5
Springhead Ent Pk DA11 . 35 C7
Springhead Rd
Erith DA8 .... 14 F8
Northfleet DA11 .... 35 C7
Spring Head Rd TN15 .... 76 F2
Spring Hill TN11, TN3 .... 157 A7
Springholm Cl TN16 ...... 72 C1
Spring La
Bidborough TN3 .... 142 D3
Oldbury TN15 .... 94 B5
Spring Lodge 3 BR5 ..... 44 C4
Springrove Cotts TN12 .. 148 B5
Springshaw Cl TN13 ...... 91 D4
Spring Shaw Rd BR5 ..... 44 A8
Springvale ME8 .... 69 C6
Spring Vale
Bexley DA7 .... 14 B3
Dartford DA1 .... 32 D8
Maidstone ME16 .... 99 E4
Swanscombe DA9 .... 17 C1
Spring Vale Cl BR8 ...... 45 F8
Springvale Ct
Eltham SE12 .... 11 A3
Northfleet DA11 .... 35 C6
Spring Vale N DA1 .... 32 D8
Springvale Ret Pk 2 BR5 44 C6
Spring Vale S DA1 .... 32 D8
Springvale Way BR5 ..... 44 C6
Springview Apartments
TN2 .... 159 D6
Springwater Cl SE18 ..... 12 A6
Springwell Rd TN9 ...... 143 B8
Springwood Cl 1 ME16 .. 99 A3
Springwood Hall TN11 .. 110 D1
Springwood Rd ME16 .... 99 A3
Sprivers Gdn★ TN12 ..... 162 E4
Spruce Cl ME20 .... 82 B2
Sprucedale Cl BR8 .... 45 E7
Spruce Ho TN4 .... 158 E4
Spruce Rd TN16 .... 72 D3
Spurgeon Cl RM17 .... 18 C8
Spurgeons Cotts ME17 .. 115 E2
Spur Rd BR6 .... 58 A8
Spurrell Ave DA5 .... 31 D4
Spurway ME14 .... 101 A4
Square Hill ME15 .... 100 B4
Square Hill Rd ME15 .... 100 B4
Square The
Cowden TN8 .... 155 B6
Hadlow TN11 .... 128 E8
Hunton ME15 .... 131 D7
Leigh TN11 .... 125 F1
Lenham ME17 .... 120 D5
Sevenoaks TN13 .... 91 E5
Swanley BR8 .... 45 D6
Tatsfield TN16 .... 88 C7
Wadhurst TN5 .... 185 A4
Squerryes Ct★ TN16 ..... 105 C7
Squerryes Mede TN16 ... 105 C8
Squires Cl ME2 .... 52 B7
Squires Field BR8 .... 45 F8
Squires Ho 3 SE18 ...... 12 B8
Squires Way DA2 .... 31 D4
Squires Wood Dr BR7 .... 28 F1
Squirrel Way TN2 .... 159 E5
Stable Cl ME5 .... 68 C5
Stabledene Way TN2 .... 160 D6
Stable Lane DA5 .... 31 B6
Stables End BR6 .... 57 C7
Stables The TN18 .... 194 E8
Stace Cl TN30 .... 193 C8
Stacey Cl DA12 .... 36 E3
Stacey Rd TN10 .... 127 A4
Staceys St ME14 .... 99 F5
Stackfield 1 TN8 .... 122 D3
Stack La DA3 .... 48 F4
Stacklands Cl TN15 ..... 61 E4
Stack Rd DA4 .... 47 D5
Stadium Rd SE18 .... 11 F8
Stadium Way DA1 .... 14 E2
Stadler Cl ME16 .... 99 D7
Staffa Rd ME15 .... 116 A7
Staffhurst Wood Rd TN8,
RH8 .... 121 C6
Stafford Cl DA9 .... 16 F2
Stafford Rd
Royal Tunbridge Wells
TN2 .... 159 E4
Sidcup DA14 .... 29 E4
Tonbridge TN9 .... 127 B2
Stafford St ME7 .... 54 C5
Stafford Way TN13 ..... 108 C8
Stag Rd
Chatham ME5 .... 68 B5
Royal Tunbridge Wells
TN2 .... 159 D8
Stagshaw Cl ME15 ...... 100 A2
Stag Theatre The★ TN13 .. 92 B2
Stainer House SE3 .... 11 C3
Stainer Rd TN10 .... 127 F6
Staines Wlk DA14 .... 30 C2
Stainmore Cl BR7 .... 43 D8
Stairfoot La TN13 .... 91 C5
Stair Rd TN10 .... 127 F4
Stake La ME2 .... 66 A6
Staleys Acre 7 TN15 ..... 94 F7
Staleys Rd TN15 .... 94 F7
Stalham Ct ME7 .... 69 B4
Stalin Ave ME5 .... 68 B8
Stalisfield Pl BR6 .... 57 A1
Stampers The ME15 ...... 99 D2
Stanam Rd TN2 .... 160 E6
Stanbridge Rd TN8 ...... 122 B2
Stanbrook Rd
Northfleet DA11 .... 35 F8
Woolwich SE2 .... 3 B4
Standard Ind Est E16 .... 1 F4
Standard Rd
Bexley DA6 .... 13 E3
Erith DA17 .... 4 A1
Farthing Street BR6 .... 57 A1
STANDEN 168 B5
Standen Cl ME8 .... 69 E4
Standen St
Benenden TN17, TN18 .... 190 D2
Royal Tunbridge Wells
TN4 .... 159 A5
Standen Street TN17 ..... 196 E8
STANDEN STREET 190 D1
Standings Cross TN12 ... 145 E1
Standish Ho SE3 .... 11 B3
STANDON STREET 196 D8
Stane Way SE18 .... 11 E7
Stanford Dr ME16 .... 99 C3
Stanford La TN11 .... 112 C2
Stanford Way ME2 .... 52 C2
Stangate Rd
Birling ME19 .... 81 B8
Rochester ME2 .... 52 C7
Stangrove Rd TN8 ...... 122 C1
Stanham Pl DA1 .... 15 A3
Stanham Rd DA1 .... 15 C2
Stanhill Cotts DA2 .... 31 D2
Stanhope Ave BR2 .... 42 A1
Stanhope Cl ME14 .... 99 E7
Stanhope Rd
Bexley DA7 .... 13 E5
Rochester ME2 .... 53 A7
Royal Tunbridge Wells
TN1 .... 159 C5
Sidcup DA15 .... 30 A4
Swanscombe DA10 .... 17 F1
Stanhopes RH8 .... 104 B7
Stanhope Way TN13 ...... 91 D5
Stan La ME18 .... 112 A7
Stanley Cl
Eltham SE9 .... 29 C7
Staplehurst TN12 .... 149 E4
Stone DA9 .... 16 E2
Stanley Cotts DA2 .... 33 E3
Stanley Cres DA12 .... 36 D3
Stanley Glyn Ct BR7 ...... 29 A3
Stanley Holloway Ct E16 .. 1 A7
Stanley Rd
Bromley BR2 .... 42 C5
Chatham ME5 .... 68 C6
Gillingham ME7 .... 54 C6
Grays RM17 .... 18 B8
Marden TN12 .... 148 D5
Northfleet DA11 .... 35 E7
Orpington BR6 .... 43 F1
Royal Tunbridge Wells
TN1 .... 159 B5
Sidcup DA14 .... 30 A5
Swanscombe DA10 .... 17 F1
Stanley Way BR5 .... 44 B4
Stanmore Ho SE12 .... 28 B7
Stanmore Rd DA17 .... 4 C2
Stansfeld Rd E16 .... 1 D7
STANSTED 62 F1
Stansted CE Prim Sch
TN15 .... 62 F1
Stansted Cl ME16 .... 99 D7
Stansted Cres DA5 .... 30 D7
Stansted Hill TN15 .... 63 A1
Stansted La TN15 .... 62 C1
Stanton Cl BR5 .... 44 C2
Stanton Ct
9 Bromley BR1 .... 42 C7
5 Sidcup DA15 .... 30 A5
Staple Cl DA5 .... 31 D5
Staple Dr TN12 .... 149 F4
Stapleford Ct TN13 ...... 91 F4
STAPLEHURST 149 D4
Staplehurst Ho BR5 ...... 44 C4
Staplehurst Prim Sch
TN12 .... 149 E3
Staplehurst Rd
Bogden TN12 .... 133 C2
Frittenden TN12, TN17 .... 150 D1
Staplehurst Rd *continued*
Gillingham ME8 .... 55 B3
Staplehurst Sta TN12 .... 149 E5
Staplers Ct ME14 .... 100 B8
Staples Ho E6 .... 2 A7
Staples The BR8 .... 46 B8
Stapleton Rd
Bexley DA7 .... 13 F8
Orpington BR6 .... 57 F7
Stapley Rd DA17 .... 4 A1
Starboard Ave DA9 .... 17 B1
Star Bsns Ctr RM13 .... 4 E8
Starbuck Cl SE9 .... 29 A8
Star Hill
Crayford DA1 .... 14 E2
Rochester ME1 .... 53 D5
Star Hill Rd TN14 .... 75 A2
Star Ho TN3 .... 176 B5
Star La
Gillingham ME7 .... 69 A7
Orpington BR5, BR8 ...... 44 E5
Starling Cl DA3 .... 49 B6
Star Mill Ct ME5 .... 54 D2
Star Mill La ME5 .... 54 D2
Starnes Ct 5 ME14 ...... 100 A5
Starr Cotts TN12 .... 131 C2
Starts Cl BR6 .... 57 A7
Starts Hill Ave BR6 ...... 57 B6
Starts Hill Rd BR6 .... 57 B6
Starve Goose La TN17 ... 178 E4
State Farm Ave BR6 ...... 57 C6
Stately Pk ME18 .... 113 C1
Station App
Bexley, Barnehurst DA7 .... 14 C5
Bexley, Bexleyheath DA7 ... 13 E5
Bexley, Welling DA16 ...... 13 A5
2 Borough Green TN15 .... 94 F7
Bromley BR7 .... 28 E2
Chelsfield BR6 .... 58 B5
Chislehurst BR7 .... 43 A7
Dartford DA1 .... 15 E1
Edenbridge TN8 .... 122 C2
Grays RM17 .... 18 A8
Greenwich SE3 .... 11 B4
Halling ME2 .... 66 A5
Hayes BR2 .... 42 A1
Maidstone ME16 .... 99 F3
Orpington BR6 .... 57 F8
Orpington, St Mary Cray
BR5 .... 44 B5
Otford TN14 .... 76 C3
Paddock Wood TN12 ..... 146 A7
Staplehurst TN12 .... 149 E5
Swanley BR8 .... 45 E5
Station Cotts
Gill's Green TN18 .... 188 F5
Hartley TN17 .... 178 E2
Horsmonden TN12 .... 163 B5
Station Cres SE3 .... 1 A1
Station Ct 1 TN15 .... 94 F7
Station Hill
Chiddingstone Causeway
TN11 .... 141 A8
Hayes BR2 .... 56 A8
Station Hill Cotts ME15 .. 115 A7
Station Mews 3 TN30 ... 193 A7
Station Par
Sevenoaks TN13 .... 92 A3
Sidcup DA15 .... 30 A6
Station Rd
Aylesford ME20 .... 82 E2
Betsham DA13 .... 35 A4
Bexley DA7 .... 13 E4
Borough Green TN15 ...... 94 F7
Brasted TN16 .... 90 B4
Bromley BR1 .... 42 A8
Cliffe ME3 .... 22 B3
Crayford DA1 .... 14 F1
Cuxton ME2 .... 52 C2
East Farleigh ME15 ...... 115 A7
East Tilbury RM18 .... 20 B7
Edenbridge TN8 .... 122 C2
Erith DA17 .... 4 A3
Eynsford DA4 .... 60 D7
Goudhurst TN17 .... 177 C7
Groombridge TN3 .... 171 C7
Halstead TN14 .... 74 F8
Harrietsham ME17 .... 119 D6
Headcorn TN27 .... 151 D5
Hurst Green TN19 .... 194 A3
Longfield DA3 .... 48 E6
Maidstone ME14 .... 99 F5
Meopham Station DA13 .... 50 A4
Nettlestead Green ME18 .. 113 C1
Newington ME9 .... 71 B6
Northfleet DA11 .... 18 B1
Northiam TN31 .... 197 C1
Orpington BR6 .... 57 F8
Orpington, St Mary Cray
BR5 .... 44 C5
Otford TN14 .... 76 C3
Paddock Wood TN12 ..... 145 F7
Rochester ME2 .... 53 C7
Rockrobin TN5 .... 184 C6
Sevenoaks TN13 .... 91 E7
Shoreham TN14 .... 76 A7
Sidcup DA14, DA15 .... 30 A5
Snodland ME20 .... 82 D2
Staplehurst TN12 .... 149 F5
Stone DA9 .... 17 A2
Sutton at Hone DA4 .... 47 B7
Swanley BR8 .... 45 E5
Tenterden TN30 .... 193 A7
Withyham TN7 .... 170 B5
Station Road N DA17 ...... 4 B3
Station Sq BR5 .... 43 C4
Station St E16 .... 2 B5
Steadman Cl ME3 .... 38 C6
Stede Hill ME17 .... 103 F3
STEDE QUARTER 168 E1
Stedley 10 DA14 .... 30 A4
Stedman Cl DA5 .... 31 E5
Steele Ave DA9 .... 17 A2
Steele's La DA13 .... 64 A6
Steele St ME2 .... 53 A8
Steele Wlk DA8 .... 14 B7
Steellands Rise TN5 ..... 186 F1
Steep Cl BR6 .... 57 F4
Steephill Sch DA3 .... 48 D5
Steeple Heights Dr TN16 . 72 D2
Steerforth Cl ME1 .... 53 C2
Steers Pl TN11 .... 111 E2
Stella Cl TN12 .... 148 D5
Stelling Rd DA8 .... 14 D7
Stenning Ct TN10 ...... 127 C4
Stephen Cl BR6 .... 57 F7
Stephen Rd DA7 .... 14 C4
Stephenson Ave RM18 .... 19 A6
Stephenson Ho SE2 .... 3 D1
Stephen's Rd TN4 ...... 159 B6
Stepneyford La TN17 .... 191 C7
Steps Hill Rd ME9 .... 86 D6
Sterling Ave ME16 .... 99 C5
Sterling Ho SE3 .... 11 B3
Sterndale Rd DA1 .... 32 F8
Sterry Gdns ME15 ...... 116 E7
Stevanne Ct 1 DA17 .... 4 A1
Stevedale Rd DA16 .... 13 C5
Steven Cl ME4 .... 54 A3
Stevens Cl
Dartford DA2 .... 33 E3
Egerton TN27 .... 137 F3
Joyden's Wood DA5 .... 31 D4
Snodland ME6 .... 82 A8
Stevens Cotts TN30 ..... 193 A7
Stevenson Cl
Erith DA8 .... 15 B7
Maidstone ME15 .... 99 F3
Stevenson Way ME20 ..... 81 F4
Stevens Rd ME20 .... 82 F6
Stewart Cl BR7 .... 29 B4
Stewart Ho ME3 .... 39 F6
Stewart Rd TN4 .... 159 C7
Steyning Gr SE9 .... 28 F4
Steynton Ave DA5 .... 30 D6
Stickens La ME19 .... 97 E7
Stickfast La ME17 ...... 135 D3
STICK HILL 139 A3
Stickland Rd 2 DA17 ...... 4 A2
STIFF STREET 87 E7
Stilebridge La ME17 ..... 133 A5
Stiles Cl
Bromley BR2 .... 42 F3
Erith DA8 .... 4 B1
Still La TN4 .... 142 F2
Stillwater Mews ME4 ..... 40 B2
Stirling Cl
Gillingham ME8 .... 69 E4
Rochester ME1 .... 53 A3
Sidcup DA14 .... 29 F4
Stirling Dr BR6 .... 58 B5
Stirling Ho 5 SE18 .... 2 B1
Stirling Rd ME19 .... 96 F3
Stisted Way TN27 .... 137 F3
STOCKBURY 86 E8
Stockbury Dr ME16 .... 99 D7
Stockbury Hill Wood Nature
Reserve★ ME9 .... 86 D6
Stockbury Ho 7 BR5 ..... 44 D1
Stockenbury TN12 ...... 129 F6
Stockett La ME15 .... 115 D6
Stock Hill TN16 .... 72 D2
Stock La DA2 .... 32 C4
STOCKLAND GREEN 142 C1
Stockland Green Rd
Royal Tunbridge Wells
TN3 .... 158 D8
Speldhurst TN3 .... 158 B8
STOCKS GREEN 126 B4
Stocks Green Prim Sch
TN11 .... 126 E5
Stocks Green Rd TN11 ... 126 C5
Stocks Rd TN30 .... 199 F3
Stockton Cl ME14 .... 100 B8
Stockwell Cl BR1 .... 42 B7
Stofield Gdns SE9 .... 28 D5
STOKE 25 A3
Stoke Com Sch ME3 ...... 25 C5
Stoke Rd
Allhallows ME3 .... 9 C1
Hoo St Werburgh ME3 ..... 40 F6
Kingsnorth ME3 .... 41 C8
Lower Stoke ME3 .... 24 E1
Stokesay Ct 14 DA2 ...... 16 B1
STONE 16 F2
Stoneacre★ ME15 .... 117 B7
Stoneacre Cl ME8 .... 69 D5
Stoneacre Ct 7 ME15 ... 100 A1
Stoneacre La ME15 ...... 117 B7
STONE BRIDGE 184 E6
Stonebridge Green Rd
TN27 .... 137 F4
Stonebridge Rd DA11 .... 18 B2
Stone Castle Dr DA9 ..... 17 A1
Stonechat Sq 6 E6 .... 1 E8
Stone Cotts TN3 .... 175 F4
Stone Court La TN2 ..... 160 E8
Stonecroft DA13 .... 80 A8
Stonecroft Rd DA8 .... 14 C7
Stonecrop Cl ME4 .... 40 C1
STONE CROSS
Langton Green 157 A2
Wadhurst 185 A3
Stone Crossing Sta DA9 .. 16 E2
Stonecross Lea ME5 ...... 54 C1
Stone Cross Rd TN5 ..... 185 A4
STONECROUCH 186 F6
Stone Ct DA8 .... 4 F1
Stonefield Cl DA7 .... 14 A4
Stonefield Way SE7 ...... 11 D7
Stonegate Cl BR5 .... 44 C6
Stonegate Rd TN5 ...... 185 C1
Stone Hill Rd TN27 ...... 137 F2
Stonehill Woods Pk DA14. 31 B2
Stonehorse Ct ME3 .... 39 A3
Stonehorse La ME2 .... 39 A2
Stonehouse Cnr RM19 .... 16 E8
Stonehouse La
Halstead TN14 .... 74 E8
Pratt's Bottom TN14 ...... 58 E1
Purfleet RM19 .... 16 E8
Stonehouse Rd BR6, TN14. 58 D1
Stoneings La TN14 .... 89 F8
Stone Lake Ind Pk SE7 .... 1 C2
Stone Lake Ret Pk SE7 .... 1 C2
Stoneleigh Rd
Bromley BR1 .... 43 B6
The Chart RH8 .... 104 E5
Stonely Cres 3 DA9 ...... 17 C3
Stoneness Rd RM20 ...... 17 C7
Stone Pit La TN18 .... 196 E5
Stone Place Rd DA9 ...... 16 E2
Stone Rd BR2 .... 42 A5
Stone Row TN3 .... 157 B5
Stone Row Cotts TN3 .... 157 D1
Stone St Mary's CE Prim Sch
DA9 .... 33 E8
Stones Cross Rd BR8 ..... 45 C4
Stones Rdbt ME4 .... 40 B1
Stone St
Cranbrook TN17 .... 179 D5
Gravesend DA11 .... 19 B1
Royal Tunbridge Wells
TN1 .... 159 B4
Stonestile Bsns Pk TN27 151 A7
Stonestile Rd TN27 ...... 151 A7
STONE STREET 93 E2
Stone Street Rd TN15 .... 93 E2
Stoneswood Rd RH8 .... 104 B5
Stonewall E6 .... 2 A8
Stonewall Park Rd TN3 .. 157 F3
Stone Wood DA2 .... 34 C5
Stonewood Cl TN4 ...... 159 A8
Stonewood Rd DA8 .... 4 E1
Stoney Alley SE18 .... 12 A5
Stoney Bank ME7 .... 54 F1
Stony Cnr DA13 .... 49 E6
Stonyfield TN8 .... 122 D3
Stony La ME1 .... 67 C5
Stopford Rd ME7 .... 54 D4
Storehouse Wharf ME12 .. 27 F3
Store Rd E16 .... 2 A4
Storey St E16 .... 2 A4
Stornaway Strand DA12 .. 36 F4
Stotfold BR1 .... 42 E8
Stour Cl
Orpington BR2 .... 56 C6
Rochester ME2 .... 52 F7
Tonbridge TN10 .... 127 B5
Stour Ct 21 BR5 .... 44 D1
Stour Rd DA1 .... 15 A4
Stow Ct DA2 .... 33 C8
Stowe Rd BR6 .... 58 B6
Stowting Rd BR6 .... 57 E6
Strait Rd E6 .... 1 F6
Strand Approach Rd ME7 . 54 E7
Strand Cl DA13 .... 50 A3
Strand Ct SE18 .... 2 E1
Strandfield Cl SE18 .... 2 E1
Strand L Pool & Pk ME7 ... 54 F7
Strand Rdbt The ME7 .... 54 E7
Stratfield Ho SE12 .... 28 A6
Stratford Ave ME8 .... 69 D8
Stratford Dr ME15 ...... 116 D6
Stratford House Ave BR1 . 42 E6
Stratford La 2 ME8 .... 69 F8
Stratford Rd ME19 .... 97 A8
Stratford St TN1 .... 159 C5
Strathaven Rd SE12 ...... 11 B1
Stratheden Par SE3 ...... 11 A7
Stratheden Rd SE3 .... 11 A7
Stratton Cl DA7 .... 13 E4
Stratton Rd DA7 .... 13 E4
Stratton Terr TN16 ...... 105 C8
Strawberry Cl TN2 ...... 172 E7
Strawberry Fields
Orpington BR6 .... 57 B5
Swanley BR8 .... 45 E7
Strawberry Vale TN9 .... 127 C1
Straw Mill Hill ME15 ..... 99 E1
Streamdale SE2 .... 13 B8
Stream La TN18 .... 195 A7
Stream Pit La TN18 ..... 196 B5
Streamside ME20 .... 82 B1
Stream Side TN10 ...... 127 D6
Streamside Cl
Bromley BR2 .... 42 A5
Hildenborough TN11 ..... 126 E5
Stream The ME20 .... 82 C1
Stream Way DA17 .... 14 A8
Streatfield TN8 .... 122 D1
Streatfield Ho TN16 ...... 89 C1
Street End Rd ME5 .... 54 B1
Street Farm Cotts ME3 ... 40 F6
Streetfield ME17 .... 135 F7
Streetfield Mews SE3 .... 11 A4
Streetfield Rd ME8 .... 55 F1
Street The
Ash TN15 .... 62 E5
Benenden TN17 .... 190 D6
Boxley ME14 .... 84 C3

Street The continued
Bredhurst ME7..........69 B1
Cobham DA12..........50 F6
Detling ME14..........85 A1
Egerton TN27..........137 F3
Frittenden TN17........166 E7
Hartlip ME9............70 D5
High Halstow ME23.....23 E3
Horton Kirby DA4.......47 C5
Ightham TN15..........94 D6
Maidstone ME14........101 C4
Meopham DA13.........50 A1
Mereworth ME18........112 D8
Plaxtol TN15...........110 F7
Ryarsh ME19...........80 F4
Shorne DA12...........37 E3
Sissinghurst TN17......180 B8
Smarden TN27..........153 A1
Stockbury ME9.........86 E8
Teston ME18...........114 A7
Trottiscliffe ME19......80 A5
Ulcombe ME17..........135 F7
Upper Halling ME2......65 B5
Wittersham TN30........199 D3
Strettitt Gdns TN12......129 F5
Strickland Ave DA1......15 F4
Strickland Way 5 BR6....5 F3
Strongbow Cres SE9.....11 F2
Strongbow Rd SE9......11 F2
STROOD
Rochester............52 F7
Tenterden............192 B5
Strood Ent Pk ME2......53 B7
Strood Sports Ctr ME20..52 F7
Strood Sta ME2.........53 C7
Strover St ME7..........54 C7
Struttons Ave DA11.....35 F6
Stuart Ave BR2.........42 A1
Stuart Cl
Hextable BR8...........32 A1
Maidstone ME14........100 C6
Royal Tunbridge Wells
TN2..................172 F8
Stuart Evans Cl DA16....13 C4
Stuart Mantle Way DA8...14 E7
Stuart Rd
Bexley DA16............13 B6
Gillingham ME7.........54 D3
Gravesend DA11.........19 F1
Stubbs Hill BR6, TN14...74 C6
Studios The DA3.........62 F8
Studland Cl DA15.......29 F5
Studley Cres DA3.......49 C7
Studley Ct DA14........30 B3
Stumble Hill TN11......110 C5
Sturdee Ave ME7........54 E4
Sturdee Cotts ME3......41 A6
Sturges End E4..........9 C2
Sturla Rd ME4..........54 D2
Sturmer Ct ME19........97 A2
Sturry Way ME5.........55 C2
STYANTS BOTTOM
Styants Bottom Rd TN15..93 F5
Style Cl ME8...........69 E4
Styles Cl TN8..........123 B5
Styles Cotts TN8.......123 B5
Styles Ct TN12.........145 F7
Styles La ME14..........84 C3
Sudbury E6.............2 A7
Sudbury Cres BR1.......28 A3
Suffolk Ave ME8........55 F1
Suffolk Cl 7 ME8.......55 F1
Suffolk Mews 1 TN1....159 A4
Suffolk Rd
Dartford DA1...........15 E1
Gravesend DA11.........19 D1
Sidcup DA14...........30 C2
Suffolk Way TN13.......92 C2
Sullivan Ave E16........1 D8
Sullivan Cl DA1.........32 C8
Sullivan Rd
Tilbury RM18...........19 A6
Tonbridge TN10........127 E5
Sultan Mews ME5.......68 C2
Sultan Rd ME5..........68 C2
Summer Cl TN30........183 C1
Summerfield
6 Bromley BR1........42 B8
Marden TN17...........164 B6
Summerfield St 5 SE12..28 A8
Summerhill ME7........151 A6
Summer Hill BR7........43 A7
Summerhill Ave TN4.....142 F1
Summerhill Cl BR6......57 E7
Summerhill Rd
Bogden TN12..........133 C1
Dartford DA1..........32 D8
Summerhill Villas BR7...43 B8
Summerhouse Dr DA2,
DA5...................34 A4
Summerlands Lodge BR6..57 A6
Summerson Cl ME1......53 C1
Summerton Way SE28....3 D7
Summervale Rd TN4.....158 E1
Sumner Cl
Orpington BR6.........57 C6
Rolvenden TN17........191 F3
Sunburst Cl TN12.......148 D5
Sunbury St SE18........1 F3
Sun Ct DA8............14 F5
Sunderland Cl ME1......53 A3
Sunderland Dr ME8.....70 A8
Sunderland Ho 8 ME7...54 C7
Sunderland Point E16....2 C5

Sundew Ct 9 RM17......18 D8
Sundorne Rd SE7........1 C1
SUNDRIDGE
Brasted..............90 F3
Lewisham............28 C2
Sundridge Ave
Bexley DA16............12 C4
Bromley BR1..........42 D8
Sundridge & Brasted CE
Prim Sch TN14.........90 E2
Sundridge Cl DA1.......16 A1
Sundridge Cl B BR1....28 B1
Sundridge Dr ME5......68 A4
Sundridge Hill
Cuxton ME2............52 C3
Halstead TN14.........74 C1
Sundridge Ho BR1......28 B3
Sundridge La TN14.....74 C2
Sundridge Park Sta BR1..28 B1
Sundridge Rd ld TN14...91 B8
Sunfields Pl SE3.......11 B7
Sun Hill DA3...........62 A8
Sunhill Ct TN2.........160 C6
Sun La
Gravesend DA12........36 C6
Greenwich SE3.........11 B7
Sunland Ave DA6........13 E3
Sunningdale Cl
Erith SE28............3 E7
Gillingham ME8.........69 C6
Sunningdale Ct DA16....13 C4
Sunningdale Dr ME8.....69 C6
Sunningdale Rd BR1.....42 E4
Sunningvale Ave TN16...72 D3
Sunningvale Cl TN16....72 D3
Sunnybank ME5.........187 E3
Sunnydale BR6..........57 A8
Sunnydale Rd SE12......11 B2
Sunnyfield Rd BR7......44 A6
Sunnyfields ME8........69 E8
Sunnymead Ave ME7.....54 F5
Sunnyside TN8..........122 B3
Sunnyside Rd TN4......159 C4
Sunray Ave BR7.........42 F3
Sun Rd DA10...........17 F1
Sunrise Way ME19......97 C3
Sunset Cl DA8..........15 B7
Sunset Rd SE28.........3 A5
Sunshine Ct 1 ME8.....69 E8
Sun Terr ME5...........68 B4
Superabbey Est ME20....83 B2
Superior Dr 8 BR6......57 F4
Surlingham Cl SE28.....3 D6
Surrenden Rd TN12.....149 E3
Surrey Cl TN2..........172 F8
Surrey Rd ME15.........116 D8
Susan Rd SE3...........11 B1
Susan Wood BR7........43 A8
Sussex Cl
Royal Tunbridge Wells
TN2..................159 C1
West Kingsdown TN15...61 E3
Sussex Dr ME5..........68 A4
Sussex Mews 19 TN2....159 A2
Sussex Rd
Dartford DA1...........33 A8
Erith DA8.............14 B7
Maidstone ME15.......116 D8
Orpington BR5.........44 C3
Sidcup DA14...........30 B3
Tonbridge TN9.........143 A8
Sussex Road Prim Sch
TN9...................143 A8
Sutcliffe Pk Athletics Track..11 B2
Sutcliffe Rd
Bexley DA16............13 C5
Woolwich SE18........12 E8
Sutherland Ave
Bexley DA16............13 C5
Biggin Hill TN16.......72 E1
Orpington BR5.........43 F4
Sutherland Cl
Chalk DA12............37 B6
Stone DA9.............16 F2
Sutherland Gdns ME8...69 E6
Sutherland Ho SE18....11 F6
Sutherland Rd
Erith DA17.............4 A3
Royal Tunbridge Wells
TN1..................159 B3
Sutlej Rd SE7..........11 C7
SUTTON AT HONE.......33 A1
Sutton at Hone CE Prim Sch
DA4...................33 A1
Sutton Cl ME8..........70 A8
Sutton Ct TN12.........148 C5
Sutton Forge TN12.....148 D5
Sutton Hts ME15........116 F6
Sutton Rd
Langley ME17..........117 C5
Maidstone ME15.......116 D6
Sutton St ME14.........101 D4
SUTTON VALENCE......134 E6
Sutton Valence Castle (rems
of) * ME17.............134 C7
Sutton Valence Prep Sch
ME17..................134 C7
Sutton Valence Prim Sch
ME17..................134 E7
Sutton Valence Sch
ME17..................134 E7
Swadelands Cl ME17....120 C5
Swadelands Sch ME17...120 C5
Swaffield Rd TN13......92 C5
Swain Cl ME2...........52 F8

Swain Rd
Gillingham ME8.........69 B6
Tenterden TN30.......183 D3
Swaisland Rd DA1.......15 B1
Swaisands Dr DA1......14 F2
Swaledale Rd DA2......33 C7
Swale Rd
Crayford DA1..........15 A3
Rochester ME2.........52 C7
Swallow Cl
Bexley DA8............14 E6
Stone DA9.............16 F2
Swallow Cl 3 SE12.....28 A8
Swallow Dr TN29........159 F6
Swallowfield Rd SE7....1 B1
Swallowfields 2 ME11...35 E5
Swallow Ho 4 ME6.....99 E4
Swallow Rd ME20.......81 F2
Swallow Rise ME5......68 A5
Swallow St E6..........1 E8
Swallowtail Cl BR5.....44 D5
Swan Apartments 12
ME15..................116 E5
Swan App E6............1 E8
Swanbridge Rd DA7.....14 B6
Swan Bsns Pk DA1......15 C3
Swan Cl BR5............44 A6
Swan Cotts TN30.......199 D3
Swan La
Brandfold TN17........163 F3
Dartford DA1..........31 F8
Marplit Hill TN8........122 C4
Swanland Dr TN9.......142 F7
SWANLEY............45 E5
Swanley Ctr BR8........45 E5
Swanley La BR8.........45 F6
Swanley New Barn Railway *
BR8...................45 E8
Swanley Rd DA16.......13 C6
Swanley Sta BR8........45 E5
Swanley Tech Coll BR8..45 E6
SWANLEY VILLAGE.....46 A8
Swanley Village Rd BR8..46 B8
Swanmead Way TN9.....127 D2
Swan Rd SE18..........2 B1
Swan Ridge TN8........122 D4
SWANSCOMBE........17 D2
Swanscombe Bsns Ctr
DA10..................17 D1
Swanscombe Ho 1 BR5..44 B7
Swanscombe St DA10...17 F1
Swanscombe Sta DA10..17 F2
Swansea Ct E16........2 B4
Swan St
West Malling ME19.....97 C8
Wittersham TN30.......199 C3
SWANTON............112 A8
Swanton Rd
Erith DA8.............14 B7
Mereworth ME18.......112 A8
SWANTON STREET....87 F3
Swan Valley Com Sch
DA10..................34 F8
Swanzy Rd TN14........92 C7
Sward Rd BR5...........44 A3
Swattenden La TN17....179 B1
Swaylands Rd DA1......14 A8
Swaynesland Rd ME8...104 F1
Sweeps Hill Cl TN2.....160 D7
Sweeps La BR5..........44 D5
Sweet Briar Cl ME16...99 D5
Sweetings La TN3, TN5..175 D1
Sweet La ME19..........98 A4
Sweetlands La TN12.....150 A5
Swetenham Wlk SE18...2 C1
Sweyne Rd DA10........17 E1
Sweyn Pl SE3..........11 A5
Swievelands Rd TN16....72 D1
Swift Cl
Larkfield ME20.........82 A2
Woolwich SE28.........3 B6
Swift Cres ME5.........68 C6
Swift Ho 6 ME16.......99 E4
SWIFT'S GREEN.......152 E6
Swift La TN17..........179 D6
Swiller's La DA12......37 E3
Swinburne Gdns RM18...19 B5
Swingate Ave ME3......22 B6
Swingate Cl ME5........68 B2
Swingate Inf Sch ME5..68 C1
Swingfield Ct BR2.......42 D8
Swinton Ave ME3.......39 F5
Swires Shaw BR2........56 D6
Swithland Gdns SE9....29 A4
Syamore Mews DA8.....4 D1
Sycamore Ave DA15.....12 F1
Sycamore Cl
Gravesend DA12........36 D8
Tilbury RM18...........19 A5
Sycamore Cotts
Bidborough TN3........142 D3
Pembury TN2...........160 C6
Sycamore Cres ME16...99 C5
Sycamore Ct
Erith DA8............4 D1
Stone DA9.............33 E8
Sycamore Dr
Aylesford ME20........82 E1
Swanley BR8...........45 E7
Sycamore Gdns TN12...145 A6
Sycamore Lodge BR6...57 F8
Sycamore Rd
Dartford DA1..........32 D7
Rochester ME2.........52 E5
Sychem La TN12........145 A6
Sychem Pl TN12........145 A7
Sydenham Cotts SE12..28 C6

Sydney Cotts 11 BR5....44 C5
Sydney Rd
Bexley DA6............13 D3
Chatham ME4..........54 A3
Erith SE2.............3 D3
Sidcup DA14...........29 E4
Tilbury RM18...........19 A5
Sydney Terr TN18.......188 F3
Sylewood Cl ME1........67 B8
Sylvan Cl RH8..........104 B6
Sylvan Glade ME5.......84 A8
Sylvan Mews DA9.......17 B3
Sylvan Rd ME8..........69 C8
Sylvan Wlk BR1.........42 F6
Sylvester Ave BR7......28 C2
Sylvester Cl ME2.......66 A4
Sylvestre TN13.........91 E6
Symonds Cl TN15.......61 E5
Symonds La ME18.......130 F6
Symonds Rd ME3........22 A4
Symons Ave ME4........54 A2
Syon Lodge 11 SE12....28 A8
Syringa Ct 10 RM17....18 D8

T

Tabor Ct TN12..........163 A6
Tadburn Gn ME5........68 B2
Taddington Wood La ME5..67 E2
Tadley Cl
Gillingham ME7........54 F6
Rochester ME1.........67 C8
Tail Race The ME15....99 E2
Painter Rd TN11........111 E1
Talbot Pk TN17.........159 D5
Talbot Rd
Maidstone ME16........99 C6
The Moor TN18.........194 F8
Talehangers Cl DA6.....13 D3
Tallents Cl DA4.........33 B1
Tallis Cl E16...........1 B7
Tallis Gr SE7...........8 A1
Tall Trees Cl ME17.....118 D2
Tally Rd RH8...........104 E4
Tamar Dr ME2..........52 F7
Tamarind Cl ME7........69 A4
Tamar Rd TN10.........127 B5
Tamar St SE7...........1 C1
Tamesis Strand DA12...36 E3
Tandridge Dr BR6.......43 A1
Tandridge Pl 8 BR6.....43 D1
Tangier La TN3.........173 B6
Tangleberry Cl BR1.....42 F5
Tanglewood Cl ME8.....69 C6
Tanglewood Cl BR5.....54 F5
Tangmere Cl ME7.......54 F5
Tanhurst Wlk SE2.......3 D3
Tanker Hill ME8.........69 D6
Tanners Mead TN8.....122 C1
Tannery Rd TN9........127 C1
Tansy Cl E6............2 A7
Tanyard
Rolvenden TN17........191 E4
Sandhurst TN18........196 B5
Tanyard Cotts DA12.....37 E1
Tanyard La TN4.........142 F1
Tan Yard La DA5........31 A8
Tanyard The TN17.......179 D4
Tappan Dr ME4.........40 B2
Tapsell's La TN5.......184 D5
Tarbutts TN17..........179 D4
Target Bsns Ctr ME15..116 F4
Tarland Ho TN2.........159 D3
Tarling Cl DA14.........30 B5
Tarnwood Pk SE9.......28 F7
Tarragon Rd ME16......99 B3
Tasker Cl ME15........101 B3
Tasmania Ho RM18......19 A6
Tasman Wlk E16........1 D7
Tassell Cl ME19........82 A1
Tate Rd E16............1 F5
Tates TN18............189 A1
Tates Orch DA3........48 F3
Tatler Cl ME5..........68 D2
TATSFIELD...........88 D7
Tatsfield Cl ME8.......55 A2
Tatsfield La
Biggin Hill TN16.......88 F6
Hill Park TN16........89 A6
Tattersall Cl SE9......11 E2
Tattershall Rd ME15...100 A1
Tattlebury La TN17.....163 F1
Tattlebury Rd TN27....151 C8
Taunton Cl
Bexley DA7............14 D5
Maidstone ME15.......116 F6
Taunton Rd DA11.......18 A2
Taunton Vale DA12.....36 D5
Tavern Cl TN15.........94 F7
Tavern Cotts TN15.....93 A3
Taverners Rd ME8......69 E7
Tavistock Cl
Chatham ME5..........67 F1
Gillingham ME8........69 E7
Tavistock Rd
Bexley DA16............13 C6
2 Bromley BR2.........42 A5
Tavy Bridge SE2........3 C4
Tawney Rd SE28........3 B6
Tay Cl ME5............68 B5
Tayfields TN12.........150 C6
Taylor Cl
Harrietsham ME17......119 D6
4 Orpington BR6.......57 F6

Taylor Ct 1 TN2........159 C7
Taylor Rd ME6..........81 F8
Taylor Row DA2.........32 C5
Taylor's Bldgs SE18....2 B2
Taylors Cl DA14........29 F4
Taylor's La ME19.......79 F6
Taylor's La
Higham ME3...........38 B5
Rochester ME2.........53 B7
Taylors Pl ME19........79 E5
Taylor St TN4..........159 A8
Tea Garden La TN3.....158 C2
Teakcroft Ctr RM13.....4 D7
Teal Ave BR5...........44 D5
Teal Cl
Grain ME3............27 B5
Newham E16...........1 D8
Teal Dr ME4...........40 B2
Teapot La ME20........82 E1
Teardrop Ctr BR8......46 C4
Teardrop Ind Pk BR8...46 C4
Teasaucer Hill ME15...115 F8
Teasel Cl ME14........100 F4
Teasel Ct SE28........2 E5
Teasel Rd ME5..........67 F4
Teasels TN27..........168 A1
TEASLEY MEAD.......156 C4
Teasley Mead TN3......156 C4
Tebbs Way TN15........94 C3
Tedder Ave ME5........68 A7
Tedder Rd TN14........159 B7
Teesdale Rd DA2........33 C7
Teeswater Ct DA18......3 D3
Teign Mews SE9........28 E6
Teignmouth Rd DA16...13 C5
Teise Cl TN12..........159 D2
Tekram Cl TN8..........122 C1
Telegraph Hill ME3.....38 C3
Telemann Sq SE3.......11 B3
Telford Ho
2 Erith DA17...........4 A3
1 Maidstone ME14.....100 A6
Telford Rd SE9.........29 D6
Telscombe Cl BR6.......57 E8
Telston La TN14........75 F2
Temeraire Manor 2 ME7..54 A6
Tempest Rd ME19.......96 F3
Templar Dr
Erith SE28............3 D7
Gravesend DA11........36 A3
Templars Cl 11 TN8....122 D3
Temple Cl SE28........2 C3
Temple Gdns ME2.......53 A6
TEMPLE HILL.........16 A3
Temple Hill DA1........15 F2
Temple Hill Sq DA1.....16 A3
Temple Manor * ME2...53 A6
Temple Mill Prim Sch
ME2...................39 B1
Templemore DA14.......30 B3
Temple Rd TN16........72 D2
Temple Sch ME2........39 B2
Temple Way
Royal Tunbridge Wells
TN2..................159 C7
West Malling ME19.....81 F1
Tenby Rd DA16.........13 D6
Tenchley's La
Limpsfield RH8........104 D4
The Chart RH8.........104 E4
Tenney Ho RM17........18 B7
Tennison Way ME15....116 D6
Tennyson Ave ME6......39 E7
Tennyson Cl DA16......12 F6
Tennyson Ho 2 DA17...3 F1
Tennyson Rd
Dartford DA1..........16 A2
Gillingham ME7........54 C3
Tennyson Wlk
Northfleet DA11.......35 D5
Tilbury RM18...........19 B5
Tenor Dr ME3..........40 E6
Tensing Ave DA11......35 E5
TENTERDEN..........193 C8
Tenterden CE Jun Sch
TN30..................193 B8
Tenterden Cl SE9.......28 A7
Tenterden & District Mus *
TN30..................193 B7
Tenterden Inf Sch TN30..193 B7
Tenterden L Ctr TN30...193 B7
Tenterden Rd
Biddenden TN27.......182 B3
Chatham ME5..........68 B5
Fosten Green TN27....181 F4
Rolvenden TN17........192 A8
Tenterden Station Est
TN30..................193 B8
Tenterden Town Sta *
TN30..................193 B8
Tenterden Vineyard *
TN30..................193 C8
Tent Peg La BR5........43 C4
Tenzing Ct SE9.........28 E6
Terrace Butler Ave ME2..53 E8
Terence Cl
Chatham ME4..........54 A2
Gravesend DA12........36 F6
Terence Ct 6 DA17.....13 F6
Terminus Rd ME16......99 A2
Tern Cres ME2..........52 C6
Terrace Rd ME16........99 E1
Terrace St DA12........19 E3
Terraces The DA2.......33 C8

Terrace The
Chatham ME4. . . . . **53** F7
23 Gravesend DA12 . . . . . . **19** B1
Rochester ME1 . . . . **53** C5
Sevenoaks TN13 . . . . **91** D5
Terry's Lodge Rd TN15 . . . **78** C6
Terry Wlk ME19 . . . . **81** E2
Testers Cl RH8. . . . . **104** B3
TESTON **114** A8
Teston Ho ME18 . . . . **114** A7
Teston La ME15, ME18 . . . . **114** C7
Teston Rd
Kings Hill ME19 . . . . **97** B5
Offham ME19 . . . . **96** C7
Red Hill ME18 . . . . **97** A6
Wateringbury ME18 . . . . . . **97** A6
Tetley Mews TN2 . . . . **159** D4
Tetty Way BR1, BR2 . . . . . . **42** A7
Teviot Cl DA16 . . . . **13** B6
Tewson Rd SE18 . . . . **2** E1

Thistlebank ME5 . . . . **68** A3
Thistlebrook SE2 . . . . **3** C4
Thistlebrook Ind Est SE2 . . . **3** C4
Thistle Ct DA1 . . . . **33** B7
Thistledown
Gravesend DA12 . . . . **36** D2
Maidstone ME14 . . . . **100** F4
Thistledown Cl ME7 . . . . . . **69** A4
Thistlefield Cl DA5 . . . . **30** D7
Thistlemead BR7. . . . . **43** B7
Thistle Rd DA12. . . . . **36** E8
Thomas Aveling Sch The
ME1. . . . . **67** C8
Thomas Cotts DA13 . . . . **35** B1
Thomas Cribb Mews E6 . . . . **2** A7
Thomas Dinwiddy Rd
SE12. . . . . **28** B6
Thomas Dr DA12 . . . . **36** D6
Thomas Dunk Almshouses **13**
TN18 . . . . **189** A2
Thomas Harris Cl ME2. . . . . **66** B4
Thomas Rider Way ME15 . . **116** B4
Thomas Shearley Ct DA5 . . **31** B8
Thomas St
Rochester ME1 . . . . **53** C3
Royal Tunbridge Wells
TN4. . . . . **159** A5
Woolwich SE18 . . . . **2** B2
Thomas Tallis Sch SE3 . . . . **11** B4
Thomas Wyatt Way **2**
TN15 . . . . **78** F3
Thompson Cl ME8. . . . . **70** A8
Thomson Cl ME6. . . . . **66** A1
THONG. **37** A2
Thong La
Basted TN15 . . . . **94** F5
Gravesend DA12. . . . . **37** A2
Thorn Cl
Bromley BR1 . . . . **43** A3
Chatham ME5. . . . . **67** D1
Thorndale BR7. . . . . **28** F1
Thorndale ME5 . . . . **67** D4
Thorndon Ct TN17 . . . . . . **198** A8
Thornden La
Rolvenden Layne TN17 . . . **198** A8
Rolvenden TN17. . . . . **192** A1
Thorndike Cl ME4 . . . . **67** F8
Thorndike Ho ME4 . . . . **67** F8
Thorndon Cl BR5 . . . . **43** F7
Thorndon Rd BR5 . . . . **43** F7
Thorndyke Way **1** TN15. . . **78** F3
Thorne Cl
Erith DA8. . . . . **14** B8
Newham E16 . . . . **1** A7
Thornet Wood Rd BR1 . . . . **43** A6
Thorneycroft Cl ME17 . . . . **118** D2
Thornfield Gdns TN2 . . . . . **159** F5
Thornham Rd ME8 . . . . **55** C3
Thornhill Ave SE18 . . . . **12** E7
Thornhill Pl ME14 . . . . **100** A6
Thorn Rd TN12. . . . . **148** E4
Thorn's Mdw TN16 . . . . **90** C4
Thornton Dene DA14 . . . . . . **30** A3
Thornton Rd
Bromley BR1 . . . . **28** A3
Erith DA17. . . . . **3** E1
Thorntree Prim Sch SE7 . . . **1** D1
Thorntree Rd SE7 . . . . **1** D1
Thorold Rd ME5 . . . . **54** B3
Thorpe Ave TN10 . . . . **127** C5
Thorpe Cl BR6 . . . . **57** E8
Thorpe Wlk ME8 . . . . **69** D3
Thrale Way ME8 . . . . **69** E4
THREE CHIMNEYS **167** B2
Three Corners DA7. . . . . . . **14** B5
Three Elm La TN11 . . . . . . **128** D5
Three Gates Rd DA3. . . . . . **48** A2
THREE LEG CROSS **186** C3
Three Leg Cross Rd TN5 . . **186** D3
Three Oaks La TN5 . . . . . . **184** D7
Thresher Field TN8 . . . . . . **140** A6
Threshers Dr ME14. . . . . . . **100** E5
Thrift La TN14 . . . . **73** E2
Thrift The DA2. . . . . **34** C5
Throckmorton Rd E16. . . . . . **1** B7
Throwley Cl SE2 . . . . **3** C3
Thrush Cl ME5 . . . . **68** B7
Thunderer Rd RM9 . . . . **3** F8
THURNHAM **101** D8
Thurnham CE Inf Sch
ME14. . . . . **101** A4
Thurnham La **5** BR5. . . . . . **44** D1
Thurnham La ME14 . . . . . . **101** C7
Thurrock Bsns Ctr RM20 . . **16** E8
Thurrock Park Way RM17 . **18** A8
Thursland Rd DA14 . . . . . . **30** E3
Thursley Rd SE9 . . . . **28** F5
Thurston Dr ME2 . . . . **52** D7
Thurstone Ct ME14. . . . . . . **99** F6
Thwaite Cl DA8 . . . . **14** C8
Thyer Cl SE9 . . . . **57** C6
Thyme Cl SE3 . . . . **11** C4
Thyme Wlk ME15 . . . . **99** B3
Tibbs Court La TN12 . . . . . **162** A6
TICEHURST **186** E2
Ticehurst Cl BR5. . . . . **30** A1
Tichborne Cl ME16 . . . . **99** C6
Tickford Cl SE2 . . . . **3** C4
Tidal Basin Rd E16 . . . . **1** A6
Tidebrook Cl **1** BR5 . . . . . . **44** C5
Tidelock Ho SE10 . . . . **1** E3
Tideside Ct SE18 . . . . **1** E3
Tideway The ME1 . . . . **67** C8
Tidford Rd DA16 . . . . **12** F5
Tiger La BR2 . . . . **42** B5
Tilbrook Rd SE3 . . . . **11** D4
TILBURY **19** B4

Tilbury Cl BR5 . . . . **44** B7
Tilbury Fort ★ RM18 . . . . . **19** C3
Tilbury L Ctr RM18 . . . . . . **19** B5
Tilbury Manor Inf Sch
RM18 . . . . **19** B7
Tilbury Manor Jun Sch
RM18 . . . . **19** B7
Tilbury PRU RM18 . . . . **18** F6
Tilbury Town Sta RM18 . . . **18** F5
Tilden Cl TN26 . . . . **183** D7
Tilden Ct TN26. . . . . **183** E7
Tilden Gill Rd TN30 . . . . . . **193** C7
Tilden La TN12 . . . . **132** C3
Tilden Rd TN26 . . . . **192** F7
Tilebarn Cnr TN10 . . . . **127** E4
Tile Farm Rd BR6 . . . . **57** D7
Tile Fields ME17 . . . . **102** D2
Tile Fields ME17 . . . . **102** D2
Tilehurst Point **2** SE2. . . . . **3** D1
Tile Kiln La
Coldblow DA5. . . . . **31** C6
Dartford DA5, DA5. . . . . . . **31** F5
Tilghman Way ME6 . . . . . . **66** B1
Till Ave DA4 . . . . **46** F2
Tilley Cl ME3 . . . . **34** B3
Tillingbourne Gn BR5 . . . . . **44** A5
Tillmans TN15 . . . . **95** A7
Tilmans Mead DA4 . . . . **47** A2
Tilton Rd TN15. . . . . **94** F7
Tinker Pot La TN15 . . . . **77** D6
Tinkerpot Rise TN15 . . . . . . **77** C5
Tinker's Alley ME1 . . . . **53** F7
Tinkers La TN5 . . . . **186** E3
Tintagel Gdns ME2 . . . . . . **52** F7
Tintagel Manor **6** ME7. . . . **54** C6
Tintagel Rd BR5 . . . . **44** C1
Tintern Rd ME16 . . . . **99** D7
Tippens Cl TN17 . . . . **179** D4
Titan Rd RM17. . . . . **18** B8
Titchfield Cl **6** ME15 . . . . . **116** F6
Titchfield Rd ME15 . . . . . . **116** F6
Tithe Yd ME17 . . . . **120** D5
Titmuss Ave SE28 . . . . **3** B6
TITSEY. **88** B2
Titsey Cnr RH8. . . . . **104** B7
Titsey Hill CR6, RH8. . . . . . **88** B4
Titsey Pl ★ RH8 . . . . **88** B3
Titsey Rd
Limpsfield RH8. . . . . **104** B8
Titsey RH8 . . . . **88** B1
Tiverton Dr SE9 . . . . **29** C7
Tivoli Gdns
Gravesend DA12 . . . . **36** B7
Woolwich SE18 . . . . **1** E2
Toad Hall Ccts ME3 . . . . . . **40** A4
Tobruk Way ME15 . . . . . . **103** A8
Toby Gdns TN11 . . . . **128** E8
Tockwith Ct TN13 . . . . **92** D4
Toddington Cres ME5 . . . . . **67** D1
Toke Pl ME17 . . . . **132** E8
Tolcairn Ct **2** DA17 . . . . **4** A1
Tolgate La ME2 . . . . **53** B7
Tolgate Way ME14 . . . . **83** E4
Tolhurst Rd TN12 . . . . **145** A7
TOLLGATE. **95** A8
Tollgate Mews TN15 . . . . . . **95** A8
Tollgate Pl TN27 . . . . **151** E5
Tollgate Rd
Dartford DA1 . . . . **33** D8
Newham E6 . . . . **1** F8
Tolsey Mead TN15 . . . . **95** A8
Tom Coombs Cl ME7 . . . . . **11** E3
Tom Cribb Rd SE28 . . . . **2** D3
Tom Jenkinson Rd E16. . . . . **1** A5
Tom Joyce Cl ME6 . . . . **81** F7
Tomlin Cl
Snodland ME6 . . . . **82** A8
Staplehurst TN12. . . . . . . **149** E4
Tonbridge
TONBRIDGE. **127** A2
Tonbridge By-Pass
Tonbridge, Stocks Green TN11,
TN9, TN4, TN11, TN15 . . **126** B5
Tonbridge TN4, TN9, TN11 **143** C6
Tonbridge Castle ★ TN9 . . **127** B2
Tonbridge Chambers **10**
TN9 . . . . **143** B8
Tonbridge Cottage Hospl
TN11. . . . . **143** C6
Tonbridge Ct ME16 . . . . **99** D3
Tonbridge Gram Sch
TN9. . . . . **143** C7
Tonbridge Ho ME2 . . . . **39** C1
Tonbridge Rd
Hadlow TN11 . . . . **128** C2
Ightham TN15 . . . . **94** C3
Little Mill TN11, TN12, TN12 **131** D3
Maidstone, East Barming
ME16. . . . . **98** E1
Maidstone, Upper Fant
ME16. . . . . **99** C3
Pembury TN2 . . . . **160** A7
Sevenoaks TN13, TN15 . . . **108** D7
Tonbridge TN11 . . . . **126** E5

Tonbridge Rd continued
Wateringbury ME18. . . . . . **113** C8
Tonbridge Sch TN10. . . . . . **127** C3
Tonbridge Sta TN9 . . . . . . **127** B1
Tonbridge Swim Pool
TN9 . . . . **127** B2
Tong La TN12 . . . . **162** B2
Tong Rd TN12, TN3 . . . . . . **162** A4
Tongswood Dr TN18 . . . . . **189** C1
Tony Law Ho SE12 . . . . **11** A2
Tooley St DA11 . . . . **35** D8
Topcliffe Dr BR6 . . . . **57** D6
Top Dartford Rd BR8, DA2. . **32** A2
Topley Dr ME23 . . . . **23** E3
Topley St SE9 . . . . **11** D3
Torbay Rd TN12 . . . . **130** B5
Torbrook Cl DA5 . . . . **13** E1
Tor Gr SE28 . . . . **2** E5
Tormount Rd SE18 . . . . **12** E8
Toronto Rd
Gillingham ME7 . . . . **54** E4
Tilbury RM18 . . . . **19** A5
Tor Rd DA16 . . . . **13** C6
Torrens Wlk DA12 . . . . **36** E3
Torrington Cl ME18 . . . . . . **112** D8
Torver Way BR6 . . . . **57** D7
Totnes Rd DA16. . . . . **13** C7
Tovey Sq ME7 . . . . **54** F6
TOVIL. **99** E1
Tovil Gn ME15 . . . . **99** E2
Tovil Green Bsns Pk
ME15. . . . . **99** E1
Tovil Hill ME15. . . . . **99** E2
Tovil Rd ME15 . . . . **99** F2
Tovil Sch ME15 . . . . **99** D2
Tower Cl
Gravesend DA12 . . . . **36** E3
Orpington BR6. . . . . **57** F7
Tower Croft DA4 . . . . **60** E8
Towerfields ME6 . . . . **56** E6
Tower Gdns ME14 . . . . . . **101** B4
Tower Hill ME19 . . . . **96** D7
Tower Ind Est TN15 . . . . . . **78** D5
Tower La ME14 . . . . **101** B4
Tower Park Rd DA1 . . . . . . **14** F2
Tower Rd
Bexley DA7 . . . . **14** A3
Dartford DA1 . . . . **15** C1
Erith DA17. . . . . **4** C2
Orpington BR6. . . . . **57** F7
Tower Ret Pk DA1 . . . . **14** F2
Towers Point ME1 . . . . **53** B4
Towers Wood DA4 . . . . **47** D8
Towerzey Way ME19 . . . . . **97** B3
Town Acres TN10 . . . . **127** C4
Towncourt Cres BR5 . . . . . **43** D5
Towncourt La BR5 . . . . **43** D2
Townfield Cnr DA12. . . . . . **36** D7
Towngate Wood Park Mobile
Home Pk TN10 . . . . **127** E2
Town Hill
Lamberhurst TN3. . . . . . . **176** A4
West Malling ME19 . . . . . . **81** C1
Town Hill Cl ME19 . . . . **81** C1
Townland Cl TN27 . . . . **168** A2
Townlands Rd TN5 . . . . . . **184** F4
Townley Gram Sch for Girls
DA6. . . . . **13** F2
Townley Rd DA6 . . . . **13** F2
Town Lock Ho **4** TN9 . . . . **127** C2
Town Mdw TN17 . . . . **179** D4
Town Pier Sq **5** DA11 . . . . **19** B1
Town Rd ME3. . . . . **39** A6
Townsend Rd ME6 . . . . **81** F8
Townsend Sq ME19 . . . . . . **97** A2
Townshend Cl DA14. . . . . . **30** B2
Townshend Ho ME **14** SE18 . . . **1** F2
Townshend Rd BR7. . . . . . . **29** B3
Town Sq ME18 . . . . **14** E8
Town Square Cres DA9. . . . **33** F8
Town Station Cotts TN8 . . **122** D1
Toynbec Cl BR7. . . . . **29** B4
TOY'S HILL **106** C3
Toy's Hill TN16, TN8 . . . . . **106** C3
Tracies The ME9 . . . . **71** C6
Trader Rd E6 . . . . **2** B7
Tradescant Dr DA13. . . . . . **50** B3
Trafalgar Rd
Dartford DA1 . . . . **32** E6
Gravesend DA11 . . . . **36** A8
Wouldham ME1 . . . . **66** C5
Trafalgar St ME7. . . . . **54** C2
Tramways ME5 . . . . **54** C2
Tranquil Rise DA8. . . . . **4** E1
Transfesa Rd TN12. . . . . . **146** A7
Transmere Cl BR5 . . . . **43** C3
Transmere Rd BR5 . . . . **43** C3
Transom Ho **3** ME1 . . . . . . **53** C1
Trapfield Cl ME14 . . . . **101** C4
Trapfield La ME14 . . . . **101** C4
Trapham Rd ME16 . . . . **99** D5
Trasa Cl **3** ME17 . . . . **18** C8
Travers Gdns ME9. . . . . **87** F5
Travertine Rd ME6 . . . . **68** B1
Trebble Rd DA10. . . . . **17** E1
Trebilco Cl TN12 . . . . **159** D7
Tredegar Rd DA2 . . . . **32** A5
Tredwell Cl BR1 . . . . **42** E5
Treebourne Rd TN16 . . . . . **72** C1
Tree La TN15 . . . . **110** E8
Tree Rd E16 . . . . **1** C7
Treetops
Gravesend DA12 . . . . **36** B4
Kemsing TN15 . . . . **77** A2
Tonbridge TN9 . . . . **143** B7
Treetops Cl SE2 . . . . **3** E1
Treewall Gdns BR1. . . . . . . **28** B4

Trefoil Ho
Erith DA18 . . . . **3** E4
Grays RM17. . . . . **18** B7
Tregony Rd BR6 . . . . **57** F6
Trelawn Cres ME5 . . . . **68** B2
Trellyn Cl ME16 . . . . **98** F2
Trench Rd TN10. . . . . **127** C6
TRENCH WOOD **127** B7
Trenear Cl BR6 . . . . **58** A6
Trentham Dr BR5 . . . . **44** A5
Trenton Cl ME16 . . . . **99** B7
Trent Rd ME5 . . . . **68** B5
Trevale Rd ME1 . . . . **53** B1
Trevelyan Cl DA1 . . . . **15** F3
Trevereux Hill RH8 . . . . . . **104** F4
Trevino Dr ME5 . . . . **67** F2
Trevithick Dr DA1. . . . . **15** F3
Trevor Cl BR2 . . . . **42** A2
Trevor Dr ME16 . . . . **99** C5
Trewin Cl ME20 . . . . **82** D2
Trewsbury Ho **2** SE2. . . . . . **3** D4
Triangle Cl E16 . . . . **1** C8
Triangle The DA15 . . . . **30** A8
Tricorn Ho SE28 . . . . **2** D5
Trident Cl ME2 . . . . **53** E7
Trinity Cl
Orpington BR2. . . . . **42** E1
Royal Tunbridge Wells
TN2. . . . . **159** D4
Trinity Ct
Dartford DA1 . . . . **33** B1
Eltham SE9. . . . . **12** B1
Forstal ME20 . . . . **83** A3
Trinity Gdns DA1. . . . . **15** D1
Trinity Mews SE9 . . . . **12** D1
Trinity Pl DA6. . . . . **13** F3
Trinity Rd
Gillingham ME7 . . . . **54** C6
Gravesend DA12 . . . . **36** C8
Trinity Sch ME1. . . . . **53** D4
Trinity Sch, Belvedere
DA17. . . . . **4** C2
Trinity St **12** E16 . . . . **1** A8
Trinity Theatre & Arts Ctr ★
5 TN1. . . . . **159** A4
Tristan Gdns TN4 . . . . **158** D4
Triton Lodge **9** DA8 . . . . . . **4** E1
Triumph Rd E6 . . . . **1** F7
Trivett Cl DA9 . . . . **17** A2
Trolling Down Hill DA2. . . . **33** C6
Troodos Hill ME14 . . . . **99** F8
Troon Cl SE28 . . . . **3** D7
Trosley Ave DA11 . . . . **36** B6
Trosley Ctry Pk ★ ME19,
DA13. . . . . **80** A7
Trosley Ctry Pk Visitor Ctr ★
DA13. . . . . **79** E7
Trosley Rd DA17 . . . . **14** A8
TROTTISCLIFFE. **80** A5
Trottiscliffe CE Prim Sch
ME19. . . . . **80** A5
Trottiscliffe Rd ME19. . . . . **80** D3
Trotts La TN16 . . . . **105** C8
Trotwood Cl ME5 . . . . **84** A8
Troughton Rd SE7 . . . . **1** B1
Troutbeck Ho ME20 . . . . . . **82** C1
Troy Ct **6** SE18 . . . . **2** B2
Troy La TN8 . . . . **121** F4
Troy Mews ME1. . . . . **53** C4
Troys Mead ME17 . . . . **102** D2
TROY TOWN
Langhurst. **121** F5
Rochester **53** C5
Trubridge Rd ME3 . . . . **40** E5
Truro Cl ME8 . . . . **55** D3
Truro Rd DA12. . . . . **36** D5
Truro Wlk TN10. . . . . **127** D5
Trusedale Rd E6 . . . . **1** F7
Trycewell La TN15 . . . . **94** D6
Tuam Rd SE18 . . . . **12** D8
Tubbenden Cl BR6 . . . . **57** E7
Tubbenden Dr BR6 . . . . **57** D6
Tubbenden Inf & Jun Sch
BR6. . . . . **57** D6
Tubbenden La BR6 . . . . **57** E7
Tubbenden Lane S BR6. . . . **57** D5
Tubs Hill TN13 . . . . **92** B3
Tubs Hill Par TN13 . . . . **92** A3
TUDELEY **144** B7
TUDELEY HALE. **128** C1
Tudeley La
Tonbridge TN9 . . . . **143** D7
Tonbridge, Tudeley TN11,
TN9. . . . . **144** B8
Tudeley Woods Nature
Reserve ★ TN11 . . . . **144** B4
Tudor Ave ME14 . . . . **100** B6
Tudor Cl
Bromley BR7 . . . . **42** F8
Dartford DA1 . . . . **15** B1
Northfleet DA11. . . . . **35** E7
Tudor Cres TN14. . . . . **76** D3
Tudor Ct
Biggin Hill TN16 . . . . **72** E2
Crockenhill BR8. . . . . **45** C2
Royal Tunbridge Wells
TN2. . . . . **158** E1
Sidcup DA14. . . . . **30** A5
Tudor Dr TN14. . . . . **76** C3
Tudor Gr
Chattenden ME3 . . . . **39** F4
Gillingham ME8 . . . . **69** E8
Tudor Par SE9 . . . . **11** E3
Tudor Way BR5 . . . . **43** D3
Tudor Wlk DA5 . . . . **13** E1

Tudway Rd SE3 . . . . 11 C3
Tufa Cl ME5 . . . . 68 B1
Tuffs Cotts ME3. . . . . 25 C3
Tufnail Rd DA14 . . . . 15 F1
Tufton Rd ME8. . . . . 63 A6
Tufton St ME14 . . . . 100 A4
Tugboat St SE28 . . . . .2 E4
Tugmutton Cl BR6 . . . . 57 B6
Tulip Cl ⑤ E6 . . . . .1 F8
Tulip Tree Cl TN9 . . . . 143 B8
Tumblefield Est TN15 . . . . 78 F8
Tumblefield Rd TN15. . . . . 78 E7
Tumblers Hill ME17 . . . . . 106 E3
Tunbridge Wells Girls' Gram
Sch TN4 . . . . 159 A6
Tunbridge Wells Gram Sch
for Boys TN4 . . . . 159 A7
Tunbridge Wells High Sch
TN2 . . . . 159 F5
Tunbridge Wells Mus & Art
Gall★ TN1 . . . . 159 B4
Tunbridge Wells Nuffield
Hospital The TN2 . . . . . 159 D3
Tunbridge Wells Sta
TN1 . . . . 159 A3
Tunbridge Wells Trad Pk
TN2 . . . . 159 D8
Tunbridge Wells West Sta★
TN2 . . . . 158 F1
Tunbury Ave ME5 . . . . 67 F1
Tunbury Avenue S ME5 . . . 67 F1
Tunbury Prim Sch ME5 . . . 67 F1
Tunnan Leys E6 . . . . .2 A7
Tunnel Ave ❶ SE10. . . . . . . .1 A1
Tunnel Cotts RM20 . . . . . . 17 A8
Tunnel Est RM20 . . . . 16 F8
Tunnel Rd TN1 . . . . 159 B4
Tunstall Ct BR6 . . . . 57 E6
Tunstock Way DA17 . . . . . . .3 E3
Tupman Cl ME1 . . . . 53 B4
Tuppy St SE28 . . . . .2 C3
Turgis Cl ME17 . . . . 117 E4
Turks Hall Pl ME2 . . . . 65 E5
Turley Cotts TN3 . . . . 158 A8
Turnberry Way BR6 . . . . . . 51 E5
Turnbull Cl DA9 . . . . 33 E8
Turnbury Cl SE28 . . . . .3 D7
TURNDEN 179 B4
Turnden Rd TN17 . . . . 179 A3
Turner Ave TN17 . . . . 179 D3
Turner Cl TN16 . . . . 72 C7
Turner Ct DA1 . . . . 15 C2
Turner Ho
Gravesend DA12 . . . . 36 C6
⑤ Greenwich SE7. . . . . . 11 B8
Turner Rd
Bean DA2. . . . . 34 B5
Tonbridge TN10 . . . . 127 E5
Turners Ave TN30 . . . . . . 193 B8
Turners Gdns TN13. . . . . . 108 C7
TURNER'S GREEN 184 F6
Turners Green La TN5 . . . . 184 F6
Turners Green Rd TN5 . . . 184 F6
Turner's Oak DA3 . . . . 62 E7
Turners Pl DA4 . . . . 47 C8
Turner St ME3 . . . . 22 B5
Turnpike Ct DA6 . . . . 13 D3
Turnpike Dr BR6 . . . . 58 D2
Turnpike La ME18 . . . . 119 C8
Turnstone DA3 . . . . 49 A7
Turnstone Rd ME5 . . . . 68 C1
Turnstones The DA12 . . . . . 36 D6
Turpington Cl BR2 . . . . 42 E2
Turpington La BR2 . . . . 42 E3
Turpin La DA8 . . . . 15 A8
Turpin Rd ❺ SE28 . . . . 12 B8
Tuscan Dr ME5 . . . . 68 C1
Tuscan Rd SE18 . . . . .2 D1
Tutsham Way TN12 . . . . . 145 F6
Tuxford Rd TN4 . . . . 158 B5
Tweed Rd TN10 . . . . 127 C5
Tweedy Rd BR1 . . . . 42 A8
Twigg Cl DA8 . . . . 14 E7
Twin Tumps Way SE28 . . . . .3 A6
Twisden Rd ME19 . . . . 97 F8
Twiss Ho ⑤ SE18 . . . . .2 B1
Twistleton Ct ❼ DA1. . . . . 15 D1
TWITTON. 75 E4
Twitton La TN14 . . . . 75 E3
Twitton Mdws TN14 . . . . . 75 E3
Two Gates Hill ME7 . . . . . . 38 F5
Twydall Cl 55 B2
Twydall Ent Ctr ME8 . . . . . 55 C2
Twydall Gn ME8. . . . . 55 B3
Twydall Inf Sch ME8 . . . . . 55 B2
Twydall Jun Sch ME8 . . . . . 55 B2
Twydall La ME8. . . . . 55 B2
Twyford Ct ME14. . . . . 100 D6
Twyford Rd TN11 . . . . 111 E1
Twysden Cotts TN3 . . . . . 196 A4
Twysden Rd ME15 . . . . . . 106 F2
Tye La BR6 . . . . 57 C5
Tyeshurst Cl SE2 . . . . .3 E1
Tyland Barn Wildlife Park★
ME14 . . . . 83 E3
Tyland La ME14 . . . . 83 F3
TYLDEN 168 E7
Tyler Cl
❶ East Malling ME19. . . . 97 F8
Erith DA8 . . . . 14 B7
Tyler Dr ME8 . . . . 69 E4
Tyler Gr DA1 . . . . 15 F3
Tylers Green Rd BR8 . . . . . 45 C2
Tylney Rd BR1 . . . . 42 D7
Tyndall Rd DA16 . . . . 12 F4

Tyne Cl ME5 . . . . 68 C5
Tynedale Cl DA2. . . . . 33 D7
Tynemouth Cl E6 . . . . .2 B7
Tynemouth Rd SE18. . . . . . .2 E1
Tyne Rd TN10. . . . . 127 B5
Typhoon Rd ME19. . . . . . . 96 F3
Tyron Way DA14 . . . . 29 F3
Tyrrel Ave DA16 . . . . 13 B2
Tyrrells Hall Cl ❸ RM17 . . 18 D8
Tyrwhitt–Drake Mus of
Carriages★ ⑨ ME15 . . . 100 A3

U

Uckfield La TN8. . . . . 139 D4
Udall Cotts DA15. . . . . 29 E5
Ufton Cl ME15 . . . . 100 E1
ULCOMBE 135 F7
Ulcombe CE Prim Sch
ME17. . . . . 135 F6
Ulcombe Hill ME17. . . . . . 118 F1
Ulcombe Rd
Headcorn TN27 . . . . 151 C6
Langley Heath ME17. . . . 117 E3
Ullswater Ho ⑥ ME15 . . . 116 E7
Underdown Ave ME4. . . . . 53 F1
UNDERLING GREEN 132 F2
Underlyn Ind Est TN12. . . 132 F2
Underlyn La TN12. . . . . . . 132 D1
UNDERRIVER 124 C4
Underriver House Rd
TN15 . . . . 109 D5
Underwood ME15 . . . . 96 D7
Underwood Cl ME15 . . . . . 99 F2
Underwood Rise TN2 . . . . 158 F1
Underwood The SE9 . . . . . 28 F6
Unicorn Wlk DA9 . . . . 16 F2
Unicumes La ME16. . . . . . . 99 C2
Union Mill The★ TN7 . . . . 179 D4
Union Ple ME15 . . . . 116 F4
Union Pl ME4 . . . . 54 A4
Union Rd BR2. . . . . 42 D4
Union Sq ㉒ TN2 . . . . 159 A2
Union St
Chatham ME4. . . . . 54 A3
Flimwell TN5 . . . . 187 B3
Maidstone ME14 . . . . . . 100 A5
Rochester ME1 . . . . 53 C5
UNION STREET 187 B3
Unity Way SE18. . . . . .1 D3
University Gdns DA5 . . . . . 30 F8
University Pl DA8 . . . . 14 C7
University Way
Dartford DA1. . . . . 15 E4
Woolwich E16 . . . . .2 B6
Univ for the Creative Arts at
Maidstone ME16. . . . . . . 99 C3
Univ for the Creative Arts at
Rochester ME1 . . . . 53 E4
Univ of East London E16 . . .2 A6
Univ of Greenwich Avery Hill
Campus (Mansion Site)
SE9 . . . . 12 C1
Univ of Greenwich Avery Hill
Campus (Southwood Site)
SE9 . . . . 29 D8
Univ of Greenwich Medway
ME4. . . . . 54 B8
Univ of Kent (Universities at
Medway Campus) ME4 . . 54 B8
Unwin Cl ME20 . . . . 83 A3
Upbury Way ME4 . . . . 54 A4
Upchat Rd ME2, ME3. . . . . 39 F3
Updale Rd DA14 . . . . 29 F4
Upland Prim Sch DA7 . . . . 13 F4
Upland Rd DA7 . . . . 13 F4
Uplands SE18 . . . . .2 B1
Uplands Cl
Rochester ME2 . . . . 52 D6
Sevenoaks TN13 . . . . 91 F4
Uplands Com Coll TN5 . . 185 A4
Uplands Rd BR6 . . . . 44 B1
Uplands Way TN13. . . . . . . 91 F4
Upnor Castle★ ME2 . . . . . 39 E7
Upnor Ho ME15 . . . . 116 E8
Upnor Rd ME2 . . . . 39 E2
Upper Abbey Rd DA17 . . . . .4 A2
Upper Austin Lodge Farm
Cotts DA4 . . . . 60 E3
Upper Austin Lodge Rd
DA4. . . . . 60 D4
Upper Ave DA13 . . . . 49 E8
Upper Barn Hill ME15 . . . 114 E3
Upper Britton Pl ME7 . . . . 54 B5
UPPER BUSH 51 F2
Upper Bush Rd ME2 . . . . . 51 F2
Upper Church Hill DA9 . . . 16 E2
Upper Cumberland Wlk
TN1 . . . . 159 B1
Upper Dr TN16. . . . . 72 C1
Upper Dunstan Rd TN4 . . 159 B6
Upper East Rd ME4. . . . . . . 54 B8
UPPER FANT. 99 E3
Upper Fant Rd ME16 . . . . . 99 D2
Upper Green La TN11. . . . 110 D5
Upper Green Rd TN11 . . . 110 D5
Upper Grosvenor Rd TN1,
TN4 . . . . 159 B3
Upper Grove Rd DA17 . . . . 13 F8
UPPER HALLING 65 E5
UPPER HARVEL 64 C3
UPPER HAYESDEN 142 C6
Upper Haysden La TN11,
TN9 . . . . 142 E6
Upper Holly Hill Rd DA17 . .4 B1
Upper Hunton Hill ME15 . 115 A3
Upper Luton Rd ME5 . . . . . 54 C2

Upper Mill
East Malling ME19. . . . . . 97 F7
Wateringbury ME18. . . . 113 D8
Upper Nellington TN3 . . . 158 B4
Upper Park Rd
Bromley BR1 . . . . 42 C8
Erith DA17 . . . . .4 B2
Upper Platts TN5 . . . . 186 F1
Upper Profit TN3 . . . . 158 A3
Upper Rd ME15 . . . . 100 B2
UPPER RUXLEY 31 A2
Upper Ruxley Cotts DA14 . 31 A1
Upper Sheridan Rd DA17. . .4 A1
Upper Spring La TN15. . . . 94 B5
Upper St
Hollingbourne ME17 . . . 102 C3
Leeds ME17. . . . . 117 F5
Rusthall TN4 . . . . 158 D4
Upper Stephens TN3 . . . . 158 A3
Upper Stone St ME15. . . . 100 A3
Upper Street S DA3 . . . . . . 62 F8
Upper Tarn La TN5. . . . . . 186 A2
Upperton Rd DA14 . . . . . . 29 F3
UPPER UPNOR 39 F1
Upper Wickham La DA16. . 12 C5
Upton Cl DA5 . . . . 13 F1
Upton Day Hospl DA6. . . . 13 E3
Upton Prim Sch DA6 . . . . . 13 F1
Upton Quarry TN3 . . . . . . 157 F3
Upton Rd
Bexley DA5, DA6 . . . . . . 13 E2
Woolwich SE18 . . . . 12 C8
Upton Road S DA5 . . . . . . 13 F1
Uptons TN27 . . . . 151 C6
Upton Villas ❹ DA6 . . . . . 13 E3
Upwood Rd SE12. . . . . 11 A1
Uridge Cres TN10 . . . . 127 C4
Uridge Rd TN10 . . . . 127 C4
Urquhart Cl ME5 . . . . 68 A5
Ursula Lodges DA14 . . . . . 30 B3
Usborne Cl TN12 . . . . 149 E3

V

Vaizeys Wharf SE7 . . . . .1 B3
Vale Ave
Royal Tunbridge Wells, Mount
Sion TN1 . . . . 159 A3
Royal Tunbridge Wells,
Southborough TN4 . . . . 142 F1
Vale Cl BR6. . . . . 57 A6
Vale Cotts ME9 . . . . 87 A8
Vale Ct TN4. . . . . 143 A2
Vale Dr ME5 . . . . 67 E6
Valence Ho ME15 . . . . 116 C7
Valence Rd DA8. . . . . 14 D7
Valence Sch TN16 . . . . 89 F1
Valence View TN17 . . . . . 166 E7
Valenciennes Ho ME4 . . . . 54 A4
Valentine Ave DA5 . . . . . . 30 E7
Valentine Cl ME7 . . . . 55 A1
Valentine Dr ME23 . . . . . . 23 E4
Valentine Rd ME15 . . . . . . 116 E7
Vale Rd
Bromley BR1 . . . . 43 A7
Dartford DA1. . . . . 32 B7
Hawkhurst TN18 . . . . . . 188 F3
Maidstone ME15 . . . . . . 115 E4
Northfleet DA11. . . . . . . 35 E7
Royal Tunbridge Wells, Mount
Sion TN1 . . . . 159 A3
Royal Tunbridge Wells,
Southborough TN4 . . . . 142 F1
Tonbridge TN9 . . . . 127 C1
Valerian Cl ME5. . . . . 67 E4
Valestone Ave ME15 . . . . . .67 E4
Valetta Way ME1 . . . . 53 B4
Valiant Ho ❺ SE7 . . . . .1 C1
Valiant Rd ME5 . . . . 68 C2
Valiant Way E6 . . . . .1 F8
Valley Cl DA1 . . . . 14 F1
Valley Dr
Gravesend, Riverview Park
DA12. . . . . 36 D4
Gravesend, Singlewell DA12 36 E1
Maidstone ME15 . . . . . . 115 F6
Sevenoaks TN13 . . . . 92 B1
Valley Forge Cl TN10. . . . . 127 F4
Valley Gdns DA9 . . . . 17 B1
Valley Gr SE7. . . . . .1 C1
Valley Hts DA1. . . . . 15 C1
Valley La DA13. . . . . 64 B2
Valley Industries TN11. . . 128 B7
Valley Mushroom Farm
TN16. . . . . 72 D1
Valley Park Com Sch
ME15. . . . . 100 C4
Valley Rd
Crayford DA1. . . . . 14 F1
Erith DA8 . . . . 4 D2
Fawkham Green DA3. . . . 48 C2
Gillingham ME7 . . . . 54 E4
Orpington BR5. . . . . 44 B8
Rusthall TN4 . . . . 158 D4
Valley Rise ME5. . . . . 67 F1
Valleyside SE7 . . . . 1 C1
Valley The ME17 . . . . 113 C3
Valley The (Charlton Athletic
FC) SE7 . . . . .1 C1
Valley View
Biggin Hill TN16. . . . . . . 72 D1
Royal Tunbridge Wells
TN4 . . . . 143 A2
Swanscombe DA9 . . . . . . 17 B1
Valley View ME1 . . . . 53 B1
Valley View Terr DA13. . . . 46 F1
Valliers Wood Rd DA15. . . 29 E7

Vambery Rd SE18 . . . . 12 C8
Vanbrugh Cl ❷ E16 . . . . . . .1 D8
Vanbrugh Pk SE3 . . . . 11 A7
Vanburgh Cl BR6. . . . . 43 E1
Vancouver Cl BR6. . . . . . . 58 A6
Vancouver Dr ME8 . . . . . . 55 C1
Vandome Cl E16 . . . . .1 B7
Vandyke Cross SE9. . . . . . . 11 E2
Vanessa Cl DA17 . . . . .4 A1
Vanessa Way DA5 . . . . 31 D5
Vanessa Wlk DA12 . . . . . . 36 F3
Vange Cottage Mews
ME1 . . . . 53 B4
Vanguard Cl E16 . . . . 1 A8
Vanguard Way ME2 . . . . . . 53 E8
Vanity La ME17 . . . . 115 D1
Vanoc Gdns BR1 . . . . 28 A4
Vanquisher Wlk DA12 . . . . 36 F5
Varley Rd E16 . . . . 1 B7
Varnes St ME20 . . . . 90 E7
Vaughan Ave TN10 . . . . . . 127 E6
Vaughan Cl DA1 . . . . 32 D8
Vaughan Rd DA16. . . . . . . 12 F5
Vauxhall Cl DA11. . . . . 35 F8
Vauxhall Cres ME6 . . . . . . 82 A6
Vauxhall Pl DA1. . . . . 32 B8
Vauxhall La
Bidborough TN11, TN4. . 143 B4
Tonbridge TN11, TN4 . . . 143 D6
Vauxhall Pl DA1. . . . . 32 E8
Veitchil Barn BR8 . . . . 45 F8
Veles Rd ME6. . . . . 81 F8
Venmead Ct ❹ DA17 . . . . . 4 A2
Venners Cl DA7 . . . . 14 E2
Ventnor Cl ME5 . . . . 68 C8
Venture Cl DA5. . . . . 30 E8
Venture Ct SE12 . . . . 28 A8
Venus Rd SE18. . . . . 1 F3
Verdun Rd SE18, SE2. . . . . 13 A8
Vermont Rd TN4 . . . . 158 C4
Vernham Rd SE18 . . . . 12 C8
Vernon Cl
Orpington BR5 . . . . 44 B6
West Kingsdown TN15. . . 61 F2
Vernon Rd
Royal Tunbridge Wells
TN1. . . . . 159 C6
Swanscombe DA10 . . . . . 17 F1
Verona Gdns DA12 . . . . . . 36 E4
Verona Ho DA8 . . . . 14 F7
Vert Ho RM17. . . . . 18 C7
Veryan Cl BR5 . . . . 44 C5
Vesper Ct TN27 . . . . 153 A1
Vestry Cotts
New Barn DA3. . . . . 49 C5
Sevenoaks TN4 . . . . 92 C8
Vestry Rd TN14 . . . . 92 C8
Viaduct Terr DA4 . . . . 47 C7
Via Romana DA12 . . . . 37 B7
Vicarage Ave SE3 . . . . 11 A7
Vicarage Cl
Chalk DA12 . . . . 37 A7
East Farleigh ME15 . . . . 115 B6
Hoo St Werburgh ME3. . . 40 E4
Sevenoaks TN13 . . . . 91 D8
Stoke ME3 . . . . 25 A3
Vicarage Pk SE18 . . . . 2 C1
Vicarage Rd
Coldblow DA5 . . . . 31 B7
Gillingham ME7 . . . . 54 C5
Halling ME2 . . . . 65 F5
Rochester ME2 . . . . 53 B8
Royal Tunbridge Wells
TN4 . . . . 142 F2
Woolwich SE18 . . . . .2 C1
Yalding ME18. . . . . 114 A1
Vicarage Row TN15 . . . . . . 55 E5
Vicarage Sq RM17 . . . . 18 C8
Vicarage Way TN10 . . . . . 194 A3
Vicary Way ME16 . . . . 99 D5
Vickers Rd DA8 . . . . .4 D1
Victoria Ave ❸ DA2. . . . . . 36 B8
Victoria Bglws DA14 . . . . . 30 F1
Victoria Bsns Ctr DA16. . . 13 B5
Victoria Ct
Chatham ME5. . . . . 67 C2
Edenbridge TN8 . . . . 138 C8
Victoria Cotts
Cranbrook TN17 . . . . . . 179 D5
Edenbridge TN8. . . . . . . 138 C8
Victoria Ct ❽ ME16. . . . . . 99 E3
Victoria Dock Rd E16 . . . . . 1 B6
Victoria Dr
Kings Hill ME19. . . . . 96 F1
Sutton at Hone DA4. . . . . 47 D7
Victoria Gdns TN16 . . . . . . 72 C4
Victoria Hill Rd BR8. . . . . . 46 A8
Victoria Ind Pk DA1 . . . . . 15 D2
Victoria Orch ME16 . . . . . 99 B3
Victoria Rd
Bexley DA6. . . . . 14 A3
Bromley BR2 . . . . 42 D4
Chatham, Kit Hill ME5. . . 67 E3
Chatham, Luton ME4 . . . 54 B2
Chislehurst BR7. . . . . . . 29 A3

Victoria Rd continued
Dartford DA1. . . . . 15 E2
Edenbridge TN8. . . . . . . 138 C8
Erith DA8 . . . . 14 E8
Golden Green TN11 . . . . 128 F6
Northfleet DA11. . . . . . . 35 F7
Royal Tunbridge Wells,
Southborough TN4 . . . . 142 E1
Royal Tunbridge Wells
TN1. . . . . 159 B4
Sevenoaks TN13 . . . . 92 B2
Sidcup DA15 . . . . 30 A5
Victoria Scott Ct DA1 . . . . 14 F4
Victoria St
Eccles ME20 . . . . 82 F6
Erith DA17 . . . . 3 F1
Gillingham ME7 . . . . 54 D6
Maidstone ME16 . . . . . . 99 E3
Rochester ME1 . . . . 53 D3
Rochester, Strood ME2. . 53 B7
Victoria Terr ME1 . . . . 53 A2
Victoria Way SE7 . . . . 1 B1
Victoria Wharf DA1 . . . . . . 15 E2
Victor Mills Cotts DA14. . . 31 A1
Victory Cotts TN14 . . . . . 108 C2
Victory Dr ME19 . . . . 97 D2
Victory Lodge ❿ DA8 . . . . . .4 E1
Victory Manor ❶ ME7. . . . 54 A6
Victory Pk ME2 . . . . 53 E7
Victory Terr ME17 . . . . . . 134 E8
Victory Way DA2. . . . . 16 C3
Vidal Manor ME1 . . . . 54 C5
Vidgeon Ave ME3 . . . . 40 D6
View Cl TN16 . . . . 72 C3
Viewfield Rd DA5 . . . . 30 C7
Viewland Rd SE18 . . . . 2 F1
Viewlands ME5 . . . . 54 C3
Viewlands Ave TN16 . . . . . 89 F7
Viewpoint Cl DA3 . . . . 48 F5
View Rd ME3 . . . . 39 B7
View The SE2. . . . . 3 E1
Vigilant Way DA12 . . . . . . 36 F3
Vigo Hill ME19, TN15. . . . . 79 E6
Vigo Rd TN15. . . . . 79 C7
VIGO VILLAGE 80 B8
Vigo Village Sch TN15 . . . . 80 A8
Viking Cl ME2 . . . . 52 F4
Viking Ho ❸ SE5 . . . . 1 E2
Viking Rd DA11 . . . . 35 C5
Viking Way
Erith DA8 . . . . 4 C3
West Kingsdown TN15. . . 61 E5
Villa Cl DA12 . . . . 37 B6
Villacourt Rd SE18, SE2 . . 13 A8
Villa Ct DA1 . . . . 32 C6
Village Green Ave TN16 . . 72 E2
Village Green Rd DA1 . . . . 15 A3
Village Green Way TN16. . 72 E2
Village The SE7 . . . . 11 D8
Village View ME5 . . . . 54 C2
Villa Rd ME3 . . . . 38 B3
Villas Rd SE18 . . . . 2 C2
Vincent Cl
Bromley BR2 . . . . 42 B5
Sidcup DA15 . . . . 29 E7
Vincent Rd
Kit's Coty ME20 . . . . 83 C7
Woolwich SE18. . . . . 2 B2
Vincent St E16. . . . . 1 A8
Vincent So TN16 . . . . 72 C6
Vincent St ❸ E16 . . . . 1 A8
Vine Ave TN16 . . . . 92 B3
Vine Court Rd TN13 . . . . . . 92 C4
Vine Ct
❿ Gravesend DA11 . . . . . 19 B1
Staplehurst TN12. . . . . . 149 F3
Maidstone ME14 . . . . . . 113 D8
Vine Lodge TN13 . . . . 92 C3
Vine Pavilion The
(Sevenoaks Vine CC)
TN13. . . . . 92 C3
Vine Rd BR6 . . . . 57 F4
Vineries The ME7 . . . . 54 E5
Vine The
Hildenborough TN11 . . . 109 C1
Rochester ME1 . . . . 53 C5
Vine The TN13 . . . . 92 C3
Vine Wlk TN12 . . . . 149 E3
Vineyard La TN5 . . . . 186 C2
Viney's Gdns TN30 . . . . . . 183 C1
Vinson Cl BR6 . . . . 44 A1
Vinson Ct DA15 . . . . 30 A6
Vinters Rd ME14 . . . . 100 B4
Vinters Valley Nature
Reserve★ ME14. . . . . . . 100 D5
Vintners Way ME14 . . . . . 100 E4
Viola Ave SE2. . . . . 3 B1
Violet Cl ME5 . . . . 84 A8
Violets The TN12. . . . . 146 A5
VIP Trad Est SE7 . . . . 1 C2
Virginia Rd ME7 . . . . 54 C7
Virginia Wlk DA12 . . . . . . 36 E2
Viscount Dr E6 . . . . 1 F8
Vista The
Eltham SE9 . . . . 28 E8
Sidcup DA14 . . . . 29 F3
Vixen Cl ME5 . . . . 68 C6
Voce Rd SE18 . . . . 12 D7
Vogue Ct ⓫ BR1 . . . . 42 B8
Vostry Ind Est ME14 . . . . . 92 C8
Voyagers Cl SE28 . . . . 3 C7
Vulcan Cl
Chatham ME5. . . . . 68 B7
Newham E6 . . . . 2 A7
Vyne The DA14 . . . . 14 B4
Vyvyan Cotts TN17 . . . . . 190 C3
Vyvyan Ho SE18. . . . . 12 A6

W

Wadard Terr BR8 46 C4
Wade Ave BR5 44 D2
Wadeville Cl DA17 4 A1
WADHURST 185 A4
Wadhurst Bsns Pk TN5 184 B7
Wadhurst CE Prim Sch TN5 184 F5
Wadhurst Rd TN3 173 D1
Wadhurst Sta TN5 184 C6
Wadlands Rd ME3 22 B5
Waghorn Rd ME6 82 A8
Waghorn St ME4 54 B2
Wagoners Cl ME14 100 E4
Wagon La TN12 130 C1
Wagtail Way BR5 44 D5
Waid Cl DA1 15 F1
Wainhouse Cl TN8 122 D3
WAINSCOTT 39 D3
Wainscott Prim Sch ME2 39 D2
Wainscott Rd ME2 39 D2
Wainscott Wlk ME2 39 D3
Waite Davies Rd 8 SE12 28 A8
Wakefield Cl ME2 52 D6
Wakefield Rd DA9 17 C2
Wakeford Cl DA5 30 D7
Wakehurst Cl ME17 115 B3
Wakeleys Cotts ME8 70 B8
Wakely Cl TN16 72 C1
Wake Rd ME1 67 C8
Wakerley Cl 6 E6 1 F7
Waldeck Rd DA1 16 A1
Waldegrave Rd BR1 42 F5
Walden Ave BR7 28 F4
Walden Cl DA17 3 F1
Waldenhurst Rd BR5 44 D2
Walden Par BR7 28 F2
Walden Rd BR7 28 F2
Waldens Cl BR5 44 D2
Waldens Rd BR5 44 E3
Waldens The ME17 118 E2
WALDERSLADE 67 F1
WALDERSLADE BOTTOM 67 A2
Walderslade Ctr ME5 68 A3
Walderslade Girls Sch 7 ME5 67 F5
Walderslade Prim Sch ME5 68 A3
Walderslade Rd ME5 67 F6
Walderslade Village By-pass ME5 67 F3
Walderslade Woods ME5 67 E2
Waldo Ind Est BR1 42 D6
Waldo Rd BR1 42 D6
Waldrist Way DA18 3 F4
Waldron Dr ME15 115 F6
Waldstock Rd SE28 3 A6
Walkden Rd BR7 29 A3
Walker Cl
Crayford DA1 14 F4
Woolwich SE18 2 C2
Walker Pl TN15 94 D6
Walkhurst Cotts TN17 190 F7
Walkhurst Rd TN17 190 F7
Walkley Rd DA1 15 B2
Walks The TN3 171 C8
Walk The ME17 118 E2
Wallace Cl
Erith SE28 3 D6
Royal Tunbridge Wells TN2 173 A8
Wallace Gdns DA10 17 E1
Wallace Rd ME1 67 E8
Wallace Terr TN15 62 E4
Wall Cl ME3 40 D7
WALLCROUCH 185 F1
Waller Hill TN17 166 B5
Wallers TN3 158 A8
Wallhouse Rd DA8 15 C7
Wallis Ave ME15 116 E5
Wallis Cl DA2 31 F5
Wallis Field TN3 171 B6
Wallis Oak Ave 12 ME15 116 F5
Wallis Pk DA11 18 B2
Walmer Cl BR6 57 D6
Walmer Ct 3 ME14 100 A5
Walmer Ho ME2 39 C1
Walmers Ave ME3 38 A4
Walmer Terr SE18 2 D2
Walnut Cl
Chatham ME5 68 B8
Eynsford DA4 60 D7
Paddock Wood TN12 146 A6
Yalding ME18 113 F1
Walnut Hill Rd DA13 49 E6
Walnuts L Ctr BR6 44 A1
Walnuts Rd BR6 44 B1
Walnuts Sh Ctr The BR6 44 A1
Walnut Tree Ave
Dartford DA1 32 E6
Loose ME15 116 A5
Walnut Tree Cl
Chislehurst BR7 43 C8
Westerham TN16 89 D1
Walnut Tree Ct ME20 82 B1
Walnut Tree La ME15 116 A5
Walnut Tree Rd DA8 4 E1
Walnut Tree Way DA13 50 B3
Walnut Way
Royal Tunbridge Wells TN4 159 D8
Swanley BR8 45 D7
Walpole Cl ME19 81 F1
Walpole Ho 4 BR7 43 D8
Walpole Pl SE18 2 B2
Walpole Rd BR2 42 D4
Walsham Cl SE28 3 D6
Walsham Rd ME5 67 F1
Walshaw Ho 2 ME14 100 A6
Walsingham Cl ME8 69 D3
Walsingham Ho 3 ME14 100 A6
Walsingham Pk BR7 43 D7
Walsingham Rd BR5 44 B8
Walsingham Wlk DA17 14 A8
Walter Burke Ave ME1 66 C5
Walter Burke Way ME4 54 A8
Walter's Farm Rd TN9 127 C1
WALTER'S GREEN 156 E6
Walters Green Rd TN11 156 F6
Walters Ho SE18 12 A7
Walters Rd ME3 40 E6
Walterstown Ct DA1 32 D8
Walters Yd BR1 42 A7
Waltham Cl
Dartford DA1 15 A1
26 Orpington BR5 44 D1
Waltham Rd ME8 55 C3
Walthamstow Hall Jun Sch TN13 92 B5
Walthamstow Hall Senior Sch TN13 92 C4
Walton Rd
Sidcup DA14 30 C5
Tonbridge TN10 127 F6
Walwyn Ave BR1 42 D6
WANDEN 153 B7
Wanden La TN27 153 C8
Wansbury Way BR8 46 A5
WANSHURST GREEN 149 A7
Wanstead Cl BR1 42 C7
Wanstead Rd BR1 42 C7
Wansunt Rd DA5 31 C7
Warberry Park Gdns TN4 158 E4
Warblers Cl 3 ME2 53 A7
Ward Cl
Durgates TN5 184 E5
Erith DA8 14 D8
Warden Cl ME16 99 C4
Warden Mill Cl ME18 113 E7
Warden Rd ME1 53 C2
Wardens Field Cl 2 BR6 57 F4
Warde's ME18 113 F2
Wardona Ct DA10 17 F1
Wardour Ct 11 DA2 16 B1
Ward's La TN5 185 E4
Wards Wharf App E16 1 D4
Warepoint Dr SE28 2 D4
Ware St ME14 101 A5
WARE STREET 101 B5
Warham Rd TN14 76 B3
Waring Cl BR6 58 A4
Waring Dr BR6 58 A4
Waring Rd DA14 30 C2
Warland Rd
West Kingsdown TN15 61 F2
Woolwich SE18 12 E7
WARMLAKE 117 D1
Warmlake ME17 117 F1
Warmlake Bsns Est ME17 117 E1
Warmlake Rd ME17 117 C1
Warne Pl 4 DA15 13 B1
Warner St ME4 53 F3
Warnett Ct ME6 66 A1
Warnford Gdns ME15 116 A8
Warnford Pl ME15 116 A8
Warnford Rd BR6 57 F5
Warren Ave BR6 57 F5
Warren Cl DA6 14 A2
Warren Cotts TN11 141 A3
Warren Court SE7 11 C8
Warren Ct TN15 92 C3
Warren Dr BR6 58 B5
Warren Farm La TN3 172 B4
Warren Gdns BR6 58 A5
Warren Hastings Ct DA11 18 F1
Warren La
Oxted RH8 104 A1
Woolwich SE18 2 B3
Yelsted ME9 70 C3
Warren Rd
Bexley DA6 14 A2
Dartford DA1 32 E5
Hayes BR2 56 A8
Kit's Coty ME5 83 D7
Luddesdown ME2 51 D3
Northfleet DA13 35 B3
Orpington BR6 58 C5
Sidcup DA14 30 C5
Warren Ridge TN3 173 C3
Warren Road Prim Sch BR6 57 F6
Warrens The DA3 48 F3
Warren The
Gravesend DA12 36 D4
2 Greenwich SE7 11 C8
Penshurst TN11 141 A4
Ticehurst TN5 186 E1
Warren View DA12 37 E2
Warren Wlk 1 SE7 11 C8
Warren Wood Cl BR2 56 A8
Warren Wood Com Prim Sch ME1 67 C8
Warren Wood Rd ME1 67 C7
Warrington Rd TN12 146 A6
Warrior Ave DA12 36 C4
Warrior Cl SE28 2 D5
Warsop Trad Est TN8 138 D8
Warspite Rd SE18 1 E3
Warwall E6 2 B7
Warwick Cl
Orpington BR6 58 A7
Sidcup DA5 30 F8
Warwick Cres ME1 52 F2
Warwick Ct 8 DA8 14 F7
Warwick Gdns DA13 64 A8
Warwick Pk TN2 159 B1
Warwick Pl
Maidstone ME16 99 E3
Northfleet DA11 18 B2
Warwick Rd
Bexley DA16 13 C4
4 Royal Tunbridge Wells TN1 159 A2
Sidcup DA14 30 B3
Warwick Terr SE18 12 D8
Warwick Way DA1 32 E6
Washington Ho ME15 116 E5
Washneys Rd BR6 74 B6
Washwell La TN5 184 F3
Wassall La TN17 197 E7
Watchgate DA2 33 E3
Watchmans Terr 6 ME5 54 C2
Watercress Cl TN14 92 C7
Watercress Dr TN14 92 C7
Watercroft Rd TN14 58 F1
Waterdale Rd SE2 13 A8
Waterdales DA11 35 D7
Waterdown Rd TN4 158 E1
Waterfield TN2 173 A7
Waterfield Cl
Erith DA17 4 A3
Woolwich SE28 3 B5
Waterfrets Cotts TN3 157 F5
Waterfront L Ctr SE18 2 A3
Waterfront Studios Bsns Ctr E16 1 A5
Watergate Ho 5 SE18 2 A2
Waterglade Ind Pk RM20 16 F8
Waterhead Cl DA8 14 E7
Waterhouse Cl E16 1 D8
WATERINGBURY 113 D7
Wateringbury CE Prim Sch ME18 113 E6
Wateringbury Cl BR5 44 B7
Wateringbury Rd ME19 97 F3
Wateringbury Sta ME18 113 E6
Water La
Harrietsham ME17 119 A5
Hawkhurst TN18 189 B4
Headcorn TN17, TN27 151 A4
Hunton ME15 131 D6
Kingswood ME17 118 F3
Limpsfield RH8 104 A8
Maidstone, Bearsted ME14 101 E6
6 Maidstone ME15 100 A4
Shoreham TN14 75 F6
Sidcup DA14 30 F6
Smarden TN27 152 F2
West Malling ME19 97 C8
Waterlakes TN8 138 C8
Waterloo Pl
Cranbrook TN17 179 D5
High Halston ME3 40 B8
Tonbridge TN9 143 B8
Waterloo Rd
Cranbrook TN17 179 D6
Gillingham ME7 54 C4
Tonbridge TN9 143 B8
Waterloo St
1 Gravesend DA12 36 C8
Maidstone ME15 100 A3
Waterlow Rd
Maidstone ME14 100 A6
Vigo Village DA13 79 F7
WATERMAN QUARTER 151 D2
Waterman's La TN12 146 B3
Watermans Way DA9 17 B3
Watermeadow Cl
Erith DA8 15 B6
Gillingham ME7 68 F6
Watermill Cl
Maidstone ME16 99 B5
Rochester ME2 53 C8
Water Mill Way DA4 47 B7
Watermint Cl BR5 44 D5
Waters Cotts TN5 185 A4
Waters Edge ME15 99 F2
Waters Edge Ct DA8 4 F1
Waterside
Crayford DA1 14 F2
6 Maidstone ME14 99 F4
Waterside Cl SE28 3 A6
Waterside Ct ME19 81 E2
Waterside Ct ME2 53 E6
Waterside Gate ME16 99 F5
Waterside La ME7 54 F7
Waterside Mews ME18 113 D6
Waterside Prim Sch 4 SE18 2 D1
Water Slippe TN11 111 D1
Watersmeet Cl ME15 100 A1
Watersmeet Way SE28 3 D7
Waters Pl ME7 69 A6
Waterstone Way DA9 17 A1
Waterton BR8 45 D5
Waterton Ave DA12 36 E8
Waterworks Cotts TN14 92 B6
Watery La
Heaverham TN15 93 D7
Sidcup BR5, DA14 30 B2
Watford Rd E16 1 A8
Watkins Cl TN12 149 E5
Watling Ave ME5 54 D2
Watling Ho 10 SE18 12 A8
Watling St
Bean DA2 34 D6
Bexley DA6, DA7 14 C3
Dartford DA1, DA2 33 C8
Gillingham ME5 54 D2
Watling St *continued*
Gravesend DA11, DA12 36 C2
Northfleet DA11, DA13 35 D4
Rochester ME2 52 D7
Watson Ave ME5 67 D5
Watson Cl RM20 17 A6
Watt Ho SE2 3 C1
Watts' Ave ME1 53 C4
Watts Cl
Snodland ME6 82 B8
Wadhurst TN5 184 F4
WATT'S CROSS 126 B7
Watt's Cross Rd TN11 126 B6
Watt's La BR7 43 C8
Watts' St ME4 53 E3
Wat Tyler Way ME15 100 A4
Wavell Dr DA15 12 E1
Waveney Rd TN10 127 B5
Waverley Cl
Bromley BR2 42 D4
Chatham ME5 68 D2
Coxheath ME17 115 C3
Waverley Cres SE18 12 D8
Waverley Dr TN2 159 F6
Waverley Gdns E6 1 E8
Waverley Rd SE18 2 D1
WAYFIELD 68 A8
Wayfield Com Prim Sch ME5 68 A7
Wayfield Link SE9 12 D1
Wayfield Rd ME5 68 A7
Waylands BR8 45 F5
Waylands Cl TN14 74 E4
Wayne Cl BR6 57 F7
Wayne Ct ME2 39 D2
Wayside
3 Chislehurst BR7 43 D8
Tenterden TN30 183 B2
Wayside Ave TN30 183 B3
Wayside Dr TN8 122 D3
Wayside Flats TN30 183 B2
Wayside Gr SE9 28 F4
Waystrode Manor★ TN8 154 F6
Wayville Rd DA1 33 B8
Way Volante DA12 36 E4
Weald Cl
Istead Rise DA13 35 E1
Maidstone ME15 116 C6
Orpington BR2 56 E8
Sevenoaks Weald TN14 108 C2
Weald Com Prim Sch TN14 108 B2
Weald Ct TN11 126 D6
Wealden Ave TN30 183 B1
Wealden Cl TN11 126 E5
Wealden Ct 5 ME5 54 B3
Wealden Pl TN13 92 D6
Wealden View TN17 177 E8
Wealden Way ME20 98 E7
Weald of Kent Gram Sch TN9 143 C7
Weald Rd TN13 108 B7
Weald Sports Ctr The TN17 179 C6
Weald The BR7 28 F2
Weald View
Frittenden TN17 166 E6
Paddock Wood TN12 146 E1
Turner's Green TN5 184 F6
Weald View Rd TN9 143 B7
WEARDALE 106 B5
Weardale Ave DA2 33 C7
Weare Rd TN4 159 C8
Weatherly Cl ME1 53 C4
Weathersfield Ct 1 SE9 11 F1
Weaver Cl E6 2 B6
Weavering Cl ME2 39 B2
Weavering Cotts ME14 100 E3
Weavering St ME14 100 F4
WEAVERING STREET 100 F5
Weavers Cl
Gravesend DA11 36 A7
Staplehurst TN12 149 F4
Weavers Cotts TN17 177 E8
Weavers La TN14 92 C6
Weaver's Orch DA13 35 A2
Weavers The
Biddenden TN27 168 A1
Maidstone ME16 99 B5
Webb Cl ME3 40 D6
Webb Ct 6 SE28 3 B6
Webber Cl DA8 15 B7
Webb's Mdw TN15 92 C2
Webbs Orchard TN12 161 E8
Webster Rd ME8 55 F1
Wedgewood Cl ME16 99 B5
Wedgewood Ct DA5 30 F8
Wedgewood Dr ME5 68 A7
Wedgwoods TN16 88 C6
Weeds Wood Rd ME5 67 F4
Weeks La TN27 168 A5
Week St ME14 100 A4
Weigall Rd SE12, SE3 11 A3
Weird Wood DA3 49 C6
Weir Mill ME19 97 F7
Weir Rd DA5 31 B8
Welbeck Ave
Bromley BR1 28 A4
Royal Tunbridge Wells TN4 159 C8
Sidcup DA15 30 A7
Welcombe Ct ME8 69 D8
Weld Cl TN12 149 F4
Weldstock Ho 2 SE28 2 D3
Wellan Cl DA16 13 B2
Welland Rd TN10 127 B4
Wellands Cl BR1 42 F7
Wellbrook Rd BR6 57 A6
Well Cl TN11 125 F1
Wellcome Ave DA1 15 E3
Weller Ave ME1 53 D2
Weller Pl BR6 73 A8
Weller Rd TN4 158 C4
Wellers Cl TN16 105 C8
WELLER'S TOWN 140 D5
Wellesley Cl 7 SE7 1 C1
Well Field DA3 48 F5
Well Hall Par SE9 11 F3
Well Hall Pleasaunce★ SE9 11 E3
Well Hall Rd SE18, SE9 11 F5
WELL HILL 59 B4
Well Hill BR6 59 B5
Well Hill La BR6 59 B4
Well Hill Nursery BR6 59 C4
Wellhurst Cl BR6 57 F3
WELLING 13 B4
Wellingfield Ct 1 DA16 13 A4
Welling High St DA16 13 B4
Welling Sch DA16 13 B6
Welling Sta DA16 13 A5
Wellington Ave
Sidcup DA15 13 A1
Woolwich SE18 2 B3
Wellington Cotts
Gill's Green TN18 188 E4
Meopham DA13 64 A7
Wellington Gdns SE7 1 C1
Wellington Ho 6 ME15 116 E5
Wellingtonia Way TN8 122 C2
Wellington Mews SE7 11 C8
Wellington Par DA15 13 A2
Wellington Pl
Maidstone ME14 99 F6
Sparrow's Green TN5 184 F5
Wellington Rd
Bexley DA5 13 D2
Bromley BR2 42 C5
Dartford DA1 15 C1
Erith DA17 3 F1
Gillingham ME7 54 C4
Orpington BR5 44 C3
Tilbury RM18 19 A5
Wellington St
Gravesend DA12 36 C8
Woolwich SE18 2 A2
Wellington Way ME19 96 F3
Welling Way DA16 12 D4
Wellmeade Dr TN13 108 B8
Well Penn Rd ME3 22 C3
Well Rd
Maidstone ME14 100 A5
Otford TN14 76 C3
Wells Cl
Royal Tunbridge Wells TN1 159 A3
Tenterden TN30 193 B8
Tonbridge TN10 127 D4
Westerham TN16 105 C8
Wells Cotts ME18 113 C2
Wells Ct ME2 52 D5
Wells Ho
Bromley BR1 28 B3
Royal Tunbridge Wells TN4 158 F4
Wellsmoor Gdns BR1 43 A6
Wells Rd
Bromley BR1 42 F7
Rochester ME2 52 D5
Well St
East Malling ME19 97 E6
Maidstone ME15, ME17 115 E4
WELL STREET 97 E6
Welton Cl TN9 142 F7
Welton Rd SE18 12 E7
Wemmick Cl ME1 67 D7
Wendover Cl ME2 66 B5
Wendover Ct BR2 42 B6
Wendover Rd
Bromley BR1, BR2 42 B6
Eltham SE9 11 D4
Wendover Way
Bexley DA16 13 A3
Orpington BR6 44 A3
Wensley Cl SE9 11 F1
Wents Wood ME14 100 F5
Wentworth Cl
Erith SE28 3 D7
Gravesend DA11 36 A3
Hayes BR2 56 A8
Orpington BR6 57 E5
Wentworth Dr
Cliffe Woods ME3 39 B8
Dartford DA1 15 A1
Gillingham ME8 69 E7
Wentworth Ho 3 SE3 11 A7
Wentworth Prim Sch DA1 32 A8
Wenvoe Ave DA7 14 B5
Wernbrook St SE18 12 C8
Wesley Ave E16 1 B5
Wesley Cl
Maidstone ME16 98 F3
Orpington BR5 44 C6
Wesley Ho BR1 42 D6
Wessex Dr DA8 14 E6
Wessex Wlk DA2 31 E6
West App BR5 43 C4
Westbere Ho BR5 44 C4
West Borough Prim Sch ME16 99 B3
Westbourne Rd DA7 13 E7
Westbrook Ct SE3 11 B6
Westbrook Dr BR5 44 D1

Westbrooke Cl ME4 . . . . . . 54 A2
Westbrooke Cres DA16 . . . . 13 C4
Westbrooke Rd
  Bexley DA16 . . . . 13 C4
  Sidcup DA15 . . . . 29 D6
Westbrooke Sch DA16 . . . . 13 D4
Westbrook Rd SE3 . . . . 11 B6
Westbrook Terr TN2 . . . . . 159 D1
West Brow BR7 . . . . 29 B3
Westbury Cl ME5 [5] DA14 . 30 A4
Westbury Rd ME1 . . . . 42 D8
Westbury Terr TN16 . . . . . 105 C8
Westcombe Hill SE7 . . . . . . 45 A8
Westcombe Park Rd SE3 . . 11 A7
Westcombe Park Sta SE3 . . 1 A1
Westcott Ave DA11 . . . . 36 A5
Westcott Cl BR1 . . . . 42 F4
WESTCOURT 36 E6
Westcourt Prim Sch DA12 36 E6
Westcourt Rd ME7 . . . . 54 A6
West Crescent Rd DA12 . . 19 C1
WEST CROSS 191 D4
West Cross TN30 . . . . 191 D4
West Cross Gdns TN30 . . . 192 F7
West Ct [6] ME15 . . . . 100 A1
Westdale Rd SE18 . . . . 12 E8
Westdean Ave SE12 . . . . . . 28 C7
West Dr
  Chatham ME5 . . . . 67 D5
  Sutton Valence ME17 . . . . 135 B7
Wested Farm Cotts BR8 . . 45 F2
Wested La BR8 . . . . 46 A3
West End
  Brasted TN16 . . . . 90 B2
  Kemsing TN15 . . . . 77 A2
  Marden TN12 . . . . 148 C6
Westerdale Rd [5] SE10 . . . 1 A1
Westergate Rd
  Bexley SE2 . . . . 13 E8
  Rochester ME2 . . . . 38 F1
WESTERHAM 89 C1
Westerham Cl ME8 . . . . 55 B3
Westerham Dr DA15 . . . . . . 13 C1
Westerham Hill TN16 . . . . . 89 B5
Westerham Rd
  Brasted TN16 . . . . 90 A2
  Limpsfield RH8, TN16 . . . 104 C6
  Orpington BR2 . . . . 56 D4
  Sevenoaks TN13 . . . . 91 C4
  Westerham TN16 . . . . 105 A8
Westerhill Rd ME17 . . . . . . 115 C1
Western Ave
  Chatham ME4 . . . . 54 A8
  [7] Hawkhurst TN18 . . . . . 188 D7
Western Beach Apartments
  E16 . . . . 1 A5
Western Cross Cl DA9 . . . . 17 C1
Western Gateway E16 . . . . . 1 A6
Western Rd
  Borough Green TN15 . . . . . 94 F7
  Hawkhurst TN18 . . . . 188 F2
  Maidstone ME16 . . . . 91 C5
  Royal Tunbridge Wells,
  Southborough TN4 . . . . . 143 A1
  Royal Tunbridge Wells,
  TN1 . . . . 159 C5
  Turner's Green TN5 . . . . . 184 F6
Western Way SE28 . . . . 2 E4
WEST FARLEIGH 114 D6
Westfield
  New Ash Green DA3 . . . . . 62 F6
  [1] Orpington BR6 . . . . 57 C5
  Sevenoaks TN13 . . . . 92 C5
Westfield Bsns Ctr ME2 . . 53 C7
Westfield Cl DA12 . . . . 36 C2
Westfield Cotts
  Cudham TN14 . . . . 73 D3
  West Kingsdown TN15 . . . . 61 F4
Westfield Gdns ME9 . . . . . . 71 C3
Westfield Ho ME2 . . . . 192 F7
Westfield Rd DA1 . . . . 14 C4
WESTFIELD SOLE 84 C7
Westfield Sole Rd ME5,
  ME14 . . . . 84 D8
Westfield St SE18 . . . . 1 D3
Westfield Terr TN17 . . . . . 178 F1
Westfield Villas TN12 . . . . 148 B5
Westgate Ct SE12 . . . . 28 A7
Westgate Ho [8] DA11 . . . . 11 D1
Westgate Prim Sch DA1 . . 32 D8
Westgate Rd DA1 . . . . 15 D1
West Hallowes SE9 . . . . 28 E7
Westhall Rd BR8 . . . . 45 D6
WEST HEATH 13 D8
West Heath Cl DA1 . . . . 14 F1
West Heath La TN13 . . . . . 108 B7
West Heath Rd
  Bexley SE2 . . . . 13 D8
  Crayford DA1 . . . . 14 F1
West Hill
  Biggin Hill BR6 . . . . 72 F7
  Dartford DA1 . . . . 15 D1
Westhill Cl DA12 . . . . 36 B7
West Hill Dr DA1 . . . . 15 C1
West Hill Prim Sch DA1 . . 15 C1
West Hill Rise DA1 . . . . 15 D1
Westholme BR6 . . . . 43 F2
West Holme DA8 . . . . 14 C6
Westhorne Ave SE12, SE9 . 11 C2
Westhurst Dr BR7 . . . . 29 B3
West Kent Ave DA11 . . . . . . 18 C1
West Kent Coll TN9 . . . . . . 143 A7
WEST KINGSDOWN 61 A7

West Kingsdown CE Prim
  Sch TN15 . . . . 62 A2
West Kingsdown Ind Est
  TN15 . . . . 61 F2
West La ME3 . . . . 26 F6
Westland Ho [1] E16 . . . . . . 2 A5
Westland Lodge [2] BR1 . . 42 E7
Westleigh Dr BR1 . . . . 42 E8
West Lodge Prep Sch [2]
  DA14 . . . . 30 A5
WEST MALLING 97 C7
West Malling CE Prim Sch
  ME19 . . . . 97 B8
West Malling Ind Pk
  ME19 . . . . 80 E2
West Malling Sta ME19 . . . 97 D8
Westmarsh Cl ME15 . . . . . 116 F7
Westmead DA2 . . . . 82 C4
West Mersea Cl E16 . . . . 1 B5
West Mill DA11 . . . . 18 F1
Westminster Sq ME16 . . . . 99 B4
Westmoor St [9] E3 . . . . 1 D3
Westmoreland Ave DA16 . . 12 E3
Westmoreland Pl [9] BR1 . . 42 A6
Westmoreland Rd BR2 . . . . 42 A5
Westmore Rd TN16 . . . . 88 C7
Westmorland Gn ME15 . . . 116 E7
Westmorland Rd ME15 . . . 116 E7
Westmount Ave ME4 . . . . . . 53 F3
Westmount Rd SE9 . . . . 12 A3
Weston Ave RM20 . . . . 16 F8
Weston Rd ME2 . . . . 53 A8
West Park Ave TN4 . . . . . . 142 F1
West Park Rd ME15 . . . . . . 100 B2
West Parkside SE10 . . . . 1 A2
WEST PECKHAM 112 A6
West Pk SE9 . . . . 28 E7
West Rd
  Chatham ME4 . . . . 54 A7
  Goudhurst TN17 . . . . 177 E8
  Kildown TN17 . . . . 176 F3
Westree Rd [7] ME16 . . . . . . 99 E3
Westree Rd ME16 . . . . 99 E3
Westrise TN9 . . . . 48 D7
West Shaw DA3 . . . . 48 D7
West Silverton Sta E16 . . . . 1 A5
West St
  Bexley DA7 . . . . 13 F4
  Bromley BR1 . . . . 42 A7
  Erith DA8 . . . . 4 E1
  Gillingham ME7 . . . . 54 D6
  Gravesend DA11 . . . . 19 B1
  Grays RM17 . . . . 18 A8
  Harrietsham ME17 . . . . . . 119 C6
  Hunton ME15 . . . . 131 D7
  Rochester ME2 . . . . 39 B1
  West Malling ME19 . . . . . . 97 B8
  Woodside Green ME17 . . . 120 E8
  Wrotham TN15 . . . . 78 F3
WEST STREET 18 A8
West Terr DA15 . . . . 29 E7
WEST THURROCK 17 B8
West Thurrock Prim Sch
  RM20 . . . . 17 A8
West Thurrock Way RM20 . 17 B8
WEST TILBURY 19 E8
Westview ME4 . . . . 40 B2
West View ME17 . . . . 134 E8
West View Hospl TN30 . . . 192 E6
West View Rd
  Crockenhill BR8 . . . . 45 D3
  Dartford DA1 . . . . 15 F1
  Swanley BR8 . . . . 46 A5
Westway
  Coxheath ME17 . . . . 115 C3
  Pembury TN2 . . . . 160 D7
West Way BR5 . . . . 43 D4
Westways
  Edenbridge TN8 . . . . 122 C2
  Westerham TN16 . . . . 89 C1
Westwell Cl BR5 . . . . 44 D1
Westwell Ho TN30 . . . . 192 F7
Westwell Rd ME16 . . . . 99 B3
WESTWOOD 92 D6
West Wood Cl BR1 . . . . 42 D6
Westwood Farm DA13 . . . . 34 D2
Westwood La DA16 . . . . 12 F4
Westwood Rd
  Betsham DA13 . . . . 34 E2
  East Peckham TN12 . . . . . 129 C6
  Loose ME15 . . . . 116 A7
  Rusthall TN4 . . . . 158 C5
West Wood Rd ME9 . . . . . . 86 B8
West Woodside DA3 . . . . . . 30 E7
Westwood Way TN13 . . . . . 91 F5
Westwood Wlk ME9 . . . . . . 71 B7
West Yoke TN15 . . . . 62 D7
Wetheral Dr ME5 . . . . 64 C4
Wexford Pl ME15 . . . . 116 D6
Weyhill Cl ME14 . . . . 100 C6
Weyman Rd SE3 . . . . 11 C6
Weymouth Cl E6 . . . . 2 B7
Wharfdale Sq ME15 . . . . . . 99 E1
Wharfedale Rd DA2 . . . . . . 33 C7
Wharf La ME3 . . . . 22 B6
Wharf Rd
  Gillingham ME7 . . . . 54 C7
  Gravesend DA12 . . . . 19 E1
  Grays RM17 . . . . 17 F8
  Maidstone ME15 . . . . 99 E2
Wharf Road S RM17 . . . . . . 17 F8

Wharfside Cl DA8 . . . . 4 F1
Wharncliffe Ho DA9 . . . . . . 17 B1
Wharton Rd BR1 . . . . 42 B8
Whatcote Cotts TN15 . . . . . 95 C7
Whatman ME14 . . . . 100 C6
Wheatcroft DA12 . . . . 36 C7
Wheatcroft [5] E16 . . . . 69 F7
Wheatear Way ME5 . . . . 68 B7
Wheatfield ME9 . . . . 81 E1
Wheatfield Cl TN17 . . . . . . 179 C5
Wheatfield Dr TN17 . . . . . . 179 C5
Wheatfield Lea TN17 . . . . . 179 C5
Wheatfields
  Chatham ME5 . . . . 68 D2
  Maidstone ME14 . . . . 100 D4
  Newham E6 . . . . 2 B7
Wheatfield Way TN17 . . . . 179 C5
Wheatley Cl DA9 . . . . 11 F4
Wheatley Terrace Rd DA8 14 F8
Wheatsheaf Cl ME15 . . . . . 116 B8
Wheatsheaf Hill
  Chelsfield TN14 . . . . 58 F2
  Ide Hill TN14 . . . . 106 F4
Wheatsheaf Way TN10 . . . 127 D6
Wheatstone Rd DA4 . . . . 4 D1
Wheelbarrow Park Est
  TN12 . . . . 148 B7
Wheeler Pl
  Bromley BR2 . . . . 42 B5
  Kings Hill ME18 . . . . 97 A2
Wheeler St [2] La ME17 . . . 132 E7
Wheeler St
  Headcorn TN27 . . . . 151 E5
  Maidstone ME14 . . . . 100 A5
Wheelers The ME8 . . . . 69 B6
Wheelwrights The ME17 . . 119 D6
Wheelwrites TN15 . . . . 110 E7
Whenman Ave DA5 . . . . 31 C5
Whernside Cl SE28 . . . . 3 C6
WHETSTED 129 E1
Whetsted Rd
  Five Oak Green TN12 . . . . 145 C8
  Whetsted TN12 . . . . 129 F1
Whetstone Rd SE3 . . . . 11 D6
Whiffen's Ave ME4 . . . . 53 F5
Whiffen's Ave W ME4 . . . . . 53 F5
Whiffen Wlk ME19 . . . . 2 B1
Whimbrel Cl SE28 . . . . 3 C6
Whimbrel Gn ME20 . . . . 81 F2
Whimbrels The ME4 . . . . . . 40 B1
Whimbrel Wlk ME5 . . . . 68 C1
Whinchat SE28 . . . . 2 D3
Whinfell Way DA12 . . . . 36 F4
Whinyates Rd SE9 . . . . 11 E4
Whippendell Cl BR5 . . . . . . 44 B8
Whippendell Way BR5 . . . . 44 B7
Whistler Rd TN10 . . . . 127 D6
Whitby Cl
  Biggin Hill TN16 . . . . 72 B1
  Stone DA9 . . . . 17 A2
Whitby Rd SE18 . . . . 1 F2
Whitchurch Cl ME16 . . . . . 99 E4
Whitcombe Cl ME5 . . . . 68 C3
White Ave DA11 . . . . 35 F5
Whitebeam Ave BR2 . . . . . . 43 A3
Whitebeam Cl TN15 . . . . . . 77 A2
Whitebeam Dr ME17 . . . . . 115 B3
White Bear Pas [3] TN1 . . . 159 A2
Whitebine Gdns TN12 . . . . 130 A6
Whitechapel La TN31 . . . . . 192 F7
White Cottage Rd TN10 . . 127 D6
Whitecroft BR8 . . . . 45 E7
Whitefield Cl BR5 . . . . 44 C6
Whitefield Rd TN4 . . . . 159 A6
Whitefriars TN13 . . . . 108 A8
Whitefriars Wharf TN9 . . . 127 C1
White Gate ME2 . . . . 52 F8
Whitegate Cl ME8 . . . . 69 D5
White Gates DA14 . . . . 30 A3
Whitegates Ave TN5 . . . . . . 61 E4
Whitegates La TN5 . . . . . . 184 D8
Whitehall Dr ME17 . . . . . . 118 D3
Whitehall La
  Erith DA8 . . . . 14 F5
  [5] Grays RM17 . . . . 18 A8
Whitehall Rd
  Broad Street ME14 . . . . . . 102 A6
  Bromley BR2 . . . . 42 D5
White Hart Ave SE28 . . . . . . 2 E3
White Hart Cl TN13 . . . . . . 108 C7
White Hart Par TN13 . . . . . 91 E5
White Hart Rd
  Orpington BR6 . . . . 44 A2
  Woolwich SE18 . . . . 2 E2
White Hart Wood TN13 . . . 108 C6
White Hart Yd [10] DA11 . . 11 B1
Whitehaven Cl BR2 . . . . 42 A5
Whitehaven Ct [6] DA6 . . . 13 E3
Whitehead Cl DA2 . . . . 32 C5
Whiteheads La ME14 . . . . . 101 B4
WHITEHILL 48 D7
Whitehill TN15 . . . . 79 B5
Whitehill La DA12 . . . . 36 C5
Whitehill Par DA12 . . . . 36 C5
Whitehill Prim Sch DA12 . 36 C5
Whitehill Rd
  Dartford DA1 . . . . 15 A2
  Gravesend DA12 . . . . 36 C6
  Longfield, Whitehill DA13 . 48 D8
  Meopham DA13 . . . . 48 D8
White Hill Rd ME9, ME14 . 69 D1
Whitehorse Hill ME5 . . . . . 54 B3
White Horse Hill BR7, SE9 . 29 A4
White Horse La
  Harvel DA13 . . . . 64 C2
  Otham Hole ME15 . . . . . . 117 A6

White Horse Rd DA13 . . . . 64 E1
White Horse Wood Cty
  Park☆ ME14 . . . . 85 D2
White House Cl ME3 . . . . . . 40 E4
Whitehouse Cres ME1 . . . . 83 A8
White House La TN14 . . . . 107 F5
White House Rd TN14 . . . . 107 F5
White La RH8, TN16 . . . . . . 88 B3
Whitelake Rd TN10 . . . . . . 127 C5
Whiteleaves Rise ME2 . . . . 52 B3
Whitelimes TN18 . . . . 188 D8
White Lodge TN1 . . . . 159 C4
White Lodge Cl TN13 . . . . . 92 B4
WHITE OAK 45 E7
White Oak Cl [12] TN9 . . . 143 B8
Whiteoak Ct [3] BR8 . . . . . 45 E6
White Oak Gdns DA15 . . . . 29 F8
White Oak L Ctr BR8 . . . . . 45 E7
White Oak Sq [3] BR8 . . . . 45 E6
WHITE POST 156 D7
White Post
  Four Elms TN8 . . . . 123 A6
  Hollingbourne ME17 . . . . 103 B5
White Post Hill DA4 . . . . . . 110 F5
Whitepost La DA13 . . . . 47 A2
White Post La
  Culverstone Green DA13 . . 63 F2
  Sole Street DA13 . . . . 50 B5
White Rd ME4 . . . . 54 A2
White Rock Ct ME16 . . . . . . 99 E3
White Rock Pl [7] ME16 . . . 99 E3
Whites Cl DA9 . . . . 17 C1
White's La TN18 . . . . 189 B2
White's Mdw BR1 . . . . 43 A5
Whitewall Ctr ME2 . . . . 53 D8
Whitewall Rd ME2 . . . . 53 D7
Whitewall Way DA12 . . . . . 36 F4
Whitewebbs Way BR5 . . . . . 43 F8
Whitewell La TN17 . . . . 179 D7
Whitewood Cotts TN16 . . . 88 C7
Whitewood Post La ME20 . 98 F7
Whitfield Cres [1] DA2 . . . . 33 D8
Whitfield Rd
  Bexley DA7 . . . . 13 F7
Whitings Way E6 . . . . 2 A8
Whitmore St ME16 . . . . 99 D2
Whitney Cl ME14 . . . . 100 C6
Whittaker St ME4 . . . . 54 A4
Whitworth Rd SE18 . . . . . . 12 A7
Whybourne Crest TN2 . . . 159 D1
Whyman Ave ME4 . . . . 54 A1
Wichling Cl BR5 . . . . 44 D1
Wickenden Rd TN13 . . . . . . 92 C5
Wicken Ho ME16 . . . . 99 E4
Wickens Pl ME19 . . . . 97 C8
Wickets The TN14 . . . . 100 C6
Wickham Cl ME9 . . . . 71 B6
Wickham Common Prim Sch
  BR4 . . . . 56 A6
Wickham Ct DA16 . . . . 12 E5
Wickham Field TN14 . . . . . 75 F3
Wickham Gdns TN4 . . . . . . 158 D5
Wickham La SE2, SE18 . . . 13 A8
Wickham Pl ME17 . . . . 120 D5
Wickham St
  Bexley DA16 . . . . 13 A6
  Rochester ME1 . . . . 53 D3
Wickhams Way DA3 . . . . . . 48 F4
WICK HILL 167 F8
Wickhurst Rd TN14 . . . . . . 107 F3
Wicks Cl SE9 . . . . 28 D4
Wicksteed Cl DA5 . . . . 31 D5
Widbury TN3 . . . . 157 F3
Widecombe Rd SE9 . . . . 28 E5
Widgeon Cl E16 . . . . 1 B7
Widgeon Path SE28 . . . . 1 B7
Widgeon Rd
  Erith DA8 . . . . 15 B7
  Rochester ME2 . . . . 52 D6
Widmore ME8 . . . . 42 E7
Widmore Lodge Rd BR1 . . 42 D7
Widmore Rd BR1 . . . . 42 C7
WIERTON 133 F8
Wierton Hill ME17 . . . . 133 D7
Wierton La ME17 . . . . 116 C1
Wierton Rd ME17 . . . . 133 E8
WIGMORE 69 B4
Wigmore Glade ME8 . . . . . . 69 B4
Wigmore Rd ME8 . . . . 69 B4
Wilberforce Ct [2] SE28 . . . . 3 C5
Wilberforce Rd ME17 . . . . 115 D3
Wilberforce Way DA3 . . . . 36 D3
Wilde Cl RM18 . . . . 19 C5
Wilden Park Rd TN12 . . . . 164 E7
Wilde Rd DA8 . . . . 15 A6
WILDERNESSE 92 E4
Wilderness Ave TN15 . . . . . 92 F5
Wilderness Mount TN13 . . 92 D5
Wildernesse Sch The
  TN13 . . . . 92 E6
Wilderness Mews TN2 . . . 159 C4
Wilderness Rd BR7 . . . . 29 B1
Wildfell Cl ME5 . . . . 84 C8
Wildman La ME18 . . . . 69 D3
Wildwood Cl
  Kingswood ME17 . . . . 118 E2
  [1] Lewisham SE12 . . . . . . 28 A8
Wildwood Glade ME8 . . . . . 69 B4
Wilford Ho [3] SE18 . . . . 2 B1
Wilfred St [22] DA12 . . . . . . 19 B1
Wilkinson Cl [1] DA1 . . . . . 16 A3
Wilkinson Pl ME18 . . . . 97 A2
Wilkinson Rd E16 . . . . 1 C7
Wilks Ave DA1 . . . . 32 F6
Will Adams Ct [9] ME7 . . . 54 C6
Will Adams Rdbt ME8 . . . . 54 F2
Will Adams Way ME8 . . . . . 54 F1

Will Crooks Gdns SE9 . . . . 11 D3
Willenhall Rd SE18 . . . . 2 B5
Willersley Ave
  Orpington BR6 . . . . 57 D2
  Sidcup DA15 . . . . 29 F2
Willersley Cl DA15 . . . . 29 F2
Willersley Gdns TN17 . . . . 179 D6
Willett Cotts TN3 . . . . 43 E2
Willetts Cotts TN3 . . . . . . 156 C4
Willetts La TN3 . . . . 156 C4
Willett Way BR5, BR6 . . . . 43 E2
William Baker Ho ME20 . . 98 F8
William Barefoot Dr SE9 . . 28 F6
William Foster La DA16 . . . 13 A5
William Ho [4] DA12 . . . . . 36 B8
William Judge Cl TN30 . . . 193 D7
William Luck Cl TN12 . . . . 129 E6
William Petty Way BR5 . . . 44 C2
William Rd ME2 . . . . 52 C2
William Smith Ho [10] DA17 . 4 A3
William St
  Gravesend DA12 . . . . 36 B8
  Grays RM17 . . . . 18 C8
  Royal Tunbridge Wells
  TN4 . . . . 159 A5
Williams Way DA2 . . . . 31 D6
Willicombe Ho TN2 . . . . . . 159 D4
Willicombe Pk TN2 . . . . . . 159 D4
WILLINGTON 100 E1
Willington Gn ME15 . . . . . . 116 E7
Willington St ME15 . . . . . . 100 F2
Willis Ho ME1 . . . . 53 C4
Willis Rd DA8 . . . . 4 D2
Willoughby Way SE7 . . . . . . 1 B2
Willow Ave
  Hoo St Werburgh ME3 . . . 40 E3
  Sidcup DA15 . . . . 13 A1
  Swanley BR8 . . . . 45 F5
Willowbank Ct [12] ME15 . 100 B4
Willowbank Dr ME23 . . . . . 23 E4
Willowbay Gdns ME8 . . . . . 69 E4
Willow Cl
  Bromley BR2 . . . . 42 F4
  Harrietsham ME17 . . . . . . 119 D6
  Orpington BR5 . . . . 44 B2
  Sidcup DA15 . . . . 13 F1
Willow Cres
  Five Oak Green TN12 . . . . 145 B7
  Staplehurst TN12 . . . . 149 F5
Willow Ct
  Dartford DA1 . . . . 32 C7
  Loose ME15 . . . . 116 A6
Willow Dene Sch SE18 . . . . 12 E6
Willowfields Cl [1] SE18 . . . . 2 E1
Willow Gr BR7 . . . . 29 B2
Willow Grange DA14 . . . . . . 30 B5
Willowherb Cl ME4 . . . . 40 C1
Willow Ho
  [2] Chatham ME5 . . . . 67 F5
  [8] Maidstone ME16 . . . . . 99 A3
Willow La
  Paddock Wood TN12 . . . . 146 E6
  Woolwich SE18 . . . . 2 A2
Willow Lea TN10 . . . . 127 C7
Willow Lodge TN4 . . . . 158 E4
Willowmead ME19 . . . . 81 E2
Willow Pk TN14 . . . . 75 F2
Willow Rd
  Dartford DA1 . . . . 32 C7
  Erith DA8 . . . . 15 A6
  Larkfield ME20 . . . . 81 F3
  Rochester ME2 . . . . 52 E6
Willow Rise ME15 . . . . 100 F1
Willowside ME6 . . . . 66 A1
Willows The
  Gillingham ME8 . . . . 55 E2
  Grays RM17 . . . . 18 D8
  Newington ME9 . . . . 71 B6
Willow Terr DA4 . . . . 60 E8
Willow Tree Cl DA14 . . . . . 29 F3
Willow Tree Rd TN2 . . . . . . 158 F1
Willow Tree Wlk BR1 . . . . . 42 B8
Willow Vale BR7 . . . . 29 B2
Willow Way
  Biddenden TN27 . . . . 182 D7
  Maidstone ME15 . . . . 100 B3
Willow Wents ME18 . . . . . . 96 D1
Willow Wlk
  Culverstone Green DA13 . . 63 F3
  Orpington BR6 . . . . 57 B7
  Royal Tunbridge Wells
  TN2 . . . . 159 B8
Willowwood [20] ME15 . . . 116 E5
Willow Wood Rd DA13 . . . . 63 F2
Willrose Cres SE2 . . . . 3 B1
Will Thorne Pav E16 . . . . 1 E7
Wilman Rd TN4 . . . . 159 B7
Wilmar Way TN15 . . . . 72 F7
Wilmecote Cl ME8 . . . . 69 D8
WILMINGTON 32 C4
Wilmington Ave BR6 . . . . . 58 C8
Wilmington Court Rd
  DA2 . . . . 32 A6
Wilmington Enterprise Coll
  DA2 . . . . 32 B5
Wilmington Gram Sch for
  Boys DA2 . . . . 32 B5
Wilmington Ho DA2 . . . . . . 32 D6
Wilmington Prim Sch
  DA2 . . . . 32 B5
Wilmington Way ME8 . . . . . 55 B2
Wilmot Rd DA1 . . . . 15 B2
Wilmount St SE18 . . . . 2 B2
WILSLEY GREEN 179 D7
WILSLEY POUND 179 E8
Wilson Ave ME1 . . . . 67 E7
Wilson Cl
  Maidstone ME15 . . . . 116 E7

Wilson Cl continued
Tonbridge TN11 . . . . 126 F5
Wilson Ct ME18 . . . . 114 A1
Wilson Ho 3 SE7 . . . . 11 C8
Wilson La DA4 . . . . 47 F7
Wilson Rd TN10 . . . . 127 E5
Wilsons La ME15 . . . . 115 A5
Wilsons Way DA13 . . . . . . 63 F3
Wilton Dr ME20 . . . . 98 B8
Wilton Ho 2 BR7 . . . . 43 D8
Wilton Rd SE2 . . . . 3 C2
Wiltshire Cl
Chatham ME5 . . . . 68 C8
Dartford DA2 . . . . 33 D8
Wiltshire Rd BR6 . . . . 44 A2
Wiltshire Way
4 Maidstone ME15 . . . . . 116 E8
Royal Tunbridge Wells
TN2 . . . . 159 D7
Wimborne Cl ME4 . . . . 30 B4
Wimborne Ave BR7 . . . . . . 43 F6
Wimborne Ho DA12 . . . . . . 36 D5
Wimborne Dr ME8 . . . . 49 D6
Wimpole Cl BR2 . . . . 42 C5
Winch Cl TN17 . . . . 129 D4
Winchcomb Gdns SE9 . . . . 11 D3
Winchelsea Ave DA7 . . . . . . 3 F7
Winchelsea Rd ME5 . . . . . . 68 B5
Winchester Ave ME5 . . . . . 67 F4
Winchester Cl 11 E6 . . . . . . 1 F5
Winchester Cres DA12 . . . 36 D5
Winchester Ct 14 DA17 . . . 4 A1
Winchester Gr TN13 . . . . . . 92 B4
Winchester Ho
3 Maidstone ME15 . . . . . 116 F7
Woolwich SE18 . . . . 1 C7
Winchester Pl 9 ME14 . . . 100 A5
Winchester Rd
Bexley DA7 . . . . 13 D5
Hawkhurst TN18 . . . . 189 A2
Orpington BR6 . . . . 58 C6
Tonbridge TN10 . . . . 127 D5
Winchester Way ME4 . . . . . 70 A8
WINCHET HILL 164 B6
Winch's Garth TN12 . . . . . 149 F5
Wincliff Rd TN9 . . . . 143 B8
Wincrofts Dr SE9 . . . . 12 D3
Windermere Cl
Dartford DA1 . . . . 32 B7
Orpington BR6 . . . . 57 B7
Windermere Dr ME8 . . . . . . 69 D7
Windermere Ho 4 ME15 . 116 E7
Windermere Rd DA7 . . . . . . 14 C5
Windhover Way DA12 . . . . . 36 A4
Windmill Cl ME2 . . . . 39 B1
Windmill Cotts
Cranbrook TN17 . . . . 179 D6
Lower Stoke ME3 . . . . 25 C5
Windmill Ct
Maidstone ME17 . . . . 116 B3
Royal Tunbridge Wells
TN2 . . . . 159 C3
Windmill Grange TN15 . . . 61 F3
WINDMILL GREEN 9 B2
WINDMILL HILL 36 A7
Windmill Hill
Brenchley TN12 . . . . 146 B1
Fairbourne Heath ME17 . . 119 B1
Platt TN15 . . . . 95 D7
Pye Corner ME17 . . . . 136 B7
Wrotham Heath ME1 . . . . 101 B4
Windmill La
Cousley Wood TN5 . . . . . . 185 C8
Durgates TN5 . . . . 184 E4
Keston BR2 . . . . 56 C6
Wrotham Heath TN15 . . . . 95 B8
Windmill Lane E ME19 . . . 97 C6
Windmill Lane W ME19 . . . 97 C6
Windmill Manor ME7 . . . . . 54 C4
Windmill Pk TN15 . . . . 95 E7
Windmill Rd
Gillingham ME7 . . . . 54 C4
Sevenoaks TN13 . . . . 108 B2
Sevenoaks Weald TN14 . . 108 B2
Windmill Row ME17 . . . . . 117 D2
Windmill St
Gravesend DA12 . . . . 36 B7
12 Gravesend DA12 . . . . . 36 B8
Rochester ME2 . . . . 39 B1
Royal Tunbridge Wells
TN2 . . . . 159 C3
Windrush Cl ME19 . . . . 4 E1
Windrush Prim Sch SE28 . . . 3 B6
Windsor Ave ME4 . . . . 53 F2
Windsor Cl
Chislehurst BR7 . . . . 29 B3
Maidstone ME14 . . . . 100 B6
Windsor Ct
1 Bromley BR1 . . . . 42 E6
Gillingham ME7 . . . . 54 D5
18 Sidcup DA14 . . . . 30 A5
Windsor Dr
Dartford DA1 . . . . 15 A1
Orpington BR6 . . . . 58 A4
Windsor Hall E16 . . . . 1 B5
Windsor Rd
Bexley DA6 . . . . 13 E3
Gillingham ME7 . . . . 54 D5
Gravesend DA12 . . . . 36 B4
Chatham ME5 . . . . 53 C1
Hawkhurst TN18 . . . . 189 A2

Wingfield Prim Sch ME3 . . 11 B4
Wingfield Rd DA12 . . . . 36 B8
Wingham Cl
Gillingham ME8 . . . . 55 C3
Maidstone ME15 . . . . 116 F7
Wingrove Dr
Maidstone ME14 . . . . 100 E5
Rochester ME2 . . . . 53 C7
Winifred Rd
Dartford DA1 . . . . 15 B2
Erith DA8 . . . . 4 E1
Maidstone ME15 . . . . 100 F3
Winifred St E16 . . . . 1 F5
Winn Common Rd SE18 . . 12 E8
Winnipeg Dr 3 BR6 . . . . . . 57 F4
Winn Rd SE12, SE9 . . . . 28 B7
Winser Dr TN17 . . . . 192 A1
Winsor Prim Sch E6 . . . . 2 A7
Winsor Terr E6 . . . . 2 A8
Winston Ave ME19 . . . . 97 B3
Winston Cl DA9 . . . . 16 F1
Winston Ct 10 BR1 . . . . . . 42 A8
Winston Dr
Biggin Hill TN16 . . . . 72 D2
Rochester ME2 . . . . 39 D2
Winstone Scott Ave TN3 . 157 E4
Winston Rd ME2 . . . . 52 D5
Winterborne Ave BR6 . . . . 57 D7
Winterfield La ME19 . . . . . . 97 E8
Wintergarden Cres DA3 . . 34 A8
Wintergreen Cl
1 Newham E16 . . . . 1 E8
St Mary's Island ME4 . . . . 40 C1
Winters Croft DA12 . . . . . . 36 D2
Winterton Ct 8 TN16 . . . . . 89 D1
Winton Rd BR6 . . . . 57 B6
Winton St SE9 . . . . 44 C5
Wireless Rd TN16 . . . . 72 D4
Wirrals The ME5 . . . . 68 A4
Wirral Wood Cl BR7 . . . . . . 29 A2
Wiseacre TN3 . . . . 176 A3
Wise Ho SE18 . . . . 12 A7
Wise's La TN15 . . . . 62 E2
Wishart Rd SE3 . . . . 11 D5
Wish Valley Mews TN18 . . 194 F8
Wisley Rd BR5 . . . . 30 B1
WISSENDEN 169 F7
Wissenden La TN27 . . . . . . 153 D1
Wistaria Cl BR6 . . . . 57 B8
Wisteria Gdns BR8 . . . . 25 D7
Wisteria Ho 11 ME15 . . . . 116 F7
Witches La TN13 . . . . 91 D4
Witham Way ME2 . . . . 52 F7
Withens Ct BR5 . . . . 38 B8
Witherston Way SE9 . . . . . 29 A5
WITHYHAM 170 A3
Withyham Rd TN6 . . . . 171 B7
WITTERSHAM 199 D3
Wittersham CE Prim Sch
TN30 . . . . 199 D2
Wittersham Cl ME5 . . . . . . 68 B5
Wittersham Ho 2 BR5 . . . . 44 D1
Wittersham Rd
Wittersham, Potman's Heath
TN17, TN30 . . . . 198 D4
Wittersham TN30 . . . . . . 198 C6
Wixom Ho SE3 . . . . 11 C3
Woburn Cl ME16 . . . . 91 D6
Woburn Ct 1 ME18 . . . . 3 D7
Woburn Ct 11 BR6 . . . . 51 C8
Wodehouse Cl ME20 . . . . . 81 F4
Wodehouse Rd DA1 . . . . . . 16 A3
Woldham Pl BR2 . . . . 42 C5
Woldham Rd BR2 . . . . 42 C5
Wolds Dr BR6 . . . . 57 A6
Wolfe Cl BR2 . . . . 42 A3
Wolfe Cres SE7 . . . . 1 D1
Wolfe Rd ME16 . . . . 99 B2
Wolf Ho ME4 . . . . 54 B8
Wolf's Cnr RH8 . . . . 104 A5
Wolf's Hill RH8 . . . . 104 A4
Wolf's Rd RH8 . . . . 104 B5
Wolf's Row RH8 . . . . 104 A5
Wolfs Wood RH8 . . . . 104 A3
Wollaston Cl ME8 . . . . 49 D3
Wolseley Rd TN4 . . . . 159 C7
Wolsey Cl SE28 . . . . 3 D4
Wolsey Ct 9 DA9 . . . . 17 A1
Wolsey Cl 11 . . . . 11 F1
Wolsey Mews BR6 . . . . 57 F5
Wolsey Cl DA1 . . . . 14 E2
Wolsey Ho DA1 . . . . 14 E2
Wolvercote Rd SE2 . . . . 3 D4
Wombwell Gdns DA11 . . . . 35 C6
WOMBWELL PARK 35 D6
Woodbine Cotts ME2 . . . . . 65 E5
Woodberry Dr DA15 . . . . . . 31 D5
Woodbine Rd DA15 . . . . . . 29 E7
Woodbrook Rd SE2 . . . . . . 13 B8
Woodbury Cl
Biggin Hill TN16 . . . . 72 F1
2 Royal Tunbridge Wells
TN4 . . . . 159 A5
Woodbury La SE12 . . . . 28 B4
Woodbury La TN30 . . . . . . 193 A7
Woodbury Park Gdns
TN4 . . . . 159 B5
Woodbury Park Rd TN4 . . 159 B5
Woodbury Rd
Chatham ME5 . . . . 67 F1
Hawkhurst TN18 . . . . 189 A2
Woodchurch Cl
Chatham ME5 . . . . 68 B5
Sidcup DA14 . . . . 29 D5
Woodchurch Cres 1 BR5 . 44 C4
Woodchurch Dr BR1 . . . . . . 28 D1

Woodchurch Ho ME8 . . . . . 55 C2
Woodchurch Rd TN30 . . . . 193 D8
Wood Cl
Ditton ME20 . . . . 98 E8
Joyden's Wood DA5 . . . . . 31 E5
Woodcliffe Dr BR7 . . . . 43 A7
Woodcock La
Grafty Green ME17 . . . . . 136 E5
Iden Green TN17 . . . . 190 B3
Woodcocks
Headcorn TN27 . . . . 151 D5
Newham E16 . . . . 1 D8
Woodcote Dr BR6 . . . . 43 D2
Woodcroft SE9 . . . . 28 F5
Woodcut ME14 . . . . 100 A8
Wood Dr
Bromley BR7 . . . . 28 E2
Sevenoaks TN13 . . . . 91 F1
Wood End BR8 . . . . 45 C5
Woodfall Dr DA1 . . . . 14 F3
Woodfalls Ind Est ME18 . 130 D6
Woodfield Ave
Gravesend DA11 . . . . 36 B6
Tonbridge TN11 . . . . 126 E5
Woodfield Rd TN9 . . . . 143 B8
Woodfields TN13 . . . . 91 D4
Woodfield Way ME3 . . . . . . 39 E4
Woodford Gr ME19 . . . . 97 B3
Woodford Ho 10 SE18 . . . . 12 B8
Woodford Rd ME16 . . . . 99 B2
Woodgate La ME9 . . . . 71 C2
Woodgate Rd ME9 . . . . 80 D4
Woodgates Cl TN26 . . . . . 183 D7
Woodgate Way
TN11 . . . . 143 E7
Woodgers Gr BR8 . . . . 45 F7
Woodget Cl E6 . . . . 1 E7
Woodgreen Rd E6 . . . . 1 E8
Woodhayes BR7 . . . . 29 B2
Woodhead Dr BR6 . . . . 57 E8
Woodhill SE18 . . . . 1 E2
Woodhill Pk TN2 . . . . 160 C6
Woodhill Prim Sch SE18 . . 1 E2
Woodhurst ME5 . . . . 67 D4
Woodhurst Ave BR5 . . . . . . 43 C3
Woodhurst La ME17 . . . . . 52 B2
Woodhurst Rd SE2 . . . . 3 A2
Woodington Cl SE9 . . . . 12 A1
Woodknoll Dr BR7 . . . . 42 F8
Wood La
Dartford DA2 . . . . 33 F4
East End TN17 . . . . 181 C3
Swanley Village BR8 . . . . . 46 D8
Woods Terr DA12 . . . . 36 C5
Woodstock Cl DA5 . . . . 30 F7
Woodstock Ct SE12 . . . . . . 11 A1
Woodstock Rd ME2 . . . . . . 53 A7
Woodvale Cl BR1 . . . . 42 B8
Woodview Cl BR5 . . . . 57 C8
Woodview Cl TN15 . . . . 61 E3
Woodview Cres TN11 . . . . 126 F5
Woodview Rd BR8 . . . . 45 D7
Woodview Rise ME2 . . . . . . 38 F1
Woodville SE3 . . . . 11 B6
Woodville Cl SE12 . . . . 11 A2
Woodville Gr 2 DA16 . . . . . 13 A4
Woodville Halls 14 DA12 . 36 B8
Woodville Pl 2 DA12 . . . . . 36 B8
Woodville Rd ME15 . . . . . . 100 A2
Woodville St 18 SE18 . . . . . 1 E2
Woodward Terr DA9 . . . . . . 16 E1
Wood Way BR6 . . . . 57 A8
Woodyates Rd
Eltham SE12 . . . . 28 B8
Lewisham SE12 . . . . 11 A1
Woolacombe Rd SE3 . . . . . 11 C5
Woolaston Cl ME15 . . . . . . 99 F1
Woolbright Cl ME8 . . . . 14 E1
Wooldeys Rd ME8 . . . . 55 F2
Woolf Cl SE28 . . . . 3 B5
Woolf Wlk RH18 . . . . 19 C5
Woollett Cl DA1 . . . . 15 A3
Woollett St ME14 . . . . 100 A5
Woolley Cl TN4 . . . . 142 F1
Woolley Rd
Maidstone ME15 . . . . 116 F7
Royal Tunbridge Wells
TN4 . . . . 142 F1
Woolpack Cnr TN27 . . . . . 182 A7
Woolpack Cotts TN27 . . . 182 A7
WOOLWICH 2 B3
Woolwich Arsenal Sta
SE18 . . . . 2 B2
Woolwich Church St SE18 . 1 E3
Woolwich Cl SE12 . . . . 11 B1
Woolwich Comm SE18 . . . . 12 A8
Woolwich Dockyard Ind Est
SE18 . . . . 1 E3
Woolwich Dockyard Sta
SE18 . . . . 1 F2
Woolwich High St SE18 . . . 2 A3
Woolwich Manorway E16 . . 2 B4
Woolwich Manor Way E6 . . 2 A7
Woolwich New Rd SE18 . . . 2 B2
Woolwich Polytechnic Sch
SE18 . . . . 3 A5
Woolwich Rd
Bexley DA7 . . . . 14 A4
Erith SE2 . . . . 3 E1
Greenwich SE10, SE7 . . . . . 1 C2
Woolwich Tramshed The ★
9 SE18 . . . . 2 B2
Wootton Gn ME8 . . . . 55 D3
Wootton Ho SE9 . . . . 12 D1
Wopsle Cl ME1 . . . . 67 D7
Worcester Cl
Istead Rise DA13 . . . . 35 F1
Rochester ME2 . . . . 52 E8

Worcester Cl continued
Swanscombe DA9 . . . . 17 B3
Worcester Rd ME15 . . . . . 116 D7
Wordsworth Cl
Chatham ME5 . . . . 68 C7
Tilbury RM18 . . . . 19 C5
Wordsworth Ho 15 SE18 . 12 A8
Wordsworth Rd
Bexley DA16 . . . . 12 E6
Maidstone ME14 . . . . 100 B7
Wordsworth Way
Dartford DA1 . . . . 16 A3
New Hythe ME20 . . . . 82 A4
Workhouse La
Chartway Street ME17 . . . 118 A1
Coxheath ME15 . . . . 115 C4
Sutton Valence ME17 . . . 135 A8
Workhouse Rd ME19 . . . . . . 80 F4
Worlds End La BR6 . . . . 58 B3
Worleys Dr BR6 . . . . 57 D6
Wormdale Hill ME9 . . . . 71 B3
Wormdale Rd ME9 . . . . 71 B4
WORMS HILL 164 B5
Worsenden TN27 . . . . 167 E1
WORSENDEN GREEN 167 D2
Worsfold Ct 3 ME15 . . . . . 100 A1
Worships Hill TN13 . . . . . . 91 E4
Worth Cl BR6 . . . . 57 E6
Worthing Cl RM17 . . . . 17 E8
Wotton Cl ME15 . . . . 116 C5
Wotton Gn BR5 . . . . 44 D5
WOULDHAM 66 D5
Wouldham CE Prim Sch
ME1 . . . . 66 C5
Wouldham Ct ME1 . . . . 66 C5
Wouldham Rd
Grays RM17, RM20 . . . . . . 17 E8
Rochester ME1 . . . . 52 E1
Wouldham Terr 3 BR5 . . . . 44 B6
Wrangleden Cl ME15 . . . . . 116 C5
Wrangleden Rd ME15 . . . . 116 C5
Wrangling La DA13 . . . . 64 F3
Wrekin Rd SE18 . . . . 12 C7
Wren Cl
Larkfield ME20 . . . . 81 F1
Orpington BR5 . . . . 44 D6
Wren Ind Est ME15 . . . . . . 116 F4
Wren Path SE28 . . . . 2 D4
Wren Rd DA14 . . . . 30 C5
Wrens Croft DA11 . . . . 35 E4
Wren's Cross ME15 . . . . . . 100 A3
Wren Way ME5 . . . . 68 B6
Wren Wlk RM18 . . . . 19 B7
Wricklemarsh Rd SE3 . . . . 11 B6
Wright Cl
Gillingham ME8 . . . . 55 C2
Swanscombe DA10 . . . . . . 17 D1
Wrights Cl TN30 . . . . 193 A8
WROTHAM 78 F2
WROTHAM HEATH. 80 A1
Wrotham Hill Rd TN15 . . . . 79 A6
Wrotham Rd
Bexley DA16 . . . . 13 C6
Borough Green TN15 . . . . 95 A8
Gravesend DA11, DA13 . . 36 A4
Meopham Station DA13 . . 50 A3
Wrotham Road Prim Sch
DA11 . . . . 36 B8
Wrotham Sch TN15 . . . . 79 E5
Wrotham Water La ME19,
ME19 . . . . 79 E4
Wrotham Water Rd TN15,
ME19 . . . . 79 E4
Wrottesley Rd SE18 . . . . . . 12 C8
Wrott & Hill Cl DA4 . . . . 47 B8
Wroxham Rd SE28 . . . . 3 D6
Wulfred Way TN15 . . . . 77 B1
Wyatt Cl TN15 . . . . 94 F7
Wyatt Ho 1 ME2 . . . . 53 A7
Wyatt Pl ME2 . . . . 53 A7
Wyatt Rd DA1 . . . . 26 A8
Wyatt St ME14 . . . . 100 A4
Wyke Manor Rd ME14 . . . 100 A4
Wyles St ME4 . . . . 54 A7
Wyles St ME7 . . . . 54 C7
Wylie Ho ME3 . . . . 39 F6
Wylie Rd ME3 . . . . 34 C2
Wyncham Ave DA15 . . . . . . 29 F7
Wyncroft Cl BR1 . . . . 42 F6
Wyndcliff Rd SE3, SE7 . . . . 11 B8
Wyndham Ave TN11 . . . . . 125 F1
Wyndham Cl
Leigh TN11 . . . . 125 F1
Orpington BR6 . . . . 43 C1
Wyndham Rd ME4 . . . . 53 E2
Wynford Gr BR5 . . . . 44 B6

Wynford Pl DA17. . . . . 14 A8
Wynford Way SE9. . . . . 28 F5
Wynn's Ave DA15. . . . . 13 A2
Wytchlings The ME17. . . 118 D2
Wythens Wlk SE9. . . . . 12 B1
Wytherling Cl ME14. . . . . 100 F5
Wythes Cl BR1. . . . . 42 F7
Wythes Rd E16. . . . . .1 E5
Wythfield Rd SE9. . . . . 11 F1
Wyvern Cl
  Dartford DA1. . . . . 32 C8
  Orpington BR6. . . . . 58 B7
  Snodland ME6. . . . . 82 A7
Wyvern Ho 3 RM17. . . . . . 18 B8
Wyvill Cl ME8. . . . . 69 E5

Y

YALDING. 113 F1
Yalding Cl ME2 . . . . 39 B1
Yalding Gr BR5 . . . . 44 D5
Yalding Hill ME18. . . . . . 114 A3
Yalding Organic Ctr★
  ME18. . . . . 130 F7
Yalding St Peter & St Paul
  CE Prim Sch ME18. . . . . 114 A1
Yalding Sta ME18 . . . . . . 113 D1
Yantlet Dr ME2 . . . . 52 C7
Yardley Cl TN9. . . . . 127 D3
Yardley Park Rd TN9. . . 127 D3
Yard The ME5 . . . . 68 B3
Yarnton Way SE2, DA18. . . . .3 E4
Yarrow Cres E6. . . . . .1 E8
Yarrow Ct ME14. . . . . 100 F5
Yarrow Rd ME5. . . . . 67 F4
Yateley St SE18 . . . . 1 D3
Yaugher La ME9 . . . . 70 C3
YELSTED 70 A1
Yelsted La
  Chatham ME14. . . . . 84 D7
  Yelsted ME9. . . . . 70 A1
Yelsted Rd ME9 . . . . 86 A7
Ye Olde Tudor Ct BR7. . 29 B3
Yeoman Cl E6. . . . . .2 B6
Yeoman Ct ME14. . . . . . . 101 B3
Yeoman Dr ME7 . . . . 54 F1
Yeoman Gdns TN12 . . . 145 F6
Yeoman Ho ME1. . . . . . . 53 D4

Yeoman La ME14. . . . . . . 101 B4
Yeoman Pk ME15 . . . . . . 101 A2
Yeoman's Mdws TN13. . . 92 A1
Yeoman Way ME15. . . . . 101 A2
Yeovil Cl BR6. . . . . 57 E8
Yester Dr BR7 . . . . 28 E1
Yester Pk BR7 . . . . 28 F2
Yester Rd BR7 . . . . 28 F1
Yew Rd ME3 . . . . 40 E3
Yews The DA12 . . . . 36 D7
Yew Tree Cl
  Aylesford ME20. . . . . 82 E1
  Bexley DA16 . . . . 13 A6
  Chatham ME5. . . . . 68 D1
  New Barn DA3. . . . . 49 D7
  Sevenoaks TN13 . . . . 91 D4
Yew Tree Cotts
  Groombridge TN3 . . . . . 171 F8
  Halstead TN14. . . . . 74 F7
  Sandling ME14. . . . . 83 F1
YEWTREE GREEN. 147 B1
Yew Tree Green Rd
  TN12 . . . . 147 A1
Yewtree Ho 2 ME1. . . . . 53 D4
Yewtree Ind Est ME20. . 82 D2
Yew Tree Mews TN16 . . 105 D8

Yew Tree Pl ME7. . . . . 69 B1
Yew Tree Rd TN4 . . . . . . 159 B8
Yoke Cl ME2. . . . . 53 B8
Yokosuka Way ME7 . . . . . 55 A7
Yolande Gdns SE9 . . . . . . 11 E2
Yopps Gn TN15 . . . . 94 E1
YOPPS GREEN 94 E1
York Ave
  Chatham ME5. . . . . 67 F3
  Gillingham ME7. . . . . 54 C4
  Sidcup DA15 . . . . 29 F6
York Cl E6. . . . . .1 F7
York Hill ME5. . . . . 54 C2
Yorkland Ave DA16. . . . . . 12 F3
York Par TN10. . . . . 127 C6
York Pl RM17. . . . . 18 A8
York Rd
  Biggin Hill TN16. . . . . . . 88 B8
  Dartford DA1. . . . . 32 F8
  Gravesend DA12 . . . . 36 C5
  Maidstone ME15 . . . . . . 100 C2
  Northfleet DA11. . . . . 35 D8
  Rochester ME1 . . . . 53 C3
  Royal Tunbridge Wells
    TN1. . . . . 159 A4
  Tonbridge TN10 . . . . . . 127 D5

York Rise BR6 . . . . 57 E8
York Road Jun Sch 4
  DA1. . . . . 32 F8
York Terr DA8 . . . . 14 C6
Youens Pl ME3. . . . . 38 B3
Young Rd E16 . . . . .1 C7

Z

Zambra Way TN15 . . . . . . 92 F7
Zangwill Rd SE18, SE3 . . . 11 D6
Zealand Ho SE18. . . . . .1 E2
Zelah Rd BR5. . . . . 44 C2
Zetland Ave ME7. . . . . 54 E2
Zillah Gdns ME8 . . . . 69 C6
Zion Pl DA12. . . . . 36 B8
Zion St TN15. . . . . 92 F6